SOCIAL ISSUES
and Contradictions
IN CANADIAN SOCIETY

SOCIAL ISSUES
and Contradictions
IN CANADIAN SOCIETY

THIRD EDITION

B. SINGH BOLARIA
University of Saskatchewan

HARCOURT
BRACE
CANADA

Harcourt Brace & Company, Canada

Toronto Montreal Fort Worth New York Orlando
Philadelphia San Diego London Sydney Tokyo

Canadian Cataloguing in Publication Data

Main entry under title:
   Social issues and contradictions in Canadian society

3rd ed.
Includes bibliographical references and index.
ISBN 0-7747-3615-1

1. Canada—Social conditions—1971– . I. Bolaria, B. Singh, 1936– .

HN103.5.S623 2000   971.064   C98-932220-3

New Editions Editor: Megan Mueller
Developmental Editor: James Bosma
Production Editors: Carolyn McLarty and Semareh Al-Hillal
Senior Production Co-ordinator: Sue-Ann Becker

Copy Editor: Tilman Lewis
Cover Design: Sonya V. Thursby, Opus House Incorporated
Interior Design: Dave Peters
Typesetting and Assembly: Janet Zanette
Printing and Binding: Transcontinental Printing Inc.

Cover Art: Kathy Ruttenberg, *Waiting for the Light* (1994). Oil on linen. 60" × 48". Image provided by Gallery Henoch, New York. Reproduced with permission of the artist.

Harcourt Brace & Company Canada, Ltd.
55 Horner Avenue, Toronto, ON, Canada M8Z 4X6
Customer Service
Toll-Free Tel.: 1-800-387-7278
Toll-Free Fax: 1-800-665-7307

This book was printed in Canada.

1 2 3 4 5   04 03 02 01 00

PREFACE

This third edition came about in response to a continuing demand for a text detailing the major issues and contradictions in Canadian society. All the articles in this volume have been revised and updated and incorporate the contemporary theoretical debates and current empirical data relative to specific social issues and problems. Obviously this resource cannot cover an exhaustive list of topics but, rather, examines what the editor believes to be the most important issues affecting Canadian society today.

The social issues that concern the public change from time to time. Early sociologists were preoccupied, for the most part, with matters of social stability and social harmony. They focussed on issues of deviance and other behaviour patterns considered to be disruptive of social order. Issues of "morality," such as prostitution, homosexuality, and abortion, were topics commonly discussed in texts on social problems. One of the assumptions often made by early sociologists was that these problems resulted from "defective" individuals—mentally deficient persons or social misfits. While some of these issues are still included in texts on social problems, they are no longer analyzed solely in terms of the "personal deficiencies" of individuals. For example, the question of homosexuality has largely been transformed from one of "deviant" or "sinful" behaviour to an issue of human rights—of discrimination and oppression based upon sexual orientation.

The issues that receive the most attention at any given time are determined by many different causes, including shifts in the values and norms of the society and social and political movements. For example, environmental degradation and pollution have not always been major social concerns. Environmentalists have helped raise the public consciousness and heighten awareness of hazardous chemicals, carcinogens, and toxic waste. The civil rights and feminist movements that began in the 1960s have brought into focus the issues of racism and sexism. Currently, the issues of social, economic, and political inequality, based upon the status ascribed to attributes such as gender, race, or other criteria, are receiving considerable attention from the general public, politicians, and the academic community. First Nations land claims and demands for self-government have helped focus attention on the historical and contemporary issues now facing the indigenous population.

Empirical evidence indicates that many individuals and groups continue to encounter inequality of conditions (for example, differential distribution of income and wealth) and inequality of opportunity (for example, differential access to education and health care). Political, economic, and social stratification are fundamental aspects of Canadian society. Thus, a number of essays in this volume are devoted to the issue of inequality and its consequences.

Sociologists interested in this area approach and examine these essential topics and issues from various theoretical perspectives and paradigms, and use varying levels of analysis. Although the issues are diverse, the underlying contradictions of society are major determinants of all these issues and problems. Sociologists with critical orientation tend to focus on structural conditions and contradictions, and on the institutional arrangements that produce and perpetuate social problems. In short, the focus is on the social structure and its primary and secondary contradictions, rather than on the personal pathologies of the problematic populations. The social issues in this volume are analyzed largely in terms of various structural contradictions.

A final note may be added here. Critical sociology in its various forms has proved its utility in the analysis of a wide range of social phenomena. More recently, in the areas of gender studies and racial and cultural studies, the works of feminist scholars and racial minority scholars have made significant contributions to the literature in critical sociology, which is characterized by its focus on class relations and class contradictions under capitalism. These and other developments have helped "make the case" for critical social analysis. Critical sociology's contributions to a number of substantive areas in sociology are now well recognized and accepted by the academic community. It is hoped that the essays in this volume will make a contribution to the critical analysis of social issues and social problems.

Acknowledgements

A number of people have contributed to the completion of this book. First, I would like to express my appreciation to the contributing authors who accepted my invitation to write chapters for this volume or the first two editions.

Of course, I wish to thank a number of people at Harcourt Brace & Company, Canada, particularly Heather McWhinney, Megan Mueller, James Bosma, and Carolyn McLarty, who, with their colleagues, bore the responsibility to see this book through to its completion. I am grateful to all of them for their professional guidance, enthusiasm, and support for this project. I would also like to thank Tilman Lewis for copy editing this book. I also wish to thank my family for their patience, understanding, and support—especially Rosemary and Kiran, who provided considerable academic and intellectual support to clarify my ideas, and editorial and research assistance in completing this book.

Finally, I wish to thank the following reviewers, whose comments and suggestions proved extremely helpful in the development of this new edition: G.S. Basran, University of Saskatchewan; Robert Biezenski, University of Regina; Sinnika Dixon, Canadian University College; Leslie Laczko, University of Ottawa; and Dorothy Pawluch, McMaster University.

B. Singh Bolaria
University of Saskatchewan

A Note from the Publisher

Thank you for selecting *Social Issues and Contradictions in Canadian Society*, Third Edition, by B. Singh Bolaria. The author and publisher have devoted considerable time to the careful development of this book. We appreciate your recognition of this effort and accomplishment.

We want to hear what you think about *Social Issues and Contradictions*. Please take a few minutes to fill in the stamped reader reply card at the back of the book. Your comments and suggestions will be valuable to us as we prepare new editions and other books.

CONTENTS

1 - Power + change

Part IV Institutional Structures and Inequality

Part V Environment and Urbanization

Part VI Health and Illness

Part VII The Welfare State and Social Policy

CHAPTER 1

An Introduction to Social Issues and Contradictions: Sociological Perspectives

B. Singh Bolaria

Learning Objectives

After studying this chapter, you should be able to
- Appreciate the distinction between **personal troubles** and **social issues**.
- Understand some of the salient aspects of theoretical and conceptual debate in the study of social issues and **social problems**.
- Understand the individualistic, cultural, and structural perspectives in the study of social inequality and social issues.
- Understand social problems and issues as structural features of Canadian society and not just as a personal trouble of individuals.

Introduction

The social issues and social problems that concern the public and the academic community change over time. Early sociologists concerned themselves mainly with issues of deviance and behaviour considered disruptive to social stability, social harmony, and the social and moral order (Coleman and Cressey 1984; Eitzen and Zinn 1989). It was commonly assumed that many of these problems resulted from maladjusted, abnormal individuals who had some mental deficiency or disorder, or social misfits who had been inadequately socialized into societal norms and values. The "medical model" of deviance, expressed in clinical language, was dominant in the analysis of social ills. Over time, there has been a shift in both the conceptualization and the analysis of social problems. These issues are no longer analyzed solely with reference to personal pathologies of individuals. Sociologists with critical orientation tend to focus on social, political, and economic conditions, and institutional arrangements, that produce social problems.

Changes in the social issues that receive the most attention have many different causes. These may include shifts in the values and norms of the society as well as social and political movements (Coleman and Cressey 1984). For example, environmental degradation and pollution have not always been important social issues. Environmentalists are largely responsible for heightened public awareness in this regard. The civil rights and feminist movements that began in the sixties have brought into focus the issues of racism, sexism, and racial and gender inequalities. Issues related to inequality, whether based on factors of social ascription such as gender or race, or on other criteria, have dominated public and academic debates in recent years. While there has been increasing awareness of these inequalities and a growing consciousness of the right to equality shared by all Canadians, many individuals and groups continue to encounter **inequality of conditions** and **of opportunities**. These inequalities create different opportunities and **life chances** for individuals, which are reflected in such measures as their level of education, health status, nutrition, and treatment by the justice system.

Because of the prominence of social, political, and economic stratification in Canada, the primary focus of this book is on inequality and its consequences. These and other issues are analyzed for the most part in terms of various systemic structural contradictions.

The purpose of this chapter is, by way of introduction, to outline some of the salient aspects of theoretical and conceptual debate in the study of social issues and social problems. More specifically, this chapter treats the topics of the definition and etiology of personal troubles and public issues, and individualistic and structural explanations. The fundamental question is, who or what is to be "blamed"—"defective" individuals or "faulty" structures. Wherever appropriate, examples from various subdisciplines of sociology are used to illustrate the relative aspects of the debate. It is hoped that this discussion will put into context the analyses presented in various essays in this book.

Personal Troubles and Public Issues

Many people tend to individualize such issues as poverty and unemployment as personal problems of the poor and unemployed, rather than regarding them as social problems. This distinction between personal and social problems is a crucial one, since it is germane to the question of who or what is at fault (Lauer 1978; Eitzen and Zinn 1989). For instance, is poverty due to the laziness or other "defects" of the poor individuals? Or is it due to the maldistribution of wealth and differential opportunity structures in society? Lauer defines a **personal problem** as "one whose causes and solutions lie within the individual and the individual's immediate environment," and a social problem as "one whose causes and solutions lie outside the individual and his or her immediate environment" (1978, 3).

C. Wright Mills, in *The Sociological Imagination*, made a crucial distinction between "the personal troubles of milieu" and the "public issues of social structure." Mills (1959, 8) states: "Troubles occur ... within the range of [the individual's] immediate relations with others; they have to do with [individual] self and with those limited areas of social life of which [the individual] is directly and personally aware.... A trouble is a private matter." On the other hand, "issues have to do with matters that transcend these local environments of the individual and the range of his [or her] inner life. They have to do with the organization of many such milieux into the institutions of an historical society.... An issue is a public matter." Mills states further that "it is the very nature of an issue, unlike even widespread trouble, that it cannot very well be defined in terms of the immediate and everyday environments of ordinary men [or women]. An issue, in fact, often involves a crisis in institutional arrangements, and often too it involves what Marxists call 'contradictions' or antagonisms" (1959, 8–9).

Mills provides a number of illustrations of the difference between the two. If an individual is unemployed, that is his personal trouble. The individual may lack skills, have flaws in his character, and may lack motivation. But if millions of workers are unemployed and high unemployment rates persist year after year, then it is a public issue, not just a question of immediate opportunities for an individual. Mills (1959, 9) states: "The very structure of opportunities has collapsed. Both the correct statement of the problem and the range of possible solutions require us to consider the economic and political institutions of the society, and not merely the personal situation and character of a scatter of individuals." Similarly, inside a marriage a couple may experience personal troubles and ultimately get a divorce. If this couple is only one of the very few marriages that experience such problems then one may conclude that the couple has entirely personal problems or troubles. But if the divorce rate is high and millions of marriages break up, affecting millions of couples and children, it is no longer a "personal trouble." Then the question is not what is wrong with a particular couple but rather what has happened to the institutions of marriage and the family. According to Mills, "this is an indication of a structural issue having to do with the institutions of marriage and the family and other institutions that bear upon them" (1959, 9).

If the current economic arrangements produce high unemployment and cyclical boom and bust periods, then the problem of unemployment becomes incapable of personal solutions. However, sociological discussions often lack analysis of the economic institutions and the way they affect other areas of social and individual life. In

---

Sociological Imagination

What we experience in various and specific milieux, I have noted, is often caused by structural changes. Accordingly, to understand the changes of many personal milieux we are required to look beyond them. And the number and variety of such structural changes increase as the institutions within which we live become more embracing and more intricately connected with one another. To be aware of the idea of social structure and to use it with sensibility is to be capable of tracing such linkages among a great variety of milieux. To be able to do that is to possess the sociological imagination.

Source: C. Wright Mills, *The Sociological Imagination* (New York: Oxford University Press, 1959), pp. 10–11.

part, sociologists continue to have difficulty appreciating the connection between personal troubles and public issues (Fry 1984).

In one sense, to those who are affected, it makes no difference whether a particular situation is defined as a personal or a social problem. The consequences for the unemployed and the divorced are still the same in terms of individual suffering. But in other respects, whether a problem is defined as "personal trouble" or a "social issue" is of crucial significance. This distinction determines the causes, consequences, and solutions to the problems (Lauer 1978).

"Defective" Individuals or "Faulty" Structures

In their study of social issues and social problems, generations of sociologists have used different conceptual frameworks and perspectives. Also, a debate continues over the unit of analysis, that is, whether the focus of analysis ought to be the individual or the social structure. A corollary of this is the matter of who is to be "blamed" for such issues as poverty, and for race, class, and gender inequalities. There is continuing debate as to whether these inequalities emanate from the personal pathologies and inadequacies of the individuals (individualistic explanations)—or from structured inequalities of the system (structural explanations)—in other words, whether minorities or other disadvantaged groups are themselves the problems or victims of the system. A discussion of selective examples helps to illuminate the basic arguments involved in the study of social issues.

Why is there poverty in the midst of plenty? Explanations of poverty tend to fall within three areas: personal, cultural, and economic.

One persistent element in our ethos is the belief that everyone in this society has equal opportunities. Consequently, success or failure is thought to depend upon individual characteristics. Belief in the value of hard work and competition tends to promote the thinking that each individual is responsible for his or her destiny. Joe Feagin (1975, 91–92) has summarized the basic contents of what he characterizes as the "**ideology of individualism**" as follows:

1. Each individual should work hard and strive to succeed in competition with others.
2. Those who work hard should be rewarded with success (seen as wealth, property, prestige, and power).
3. Because of widespread and equal opportunity, those who work hard will in fact be rewarded with success.
4. Economic failure is an individual's own fault and reveals lack of effort and other character defects.

Poverty, then, is a consequence of "defective" personal traits of individuals. People are poor because of some personal deficiency, which is either innate inferiority (biological or intellectual) or cultural inferiority (the **culture of poverty**). Proponents of Social Darwinism, like the nineteenth-century sociologist Herbert Spencer, have argued that the poor are unfit: "Poverty was nature's way of 'excreting' ... unhealthy, imbecile, slow, vacillating, faithless members of society in order to make room for the 'fit'" (Eitzen and Zinn 1989, 178). Arthur Jensen (1969; 1980) and Richard Herrnstein (1971; 1973) have argued that certain groups lack intellectual endowment—for instance, blacks as compared to whites—and that intelligence is primarily inherited. Poor performance in school and subsequent failure are attributed to low intelligence rather than the differential educational opportunities, culturally biased IQ tests, and advantages and disadvantages of class background and inheritance (Eitzen and Zinn 1989, 179). William Ryan (1976, 54) states: "Arthur Jensen and Richard Herrnstein confirm regretfully that Black folks and poor folks are born stupid, that little rich kids grow up rich adults, not because they inherited Daddy's stock portfolio, but rather because they inherited his brains."

While the personal approach locates the source of poverty within the individuals themselves—"defective" individuals—the "culture of poverty" hypothesis locates poverty in poor people's way of life—"defective" culture. Poverty in both instances is a consequence of "defective" behaviour of the individuals. Anderson and Gibson (1978, 168) state:

> The cultural account is similar to the personal account in that both attribute the causes of poverty to the defective behaviour of the individual, but differs in that the cultural account, rather than tracing the deficiencies of the poor individual to independent sources within the individual, explains poverty-producing deficiencies as originating in a lower class way of life.

The "culture of poverty" was given its most systematic treatment by Oscar Lewis (1966). Cultural traits he attributes to the poor include low aspirations, impulsiveness, lack of moral values, present orientation, resignation, and fatalism. Others, such as Banfield (1977), Kluckhohn and Strodtbeck (1961), and Sowell (1981), add to the list of cultural traits with which they explain the disadvantaged status of some groups; they cite devaluation of education, present time orientation, low motivation, language difficulties, dependency, and lack of achievement orientation.

Because poor individuals are blamed for their condition, a stigma is attached to being poor (Coleman and Cressey 1984, 166). They get labelled as "disreputable" (Matza 1966). This stigmatization and labelling further strengthens negative images of the poor, such as lazy, unwilling to work, and "welfare bums." Poor parents are also blamed for the poverty of their children, through the transmission of defective "culture of poverty" traits to the next generation. In other words, it is the "culture of poverty" that is the cause of the cycle of poverty rather than the economic system and the differential opportunity structures. However, opponents of this thesis, such as Anderson and Gibson (1978), have argued that the economic system that has made one generation of individuals poor will usually do the same kind of job on their children. Mills (1956, 111) states: "The accumulation of advantages at the very top parallels the vicious cycle of poverty at the very bottom." Liebow, in his attempt to clarify the distinction between culturally transmitted poverty and poverty produced anew in each generation, explains that

> the son goes out and independently experiences the same failures, in the same areas, and for much the same reasons as his father. What appears as a dynamic, self-sustaining cultural process is, in part at least, a relatively

> simple piece of social machinery which turns out, in rather mechanical
> fashion, independently produced look-alikes. (1967, 223)

The "culture of poverty" thesis is criticized on other grounds as well. Valentine (1968) argues that the conditions of the poor described by Lewis are imposed on them from outside rather than being the product of the "culture of poverty." Lifestyles of the poor, Roach and Gursslin (1967) argue, are an adaptation to poverty rather than the cause of poverty.

Whether the poor are defined as poor because of "defective" individual traits or their "defective" way of life, in either case they are objects of what Ryan (1971) has called "blaming the victim." Parenti (1978, 24) comments: "Focusing on the poor and ignoring the system of power, privilege, and profit which makes them poor, is a little like blaming the corpse for the murder."

This focus on individuals and their way of life is not confined to the analysis of poverty alone. Individual lifestyles and consumption patterns are widely invoked to explain the increase in many diseases. The inadequate or improper use of medical services by the poor is often attributed to their lack of knowledge, lack of readiness to use services, lack of positive values toward health, and cultural impediments to the use of services. Though it is phrased somewhat differently, again the analysis shifts the responsibility for not benefiting from services onto the individual—it blames the victim (Bolaria 1988). This focus on individual lifestyles and self-imposed risks tends to downgrade the importance of social and environmental factors in the production of illness and the differential availability of health services to different groups (Bolaria 1994; Bolaria and Bolaria 1994).

With few exceptions, sociological studies of racial minorities are guided by the traditional "race relations cycle" perspective and its many present-day variations of assimilation theories. One can hardly avoid the literature dealing with cultural distinctiveness, cultural patterns and orientations, adaptation, integration, accommodation, identity, assimilation, and so forth. In addition, the tendency has been to examine the "problems" of non-Europeans. Studies of racial minorities, for the most part, tend to degenerate into more-or-less socio-psychological examinations of "ethnic problems" or "identity crises," of "adaptation problems" or "assimilation problems," of "race problems" or "family problems." In short, they highlight personal and social pathologies of racial minorities and their institutions (Bolaria 1983; Bolaria and Li 1988). The disadvantaged position of racial minorities is often explained by biological and cultural deficiency theories in which the organization of the society along racial lines, institutional racism, and differential power relations are typically overlooked (Eitzen and Zinn 1989; Bolaria and Li 1988).

The sociology of deviance has often concentrated on what Davis (1980) characterizes as the unconventional and problematic aspects of life (for example, crime, alcoholism, and prostitution) and other social and personal "failures." Davis (1980, 9) further observes: "In its unreflective form, the field has focused exclusively on the victims of social change, rather than on the structural sources of change and social problems, thus turning human tragedy into the bread and butter issues for sociologists of deviance."

Many studies in this area focus on the "antisocial" individuals and their maladjustments, personal failures, and pathologies, rather than on social conditions and class, race, and gender inequalities in the legal structure and the justice system (Davis 1980; Eitzen and Zinn 1989; Samuelson 1995).

Another illustration of the debate in sociology comes from the study of gender inequality. In this area, two approaches can be identified: the gender-role socialization approach and the structural approach. The first approach focusses on individuals and the characteristics they acquire in the process of socialization (for example, mascu–line–feminine roles, independent and dependent behaviours); the second one focusses on factors external to the individuals, such as differential opportunity structures for men and women, inequality of power, and so forth (Eitzen and Zinn 1989; Glazer and Waehrer 1977). While socialization may "produce differences in the personalities, behaviors, and motivations of women and men, essentially gender stratification is maintained by societal forms" (Eitzen and Zinn 1989, 250). Uncritical use of the socialization perspective, Peterson and Enarson (1974) contend, diverts attention from the structured inequalities of the system: "Misuse of the concept of socialization plays directly into the Blaming the Victim ideology, by focusing on the victim; responsibility for 'the woman problem' rests not in the social system with its sex structured distribution of inequality, but in socialized sex differences and sex roles" (1974, 8).

The individualization of social problems and its accompanying focus on the personal pathologies of the victim are prevalent in numerous areas of study. Ryan (1971, 5) states:

> the miserable health care of the poor is explained away on the grounds that the victim has poor motivation and lacks health information. The problems of slum housing are traced to the characteristics of tenants who are ... not yet "acculturated" to life in the big city. The "multiproblem" poor, it is claimed, suffer the psychological effects of impoverishment, the "culture of poverty," and the deviant value system of the lower classes; consequently, though unwittingly, they cause their own troubles.

This focus on "problematic individuals" or "problematic groups" and on "blaming the victim" tends to strengthen "the ideological construct of bourgeois individualism by which one is responsible for one's own wealth or lack of it, for one's own work or lack of it, and for one's own health or lack of it" (Navarro 1978, 206). Thus it masks the structural conditions in the society that produce inequality, unemployment, and ill health. Among other consequences, the "blaming the victim" approach—what Eitzen and Zinn refer to as the person-blame approach—absolves institutions of any blame and justifies Social Darwinism (Eitzen and Zinn 1989, 18).

The structural approach, or what Eitzen and Zinn refer to as the system-blame approach, tends to focus on "system pathologies" rather than individual pathologies.

In contrast to the individual and cultural deficiency approaches, a structural explanation of poverty, for instance, locates its causes in the social-structural conditions that produce high unemployment, low-paying jobs, and unequal opportunity structures. Michael Harrington, in his book *The Other America*, states that "the real explanation of why the poor are where they are is that they made the mistake of being born to the wrong parents, in the wrong section of the country, in the wrong industry, or in the wrong racial or ethnic groups" (1963, 21). He points to the social-structural conditions in capitalist society that produce inequality.

The basic tenet of capitalism—the profit motive—produces inequality and poverty in several ways. To maximize profits, capitalists use every means to reduce labour costs. Such reductions are accomplished by maintaining a surplus of labour, which depresses wages, allowing employers to benefit from paying workers the lowest possible wages, and from the rotation of labourers and other measures (Eitzen and Zinn 1989, 185; Teeple 1994).

Labour market characteristics are particularly important in any discussion of poverty. The type of job, the pattern of demand for workers in it, and their bargaining power vis-à-vis their employer are very important in relation to earnings. For instance, those in managerial and professional jobs are less likely to be poor than are workers in service industries and fishing. It should be noted that service industries are heavy employers of women (National Council of Welfare 1988; 1987). Moreover, the Canadian labour market is segmented along occupational, gender, ethnic, and racial lines. Many women and minorities end up in secondary and marginal sectors that offer poor working conditions and low wages (Trumper and Wong 1997; Bolaria and Bolaria 1997).

Illustrations from other areas illuminate the distinction between individualistic and structural explanations. In medical sociology, rather than focussing on individual lifestyles, behaviour, and consumption patterns, recent studies from the perspective of historical materialism have focussed on illness-generating conditions. Several social conditions that generate illness and are associated with high levels of mortality are the focus of this approach. Social class, economic cycles, socially produced stress, production processes, the nature of work, and measures taken to increase profits are all analyzed (Waitzkin 1983; Navarro 1986). It is well known that cancer and other chronic diseases are related to environmental factors and the workplace (Harding 1994; Shields and Dickinson 1994). Evidence also links incidence of illness to economic cycles and levels of employment. Disruption of stable community relations has consistently led to an increase in rates of hypertension. (For a review of studies linking social status and health status, see Hay 1994.)

Rather than focussing on the individual life cycle and its relation to stress, "historical materialist epidemiology shifts the level of analysis to stressful forms of social organization connected to capitalist production and industrialization" (Waitzkin 1983, 63). Studies in the area of occupational health and safety provide persuasive evidence that links work environment to illness and disease, and points to basic contradictions between profit and safety. If it is expected to interfere with profits, a health- or safety-related improvement in the workplace is not likely to be implemented. Waitzkin (1983, 9) writes:

> Safety in the workplace, in almost all instances, means increased cost of production and, as a result, decreased profits. The technical improvements necessary to protect workers from dust, fumes, radioactivity, accidents, and stress entail inevitable expenses.... The constraint of private profit is a structural basis for resistance to changes in production that would assure occupational health and safety.

The contradiction between profit and safety also accounts for environmental degradation. The safe disposal of the waste products of industrial production would be costly indeed. Profit considerations encourage dumping of hazardous waste without regard to the environment or the health and safety of the public (Clow and Felt 1995). The analysis of illness, work, and the environment in the light of these and other features of capitalism (for example, class conflict and exploitation) points to the fact that inequalities in health are closely linked to the structural contradictions of the system. The focus on individuals' lifestyles, behaviours, and their "accident proneness" tends to obfuscate the social causes of disease. As well, it diverts attention from unhealthy and unsafe workplaces and environments, obscures the extent to which health and illness depend upon socially determined ways of life, shifts responsibility for health and illness back onto the individual, and so individualizes the problem of inequality in health status (Bolaria and Bolaria 1994).

Similarly, in contrast to the biological and cultural deficiency theories that put the blame on racial minorities, and others that blame individual racism for the disadvantaged position of minorities, the structural theories focus on institutional patterns and **structural inequalities**, which perpetuate racial inequality and racial oppression independently of prejudicial attitudes (Bolaria and Li 1988; Satzewich 1994). Carmichael and Hamilton (1967, 4–5) discuss both types of racism. Individual racism "consists of overt acts by individuals, which cause death and injury, or the violent destruction of property," and institutional racism "originates in the operations of established and respected forces in the society."

The normal daily operations of our respected institutions continue to perpetuate racial inequality. Racial ideology and practices reach far back into the Canadian past. Colonization of the Native population, racist immigration policies and practices against Chinese and South Asians, internment of Japanese—all attest to the racist policies and practices of the Canadian state and other institutions. These past policies and practices continue to affect the current status of racial minorities in this country. Institutional inequality and racism are manifested in various exclusionary practices in the social, political, and economic spheres. While patterns and practices of discrimination have changed over time, racial domination and racial discrimination remain a permanent feature of Canadian society (Bolaria and Li 1988; Satzewich 1995).

Like the racial minorities, a large proportion of women face discrimination in the workplace and end up in dead-end jobs and low-paying segments of the labour market. Their location in the labour market primarily accounts for their poverty and social subordination. Women of colour face both racial and gender discrimination and exploitation (Bolaria and Li 1988; Trumper and Wong 1997; Bolaria and Bolaria 1997).

Because institutions are interrelated, exclusion of minorities from one institution is likely to influence their opportunities in other institutions (Eitzen and Zinn 1989). Inadequate income and poverty, for instance, affect individual life chances as manifested in health status, nutrition, and educational levels, which in turn will affect job opportunities and income levels. These inequalities are cumulative. Inequality of conditions produces differential opportunity structures, which in turn produce differential conditions. As Benokraitis and Feagin (1974, 6) put it, "unequal resources will produce unequal qualifications to compete for goods and services, unequal qualifications will limit access to goods and services and unequal access to goods and services will result in unequal resources."

In summary, an analysis of social institutions and of the structural contradictions inherent in the current political-economic and social arrangements illuminates how these institutions and arrangements cause and perpetuate inequalities and differential opportunity structures. This approach locates the cause of the "problems" in the defective system rather than in the deficiencies of the individuals and their "defective" way of life.

The Capitalist Economy, Inequality, and the Capitalist State

To fully appreciate the social structural conditions that produce economic inequality in capitalist societies, it is important to further consider the basic features of capitalism and the capitalist economy.

Capitalism is one type of production system, with corresponding sets of social relationships. Some basic features of capitalism distinguish it from other systems of production: Under capitalism, commodities are produced primarily for sale rather than for consumption, means of production are privately owned, there is a free market, and production is for profit and capital accumulation (Li and Bolaria 1994, xix).

Certain social relationships within capitalist societies correspond to these basic features of capitalism. For example, most people under capitalism sell their labour power for a wage. The necessity of wage labour to capitalist production has led to increasing proletarianization of the population, that is, to its conversion to the working class. Correspondingly, ownership of the means of production has become increasingly concentrated in the hands of fewer people through their control of multinational corporations (Li and Bolaria 1994).

Teeple (1994) argues that there are two main defining elements of a capitalist economy from which other common features can be deduced. The two main elements are commodification of production (production for exchange), and an underlying motive for production of profit and capital accumulation, not of immediate satisfaction of material needs. Arising from these features is another common characteristic of capitalist societies, namely, economic inequality. Teeple argues that "such inequality is intrinsic to the system for it is a necessary and recurrent consequence of production for profit and of the commodity form of goods and services" (Teeple 1994, 104).

In addition to the structural social characteristics of the capitalist economy, the state's role in a capitalist society is essential. State policies and programs relate to social issues and to the economy because social policy decisions are made not in a vacuum but in a particular political and economic context.

A large body of literature addresses the nature of the state and state power (for review see Knutilla 1994; Teeple 1994). Two major perspectives—pluralist and Marxist—help to illuminate the contrasting views of the state and its role in capitalist society. The pluralists see the state as class-neutral, mediating and responding to the pressures of multiple interest groups, rather than of one dominant group or class; political power as dispersed through a one-person one-vote electoral system; and state actions and policies as reflecting common public interests. Pluralism is essentially a democratic view of society, politics, and the state.

On the other hand, the common theme running through the Marxist tradition is that the state in the capitalist society is dominated by the interests of the capitalist class.

The policies and actions of the state, then, rather than being in the common public interest, represent the common interests of the dominant economic class. This influence on the political process and public policy is manifested through various mechanisms, such as direct links between the economic and the political elites, lobbying, and threats to disinvest and relocate production plants (Knutilla 1994; Teeple 1994).

Pluralist claims, it turns out, do not correspond to empirical reality. Teeple's (1994) review of historical and contemporary data indicates a close link between the state and the economy. Essentially, the state has created favourable conditions for free enterprise, and continues to provide substantial economic aid to corporations in the form of direct loans and grants, tax exemptions, infrastructure to facilitate corporate operations, privatization of state enterprises, and regulation of the capitalist labour market and capital–labour relations to facilitate capital accumulation. Corporate welfare programs are often hidden in state budgets and are frequently referred to as business incentives to increase investments and employment opportunities, while social welfare programs are blamed for fiscal cuts and budgetary deficits.

Teeple (1994) also notes that due to changes in the nature of the economy there has been a shift in the form of state intervention in the economy. By the late 1970s, postwar Keynesian policies, which included state expenditures on public works to relieve unemployment and stimulate economic demand, were being replaced by monetary policies that included control over money supply through interest rates and taxation policies (lower taxes) to encourage investment by corporations. Neo-conservative policies (monetarism and supply-side economics) were introduced by individual nation-states in response to the demands of global capital. The adoption of neo-conservative government policies has also hastened the diversion of state priorities and resources from social and human services to the enhancement of labour productivity and capital accumulation. There has also been a sustained attack on welfare programs and social services, which, it is claimed, adversely affect government deficits, individual initiatives, and labour productivity at a time when Canada needs to become more competitive internationally. In the 1980s, the federal and provincial governments began to overhaul welfare, unemployment insurance, and other social programs, imposing tighter eligibility requirements and spending ceilings.

These and other measures to reduce social wages are likely to exacerbate inequality, and the state may find it difficult to harmonize contradictions between capital accumulation and legitimization.

This intrinsic inequality of the system leads to society's division into classes and subclasses of individuals defined by their relationships to the means of production and ownership of private property (Teeple 1994). Members of each class share common interests, which are often the primary source of the ongoing struggle between the classes. For instance, the capitalist class (owners of means of production) use every means to reduce the costs of production, including labour costs, to maximize profits and capital accumulation. On the other hand, the workers, without ownership of the means of production, are compelled to sell their labour power for wages in order to exist. Their interest lies in maintaining and even striving to increase the levels of their wages and other benefits. These contradictory interests form the primary basis of antagonistic and hostile relationships between classes.

The primary motives of capitalist production—profits and capital accumulation— produce inequality and poverty in several ways. Numerous strategies are used to

The Capitalist Economy

The word "capitalism" is used to designate a type of economic system whose main principle is private property.

There are two main characteristics of the capitalist economy about which there is little or no disagreement and from which many other common features can be deduced. First, everything produced in this system is produced as a commodity, that is, as a form of private property for exchange. Implied in this is the fact that the labour power necessary to produce these commodities is itself a commodity, something that can be sold, albeit only for periods of time. It follows that the sale and purchase of labour power and its products takes place as in a market, every owner competing against every other.

The second characteristic of the capitalist economy is that the direct purpose and underlying motive of production is to make a profit. The satisfaction of certain material needs is, of course, why production takes place at all, but this is not the immediate goal of production under capitalism. Here the producers remain indifferent to the effects of their products, for the accumulation of private property is the sole aim of production.

Arising from these defining elements there is another feature common to all capitalist societies, namely, economic inequality. Such inequality is intrinsic to the system for it is a necessary and recurrent consequence of production for profit and of the commodity form of goods and services. The reason lies in the fact that private property is the exclusive right or enforceable claim to things, that is, the right to use and dispose of things in one's own self-interest. Because private property is a legally defined *exclusive* power over things, it follows that those with more wealth in this form will have more economic power in society. In capitalism, there is in effect only more or less wealth in this form, hence economic inequality.

Source: Gary Teeple, "Capitalist Economy and the State," in Peter S. Li and B. Singh Bolaria, eds., *Essentials of Contemporary Sociology* (Toronto: Copp Clark, 1994), pp. 104–105.

reduce labour costs, including increasing labour productivity; maintaining a surplus of labour (unemployed and reserve army of labour), which threatens wage levels; threatening to relocate production to low-wage areas; labour rotation; and other labour procurement measures (Eitzen and Zinn 1989; Teeple 1994; Bolaria and Bolaria 1994). Organization of production, the labour process, and the structure of the labour market also contribute to economic inequality. Labour market segmentation and one's location within the market (i.e., one's type of job), patterns of labour demand, and bargaining position are very important in relation to wage levels. At the broader level, the capitalist economy is divided into two economic sectors that have different characteristics, working conditions, and rewards for workers. The primary sector is characterized by large organizations, stable production, well-paid jobs, and stable employment and career patterns. The secondary sector is composed of marginal firms, typically with poorly paid labour, a poor work environment, a lack of job security, and unstable employment patterns (Gordon, Edwards, and Reich 1982; Bonacich 1972; Piore 1975). This duality of the labour market perpetuates economic inequalities and racial, ethnic, and gender divisions in the labour force. Labour market segmentation at the structural level is a major obstacle not only to economic equality, but also to working-class unity on a political level.

Social Structure and Life Chances

The division into an individualistic structural dichotomy may be a simplification of a complex phenomenon, but it does allow for some enlightening perspectives on social issues. It also helps clarify the distinction between the types of explanations used by sociologists and others. Whether social problems are considered to emanate from the personal "pathologies" of individuals or from systemic structural contradictions has important consequences for the individual (Lauer 1978). For example, if we define a "personal situation" as one that is due to our own failure or inadequacies, we are likely to blame ourselves and perhaps even passively accept the situation. Sennett and Cobb, in *The Hidden Injuries of Class*, tell of the "self-accusation ... of a nearly illiterate" garbage collector, who states: "Look, I know it's nobody's fault but mine that I got stuck here where I am, I mean ... if I wasn't such a dumb shit ... no, it ain't that neither ... if I had applied myself, I know I got it in me to be different, can't say anyone did it to me" (1973, 96). This self-blame is not surprising in the face of the dominant ideology of individualism, equality of opportunity, and fair competition. It is an ideology that tends to promote the idea that only individual qualities such as hard work, motivation, initiative, and intelligence determine one's station in life.

While this ethos is used to justify the inequalities in our society, the empirical reality is quite different. One's location in the social structure has important bearing on one's opportunities in life. Max Weber saw class position as closely linked to people's life chances, that is, their chances to acquire material goods and other amenities (Gerth and Mills 1958). As noted above, a number of studies indicate that economic inequalities produce inequalities in opportunities and life chances, which are reflected in such measures as education, health, and consumption patterns (Wotherspoon 1987; Bolaria and Dickinson 1988; Chossudovsky 1983). Racial ascriptive status continues to be an important determinant of the life chances of racial minorities (Bolaria and Li 1988). A royal commission report, *Equality in Employment,* says of Canada's Native people that

> their economic plight has taken its inevitable toll on social conditions. Native people are angry over the disproportionate numbers of native people who drop out of school, who are in prison, who suffer ill health, who die young, who commit suicide. They are saddened by the personal, communal, and cultural dislocation of their people. (Abella 1984, 33)

Other factors of social ascription, such as gender, continue to be important determinants of inequalities of conditions and opportunities (Abella 1984). These examples signify the importance of structural analysis in the study of gender and racial inequality and the link between individuals' location in the social structure and their life chances.

The analysis of the social system and structured inequalities, and their impact on individuals, is the appropriate domain of sociology. The insights of the "sociological imagination" have been increasingly significant in understanding institutional structures and how they interrelate, and the connection between personal troubles and social issues.

Organization of the Book

Despite the optimistic prognosis by some social thinkers that with industrialization and modernization the traditional social ascriptive bases for systems of inequality, such as gender and race, would no longer be relevant, empirical reality indicates that they continue to be important determinants of social, political, and economic inequalities in Canada. These inequalities produce differential access to opportunity structures, and hence different life chances for various social groups in this society.

In Part I, entitled "Capital, Labour, and Class," the contradictions of economic and social relations of production, class contradictions, class inequality and poverty, and the state's role in the structuring and mediation of capital–labour relations and regulation of the labour market are discussed. The underlying theme of these essays is that unemployment, capital–labour relations, and conditions of work are all social issues, and that the capitalist state structures and mediates capital–labour relations in the interests of the class it represents. This theme is highlighted in the discussions on restructuring of the production process, linkages between the nature and organization of work and unemployment in capitalist societies, and the procurement of foreign labour to meet labour force needs in Canada. The last reading in this section focusses on a structural social problem produced by the contradictions of the capitalist economy, that is, vast economic disparities produced primarily by production for profit and capital accumulation. Specifically, the linkage between income inequality and life chances is discussed, with particular emphasis on the emergence and persistence of food banks as a response to hunger.

In Part II, "Gender and Family," two essays address the issues of gender relations and gender inequality in both the domestic and public spheres. These essays present an analysis of the historical and contemporary structural basis of gender inequality, with the underlying theme that gender inequality is rooted in the ideology and social construction of patriarchal gender relations, the cult of domesticity, the bourgeois family ideal, and capitalist class relations. These readings discuss various theoretical perspectives on inequalities between men and women, elaborate on specific processes that place women in subordinate social roles, and examine the structural barriers that produce and reproduce gender inequality.

Like gender, racial ascriptive status forms an important basis of social, political, and economic inequality. Essays in Part III, "Race and Ethnicity," address the issues of racism, racial inequality, economic exploitation of racial minorities, and the institutional and structural arrangements and social contradictions that continue to sustain these inequalities. The underlying theme of these essays is that racism and racial inequality are structural aspects of both the past and the present operation of Canada as a capitalist society. Specific processes involved in the racial subordination and economic exploitation of racial minority immigrant groups and the First Nations are discussed, as well as Canada's multiculturalism policy and its limitations.

Part IV, "Institutional Structures and Inequality," examines the impact of structured inequalities on the life chances of individuals and social groups. Differential access to opportunity structures and life chances is reflected in unequal education and involvement in and treatment by the justice system. These inequalities are correlated with gender, class, and race.

There is growing awareness of and concern about the impact of environmental degradation on human existence and survival. The concerns are not only about chemicals and air pollutants, but also about the quality of the social environment. Damage to the ecosystem causes human illnesses and deaths arising from extensive and prolonged exposure to various pollutants. Social environmental factors primarily associated with urbanization, such as population density, violence and crime, social disorder, and social conflicts, also have an impact on human quality of life. The two essays in Part V, entitled "Environment and Urbanization," address these issues.

Part VI, "Health and Illness," examines health care issues with particular focus on aging and mental illness. It treats the link between demographic and epidemiological transitions and the resulting demands on health services; differential accessibility and utilization of health services by socio-economic status and age; social determinants of health and illness; sociological and psychological analyses of mental illness; and the importance of social, structural, and contextual factors in the study of mental illness.

Part VII, "The Welfare State and Social Policy," examines policies and programs intended to ameliorate inequalities and solve social problems. The first essay discusses the development of the welfare state and its current contradictions. The welfare state, which at one time was viewed as the most important institution for solving social problems, has itself become a problem that requires fixing. The confrontation between social welfare policy and the politics of deficit can be expected to reduce and limit welfare benefits for the needy and produce unfavourable changes in state policies and priorities. The social welfare constraints that result are likely to sharpen social contradictions and escalate social problems.

The concluding chapter examines the policy implications of interpreting and analyzing social issues within an individualistic or structural framework, and constraints imposed on social programs and social policy by global capital. It is argued that a strictly individualistic approach absolves the political, economic, and social structures of responsibility for social ills; its consequence is the orientation of policy toward changing the individual's "defective" way of life. In contrast, within a structural framework the solutions are seen to lie in transforming the basic structures and institutions that produce and reproduce deleterious social conditions. Furthermore, alternative social policy choices are greatly affected by global corporate demands, increasing pressure toward harmonization of social programs, and reducing national sovereignty and political leverage on public policy.

Summary

- This chapter examines the definition and etiology of personal troubles and public issues, and offers individualistic and structural explanations.
- Examples from various subdisciplines of sociology are used to illustrate aspects of the debate on the fundamental question of who or what is to be "blamed"—"defective" individuals or "faulty" structures.
- It is argued that the analysis of the social system and structural inequalities, and their impact on individuals, is the appropriate domain of sociology.
- The importance of structural analysis and the link between individuals' location in the social structure (inequality of conditions) and their life chances (differential opportunities) are highlighted.
- It is concluded that the insights of the "sociological imagination" are significant in understanding institutional structures and their interrelationship, and the connection between personal troubles and social issues.

Questions to Consider

1. Discuss the distinction between personal troubles and social issues.

2. Discuss the individualistic, cultural, and structural perspectives in the study of social inequality.

3. Outline the basic contents of the "ideology of individualism" and discuss how this ideology supports the status quo.

4. Provide evidence to demonstrate the relationship between individuals' location in the institutional structures and their life chances.

5. Discuss the implications of whether social problems are considered to emanate from the personal pathologies of individuals or from systemic structural contradictions for individual and institutional changes.

Suggested Readings

Bolaria, B. Singh, and Peter S. Li. *Racial Oppression in Canada.* 2d ed. Toronto: Garamond Press, 1988.

Fry, John A., ed. *Contradictions in Canadian Society.* Toronto: John Wiley and Sons, 1984.

Li, Peter S. *The Making of Post-War Canada.* Toronto: Oxford University Press, 1996.

Mills, C. Wright. *The Sociological Imagination.* New York: Oxford University Press, 1959.

Samuelson, L., ed. *Power and Resistance: Critical Thinking about Canadian Social Issues.* Halifax: Fernwood Publishing, 1994.

Satzewich, Vic. *Racism and Social Inequality in Canada.* Toronto: Thompson Educational Publishing, 1998.

Vorst, Jesse, et al. *Race, Class, Gender: Bonds and Barriers.* Toronto: Garamond Press and Society for Social Studies, 1991.

Wotherspoon, Terry. *The Sociology of Education in Canada: Critical Perspectives.* Toronto: Oxford University Press, 1998.

Glossary

culture of poverty A set of cultural traits attributed to the poor, such as low aspirations, impulsiveness, present orientation, resignation, and fatalism, which are considered causes of poverty.

ideology of individualism An ideology that tends to promote the idea that only individual qualities such as hard work, motivation, initiative, and intelligence determine one's station in life.

inequality of conditions Differential access to and availability of valued resources.

inequality of opportunities Differential access to opportunity structures because of inequality of conditions.

life chances The opportunities that people have to acquire material goods, services, and desirable living conditions.

personal problem A problem whose causes and solutions lie within the individual and his or her immediate environment.

personal trouble A private matter that occurs within the range of the individual's immediate environment and relations with others.

social issue A public matter that often involves a crisis in institutional arrangements and social contradictions.

social problem A problem whose causes and solutions lie outside the individual and his or her immediate environment.

structural inequality An arrangement of social positions whereby one's location in the social structure has important bearing on one's opportunities in life (life chances).

References

Abella, R.S. 1984. *Equality in Employment.* Ottawa: Minister of Supply and Services.

Anderson, C.H., and J.R. Gibson. 1978. *Toward a New Sociology.* 3d ed. Homewood, IL: Dorsey Press.

Banfield, E. 1977. *The Unheavenly City Revisited.* Boston: Little, Brown.

Benokraitis, N., and J.R. Feagin. 1974. "Institutional Racism: A Review and Critical Assessment of the Literature." Paper presented at the American Sociological Association, Montreal, August. Cited in Eitzen and Zinn, *Social Problems.* 217–18.

Bolaria, B.S. 1983. "Dominant Perspectives and Non-White Minorities." In *Racial Minorities in Multicultural Canada,* ed. P.S. Li and B.S. Bolaria. Toronto: Garamond Press. 157–69.

———. 1988. "The Politics and Ideology of Self-Care and Lifestyles." In *Sociology of Health Care in Canada*, ed. B.S. Bolaria and H.D. Dickinson. Toronto: Harcourt Brace Jovanovich. 537–49.

———. 1994. "Lifestyles, Material Deprivation and Health." In *Racial Minorities, Medicine and Health*, ed. B.S. Bolaria and R. Bolaria. Saskatoon: Social Research Unit and Halifax: Fernwood Publishing. 67–84.

Bolaria, B.S., and R. Bolaria. 1994. "Inequality and Differential Health Risks of Environmental Degradation." In *Racial Minorities, Medicine and Health*, ed. B.S. Bolaria and R. Bolaria. Saskatoon: Social Research Unit and Halifax: Fernwood Publishing. 85–94.

Bolaria, B.S., and R. von Elling Bolaria. 1997. "Capital, Labour Migrations." In *International Labour Migrations*, ed. B.S. Bolaria and R. von Elling Bolaria. New Delhi: Oxford University Press. 1–17.

Bolaria B.S., and H.D. Dickinson. 1988. *Sociology of Health Care in Canada.* Toronto: Harcourt Brace Jovanovich.

Bolaria, B.S., and P.S. Li. 1988. *Racial Oppression in Canada.* 2d ed. Toronto: Garamond Press.

Bonacich, E. 1972. "A Theory of Ethnic Antagonism: The Split Labour Market." *American Sociological Review* 37: 547–59.

Carmichael, S., and C.W. Hamilton. 1967. *Black Power: The Politics of Liberation in America.* New York: Vintage.

Chossudovsky, M. 1983. "Underdevelopment and the Political Economy of Malnutrition and Ill Health." *International Journal of Health Services* 3, no. 1: 69–87.

Clow, M. and L.F. Felt. 1995. "Industrial Development and Environmental Integrity: Contradiction or Co-existence." In *Social Issues and Contradictions in Canadian Society*, 2d ed., ed. B.S. Bolaria. Toronto: Harcourt Brace & Company, Canada. 247–64.

Coleman, J., and D. Cressey. 1984. *Social Problems.* 2d ed. New York: Harper and Row.

Davis, N.J. 1980. *Deviance.* 2d ed. Dubuque, IA: Wm. C. Brown.

Eitzen, D.S., and M.B. Zinn. 1989. *Social Problems.* 4th ed. Boston: Allyn and Bacon.

Feagin, J.R. 1975. *Subordinating the Poor: Welfare and American Beliefs.* Englewood Cliffs, NJ: Prentice-Hall.

Fry, J.A. 1984. *Contradictions in Canadian Society.* Toronto: John Wiley and Sons.

Gallup Report. 1985. "Poverty." No. 234 (March): 21–25.

Gerth, H.H., and C.W. Mills. 1958. *Max Weber: Essays in Sociology.* New York: Galaxy.

Glazer, N., and H.Y. Waehrer, eds. 1977. *Women in a Man-Made World.* Chicago: Rand McNally.

Gordon, D.M., R.L. Edwards, and M. Reich. 1982. *Segmented Work, Divided Workers.* Cambridge: Cambridge University Press.

Harding, J. 1994. "Environmental Degradation and Rising Cancer Rates: Exploring the Link in Canada." In *Health, Illness and Health Care in Canada*, 2d ed., ed. B.S. Bolaria and H. Dickinson. Toronto: Harcourt Brace. 649–67.

Harrington, M. 1963. *The Other America: Poverty in the United States.* Baltimore: Penguin Books.

Hay, D.I. 1994. "Social Status and Health Status: Does Money Buy Health." In *Racial Minorities, Medicine and Health,* ed. B.S. Bolaria and R. Bolaria. Saskatoon: Social Research Unit and Halifax: Fernwood Publishing. 9–52.

Herrnstein, R. 1971. "I.Q." *Atlantic* 228 (September): 43–64.

———. 1973. *I.Q. in the Meritocracy.* Boston: Little, Brown.

Jensen, A.R. 1969. "How Much Can We Boost IQ and Scholastic Achievement?" *Harvard Educational Review* 39 (Winter): 1–123.

———. 1980. *Bias in Mental Testing.* New York: Free Press.

Kluckhohn, F., and F.L. Strodtbeck. 1961. *Variations in Value Orientations.* New York: Harper and Row.

Knutilla, M. 1994. "The State and Social Issues: Theoretical Considerations." *Power and Resistance: Critical Thinking about Canadian Social Issues*, ed. L. Samuelson. Halifax: Fernwood Publishing. 1–18.

Lauer, R.H. 1978. *Social Problems and the Quality of Life.* Dubuque, IA: Wm. C. Brown.

Lewis, O. 1966. *La Vida.* New York: Random House.

Li, P.S., and B. Singh Bolaria. 1994. "Introduction." In *Essentials of Contemporary Sociology*, ed. P.S. Li and B.S. Bolaria. Toronto: Copp Clark. xviii–xx.

Liebow, E. 1967. *Tally's Corner.* Boston: Little, Brown.

Matza, D. 1966. "The Disreputable Poor." In *Class, Status, and Power.* 2d ed, ed. R. Bendix and S.M. Lipset. New York: Free Press. 289–302.

Mills, C.W. 1943. "The Professional Ideology of Social Pathologists." *American Journal of Sociology* 49, no. 2: 65–180.

———. 1956. *The Power Elite.* New York: Oxford University Press.

———. 1959. *The Sociological Imagination.* New York: Oxford University Press.

Muszynski, A. 1995. "Social Stratification: Class and Gender Inequality." In *Social Issues and Contradictions in Canadian Society,* 2d ed., ed. B.S. Bolaria. Toronto: Harcourt Brace. 19–40.

National Council of Welfare. 1988. *Poverty Profile 1988.* Ottawa: Supply and Services Canada.

———. 1997. *Poverty Profile 1995.* Ottawa: Supply and Services Canada.

Navarro, V. 1978. "The Crisis of the Western System of Medicine in Contemporary Capitalism." *International Journal of Health Services* 8, no. 2.

———. 1986. *Crisis, Health, and Medicine.* New York: Tavistock Publications.

Parenti, M. 1978. *Power and the Powerless.* 2d ed. New York: St. Martin's Press.

Peterson, L., and E. Enarson. 1974. "Blaming the Victim in the Sociology of Women: On the Misuse of Concept of Socialization." Paper presented at the Pacific Sociological Association Meetings, San Jose, California, March. Cited in Eitzen and Zinn, *Social Problems.* 259–60.

Piore, M.J. 1975. "Notes for a Theory of Labour Market Segmentation." In *Labour Market Segmentation,* ed. R.L. Edwards et al. Lexington, Man.: Heath. 125–50.

Roach, J.L., and O.R. Gursslin. 1967. "An Evaluation of the Concept 'Culture of Poverty.'" *Social Forces* 45: 383–92.

Ryan, W. 1971. "Postscript: A Call to Action." *Social Policy* 3 (May–June).

———. 1976. *Blaming the Victim.* New York: Random House.

Samuelson, L. 1995. "The Canadian Criminal Justice System: Inequalities of Class, Race and Gender." In *Social Issues and Contradictions in Canadian Society*, 2d ed., ed. B.S. Bolaria. Toronto: Harcourt Brace. 449–80.

Satzewich, V. 1995. "Social Stratification: Class and Racial Inequality." In *Social Issues and Contradictions in Canadian Society*, 2d ed., ed. B.S. Bolaria. Toronto: Harcourt Brace. 98–121.

Sennett, R., and J. Cobb. 1973. *The Hidden Injuries of Class.* New York: Vintage Books.

Shields, J., and H.D. Dickinson. 1994. "Health for Sale: The Political Economy of Occupational Health and Safety." In *Health, Illness and Health Care in Canada,* 2d ed., ed. B.S. Bolaria and H.D. Dickinson. Toronto: Harcourt Brace. 668–83.

Sowell, T. 1981. *Ethnic America: A History.* New York: Basic Books.

Teeple, G. 1994. "The Capitalist Economy and the State." In *Essentials of Contemporary Sociology,* ed. P.S. Li and B.S. Bolaria. Toronto: Copp Clark. 104–26.

Trumper, R., and L.L. Wong. 1997. "Racialization and Genderization: The Canadian State, Immigrants and Temporary Workers." In *International Labour Migrations*, ed. B.S. Bolaria and R. von Elling Bolaria. New Delhi: Oxford University Press. 153–91.

Valentine, C.A. 1968. *Culture and Poverty: Critique and Counter-Proposals.* Chicago: University of Chicago Press.

Waitzkin, H. 1983. *The Second Sickness.* New York: Free Press.

Wotherspoon, T., ed. 1987. *The Political Economy of Canadian Schooling.* Toronto: Methuen.

PART I

Capital, Labour, and Class

INTRODUCTION

Capitalism is characterized by certain basic features that distinguish it from other modes of production, namely private ownership of the means of production, production of commodities for sale rather than for consumption, a market economy, and production for profit and capital accumulation. Corresponding to these basic features are certain social relationships of capitalist societies. For example, waged labour is one of the distinct social features of capitalism, that is, most people sell their labour for a wage.

Material production requires labour power. For a capitalist economy to function, its labour force has to be produced, maintained, and renewed. In the process of consuming labour power, the capitalist is able to realize a gain in value beyond the wages paid to the labourer. The value beyond that required to purchase the labour is known as *surplus value*.

The amount of the wage paid to labour—what it costs the capitalist to buy labour power—is influenced by many factors, and may range from what is needed for mere subsistence to a level sufficient to maintain a traditional standard of living. The size of the industrial "reserve army of labour," the unemployed or irregularly employed who compete with workers for their jobs, contributes to the variations in wage level. Capitalists seek every means to reduce labour costs and to increase the output of their workers so that they can realize an even larger surplus. There is an inherent conflict of interest over surplus value between the capitalists and the workers; surplus value and wages are inversely related.

Capitalist relations of production are characterized by a specific set of class relations, the transformation of labour into a commodity, and the appropriation of surplus value by the capitalist class. It may be noted that under other social forms—slavery and feudalism—a ruling class also appropriated a surplus from the working population. Yet, in a capitalist society, the way in which a surplus is appropriated takes a special form: the capitalists exercise direct control over all the processes of labour and production through their ownership of the means of production. To be sure, the organization of work and the control of production is primarily a product of the outcome of the historical struggle between labour and capital. Labour has had some victories, but the production process under capitalism remains characterized by the primacy of management control. The institutionalization of this control varies with the nature of the production process. In the case of low-cost labour, management's control rests primarily on the powerlessness of the workers.

The state plays a crucial role in structuring capital–labour relations and capital accumulation. The capitalist system of production and exploitation is secured by the capitalist state, which has a monopoly over the legitimate use of force; this coercive force is embodied in law and legal institutions. Collective bargaining procedures, the enforcement of labour laws, "back to work" legislation, and minimum wage levels are all examples of state intervention and institutionalization of capital–labour relations.

In sum, the extraction of surplus from workers in the process of production is an act of power by the capitalist class exercised through the capitalist state.

In capitalist countries, a number of contradictions arise out of the economic and social relations of production and conflicting class interests. The state plays an important role in structuring, or "mediating," labour capital and property relations. The issues that are the outcomes of these contradictions are discussed in this section.

Harley D. Dickinson, in the chapter entitled "Work and Unemployment as Social Issues," argues that unemployment is best understood as a social issue rather than as a personal problem. Further, he argues that an adequate understanding of unemployment requires that it be analyzed in relation to the nature and organization of employment. Dickinson divides his chapter into four main sections. In the first section, he states that unemployment becomes a major social issue only in the context of societies where the capitalist mode of production is dominant and the majority of people are dependent on wages and other forms of employment income for their livelihood. In the second section, he outlines a theory of the capitalist labour process, arguing that the changing nature of both employment and unemployment is a consequence of capitalist employers attempting to increase worker productivity and decrease the costs of production in order to maximize profitability. More specifically, the extension of the occupational division of labour and the development of productivity-enhancing and labour-saving technology contribute to contradictory tendencies: an increased demand for wage labour of some categories of workers and a decreased demand for the labour of others. These tendencies result in different experiences of employment and unemployment for different categories of workers.

In the third section, Dickinson examines some of the ways in which the capitalist labour process has had an effect on workers in the goods-producing sector of the economy. The major trends that he describes strongly suggest that attempts by employers to increase workers' productivity and reduce the costs of production have resulted in decreased wages and incomes, declining union membership, and increased frequency and duration of unemployment for certain categories of workers—women, the young, and the elderly. Then he looks at the same processes in the services-producing sector of the economy, where similar forms of productivity enhancement and cost reduction affect different categories of workers. Finally, he discusses the growth and trends in self-employment.

In conclusion, Dickinson states that the experience of intermittent unemployment is likely to be increasingly common for a growing number of workers. The problem of unemployment, he argues, requires a political solution.

Even when some segments of the labour force face high levels of unemployment, Canada continues to import foreign workers to supplement the labour pool and meet the demand for labour in some sectors of the economy. Immigrant labour has always been crucial for Canadian development and capital accumulation. As capitalism has become increasingly global in character, the internationalization of capital has been accompanied by the internationalization of labour. Global disparities allow the advanced capitalist countries, including Canada, to have access to the international labour pool. The flow of this labour to the labour-importing countries is regulated by the state through immigration laws.

In his chapter on the international migration of workers to Canada, "Capital Accumulation and State Formation: The Contradictions of International Migration,"

Vic Satzewich argues that these migratory flows are structured by a dialectic of economic, political, and ideological relations. These relations, he notes, are by no means complementary or consistent. Immigration levels and the ethnic composition of immigrant groups are continuously being shaped by contradictory forces. Satzewich identifies three sets of issues associated with international migration to Canada. These are contradictions between migration as an aspect of capital accumulation and migration as an aspect of state formation, political and ideological constraints faced by the state in using immigration to solve demographic and fiscal problems associated with the declining fertility and aging of its population, and the question of whether migration contributes to economic development in labour-exporting countries or whether it is a new form of postcolonial exploitation.

Satzewich argues that immigration and migration controls are the outcome of a contradiction between the process of capital accumulation and the process of state formation. This is demonstrated by the data on overall immigration to this country and restrictive and exclusionary policies with respect to certain categories of immigrants. Canada has sought out not simply inexpensive labour, but also labour that could become part of the Canadian "imagined community." Some workers may be desirable from an accumulation standpoint, but may not be considered as good potential citizens because of racial or other characteristics.

Satzewich observes that future socio-economic problems associated with population aging and declining fertility could be resolved by increasing the level of immigration to Canada. However, racism and the continued salience of race ("white country") in the definition of Canada as a nation may preclude the use of immigrant labour from non-traditional source countries to resolve Canada's social and economic problems.

Social and economic contradictions are being managed partly through immigration regulations. Through restrictions on entry, the Canadian state has been successful in converting what otherwise might have been permanent settlers into lower-cost migrant contract labour. Immigration laws allow foreign labour to be admitted without granting the workers the legal status of regular immigrants. Since the introduction of the Employment Authorization Program in 1973, thousands of workers, ranging from professionals to unskilled labourers, have been admitted as temporary workers. A case in point is the seasonal agricultural workers' program by which Caribbean workers are admitted to work on farms without being granted landed immigrant status and subsequent citizenship rights. The evidence presented in this chapter also indicates that, contrary to the claims of the Canadian government, the earnings by Caribbean workers mostly have a "consumption effect" rather than producing modernization and economic development in the Caribbean. The admission of these workers under contractual arrangements allows the exploitation of their labour by employers in Canada, without any threat to the Canadian "imagined community."

As noted earlier, capitalist production is primarily for profit and capital accumulation. This and other features of capitalism produce vast economic disparities in capitalist societies that have numerous negative consequences for disadvantaged groups.

Poverty, malnutrition, and hunger are generally thought of as problems of Third World countries. While the significance and concentration of these problems in the Third World cannot be overstated, the advanced capitalist countries have not eliminated them, either. The chapter entitled "Income Inequality, Poverty, and Hunger," by B. Singh Bolaria and Terry Wotherspoon, addresses these issues.

Inequalities of income produce inequalities of life chances—chances for material and social rewards. Poverty translates into homelessness, poor health, low life expectancy, malnutrition, hunger, and other hardships.

Income distribution in Canada—one of the dimensions of inequality—is highly skewed; there has been very little change over the past four decades. The gap between the rich and the poor would be even wider were it not for government transfer payments. Poverty is a persistent phenomenon, affecting disproportionate numbers of certain social groups—women and the elderly, for example. Selected data on the links between income inequality and life chances are discussed in this chapter, with particular emphasis on the emergence and persistence of food banks as a response to hunger. The implications of this private, volunteer-based solution to a structural social problem produced by the contradictions of the capitalist economy are explored in the context of the social welfare restraint being advocated to reduce federal and provincial deficits.

CHAPTER 2

Work and Unemployment as Social Issues

Harley D. Dickinson

Learning Objectives

After studying this chapter, you should be able to
- Understand the relationships between work and unemployment in capitalist societies in general and in Canada in particular.
- Understand how the extension of the division of labour is related to the expansion of both employment and unemployment.
- Understand the origins of labour-saving and productivity-enhancing technologies and their consequences for employment and unemployment.
- Recognize that the nature, duration, and consequences of unemployment vary according to factors such as gender, marital status, and age.
- Understand unemployment as a structural feature of capitalist societies and not just as a personal problem of the unemployed.

Introduction

Unemployment is accepted as an inevitable characteristic of life in modern societies. In this chapter, I argue that unemployment is appropriately understood as a social issue—and not just as a personal problem (Mills, 1959). Unemployment is largely a consequence of contradictions in the nature and organization of employment, or the characteristics of work processes, in modern capitalist societies. Unemployment cannot adequately be understood in terms of the personal characteristics of unemployed individuals. Having said that, however, it must be recognized that the experience of unemployment has profound consequences for individuals.

If we accept the proposition that unemployment cannot be understood in isolation from employment, it follows that the causes and conditions of unemployment are as heterogenous as the terms and conditions of work. That is, the terms and conditions of employment, as well as the duration and extent of unemployment, vary over time by industry and occupation, and by category of worker. Thus, the reporting of official

The Effects of Unemployment on Identity

The various positions one occupies in life form the raw materials from which we construct our personal identities. In this regard, occupation, or the type of work we do, is an important factor. In a study on the effects of unemployment on one's identity, Patrick Burman provides the following insights.

How did informants manage their discreditable stigmas? There was always the risk of chance encounters with acquaintances, or old high school friends, somewhere in the city. One woman found it hard to run into someone she had known from high school. Sooner or later, out came the dreaded question: "What are you doing now?" She had to answer, "Well, I'm ... staying at home." When called upon to announce one's social identity, one was at a loss. That this incoherence directly impacted upon personal identity was evident in this expression by young Terrence:

> *It's very hard for me to tell somebody, 'cause it's not like me.... I feel guilty in a way. I feel bad. Everyone has to do something in this world.*

He not only described the stigma of being unemployed in an affluent city; he also accepted the cultural bias against which the stigma offended, that is, the link between moral injunction to "do something in this world" with employment.

Some coped with the stigma by withholding themselves from the social round. Simon commented:

> *I'm not quite so outgoing. I'm not so interested in meeting old friends because then I have to say, "Well, I'm not working." And then, "Well, why aren't you working?" And then.... There has been that negative aspect in my social life.*

Others concealed the truth by deflecting The Question in some artful way. Another tactic was to lie or shade the truth: for example, to call oneself "self-employed." Dick, a young man, had mostly employed friends, which made him feel like "one of the unfortunate ones." There was something of the performance in his meetings with these friends:

> *They ask me, "Oh well, what are you up to?" I say, "Well, I'm unemployed, but I'm doing this and that." I say, "I do this and that" but I never really get around to it—'cause I got to make it sound good, right? "Oh no, I'm unemployed, so I don't know what I'm going to do now." You know what that's going to sound like.*

He was never sure if they "bought" this: "It's hard to say what they're really thinking."

(continued)

(continued)

Dick and other informants, ejected from the usual round of getting and spending, began to notice something about conversations: they seemed to be either "discourses of shop talk" or "of consuming." Lorne said of his friends: "A lot of them have jobs, you know. It's hard. They'll sit there and talk about their work, and they'll ask you how your work's going. And you'll tell them. And they'll ask you how to get your money. And ... when you say you get your money from Welfare, they really don't think too highly of you." Heather found that her employed friends were not only busy, but were preoccupied with how busy they were. They talked about the things they did and the places they saw. "And they're always chatting about people they're working with.... And I wonder if they're mentioning us to their friends. How she's only staying at home, how she's not working." Having no work to talk about with her friends, "I withdraw from them. I don't say as much. They're going to think I'm boring, so I don't talk to them." A few informants reported friends who will nag at them, "Haven't you got a job yet? Why haven't you found work yet?"—as though urging them to make themselves alive and knowable in the contemporary idiom.

These questions and the "What do you do?" question suggested that "shop talk" was a key way of expressing modern social identities. Gail made a point of taking an interest in her employed friends, listened sympathetically to their job gripes, tried to stay in the flow—even when she could not contribute much. Informants told how much they missed participating in the great outpouring of shop talk. Dorothy, the partially-sighted teacher, suggested that unemployment withdrew the tools a person needed to become articulate within the culture.

> *The whole feeling I had ... that nobody really understood where I was, what I was going through, what I cared about, what was important to me. Because I was no longer talking about my job as a teacher, in fact I wasn't talking about my job as anything. I had a very strong sense of not fitting in.*

Dorothy's analysis took it down to identity: "So much of what we do in our jobs seems to identify us, and sometimes we don't realize how strongly we identify with our occupations. We don't realize that until we don't have one anymore." Constructing identity, then, with little help from society, becomes the unemployed person's burden.

The second prevailing conversation through which social identities were amplified and displayed was the "discourse of consuming." When Matthew had employed friends over, they talked about "the rent they are paying, ... the new cars, the movies, the restaurants they've gone out to. It really bothers me. They can't seem to relate to the fact that.... Where am I going to get enough money to get, you know, eggs, bread, for next week." He has tried to talk to them but "they don't really understand." Heather, who wanted to keep a connection with her employed friends, steeled herself to listen to the excited talk about new purchases, a new home. Having material ambitions herself, she derided the slow progress of her own "consumption career" when compared with that of her friends:

(continued)

(continued)

> *Oh my God, they're going so much ahead of us, and here we are sitting back and ... nothing's changing in my life, compared to theirs.... They're saying "We're doing this and that," and I'll think, "We're not going to be doing that for a while."*

Source: Excerpt from Patrick Burman, *Killing Time, Losing Ground: Experiences of Unemployment* (Toronto: Thompson Educational Publishing, 1988), pp. 111–13.

unemployment rates, which include everybody in the labour force, obscures differences among categories of workers, in various industries, at different times. In this chapter, labour process theory is used to examine some of these differences.

The chapter is divided into four sections. The first provides a general overview of the rise to dominance of the capitalist mode of production. I argue that the specific nature of capitalist class relations creates the circumstances within which unemployment emerges as a major social issue. The second section consists of a brief outline of labour process theory. It shows how the pursuit of employer interests results in unemployment. The third section examines some of the ways in which the transformation of work results in changes to the structure of the economy and the nature of both employment and unemployment. Other consequences of the pursuit of employer interests, such as the growth in part-time work and the reduction in average incomes, especially among certain segments of the population, are also discussed in this section. In the fourth section, I conclude that the solution to unemployment is to be found in the political realm and demands the reorganization of the social relations of work.

The Capitalist Mode of Production and Wage Labour

Dependence on employment income for survival results in unemployment being both a personal problem and a social issue. A central feature of modern capitalist societies is that many people do not have access to alternative sources of livelihood. This state of affairs is relatively recent; the creation of the modern wage-earning class characteristic of all modern capitalist societies is a process that is still going on.

Many, if not most, socially necessary goods and services in capitalist societies are produced for exchange (sale) on various **commodity** markets by people working for wages or salaries. The incomes derived from those wages and salaries are in turn used to purchase goods and services in the marketplace. In order for the capitalist system of production to expand, people must be freed from any social relationships, duties, obligations, commitments, or alternative sources of earning a living, so that they are available, willing, and able to work as part of the wage-earning class. Much social policy is directed toward achieving this end. Under these circumstances, wage earners are dependent upon employers for jobs.

Although it is beyond the scope of this chapter to examine the making of the modern **working class** in Canada, a growing body of literature exists on this topic.

According to Pentland (1981) and others (Kealey 1979; 1980; Palmer 1979; 1980), the later decades of the nineteenth century saw the rise to dominance of industrial capitalism in Canada. This corresponded to the transformation of an increasing proportion of the population into members of the wage-earning class. In 1997 about 13.9 million workers were in the labour force. This represents an increase of over 1.9 million workers since 1981 and the continuation of a long-term trend of growth in the absolute size of the labour force (see Table 2.1 on page 35).

The growth in the labour force and the concomitant process of integration into the working class occurs unevenly. Thus, different categories of people, at different times, are differentially integrated into or excluded from participation in the wage relation. More concretely, this means that different categories of people, such as women, the young, the elderly, and members of ethnic minorities perform different types of jobs under different working conditions, for different levels of pay and with different consequences. One consequence, of course, is a different probability and duration of unemployment.

Labour Process Theory and Unemployment

All societies must solve the problems of producing and distributing wealth. At a more concrete level, this is manifested as the problem of production and distribution of the goods and services required for a socially acceptable standard of living. The different ways of solving these problems give rise to different types of societies and different types of individuals. Capitalist societies are those in which the capitalist mode of production and circulation is dominant. This is not to say that no other modes of production and circulation exist in those societies, but rather that the noncapitalist modes are less significant in terms of the quantity of economic activity accounted for, or the proportion of the population involved.

As mentioned above, one of the identifying features of capitalism is its specific class composition and the nature of its class relations. The necessary classes for capitalism to exist are, of course, the capitalist class and the working class. This does not mean that other classes do not exist. Rather, it means that those other classes are not necessary for capitalism, considered as a mode of production, to exist. The capitalist class and the working class exist only in relation to each other. That is, the capitalist class consists of those members of society who own and control the means of production, and who employ others. The working class consists of those members of society who do not own any means of production and who sell their labour power—their mental and physical capacity to do work—for wages or salaries to those who own the means of production. The **means of production** consist of those things that are necessary for production to take place. This includes plant equipment, machinery, raw materials and everything else, exclusive of **labour power**, that is needed for the production of goods and services.

The relationship between employers and employees consists of mutual, but unequal, dependence: Capitalist employers are dependent on an adequate supply of people who are available, willing, and able to perform the tasks and functions required by the nature and organization of existing labour processes. Members of the working class are dependent on capitalist employers for wage work that will provide them and their dependants with the income needed to purchase goods and services. Within the context of this mutual dependence, the working class is economically, socially, and politically subordinate to the capitalist class. Members of the capitalist class—employers, that is—use their dominant position to secure their own interests and objectives.

The primary objective of capitalist production is to earn profits for business owners. Capitalist employers attempt to increase profits by securing control over labour processes in order to increase worker productivity and decrease the costs of production. Those capitalists who are successful in lowering their costs of production below those of their competitors generally lower the selling price of their goods or services and, thereby, attempt to secure a larger share of the market. One of the contradictions of capitalism is the tendency for free-market competition of this type to lead to market monopolies. Monopolies are notorious for providing consumers with overpriced, low-quality goods and services, unless they are highly regulated. A second consequence of competition-driven attempts to reduce production costs and increase productivity is the transformation of the terms and conditions of work of employees. I will limit discussion to the second point.

Historically the reduction of costs of production has been achieved in absolute or relative terms. **Absolute reductions in the costs of production** are achieved through reductions in real wages. This can be done in at least two ways. First, wage and salary rates can be reduced per time period. Second, workers can be employed for fewer hours. In Canada, and throughout the capitalist world in recent years, both techniques have been tried. The first may result in lower real earnings for individuals, although individual workers may counter this potential by working more hours or working at multiple jobs. The number of multiple job holders, for example, increased from one in forty workers in 1977 to one in twenty in 1993 (Statistics Canada 1998a, 191). This suggests that workers are reacting to unemployment or lower wages by working more.

Relative reductions in the costs of production are achieved by increasing worker productivity so that the cost per unit produced decreases at a rate faster than the costs of production increase. Historically this has been achieved in two ways. The first is the extension of the occupational division of labour and the replacement of high-wage workers with low-wage workers. Thus, the extension of the capitalist division of labour not only reduces the costs of production in absolute terms, it also contributes to decreased costs of production in relative terms, because it results in increased worker productivity. The second way relative reductions in production costs are achieved is through the development and application of productivity-enhancing and labour-saving technologies in the workplace.

These two employer strategies are characterized by certain contradictory consequences. The extension of the occupational division of labour, for example, is generally recognized as contributing to increased worker productivity and reduced costs of production. It also requires expansion of the pool of people who are available, willing, and able to perform employer-defined work tasks. The application of labour-saving technologies, on the other hand, results in a reduction in employment, or an increase in unemployment, at least to the extent that new technology enables fewer workers to produce more in less time. These processes are examined in more detail below.

The Capitalist Division of Labour and Work

The development and extension of the capitalist division of labour results in the need for increased numbers of wage labours. This is because the master principle underlying the development and extension of the capitalist division of labour consists of breaking down any given labour process into its constituent tasks and then assigning each of those separate tasks, or some small combination of those tasks, to individual workers and occupational groups. When Adam Smith described this capitalist process of "dividing labour" in order to show how it results in increased productivity, he chose as his example pin manufacturing.

Smith (1965) showed how pin manufacturing, which in precapitalist societies was undertaken by a single craftsperson performing all the required functions himself or herself, with perhaps a small number of assistants, came to be a labour process characterized by eighteen distinct operations and categories of workers under the capitalist mode of production. Smith argued that the increased productivity that resulted from dividing labour in this way was the result of three "circumstances": first, productivity rises because of the increased facility and speed of operation that results from the repetition of tasks; second, it rises because of the time saved when workers specialize, rather than moving from one type of task to another; and, third, worker productivity increases because of the invention of machinery that enables one worker to do the work of many (that is, because of the development of productivity-enhancing and labour-saving technology and its application in the form of machinery). In fact, only the first two reasons for increased productivity can properly be seen to result from the extension of the occupational division of labour described. I will return to this point.

The development of the capitalist division of labour has consequences other than increased productivity. The division of a work process into its constituent tasks and the assignment of each one to an individual worker has the result of reducing the skill levels required. Reduced skill requirements in turn result in lower wages. Deskilled workers often are less able to find alternative employment because the skills they possess are often industry- or even firm-specific. This results in fewer opportunities for these workers, which in turn results in a deterioration of their bargaining position compared to that of the employer. That is, it is generally easier for employers to recruit relatively unskilled labour than it is for unskilled labour to find alternative employment. Thus, the extension of the capitalist division of labour facilitates reductions in the costs of production in both absolute and relative terms. The reduction of the costs of production in absolute terms, through the extension of the capitalist division of labour, has been referred to as the Babbage Principle (Braverman 1974). The Babbage Principle refers to an observation made by Charles Babbage in 1832. He observed that the list of advantages of the division of labour noted by Adam Smith was incomplete because it failed to include the recognition that subdividing a labour process into its component tasks, each requiring different degrees of skill and strength, enabled employers to employ workers with the minimum skills required to perform the fragmented tasks and, accordingly, to pay them lower wages.

Not surprisingly, workers have resisted the tendency toward the deskilling of work and the devaluation of wages associated with the capitalist extension of the occupational division of labour. Historically this has been one of the major forms of class struggle in capitalist societies. The results of these struggles have been uneven over time; they have varied by country, industry, and occupation. That is, different occupations have been more or less opposed, and more or less successful in their opposition, to various employer attempts to deskill work, disempower workers, and devalue labour power (Dickinson 1991).

Those occupational groups that have been relatively unsuccessful in their resistance to employer initiatives of this type are often faced with relatively poor working conditions, low pay, and high job insecurity. This often translates into more frequent and longer periods of unemployment. Those individual workers and occupational groups that have been more successful in resisting these employer initiatives are able to transform their relative position of strength vis-à-vis the employer into better working conditions, often with higher pay and greater job security. Among other things, this translates into less frequent and shorter periods of unemployment.

Productivity-Enhancing and Labour-Saving Technology

Capitalist employers, under the perpetual pressure of intercapitalist competition and worker resistance, must find ways other than the division of labour to increase worker productivity and reduce the costs of production. The development of new scientific and technical knowledge and its application to the workplace in the form of productivity-enhancing and labour-saving machinery is the other major mechanism for increasing profits. The term *labour-saving* is, in certain respects, misleading. It suggests that new technology has the consequence of making work easier—a common misunderstanding. Of course, in some circumstances, and to a certain degree, this is a correct interpretation. More importantly, however, labour-saving technology is labour-saving from the point of view of the employer, not the employee. From the employer's point of view, technology is labour-saving if and when it enables one worker to produce more in a given time period than he or she could without the technology. This is the third circumstance that Adam Smith claimed led the extension of the division of labour to result in increased productivity. Although the development and implementation of new technology in the form of machinery is related to the development of new divisions of labour, more often than not, technological innovations are developed to replace those well-paid occupations that have been able successfully to resist the breakdown of their skills through organizational and political means. And although it is often claimed that new technology, especially new automatic technology, will enable people to be freed from the dirty, dangerous, and dull jobs of modern industry, usually it is those types of jobs that are not replaced with new technology. This is at least partly because the dirty, dangerous, and dull jobs are the least well paid and can be filled with unskilled domestic, immigrant, or migrant labour, especially during periods of high unemployment.

The Changing Nature of Employment and Unemployment

In aggregate, decisions taken by individual employers in order to increase productivity, reduce costs, and maximize profits contribute to changes in the structural characteristics of the economy. If we look at the Canadian economy in the post–Second World War period we find some interesting developments. We see, for example, a relative and, in recent years, a real decline in the goods-producing sector of the economy and an increase in the services-producing and self-employment sectors of the economy,[1] at least in terms of employment patterns.

As Table 2.1 shows, between 1951 and 1997 the services-producing sector of the economy grew from about 2.5 million workers to about 10.2 million. During the same period, the labour force in the goods-producing sector increased from 2.8 million workers to about 3.8 million. Following the major restructuring of capital that culminated in the recessions of the early 1980s and 1990s, employment in the goods-producing sector decreased in real terms. Thus, by 1997 there were about 29 400 fewer workers employed in the production of goods than there had been in 1981. In contrast, the services-producing sector employed about 2.23 million more workers in 1997 than it had in 1981. If we examine these developments in more detail, we see some interesting trends.

After the recession of the early 1980s, many jobs in the goods-producing sector of the economy were permanently lost to relocation and labour-saving technology in the form of mechanized and automated production processes. Picot and Wannell (1987, 90), reporting the findings of a survey conducted in January 1986, found that of the one million workers who lost full-time jobs and who were not recalled during the 1981 to 1984 period, the largest proportion—36 percent—cited plant closure or relocation as the cause. Plant closure and relocation are most often caused by bankruptcy, technologically based changes to production processes (mechanization or automation), or by the export of capital to low-wage areas. The jobs that were permanently lost during the 1981 to 1984 time period were concentrated in construction and mining, and parts of the manufacturing sector. This finding lends support to the contention that changes to the occupational division of labour and the development of new technology are underlying causes of the permanent job loss experienced in the goods-producing sector of the economy since the early 1980s.

Although Picot and Wannell (1987, 90) show that it was younger workers (aged 20 to 34 years) and workers with less than three years of tenure in their jobs who had the highest incidence of permanent job loss, it was older workers who, following unemployment, had the greatest difficulty finding new jobs. Those workers aged 55 years and over who were permanently laid off, for example, experienced job searches that were longer than average, and had a higher rate of unemployment at the time the survey was conducted. Those who did find jobs took above-average pay cuts. The unemployment rate for all those surveyed, regardless of age, was 25 percent. This was more than twice the rate for the labour force as a whole (1987, 91). For older workers, the unemployment rate was higher yet. Picot and Wannell (1987, 150, Table 13) show that, similarly, of all those workers who were laid off from manufacturing jobs between 1981 and 1984 but who found new manufacturing jobs, the average weekly wage, not accounting for inflation, had decreased by more than 7 percent. Again, for older workers the average cut in wages was even higher.

Table 2.1   Labour Force by Sector, Canada, Selected Years, 1951–1997

	Labour force (000s)				
	1951	**1961**	**1971**	**1981**	**1997**
Total labour force	5 286	6 472	8 627	12 005	13 941
Goods-producing sector	2 806	2 861	3 276	4 063	3 769
Services-producing sector	2 480	3 611	5 351	7 942	10 172

	Percent distribution				
	1951	**1961**	**1971**	**1981**	**1997**
Total labour force	100	100	100	100	100
Goods-producing sector	53.1	44.2	38	33.8	27
Services-producing sector	46.9	55.8	62	66.2	73

Sources: Adapted from W.G. Picot, "The Changing Industrial Mix of Employment, 1951–1985," *Canadian Social Trends*, Cat. no. 11-008 (Spring 1987): 11; *Labour Force Annual Averages, 1981–1988*, Cat. no. 71-529; *Labour Force Annual Averages, 1992*, Cat. no. 71-220; and <http://www.statcan.ca:80/english/Pgdb/People/Labour/labour212.htm>.

As Picot and Wannell have shown, older workers are less likely than younger workers to be laid off permanently, but once laid off they are less likely to find new jobs. This is what one would expect, especially in the goods-producing sector of the economy, which historically has been relatively highly unionized, relatively highly paid, and male dominated. Unionization traditionally has been one way in which workers have organized to pursue their interests in securing higher incomes, better working conditions and benefits, and increased job security. The lower rate of permanent layoff among older workers is possibly a reflection of the relative success of unions in achieving increased job security for their members in the form of collective agreements that contain seniority clauses. In general terms, the relative success of unions in protecting the interests of their members against employer attempts to deskill work and reduce wages has led employers and their political allies to claim that union insistence on seniority rights and wage protection results in "rigidities" that reduce the capacity of firms to respond to changing market conditions and competition. Employer attacks on unions on the economic level, in the form of organizational and technological change, have been accompanied at the political level by changes in labour legislation that effectively limit union rights and powers. These economic and political initiatives have been accompanied at the ideological level by claims that economic prosperity, if not survival, depends upon increased "flexibility" and "adaptability" on the part of workers. Together these terms can be understood, at least in part, as being a code for reduced capacity to resist effectively employer initiatives aimed at increasing worker productivity and reducing the costs of production.

In order to facilitate flexibility among the unionized work force, many older male workers, especially those covered by collective agreements with seniority clauses and receiving relatively high wages, have been offered the choice of taking early retirement or permanent layoff, or being fired. This has resulted in a dramatic decrease in the labour-force participation rate of men between the ages of 54 and 65 years. In 1975 the participation rate of men between those ages was about 76 percent; in 1996 their participation rate was down to 55 percent. This means that in 1996, 45 percent of men aged 55 to 64 years of age were not in the labour force (Lindsay 1987; Statistics Canada 1997a).

This continues a trend commented on by Lindsay (1987). Lindsay shows that between 1975 and 1985, the major reason for men in this age group not to participate in the labour force was early retirement: "the number of men aged 55–64 who were no longer in the labour force, after retiring from their last job, increased almost 200 percent, from 33,000 to 98,000" (1987, 13). During the same period, the increase in the total male population in that age group was only 23 percent. Combining those who chose early retirement with those who were unable to find work after having been permanently laid off or fired from their last job accounts for 40 percent of the increase in unemployment for men in this age group between 1975 and 1985. As Lindsay points out, most of the rest of the increase is accounted for by those who had been out of the labour force for the last five years or who had never been in the labour force (1987, 14). Many, if not most, of those who had not been in the labour force within the last five years, of course, were men who had already taken an early retirement option or else who previously had been laid off and were unable to find new work.

In addition to this trend toward permanent withdrawal from the labour force by categories of people who have traditionally had high participation rates, we see a trend toward increases in the incidence and rate of long-term unemployment. In 1985, for example, those who were unemployed for a year or more made up 10 percent of the total number of unemployed. In 1980 the figure had been 4 percent. The pattern is similar for those unemployed from six to twelve months. In 1985 these people accounted for 17 percent of the unemployed, compared to 13 percent in 1980 (Parliament 1987, 17).

The experience of long-term unemployment, like permanent withdrawal from the labour force, is not evenly distributed among all workers. Older male workers, that is, those over 45 years of age and especially those between the ages of 55 and 64, bear the brunt of the increase in long-term unemployment. In 1985, 46 percent of unemployed men 55 years and older, and just about 40 percent of those aged 45 to 55 years old, were unemployed for six months or more. In addition, in 1985, 21 percent of unemployed men aged 55 years and older, and 20 percent of those between 45 and 54 years, had been unemployed for more than a year (Parliament 1987, 17).

For many of the older, unionized male workers who stayed in the labour force and who remained employed, flexibility and adaptability to organizational and techno-logical change was made more appealing by pay increases. Myles, Picot, and Wannell (1988, 89), for example, show that between 1981 and 1986 there was an upward shift in the wage distribution among workers over the age of 35 years. This upward shift in the wage distribution was greatest for males 50 years and older (see Table 2.2).

On the Road with the Unemployed

Employment must be understood as a social issue; however, it must also be understood as a personal problem. The following excerpt is taken from the first-hand experiences of Alan Mettrick, who, between 1981 and 1983, took to the road with the unemployed in search of work. The resultant book, entitled Last in Line: On the Road and Out of Work ... A Desperate Journey with Canada's Unemployed, *provides a disturbing insight into a world that too many know from personal experience.*

I thought, as I had thought a hundred times before in the past couple of years: Why doesn't somebody do something? Why doesn't the director, or welfare, or somebody, go out and help this 86-year-old man with a hernia find somewhere to live? Why don't they get off their butts and do it? Why don't I?

Instead the problems of individuals seemed to go round and round like birds, always coming back to roost. So many rules and regulations, so many departments and budgets, and nobody to show an 86-year-old man with a hernia to a room where he could live in peace.

The thoughts, probably naïve, are recorded as they came, and demonstrate my increased anger and agitation as my exposure to the havoc around me increased. What began as a fairly objective odyssey had embittered me, as the recession was embittering so many others.

A group was marching the length of the island to protest unemployment. Meanwhile, hundreds lined up for hours outside the Victoria employment centre because they had heard they could apply for jobs at a new company—only to have their hopes dashed when the company doors opened. They were only taking names and addresses today, and that job application forms could be mailed out. There would be no interviews. There had been no need to queue. There were, as yet, no jobs. Oops, sorry folks, just another little gaffe.

Back in 1932, in "The Experiences of a Depression Hobo," an anonymous writer said: "My spirit is by no means broken, I just feel angry, and the more Canada kicks me the more I'll retaliate ...

"Until such time as I get a decent job I intend to live well, dress respectably, eat all that's good for me, keep myself clean and have clean clothes. Canada will pay for this. I will obtain what I need by bumming and other comparatively honest methods. If my ways and means should fail, I shall resort to thieving and other criminal ways ..."

In the spring of 1983 I walked the waterfront through the night with a homeless transient who told me he had already robbed one bank during the recession and was planning to rob another.

"I want to work," he said. "I don't like stealing. But I'll take it any way I can. I'm not going to be a bum."

In the dawn we saw men going to work on the fishing boats, getting the boats in shape for the season. Working for nothing, in the hopes of landing a deckhand job.

One way or another, the survival instinct showed itself, as it had not done since the thirties.

(continued)

(continued)

To eat was the prime concern, and Victoria churches had rallied to aid the unemployed in a far more vigorous way than their counterparts in Vancouver. In the mornings there was bread and soup in the basement of St. Andrews Cathedral. They called it the 9–10 Club. Three nights a week there was a soup line at another downtown church. This was in addition to the Upper Room (where I had once eaten Christmas dinner with the Frenchman, Jean), the Mustard Seed street church, which now ran a food bank, and the St. Vincent de Paul Society, which was also giving away bags of groceries.

Every soup kitchen was full every day, and the volunteers who staffed them did a sensitive job. No religion was forced on the jobless here—only food. Nothing was moving out of the once-busy labour pool. The men spoke of weeks between temporary jobs. After I finished on the daffodil farm I sat in the pool every morning for a week. It was now housed in a much smaller building. I started off with priority number 38 and barely moved. After a week I just gave up. Many others did so, too. The better weather was coming. People were talking about riding freights.

Source: Excerpt from Alan Mettrick, *Last in Line: On the Road and Out of Work ... A Desperate Journey with Canada's Unemployed* (Toronto: Key Porter Books, 1985), pp. 198–99.

Thus, increasingly throughout the 1980s we saw fewer older male workers actually working, but those that were employed were making more money on average. This pattern continued through to 1995 with average annual earnings for men over 50 years of age increasing by 6 percent. For women workers over the age of 45, the increase in average annual income between the late 1970s and 1995 was about 25 percent (Picot 1997, 74).

TABLE 2.2   Percentage Change in Relative Mean Wage, by Age Group and Region, 1981–1986

	Atlantic Provinces	Quebec	Ontario	Manitoba and Saskatchewan	Alberta	British Columbia
16–24 years	−13.7	−12.1	−19.2	−14.4	−23.4	−15.9
25–34 years	−8.5	−4.6	−6.9	−4.5	−3.9	−7.8
35–49 years	5.4	3.7	4.5	0.9	6.5	4.7
50–64 years	6.3	−1.0	10.0	8.7	7.6	6.4

Source: Adapted from J. Myles, G. Picot, and T. Wannell, "The Changing Wage Distribution of Jobs, 1981–1986," *The Labour Force*, Cat. no. 71-001 (October 1988): 111.

The situation is the opposite with regard to younger workers. Those between the ages of 16 and 34 years of age experienced a downward shift in wage distributions over the same period, with the youngest workers experiencing the most dramatic decline.

It is not unexpected that reduced hourly wages and earnings for younger workers correspond to significant declines in the percentage of unionized workers in the younger age groups between 1981 and 1986. In the manufacturing sector, the percentage of unionized jobs held by younger workers dropped to 28 percent in 1986 from 35 percent in 1981. In resource-based industries the drop was from 52 percent to 30 percent, in construction the drop was from 26 to 15 percent, and in social services it was from 49 to 40 percent (Myles, Picot, and Wannell 1988, 126).

This pattern held through to 1995. Between 1989 and 1995, for example, average annual earnings for those between the ages of 25 and 34 years decreased by 10 percent. Average annual earnings for young women during that time period remained constant (Picot 1997, 74).

A closer look at patterns within the manufacturing sector reveals some other trends. Table 2.3 shows that the restructuring of capital, which culminated in the recession of the early 1980s, resulted in a decline of about 200 000 workers in the total full-time male manufacturing labour force between 1981 and 1983. Although the number of male full-time workers in manufacturing fluctuated throughout the rest of the 1980s, since the beginning of the 1990s numbers have dropped quite markedly, so that in 1992 there were about 72 000 fewer full-time male workers in the manufacturing sector than there had been in 1983, the worst year of the recession. By 1996, this trend had reversed and there were 1.6 million men working in the manufacturing sector, 67 000 more than were working in 1983, but still 30 000 fewer than had been working in 1981.

Full-time employment of female workers in manufacturing shows similar patterns. For female full-time workers in the manufacturing sector, 1982 was the worst year. Despite gains since then, the number of females in full-time manufacturing jobs in 1992 was 15 000 fewer than it had been in 1982. By 1996, these losses had been regained, but there were still 4000 fewer women working full-time in manufacturing than there had been in 1981.

If we look at the part-time labour force in manufacturing, we see that for both males and females it increased in size between 1981 and 1996, with some fluctuation. Combined with the slight shift in the gender composition and the age composition of the manufacturing labour force, this increase in the use of part-time workers seems to support the conclusion that less expensive workers are being employed to replace more expensive, older, unionized workers. Although many of the postrecession workers are doing the "same" jobs as the prerecession workers, they are doing them for less money, and under conditions of decreased job security. That is, postrecession workers are more "flexible" and "adaptable" than prerecession workers.

The major trends in the goods-producing sector described above strongly suggest that various employer attempts to increase worker productivity and reduce the cost of production have resulted in decreased wages, and increased frequency and duration of unemployment for certain categories of workers. Although the growth in the services-producing sector of the economy is characterized by similar processes of productivity enhancement and cost reduction, different categories of workers are affected.

TABLE 2.3 Estimates of Manufacturing Labour Force, Annual Averages, Canada, 1981–1996 (000s)

| | Manufacturing labour force | | | Employment | | | | | | | | | | Unemployment | | | | | |
| | | | | Total employment | | | Full-time employment | | | Part-time employment | | | Total unemployment | | | Unemployment rate (%) | | |
	Total	Male	Female	Total	Male	Female	Total	Male	Female	Total	Male	Female	Total	Male	Female	Total	Male	Female
1981	2305	1633	642	2124	1 552	571	2052	1523	529	72	29	42	181	110	71	7.90	6.60	11.00
1982	2225	1603	622	1928	1 404	523	1856	1377	479	72	28	44	298	199	99	13.40	12.40	15.90
1983	2159	1536	622	1879	1 347	532	1807	1319	488	72	28	44	280	189	91	13.00	12.30	14.60
1984	2195	1557	638	1954	1 403	551	1886	1374	512	68	29	39	241	154	87	11.00	9.90	13.60
1985	2180	1554	626	1960	1 416	544	1887	1387	500	73	29	44	220	138	82	10.10	8.90	13.10
1986	2180	1537	643	1989	1 417	572	1917	1390	526	72	27	45	192	120	72	8.80	7.80	11.10
1987	2202	1552	650	2018	1 442	576	1946	1411	535	72	31	42	184	111	74	8.40	7.10	11.30
1988	2271	1603	669	2104	12 504	600	2026	1472	554	78	32	46	168	99	68	7.40	6.20	10.20
1989	2294	1536	674	2141	1 525	609	2043	1483	559	84	34	49	170	103	65	7.60	7.20	8.10
1990	2198	1547	651	2001	1 425	576	1932	1396	535	69	29	40	197	122	75	9.00	7.90	11.50
1991	2122	1497	625	1865	1 331	534	1793	1302	491	72	29	43	257	166	92	12.10	11.10	14.60
1992	2046	1448	598	1788	1 276	512	1710	1247	464	78	30	48	258	172	86	12.60	11.90	14.40
1996	2244	1603	638	2082	1 495	587	1975	1442	532	194	48	55	159	108	51	7.10	6.70	8.00

Sources: Adapted from *Labour Force Annual Averages, 1981–1988*, Cat. no. 71-529, Table 10; *The Labour Force, 1989*, Cat. no. 71-001, Vol. 45, Nos. 1–12; and *Labour Force Annual Averages, 1990, 1991, 1992, 1996*, Cat. no. 71-529.

The Growth of the Services-Producing Sector

The growth of employment in the services-producing sector of the economy is large-ly the result of the creation of new industries, or the greatly expanded scope of oper-ation of already existing industries that are providing new services in new ways to new consumers. The creation of new industries or the expansion of already existing industries, of course, requires a pool of people who are available, willing, and able to perform the new employer-defined work tasks. To a large extent, the creation and expansion of the services-producing sector has relied upon the recruitment of youth working part-time and women aged 25 and older to the labour force (Statistics Canada 1992, A-2).

As one would expect, the labour-force participation rate for separated and divorced women, especially between the ages of 25 and 44, is quite high. One effect of the liberalization of divorce law in 1968 was an increased divorce rate. The crude divorce rate per 100 000 persons in Canada in 1966 was 51.2; this increased to 54.8 in 1968, to 139.8 in 1970, to over 200 in 1974, and it continued a steady rise until 1982 when it peaked at 285.9. Although since then there has been a decline in the crude divorce rate, the total number of separated and divorced women who are employed has continued to rise throughout the 1980s and 1990s.

If we turn our attention to labour-force participation of married women, we see that it has been rising steadily throughout most of this century, and particularly since the Second World War. Between 1921 and 1941, for example, the labour-force par-ticipation rate for married women rose from 2.16 to 3.74 percent. By 1951 it had increased to 11.2 percent (Skoulas 1974, 9). It has continued to increase, with slight fluctuation, into the 1990s. In 1996 the labour-force participation rate for married women was 61.6 percent (Statistics Canada 1997a). It seems clear that since the Second World War in particular, conditions that make it desirable or necessary for married women to enter the waged labour force have become increasingly prevalent (Li 1996).

Knowledge about the factors that encourage or discourage labour-force participa-tion among various categories of people is crucial for policy-makers concerned with economic and social planning. On the basis of his research, Skoulas (1974, 87–89) described a number of factors that affected the labour-force participation of married women. He found that, among other things, lower family income (excluding the wife's) increased the wife's labour-force participation, as did an unemployed hus-band. The strength of this last relationship, he pointed out, "depends on the duration of husband's unemployment, his weekly earnings, and the 'normal' level of family income excluding wife's earnings" (1974, 87). As we have seen, lower earnings and insecure conditions of employment have been created in recent years as a result of employer initiatives facilitated by government policy. Increased labour-force partici-pation by married women is one way families have attempted to offset the downward trend in individual wages and incomes. Increases in the number of working family members, combined with smaller families, have contributed to rising family income simultaneously with declining mean wages for individuals in certain age groups.

The growth in the services-producing sector of the economy, increased female labour-force participation, and the expansion of part-time work are all related.

Lévesque (1987) examined the growth of part-time work in Canada between 1975 and 1986. Over that period, part-time employment as a proportion of full-time employment rose by 7.76 percent, from 10.6 to 18.36 percent of the labour force. By 1996, with some slight variation, it had increased to 23.4 percent (see Table 2.4). On the basis of his study, however, Lévesque (1987) found that only 20 percent of the growth in part-time employment could be explained by the changing structure of the economy—the growth of employment in the services-producing sector and the relative decline in the growth of employment in the goods-producing sector. Eighty percent of the growth in part-time employment was accounted for by changes occurring within industries. That is, all industries, whether goods-producing or services-producing, are relying more on part-time workers now than in the past.

As we have seen, the growth of part-time employment is at least partly a result of employer attempts to reduce the costs of production. The growth of part-time work can be understood as a logical extension of the Babbage Principle. The Babbage Principle recognizes that reductions in the costs of production are realized as a consequence of the capitalist division of labour because the fragmentation of work processes into their constituent tasks and their allocation to different workers or occupational groups enables employers to hire workers who possess only those skills and abilities required to perform a certain aspect of the entire work process; this reduces overall wage costs. Thus, the development and extension of the capitalist division of labour is partly an attempt by employers to ensure that they are paying for only the minimum amount of skill required to perform certain aspects of a divided labour process. Similarly, the division of the working day, week, month, or year into component parts helps employers ensure that they are paying wages to workers to perform tasks for only the minimum amount of time required for their completion. The growth of part-time work helps employers ensure that when an employee cannot be kept busy on a continuous basis performing specified tasks, he or she is let go to be recalled when, and if, enough work is available. Thus, the logic underpinning the development and extension of the capitalist division of labour is that labour processes are broken down into component tasks that are doled out to individual workers on a piecemeal basis, and that working time is increasingly being partitioned into periods of employment interspersed with frequent periods of unemployment, depending on the needs of employers.

The reduction in the costs of production associated with the shift toward part-time work by employers is facilitated by government policy. Under current laws employers are not required to make compulsory contributions for part-time workers—or at least not at the full-time rate—to supplementary income plans such as health and welfare schemes, pension plans, workers' compensation, and unemployment insurance funds. As we have seen, wages and incomes have declined in recent years under the pressure of employer cost-reduction initiatives. The cost of labour to employers, however, is not restricted to wages and salaries. The contributions mentioned above represent supplementary labour costs. If we divide labour-related employer costs into the two components—wages and salaries, on the one hand, and supplementary labour costs, on the other hand—we see some interesting trends. Wong (1988) examines these two aspects of labour income in Canada for the years between 1975 and 1987.

The wages and salaries component of labour income accounts for just over 90 percent of labour income. Wong (1988, 97) shows that between 1975 and 1977, real

Table 2.4 Full-Time and Part-Time Employment by Sex and Age, Canada, Selected Years (000s)

	Both sexes				Males			Females		
	Total	Full-time	Part-time	Part-time as proportioin of full-time employment	Full-time	Part-time	Male part-time as proportion of male full-time employment	Full-time	Part-time	Female part-time as proportion of female full-time employment
1981										
Canada	11 001	9 515	1 486	0.1561	6 144	413	0.0672	3 372	1 074	0.3185
15–24 years	2 667	2 015	652	0.3235	1 118	298	0.2665	897	354	0.3946
25–44 years	5 318	4 828	490	0.1014	3 142	42	0.0133	1 686	448	0.2657
45+ years	3 016	2 672	344	0.1287	1 883	73	0.0387	788	272	0.3451
1984										
Canada	10 932	9 263	1 668	0.1801	5 826	482	0.0827	3 438	1 187	0.3453
15–24 years	2 341	1 624	717	0.4415	883	324	0.3669	741	393	0.5304
25–44 years	5 628	5 052	576	0.111	3 151	73	0.0232	1 901	503	0.2646
45+ years	2 963	2 588	375	0.1449	1 792	85	0.0474	796	290	0.3643
1986										
Canada	11 531	9 742	1 789	0.1836	6 053	514	0.0849	3 689	1 274	0.3453
15–24 years	2 367	1 604	762	0.475	875	343	0.392	730	419	0.5739
25–44 years	6 132	5 491	640	0.1165	3 362	81	0.024	2 130	559	0.2624
45+ years	3 033	2 647	386	0.1458	1 816	90	0.0495	830	297	0.3578
1990										
Canada	12 572	10 640	1 932	0.182	6 387	561	0.088	4 253	1 371	0.322
15–24 years	2 254	1 459	795	0.545	800	365	0.546	660	429	0.65
25–44 years	6 934	6 239	695	0.111	3 669	93	0.025	2 570	602	0.234
45+ years	3 383	2 942	442	0.15	1 918	103	0.054	1 024	339	0.331

(continued)

Table 2.4 *(continued)*

	Both sexes				Males			Females		
	Total	Full-time	Part-time	Part-time as proportion of full-time employment	Full-time	Part-time	Male part-time as proportion of male full-time employment	Full-time	Part-time	Female part-time as proportion of female full-time employment
1992										
Canada	12 240	10 182	2 058	0.202	6 954	618	0.089	4 128	1 440	0.349
15–24 years	1 989	1 166	823	0.701	634	379	0.56	533	444	0.833
25–44 years	6 750	5 988	762	0.127	3 498	122	0.035	2 490	639	0.257
45+ years	3 501	3 028	473	0.156	1 923	117	0.061	1 106	356	0.322
1996										
Canada	13 676	11 087	2 589	0.2335	6 678	801	0.1199	4 409	1 788	0.4055
15–24 years	2 040	1 110	929	0.8369	646	406	0.6285	464	523	1.1272
25–44 years	7 496	6 495	1 001	0.1541	3 833	206	0.0537	2 662	794	0.2983
45+ years	4 141	3 481	659	0.1893	2 199	188	0.0855	1 282	471	0.3674

Note: Full-time employment consists of persons who usually work 30 hours or more per week, plus those who usually work fewer than 30 hours but consider themselves to be employed full-time (e.g., airline pilots); part-time employment consists of all other persons who usually work fewer than 30 hours per week.
Sources: Adapted from *Labour Force Annual Averages, 1981–1988*, Cat. no. 71-529; *Labour Force Annual Averages, 1989–1994*, Cat. no. 71-529; *Labour Force Annual Averages, 1992*, Cat. no. 71-220; and *Labour Force Annual Averages, 1996*, Cat. no. 71-220.

wages and salaries grew by 5.6 percent. In 1978 they began a downward trend, which, by 1987, amounted to a 6.2 percent real decline. This decline in average labour income would have been more precipitous had it not been for a real increase of 32.7 percent in supplementary incomes from 1975 to 1987. Wong (1988, 92) points out that some components of supplementary labour income are universal and some are not. Fewer than 40 percent of all paid workers in Canada, for example, were covered by private pension plans and health and welfare benefits, which, nevertheless, accounted for about 60 percent of supplementary labour income. Canada and Quebec pension plans, unemployment insurance, and workers' compensation plans, however, are universal. One can see that employers would have an interest in employing a smaller proportion of workers for whom they had to make payments into various supplementary income plans relative to those workers for whom they did not have to make such payments. The 40 percent of workers covered by private pensions and benefits roughly corresponds to the proportion of the labour force that is unionized. From this perspective one can see that part-time workers are doubly attractive insofar as they are usually not unionized and, under current laws, even when it comes to universal labour-income plans, employers are not required to make contributions on their behalf, at least not at the same level as for full-time workers. When this is combined with the fact that part-time wage rates are generally lower than full-time rates, one would expect, all things being equal, that the trend toward increased reliance on part-time workers will continue.

It is important to point out that although most of the increase in part-time employment is voluntary—that is, the workers involved choose to work part-time for reasons of their own—the proportion of involuntary part-time workers is substantial. In 1975, 11 percent of part-time workers reported they were working part-time only because full-time employment was unavailable. This reached a high of just over 30 percent in 1984, falling to about 24 percent in 1988 and rising again to about 30 percent in 1997 (Akyeampong 1987; Statistics Canada 1997a; 1998b).

With regard to unemployment among part-time workers, Clemenson (1987, 32) found that between 1980 and 1986 the unemployment rate for males was 14.6 percent, while for females it was 10.6 percent. This is the opposite of male and female experiences of unemployment in the full-time labour force, where the unemployment rate for males was 10.2 percent and for females it was 13.6 percent for the same years.

The Growth of Self-Employment

As we have seen above, the nature of the Canadian economy has been changing for the past several decades. The growth in the service sector over the course of this century has resulted in a dramatic alteration in the industrial structure of the Canadian economy and consequently in the types and conditions of employment available. In 1911, for example, two-thirds of employment in Canada was in the goods-producing sector of the economy, most of which involved agriculture. By 1996, less than one-quarter of Canadian employment was in this sector and two-thirds was in the services-producing sector (Statistics Canada 1997b).

In addition to this structural shift from a predominantly goods-producing to a predominantly services-producing economy, the level of self-employment has risen. The number of the self-employed, both incorporated and unincorporated, has increased from 1 048 000 in 1976 to 2 266 600 in 1996 (Statistics Canada 1997b). The self-employed accounted for about 17 percent of the labour force in 1996 (Statistics Canada 1998a).

In 1989, about 45 percent of the self-employed were also employers. Over the 1990s this fell, and by 1996 only about 37 percent of the self-employed hired workers (Statistics Canada 1997b). This is significant because of the fact that in recent years "the vast majority of employment gains have been attributed to small businesses," which are generally operated by self-employed working owners (Statistics Canada 1988, 5). Current patterns of corporate and government "downsizing" support the widespread contention that it is small and medium-sized business that will generate the increased employment opportunities of the foreseeable future. Thus, there appears to be a contradiction between the rhetoric and the reality of small business and employment.

Any economic or labour-market policy that intends to deal with the problems of economic growth and unemployment by expanding self-employment and small and mid-sized business should be sensitive to the numerous forces at work contributing to the failure of many such enterprises. The number of business bankruptcies provides an indication of this; between 1978 and 1996, for example, the number of business bankruptcies increased from 5546 to 12 200 (Consumer and Corporate Affairs Canada 1978; Industry Canada 1998).

These figures suggest that the growth of self-employment and the number of small and mid-sized employers may not be a panacea for the problems of unemployment and slow economic growth. To the extent that these solutions reproduce the contradictions of capitalist economic practices that have been discussed above, they can at least be short-term, incomplete answers.

Conclusions

Given the changing structure of the economy and an increasingly rapid rate of organizational and technological change resulting from intensified intercapitalist competition, unemployment is likely to become a normal experience for workers. Policy-makers and planners throughout the capitalist world have been preparing us for this for some time. The culturally normal pattern of schooling, work, and retirement, we are told, is, or is soon to be, an anachronism. Workers of the future—and for many the future is now—are not to expect to pursue a lifelong career. Workers are to expect a series of jobs interspersed with periods of unemployment, during which they are to undertake to retrain themselves so as to acquire the skills required by employers. The ideology of "learning for life" is an attempt to sell this new vision of working life to people (National Advisory Panel 1984). In reality, retraining does not affect the re-employment rate for the unemployed and constitutes a significant expense (Picot and Wannell 1987). Retraining may also require individuals and their families to relocate, given that most institution-based vocational and skills-training programs are concentrated in particular areas.

Unemployment is a permanent and growing feature of societies where the capitalist mode of production is dominant. Although we have seen that the form and experience of employment and unemployment differ at various times and places for different categories of people, we can be assured that for many, if not for most, unemployment will be a part of the future. The solution to the problem of unemployment resides in the political realm, and will require a transformation of the interests underpinning economic decision making and resource mobilization and allocation.

Summary

- This chapter examined work and unemployment as social issues.
- Using labour process theory, it was shown that the nature and organization of work in capitalist societies produces tendencies towards both expanded employment and unemployment.
- Data were presented that showed how the changing nature of employment and unemployment affects different categories of people.
- It was concluded that the solution to the problems of unemployment resides in the realm of social and economic policy.

Questions to Consider

1. What effect does labour-force participation of married women with children have on family size? What effect will this have on future recruitment to the labour force?

2. If unemployment results from the class interests of employers, what is the solution, if any, to the problem?

3. What is the relationship between decreasing labour incomes and unemployment?

4. What are the obstacles to the unemployed organizing to pursue their collective interests?

5. Are the employed and the unemployed political allies or adversaries? Why?

Suggested Readings

Braverman, Harry. *Labor and Monopoly Capital: The Degradation of Work in the Twentieth Century.* New York: Monthly Review Press, 1974.

Burman, Patrick. *Killing Time, Losing Ground: Experiences of Unemployment.* Toronto: Thompson Educational Publishing, 1988.

Li, Peter S. *The Making of Post-war Canada.* Toronto: Oxford University Press, 1996.

Wong, Fred. "Trends in Labour Income." In *The Labour Force, September 1988*. Ottawa: Statistics Canada. 87–116.

Glossary

absolute reductions in the costs of production The technique used by employers to reduce the costs associated with the production of commodities. Absolute reductions generally involve lowering workers' wages, which constitutes the majority of the costs of production. This takes the form of involuntary rollbacks and negotiated concessions.

commodities Goods and services produced for exchange (sale) on the market, rather than for immediate consumption by producers.

labour power A person's physical and mental capacity to perform work.

means of production Everything that is necessary for contemporary commodity production to take place. It includes plants, equipment, machinery, technology, and raw materials. Increasingly, it is being argued that the means of production also includes information or knowledge.

relative reductions in the costs of production The technique used by employers to increase the amount produced in a given time period by increasing worker productivity, thereby decreasing the cost per unit produced. This is often accomplished through extension of the occupational division of labour and/or the development and application of labour-saving technology.

working class Within capitalist societies, the working class consists of those individuals who must sell their labour power for wages or salaries to employers who own and control the means of production.

Notes

1. For analytical purposes the economy is often divided into two sectors: the goods-producing sector and the services-producing sector. The services-producing sector is often subdivided into commercial and non-commercial (largely government) services. Commercial services, the largest sector of the economy, are further subdivided into three parts: distributive, producer, and consumer services. Below is a list of the industries contained within each sector.

   Goods-producing sector: agriculture, manufacturing, construction, mining, oil and gas extraction, utilities, forestry, fishing

   Services-producing sector:
   1. Commercial services:
      a. Distributive services: transportation and storage, communication, wholesale and retail trade
      b. Consumer services: accommodation and food services, personal services, amusement and recreational services, other miscellaneous services
      c. Producer services: services for business management (for example, accounting, engineering, and legal and management consulting), finance, insurance, estate
   2. Non-commercial services: education, health and welfare, religious organizations, public administration (government)

   These definitions and classifications are taken from W. Garnett Picot, "The Changing Industrial Mix of Employment, 1951–1985," *Canadian Social Trends* (Statistics Canada) (Spring, 1987): 8.

References

Akyeampong, E.B. 1987. "Involuntary Part-Time Employment in Canada, 1956–1986." *Canadian Social Trends* (Statistics Canada) (Autumn): 26–29.

Braverman, H. 1974. *Labor and Monopoly Capital: The Degradation of Work in the Twentieth Century.* New York: Monthly Review Press.

Clemenson, H.A. 1987. "Unemployment Rates for the Full-Time and Part-Time Labour Forces." *Canadian Social Trends* (Statistics Canada) (Autumn): 30–33.

Consumer and Corporate Affairs Canada. 1978. *Annual Statistical Summary for the 1978 Calendar Year.*

———. 1991. *Annual Statistical Summary for the 1991 Calendar Year.*

Dickinson, H.D. 1991. "The Three Ds of Vocational Training: Deskilling, Disempowerment and Devaluation." In *Hitting the Books: The Politics of Educational Retrenchment*, ed. T. Wotherspoon. Toronto and Saskatoon: Garamond Press and Social Research Unit, Department of Sociology. 101–18.

Industry Canada. 1998. *Annual Statistical Summary for the 1997 Calendar Year.* Office of the Superintendent of Bankruptcies.

Kealey, G.S. 1979. "H.C. Pentland and Working Class Studies." *Canadian Journal of Political and Social Theory* (Spring/Summer).

———. 1980. *Toronto Workers Respond to Industrial Capitalism, 1867–1892.* Toronto: University of Toronto Press.

Lévesque, J.-M. 1987. "The Growth of Part-Time Work in a Changing Industrial Environment." *The Labour Force, May 1987.* Ottawa: Statistics Canada/Supply and Services Canada. 87–107.

Li, Peter S. 1996. *The Making of Post-war Canada.* Toronto: Oxford University Press.

Lindsay, C. 1987. "The Decline in Employment among Men Aged 55–64; 1975–1985." *Canadian Social Trends* (Statistics Canada) (Spring): 12–15.

Mills, C. 1959. *The Sociological Imagination.* London: Oxford University Press.

Myles, J., G. Picot, and T. Wannell. 1988. "The Changing Wage Distribution of Jobs, 1981–1986." *The Labour Force* (October). Ottawa: Statistics Canada/Supply and Services Canada. 85–138.

National Advisory Panel on Skill Development. 1984. *Learning for Life: Overcoming the Separation of Work and Learning.* Ottawa: Supply and Services Canada.

Palmer, B. 1979. *A Culture in Conflict: Skilled Workers and Industrial Capitalism in Hamilton, Ontario, 1860–1914.* Montreal and Kingston: McGill-Queen's University Press.

———. 1980. "Working-Class Canada: Recent Historical Writing." *Queen's Quarterly*, 87.

Parliament, J.-A. 1987. "Increases in Long-Term Unemployment." *Canadian Social Trends* (Statistics Canada) (Spring): 16–19.

Pentland, H. 1981. *Labour and Capital in Canada: 1650–1860.* Toronto: James Lorimer and Company.

Picot, W.G. 1987. "The Changing Industrial Mix of Employment, 1951–1985." *Canadian Social Trends* (Statistics Canada) (Spring): 8–11.

———. 1997. "What Is Happening to Earnings Inequalities in Canada in the 1990s?" *Canadian Business Economics.* Vol. 6, No. 1 (Fall 1997): 65–107.

Picot, W.G., and T. Wannell. 1987. "Job Loss and Labour Market Adjustment in the Canadian Economy: Findings from a Special Survey." *The Labour Force* (March). Ottawa: Statistics Canada/Supply and Services Canada. 85–150.

Skoulas, N. 1974. *Determinants of the Participation Rate of Married Women in the Canadian Labour Force: An Econometric Analysis.* Ottawa: Statistics Canada/Industry, Trade and Commerce.

Smith, A. 1965. *The Wealth of Nations.* New York: Random House.

Statistics Canada. 1984a. *Women in the Work World.* Ottawa: Supply and Services Canada.

———. 1984b. *Changes in Income in Canada, 1970–1980.* Ottawa: Supply and Services Canada.

———. 1984c. *Labour Force Annual Averages, 1975–1983.* Ottawa: Supply and Services Canada.

———. 1987. *Income Distribution by Size in Canada. 1986.* Ottawa: Supply and Services Canada.

———. 1988. *Enterprising Canadians: The Self-employed in Canada.* Ottawa: Supply and Services Canada.

———. 1989a. *Labour Force Annual Averages 1981–1988.* Ottawa: Supply and Services Canada.

———. 1989b. *The Labour Force, 1989.* Vol. 45, Nos. 1–12. Ottawa: Supply and Services Canada.

———. 1990. *Women in Canada: A Statistical Report.* 2d ed. Ottawa: Minister of Supply and Services.

———. 1991. *Labour Force Annual Averages, 1990.* Ottawa: Supply and Services Canada.

———. 1992. *Labour Force Annual Averages, 1991.* Ottawa: Supply and Services Canada.

————. 1993. *Labour Force Annual Averages, 1992*. Ottawa: Supply and Services Canada.

————. 1997a. *Labour Force Annual Averages, 1996*. Ottawa: Minister of Industry.

————. 1997b. "The Self Employed." *Labour Force Update*. Vol. 1, No. 3 (Autumn). Ottawa: Minister of Industry.

————. 1998a. *Canada Year Book, 1997*. Ottawa: Minister of Industry.

————. 1998b. "An Overview of the 1997 Labour Market." *Labour Force Update*. Vol. 2, No. 1 (Winter). Ottawa: Minister of Industry.

————. <http://www.statcan.ca:80/english/Pgdb/People/Labour/labour212.htm>.

Wong, F. 1988. "Trends in Labour Income." *The Labour Force* (September). Ottawa: Statistics Canada/Supply and Services Canada. 87–116.

CHAPTER 3

Capital Accumulation and State Formation: The Contradictions of International Migration

Vic Satzewich

Learning Objectives

After studying this chapter, you should be able to
- Outline the contradictory forces that have influenced the direction and content of immigration policies in Canada.
- Understand the links between the process of migration and the capitalist mode of production.
- Understand the important demographic trends in the country, and the potential that immigration has to counteract such trends.
- Understand the role that migration plays in the socio-economic development of developing countries.

Introduction

> It is the very qualities (real or imagined) that make certain groups particularly suitable for their role as workers that make them unsuitable for membership in the receiving society. Shared by all classes and strata in the receiving society, these integrative concerns, whether expressed in manifestly xenophobic ideologies or by way of euphemistic codes, universally impinge upon the determination of immigration policy. The conflicting interests of industrial societies—to maximize the labour supply and to protect cultural integrity—can be thought of as a dilemma to which a limited number of solutions are possible. (Zolberg 1981, 15)

The spatial relocation of labour across international boundaries has been a fundamental aspect of capitalist development since the Industrial Revolution. The forms of migration have varied. They range from the forced migrations associated with indentured servitude, slavery, and contract labour to the comparatively "free" migrations of wage labourers, capitalists, and highly skilled professionals. But, despite differences in form, there is an important link between capitalism and migration (Sassen-Koob 1981).

This chapter argues that migration flows are structured by a dialectic of economic, political, and ideological relations. These relations are by no means complementary or consistent with one another; indeed, in many cases contradictions exist between the various forces that shape systems of immigration control. Three sets of issues associated with the process of **international migration** to Canada are identified. First, this chapter suggests, in light of Zolberg's comment on the previous page, that there is a contradiction between migration as an aspect of **capital accumulation** and migration as an aspect of **state formation**. It demonstrates that migration control in Canada results from the interaction of these two processes. Second, it suggests a political and ideological limit to the degree to which the state can use immigration to solve demographic, fiscal, and accumulation problems associated with the aging of Canada's population. Third, it examines whether migration contributes to economic development in sending countries—those countries where migrants originate—or whether it is but a new form of postcolonial exploitation.

Migration, Accumulation, and State Formation

People migrate mainly, but not exclusively, because of economic reasons. As such, the process of migration is structured by the dynamics of the supply of and demand for labour. These dynamics are rooted in the process of capital accumulation and the formation and reproduction of **relative surplus populations** (Wood 1982).

As part of the broader process of the origin and development of capitalist relations of production, the process of capital accumulation contributes to the formation of relative surplus populations. Relative surplus populations consist of people whose labour power is not required within a particular national economy, and as such they are either unemployed or irregularly employed. Such populations play an important role in capitalist economies because these people are available for sudden increases in the demand for labour and hence ensure that employers never run short of labour. Surplus populations serve to keep wages low by broadening the pool of potential workers that employers can hire during upturns in the economy. Additionally, a pool of unemployed workers has the potential to take jobs away from already employed workers, hence acting as a disciplinary force over the working class.

Migration is both a cause and consequence of the process of capital accumulation (Wood 1982). Capital accumulation initially propels, or forces, certain groups of people to join the relative surplus population and to migrate because of its associated economic dislocations. The penetration of capitalist social relations into agricultural regions of the world economy displaces workers from the production process. Marx (1967 [1867], 640–43) refers to this as the formation of a latent surplus population.

The process of capital accumulation also induces migration for those who work in industrial sectors of production already characterized by the presence of capitalist relations of production. Workers are replaced by machines through technological innovations such as the computerization of the workplace or the mechanization of jobs that were previously done by hand. With the restructuring associated with accumulation, workers are displaced from the production process. Marx refers to these people as the floating surplus population.

Capital accumulation is also a stimulus to migration in that it creates the conditions that give rise to labour demand. While, as noted above, the process of capital accumulation can throw people out of the production process, it can display a counteracting tendency to increase the demand for labour. This can occur, for example, when the amount of surplus value invested in new machinery or a new plant is sufficiently great, or when the process of investment deskills the work force and replaces relatively expensive skilled labour with relatively cheap unskilled labour (Miles 1986). Thus, to the extent that migration replenishes the reserve army of labour, migration contributes to the process of capital accumulation by increasing the supply of potential workers and by reducing pressures for wage increases when the demand for workers increases.

Thus, the process of accumulation can help explain the formation of labour pools, the broad structural pressures that force people into migrating, and the reasons states sanction and help organize the importation of foreign-born labour. But a more specific account is necessary. A singular focus on the process of accumulation cannot explain why particular groups of workers are allowed to cross the boundaries of the state to sell their labour power for wages, how they are incorporated into sites in production relations, and why they end up in the jobs they do (Thomas 1985, 12). It is therefore necessary to recognize that migration is also an aspect of nation-state formation.

The world is today divided into states. One of the prerogatives of modern states is their ability to control their borders and determine who can cross the physical and symbolic boundaries of the state. Given a shortage of labour and the existence of a globally dispersed relative surplus population, why are certain groups of people allowed to cross the national boundary to sell their labour power for wages, and others not? Such considerations, I suggest, are based on assessments of whether members of certain other nations can eventually become part of the community of the receiving state. The criteria used to define particular nations are fundamental aspects of the process of migration control.

Thus, assessments of potential migrants are based not only on their expected capacity to expend labour power, but also on whether they can become part of the nation's imagined community. It is these assessments over and above those associated with the capacity to labour that constitute the fundamental contradiction of immigration control. Some groups who may be good workers may not be defined as good potential citizens.

This means that immigration control is subject to a set of contradictory pressures and processes. The remainder of this chapter examines how immigration controls have responded to these contradictory pressures.

Immigration Control in Canada

As a settler capitalist state, Canada has seen migration play an important role in the initial formation of capitalist relations of production (see Pentland 1981; Denoon 1983; Ehrensaft and Armstrong 1981). In the initial absence of a class of free wage labour, migration, along with natural population growth, contributed to the formation of a pool of labour that employers could draw upon (Pentland 1959).

Since the establishment of capitalist relations of production in Canada around the middle of the nineteenth century (Pentland 1981; Palmer 1984), migration has continued to play an important role in the economic and social development of the country, especially in terms of the growth in the labour force and the reproduction of the active and reserve armies of labour. Migration to Canada has been broadly linked to the business cycle (although the correlation is not perfect): it has been structured by employers' demands for labour power to fuel the process of accumulation (Avery 1979, 37). Immigration levels were comparatively low during the 1930s, which was a period of recession. Conversely, during periods of economic expansion (1898–1916 and 1947–73) immigration levels tended to be comparatively high. The statistical dimensions of migration to Canada since Confederation are given in Table 3.1.

The contribution of **net migration** to labour-force growth is given in Table 3.2. The figures in this table demonstrate that during the first decade of the twentieth century, the excess of immigration over emigration contributed to 62.3 percent of the growth in the Canadian labour force. The contribution of net immigration to labour-force growth has declined since then, but is still substantial. Between 1951 and 1961,

TABLE 3.1 Immigration to Canada, by Ten-Year Intervals, 1867–1994

Year	Number of immigrants
1867–1876	273 556
1877–1886	682 104
1887–1896	539 207
1897–1906	907 719
1907–1916	2 227 245
1917–1926	996 011
1927–1936	693 367
1937–1946	193 314
1947–1956	1 315 457
1957–1966	1 311 587
1967–1976	1 699 975
1977–1986	1 066 637
1987–1994[a]	1 683 565

[a] Figure is for eight years only.
Source: Reproduced from "Immigration Statistics" and from "Historical Statistics of Canada," published by Citizenship and Immigration Canada. Reproduced with the permission of the Minister of Public Works and Government Services Canada, 1998.

net migration contributed to 39.5 percent of the growth of the labour force, and between 1966 and 1986, 23 percent of the growth in the labour force was due to net migration (Beaujot 1992, 55).

Despite large-scale migration to the country since Confederation and the important contributions that net migration has made to the growth in the labour force, migration has not been solely a spontaneous reaction to labour demand. Since Confederation, immigration controls have also been shaped by pressures associated with the formation and maintenance of a nation-state. It was expected and hoped that people who migrated to Canada would settle permanently. Permanent settlers were sought because they would contribute to the process of accumulation via the settlement of land and the expansion of the domestic market for consumer commodities. But they were also to be participants in the bourgeois democratic political process. In other words, immigrants were also to become *citizens* of a nation-state. Not all peoples of the world were defined as capable of becoming citizens of such a nation; accordingly, immigration control has been structured by this concern.

These concerns have taken a number of forms. Sears (1990), in his study of early-twentieth-century medical inspection in Canada, suggests that medical inspections of potential immigrants made use of a broad conception of health that encompassed the physical, mental, and moral well-being of the individual. Medical inspections were seen to be a crucial means by which the "interests of the nation" were to be furthered.

Similarly, Whitaker (1987) has documented the political biases that underlay the selection of postwar refugees and the granting of citizenship. In an insightful analysis of postwar immigration controls, he argues that the political selection of immigrants to the country was premised on the perceived existence of an external enemy.

TABLE 3.2 Immigration and the Growth of the Labour Force, 1901–1961

Decade	Total labour force increase		Domestic supply component of increase		Contribution of net migration	
	Number (000s)	%	Number (000s)	%	Number (000s)	%
1901–11	910	100.0	343	37.7	567	62.3
1911–21	503	100.0	440	87.5	63	12.5
1921–31	736	100.0	694	94.3	42	5.7
1931–41	604	100.0	693	114.7	−89	−14.7[a]
1941–51	598	100.0	557	93.1	41	6.9
1951–61	1386	100.0	838	60.5	548	39.5

[a] Net migration was negative during this decade. Net migration therefore contributed to a 14.7 percent decline in the labour force.

Source: Reproduced from "Immigration Statistics" and from "Historical Statistics of Canada," published by Citizenship and Immigration Canada. Reproduced with the permission of the Minister of Public Works and Government Services Canada, 1998.

This enemy was defined primarily in terms of "communism." Immigration controls were structured by the desire to keep external enemies external—in other words, to prevent the formation in Canada of an enemy within. Again, the perceived existence of an enemy within was defined as a threat to the ability of Canada as a nation-state to reproduce itself.

These bases of immigration control and selection also reflected the dual nature of immigration. Even though medical selection was structured by the desire to have a healthy and productive work force that would be able to provide employers with labour power when it was required, political, racial, and medical selection were also linked to the reproduction of the nation-state as a whole. Thus, selective immigration controls have also been directed at those who have been deemed unable to participate as members of civil and political society. Simply put, sick or politically active left-leaning immigrants were seen as neither good workers nor good citizens.

In spite of the anguish displayed by Canadian literati over the apparent absence of a truly Canadian identity, the history of immigration control in Canada suggests that the imagined community that constituted the Canadian nation has been defined, at least in part, in terms of race. Immigration restrictions suggest that the Canadian nation was conceived by its ruling groups as not only a capitalist country, but also a "white country." Racist immigration controls have been based on the assumption that certain groups of people, because of their "race" and "culture," are unable to partici-pate in Canadian economic, political, and social processes.

The contradiction between migration as an aspect of capital accumulation and migration as an aspect of state formation was especially sharp in British Columbia. During the latter part of the nineteenth century, it was recognized that shortages of labour hindered the process of capitalist economic development in the province. One of the ways to promote such development was to foster the immigration of large amounts of cheap labour. But British Columbia (and Canada, more generally) was also regarded as an outpost of the British Empire. This meant that what was required in the province was not just labour, but certain types of labour: labour that would also take on the rights and duties of citizenship.

Immigration, Race, and the Canadian State

Whether South Asians, in particular women, have come to Canada or not, when they came and what socio-economic grouping came, are all determined by the immigration policy as developed by the needs in the economy, specifically the needs of a capitalist system. Immigration statistics clearly show that the immi-gration flow has been turned on and off depending on the specific need for cheap labour, whether it was for building of railways or for logging in earlier years, or for factory and farm labour in postwar years.

Racism as an ideology which subordinates a people on the basis of skin colour, ethnicity or religion proved to be very effective in maximizing the capi-talist drive for profits. Economically speaking, racism rationalizes the super-

(continued)

(continued)

exploitation of South Asian men and women by perpetuating dangerous working conditions and inhuman labour processes. Racist ideology includes the labelling of such labourers as "unskilled," "uneducated," or "inferior" and therefore "cheap." On the other hand, politically, racism encourages the reproduction of a dual labour market, based on a division between white, male, "skilled," unionized workers and female, "unskilled," unorganized workers of colour who can be exploited at different rates. This kept the working class divided and disempowered to challenge the common exploiters. Racist hostility reproduces the silence and intimidation of workers who fear being fired or deported, the latter threat being enforced through immigration and refugee policies.

The Canadian state has been an interventionist one since historically it has taken part in the process of capital accumulation and profit-making by ensuring a steady stream of immigrants, through its immigration and refugee policies. Also, it has played its coercive function through these same policies in the form of deportation clauses, exclusionary measures, the denial of family reunification and the imposition of head taxes (as in the case of Chinese immigrants) and the use of police and military forces.

The state's ideological role by imposing control through consensus, by the preservation of hegemony is also worth noting.… It is noteworthy that the government was able to practice covert racism, such as implementing the "continuous journey" stipulation, voting rights and excluding women, all due to popular racist sentiments among white Canadians in general. These actions provided a ready climate in which to deny basic human rights to South Asian men and women immigrants.

Gender and State

Gender relations are also socially organized in the South Asian community, particularly in the early years. The exclusion of female immigrants from South Asia meant that South Asian families in Canada were destined to be "bachelor," male-oriented families. Racism is implied here as well, since the exclusion of females ensured the non-permanence of the immigrant communities from South Asian countries. They were the predecessors to the guest-workers in Europe today.

In the post-1967 period, the points system reinforced the male-dominated, nuclear-family form. Females could come primarily as "sponsored" immigrants and therefore as "legally dependent" immigrants, since their second-class status in the home countries prevented their qualification as "independents" in most cases. Their past status continues after immigration. This reinforces patriarchal family norms and practices within South Asian families, with certain cultural peculiarities (e.g., the significances of age hierarchies). In contradiction, the family was also a safe haven in the settlement period, an oasis in the stressful journey towards survival. Even though the family as an institution has been less than egalitarian to most South Asian women, the principle of family reunification has been one of the most important political demands from the comm... ty, predominantly voiced by men.

Source: Tania Das Gupta, "Political Economy of Gender, Race an... South Asian Women in Canada," *Canadian Ethnic Studies* 26 (19...

This sense of the contradictory nature of immigration was evident in the 1885 report of the Royal Commission on Chinese Immigration to Canada (xxvii). One of the commissioners rather eloquently described the nature of this contradiction in the following terms:

> A government cannot look at a citizen of a free country as a mere tool in the hands of capital. The jade is much more docile than the charger, and each is useful in its place. A country is not developed merely by work. The character and habits of the workers are of importance, as well as the incidents attaching to the labour.

This same theme was echoed in the 1902 report of the Royal Commission to Investigate Chinese and Japanese Immigration (277–78):

> If the end to be sought is building up the nation, and not the exploitation of these resources, the vital interest to be secured above all others is an immigration of settlers of whom we may hope to make good Canadians, in the best sense of the word. That this object ought to be the one in view is supported by the recent public utterance of a very distinguished personage when he said: "No one who has the privilege which we have had during our tour could fail to be struck with one all-prevailing and pressing demand—the want of population. Even in the oldest of our colonies were abundant signs of this need—boundless tracts of country yet to be explored, hidden mineral wealth calling for development, vast expanses of virgin soil ready to yield profitable crops to the settler; and these can be enjoyed under conditions of healthy living, liberal laws, free institutions, in exchange for the overcrowded cities and the almost hopeless struggle for existence which, also, too often is the lot of many in the old country. I would go further and appeal to my fellow countrymen at home to prove the strength of the attachment of the motherland to her children by sending them only the best. By this means we may still further strengthen, or at all events pass on unimpaired, that pride of race, that unity of sentiment and purpose, that feeling of common loyalty and obligation which, knit together, alone can maintain the integrity of our Empire."

This dual theme associated with immigration control is also evident in the postwar period. Mackenzie King, in his now well-known statement in the House of Commons in 1947, suggested that while the immigration program should be structured by the interests of "the national economy," it should also select those who would be desirable "future citizens" (Rawlyk 1962, 289).

The 1952 Immigration Act concretized these criteria. Under the terms of the act, the minister of Citizenship and Immigration was given the power to limit or prohibit the entry of immigrants for any of the following reasons:

nationality, citizenship, ethnic group, occupation, class, or geographical area of ... in;

customs, habits, modes of life, or methods of holding property;

3. unsuitability, having regard to the climatic, economic, social, industrial, educational, labour, health, or other conditions, or requirements existing in Canada, temporarily or otherwise;
4. probable inability to become readily assimilated or to assume the duties and responsibilities of Canadian citizenship within a reasonable time after admission (Rawlyk 1962, 292–93).

These twin concerns resulted in a highly skewed flow of people to the country. Very generally, people defined as "non-white," which included people from Asia, Africa, and the Caribbean, were defined as unsuitable as permanent citizens and thus restricted from entering the country. As the minister of Citizenship and Immigration noted in 1952:

> in light of experience it would be unrealistic to say that immigrants who have spent the greater part of their life in tropical countries become readily adapted to the Canadian mode of life, which to no small extent, is determined by climatic conditions. It is a matter of record that natives of such countries are more apt to break down in health than immigrants from countries where the climate is more akin to that of Canada. It is equally true that, generally speaking, persons from tropical countries or subtropical countries find it more difficult to succeed in the highly competitive Canadian economy. (Satzewich 1988b, 225)

Table 3.3 demonstrates that, between 1950 and 1955, 94.3 percent of immigrant arrivals were from Europe and the United States, while 3.2 percent of immigrant arrivals originated in Africa and Asia. Between 1956 and 1961, 92.5 percent of immigrant arrivals were from Europe and the United States, and 3.7 percent were from Asia and Africa (see Bolaria and Li 1988, for a more detailed history of racist immigration controls in Canada).

Since 1962, there has been a formal **deracialization** of immigration control in the country. Explicitly racist immigration controls became increasingly embarrassing for government officials who wanted to see Canada become a legitimate actor on the world stage. Also, there was a shift in labour-force requirements. The numbers of highly skilled workers that were in demand in Canada were unavailable in traditional "white" source countries, and Canada was forced to broaden recruitment to "non-white" countries in order to fill this demand (Hawkins 1974, 146). This has resulted in an increased flow of immigrants from non-traditional source countries. Between 1962 and 1967, 9.4 percent of total immigrant arrivals originated in Africa and Asia, whereas the European and American contribution decreased to 83.9 percent. Between 1968 and 1973, 65.1 percent of all immigrant arrivals came from Europe and the United States, while 20.1 percent came from Asia and Africa. By the 1980s, the European and American contribution dropped to 28.5 percent, whereas the Asian and African contribution increased to 54.2 percent of the total flow of immigrants to the country. Table 3.4 puts this issue in slightly different perspective. It shows that nearly 40 percent of all immigrants who lived in Canada in 1991 came from the United Kingdom, Italy, United States, Poland, and Germany; however, of immigrants who arrived in Canada between 1981 and 1991, nearly 30 percent came from Hong Kong, the People's Republic of China, India, Vietnam, and the Philippines.

TABLE 3.3   Distribution of Immigrants, by Source Area, 1950–1991

Area	1950–55	1956–61	1962–67	1968–73	1974–79	1980–85	1986–91
Africa	0.4%	1.0%	2.2%	3.3%	4.9%	3.7%	6.0%
Asia	2.8	2.7	7.2	16.8	28.6	42.7	48.2
Europe	88.0	84.8	73.5	49.9	36.3	30.2	24.2
North and Central America (except United States)	0.7	1.0	2.8	8.4	10.4	9.1	10.9
United States	6.3	7.7	10.4	15.2	11.1	7.8	4.3
South America	0.8	1.3	1.6	3.6	6.3	4.8	5.3
Other	1.0	1.5	2.3	2.8	2.4	1.6	1.2
Total[a]	100.0	100.0	100.0	100.0	100.0	99.9	100.1

[a] Percentage may not sum to 100 because of rounding.

Source: Reproduced from "Immigration Statistics" and from "Historical Statistics of Canada," published by Citizenship and Immigration Canada. Reproduced with the permission of the Minister of Public Works and Government Services Canada, 1998.

Even though the category of "race" is no longer a formal criteria of immigration control in Canada, and even though there are increasing numbers of immigrant arrivals from outside of Europe, questions remain regarding the informal influence that racism has on the process of immigration control. Simmons (1998) argues that Canadian immigration policy and selection is neither explicitly racist nor anti-racist; instead, he argues that the immigration policy field has within it the space for the expression of **neo-racism** to influence who gets into Canada. Proposed changes to Canada's immigration policy, which would see a greater emphasis on the selection of immigrants on the basis of their ability to speak either English or French, are, for example, interpreted by some as a way that the government is trying to cloak racial selectivity under the facade of more politically acceptable criteria. The impact that racism continues to play in shaping the process whereby immigrants are selected to come to Canada needs to be assessed more fully.

Aging, Immigration, and Racism

For the next several decades, Canada will be facing two demographic processes that are expected to have implications for future immigration levels. First, Canada's fertility rate is declining. The total fertility rate that is currently required for population replacement in the country is 2.1 children per woman. However, the actual total fertility rates of Canadian women have been steadily declining, and at present are below the replacement rate. It is projected that they will continue below this level in the future. The total fertility rate in Canada declined from 3.9 in 1956 to 1.7 in 1983

TABLE 3.4   Top Ten Countries of Birth for All Immigrants and Recent Immigrants, Canada, 1991

All immigrants			Recent immigrants[a]		
Country of birth	Number	%	Country of birth	Number	%
1. United Kingdom	717 745	16.5	1. Hong Kong	96 540	7.8
2. Italy	351 620	8.1	2. Poland	77 455	6.3
3. United States	249 080	5.7	3. People's Republic of China	75 840	6.1
4. Poland	184 695	4.3	4. India	73 105	5.9
5. Germany	180 525	4.2	5. United Kingdom	71 365	5.8
6. India	173 670	4.0	6. Vietnam	69 520	5.6
7. Portugal	161 180	3.7	7. Philippines	64 290	5.2
8. People's Republic of China	157 405	3.6	8. United States	55 415	4.5
9. Hong Kong	152 455	3.5	9. Portugal	35 440	2.9
10. Netherlands	129 615	3.0	10. Lebanon	34 065	2.8
Total	4 342 890	100.0	Total	1 238 455	100.0

[a] Immigrants who came to Canada between 1981 and 1991.

Sources: Jane Badets and Tina Chui, *Canada's Changing Immigrant Population* (Toronto: Prentice Hall Canada, 1996). Reprinted with permission of Prentice Hall Canada Inc.; Statistics Canada, *Canada's Changing Immigrant Population,* Cat. no. 96-311E, p. 14.

(Hersak and Francolini 1987, 3). If present trends continue, and net migration stands at zero, the population of Canada will begin to decline by the early twenty-first century.

The second demographic process is the aging of Canada's population. Again, if current trends continue, there will be relatively fewer people of working age to support relatively greater numbers of retired people. Projections indicate that the proportion of the total population of the country 65 years and older is expected to increase from 8.7 percent in 1976 to 20.2 percent in 2031.

These two demographic processes are expected to have serious social and economic consequences in Canada. It is anticipated that employers will face an accumulation crisis to the extent that sources of labour from within Canada will decline and result in upward pressures on wages. It is additionally expected that this will put more strain on the welfare state and accentuate the fiscal crisis. The tax base of the population is expected to decline, but state expenditures on the elderly are projected to increase (Myles and Boyd 1982).

One of the ways to get around the potential social and accumulation problems associated with **population aging** and declining fertility is to expand Canada's immigration program, especially if it is focussed on the recruitment of young workers (Foot 1986; Hersak and Francolini 1987). In 1991, the overall dependency ratio (the number of children and elderly per 100 population of those economically active) for immigrants was 29.8 compared with 52.9 for those born in Canada (Badets and Chui

1996, 35). In allowing the entry of more immigrants, it is possible to enlarge the tax base and the pool of workers that employers in Canada can draw on.

Projections suggest that in order for migration to offset the effects of declining fertility and the aging of the population, immigrant intakes will have to expand well beyond current levels and even beyond the high levels of the 1950s. During the postwar economic boom in Canada, which peaked between 1950 and 1962, immigration levels averaged about 147 000 per year. One estimate suggests that if the total fertility rate remains at 1.7 children per woman and if emigration is 75 000 per year, by the year 2000, as many as 275 000 immigrants would have to be admitted to Canada per year in order to achieve a population growth rate of 1 percent. If the total fertility rate drops to 1.4, again assuming an emigration flow of 75 000 people, the number of immigrants required for a 1-percent rate of population growth would be 325 000 per year by the year 2000 (Romaniuc 1988, 94–95).

The central issue here is whether these immigration levels can be achieved, given the historical legacy of racism in Canada and a lingering sense on the part of some Canadians that non-European immigrants are a potentially problematic population. The traditional source countries of America and Western Europe are drying up as pools of immigrants. Rising standards of living mean that Europeans are less willing to move to sell their labour power for wages. Contrary to still-popular myths, Canada is no longer defined by Europeans as the land of opportunity.

In order to achieve immigrant intake levels of over 200 000 per year, policy-makers and immigration analysts recognize that, increasingly, recourse will have to be made to non-traditional source countries: that is, Asia, Africa, the Caribbean, and Central America (Foot 1986, 16–17). The dilemma is that there continues to be hostility on the part of at least some Canadians to "non-white" immigration, and a continued imagining of the Canadian nation in terms of the "white race."

A study of Canadian attitudes toward minority ethno-cultural groups undertaken in the mid-1970s brings forth evidence that "race" is an issue in people's social acceptance or rejection of groups of people (Berry, Kalin, and Taylor 1977, 245). Attitudes toward minorities and their acceptance or rejection form a continuum based upon perception of their degree of "racial" differences. More recently, a 1989 Gallup poll indicated that 54 percent of Canadians believed that racial intolerance had increased over the past five years. This was a marked increase over the findings of a 1982 study done by Gallup, which suggested that only 42 percent of the Canadian public believed that racial intolerance was increasing. Furthermore, the same 1989 poll indicated that 27 percent of Canadians experienced some type of discrimination, and of that total, approximately one-quarter of respondents who reported that they were the victims of discrimination were the victims of racial discrimination (Gallup Poll 1989).

As the 1993 federal election campaign demonstrated, some right-wing politicians were caught in a contradiction when it came to their views on immigration. As representatives of corporate interests, they saw immigration as an essential source of labour, and, in the case of business immigrants, capital. However, some were unable to resist playing the "race" card in order to win votes. They tapped into some people's anxieties about the future of Canada as a "white country" by problematizing what are seen as excessive levels of immigration in recent years. In that election, the Reform Party's (and others') concern over immigration was arguably a euphemism for objection to

Notes from the Front

There is no doubt that being on the frontline in the immigration business affects one's view of the human panorama. The first time I realized the full gravity of this situation was in a case involving the deportation of a young man from India, who broke down in front of me and begged me not to send him back to New Delhi. He was dripping with fear. He was so distraught that he went limp and collapsed.

I was stunned and dumbfounded by his response. The first thing I surmised was that New Delhi must be some kind of hell-hole to elicit this type of reaction. At one point the young man, who was being detained in Toronto's Don Jail on an immigration hold, pleaded with me to leave him in "The Don"—as if, as an alternative to the plane ride, I, or other immigration authorities, could just leave him in jail for the rest of his life and save the price of the ticket back to India for the Canadian taxpayers. This young man would rather have spent the rest of his life in a Canadian jail than live in New Delhi.

The fact that he preferred the Don Jail was really astounding. As an immigration officer, I had been to a number of jails—Toronto East and West Detention Centres, Mimico, even Collins Bay. Compared to the Don Jail, the others are almost vacation resorts. Prisoners in the Don are crammed in, stacked up and dispirited. They have to compete with rats and cockroaches for sleeping space. The place is a health hazard. In 1990, the place was so jam packed, and presented such a high security risk, that the guards went on strike. This is the place that the young man from New Delhi was willing to spend the rest of his life.

Only later did it occur to me that it's probably not that New Delhi is so bad, but rather that, for this young man, Canada is the promised land. Outside the walls of the Don Jail lies his paradise, his forbidden fruit. Inside the Don Jail, in the exercise court, he could at least smell the sweet fragrance of Canada. In the Don Jail he could at least dream about window shopping on Yonge Street, and maybe stopping at an outdoor cafe for a hot creamy cappucino or a cold beer. In the Don Jail, he could almost taste the heavenly fruit of Canada. But in New Delhi the dream becomes a pipedream—indistinct, amorphous and ephemeral; the promised land becomes a wasteland and a no-man's land.

Imagine Canada as the promised land. It is sometimes difficult for those who have been born and bred in this country to understand that for many "outlanders" Canada is like a heaven on earth. It is a place in which one can choose to stand or lie or sit. We complain about useless politicians, traumatizing taxes, the lack of an identity and the seemingly endless search for a viable federalism. Outsiders, on the other hand, see something akin to the garden of Eden. Viewed from the outside Canada epitomizes possibility, a prolific and golden place untainted by old poisons. For the clamouring horde, this is more than mere metaphor. The world still has more mud huts than two-bedroom condos. And sticks and rocks serve the "mud tribes" as major home appliances. Clearly, outsiders often don't see anything to complain about, and they would give anything to join one of the "electric tribes."

Source: Lorne Foster, *Turnstile Immigration: Multiculturalism, Social Order and Social Justice in Canada* (Toronto: Thompson Educational Publishing, 1998), pp. 24–25.

non-European immigration to Canada. To put the matter in the terms of John Oostrom, a Tory MP who sat on the House of Commons Immigration Committee in 1987, Canadians "are telling the Commons immigration committee ... that if there have to be immigrants, they should be trained immigrants from Europe." Mr. Oostrom is also reported to have defended this with the claim "that's not racism ... rather, Canadians are merely seeking people who can adjust to this climate" (*Globe and Mail,* March 6, 1987).

Recent governments have displayed an ambiguous attitude toward the issue of racism. Some have argued that the 1973 Liberal government's emphasis on the "novel and distinctive features" of the recently arriving non-white immigrants, stated in its Green Paper on Immigration, provided the opportunity for Canadians to articulate, within a legitimate public forum, anti-immigrant and racist diatribes (Bolaria and Li 1988, 175). Because it was the beginning of what was to become a long recessionary period in the country, this may have been intended to prepare the way for the reintroduction of racist immigration controls.

Since that time, various governments and the Canada Employment and Immigration Commission appear to be aware of the potential of racism to hinder the process of accumulation in the future by restricting the flow of immigrants to the country. Indeed, the Canadian government conducts regular polls to try to tap the nature and extent of hostility expressed toward immigration to this country. Part of their strategy seems to be focussed on efforts to convince Canadians that immigrants make "positive contributions" to the country. The 1987 *Annual Report to Parliament on Future Immigration Levels*, for example, contains an entire section on the benefits of immigration for Canada. The benefits cited range from positive effects on employment through increased domestic markets, increased consumption, and the resolution of labour-market bottlenecks, to more general notions of improved "openness" of Canadian society and improving the cultural diversity of the nation. Immigration also apparently enhances Canadian political and economic links with other regions of the world economy (Employment and Immigration Canada 1987, 28–34).

The government also appears to be in the process of establishing institutional structures to mediate the expected increase in racial hostility that will likely accompany the increase of "non-white" immigrants. Within the federal government, greater political priority is being given to matters of "race relations." For a brief time in the early 1990s, multiculturalism was elevated from the status of a directorate to the status of a full government department with representation at cabinet level. This priority is also evident in the formation of a "race relations" section within the multiculturalism directorate and the passage into law of the Canadian Multiculturalism Act in July 1988. While these are laudable initiatives that may represent important gains for visible minority workers in Canada, they are motivated not so much out of a concern for the well-being of immigrants and their families but rather out of the potentially negative economic impact that uncontrolled racism will have on the Canadian economy.

Thus, the crucial dilemma that policy-makers face is the extent to which they are going to pander to the racist concerns of an increasingly vocal minority of Canadians. Will the economic and social contradictions associated with aging and declining fertility not be resolved because of racism?

Economic Development or Postcolonial Exploitation?

Despite attempts to convince Canadians of the benefits of immigration and Canada's apparent interest in enlarging the flow of permanent settlers to the country, the government continues to allow the entry of workers to the country on a seasonal, contractual basis—as **migrant labour**.

Table 3.5 provides information on the number of immigrants admitted to Canada who are destined to the labour force, and the number of employment authorizations issued to temporary workers. Employment authorizations provide non-residents of Canada the right to employment in Canada, usually in a specific job for a specific period of time. Employment authorizations are multifaceted in nature (Boyd, Taylor, and Delaney 1986) and are required for those who are only temporary additions to the labour force—foreign university students who wish to take up part-time employment while undertaking their studies in Canada, and visiting professors who come to give paid lectures or teach occasional courses at universities. Authorizations are also required for migrant farm workers (to be discussed in more detail below) and domestic servants, two categories of workers that are now permanently part of the labour force. The advantage of admitting temporary workers to fill specific kinds of jobs is that when those jobs end, the workers must leave the country.

Table 3.5 indicates that during the relatively good economic times of the mid- to late 1980s, the Canadian government admitted between three and four times more migrant than immigrant workers to the country. Since then, the ratio of migrant to immigrant workers admitted has decreased. Nevertheless, in 1990, over 200 000 employment authorizations were issued to foreign workers for employment in Canada.

One of the most significant groups of foreign workers admitted to Canada on a temporary basis are workers from the Caribbean and Mexico who work in fruit and vegetable production in southern Ontario and in the sugar beet industry in southern Manitoba and Alberta. The statistical dimensions of this migration are given in Table 3.6. While this type of migration had relatively modest beginnings in 1966, when only 264 Caribbean workers were admitted, this migration stream has grown to the point that, in 1991, over 12 000 migrant workers were admitted to Canada on a seasonal-contractual basis. The volume of the flow of this category of migrant worker has increased over the years despite downturns in the Canadian economy.

Since the end of the Second World War, Ontario farmers' organizations and representatives of a number of Caribbean governments have pressured Canadian government officials to allow importation of workers from the Caribbean on a seasonal, migrant-labour basis. The historical origins of this migration are documented elsewhere (Satzewich 1988b), but evidence suggests that Canadian officials resisted such a proposal for nearly twenty years. Between 1947 and 1965, government officials did not allow Ontario farmers the opportunity to exploit the labour power of Caribbean workers, in part because of the belief that they would cause a "race relations" problem in this country. Canadian officials were especially concerned about the admittance of "black workers" from the Commonwealth, because "once they were here, and [because they] are members of the Commonwealth [they] would apply to remain

TABLE 3.5 Immigrant and Non-immigrant Workers Admitted to Canada, 1973–1991

Year	Immigrant workers[a]	Non-immigrant workers	Non-immigrants as a % of immigrants
1973	92 228	83 912	91.0
1974	106 083	86 183	81.2
1975	81 189	96 045	118.3
1976	61 461	91 103	148.2
1977	47 625	89 120	187.1
1978	35 080	63 320	180.5
1979	47 939	94 420	197.0
1980	63 403	108 871	171.7
1981	56 978	126 583	222.2
1982	55 482	125 901	227.0
1983	37 119	130 717	352.2
1984	38 500	143 979	374.0
1985	38 453	177 165	460.7
1986	48 200	205 747	426.9
1987	76 712	231 576	301.9
1988	76 350	196 678	257.6
1989	98 227	187 989	191.4
1990	114 091	191 810	168.1
1991	131 580	202 410	153.8

[a] Consists of those destined for the labour force.

Sources: **1973–1984**: Employment and Immigration Canada, *Immigration Statistics, 1984* (Ottawa: Minister of Supply and Services, 1985), pp. 53, 87; **1985**: Employment and Immigration Canada, *Immigration Statistics, 1985* (Ottawa: Minister of Supply and Services, 1986), pp. 54, 73; **1986**: Employment and Immigration Canada, *Immigration Statistics, 1986* (Ottawa: Minister of Supply and Services, 1987), pp. 66, 80; **1987–1991**: Canada Employment and Immigration Commission, *Immigration Statistics, 1985–91* (Ottawa: Minister of Supply and Services, 1992).

permanently and pressurize [sic] us to that end." This is consistent with the assessment of the government's resistance to this proposal expressed in the *Financial Times* of London (England). In a 1965 article, it was suggested that

> the colour problem appears to be one of the main worries of the Ottawa government.... Since the Jamaicans are British subjects, they could make life difficult if they decided to stay in Canada once the harvest was over in the autumn. The government could expect a full scale row in the House of Commons if it were forced to explain why it has ejected a group of Her Majesty's subjects. (Satzewich 1988a, 278)

TABLE 3.6   Caribbean and Mexican Seasonal Labour Arrivals in Canada, 1966–1993

Year	Seasonal agricultural worker arrivals
1966	264
1967	1 077
1968	1 258
1969	1 449
1970	1 279
1971	1 271
1972	1 531
1973	3 048
1974	5 537
1975	5 966
1976	5 455
1977	4 929
1978	4 984
1979	4 968
1980	6 001
1981	5 798
1982	5 510
1983	4 564
1984	4 502
1985	5 005
1986	5 166
1987	6 337
1988	8 539
1989	12 237
1990	12 510
1991	12 131
1992	11 115
1993	11 212

Note: Figures for 1966–73 include Caribbean worker arrivals only. Figures for 1974–93 include both Caribbean and Mexican seasonal workers.
Source: "Worker Arrivals by Country and Year," Human Resources Investment Branch, Human Resources Development Canada, 1998.

The Canadian state's position on this matter reflects, in a larger sense, its historically ambiguous commitment to the Commonwealth, especially as it applies to non-European migration.

Temporary migration was eventually sanctioned by government officials in 1966 because of conditions in the labour market. But it was also an attempt to stem the flow of non-European permanent settlers to the country, which had begun as a result of the deracialization of immigration control in 1962 (Satzewich 1988a).

In an effort to convince his cabinet colleagues that workers from the Caribbean should be let in on a temporary basis for the Ontario harvest, and at the same time deflect potential criticisms that such a program was simply a way that Canadian farmers could acquire "cheap labour," the minister of Citizenship and Immigration presented it as part of the government's package of development aid in the Caribbean. According to the memorandum to cabinet on the matter, submitted by the minister of Citizenship and Immigration, "the bringing in of labour from this source would fit in with the Government's general program of aid and cooperation with the West Indies" (Satzewich 1988a, 280).

If we accept for the moment what appears to have been a rather flimsy justification, to what extent has this migration contributed to the economic development of the region? Migrant labour is hypothesized to have several important effects on economic development in developing regions of the world economy. The *Daily Gleaner,* Jamaica's most influential newspaper in the 1960s, summed up rather eloquently the positive role that migrant labour could play. In addition to the direct economic benefit to be had by allowing workers to earn foreign currency, it also suggested that

> there are also indirect benefits to the West Indies on which a specific cash value cannot be placed: the value of the contact by thousands of men from the small West Indian territories with ... America and the American way of life. The workers not only see some of the bright lights of the cities and vast stretches of agricultural lands under production but they also see new techniques, methods and procedures on the farm. They also observe how the American farmer, even though he may be several financial strata above his employee—American or foreign—is still willing and able to work side by side with the humblest of labourers so as to get the task done. (quoted in Segal n.d., 7)

It is difficult to measure many of the subjective changes that have occurred in the workers' world view pertaining to modernization. Therefore, what I concentrate on are the direct economic implications for development and the use to which the funds earned in Canada are put.

Evidence from a sample survey of Caribbean farm workers suggests that little of the funds earned by workers contributes to economic development in the region (Whyte 1984). Since the start of the migration in 1966, Caribbean workers have earned considerable amounts of money from seasonal employment in the Ontario fruit and vegetable industry. Between 1966 and 1985, it is estimated that the gross earnings of Caribbean workers were $132 325 117. There are two components of Caribbean worker earnings. The first is the workers' weekly wage, which they can spend as they see fit. Another component consists of compulsory savings—savings that workers are required to remit directly to a bank in the Caribbean. Compulsory savings constitute about 19 percent of the workers' total earnings less the contribution made to their transportation by air to Canada.

Whyte's evidence suggests that the major use to which Canadian earnings are put is the purchase of goods in Canada. The main goods that the workers Whyte studied bought in Canada were clothing for the worker's family, electronic equipment, toiletries, appliances, and food. Few farm workers purchased equipment and tools that could help them in their work in the Caribbean.

Most of the money taken home at the end of the season is expended in two ways: paying general living expenses for the family and buying or improving a family home. Investment of these earnings in land, technology, or education is rare.

The pattern of expenditure of compulsory savings is slightly different. Approximately 45 percent of the workers interviewed stated that they would save their compulsory remittances; only 4 percent reported that they would use the money to invest in education, land, or machinery; the remainder reported that they would use the savings to support their family, purchase clothes or appliances, or make home repairs (Whyte 1984, 28).

Thus it appears that much of the money earned by the workers is expended to sustain their capacity to work while in Canada (because they are responsible for their own cooking, clothing, and so on). Part of the earnings of the workers finds its way to Canadian merchants near the areas where they are employed. It appears that the funds earned through employment in Canada have had little impact on development in the Caribbean. These findings are consistent with those of other studies, which show that migrant labour remittances play a minimal role in development. Government claims that these monies promote development appear to be little more than rhetoric. In reality, the importation of Caribbean workers under contract allows Canadian employers the opportunity to exploit the labour power of Caribbean workers without threatening the imagined community of the Canadian nation, which continues to be defined, in part, in terms of the "white race."

Conclusions

Immigration has been central to the economic and social development of Canada. Immigrants have an important economic role to play in the process of capital accumulation. Immigrants have contributed to the initial formation of a class of free wage labour, and have subsequently contributed to the reproduction of the working class. But because Canada is a settler capitalist nation, immigration has also been a crucial aspect of state formation. This has meant that there have been conflicting and contradictory pressures placed on state officials with respect to immigration. Canada has not simply sought out immigrant labour that was inexpensive for capitalists to purchase, but labour that could also become part of the Canadian imagined community.

The continued representation of the Canadian nation in terms of the "white race" on the part of some Canadians might mean that immigration will not be used to solve the social and economic contradictions associated with the aging of the population and its declining fertility. Racism may preclude the importation of immigrant workers from non-traditional source countries. Racism continues to structure immigration control in the country to the extent that Caribbean seasonal workers are admitted to work in the Ontario fruit and vegetable harvest without being given settlement and subsequent citizenship rights.

Summary

- International migration is linked in large part to the process of capital accumulation; however, since migration is also an aspect of state formation, a variety of other non-economic factors influence who is allowed to migrate to another country. One such factor is how ruling groups imagine the nation.
- Immigration control in Canada has historically been characterized by a tension between economic factors and racism. While some groups of immigrants and potential immigrants were seen by some people as potentially useful additions to the labour force, they were seen by others as threats to the future of Canada as a "white country." Political and medical factors also shape who has been allowed to enter Canada as an immigrant.
- Canada will be facing two demographic challenges during the next several decades. One is the aging of the population; the other is the low fertility rate. This means that, other things being equal, there will be proportionately fewer workers in the total population. Without international migration, employers may face serious shortages of workers. International migration is one way to offset the aging of the population, but there are political and ideological limits to how many immigrants are let into Canada as a way of altering demographic tendencies.
- To what extent does the movement of migrant workers to Canada actually assist the countries from which migrants come? Some believe that the migration of Mexican and Caribbean seasonal agricultural workers to Canada is a form of development aid. On balance, though, it appears that such migrant labour streams are of more benefit to Canadian employers than they are to poor countries.

Questions to Consider

1. What is the nature of the contradiction inherent in the process of migration?

2. What is the link between capital accumulation and the international migration of relative surplus populations?

3. Do systems of migrant labour contribute to the process of development in developing countries?

4. What two demographic factors will be crucial in Canada's future? How can immigration help solve the social and economic problems associated with these demographic processes? What factors will determine whether migration will be used to solve these problems?

Suggested Readings

Avery, Donald. *Reluctant Host: Canada's Response to Immigrant Workers*. Toronto: McClelland and Stewart, 1995.

Castles, Steven, and G. Kosack. *Immigrant Workers and Class Structure in Western Europe.* London: Oxford University Press, 1973.

Economic Council of Canada. *Economic and Social Impacts of Immigration.* Ottawa: Minister of Supply and Services, 1991.

Foot, D. *Population Aging and Immigration Policy in Canada: Implications and Prescriptions.* Ottawa: Canada Employment and Immigration Commission, 1986.

Miles, Robert. "Labour Migration, Racism and Capital Accumulation in Western Europe Since 1945." *Capital and Class* 28 (1986): 49–86.

Simmons, Alan. "Racism and Immigration Policy." In *Racism and Social Inequality in Canada,* ed. V. Satzewich. Toronto: Thompson Educational Publishers, 1998.

Glossary

capital accumulation The most important imperative or driving force of the bourgeois society. It refers, in part, to the process whereby economic enterprises become concentrated and centralized into fewer and fewer hands.

deracialization The process in which explicitly racist terms and concepts are replaced with apparently non-racist ones, but with the meanings remaining intact.

international migration The movement of people across international boundaries. It is both a cause and a consequence of capital accumulation.

neo-racism The cloaking of racism under the facade of more politically acceptable criteria.

net migration The difference in a country's rate of immigration and emigration.

migrant labour International migrants who are given the right of temporary work and entry to a country.

population aging An increase in the relative proportion of older people in a total population.

relative surplus populations People who are economically displaced by the process of capital accumulation and who are therefore unemployed or irregularly employed.

state formation The sociogenesis of state structures.

References

Anderson, A., and J. Frideres. 1981. *Ethnicity in Canada: Theoretical Perspectives.* Toronto: Butterworths.

Anderson, B. 1983. *Imagined Communities: Reflections on the Origins and Spread of Nationalism.* London: Verso.

Avery, D. 1979. *Dangerous Foreigners: European Immigrant Workers and Labour Radicalism in Canada, 1896–1932.* Toronto: McClelland and Stewart.

Badets, J., and T. Chui. 1996. *Canada's Changing Immigrant Population.* Toronto: Prentice Hall.

Beaujot, R. 1992. "The Socio-Demographic Impact of Immigration." In *The Immigration Dilemma,* ed. S. Globerman. Vancouver: The Fraser Institute.

Berry. J., R. Kalin, and D. Taylor. 1977. *Multiculturalism and Ethnic Attitudes in Canada.* Ottawa: Supply and Services Canada.

Bolaria, B.S., and P. Li. 1988. *Racial Oppression in Canada.* 2d ed. Toronto: Garamond Press.

Boyd, M., C. Taylor, and P. Delaney. 1986. "Temporary Workers in Canada: A Multifaceted Program." *International Migration Review* 20: 929–50.

Denoon, D. 1983. *Settler Capitalism.* London: Oxford University Press.

Department of Manpower and Immigration. 1974–1976. *Immigration Statistics.* Ottawa: Supply and Services Canada.

Ehrensaft, P., and W. Armstrong. 1981. "The Formation of Dominion Capitalism." In *Inequality: Essays in the Political Economy of Social Welfare,* ed. A. Muscovitch and G. Drover. Toronto: University of Toronto Press. 98–155.

Employment and Immigration Canada. 1977–1978. *Immigration Statistics.* Ottawa: Supply and Services Canada.

———. 1987. *Annual Report to Parliament on Future Immigration Levels.* Ottawa: Supply and Services Canada.

Foot, D. 1986. *Population Aging and Immigration Policy in Canada: Implications and Prescriptions.* Ottawa: Canada Employment and Immigration Commission.

Gallup Poll. 1989. "Large Increase in Racial Intolerance Perceived." March 20. Toronto: Gallup Canada.

Hawkins, F. 1974. "Canadian Immigration Policy and Management." *International Migration Review* 7: 141–53.

Hersak, G.A., and S. Francolini. 1987. *Immigration of Children as a Response to Demographic Concerns.* Ottawa: Supply and Services Canada.

Marx, K. 1967 [1867]. *Capital.* Vol. 1. New York: International Publishers.

Miles, R. 1986. "Labour Migration, Racism, and Capital Accumulation in Western Europe Since 1945." *Capital and Class* 28: 49–86.

———. 1987. "Recent Marxist Theories of Nationalism and the Issue of Racism." *The British Journal of Sociology* 38: 24–43.

Myles, J., and M. Boyd. 1982. "Population Aging and the Elderly." In *Social Issues: Sociological Views of Canada,* ed. D. Forcese and S. Richer. Scarborough, ON: Prentice-Hall. 258–85.

Palmer, B. 1984. "Social Formation and Class Formation in North America, 1800–1900." In *Proletarianization and Family History,* ed. D. Levine. New York: Academic Press. 229–309.

Pentland, H.C. 1959. "The Development of a Capitalist Labour Market in Canada." *Canadian Journal of Economics and Political Science* 25: 450–61.

———. 1981. *Labour and Capital in Canada*, 1650–1860. Toronto: Lorimer.

Rawlyk, G. 1962. "Canada's Immigration Policy, 1945–1962." *Dalhousie Review* 42 (Spring): 287–300.

Rex, J., and S. Tomlinson. 1979. *Colonial Immigrants in a British City.* London: Routledge and Kegan Paul.

Romaniuc, A. 1988. *Fertility in Canada: From Baby Boom to Baby Bust.* Ottawa: Statistics Canada.

Royal Commission on Chinese Immigration. 1885. *Report.* Ottawa: Queen's Printer.

Royal Commission on Chinese and Japanese Immigration. 1902. *Report.* Ottawa: Queen's Printer.

Sassen-Koob, S. 1981. "Towards a Conceptualization of Immigrant Labour." *Social Problems* 29: 65–85.

Satzewich, V. 1988a. "Modes of Incorporation and Racialization: The Canadian Case." Ph.D. thesis. University of Glasgow.

———. 1988b. "The Canadian State and the Racialization of Caribbean Migrant Farm Labour, 1947–1966." *Ethnic and Racial Studies* 11: 282–304.

Sears, A. 1990. "Immigration Controls as Social Policy: The Case of Canadian Medical Inspection." *Studies in Political Economy* 33: 91–112.

Segal, A. n.d. *Politics and Population in the Caribbean.* Rio Piedras: Institute of Caribbean Studies.

Simmons, A. 1998. "Racism and Immigration Policy." In *Racism and Social Inequality in Canada,* ed. V. Satzewich. Toronto: Thompson Educational Publishers.

Thomas, R. 1985. *Citizenship: Gender and Work.* Berkeley: University of California Press.

Urquhart, M.C., and K. Buckley. 1983. *Historical Statistics of Canada.* 2d ed. Ottawa: Statistics Canada.

Whitaker, R. 1987. *Double Standard: The Secret History of Canadian Immigration.* Toronto: Lester and Orpen Dennys.

Whyte, A. 1984. *The Experience of New Immigrants and Seasonal Farm Workers from the Eastern Caribbean in Canada.* Toronto: Institute of Environmental Studies.

Wood, C. 1982. "Equilibrium and Historical-Structural Models of Migration." *International Migration Review* 16: 298–319.

Zolberg, A. 1981. "International Migrations in Political Perspective." In *Global Trends in Migration,* ed. M. Kritz, C.B. Keeley, and S.M. Tomasi. New York: Center for Migration Studies.

CHAPTER 4

Income Inequality, Poverty, and Hunger

B. Singh Bolaria and Terry Wotherspoon

Learning Objectives

After studying this chapter, you should be able to
- Understand the definition and dimensions of **poverty** in Canada.
- Analyze poverty in relation to structures of **income inequality** and unequal **life chances**.
- Examine the consequences of poverty for differences in consumption patterns, lifestyle, health, and well-being.
- Understand the emergence and role of **food banks** in Canada since the early 1980s.
- Analyze the diverse consequences of food banks for different groups, and examine critically the extent to which they are an adequate response to problems associated with income inequality and poverty.

Introduction

Poverty, malnutrition, hunger, and disease have come to be identified with developing Third World countries. We see television images of famine and starvation in Africa and Asia almost daily. Charities constantly invoke images of frail, empty-bellied children to collect funds to help the famine-stricken populations in other countries. These images help reinforce the view that such problems exist only in Third World nations.

While the significance and concentration of poverty in the Third World cannot be overstated, neither have the advanced capitalist countries eliminated economic inequalities and poverty. The inequalities of wealth and income produce unequal life chances—that is, chances for material and social rewards. Poverty translates into homelessness, ill health, short life expectancy, malnutrition, and hunger, to mention only a few of its effects.

Canada is a highly stratified society. There are wide disparities in wealth, income, power, and prestige. These inequalities are not mere statistical categories used to classify people for social analysis; they have important implications for people's lives.

In this chapter we confine our discussion to only one dimension of inequality: disparities of income. Selective data are presented on the linkages between income inequalities and life chances. This chapter also explores the links between inequality, poverty, and hunger in this country, with particular emphasis on the emergence and persistence of food banks as a response to hunger. In the concluding section, the implications of this "private-voluntary solution" to a structurally produced social problem are explored in the context of the social expenditure restraint that is being advocated to eliminate budget deficits and to scale down the welfare state.

Income Inequality and Poverty

Income inequality is an important dimension of social stratification. An examination of income distribution data reveals wide income disparities among Canadians. These data also show the meagre extent of change in the share of income held by Canadians in different income categories over time (National Council of Welfare 1988; 1989; 1990; 1992). For instance, families in the lowest quintile had only 6.1 percent of the total income in 1951 and 6.3 percent in 1986. The corresponding figures for the highest quintile were 41.1 percent and 39.4 percent—over six times the lowest quintile's share. The figures for unattached individuals reveal that in 1986 the lowest quintile had 5.3 percent of the total income. In contrast, the highest quintile had 44.7 percent of the total income—over eight times the bottom group's share. The income distribution for unattached individuals was even more skewed in 1951 (National Council of Welfare 1988). Income inequalities continue to persist in Canada.

A significant number of Canadians live in poverty. The most common measure used to establish the poverty line is the low-income cutoffs used by Statistics Canada. These cutoffs are set at levels at which, on average, 56.2 percent of income is spent on the necessities of life: food, clothing, and shelter (National Council of Welfare 1997). There is no single cut-off line for all of Canada, because living costs vary by family size and place of residence. It should also be noted that "poverty lines only establish the upper limit of the low income population. Most poor Canadians live on incomes that are hundreds and more often thousands of dollars under the poverty line" (National Council of Welfare 1989, 5).

Poverty figures fluctuate with economic conditions. While poverty declined in Canada in the 1970s, it increased substantially during the first half of the 1980s as a result of the 1981–82 recession (National Council of Welfare 1988). Despite some movement, by the late 1980s the poverty rates had not returned to prerecession levels.

Table 4.1 shows national trends in poverty from 1980 to 1995. In 1980, the number of people living in poverty was little over 3.6 million and the poverty rate was just over 15 percent. Both the number of people who lived in poverty and the poverty rate fluctuated throughout the 1980s. These figures rose from 1982 to 1984, declined from 1985 till 1989, and rose again in the 1990s. Since 1989, poverty rates have increased amid high unemployment rates; economic restructuring that has forced job losses and wage reductions; and cutbacks in government programs, services, and social assistance rates.

TABLE 4.1   Poverty Trends, All Persons, 1980–1995

Year	Number of persons living in poverty	Poverty rate (%)
1980	3 624 000	15.3
1981	3 643 000	15.3
1982	3 951 000	16.4
1983	4 406 000	18.2
1984	4 397 000	18.1
1985	4 170 000	17.0
1986	3 976 000	16.0
1987	3 912 000	15.6
1988	3 744 000	14.8
1989	3 487 000	13.6
1990	3 821 000	14.6
1991	4 227 000	16.0
1992	4 320 000	16.1
1993	4 775 000	17.4
1994	4 795 000	16.6
1995	5 070 000	17.4

Source: *Poverty Profile 1995* (Ottawa: National Council of Welfare, Spring 1997). Reproduced with permission of the Minister of Public Works and Government Services Canada, 1998.

As Table 4.2 shows, child poverty figures followed the same general pattern as statistics for the general population. Child poverty increased in the early part of the 1980s, declined during the next few years and rose again in the 1990s. While considerable optimism that these levels would decline with the economic recovery of the mid-1980s was reinforced by subsequent commitments by the federal government to eradicate child poverty, the poverty rate for children exceeded 20 percent a decade later. Nearly 1.5 million, or more than one in five, Canadian children are poor.

Certain groups face a high risk of poverty. These include families headed by women, unattached or elderly women, unemployed, persons whose participation in the labour force is irregular, and those with low educational levels (National Council of Welfare 1992). Women overall face a much higher risk of poverty than men, a phenomenon that has come to be known as the "feminization of poverty" (National Council of Welfare 1990).

Because a vast majority of Canadians earn their income from wage employment, labour-market characteristics that determine which jobs are well paid are particularly important in any discussion of poverty. For instance, those in managerial and professional occupations and their families are unlikely to live in poverty, as compared to those in the service industries. Occupations with an above-average risk of poverty include farming, fishing, forestry, sales, clerical work, and services (National Council of Welfare 1997).

TABLE 4.2 Poverty Trends, Children under 18, 1980–1995

Year	Number of children under 18 living in poverty	Poverty rate (%)
1980	984 000	14.9
1981	998 000	15.2
1982	1 155 000	17.8
1983	1 221 000	19.0
1984	1 253 000	19.6
1985	1 165 000	18.3
1986	1 086 000	17.0
1987	1 057 000	16.6
1988	987 000	15.4
1989	934 000	14.5
1990	1 105 000	16.9
1991	1 210 000	18.3
1992	1 218 000	18.2
1993	1 415 000	20.8
1994	1 334 000	19.1
1995	1 441 000	20.1

Source: *Poverty Profile 1995* (Ottawa: National Council of Welfare, Spring 1997). Reproduced with permission of the Minister of Public Works and Government Services Canada, 1998.

Income Inequality, Life Chances, and Consumption

Income inequality and poverty have an important influence on the lives of individuals. Max Weber saw class as closely linked to people's life chances, that is, their chances to acquire material goods and other amenities (Gerth and Mills 1958). Economic and social inequalities produce inequality of opportunities and life chances, which are reflected in such measures as education, living standards, housing, health, and consumption patterns. A number of chapters in this volume attest to these inequalities and differential opportunity structures and life chances.

Most relevant to the discussion in this chapter is the link between income inequalities and consumption patterns. Chossudovsky points to "the dual and divided structure of social consumption and of consumer goods markets between necessary subsistence goods on the one hand and luxury and semi-luxury goods consumed by the privileged upper-income groups on the other hand.... This duality in the structure of social consumption, while more pronounced in peripheral social formations, is also present in the advanced capitalist countries" (1983, 76).

In addition to the differences in the goods they consume, persons with different income levels devote a different percentage of their income to necessary subsistence goods. Families and unattached individuals in the lowest quintile spend 57.5 percent

Mothers' Hunger Pangs Studied

One in four mothers turning to food banks for groceries sometimes suffer from severe hunger, a study by researchers in the University of Toronto's faculty of medicine says.

The study of 153 women with children using food banks found that 26.8 percent of the mothers reported experiencing "severe food deprivation" sometime during the past year, with 21.6 percent suffering from hunger within the past month.

Commissioned by Health Canada, the study narrowed its focus to women with children because, in families living in poverty, mothers are regarded as most likely to deprive themselves in order that their children can eat, so they are most vulnerable to household food shortages.

"While the food assistance [that food banks] provide undoubtedly helps poor families, it does not prevent them from going hungry," the study says. "Furthermore, continued reliance on such a highly stigmatized and woefully inadequate system of assistance appears to have long-term physical and psychological health consequences."

The researchers found that the women's nutrition was poor, with grossly inadequate levels of iron, magnesium, vitamin A and folate in their diets. Only 38 percent of the women surveyed considered their health to be very good or excellent.

Seventy percent of the women were surviving on social assistance alone, at an average level of income representing 52.8 percent of Statistics Canada's low-income cutoff, widely used as a poverty line.

The report concludes that food banks are failing even to stave off basic hunger in the country's poorest families.

"Clearly, the use of charitable food assistance does not make the difference between hunger and an adequate diet for women who live so far below the poverty line," said Valerie Tarasuk, assistant professor of nutritional sciences and the study's principal investigator.

Source: Margaret Philp, "Mothers' Hunger Pangs Studied," *The Globe and Mail,* April 4, 1998, p. A5.

of their income on the necessities of life. The corresponding figure for the second-lowest quintile is 45.6 percent. With each higher quintile, the percentage of income spent on necessities is lower. The family units in the highest quintile spend 33 percent of their income on the necessities of life (National Council of Welfare 1989, 13). Data from the United States indicate that those in the lowest income decile spend over 40 percent of their income on food alone, as compared to only 11 percent for the highest decile (Blumberg 1980, 181).

Chossudovsky notes that "food is by far the most important component of necessary consumption." Adequate production and supply of food in themselves do not assure adequate levels of food consumption and nutrition. Consumption levels are influenced by the social distribution of food to different groups in the population (Chossudovsky 1983), which itself is a function of income distribution. A number of studies show the relationship between low incomes and inadequate diets (Nutrition

Canada 1975; Myres and Kroetsch 1978; Reid and Miles 1977). Millions of poor Americans suffer from malnutrition and hunger (Kotz 1984; Physicians' Task Force on Hunger in America 1985; Wilkinson and Sidel 1986).

Poverty, nutrition, and hunger are also closely linked to health status (Epp 1986; Statistics Canada and Health and Welfare Canada 1981; Wilkins and Adams 1983; Wigle and Mao 1980). A report published by the Minister of Health revealed that "men in the upper income group live six years longer than men with a low income." The same report also indicated that "men in upper income groups can expect fourteen more disability-free years than men with a low income; in the case of women, the difference is eight years" (Epp 1986, 398). Other evidence associates poverty with malnutrition, psychomotor and growth retardation, emotional disturbances, and visual difficulties. These problems are even more acute among Native people (Special Senate Committee on Poverty 1971; Shah and Farkas 1985).

The adverse health effects of poverty for children have their start during pregnancy; they have significant impact on complications during pregnancy, low birth weight

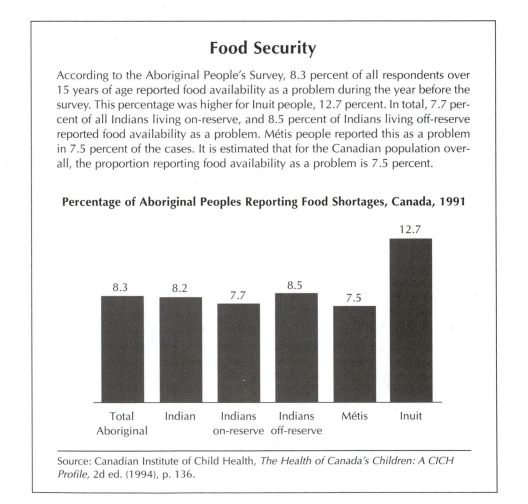

Food Security

According to the Aboriginal People's Survey, 8.3 percent of all respondents over 15 years of age reported food availability as a problem during the year before the survey. This percentage was higher for Inuit people, 12.7 percent. In total, 7.7 percent of all Indians living on-reserve, and 8.5 percent of Indians living off-reserve reported food availability as a problem. Métis people reported this as a problem in 7.5 percent of the cases. It is estimated that for the Canadian population overall, the proportion reporting food availability as a problem is 7.5 percent.

Percentage of Aboriginal Peoples Reporting Food Shortages, Canada, 1991

Source: Canadian Institute of Child Health, *The Health of Canada's Children: A CICH Profile,* 2d ed. (1994), p. 136.

of children, handicaps, poor growth, and intellectual and emotional disorders (National Council of Welfare 1975; Ross and Rutter 1978; Vernon 1979; Perkins 1974; Bradley, Ross, and Warnyca 1978; Brown 1978). Child mortality rates are higher for poor children than their wealthy peers (Fine 1989). Hess (1989, 5) outlines how children living in poverty face both direct and indirect risks to their physical and mental well-being due to greater likelihood of "substandard housing, overcrowding, exposure to toxic substances, high traffic-density, neighbourhood crime, and insufficient recreational facilities," among other things.

The cumulative effect of poverty, malnutrition, hunger, and ill health is the extensive reproduction of poverty. All of these things influence poor children's learning ability and performance in school (Chu 1989; National Council of Welfare 1975), which subsequently affect job prospects, employment patterns, and earnings. As a report by the National Council of Welfare (1975, 1) states: "To be born poor in Canada does not make it a certainty that you will live poor and die poor—but it makes it very likely."

Food Banks: Voluntary Response to a Public Problem

The contradictions associated with "hunger in the midst of plenty" are starkly illustrated by the rise of food banks across Canada in the 1980s. Since the first food bank opened in Edmonton in 1981, food banks and similar organizations have been established in many towns and cities across Canada (Canadian Association of Food Banks 1989; Riches 1986; Oderkirk 1992; Webber 1992). As Table 4.3 indicates, by 1984

The Health of Poor Children in Canada

Poor children do not share the same level of health as children who are not poor:

- The infant death rate is about twice as high in poor neighbourhoods as in rich neighbourhoods.

- The low birth weight rate is 1.4 times higher in poor neighbourhoods than in rich neighbourhoods.

- Poor children are more likely to die from injuries than non-poor children.

- Poor children are more likely to have chronic health problems and to be admitted to hospital than non-poor children.

- Poor children are more likely to have problems at school and psychiatric problems than non-poor children.

- Poor children are less likely to feel good about themselves than non-poor children.

Source: Canadian Institute of Child Health, *The Health of Canada's Children: A CICH Profile,* 2d ed. (1994), p. 128.

there were 75 food banks in Canada, mostly in the western provinces. The number of food banks continued to increase through the 1980s. By 1991, there were 292 food banks in various parts of Canada; by 1997, 508 communities had one or more food banks. This growth continues as the economy further experiences the effects of economic recession, restructuring, and unemployment.

It is estimated that two million Canadians used food banks in 1991. By 1997, in one month alone (March of that year), there were 669 877 Canadians who received emergency food assistance (Canadian Association of Food Banks 1997, 1). Children account for a large number of food-bank users. While 25 percent of the Canadian population was under age 18, over 40 percent of the food-bank beneficiaries in 1997 were in this age group (Canadian Association of Food Banks 1997, 1). For over two-thirds (68 percent) of the food-bank users, welfare was the primary source of income (Oderkirk 1992). It is evident that many Canadians depend upon food banks and other charitable meal operations for their daily food.

It is important to recognize that food-bank services operate separately from food hamper distribution and meal programs offered by other agencies such as soup kitchens, church and school programs, community friendship centres, and Salvation Army centres (Riches 1986, 13). Whereas the latter programs have operated for several decades, food-bank services constitute a relatively recent phenomenon. Charitable operations tend to serve a relatively specific clientele, such as older male indigents or children in low-income areas. By contrast, food banks do not usually

TABLE 4.3   Food Banks in Canada, 1981–1997, Selected Years[a]

	1981	1984	1988	1989	1990	1991	1997
Newfoundland	0	0	1	1	1	17	30
Prince Edward Island	0	0	2	2	2	3	3
Nova Scotia	0	2	8	14	14	27	33
New Brunswick	0	2	27	34	35	40	48
Quebec	0	2	5	5	5	11	446
Ontario	0	4	19	33	35	88	174
Manitoba	0	1	1	3	3	4	13
Saskatchewan	0	5	5	5	8	11	21
Alberta	1	12	16	26	24	40	63
British Columbia	0	47	42	36	34	51	71
Canada	1	75	126	159	161	292	905[b]

[a] Estimates from 1988 to 1991 from the Canadian Association of Food Banks do not include Salvation Army Family Services Divisions food banks. Growth during this period can be attributed to the creation of new food banks and to the registration of existing food banks with the association.

[b] Includes 1 in the Yukon and 2 in NWT. The actual number of food banks is much higher because some food banks collect food on behalf of, and distribute food to, a number of smaller member agencies or affiliates in a given geographical area.

Source: J. Oderkirk, "Food Banks," *Canadian Social Trends* 24, Cat. no. 11-008 (Spring 1992): 6–14.

target selected groups, but rather provide food parcels for any individuals and families who appear voluntarily or are referred by agencies when their cash or food supplies are inadequate. The very existence of food banks and their proliferation in food-producing regions of Canada indicate the extent to which hunger and poverty have become regular features of advanced industrial societies. The growing demand for their services has forced food banks to expand beyond their own distribution centres in order to distribute food through programs and centres such as community kitchens, women's shelters, and AIDS service organizations that feed specific client groups (Greater Vancouver Food Bank Society 1998, 1, 3).

Food banks originated as an emergency response to a situation in which people did not have sufficient welfare and other income to provide food and necessities for themselves and family members. The guiding principle on which most food banks operate is summarized by the Greater Vancouver Food Bank Society (1989, 1–2) as follows: "The food bank does not represent a long-term solution to the problem of hunger in our community; rather we see ourselves as meeting a crisis situation when government aid to the needy is diminishing." Nonetheless, they are becoming more than a temporary reality.

In other words, food banks constitute a response to shifts in both the economy and state policy. They first appeared in western Canada during the severe economic crisis of the early 1980s, in which national unemployment rates nearly doubled from 7 percent in July 1981 to 12.8 percent in December 1982; the highest increases were in Alberta, British Columbia, and other parts of western Canada. At the same time, the adoption of neoconservative government policies hastened the diversion of state priorities and resources from social and human services to the enhancement of labour productivity and capital accumulation. The Canadian Association of Food Banks (1997, 6), commenting on the "serious deterioration in household food security in Canada" in the 1990s, observes that "it is certainly not accidental that this worsening situation coincided with a regime of high unemployment coupled with federal and provincial cuts to social programs."

This constituted a reorganization of the state, one of whose consequences has been a sustained attack on welfare programs and social services. Business and political organizations claimed that welfare expenditures were contributing to government deficits and impeding individual initiative and labour productivity at a time when Canada needed to become more competitive internationally. In the 1980s, the federal and provincial governments began to overhaul welfare, unemployment insurance, and other social programs, imposing tighter eligibility requirements and spending ceilings. The theme that all Canadians must take greater individual responsibility for their own and their families' welfare, and that of the nation as a whole, resounded as a common refrain.

Through the ideology and practice of restraint, we have come to expect that employment discontinuities in the form of job losses or career shifts will accompany economic restructuring. Food banks are commonly accepted as one way of sharing the burden of temporary displacement through appeals to persons with steady incomes to donate food for distribution to those less fortunate than themselves. In this sense, food banks are seen as a temporary measure designed to alleviate crisis conditions for the hardest hit victims of recession and economic reordering. Their creation as voluntary organizations supported by contributions of food, money, and time from community members reinforces the notion that we all have a responsibility to others without placing excessive dependence on the state or other agencies.

At the same time, however, a **victim-blaming ideology** aligned with the emphasis on individual initiative implies that food-bank recipients are not merely innocent casualties of economic change. The attacks on welfare and the glorification of productive private enterprise are designed to leave the impression that persons who require social assistance and food-bank support have failed to contribute to the capitalist system, not that they have been failed by it. The criticism implies that it is not so much that food banks and meal-distribution programs are a necessary evil in Canada but that recipients are lazy, unmotivated, uneducated, or incapable of caring for themselves. The image that hunger is an anomaly in contemporary society is buttressed by statements from prominent public officials. The premier of British Columbia claimed that children were going to school hungry because their parents were playing bingo and drinking excessively; the minister of families in Saskatchewan put it this way: "You're dealing with people, a lot of them are illiterate, as a result they don't know how to shop properly, they can't get the best buys on food. All that sort of thing" (Burton 1989).

A closer examination dispels the popular notion that food banks are a temporary measure to serve less-than-desirable segments of the population. Their number and the range of clients have grown substantially since programs began operation. In Vancouver, for example, the food bank provided food aid to up to three thousand households (about 8300 persons) per week in 1989, compared with two hundred households in 1982. In Nanaimo, British Columbia, the number of registered food-bank users in December 1989 was 5569, or nearly 11 percent of the city's population, and was expanding with an average of twenty new registrations per week. The Calgary Inter-Faith Food Bank distributed food hampers to 3175 recipients in November 1989, an increase of 22 percent from one year earlier. The Saskatoon food bank served 24 083 families in 1988 compared with 8724 in 1985. An average of 679 food hampers were distributed monthly in 1989 by an agency in the Kitchener-Waterloo area, compared with 409 per month in 1988; and in Metropolitan Toronto, the Daily Bread Food Bank served about 80 000 persons per month in 1989 compared with about 500 in 1984 (Braungart 1989; Greater Vancouver Food Bank Society 1989; Robinson 1989; *Star-Phoenix* [Saskatoon], December 15, 1989, D14; *Star-Phoenix,* August 30, 1989).

Other charitable agencies have also supplied growing numbers of meals. In Regina, for instance, agencies that distribute several thousand meals and snacks to school children and adults monthly reported increases of between 20 and 33 percent in the use of their services between 1988 and 1989, while in several other cities, schools have begun or expanded regular meal and snack distribution to hungry children in recent years (Regina 1989, 9–10; York 1989). In all, based on data from March 1989, over 1.1 million meals were served that month by more than 1100 grocery programs and 400 meal programs across Canada (Canadian Association of Food Banks 1989, 2–3).

In all cases—when supplies are available—food banks distribute parcels that include basic foods such as bread, peanut butter, canned meat and fish, powdered milk, pablum, and infant formula. In other words, they provide essential nutrition, not unnecessary or extravagant items. These foods cannot always be assured; food banks depend upon whatever food items are donated and what can be purchased with cash donations. Their ability to provide adequate services is reliant upon the success of regular appeals to the public and various agencies for food, resources, and volunteer labour. In several instances, they have had to turn away people seeking their services. Moreover, several thousand more potential recipients do not receive or are not able to receive food from food banks (Canadian Association of Food Banks 1989, 4; Regina 1989, 36).

Traditionally, soup kitchens and other charitable food services have catered to older men and transients, but food banks tend to have a younger, more diverse clientele, as shown by the food items they distribute. Data on food-bank recipients present a composite picture of persons who, in their prime working years and often supporting children, have limited access to jobs and labour-force income. In Toronto, the proportion of food-bank recipients who were employed increased from 13 percent in late 1987 to 18 percent in early 1989 (Stefaniuk 1989). In 1988–89, 40 percent of food-bank recipients across Canada, with little regional variation, were children under the age of 18 (Canadian Association of Food Banks 1989, 2). As reported earlier, children have continued to be highly over-represented among recipients of food bank assistance.

The overwhelming majority of food-bank users continue to be people on welfare. Many argue that these trends provide strong evidence that incompetent or unenterprising persons, most of them welfare recipients, are more inclined to squander their "unearned" money when they know that they can receive food handouts from volunteer agencies. But these people are by no means just lazy or irresponsible. Stated simply, people who receive food-bank services, with few exceptions, do so because they cannot survive in capitalist societies without those services. Officials with food banks and other charitable meal organizations are particularly concerned about the recent trend toward large numbers of "non-traditional unemployed" who have become reliant on welfare and food-bank services because jobs have disappeared in their white-collar occupations (Greater Vancouver Food Bank Society 1989, 3; York 1989). Although the measure of the poverty line must be interpreted with caution, as noted earlier in the chapter, nearly one in five Canadians lived below the poverty line in 1995. Nonetheless, welfare and social assistance rates are not keeping pace with increases in the cost of basic needs, including food, clothing, and shelter. Moreover, as the National Council of Welfare (1987, 49) observes, "In all provinces, the definition of basic requirements is so stringent that the welfare benefit levels calculated according to these standards permit only an impoverished existence." Cutbacks in social service expenditures, particularly for single employable persons, exacerbate personal crisis to the extent that, in order for recipients to pay for some minimal necessities such as rent, clothing, heating, and transportation, other necessities such as food often have to be forgone. Analysis by the Social Planning and Research Council of British Columbia (1989, 32), for example, reveals that persons in all categories receiving income assistance experience a shortfall in total income relative to daily living costs ranging from 29 percent monthly for a single parent with one child living in a one-bedroom apartment to 83 percent for a single male.

Changing employment patterns make it difficult, if not impossible, for many potential workers to find work; extensive unemployment, underemployment, and low-wage work make people reliant on welfare and other forms of social assistance; and restrictive social assistance practices and low rates force people to turn to food banks and other charitable support. These points are reinforced in an inquiry into hunger in Regina, which stresses that virtually all respondents, including food-bank agencies, recipients, community organizations, and public officials agree that hunger is caused by poverty, which in turn is associated with

- minimum wage rates that are too low;
- high unemployment and only low-paying or part-time jobs, particularly for certain categories of people such as youth, women with young children, people with mental illnesses, and Native people;
- high-cost, poor-quality housing that forces people to spend much of their income, sometimes 50 percent or more, on shelter;
- inadequate support services including child care, home economic skills, and supportive living facilities;
- inadequate welfare allowances and inadequate financial supports for the working poor (Regina 1989, 14).

These trends force us to rethink widely accepted notions that recipients are the major beneficiaries of food-bank services. It is important to stress that unlike relatively fixed costs, such as rent and utilities, for which non-payment makes persons subject to eviction or loss of services, food and other consumption purchases are more "voluntary" in the sense that they have attached to them no deadlines or compulsion by external agencies. In other words, people who turn to food banks when they have no income left for food have already spent their available funds on shelter and other necessary goods and services. Under these circumstances, it is rental unit owners, utility companies, and other businesses that are in a position to gain from the "subsidized" costs of food-bank services, which would otherwise have to be purchased by recipients. Food banks are not the only form of social assistance that benefits capital. As Swanson (1989) observes, welfare policy in general "can also help business by providing direct wage subsidies to employers and direct rent subsidies to landlords." In this way, programs that allegedly operate to alleviate hunger and poverty actually help perpetuate these phenomena by fuelling the conditions under which they are produced.

Because most public attention directed toward food banks emphasizes food donations and the needs of recipients, issues of hunger and food banks tend to be depoliticized. We think less in terms of structured inequalities and the systemic creation of poverty than of "fortune," with the "better-off" sectors of society being called on to help the "less fortunate." It is clear that food banks and other voluntary and charitable meal operations provide a valuable service by feeding people on a day-to-day basis and enlightening many persons, such as their volunteers who encounter directly the problems of hunger and its consequences. We must also recognize, though, that these solutions to immediate problems deflect attention away from the real causes of hunger and poverty and may actually encourage government and business to distance themselves further from taking an active role in promoting the welfare of the general population. As Riches (1986, 117) concludes, the issues associated with food banks cannot be divorced from the wider contradictory realities of the **welfare state**:

> On the one hand, food banks, like the welfare state, can be seen as meeting the needs of capital and the state by acting as a means of social control. On the other hand, they can be viewed as forms of voluntarist social endeavor which could, in a number of ways, act as catalysts for progressive change.

Conclusions

Wide income disparities continue to exist among Canadians. Many Canadians continue to live in poverty. Groups at a high risk of being poor include women, families headed by women, those with low educational levels, those working in the marginalized sector of the labour market, and part-time workers.

Although poverty has fluctuated with economic cycles, it is a constant presence in Canadian society. Income transfer payments and tax credit programs have helped mitigate the impact of poverty and inequality; still, they have done little to redistribute incomes in this country more equitably.

Economic and social inequalities produce inequality of opportunities, differential life chances, and different social consumption patterns. A duality of social consumption patterns is linked to income levels—while upper-income groups have disposable income for luxury and semi-luxury goods, at the other extreme, lower-income groups are often unable to purchase even necessary subsistence goods, including food. The malnutrition and hunger that are associated with poverty have serious effects on the health and performance of individuals. The emergence of food banks has alleviated hunger for thousands of Canadians, but any permanent and long-range solutions require the elimination of economic and social inequality and poverty. This in turn requires a consideration of the causes of inequality and poverty.

Why is there poverty in the midst of plenty? One answer blames the poor themselves for some personal deficiency, either innate (biological or intellectual) or cultural. Followers of the nineteenth-century sociologist Herbert Spencer, along with other Social Darwinists, have argued that the poor are poor because they are unfit; others argue that certain groups lack intellectual endowment, a trait that they claim is primarily inherited (Herrnstein 1971; 1973; Herrnstein and Murray 1994; Jensen 1969; 1980).

Irrespective of any flaws in their formulation and evidence, these perspectives have important social policy implications. In the case of Social Darwinism, the implication is that the poor should not be helped because that would interfere with "natural selection," while in the case of biological arguments, like those of Jensen and Herrnstein, the implication is that the poor cannot be helped since they are "uneducatable" (Eitzen and Zinn 1989, 178–79). The "culture of poverty" hypothesis locates poverty in poor people's "defective" cultural values, such as lack of motivation, low aspirations, inability to defer gratification, lack of moral values, and fatalism (Lewis 1966). Therefore, the poor are poor either because they are "defective individuals" or they have a "defective" way of life. In either case, they are the objects of what Ryan (1971) has called "blaming the victim." In contrast to the individual and cultural deficiency approaches, a structural explanation of poverty locates its cause in the social structural conditions of capitalism, which produce high unemployment, low-paying jobs, and unequal opportunity structures. The basic tenet of capitalism—the profit-motive—leads capitalists to use every means to reduce labour costs. They accomplish this by maintaining a surplus of labour, which depresses wages and allows employers to rotate their labourers and take other measures to benefit themselves (Eitzen and Zinn 1989, 185).

Because a vast majority of Canadians earn their income in a form of wages from employment, labour-market characteristics that determine which jobs are well paid are particularly important in any discussion of poverty (Osberg 1981). Consider the following:

- Families headed by persons in managerial and professional occupations are unlikely to live below the poverty line.
- Occupations with an above-average risk of poverty include farming, fishing, forestry, sales, clerical work, and services.
- The poverty rate for families headed by workers in service industries—a heavy employer of women—increased from 16.2 percent in 1980 to 22.5 percent in 1995 (National Council of Welfare 1997, 39).

Because unemployment, underemployment, and marginalized jobs all contribute to inequality and poverty, the solution to poverty lies in the alteration of these conditions. However, the continuing high unemployment levels and labour-market segmentation do not lead to optimism. Not only are unemployment rates in Canada high, they are accompanied by increases in long-term unemployment (that is, lasting six months or longer). The number of Canadians experiencing long-term unemployment more than tripled between 1980 and 1983, and by 1985, 28 percent of unemployed Canadians were in the long-term unemployed category (Parliament 1987). Moreover, the Canadian labour market is segmented along occupational, gender, and ethnic lines. Many women and minorities end up in secondary and marginal sectors, which offer poor working conditions and low wages.

While the roots of poverty lie in the structural conditions just discussed, prominent sectors of the political and business elite continue to adhere to a victim-blaming strategy. The poor are blamed not only for their own poverty, but also for the fiscal crisis and budgetary deficits. It is argued that excessive social expenditures are responsible for deficits and need to be cut back in order to avert economic crisis. As Minkler (1983, 155) states, "A hallmark of the current politics of retrenchment has been the tendency by many policy makers to scapegoat the poor and the elderly as 'causes' of the 'fiscal crisis.'"

The scapegoating rhetoric has coincided with "a resurgence of the ideology that individuals create their own conditions and opportunities, and that they are to be held accountable for their predicament" (Estes 1982, 575). The rhetoric of victim blaming, fiscal crisis, and individual responsibility combine to justify cutbacks to welfare and other social programs. Large deficits are said to make it impractical to continue to support social expenditures—since we "cannot afford it," or there are "limits of the possible." As Piven and Cloward (1982, 134) state, "Fiscal austerity will not appear to be political: it will appear to be the inevitable adaptation of a responsible government to the constraints imposed by limited resources."

While "responsible governments" are implementing cutbacks in social expenditures that mostly affect the poor, public funds are being channelled to private-sector interests through the privatization of state services and other measures that strengthen the capitalist class and subsidize corporations. Concomitantly, we have seen the resurrection of the notion that individual-voluntaristic ameliorative programs, such as food banks, are the best way to help the unfortunate among us. This situation relieves the state of the responsibility to provide social assistance programs. Remaining public-sector assistance programs are explicitly targeted toward specific groups and specific problems and, therefore, tend to be "exceptionalistic" rather than "universalistic" in nature.

While transfer payments have not led to any redistribution of incomes, if it were not for state-provided social assistance programs, the gap between the rich and the poor would be even wider than it is now. Furthermore, a majority of poor families now rely on government transfer payments for the major part of their income. Therefore, any reductions in social programs will adversely affect those who most need them.

In conclusion, voluntary programs, such as food banks, are simply treating the symptoms rather than the disease. In order to eliminate the basic causes of hunger, which are inequality and poverty, a basic alteration of the structural and social condition is required. In the absence of any fundamental transformation and in view of the current attacks on the welfare state, and proposals to restructure it, it appears that a large segment of the population is likely to have to manage on its own or depend on the charity and good will of individual-voluntaristic assistance provided by the shrinking numbers of the "fortunate" among the population.

Summary

- Despite its association with Third World nations, poverty is also widespread in Canada and other advanced capitalist societies.
- Over five million Canadians, or just under one-fifth of the population, live below the poverty lines defined in relation to income requirements to meet basic living costs.
- The perpetuation of poverty is a consequence of deeply rooted social and economic inequalities in our society.
- Poverty and hunger are closely associated with major risks to physical and social well-being.
- Food banks have been opened in several centres across Canada as a voluntary response to the urgent need for basic sustenance among over two million Canadians.
- Food bank recipients include many people dependent on social assistance, but they also increasingly include children, young persons, and the working poor who are not welfare recipients.
- While food banks provide a crucial service to those who need them, they also benefit, directly or indirectly, many employers, businesses, and state agencies.

Questions to Consider

1. Discuss the linkages between income inequality and life chances. In your answer, include material from other chapters in this volume.

2. Discuss the relationships among inequality, poverty, hunger, and health.

3. "To be born poor in Canada does not make it a certainty that you will live poor and die poor but it makes it very likely." Discuss this statement.

4. From all evidence, there is no world-wide shortage of food. Why is it, then, that millions of people go hungry every day and thousands face famine and starvation?

5. Canada is one of the richest countries in the world, and it certainly produces abundant food. How, then, can we explain hunger in this country and the emergence and persistence of food banks?

6. Compare and contrast "victim-blaming" approaches with structural explanations of inequality, poverty, and hunger.

7. Identify and discuss the major contradictions associated with voluntary programs, such as food banks, that address hunger, and other social problems in this country.

Suggested Readings

Gunderson, Morley, and Leon Muszynski. *Women and Labour Market Poverty*. Ottawa: Canadian Advisory Council on the Status of Women, 1990.

Lappé, Frances Moore, and Joseph Collins. *World Hunger: Twelve Myths*. York: Gore Press, 1986.

Moscovitch, Alan, and Jim Albert, eds. *The "Benevolent" State: The Growth of Welfare in Canada*. Toronto: Garamond Press, 1987.

Oderkirk, J. "Food Banks." *Canadian Social Trends* 24, no. 6 (1992): 6–14.

Piven, F.F., and R.A. Cloward. *The New Class War: Reagan's Attack on the Welfare State and Its Consequences*. New York: Ballantine Press, 1982.

Riches, Graham. *Food Banks and the Welfare Crisis*. Ottawa: Canadian Council on Social Development, 1986.

Warnock, John W. *The Politics of Hunger*. Toronto: Methuen, 1987.

Glossary

food banks Voluntary agencies, sustained by donations of time, food, and money, established in order to distribute food to the hungry.

income inequality A pattern of income distribution in which there are consistent disparities in the relative share of income received by different segments of the population.

life chances The opportunities that people have to acquire material goods, services, and desirable living conditions.

poverty A social condition in which people lack the means to sustain themselves at or beyond minimal standards of living.

victim-blaming ideology The belief that people are responsible for their own problems and inadequacies, irrespective of social, economic, or political circumstances that may have caused these problems.

welfare state A framework of government policies, programs, and measures oriented to the preservation of basic living standards and opportunities for all people within a nation, regardless of their circumstances. It is based on the view that the state should act in the public interest on the basis of our shared responsibilities.

References

Blumberg, P. 1980. *Inequality in an Age of Decline.* New York: Oxford University Press.

Bradley, C.F., S.E Ross, and J.M. Warnyca. 1978. "Parent's Choice: A Comprehensive Perinatal Programme." Vancouver Perinatal Health Project, November.

Braungart, S. 1989. "Food Hampers Key to Survival for the Needy." *Calgary Herald,* December 16, A1.

Bronson, H.E. 1984. "Multinational Corporations, Food, and Energy." In *Contradictions in Canadian Society,* ed. J.A. Fry. Toronto: John Wiley and Sons. 43–62.

Brown, J.C. 1978. *Prevention of Handicap: A Case for Improved Prenatal and Perinatal Care.* Ottawa: Canadian Institute of Child Health.

Burton, R. 1989. "Social Workers to Help Battle Hunger in Schools." *Star-Phoenix* (Saskatoon), December 2, A3.

Canadian Association of Food Banks. 1989. *Canadian Hungercount, 1989.* Summary. Toronto: Canadian Association of Food Banks.

———. 1997. *Hunger Count 1997: A Report on Emergency Food Assistance in Canada.* Toronto: Canadian Association of Food Banks.

Chossudovsky, M. 1983. "Underdevelopment and the Political Economy of Malnutrition and Ill Health." *International Journal of Health Services* 13, no. 1: 69–87.

Chu, C. 1989. "Malnutrition Affects Learning Ability of the Poor." *Star-Phoenix* (Saskatoon), November 7: C4.

Eitzen, S., and M.B. Zinn. 1989. *Social Problems.* 4th ed. Boston: Allyn and Bacon.

Epp, J. 1986. "Achieving Health for All: A Framework for Health Promotion." *Canadian Journal of Public Health* 77, no 6: 393–407.

Estes, C.L. 1982. "Austerity and Aging in the United States: 1980 and Beyond." *International Journal of Health Services* 12, no. 4: 573–84.

Fine, S. 1989. "Poor Children More Likely to Die Than Wealthy Peers, Study Finds." *Globe and Mail,* July 25, A5.

Gerth, H.H., and C.W. Mills. 1958. *From Max Weber: Essays in Sociology.* New York: Oxford University Press.

Greater Vancouver Food Bank Society. 1989. "Food Bank Information Kit." Vancouver: Greater Vancouver Food Bank Society.

———. 1998. *Food Bank News* 2, no. 2 (Winter/Spring).

Herrnstein, R. 1971. "I.Q." *Atlantic* 228 (September): 43–64.

———. 1973. *I.Q. in the Meritocracy.* Boston: Little, Brown.

Herrnstein, R., and C. Murray. 1994. *The Bell Curve: Intelligence and Class Structure in American Life.* New York: The Free Press.

Hess, M. 1989. *Children, Schools and Poverty.* Ottawa: Canadian Teachers' Federation.

Jensen, A.R. "How Much Can We Boost IQ and Scholastic Achievements?" *Harvard Educational Review* 39 (Winter): 1–123.

———. 1980. *Bias in Mental Testing.* New York: The Free Press.

Kotz, N. 1984. "The Politics of Hunger," *New Republic* 190 (April): 19–23.

Lewis, O. 1966. *La Vida.* New York: Random House.

Minkler, M. "Blaming the Aged Victim: The Politics of Scapegoating in Times of Fiscal Conservatism." *International Journal of Health Services* 13, no. 1: 155–68.

Myres, A.W., and D. Kroetsch. 1978. "The Influence of Family Income on Food Consumption Patterns and Nutrition Intake in Canada." *Canadian Journal of Public Health* 69, no. 3: 208–21.

National Council of Welfare. 1975. *Poor Kids.* Ottawa. Supply and Services Canada.

———. 1987. Welfare: *The Tangled Safety Net.* Ottawa: Supply and Services Canada.

———. 1988. *Poverty Profile 1988.* Ottawa: Supply and Services Canada.

———. 1989. *Poverty Lines.* Ottawa: Supply and Services Canada.

———. 1990. *Women and Poverty Revisited.* Ottawa: Supply and Services Canada.

———. 1997. *Poverty Profile 1995.* Ottawa: Supply and Services Canada.

Nutrition Canada. 1975. *Survey Report on Indians and Eskimos.* Ottawa: Information Canada.

Oderkirk, J. 1992. "Food Banks." *Canadian Social Trends* 24, no. 6: 6–14.

Osberg, L. 1981. *Economic Inequality in Canada.* Toronto: Butterworths.

Parliament, J. 1987. "Increase in Long-Term Unemployment." *Canadian Social Trends* (Statistics Canada) (Spring): 8–11.

Perkins, S. 1974. "Malnutrition and Mental Development." International Union of Child Welfare Conference.

Physicians' Task Force on Hunger in America. 1985. *Hunger in America: The Growing Epidemic.* Middletown, CT: Wesleyan University Press.

Piven, F.F., and R.A. Cloward. 1982. *The New Class War: Reagan's Attack on the Welfare State and Its Consequences.* New York: Pantheon Books.

Regina Mayor's Board of Inquiry. 1989. *An Inquiry into Hunger in Regina.* Regina: The Mayor's Board of Inquiry.

Reid, D.L., and J.E. Miles. 1977. "Food Habits and Nutrition Intakes of Non-Institutionalized Senior Citizens." *Canadian Journal of Public Health* 68, no. 2: 154–58.

Riches, G. 1986. *Food Banks and the Welfare Crisis.* Ottawa: Canadian Council on Social Development.

Robinson, A. 1989. "Richards Has to Face Burning Issue in New Job." *Star-Phoenix* (Saskatoon), September 25, A3.

Ross, S.E., and A.C. Rutter. 1978. "Healthiest Babies Possible: An Outreach Program." Vancouver Perinatal Health Project.

Ryan, W. 1971. *Blaming the Victim.* New York: Pantheon Books.

Shah, C.P., and C.S. Farkas. 1985. "The Health of Indians in Canadian Cities: A Challenge to the Health-Care System." *Canadian Medical Association Journal* 133: 859–63.

Social Planning and Research Council of British Columbia. 1989. *Regaining Dignity: An Examination of Costs and the Adequacy of Income Assistance Rates (CAIN) in British Columbia.* Vancouver: Social Planning and Research Council of British Columbia.

Special Senate Committee on Poverty. 1971. *Poverty in Canada.* Ottawa: Information Canada.

Statistics Canada and Health and Welfare Canada. 1981. *The Health of Canadians: Report of the Health Survey.* (Cat. 82-538E). Ottawa: Supply and Services Canada.

Stefaniuk, W. 1989. "More Working People Using Food Banks, Survey Finds." *Toronto Star*, March 22, A21.

Swanson, J. "If Welfare 'Helps,' Why Doesn't It Help the Poor?" *Vancouver Sun,* November 18, B5.

Vernon, P.E. 1979. *Intelligence: Heredity and Environment.* San Francisco: W.H. Freeman.

Webber, M. 1992. *Food for Thought.* Toronto: Coach House Press.

Wigle, D.T., and Y. Mao. 1980. *Mortality by Income Level in Urban Canada.* Ottawa: Health and Welfare Canada.

Wilkins. R., and O. Adams. 1983. *Healthfulness of Life.* Montreal: Institute on Public Policy.

Wilkinson, W.H., and V.W. Sidel. 1986. "Hunger in America," *Social and Health Review* 3: 59–64.

York, G. 1989. "Soup Kitchens Try to Ease Hunger for Regina's Children of Poverty." *Globe and Mail,* October 9, A5.

PART II

Gender and Family

INTRODUCTION

Canada is a "vertical mosaic" of different social groups and categories. These groups are not equal in income, power, and status. While there has been an increasing awareness of these inequalities and a growing consciousness that all Canadians possess the right to equality, many groups continue to encounter unequal opportunities and differential life chances. These inequalities and life chances are correlated with gender, class, and race.

Essays in this section address the issue of gender inequality and gender relations encompassing both the public and the private spheres. While the Charter of Rights and Freedoms proclaims the principle of equality before the law regardless of factors such as race, gender, or age, the reality is that inequalities based on gender and race, structured into society itself, prevent people from participating as equal members of Canadian society. Gender inequality is rooted in a history that includes legal inequalities, feudalism, gender stereotyping, capitalist class relations, and patriarchal gender relations. While the nature of exploitative relations and the patterns of exploitation have changed over time, the basic inequality remains. While women have made significant gains in abolishing discriminatory laws, the economic reality has been much more difficult to change. Class relations continue to embody patriarchal principles. Empirical evidence shows the growing proletarianization of women and their increasingly disadvantaged position in economic relations—the "feminization of poverty."

The first reading in this section, entitled "The Social Construction/Deconstruction of Sex, Gender, Race, and Class," provides a comprehensive analysis of various theoretical perspectives on inequalities between men and women, and the role of discourse analysis in the social construction of categories such as race and gender. The liberal feminist perspective focusses on inequalities between men and women and contends that change is possible within existing institutional structures and institutions. According to this perspective, gender is a social construction and thus gender roles can be changed through state intervention, legal reforms, socialization, and education. In this perspective little attention is paid to class and race.

The socialist feminist perspective draws attention to the intersection of class and gender. Informed by the works of Marx and Engels, the relationship between patriarchy and capitalism and the social construction of race are incorporated in the discussion of inequalities between men and women. This perspective calls for going beyond reforms to a radical societal transformation.

Structuralist explanations further uncover inequalities inherent in capitalist structures and the impact of these structures on individuals that guide their lives. Poststructuralists both extend and challenge such analyses and point out how, for example, power is exercised by means other than societal structures. Postmodernists further challenge modernist theories and question their fundamental assumptions of an objectively constructed reality and the universality of concepts. Postmodernists argue that instead of it being possible to know the world in an objective fashion, everything depends upon the discourse used. They argue, for example, that the realities of sex, gender, race, and class are constructed through discourses. Thus, while liberal and socialist feminists address structural features of modern capitalist societies, poststructuralists and postmodernists question the philosophical foundation and basic assumptions of these perspectives. As Alicja Muszynski further points out, postmodernists move from the social construction of sex, gender, race, and class—part of the modernist critique of colonialism, capitalism, and patriarchy—into a deconstruction of what are now called the discourses of sex, gender, race, and class.

The next article in this section, by Leslie J. Miller, critically examines "Family Problems and Problem Families," arguing that the study of family problems is the study of the historical and political process whereby one community tries to impose its version of the good family upon other less powerful communities. The family forms designated as problems are usually those that do not conform to the ideal construct of the powerful. Miller shows how the emergent bourgeois family ideal—the patriarchal "cult of domesticity"—provided the standard against which all familial arrangements have come to be measured. She suggests that the family problems (and the "problem families") of the nineteenth and much of the twentieth century—from the "slum" family to the "blended," homosexual, or communal one—are precisely those whose arrangements appear to diverge from the ideal. Miller's discussion is informed by insights emerging from the fields of feminist scholarship and the sociology of deviance and social control.

In the first part of the chapter, Miller outlines the historical roots of the modern ideal family and the picture of the "fit" family it implies, and reviews attempts to enforce it by regulating alternative or "unfit" forms. Different mechanisms have been used to reform the "unfit" family over time. Still, it is considered necessary to invoke the image of the "normal" family regularly to justify the social control of a whole range of more-or-less discredited alternatives. The discredited family types discussed in this section are the "slum" family, the family with a "working" (i.e., employed) mother, and the lesbian family. Despite the variety of alternative arrangements that have emerged in the recent past, the ideal family type is still held up as the norm against which these alternative forms should be judged. Feminist scholars have argued that the labelling of such alternative arrangements as immoral, evil, or unhealthy be abandoned. As Miller notes, however, such core images in the culture cannot simply be argued away; they demonstrate a remarkable persistence, and various formal and informal mechanisms are used to enforce their moral authority.

One consequence of the rise of the domestic ideal was to focus attention on families that failed to measure up. A second important consequence was the protective cloak of secrecy that enclosed modern family life. This norm of privacy obscured not only women's contributions, but also the inequalities and abuses they and their children suffered. Miller emphasizes that these long-hidden aspects of family life represent forms of conduct that are now in the process of being "problematized"—that is, "discovered" as social problems. Such family realities as the unrecognized and unpaid labour of housewives, the "normal" violence of routine family life, and the structural impoverishment of women are being targeted by various groups wanting to raise their visibility and thus their recognition as urgent social problems requiring intervention and social control. Miller discusses some of these not-yet-problematized or newly problematized aspects of the family and the various socio-cultural factors that have kept them beneath the threshold of attention for so long.

In the concluding section, Miller notes some of the contradictions and ambiguities associated with the demand for social intervention into family life. If the families that fail to measure up to the bourgeois ideal can be thought of as constituting the family problems of yesterday and today, then the inequalities hidden by this same ideal are the problems of tomorrow. For feminists, the first set of problems has suffered from too much intervention; the second set, from too little. Though not always consistent, feminists generally aim to shift the state's power, so that it may be used not to perpetuate the injustices of patriarchy but to redress them.

CHAPTER 5

The Social Construction/ Deconstruction of Sex, Gender, Race, and Class

Alicja Muszynski

Learning Objectives

After studying this chapter, you should be able to
- Outline the relevant theoretical perspectives—liberal feminism; socialist feminism; and structuralism, **poststructuralism**, and **postmodernism**—and the key figures behind them.
- Explain how each perspective explains gender inequality, class inequality, **racism**, and **sex and sexuality**.
- Understand the concept of **gender** as a social construction.
- Outline the historical background of liberal feminism and understand the connections between liberal feminism and liberal philosophy.
- Differentiate between Marxist feminism and socialist feminism.

Introduction

In the two previous editions of this book, I began this chapter with a discussion of the structural inequality between men and women in Canadian society. I pointed out that its existence was a paradox given the principles stated in the Canadian Charter of Rights and Freedoms (1982): "every individual is equal before and under the law and has the right to equal protection and equal benefit of the law without discrimination and, in particular, without discrimination based on race, national or ethnic origin, colour, religion, sex, age, or mental and physical disability" (Article 15, Subsection 1). I then proceeded to demonstrate how women fought for inclusion of the word "sex" in this part of the Charter (Prentice et al. 1996, 448–50). Similarly, First

Nations struggled for recognition of aboriginal and treaty rights (Article 35), with limited success (Berger 1982, 250). The original introduction concluded:

> The lack of equal treatment because of one's race or gender points not only to the existence of individual prejudiced attitudes against, for example, aboriginal peoples or women, but also to institutional racism and sexism (Bolaria and Li 1985, 21). The very institutions that are supposed to enforce equality, which include our legal and parliamentary systems, often serve in practice to perpetuate inequality. This is a fundamental contradiction in our society.

Revisiting these words half a decade later, they strike me as being overly simplistic. While I still believe that fundamental structural inequalities exist and that we as Canadians must commit ourselves to overcoming them, how we are to do this has become a more complicated question as more "minority groups" become politically engaged and articulate their own particular standpoints, which challenge both the political and the theoretical status quo.

In the previous editions I presented one theoretical perspective, basically a socialist feminist one that extended the liberal democratic commitment to equality for all individual citizens. I tried to demonstrate the contradictions inherent in such a commitment when inequalities are structured into groups along the lines of gender, race and ethnicity, and class. For undergraduate students beginning their journey through the thicket of sociological theories, this was already quite a challenge. Now I will be asking you to explore a range of perspectives, each of which takes a different spin on the structured inequalities of gender, race, and class, and throws sex and sexuality into the mix as well.

Beginning with the theories that seek to explain and demonstrate such structured inequalities, we move through to those theories that do not so much deny their existence as question the foundation upon which the theories are themselves constructed and the type of world view they assume. I want to take you through these various "spins" and let you decide for yourselves how and if any of them challenge your own world view and basic ideas about how the world operates. Hopefully, the experience will open your eyes to new ways of seeing, although you may be left with more questions than answers. An undergraduate student in one of my upper-level theory classes, on hearing another student ask me a question, replied that after four years he had learned that in sociology most questions are given the response "It depends."

Unlike teachers in most undergraduate science and engineering classes, sociologists often begin with ambiguities. Nothing is as it appears to be. And there are no easy explanations for how the social world works, never mind why it works the way it does. But for me this is what makes sociology fascinating—there are no fixed truths to be memorized and retained forever. Instead we are asked to sharpen our critical faculties and to question precisely those truths and realities that appear to be most self-evident. Sex, gender, and race are three such taken-for-granted factual realities. In the presentation that follows, I will take you through a theoretical journey beginning with the perspective that tends to take the previous conclusion at face value, and ending with those that blow it apart.

Liberal Feminism

Historical Background

The liberal feminist perspective deals with women's rights within the context of a liberal democracy, like Canada. The underlying philosophy upon which it builds is called liberalism, a philosophy extending back to the period of the Enlightenment (ca. 1690–1790), the Age of Reason sparked by Descartes' philosophy (Cartesianism), the scientific discoveries of Galileo, and Newton's establishment of the science of physics based on the principles of mathematics. In this revolution of ideas, reason displaced God as the fundamental conduit to knowledge about the world. The ascendancy of scientific knowledge in turn helped to produce a global economic transformation, the Industrial Revolution (beginning in Great Britain around the middle of the eighteenth century). And the ideas inherent in liberal philosophy also led to two political revolutions, the American Revolution in 1776–83 and the French Revolution in 1789 (LeGates 1996, 117–55). The political rights of citizens (initially confined to white property-holding men) were enshrined in the American Declaration of Independence and the French Declaration of the Rights of Man and the Citizen.

In Canada, the British North America Act of 1867 reflected a more peaceful separation of a British colony than had taken place in the United States. Eventually, in 1982, the Canadian Constitution was repatriated and the Canadian Charter of Rights and Freedoms was enshrined in it. These political–legal acts are all extensions of the political principles enunciated two centuries ago.

While the political revolutions were to liberate "man" from monarchic rule, the term "man" did not extend to all men or to any women (there were occasional exceptions to certain classes of women who held property, but even these rights were eventually removed). Non-white races were excluded. The institution of slavery (in 1629, the first slave came directly to Canada, then New France, from Africa) was not officially abolished until the nineteenth century in Great Britain (Britain abolished the slave trade in 1807) and by extension in its Canadian colony (Wolf 1982, 201). Slavery continued to be practised in the United States until the Emancipation Proclamation of 1863 (Henry et al. 1995, 64–66).

In 1876 the Canadian government legislated the Indian Act, creating an official government category of status Indians who, being wards of the state, did not acquire the right to vote in federal elections until 1960. In addition to the creation of "races" of people who were denied the rights accorded to white Anglo-Saxon citizens, the issues of class also became relevant. One purpose of creating a Canadian state was to develop an indigenous form of capitalism, which required a large population of wage labourers forced to seek employment or starve. For Canada, this has required encouraging immigration from other countries to create a labour pool. The paradox of the "modern age" has been a growing conviction that reason can be applied to know, to understand, and to change the world of nature and the world of man for the betterment of mankind in general, alongside a restricted application of political and economic benefits that creates inequalities along the cleavages of class (employer/worker), gender (man/woman), and **race** (white/other).

Marlene LeGates, in her history of Western feminism entitled *Making Waves* (1996), argues that women were unable to organize as a cohesive group around women's rights until the modern age was in place. She argues that preceding movements for the rights of particular groups, like women, there had to be a generalized public recognition that, in principle at least, all individuals are entitled to certain fundamental freedoms. In liberal democracies, these freedoms are granted to citizens and are formally recognized in the right to vote for a leader and political party who represent the will of the majority.

That women had been in a position of inequality for centuries in Europe is well documented (and called patriarchy). Men as fathers and as husbands had authority over their daughters and wives encoded in law. During the French Revolution, feminists (including men like Condorcet) emerged to make the case that women had the same political rights as men. However, these voices were in the minority and were silenced by the backlash that followed. The Napoleonic Code of 1804

> deprived married women of control over property and compelled them to acquire their husbands' citizenship, thus eliminating the basis for an independent public life. Whereas some women in the ancien régime had enjoyed certain privileges, such as voting, by virtue of their class position, now all women were categorically distinguished from men and discriminated against on that basis. French women would have to wait almost 150 years for the right to vote. (LeGates 1996, 140)

In England, Mary Wollstonecraft published *A Vindication of the Rights of Woman* in 1792, challenging Rousseau's portrayal in his 1762 book on education, *Emile*, of woman as the natural subordinate to man, who alone possessed the ability to reason. Condorcet and Wollstonecraft argued that woman also had the capacity to reason, but where this placed her in terms of public life remained ambiguous. Although she argued for woman's independence and the need for women to be educated, Wollstonecraft, like Condorcet, still saw women as basically confined to the home; while "women's 'first duty is to themselves as rational creatures,' … their civic duty was to manage their families, educate their children, and assist their neighbours" (LeGates 1996, 142).

In the United States, feminists also emerged to champion women's rights, and were connected in various ways to the abolitionist movement. "Black women had welcomed white women in their antislavery organizations but the reverse was not always true, although white women may have had a better record than white men did. Nevertheless, racism and racial inequality were acceptable to some white women even as they condemned slavery" (LeGates 1996, 178). Organized feminism emerged around the issue of acquiring the vote for women, or the question of extending suffrage to women (the larger question of universal suffrage leaving in place issues of racism and class inequality) in Great Britain, the United States, and Canada. In 1848 American women met at Seneca Falls to adopt the Declaration of Sentiments, similar in tone to the Declaration of the Rights of Woman issued by Olympe de Gouges in 1791 in France and modelled on the French Declaration of the Rights of Man and the Citizen (LeGates 1996, 178).

The stage was thus set for the movement that has come to be known as liberal feminism. From the foregoing, I hope that you can see why this movement, centred around women's political and civic rights, is part of the modernist project that stems historically from the Enlightenment. Women's rights' advocates, like Mary Wollstonecraft, argued that women were "reasonable creatures." And it was the ability to reason that set humans apart from the other animal species and gave them an avenue to knowledge and control of the world around them, including the society in which they lived.

The whole issue of race would, like the issue of gender, become a topic for scientific debate and inquiry, especially given the new respect accorded to scientific knowledge. Just as it was asked whether women were as intelligent as men and whether intelligence could be established scientifically as having been imprinted into one's sex before birth, the same questions were formulated concerning race. Was there a hierarchy of races with the most intelligent race at its apex? This question reflects the extension of "race" to what Miles (1989, 2) calls "scientific racism." In Canada, from 1885 to 1945, this question was linked to the eugenics movement centred around extending scientific study with the aim of improving the race (McLaren 1990, 14–16).

Maternal Feminism or Welfare State Liberalism?

Liberal philosophy has been further refined in terms of what rationality implies for the individual and for society as a whole:

> Liberals have attempted to define reason in various ways, stressing either its *moral* aspects or its *prudential* aspects. When reason is defined as the ability to comprehend rational principles of morality, then the value of individual autonomy is stressed. In contrast, when reason is defined as the ability to calculate the best means to achieve some desired end, then the value of self-fulfilment is stressed. Whether liberals define reason largely in moral or prudential terms, they nevertheless concur that a just society allows individuals to exercise their autonomy and to fulfil themselves. (Tong 1989, 11)

The result is two versions of liberalism that assign very different roles to the state. Classical liberals argue that the state exists to protect civil liberties "(for example, property rights, voting rights, freedom of speech, freedom of religion, freedom of association) and, instead of interfering with the free market, simply provides all individuals with an equal opportunity to determine their own accumulations within that market" (Tong 1989, 12). In this view, capitalism is the ideal economic system to encourage those individuals with the best abilities to realize their potential, thus benefiting both themselves and society as a whole. Society is viewed as a meritocracy: those most deserving will get ahead by means of their own best efforts, and in the process of serving their own interests also serve the ends of a capitalist economy. It was Herbert Spencer, a sociologist, who coined the term "survival of the fittest." The less government interferes in the economy, the better. In Canada, the Progressive Conservative parties have generally taken this stance; for example, in the two-term reign of prime minister Brian Mulroney as well as the provincial governments of Ralph Klein in Alberta and Mike Harris in Ontario.

The second version of liberalism promotes the welfare state. These liberals recognize that certain portions of the population do not profit by aggressive capitalist competition, so the state is called upon to provide more than a guarantee of fundamental rights. It must also intervene directly in the economy by providing various services to those most in need. In Canada, the welfare state emerged as a result of the widespread poverty and discontentment of the unemployed during the Great Depression of the 1930s as well as the regulated economy necessary to supply the Allies during the Second World War. As Jane Ursel (1992) demonstrates, the provision of social services like mothers' allowances, universal health care, and welfare were victories won by the organized working poor and the unemployed. In other words, those who were most in need of these services had to fight for them. The liberals in power had to be challenged to put into practice the philosophy they promoted (labelled by those without power as an **ideology**).

Wollstonecraft and those feminists who argued that women's place remained in the home, that women were morally superior to men and should thus be educated in order to be good wives and mothers, fit the first model. For them, the issue of ensuring a moral order in a society transformed by the economic excesses of capitalism was primary. Radical, or cultural, feminists would also enter this debate around the issue of woman's nature being morally superior to that of man, leading to the critique that these feminists were **essentializing** women by seeing all women as the same, and reproducing the dichotomization of male and female natures as being fundamentally different from one another. Nineteenth-century Canadian pioneers like Nellie McClung have been called maternal feminists for their insistence on the complementarity of women's and men's roles, with women assuming the functions of the moral education of men and children. And finally, antifeminists also borrow some of these arguments in denouncing those feminists who would proclaim women's equality to men in all spheres, especially in paid labour, politics, and religion.

In Canada, one of the most vocal and best organized of the antifeminist groups is REAL (realistic, equal, active, and for life) Women, established in 1983. It challenges traditionally liberal organizations like the National Action Committee on the Status of Women (NAC), which lobbies the federal government for funding on behalf of smaller groups—over 500 groups in 1993 (Prentice et al. 1996, 457)—dispersed across the country.

> [REAL Women] opposed abortion, universality of social services, the equality clauses of the Charter of Rights, no-fault divorce, legislation on equal pay for work of equal value, publicly funded daycare, affirmative action in employment, and legal protection of the rights of homosexuals. Given the dependence of Canadian women's groups on public funding, REAL Women represented a genuine threat. They provoked a government review of the Women's Program in the Secretary of State. Although the review vindicated the program, its funding was cut substantially under the Progressive Conservative governments of the 1980s. (Prentice et al. 1996, 452)

While the NAC represents the second version of liberalism, supporting the welfare state, REAL Women represents the first version. Most liberal feminists in Canada today adopt the model of welfare state liberalism. It appears, moreover, that it is not only self-proclaimed feminists (for example, those who attend the annual NAC convention) who embrace this second version of liberalism. In December 1997, Angus Reid conducted a poll examining differences in how men and women viewed the Ontario government. If Premier Harris represents the first, laissez-faire form of liberalism, it appears from the results of the poll that twice as many men (48 percent) as women (28 percent) accept this approach. Meanwhile, the federal Liberal party tends to be identified with the welfare state form of liberalism, and here we find far more women (51 percent) than men (34 percent) supporting the Liberals. There is also a 5 percent greater support of the New Democrats among women compared with men. The "gender gap" thus indicates that differences in how women and men understand liberal democracy translate into differences in their support for political parties and social programs.

The Gender Gap

Ontario's Progressive Conservative government is searching for ways to boost support among women voters and reduce a huge gender gap that has Premier Mike Harris and his senior strategists extremely worried.

Throughout the past year, public opinion polls and political focus groups have shown that women in general are much more unhappy with the Tory government than are men. Fewer than one in three women voters would support the Conservatives, according to polls conducted this month.

Changes in health care, education and social services are major factors, say senior Conservatives, their political opponents and political analysts interviewed this month, all of them women.

"If there's a guns–butter tradeoff, women are usually on the butter side and men are more on the guns," said Sylvia Bashevkin, a political-science professor at the University of Toronto.

The current gender gap facing the Tories is "as big as they get," said Lisa Young, assistant professor of political science at the University of Calgary. Like Ms. Bashevkin, she has spent several years looking at the phenomenon of gender gaps that arise when governments cut key services.

The Conservatives have initiated some of the moves political parties traditionally resort to when faced with a lack of support among women voters.

Mr. Harris has promoted strong women to major cabinet portfolios and to senior positions in the public service. The government is trumpeting programs designed to appeal to women, such as those to help shelters for battered women or boost the health of newborns.

Environics Research Group also has been pointing to the gender gap for several months. Its most recent survey of voting intentions, conducted between December 11 and December 17, 1997, showed that overall, the Conservatives trail the Liberals largely as a result of the party's lack of support among women.

(continued)

(continued)

Among all decided voters, 48 percent said they would vote Liberal, 35 percent picked the Conservatives and 13 percent opted for the New Democrats, which marked a gain of three percentage points by the Tories at the expense of the NDP since a similar poll in October. Four percent would pick another party.

When the poll was broken down along gender lines, men were virtually divided between the Conservatives (43 percent) and the Liberals (42 percent). However, women were almost twice as likely to pick the Liberals (54 percent) as the Tories (28 percent).

For some analysts, the easy explanation is that the premier's image as a strong-willed ex-jock who moved from running a small business into being a full-time politician is more likely to appeal to men than women.

At Queen's Park, the government's political opponents point to the cuts in services, and the direct impact on women, as the source of discontent among women voters.

New Democrat Marion Boyd (London Centre) worked to provide services for women before first being elected in 1990. "It's women who largely are taking on the role of caregiver," as the government shuts hospital beds and cuts home-care services, she said.

"The attack on pay equity, on employment equity, on child-care resources, certainly on education, all have had a disproportionate effect on women," Ms. Boyd said.

Liberal Sandra Pupatello (Windsor-Sandwich) also spoke of the direct impact cuts in services have on women. "Women are more likely to stay home with the sick. They are the ones that have to leave their job [when a child is sick at school]."

She argued that boosting the economy doesn't result in quick dividends for women as much as it does for men. "If this government has been good for business, that, unfortunately, is still led by men. I think that just by virtue of the makeup of the business community, it is more men. And you'll find them to be more supportive of the government because their bottom line is better....

"It's economic issues that are actually creating these gender gaps. Where you see gender gaps, chances are you've got a polarization of the parties around these economic kinds of issues," such as reducing services to fight the deficit.

In the Republican case, to reduce the gender gap, she said the party "would write off certain segments of the female electorate. They would say 'Really liberal, usually younger, single women are never going to vote for us. It just isn't going to happen. But we can make targeted appeals to certain segments of women—married women in the suburbs, middle class.' Those women would be made angry by government policy, but they could be brought back through appeals basically saying that the economic well-being of their gamily was dependent on cutbacks in the size of government. So they could usually be brought back on side," Ms. Young said.

She said the Ontario Conservatives have looked to the Republicans for some of their policy ideas and for many of their examples for political strategy. "There are groups of voters that the Ontario Tories are likely writing off."

Ms. Young also predicted there would be targeted appeals to women voters. "The smartest way to do that likely would be to promise to put more money back into education."

(continued)

(continued)

She also commented on the appointments of Ms. Ecker and Ms. Witmer. "This is a typical response. Every time the Republicans faced a large gender gap, you would see more and more women appointed to very high-profile positions."

But, she warned, "There's very little evidence to suggest that it helps any."

Ms. Bashevkin at the University of Toronto also cautioned that it is not easy to win women voters with targeted policies. "This government is going to want to keep, I would imagine, its core support among certain rural and suburban interests who are still quite on side with it. When it tries to reach out to groups of women voters, it can risk offending that core constituency."

Sexes Split over Ontario's Tories

	Men	Women
In an election would vote for:		
Conservatives	48%	28%
Liberals	34	51
New Democrats	12	17
Believe government is on the right track:	62	44
Believe pace of change is too quick:	61	75
Important issues cited by voters:		
Education	50	60
Health care	20	35
Jobs and unemployment	35	29
Taxes	10	6
Believe government successful in:		
Managing issues of concern to women	44	41
Managing issues of concern to children	44	33
Providing honest and trustworthy government	55	42
Helping those most in need	46	33
Providing hope for the future	59	42

Note: Figures provided by Angus Reid Group Inc. from a December 1997 survey of 1000 voters. The margin of error varies with each question from a minimum of plus or minus 3.1 percentage points, 19 times out of 20.
Source: "Sexes Split over Ontario's Tories," December 1997. Reproduced with permission of the Angus Reid Group.

Source: Richard Mackie, "Women Spurn Ontario Tories: Strategists Seek to Win Them Over," *The Globe and Mail*, December 30, 1997, pp. A1, A4.

So what distinguishes liberal feminists from other feminists? From other women in general? Does a woman have to openly identify herself as a feminist to fight for issues like federally subsidized child care? Can men be feminists? These are all ongoing questions to which there are diverse answers. Roberta Hamilton, for example, in her book *Gendering the Vertical Mosaic*, stresses that there is a plurality of women's movements. Just because one self-identifies as a woman and is concerned about issues of equality, one is not automatically united with all women. Even the struggles women choose will vary according to their circumstances. For example, Catholic women may not support abortion. Does this then preclude them from being feminists? Aboriginal women living on reserves mired in poverty may not see that a federally subsidized child-care program is one that would benefit them, since most of these facilities are located in urban areas. For aboriginal women, employment and programs that focus on substance and sexual abuse may be far more relevant, especially if they are empowering; that is, if they are not generated and run by white experts who come for brief stays and then return to the cities. The category of **Woman** is just that, a category that can only be reflected in the lives of actual people who identify themselves as women. "Woman" is a myth created in and through language, a myth that has had powerful symbolic value (as in the myth of Eve, for example, or that of the Virgin Mary). This critique of the category of "Woman" is one best developed by postmodernist feminists, discussed later in the chapter.

Critique of the Liberal Feminist Perspective

One of the main problems with the liberal feminist perspective is that the category of **Man** is not challenged but remains in place as the norm for women's achievement of equality. Most liberal feminists struggle to have women realize the same benefits that middle-class white men enjoy as a matter of course. So the question is posed: Equal to whom? Why? Do women want to become like this small group of men? Which women are making the case? Here issues of race and class become very important. Whose issues receive media and government attention? Liberal feminists have been criticized for representing only a small fraction of women: white, Protestant, Anglo-Saxon. Of the perspectives reviewed here, liberal feminism is the one that does not challenge existing structures, seeking instead to reform them. The view is that a liberal democracy is the best framework for extending human rights and freedoms to all individuals. Rights and freedoms tend to be interpreted piecemeal, however, as we have seen in the case of slavery.

For example, liberal feminists argue that husbands and wives are equal. Women have just as much a right to be in the paid labour force as men. Further, women should have access to the same educational and training paths available to men and should be paid the same wages as men if both perform the same tasks. Table 5.1 demonstrates that the earnings ratio between men and women in 1993 was far from equal, even in the professional categories. Women still earn between approximately 60 percent and 80 percent of what men earn when both are employed full-time. The earnings ratios for part-time workers are even lower, with women earning as little as 46.3 percent of men's wages.

TABLE 5.1   Average Annual Earnings by Occupation and Gender, 1993

	Full-time, full-year workers			All workers		
	Women	Men	Earnings ratio[a]	Women	Men	Earnings ratio[a]
Managerial/administrative	$34 765	$51 680	67.3%	$30 943	$48 187	64.2%
Natural sciences	34 896	45 851	76.1	30 855	40 979	75.3
Social sciences/religion	36 235	50 766	71.4	28 680	47 443	60.4
Teaching	40 302	50 931	79.1	30 786	43 181	71.3
Medicine/health	34 408	57 743	59.6	27 185	50 590	53.7
Artistic/recreational	30 115	38 760	77.7	18 687	28 277	66.1
Clerical	25 570	32 431	78.8	19 394	24 681	78.6
Sales	24 008	37 589	63.9	16 280	29 097	56.0
Service	18 919	31 343	60.4	12 236	21 505	56.9
Agriculture	13 106	20 570	63.7	9 895	17 021	58.1
Processing	25 494	37 460	68.1	19 475	32 149	60.6
Product assembly/ fabrication/repair	22 228	35 419	62.8	17 374	29 839	58.2
Transport equipment operation	23 001	35 796	64.3	13 708	29 590	46.3
Material handling	21 295	32 446	65.6	14 724	22 762	64.7
Total	28 392	39 433	72.0	18 936	29 599	64.0

[a] Represents women's earnings as a percentage of those of men.
Source: Statistics Canada, *Women in Canada: A Statistical Report,* 3d ed., Cat. no. 13-217, p. 96.

In addition, census figures published in March 1998 indicate that occupational segregation still exists. The top ten occupations for men and women are still segregated into the stereotypical male and female occupations. For men, they are, in descending order, truck driver, retail sales clerk, janitor/caretaker, retail manager, farmer, sales rep, vehicle mechanic, material handler, carpenter, and construction labourer. The top ten occupations for women, in descending order, are retail sales clerk, office secretary, cashier, registered nurse, accounting clerk, elementary/kindergarten teacher, waitress, office clerk, babysitter, and receptionist (Mitchell 1998, A1).

At home, there is an ideology, especially among young couples, that housework and child care should be jointly shared, especially when both spouses are also in the paid labour force. Again the reality does not match the ideal. Chris Jackson (1996, 26), using Statistics Canada data, demonstrates that in 1992 Canadians spent "roughly as much time on unpaid work as on paid work." However, women, "on average, spent 78 percent more time in 1992 on unpaid work than men did." The following chart and insert detail what constitutes unpaid work and how paid and unpaid work is divided.

What happens if a couple divorces? Ross Finnie conducted a longitudinal study of Canadian tax files to measure the financial well-being of divorced men and women

What Is Unpaid Work?

A: Household Work

Meal preparation and clean-up	Examples making a pot of tea, setting the table, cooking, baking, cleaning up after meals or baking, washing/drying dishes

Other domestic work

Cleaning	mopping floors, dusting, vacuuming, making beds, taking out the garbage
Clothing care	washing laundry, hanging it out to dry, folding clothes and linen, mending clothes, sewing on buttons, shining shoes, hemming
Repairs and maintenance	painting, plastering a wall, plumbing, fixing or washing the car, renovation, mowing and watering grass, weeding, composting, raking leaves, watering house plants
Other	packing for a move or vacation, rearranging furniture, putting groceries away, feeding and grooming pets

Help and care

Child care	feeding, changing and bathing babies and other children, putting them to bed, teaching them to learn, helping with schoolwork, reprimanding, reading and talking to children, administering first aid, medicines or shots, taking temperature, playing games with children, walking or biking with them, unpaid baby-sitting by household members (not parents or guardians), visiting children in hospital
Adult care	washing and cutting hair, running bath, providing help to disabled and elderly members of the household, administering first aid, preparing and administering medicines, taking temperature

Management and shopping	paying bills, balancing chequebooks, making shopping lists, preparing tax returns, shopping for groceries, clothing, hardware, gasoline, looking for a house or apartment, getting appliances repaired

Transportation and travel	travel related to management and shopping for goods and services, taking family members to daycare, work, school, hospital and other places, other travel related to domestic work

(continued)

(continued)

B: Other Unpaid Work

Volunteer work	fundraising, answering a crisis line, delivering meals
Other help and care	helping friends, neighbours, relatives and others with housework, cooking, transportation, repairs and maintenance
Transport: other unpaid work	travel related to volunteer work and other help and care

Canadians spent roughly as much time on unpaid work as on paid work

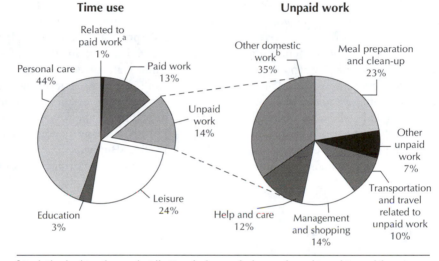

[a] Includes looking for work, idle time before and after work, and travel to and from work.
[b] Includes cleaning, laundry and ironing, clothes and shoe repair, home repair and maintenance, gardening and grounds maintenance, and pet care.
Source: Statistics Canada, *Canadian Social Trends* 42, Cat. no. 11-008 (Autumn 1996).

immediately after divorce, and then again three years later. While Finnie observed a slight difference in economic well-being between men and women immediately after divorce, three years later men tended to be better off while women suffered.

> These results paint a picture of divorce where, on average, women experience steep declines in economic well-being while men enjoy moderate increases. And while there is some recovery for women in the post-divorce years, three full years after the split they remain well below their pre-divorce levels, as well as the current levels of their ex-husbands. The gender earnings gap and low levels of spousal/child support payments are the key factors underlying these patterns. (Finnie 1996, 276)

Finnie goes on to suggest that "the welfare system probably has a positive impact on the divorce rate by facilitating men's reneging on their responsibilities to the marriage, and thus increasing the relative advantage of divorce on their part" (Finnie 1996, 278). We must remember that liberal feminists pushed for easier access to divorce as a way out of abusive marriages. Since the 1960s, divorce laws have been amended and divorces are now relatively easy to obtain. But they hold economic consequences for women, who are generally given custody of the children but who tend not to hold as well-paying jobs as their ex-spouses. Once again, we must consider class relations, since these issues (for example, child support payments) are most important for couples where the ex-spouse continues to earn a reasonable income.

To conclude this section, then, I hope you can see the main outlines of a liberal feminist perspective, in theory and in practice. When you look through a newspaper and find the latest statistics gathered by the Canadian government on issues like the wage gaps between men and women, whether divorce rates are rising or have stabilized, increased rates of child poverty, all of these "facts" (presented as statistics) lend themselves well to a liberal feminist analysis. Liberal feminists examine these at face value and use them as weapons to lobby the Canadian state to do something to improve the condition of Canadian women and children, which the "facts" show to be a social problem in need of improvement. Liberal feminists also tend to assume that the various levels of government can in fact do something to improve the living conditions of women and children, at least up to the minimum living standard established by the federal government, known as the poverty line. But what *causes* poverty? This is a question addressed directly by neo-Marxists, including critical theorists and socialist feminists.

Socialist Feminism

Frederick Engels: "The World-Historical Defeat of the Female Sex"

While welfare state liberals tend to envisage an age in which chronic poverty will eventually disappear, neo-Marxists argue that there must first be an end to capitalism. The classic work on the economic laws of capitalism and the labour theory of value is Karl Marx's *Das Kapital*. In this work, planned to appear in several volumes but unfinished at his death in 1883, Marx proposed to scientifically expose the underlying laws of capitalism. Once understood, these laws could be used as a basis for overthrowing the system. The class of proletarian workers would seize the state in preparation for a stateless and classless communist society. Marx has been accused of positivism in his insistence that the way to understand capitalism was through science; indeed, scientific Marxism reflects that strand of Marx's project (Morrow and Brown 1994, 90).

Another strand, known as critical theory, stems from Marx's earlier works, sometimes referred to as his humanist phase. These earlier writings were recovered by the Frankfurt School, founded in 1923 and relocated to New York in 1935 during the period of Nazi control in Germany (Waters 1994, 188). The Frankfurt School focussed on the elements within capitalism that provided flexibility, ways of keeping the working classes and the dispossessed from revolting against their condition. Frankfurt School theorists—for example, Herbert Marcuse in *One Dimensional Man*—examined culture and the creation of mass consumer society. The most famous contemporary theorist who was originally associated with the Frankfurt School, but has moved considerably beyond its original theoretical debates, is Jürgen Habermas.

What is the place of socialist feminists in these traditions? Marxist feminists can be identified as accepting Frederick Engels's *The Origin of the Family, Private Property and the State* as a starting point for an examination of women's unpaid labour in the home: the domestic labour debate (Hamilton and Barrett 1986). Engels and Marx worked closely together and Engels edited Marx's final work after the latter's death. Scientific Marxists tend to ignore Engels's work as heavily flawed and not truly Marxist in the scientific sense.

Basically, Engels argued that women were the first form of private property. Private property relations are fundamental to capitalism. Using Lewis Henry Morgan's study of the Iroquois, Engels described various systems of kin lineages and family formations. He traces the modern bourgeois family back to Roman law.

> Its essential features are the incorporation of unfree persons and paternal power; hence the perfect type of this form of family is the Roman. The original meaning of the word "family" (*familia*) is not that compound of sentimentality and domestic strife which forms the ideal of the present-day philistine; among the Romans it did not at first even refer to the married pair and their children but only to the slaves. *Famulus* means domestic slave, and *familia* is the total number of slaves belonging to one man. (Engels 1981, 121)

Engels, following Morgan's lead, attributed more rights to women in earlier historical periods and thus posited a collective historical defeat of women at the hands of men. Men came to assert rights over other people (slavery was one form) and over the things of nature, like land. Private property rights thus displaced rights previously held in common and required a permanent military presence to enforce, to protect, and to extend such rights through wars and conquests. Europe was divided into a series of absolute monarchies, and the basis for their overthrow was the revolutions mentioned earlier in this chapter. The liberal democratic state and the capitalist economy are intertwined. The Industrial Revolution was not only an application of scientific knowledge (for example, the steam engine, the invention of steel, railroads, and the printing press) but was largely financed by Europeans to acquire colonies and bring back to Europe the wealth found there (for example, tea, silks, and minerals like silver and gold).

Explaining Poverty

Wolf (1982) argues that the Europeans were initially weak in world trade. In 1400, the world was interconnected by trade links in which the European countries played very minor roles. But gradually, the Europeans took advantage of and came to dominate these trading networks, gaining world trade supremacy. Where once the

European countries saw their wealth drained as they paid for new commodities like tea, through a series of wars and colonial conquests wealth began to flow into Europe and Great Britain. This wealth provided further impetus for the Industrial Revolution, financing its costly technology and infrastructure (factories and the machinery housed in them, and the network of railroads and canals, for example). And capitalism allowed the emerging Western nation-states and their former white settler colonies—the United States, Canada, Australia, and New Zealand—to retain their dominant world status.

Thus, to explain poverty, we must examine the global situation as well as the Canadian context. On the world stage, Canada is a wealthy nation. But its wealth is not evenly distributed. Carstens (1991) argues that within the First World that includes Canada resides a Third World of First Nations. Far from creating a situation in which everybody becomes better off, as liberal democrats supporting the further development of capitalism argue, capitalism cannot help but generate inequalities. Table 5.2, for example, documents the extent of poverty among the First Nations. And Table 5.3 shows that the rate of child poverty in Canada is rising, from a poverty rate of 14.9 percent in 1980 to 20.5 percent in 1995. These rates reflect poverty levels for all Canadians.

While traditional Marxists focus on class (Wright 1979), others extend the analysis to demonstrate racial inequalities both within nation-states and globally (Miles 1989). Still others explore gender oppression in its complex relationship with class exploitation and racism (Muszynski 1996), adopting a socialist feminist perspective.

While socialist feminists value Engels's insights into how women as a collective group lost power, they also see his work as flawed. For example, Engels claimed that the subordination of women within the family unit was necessary so that bourgeois men could pass on their wealth to their own biological sons. In order to establish paternity, women had to be monogamous and subordinate to men. This is what Engels (1981, 120) meant by his famous phrase "the world-historical defeat of the female sex." Woman was degraded by being forced into servitude within marriage and the home. Engels called this a form of prostitution, since women were forced to marry in order to survive and forced to provide services, including sexual favours, to keep their husbands satisfied. Engels also qualified his analysis by stipulating important class differences. Among the proletariat (the working classes), everyone was forced into paid labour: men, women, and children. Thus the proletarian family no longer existed, given the long hours and brutal conditions within which all of its members were forced to live and to work. The ideal family was a creation of the bourgeoisie, where capitalists could demonstrate their newly found wealth and status by their residences, opulent homes with idle wives, well-dressed and well-mannered children, and servants.

The question Engels does not ask is why capitalism had to unfold in just this manner. There is a certain determinism and functionalism at work here. Socialist feminists have listened to radical feminist critiques of patriarchy and ask how these relations intertwine with capitalism. Much of socialist feminist work is historical, going back and exploring the types of gender and class relations found in actual specific settings and times. For example, Bettina Bradbury (1993) explores the lives of working-class families in Montreal during the latter part of the nineteenth century. Charlene Gannagé (1986) uses the case study approach to explore the lives of garment workers in Edna Manufacture, located in the Spadina garment district of Toronto. Her book is entitled *Double Day, Double Bind* to demonstrate women's double day of labour, in the paid labour force and in the household. She gives a voice to women by including excerpts from interviews, letting them speak in their own words.

TABLE 5.2   Comparing Income Levels for Aboriginal and Non-Aboriginal People, 1990

Composition of Personal Income[a] of Aboriginal and Non-Aboriginal People, 1990

	Aboriginal people[b]		Non-aboriginal people	
	Women	Men	Women	Men
Wages and salaries	74.6%	82.3%	72.9%	78.3%
Net income from self-employment	2.2	4.4	3.2	7.3
Investment income	1.4	0.6	7.7	3.7
Government transfer payments	19.8	11.0	12.7	6.3
Other income	2.0	1.8	3.5	4.4
Total	100.0	100.0	100.0	100.0
Total income ($)	13 489	20 578	17 706	30 488

[a] Includes only those with some income.
[b] Includes respondents with Indian registration who do not have aboriginal origins.

Incidence of Low Income[a] among Aboriginal and Non-Aboriginal People, by Age, 1990

	Aboriginal people[b]		Non-aboriginal people	
	Women	Men	Women	Men
Persons aged				
Under 18	35.1%	33.7%	17.0%	16.9%
18–24	41.2	30.9	22.4	17.5
35–44	28.5	20.7	14.6	11.8
45–54	24.6	21.0	11.7	9.7
55–64	33.1	26.5	17.1	13.8
65 and over	31.3	22.4	22.9	13.7
Total	32.7	27.9	16.9	13.8

[a] Includes respondents with incomes below Statistics Canada's low income cut-offs.
[b] Includes respondents with Indian registration who do not have aboriginal origins.
Source: Adapted from Statistics Canada, *Women in Canada: A Statistical Report*, Cat. no. 89-503.

TABLE 5.3   Poverty Trends, Children under 18, 1980–1995

Year	Number of children under 18 living in poverty	Poverty rate (%)
1980	984 000	14.9
1981	998 000	15.2
1982	1 155 000	17.8
1983	1 221 000	19.0
1984	1 253 000	19.6
1985	1 165 000	18.3
1986	1 086 000	17.0
1987	1 057 000	16.6
1988	987 000	15.4
1989	934 000	14.5
1990	1 105 000	16.9
1991	1 210 000	18.3
1992	1 218 000	18.2
1993	1 415 000	20.8
1994	1 334 000	19.1
1995	1 441 000	20.5

Source: *Poverty Profile 1995* (Ottawa: National Council of Welfare, Spring 1997), p. 11. Reproduced with permission of the Minister of Public Works and Government Services Canada, 1998.

Socialist Feminist Links with Radical Feminism, Anti-Racism, and Postcolonial Theories

Where socialist feminists have differed from radical feminists is in seeing patriarchy as the predominant form of oppression. Radical feminists writing in the 1960s tended to view patriarchy as universal (Firestone 1970), leading to a separatist movement where women would establish their own communities apart from men. More recently, radical feminist historians like Gerda Lerner have sought to trace the historical origins of patriarchy. But the focus has tended to be on women as forming their own class.

> Women and men have entered historical process under different conditions and have passed through it at different rates of speed. If recording, defining, and interpreting the past marks man's entry into history, this occurred for males in the third millennium BC. It occurred for women (and only some of them) with a few notable exceptions in the nineteenth century. Until then, all History was for women pre-History. (Lerner 1986, 226)

Generally, the difference between a radical feminist and a socialist feminist perspective is that radical feminists have tended to focus exclusively on women as an excluded and oppressed class, while socialist feminists have insisted on exploring the twin systems of patriarchy and capitalism as being mutually reinforcing and ever-changing to accommodate new developments. While for many radical feminists class tends to be confined to women, socialist feminists keep class separate (thus gender oppression is related to but not the same as class exploitation). And theorists like bell hooks (1984; 1994) and Patricia Hill Collins (1990) have also called attention to the dynamics of race. While for white women, the question of oppression by men can be taken for granted, the situation is far more complicated for those groups where both men and women have been completely disempowered; for example, aboriginal peoples and African-Americans/Canadians. Women in these groups cannot target men as a class because their men have also been oppressed, in ways different from those the women in their groups have experienced. Thus women experiencing racism may view anti-racist rather than feminist issues as the main axis of struggle, identifying feminism as a white middle-class women's movement that has tended to exclude them.

> Racism is another barrier to solidarity between women. The ideology of Sisterhood as expressed by contemporary feminist activists indicated no acknowledgment that racist discrimination, exploitation, and oppression of multi-ethnic women by white women had made it impossible for the two groups to feel they shared common interests or political concerns. Also, the existence of totally different cultural backgrounds can make communication difficult. This has been especially true of black and white female relationships. Historically, many black women experienced white women as the white supremacist group who most directly exercised power over them, often in a manner far more brutal and dehumanizing than that of racist white men. Today, despite predominant rule by white supremacist patriarchs, black women often work in situations where the immediate supervisor, or boss, or authority figure is a white woman. (hooks 1984, 49)

It is also bell hooks, in a later work entitled *Teaching to Transgress*, who shows us the importance of theory, not for its own sake, but as a necessary component to political action. "In many black settings, I have witnessed the dismissal of intellectuals, the putting down of theory, and remained silent. I have come to see that silence is an act of complicity, one that helps perpetuate the idea that we can engage in revolutionary black liberation and feminist struggle without theory" (hooks 1994, 66).

Theories that investigate the historical relationships whereby the Western nations created dependency in myriad ways are called postcolonial theories. The current situation of racially and ethnically disadvantaged groups is traced back to the unequal sets of power relations that established such nation-states as Canada. Aboriginal peoples experience conditions of poverty similar to those found in many of the poor countries of the world (see Table 5.2). The Royal Commission on Aboriginal Peoples reported suicide rates among them five to six times higher than those of other Canadians. "This anguish is the cumulative effect of 300 years of colonial history: lands occupied, resources seized, beliefs and cultures ridiculed, children taken away, power concentrated in distant capitals, hopes for honourable co-existence dashed over and over again" (as quoted in Bell 1995).

Socialist feminist theory, anti-racism, and postcolonial theories tend to stress historical and structural factors as crucial in explaining, for example, poverty. We cannot understand poverty today as it affects women or aboriginal peoples without understanding how these groups were formed and how they fit within the **power** structures of Canadian society (in, for example, legal systems, education, and the paid labour force). But the history that is stressed in all of these perspectives is not the "official" history generally found in elementary and high-school history textbooks. All three of these perspectives focus on the history of peoples "without history," as Wolf notes in the title of his book. The First Nations, for example, are struggling to revise the ways in which they have been portrayed and written about and are developing their own curricular material.

Recovering "herstories" has also been an important component of the feminist project. Socialist feminists are concerned with finding not only the voices of women who did not enter history until the nineteenth century, as Gerda Lerner argues, but also the voices of marginalized women: working class, poor, or stigmatized by the colour of their skin. For example, when one writes about aboriginal peoples, there must be a concern to include women's voices as well as men's. This also widens the door to include other disempowered groups: children, the elderly, and the physically and/or mentally (dis)abled, to mention a few. These newer histories and herstories also challenge the conventional and traditional view of what counts as history and how history is written: by whom? for whom? in whose interests?

The Agency/Structure Debate

Structural explanations, like those I used in previous editions, focus on interlocking systems of power by which inequalities are reproduced without anybody necessarily being aware that they are exercising power. When an official in a uniform denies a refugee from Uganda entry into Canada, he might see himself as simply doing his job. If he doesn't follow the rules and regulations laid out for him in the manuals and indoctrinated into him during his training, he will be fired. Placed within a historical and structural perspective, however, we can see this event as being located in a long series of discriminatory Canadian immigration laws in which the same rules are not applied to all applicants. Within sociology, there has been a debate over theories that over-stress either structure or agency—the agency/structure debate. Some neo-Marxist theories, like those of Louis Althusser and Nicos Poulantzas, as well as the scientific Marxism mentioned previously, favour the structural side of the controversy.

> Althusser accepts from Marx a view of the state as the object of political class struggle. Within this analysis the state has certain agencies (e.g., the police, courts, prisons, the military) which ensure the orderly operation of capitalism.... Althusser argues that the capitalist state is also much more complex than this, accomplishing reproduction not merely by the use of force but also by the manipulation of ideas.... there is therefore said to develop a plurality of "ideological state apparatuses" (ISAs) but which

traverse the boundary between the state and civil society. They include churches, schools, families, political parties, trade unions, the mass media, and cultural and recreational institutions. These institutions operate to establish an imaginary view, in the minds of individuals, of the conditions of their existence, for example, that there is no alternative to capitalism.... or that individuals make real choices about the direction of their lives. They imagine these things to be true when the reality lies elsewhere. Althusser is convinced that the key ISA in accomplishing this under contemporary conditions is the school.... No other ISA is as effective because the school has the obligatory attention of every member of society for eight hours a day, five days a week, 200 days a year, for ten years. (Waters 1994, 120)

In the "hard" structuralist view, then, individuals are created in and through the institutions and structures that guide their lives from even before the moment they are born. Althusser (1971) discusses the anticipated birth of a baby (in the middle classes) into an already constructed world made by parents, relatives, and the medical profession. The baby is given a name, and often his or her whole future is planned in advance. Indeed, the very individuality of a person is something created externally, over which he or she has no control. Thus the notion of being an individual and exercising free choice is an illusion.

For example, you may want to reflect on your days in high school and the formation of different groups, each carrying its own **identity**, displayed in clothing, for example. Students entering high school generally have a great need and desire to belong, to make friends. But in order to gain admission into the peer group, they are forced to choose and to mould themselves into what is expected of them. Even the loners are perceived in specific ways. It is as if the categories are created first, and then the person steps into that category. Of course, change does occur, but it often occurs in structured ways. For example, new fashions come on the scene and a new group forms around them. Just think of the popularity of running shoes, their expense, and how much profit companies like Nike have made selling to a teenage (and younger) market. Meanwhile, the factories in which these shoes are made are located in countries like Indonesia where the women working in them are paid a few dollars a month. If workers threaten to strike for better conditions, the company simply moves to another country with a more pliant work force, whose submissiveness is often guaranteed by the government of the country anxious to have these multinationals locate there. So, how much choice is a teenager expressing in deciding which brand of running shoes to buy? And how much choice does the female worker in the factory have? The "hard" structuralist position would answer very little if any. So how is change possible, especially if the structural conditions are not favourable (for example, a massive recession or depression in the major world economies, or a complete collapse of the world stock markets)?

Socialist feminists and critical theorists tend to adopt a "soft" structuralist position in seeing the need to identify agency on the part of the social actor. In the example just given, if teenagers are given the means of finding out about the poor working conditions involved in factories located outside Canada and producing their favourite shoes or clothing, they often act on that knowledge. Not only have teenagers boycotted brand names made by corporations that violate decent working conditions and wages, they have also taken it upon themselves to educate other teens. Their actions may not close down the corporations in question, but they do force them to be accountable, and they draw attention to the disparity between the lifestyles portrayed in their advertisements and the harsh brutality of the lives of their workers. This is one way in which the agency/structure debate is addressed.

Socialist feminists have also grappled with this dilemma of resolving the tension between the freedom of the individual to act and the constraints of the societies in which we live. One of the best known feminist theorists in this area is Dorothy Smith (1987; 1990). Part of her work has been labelled standpoint theory.

> The fulcrum of a sociology for women is the standpoint of the subject. A sociology for women preserves the presence of subjects as knowers and actors. It does not transform subjects into the objects of study or make use of conceptual devices for eliminating the active presence of subjects. Its methods of thinking and its analytic procedures must preserve the presence of the active and experiencing subject. A sociology is a systematically developed knowledge of society and social relations. The knower who is construed in the sociological texts of a sociology for women is she whose grasp of the world *from where she stands* is enlarged thereby. For actual subjects situated in the actualities of their everyday worlds, a sociology for women offers an understanding of how those worlds are organized and determined by social relations immanent in and extending beyond them. (Smith 1987, 105–106, emphasis in original)

Smith distinguishes between a sociology of women and a sociology for women. You may ask yourselves how many women founders of sociology, if any, were covered in your introductory sociology courses. For most of its history, sociology was a male enterprise that studied women in a peripheral way at best. Smith (1987, 19–22) discusses the implications of this way of studying women in a section entitled "Men's Standpoint Is Represented as Universal" in her work *The Everyday World as Problematic*. Smith links men's standpoint to what she calls "relations of ruling." These relations do not simply include individuals who make important decisions for others and thus exercise power over them; for example, parents or the prime minister or a police officer ticketing someone for a traffic violation. Relations of ruling are also "mediated by texts, by words, numbers, and images on paper, in computers, or on TV and movie screens. Texts are the primary medium (though not the substance) of power ... It is an ideologically structured mode of action—images, vocabulary, concepts, abstract terms of knowledge are integral to the practice of power, to getting things done" (Smith 1987, 17).

A sociology for women seeks not only to incorporate women's standpoints, their world views as seen through their eyes and experiences (a sociology that entails specific types of qualitative methods), it also seeks to provide women "on the margins" (to use bell hooks's phrase) with a way of seeing beyond their own life circumstances. On this point, I think both Smith and hooks would be in agreement. To empower oneself and others requires a broader understanding of the structural aspects of society that are in place and that keep women and other groups not only disadvantaged but also acquiescent in their oppression. Why is it that those without power often do not speak out? The reasons are part of the relations of ruling, and are also found in the ISAs identified by Althusser, discourses that serve to justify particular ways of seeing and make one feel helpless to change oneself, one's conditions, or the world in which one lives.

Power resides inside and between relationships. Socialist feminists and critical theorists do not define power as simply a scarce resource that is fought over by those who seek to acquire it for their own ends. We all exercise power in our daily lives— it is what allows us to function as social human beings. But the ways in which we exercise power vary.

We also exercise power over ourselves. We control our own bodies and present them to others in specific ways; for example, as gendered and/or as athletic in the clothing we might wear jogging. When certain individuals feel they have no control over anything in their own lives except over their bodies, they may act upon themselves in self-destructive ways; for example, by slashing (a practice that is fairly common among women in prison, many of whom have experienced sexual abuse that produces self-loathing) or by regulating food intake (bulimia or anorexia nervosa).

Having discussed structuralist explanations and the attempts by critical theorists and socialist feminists to overcome the agency/structure divide (dichotomous thinking in either/or terms is also a product of men's standpoint represented as universal— and tied to the project of modernism as discussed in the section on liberal feminism), let us now turn to the poststructuralist and postmodernist debates.

Poststructuralism and Postmodernism

Introduction: Precursors

Michel Foucault (1926–84) came to be friends with Louis Althusser (1918–90) in the late 1940s. Both were students at the École Normale Supérieure in Paris, although Althusser preceded Foucault. Foucault's biographer notes:

> To enter ENS is to enter a lineage as well as an elite ... In the late 1940s and the 1950s, it was still possible for a student to trace his intellectual ancestry back to 1848 through a chain of masters ... At ENS, Foucault became part of a chain which also included Louis Althusser and, through his agency, would subsequently include a younger generation of theorists such as Jacques Derrida, Etienne Balibar, Pierre Machery, and Jacques Rancière. (Macey 1994, 22)

Both men suffered from depression and came to spend extended periods of time in the school's sanitarium. Both men also had complex relationships with the French Communist Party. Macey (1994, 22) notes, "ENS also has a long history of providing a haven for quietly subversive figures," naming both Foucault and Althusser in their company. In his autobiography, Althusser describes his thirty-four years spent at the École Normale:

What did the school become? Very rapidly, from the very beginning, I ought to say, it became a real maternal cocoon, the place where I was warm and at home, protected from the outside world, the place I did not need to leave in order to see people because they passed through and came here, especially when I became famous; in short, a substitute for a maternal environment, for the *amniotic* fluid. (quoted in Macey 1994, 23)

It was also at the ENS that Foucault attended a lecture given by another theorist now seen as central in poststructuralist and postmodernist theories, especially within the French feminist movement, Jacques Lacan. Lacan (1901–81) was to revise and rework the psychoanalytic theories of Sigmund Freud and inscribe them within the postmodernist lexicon. For example, the rather crude American rendering of "penis envy" in a literal way (as in the phrase "anatomy is destiny") was rethought by Lacan and those who followed him in symbolic terms, as the power contained in the symbol of the phallus that must pass through women. Women become crucial in the process, but so does their annihilation as beings in their own right. We are here firmly on the postmodernist terrain. Judith Butler writes:

Lacan disputes the primacy given to ontology within the terms of Western metaphysics and insists upon the subordination of the question "What is/has being?" to the prior question "How is 'being' instituted and allocated through the signifying practices of the paternal economy?" The ontological specification of being, negation, and their relations is understood to be determined by a language structured by the paternal law and its mechanisms of differentiation. A thing takes on the characterization of "being" and becomes mobilized by that ontological gesture only within a structure of signification that, as the Symbolic, is itself pre-ontological.

There is no inquiry, then, into ontology per se, no access to being, without a prior inquiry into the "being" of the Phallus, the authorizing signification of the Law that takes sexual difference as a presupposition of its own intelligibility. "Being" the Phallus and "having" the Phallus denote divergent sexual positions, or nonpositions (impossible positions, really), within language. To "be" the Phallus is to be the "signifier" of the desire of the Other and to appear as this signifier. In other words, it is to be the object, the Other of a (heterosexualized) masculine desire, but also to represent or reflect that desire. This is an Other that constitutes, not the limit of masculinity in a feminine alterity, but the site of a masculine self-elaboration. For women to "be" the Phallus means, then, to reflect the power of the Phallus, to signify that power, to "embody" the Phallus, to supply the site to which it penetrates, and to signify the Phallus through "being" its Other, its absence, its lack, the dialectical confirmation of its identity. By claiming that the Other that lacks the Phallus is the one who is the Phallus, Lacan clearly suggests that power is wielded by this feminine position of not-having, that the masculine subject who "has" the Phallus requires this Other to confirm and, hence, be the Phallus in its "extended" sense. (Butler 1990, 43–44)

As you can see from this quote, poststructuralist theory is not very accessible to readers. But let me try to deconstruct some of this for you. First and foremost, note that Butler rejects the basis upon which Western philosophy is established—ontology or the possibility of an understanding of Being. Enlightenment philosophy grounds this ontology in Reason, as we have already seen. Poststructuralists reject this premise and shift rather to the structures embedded in language itself. Language provides the structures through which we construct ourselves and the reality around us. This is the grounding point, then, from the structuralist tradition; in particular, the tradition that stems from linguistics. Ferdinand de Saussure (1857–1913) provided a starting point in distinguishing between written and spoken language. Roland Barthes is seen as the founder of semiotics, extending Saussure's ideas "to all areas of social life. Not only language but also social behaviors as representations, or signs: 'Not just language, but wrestling matches are also signifying practices, as are TV shows, fashions, cooking, and just about everything else in everyday life' (Lash 1991, xi). The 'linguistic turn' came to encompass all social phenomena which, in turn, came to be reinterpreted as signs" (Ritzer 1996, 458).

Claude Lévi-Strauss (born in 1908) is a key figure of French structuralism as well as of anthropological structuralism. Lévi-Strauss argued that the incest taboo is the foundation of all cultures. The incest taboo, according to him, involves the exchange of women from one group to another. Women go outside of their groups to form new kin units and bride wealth flows the other way in recompense to the group who is losing a member. These alliances unite the two groups, but at the expense of women who are always exchanged. Combining the ideas of Lévi-Strauss and Lacan, Rubin refers to the "phallic mother." The Oedipal crisis discussed by Freud and re-interpreted by Lacan involves the "castration" of the mother "by the recognition that the phallus only passes through her, since the relationship of a male to every other male is defined through a woman" (Rubin 1975, 192).

Deconstructing Sex, Sexuality, Race, and Gender

While liberal and socialist feminists address structural features of modern capitalist societies, poststructuralists and postmodernists question the philosophical foundations of these views. Where liberal and socialist feminists argue for a social construction of gender, poststructuralists and postmodernists deconstruct not only gender, but also sex and sexuality. Because postmodernist theories are well developed in other disciplines, especially English and studies of popular culture, I will focus attention on poststructuralism here, since it both connects and disconnects with the structural theories addressed in this chapter. There is some overlap between poststructural and postmodern theories. Poststructural theories are particularly relevant to the social sciences because of their precursors in the structural theories of, for example, Talcott Parsons (structural functionalism), Althusser (structural Marxism), Jürgen Habermas (formerly a member of the Frankfurt School of critical theory), Anthony Giddens (a British sociologist who seeks to unify the structure/agency debate through his theory of structuration), and various feminist theorists. Judith Butler, cited above, works in the area of lesbian theory, challenging accepted norms of heterosexuality, a point of connection with Michel Foucault. Queer theory also pushes the envelope in terms of deconstructing sex and sexuality (Seidman 1997). The French feminists are active in postmodern and poststructuralist debates and include Luce Irigaray, Hélène Cixous, Julia Kristeva, and Monique Wittig. Their point of departure is the work of Simone de Beauvoir (1908–86), in particular, her work *The Second Sex* (1989), in which woman is defined and constructed as "Other" to "Man" (man in the generic sense as well as in the specific sense). "Man" represents both the neutral and the positive poles while "Woman" represents the negative—not man. "Man" requires the social and biological construction of "Woman" as "Other" in order to construct himself. In Canada, Dorothy Smith has pursued feminist theorizing using both the Marxian and phenomenological traditions of thought.

There is an important connection to be made with the concept of race here. A number of theorists have focussed on the social construction of race as ideology, as a **discourse**. For example, Robert Miles (1989, 73–77) develops the concept of racialization whereby a category of race was created as part of the process of colonization. Scientific theories were developed by which "race" was defined as a scientific category with a typology. The next step was to develop a hierarchy of races—each with certain innate traits—placing "Caucasians" at the apex as the most intelligent, those who developed industrialization along with civilization. Science thus became a discourse used to legitimize a certain point of view as natural, the "white man's burden" of bringing progress to other less intelligent races.

At the same time, race was used to construct an "Other" that was the opposite of "Self." The negative characteristics of "Other," Miles argues, were crucial to the identity formation of "Self," leading to a legitimation of a world order dominated by white Anglo-Saxon Protestant males. The concept of race was a necessary but insufficient condition to the establishment of racism: in the historical period of colonialism and imperialism, it involved an "othering" that produced categories of races judged to be inferior along pseudoscientific lines (such as intelligence and the capacity to reason). There are close parallels here with the dichotomous thinking that created the male/female split, although the consequences were different. For example, where did white women stand in relation to their house slaves? The concept of "Other" produces complex interlocking discourses that are used to justify the power wielded by those who do the defining. We have seen in the previous section how Dorothy Smith connects power through the use of discourse to the "relations of ruling."

Within postmodern theory, the formation of identity happens in and through us. Fundamental to this identity is our sex. Most of you probably understand the concept of sex in biological terms, as determined by combinations of XX or XY chromosomes and as visually displayed in the genitalia. Sex is assigned at birth by medical practitioners who visually inspect the baby and pronounce its male or female status. That status then underlies socialization, boys developing a masculine gender identity and girls developing a feminine gender identity. The two are seen as separate spheres of behaviour. For example, boys are said to have short attention spans, to like to play in team games, and to be good at math and spatial skills, while girls are said to be more attentive and quiet, to like to play one-on-one with a best friend, and to be good at verbal and communication skills.

Deconstructing gender then, according to this view, requires deconstructing sex as well. For example, Kessler (1994, 218) examines how physicians handle the case of "intersexed infants, babies born with genitals that are neither clearly male nor clearly female." She concludes that the medical personnel involved in making such decisions are operating with a particular conception of what is "natural."

> Although the deformity of intersexed genitals would be immutable were it not for medical interference, physicians do not consider it natural. Instead they think of, and speak of, the surgical/hormonal alteration of such deformities as natural because such intervention returns the body to what it "ought to have been" if events had taken their natural course. The non-normative is converted into the normative, and the normative state is considered natural. The genital ambiguity is remedied to conform to a "natural," that is, culturally indisputable, gender dichotomy. (Kessler 1994, 231–32)

Use of the term "deformity" is already a linguistic sign pointing to a serious problem. More subtle is the taken-for-granted naming and typing of genitalia. The word "genital" is an abstract concept applied by the physician to what he or she "sees" as belonging to the baby. For the physician to "see" a penis or a vagina as the obvious marker of a baby's sex is already part of a long process of socialization that begins with the birth of the physician.

How many sexes are there? How many genders? Gilbert Herdt has edited a thick volume entitled *Third Sex, Third Gender: Beyond Sexual Dimorphism in Culture and History* (1994). For example, Serena Nanda studies the hijras of India as both a third sex and a third gender. Meanwhile, in a reappraisal of our own Western history, historian Thomas Laqueur argues that the dichotomization of two sexes is recent, stemming from the nineteenth century. Until then, there was a one-sex model in operation. All bodies were basically or essentially male, with women seen as imperfect males. With the rise of the scientific enterprises and the emergence of medicine as a scientific profession, anatomy came to play an important role. In dissecting bodies, even female ones, anatomists drew the female genitalia as the inverted genitals of the male. The ovaries became gonads that had not dropped, while the vagina was portrayed as a hidden penis. One explanation put forward was that of the humours. Men were warm by nature, causing their genitals to drop, while the female body was cold, causing constriction (perhaps even frigidity) and a different sexual temperament. In this case, while there were two genders and woman was constructed as "other" to man, their bodies belonged to the same model with differences in degree rather than in kind.

Foucault: Sex, Sexuality, Knowledge, and Power

It is Michel Foucault who "subverts" sex and sexuality. In the *Introduction* to his *History of Sexuality* (published in three volumes but originally conceived as a much longer work, cut short by his death), Foucault begins by questioning the myth of the Victorians as a sexually repressed people. "The seventeenth century, then, was the beginning of an age of repression emblematic of what we call the bourgeois societies, an age which perhaps we still have not completely left behind" (Foucault 1980a, 17). But in his historical examination, he notes "around and apropos of sex" a "veritable

The One-Sex Model: Female Genitals as Inverted Male's

So-called biological sex does not provide a solid foundation for the cultural category of gender, but constantly threatens to subvert it. Foucault suggests an explanation when he argues that in the Renaissance and before there was no such thing as the one and only true sex and that a hermaphrodite could be regarded as having two, between which he/she could make a social and juridical choice. He is perhaps utopian in his political claim; gender choice was by no means so open to individual direction, and one was not free to change in midstream. But he is right that there was no true, deep essential sex that differentiated cultural man from woman. But neither were there two sexes juxtaposed in various proportions: there was but one sex whose more perfect exemplars were easily deemed males at birth and whose decidedly less perfect ones were labelled female. The modern question, about the "real" sex of a person, made no sense in this period, not because two sexes were mixed but because there was only one to pick from and it had to be shared by everyone, from the strongest warrior to the most effeminate courtier to the most aggressive virago to the gentlest maiden. Indeed, in the absence of a purportedly stable system of two sexes, strict sumptuary laws of the body attempted to stabilize gender—woman as woman and man as man—and punishments for transgression were quite severe.

In this world, the body with its one elastic sex was far freer to express theatrical gender and the anxieties thereby produced than it would be when it came to be regarded as the foundation of gender. The body is written about and drawn as if it represented the realm of gender and desire; its apparent instability marked the instability, indeed impossibility, of an all-male world with only male homo-erotic desire. An open body in which sexual differences were matters of degree rather than kind confronted a world of real men and women and of the clear juridical, social, and cultural distinctions between them.

Source: Thomas Laqueur, *Making Sex: Body and Gender from the Greeks to Freud* (Cambridge: Harvard University Press, 1990), pp. 124–25. Copyright © 1990 by the President and Fellows of Harvard College. Reprinted by permission of the publisher.

---

discursive explosion." What identifies Foucault as a poststructuralist is his "reading" of history as "genealogy." Rather than focussing on the official version of history and on the official events, Foucault studies how deviance came to be defined in order to establish normality as a category into which people were fitted and fit themselves, thus allowing administration by the state. To reiterate an earlier point, normality (or the social construction of "Self") has to occur through a defining and categorizing of the deviant: the insane, the criminal, and the sexually deviant; the homosexual, the masturbating child, and the hysterical woman. Foucault wrote on all of these topics, beginning with insanity and ending with sexuality (although there is no linear progression in his thought or writings).

> There is no binary division to be made between what one says and what one does not say; we must try to determine the different ways of not saying such things, how those who can and those who cannot speak of them are distributed, which type of discourse is authorized, or which form of discretion is required in either case. There is not one but many silences, and they are an integral part of the strategies that underlie and permeate discourses. (Foucault 1980a, 27)

Everyone has a sex. This "fact" was subverted to force people into their appropriate sexual orientation. It also became a means for people to come to control themselves, by controlling their bodies and their desires. It became a means for people to exercise power over themselves in conventional ways—ways dictated by experts (medical doctors, psychiatrists, and psychotherapists, and before them, Catholic priests) and institutions. (One can see here how Foucault takes Althusser's concept of ISAs and moves beyond it.) Foucault (1996, 209) responds to an interviewer's question about power and sex: "If power affects the body, it is not because it was first internalized in people's consciousness. There is a network of bio-power ... that is itself a network from which sexuality is born as a historical and cultural phenomenon within which we both recognize and lose ourselves."

In a 1980 interview entitled "Truth and Power," Foucault discusses his involvement with and rejection of Stalinism and scientific Marxism. His critique of class analysis as understood within these "discourses" (including that of the Communist Party of France in which he was involved) was that they failed to address "a whole series of questions posed by science" (Foucault 1980b, 110). Foucault's sympathy did not lie as much with the working classes of the world as with the "silenced"; for example, those incarcerated in mental asylums and prisons. He faults structuralist Marxist theories with not going far enough in the questions they pose. Those theories accept too readily a certain preconceived view of knowledge and of the "subjects" of history (for example, the proletariat as a revolutionary force).

> One has to dispense with the constituent subject, to get rid of the subject itself, that's to say, to arrive at an analysis which can account for the constitution of the subject within a historical framework. And this is what I call genealogy, that is, a form of history which can account for the constitution of knowledges, discourses, domains of objects etc., without having to make reference to a subject which is either transcendental in relation to the field of events or runs in its empty sameness throughout the course of history. (Foucault 1980b, 117)

It is quite obvious from the foregoing quotes that Foucault's discourse is not readily intelligible to the average reader. To summarize in crude form, a difficult task given Foucault's own disavowal of what he wrote as "truth," the central concepts within both a capitalist and a postmodernist society shift from the citizen of the liberal philosopher (or from the standpoint of the proletariat in Marxist discourse), to the inscription through sex and sexuality upon the body that is then formed into the citizen or the proletarian. How this inscription, or identity (and more than one identity becomes not only possible but probable: for example, black lesbian Marxist), is formed becomes the primary focus of study. Power operates not only at the level of the state or the capitalist employer. Power is diffuse and multiple, and resides across relationships. Knowledge, then, involves knowledge of how power operates. Here Foucault does not abandon the transformative project envisioned by Marx and Engels. Rather he redirects our gaze to probe even further below the surface of appearances, to look at how we as individuals come to write our identities upon ourselves, our bodies, and how they are simultaneously written for us by others. Foucault argues that the sexuality of children becomes a primary site in the exercise of power. The bodies of children are controlled (socialized) by parents as well as by a host of institutions. To test this statement, examine newspaper accounts of child poverty and child abuse. Who defines what these are? Who thereby exercises control of child custody and of solutions to the problems that are formulated? Do you find the voices of the children in these accounts? Are children silent? Power/knowledge operates on multiple levels and knowledge is power. Therein lies the transformative potential, since for Foucault, there is always a "surplus" of power that allows "subjects" to subvert the power imposed upon them.

Critique of Poststructuralism/Postmodernism

Once students overcome the verbiage and denseness associated with these "discourses," many of them become fascinated with the theories. These theories speak to our times in which media representations often appear to be more "real" than that which is represented. For example, the film *Primary Colors* is modelled upon a book by an anonymous author addressing the Clinton presidency. The movie depicts the sexual adventures of a fictional American president during his presidential campaign. But even before the movie was released, President Clinton was embroiled in the accusations made against him by Paula Jones and Monica Lewinsky. In a similar vein, the movie *Wag the Dog* depicts an American president creating a fictional war in order to divert public attention from accusations made against his personal conduct. After the movie was released, President Clinton threatened to go to war against Iraqi leader Saddam Hussein. The threat of war helped Clinton retain his popularity in the opinion polls in the face of the accusations of sexual misconduct. The link to postmodernist theories is the media preoccupation with sex and sexuality, especially deviant sexuality.

Should the sexual conduct of the leaders of nation-states be used to gauge their performance as politicians? In the case of President Clinton, who was accused of demanding sexual favours from women employed to work for him, those who pushed for impeachment claimed that the real issue was his lying and causing the women to lie under oath. But you can see that we are a long way here from the liberal philosophy covered in the first part of the chapter. Is one's private behaviour connected to one's ability to reason? Can we any longer make use of this private/public dichotomy? The irony here is that while we can ask such questions about male world leaders, women, even those who attain prominent positions in the political sphere, are still connected to the private spheres. They are still often judged by their appearance rather than by what they have to say.

The media seem to be more than a mirror for reality. Reality itself becomes dubious and unreal until it is refashioned within a medium like a newspaper or the TV newscast. The popularity of the Internet provides another forum whereby individuals can re-create themselves in totally fantasized identities in the many on-line chat rooms. Who on the Internet can know the person's "real" identity? Feminist postmodernists would also argue that it is no accident that pornography, including child pornography, has found a large audience on the Internet.

The response by those who remain unimpressed by poststructuralism and postmodernism is that people generally operate with some version of "reality." Deconstructing reality does nothing to solve problems like racism, poverty, and child abuse. In fact, these problems tend to be masked and ignored so that postmodernists in particular come to be seen as self-indulgent individualists who make everything and everyone relative by denying the existence of an external reality. For example, who has access to computers and the Internet? Are we not once again reproducing sites of privilege in First World countries that deny the economic realities of vast numbers of the world's populations? Even in Canada, as demonstrated in Table 5.3, the rate of child poverty has grown during the course of the 1990s. Postmodernists, in response, would challenge the use and construction of opinion polls and statistics. For example, go back and review the boxes and tables found in this chapter. Why are numbers and statistics so convincing?

Notwithstanding the social construction of opinion polls and statistical presentations, we see the homeless every day of the week in our major cities. There are faces attached to the poor and they are visible to anyone who cares to see them.

Summary

- The liberal feminist perspective focusses on the inequalities between men and women.
- According to this perspective, gender is a social construction and thus gender roles can be changed through socialization, education, and legal reform. Sex is biologically fixed. Little attention is paid to class and race.
- The socialist feminist perspective draws attention to the intersection of class inequalities and gender. The analyses of Marx and Engels are extended to incorporate a discussion of the relationship between patriarchy and capitalism, as well as of the social construction of race.
- Structuralist explanations within the neo-Marxist tradition uncover inequalities buried and carried within the structures of capitalism. Even the individual is just a product of structural forces that give him or her the illusion of freedom.
- Poststructuralists, like Michel Foucault, both extend and challenge such analyses, investigating, for example, how power is not only carried within societal structures, but also comes to be written on and through bodies.
- Postmodernists challenge "modernist" theories, like those of liberal and socialist feminism, arguing that we have moved into a new type of global society. Fundamental assumptions no longer hold. The factuality of two dichotomous and oppositional genders and sexes is denied. Dichotomous thinking is itself shown to be a Western construction, a product of Western philosophy.

- Instead of the possibility of knowing the world in a true and objective fashion, postmodernists argue that everything depends on the discourse used. The "realities" of sex, gender, and race are constructed through discourses and cannot be scientifically proven to exist. Science is itself a discourse created by communities of practitioners. Thus, from the social construction of sex, gender, race, and class— part of the modernist critique of colonialism, capitalism, and patriarchy—postmodernists move us into a deconstruction of what are now called the discourses of sex, gender, race, and class.

Questions to Consider

1. What are the various types of feminisms covered in this chapter? Which do you find most appealing? Why?

2. How is liberal feminism connected to liberal philosophy? What are its historical roots? What are the two types of liberal feminism discussed in this chapter?

3. What is the difference between Marxist feminism and socialist feminism? How are the two connected to the works of Marx and Engels? Where is the concept of patriarchy introduced? Why?

4. What types of Marxism are discussed? How are they connected to the agency/structure debate?

5. What is the difference between postmodernism and poststructuralism? How do they connect to structuralism? Name a key figure discussed under each heading.

6. Are we living in a modern or postmodern society? You may reject both categorizations and justify another response (for example, an advanced capitalist society). Provide examples from your own experience to explain your position.

Suggested Readings

Bannerji, Himani. *Thinking Through: Essays on Feminism, Marxism, and Anti-Racism.* Toronto: Women's Press, 1995.

Hamilton, Roberta. *Gendering the Vertical Mosaic: Feminist Perspectives on Canadian Society.* Toronto: Copp Clark, 1996.

hooks, bell. *Teaching to Transgress: Education as the Practice of Freedom.* New York: Routledge, 1994.

Rosenau, Pauline Marie. *Post-Modernism and the Social Sciences: Insights, Inroads and Intrusions.* Princeton: Princeton University Press, 1992.

Ursel, Jane. *Private Lives, Public Policy: 100 Years of State Intervention in the Family.* Toronto: Women's Press, 1992.

Glossary

discourse Discourse is a key concept within postmodernist and poststructuralist theories. It is also part of the methodology employed within these perspectives. The starting point is language and how language is expressed through words and ideas. In terms of inequality, any oppression or domination has to be internalized in order to be effective. Internalization already implies the use of words and images in understanding one's place in the world. Deconstructing these words, ideas, images, and symbols can be done in many different ways. For example, postmodernists play with language and words to show how relative they are to the context in which they are found.

essentialism This is a methodological problem found within certain strands of feminist theory. In the 1960s and 1970s, radical feminists tended to accept the argument that men and women were basically different. While malestream thinkers argued that women were inferior to men, radical feminists turned their arguments around to argue that because of their natures women were superior to men. Women's reproductive capabilities made them nurturant, peace-loving, and caring. Ecofeminists also developed this theme, drawing out the metaphor of mother nature and women's natural connection to the earth and to the environment. The problem with such connections is that they assume a fixed female and a fixed male nature, and they also essentialize nature and the environment as somehow self-evident realities. In recent decades, there has been a general consensus amongst feminists that these concepts are more complicated than first assumed.

gender Gender is generally acknowledged in feminist theories as socially constructed. This means that gender is not fixed once and for all across time or cultures. Gender is rather developed within specific cultures and reproduced through the process of socialization of children. In Western societies, there is an assumption that there are two genders and that these are linked to certain fixed biological features. Boys and girls are assumed to be different and are then brought up by parents and socialized in school, by media, and with peers to display the characteristics associated with being a girl or a boy. This socialization continues throughout life, and is especially pronounced in adolescence.

identity This is a concept that has come into popular usage in the 1990s and is linked to the methods implied in social construction. Thus, the categories of gender, sex, sexuality, race, and ethnicity are not fixed and available for study through scientific methods. Rather, the meaning of these terms must be studied in the context of the societies and cultures within which they take shape. This means that they are fluid and subject to change. Thus, a person takes on their identity in both conscious and unconscious ways that depend on that individual's cultural setting. For example, in the nineteenth century a person's class background was fixed and depended on the occupational status of one's father. In Europe, if the father was a farmer the oldest son would generally take over from the father. This has changed over the course of the twentieth century to the extent that for many people class is no longer a label that they adopt in terms of how they view themselves.

ideology This word has a very complicated history. It is used in a fairly loose way in the chapter to refer to systems of ideas that people accept to explain their world to them, such that their everyday reality comes to be taken for granted and is thus unquestioned. In this sense, then, everybody has an ideological perspective that makes sense of the world such that they can function on a day-to-day basis. Socialist feminists, postmodernists, and poststructuralists attempt to articulate these ideologies and to show what is masked or hidden behind that which is assumed by most people to be self-evident. For example, many people assume that there are only two sexes and that gender socialization is based on the biological reality of sexual difference. Postmodernists and queer theorists parody these assumptions to uncover their ideological foundations, to show that these assumptions are not part of some hard and fast reality but rather are products of certain ways of thinking about the world and the people living in it.

postmodernism and poststructuralism "Although the two are not identical, they overlap considerably and are sometimes considered synonymous. As I see it the major difference is one of emphasis more than substance. Post-modernists are more oriented to cultural critique while the post-structuralists emphasize method and epistemological matters. For example, post-structuralists concentrate on deconstruction, language, discourse, meaning, and symbols while post-modernists cast a broader net" (Rosenau 1992, 3).

power Power is another concept that has undergone rethinking in recent decades. Orthodox Marxists, for example, tended to think about power in a deterministic way. That is, power was exercised through the structures of capitalism and manifested in class exploitation. Those working for wages were made subordinate within economic and political systems controlled by the bourgeoisie. Thus, power represented power over the dispossessed. Feminist thinking and poststructural and postmodernist thinkers have rethought power in terms of how it is that individuals accept their position of inequality in various places: the workplace, the home, the state, etc. Max Weber's question of how is it that people obey even if their obedience does not benefit them has been taken up in these more recent discourses. Michel Foucault has written extensively on this topic and views power as diffuse and complex. Everybody exercises some form of power in order to survive, but how power is manifested differs in complex ways.

race and racism The way in which these two terms are treated in the chapter relates to social construction. The work of Robert Miles is used here in understanding the concept of race as one that is not fixed across time or cultures. Within Western societies, the colonial experience and the rise of the sciences have been important precedents for our thinking about race as a fixed scientific category. In this sense, then, race refers to a process of defining an "Other" in order to define one's own self and one's own group. Those who name are also those who have the power to enforce their views upon the majority of the population, including the Other. In Western societies, race has been linked to the physical marker of skin colour. Ethnicity is another way of defining self and Other through religion, national identity, language, etc. Ethnicity establishes communities of people who feel they belong because they share these common characteristics. Those who are excluded tend to be racialized as Other, and here the boundaries between ethnicity and race can become fluid (for example, racializing Jews). Racism is based on a concept of race but develops the concept in order to produce a hierarchy of races with those who do the naming at the top (whites or Caucasians or the Nordic race). Those beneath the superior race are judged by it as inferior on a number of characteristics, the most important of which is intelligence, since those who are deemed to be less intelligent by nature can then be governed by the superior race.

sex and sexuality Sex has been assumed within sociology to be a fixed characteristic best understood by the science of biology. Ethnomethodologists Suzanne Kessler and Wendy McKenna challenge the objectivity of biological science and demonstrate that biologists operate within certain assumptions about how the world operates. If there is a hidden assumption that there are two sexes, then that is what they will look for and find. Lesbian and queer theories further challenge the notion that humans have two dichotomous sexes into which they are born. Sexuality is a more diffuse concept that allows a further challenging of the essentialism of the two-sex model. Here the work of psychoanalysts has been used (Freud and Lacan) to study the ways in which sexuality and power interrelate and interconnect. Everyone has a sexuality, but how it is expressed depends on many factors, not necessarily or not only connected to one's sex and reproductive capability.

Woman/Man These are categories. Simone de Beauvoir in *The Second Sex* defined "woman" as a category "other" to man, who represents both the positive and the neutral pole (as in the generic use of the word "man" to refer to all humans). In order to define himself, man has to define who he is not—woman. Woman as a category then contains what is not man or the negative qualities from which men wish to distance themselves: emotional, lacking in reason and intelligence, nurturant, immersed in her bodily nature. Such categorization essentializes humans into two categories fixed in nature (which is also essentialized). French feminists have critiqued de Beauvoir's analysis and extended it even further (see the quote by Butler in the chapter).

References

Althusser, L. 1971. *Lenin and Philosophy and Other Essays*. Trans. B. Brewster. London: NLB.

Bannerji, H. 1995. *Thinking Through: Essays on Feminism, Marxism, and Anti-Racism*. Toronto: Women's Press.

Bell, S. 1995. "Native Suicide Rate Staggering." In *The Record* (Kitchener). June 24: F12.

Berger, T. 1982. *Fragile Freedoms: Human Rights and Dissent in Canada*. Toronto: Clarke, Irwin and Company.

Bolaria, B.S., and P.S. Li. 1985. *Racial Oppression in Canada*. Toronto: Garamond Press.

Bradbury, B. 1993. *Working Families: Age, Gender, and Daily Survival in Industrializing Montreal*. Toronto: McClelland and Stewart.

Butler, J. 1990. *Gender Trouble: Feminism and the Subversion of Identity*. New York: Routledge. Excerpt on page 118: Copyright © 1990. Reproduced by permission of Routledge, Inc.

Carstens, P. 1991. *The Queen's People: A Study of Hegemony, Coercion, and Accommodation among the Okanagan of Canada*. Toronto: University of Toronto Press.

Collins, P.H. 1990. *Black Feminist Thought: Knowledge, Consciousness, and the Politics of Empowerment*. New York: Routledge.

de Beauvoir, S. 1989. *The Second Sex*. New York: Vintage Books.

Engels, F. 1981. *The Origin of the Family, Private Property and the State*. New York: International Publishers.

Finnie R. 1996. "Women, Men, and the Economic Consequences of Divorce." In *Family Life*: Patterns and Perspectives, ed. C.J. Richardson. Toronto: McGraw-Hill Ryerson. 268–80.

Firestone, S. 1970. *The Dialectic of Sex*. New York: William Morrow and Co.

Foucault, M. 1980a. *The History of Sexuality. Volume 1: An Introduction*. New York: Vintage Books.

———. 1980b. *Power/Knowledge: Selected Interviews and Other Writings 1972–1977*. Ed. C. Gordon. New York: Pantheon Books.

———. 1986. *The History of Sexuality. Volume 2: The Use of Pleasure*. New York: Vintage Books.

———. 1988. *The History of Sexuality. Volume 3: The Care of the Self*. New York: Vintage Books.

———. 1996. *Foucault Live (Collected Interviews, 1961–1984)*. Ed. S. Lotringer. New York: Semiotext(e).

Gannagé, C. 1986. *Double Day, Double Bind: Women Garment Workers*. Toronto: Women's Press.

Hamilton, R. 1996. *Gendering the Vertical Mosaic: Feminist Perspectives on Canadian Society*. Toronto: Copp Clark.

Hamilton, R., and M. Barrett, eds. 1986. *The Politics of Diversity: Feminism, Marxism, and Nationalism*. Montreal: Book Center Inc.

Henry, F., C. Tator, W. Mattis, and T. Rees. 1995. *The Colour of Democracy: Racism in Canadian Society*. Toronto: Harcourt Brace.

Herdt, G. 1994. *Third Sex, Third Gender: Beyond Sexual Dimorphism in Culture and History*. New York: Zone Books.

hooks, b. 1984. *Feminist Theory: From Margin to Center*. Boston: South End Press.

———. 1994. *Teaching to Transgress: Education as the Practice of Freedom*. New York: Routledge.

Jackson, C. 1996. "Measuring and Valuing Households' Unpaid Work." In *Canadian Social Trends* (Autumn): 25–29. Ottawa: Statistics Canada.

Kessler, S.J. 1994. "The Medical Construction of Gender: Case Management of Intersexed Infants." In *Theorizing Feminism: Parallel Trends in the Humanities and Social Sciences*, ed. A.C. Herrmann and A.J. Stewart. Boulder: Westview Press.

Kessler, S.J., and W. McKenna. 1978. *Gender: An Ethnomethodological Approach*. Chicago: The University of Chicago Press.

Laqueur, T. 1990. *Making Sex: Body and Gender from the Greeks to Freud*. Cambridge: Harvard University Press.

Lash, S. 1991. *Sociology of Postmodernism*. London: Routledge.

LeGates, M. 1996. *Making Waves: A History of Feminism in Western Society*. Toronto: Copp Clark.

Lerner, G. 1986. *The Creation of Patriarchy*. New York: Oxford University Press.

Macey, D. 1994. *The Lives of Michel Foucault*. London: Vintage.

Mackie, R. 1997. "Women Spurn Ontario Tories: Strategists Seek to Win Them Over." In *The Globe and Mail*. December 30: A1 and A4.

Marcuse H. 1964. *One Dimensional Man*. London: Paladin.

Marx, K. 1967. *Das Kapital*. New York: International Publishers.

McLaren, A. 1990. *Our Own Master Race: Eugenics in Canada, 1885–1945*. Toronto: McClelland and Stewart.

Miles, R. 1989. *Racism*. London: Routledge.

Mitchell, A. 1998. "He's a Trucker, She Types—1990s Just Like 1950s: Sexual Divide Still Exists in Work Force, Census Shows." In *The Globe and Mail*. March 18: A1 and A6.

Morrow R.A., and D.D. Brown. 1994. *Critical Theory and Methodology*. Thousand Oaks: Sage Publications.

Muszynski, A. 1996. *Cheap Wage Labour: Race and Gender in the Fisheries of British Columbia*. Montreal and Kingston: McGill-Queen's University Press.

National Council of Welfare. 1997. *Poverty Profile 1995*. Ottawa: Supply and Services.

Prentice, A., P. Bourne, G. Cuthbert Brandt, B. Light, W. Mitchinson, and N. Black. 1996. *Canadian Women: A History*. 2d ed. Toronto: Harcourt Brace.

Ritzer, G. 1996. *Modern Sociological Theory*. 4th ed. New York: McGraw-Hill.

Rosenau, P.M. 1992. *Post-Modernism and the Social Sciences: Insights, Inroads, and Intrusions*. Princeton: Princeton University Press.

Royal Commission. 1996. *Report of the Royal Commission on Aboriginal Peoples*. Ottawa: Minister of Supply and Services.

Rubin, G. 1975. "The Traffic in Women: Notes on the 'Political Economy' of Sex." In *Toward an Anthropology of Women*, ed. R.R. Reiter. 157–210. New York: Monthly Review Press.

Seidman S. 1997. *Difference Troubles: Queering Social Theory and Sexual Politics*. Cambridge: Cambridge University Press.

Smith, D.E. 1987. *The Everyday World as Problematic: A Feminist Sociology*. Toronto: University of Toronto Press.

——. 1990. *The Conceptual Practices of Power: A Feminist Sociology of Knowledge.* Toronto: University of Toronto Press.

Statistics Canada. 1995. *Women in Canada: A Statistical Report.* 3d ed. Ottawa: Ministry of Industry.

Tong, R. 1989. *Feminist Thought: A Comprehensive Introduction.* Boulder: Westview Press.

Ursel, J. 1992. *Private Lives, Public Policy: 100 Years of State Intervention in the Family.* Toronto: Women's Press.

Waters M. 1994. *Modern Sociological Theory.* London: Sage Publications.

Wolf, E.R. 1982. *Europe and the People Without History.* Berkeley: University of California Press.

Wright, E.O. 1979. *Class, Crisis and the State.* London: Verso.

CHAPTER 6

Family Problems and Problem Families

Leslie J. Miller

Learning Objectives

After studying this chapter, you should be able to
- Understand **social problems** as conditions that are *problematized* by specific interest groups.
- See how family problems vary historically and cross-culturally.
- Identify the variety of familial arrangements in addition to the standard nuclear family.
- Understand the historical development of the patriarchal nuclear family.
- Identify factors that make some family problems less visible than others.
- Clarify the relationship between government policy on families and family problems.

Introduction

The idea that social problems are social constructs is no longer news, but the force of this insight continues to prod us into creatively questioning tacitly accepted realities around us. Two fields of scholarship—feminist studies and the sociology of deviance and social control—have located their critical edge precisely in the challenge they pose to taken-for-granted conceptions of how the world is and where its troubles reside. The goal of this chapter is to present a discussion of family problems that is responsive to the insights that have emerged from these fields of scholarship.

Social constructionists in the sociology of deviance tell us that social problems are made, not discovered (Rubington and Weinberg 1987). This means that social *conditions* (say, Quebec's declining birthrate, or increasing numbers of mothers in the labour force) do not become social *problems* until some group *makes them an issue*—that is, targets them, labels them deviant, and attempts to put them on the social agenda. The study of social problems is the study of that problematizing process. By conceptualizing it as a process, we recognize that a social problem is an interaction—

often a struggle—between society's powerful and powerless groups over whose ways are the "right" ways. Moreover, those whose ways are labelled a problem may well fail to understand why their lives need fixing—"slum" families in turn-of-the-century North American immigrant ghettos, for example, or "backward" farm families in the 1920s and 1930s, like that of Oliva Dionne, father of Ontario's famous "Quints"—and they often resent the interference of psychologists, nurses, and social welfare workers. In such cases, one group's taken-for-granted reality has become another's problem. As American sociologists Berger and Berger point out in their book *The War over the Family*, "It is not enough to say that a problem has arisen; one must also ask *whose problem it is*" (1984, 8; emphasis added). As we shall see, this insight applies with special force to women, and feminist scholars have demonstrated persuasively that the "normal" everyday realities of family life in a patriarchal society are the urgent social problems of those who see themselves victimized by that order.

In what follows, I shall argue that the family problems of this century and the last can be understood only against the backdrop of the emergent bourgeois family ideal, the patriarchal **cult of domesticity** that had the effect of sanctifying a single familial arrangement as the only proper and respectable one. This ethos, or ideal, began to develop in Northern Europe during the seventeenth century (Elias 1978 [1939]; Aries 1962) and set the standard for all other familial arrangements. In general, I shall be suggesting that the "problem families" of the nineteenth and much of the twentieth centuries, from the "slum" family to the "blended," homosexual, or communal one, are usually those whose arrangements appeared to diverge from that domestic ideal.

In the first part of the chapter, I outline the historical process that produced the modern ideal of the domestic family, and review some attempts to enforce it by regulating alternative or "unfit" forms. Though efforts to reform the "unfit" family have taken various guises over the last century and a half, the image of the "normal" family is still regularly invoked to justify the **social control** of a whole range of more-or-less discredited alternatives. Despite the variety of domestic arrangements that have proliferated since the Second World War, scholars in general agree with Barrett and McIntosh when they lament that the domestic ideal still captures "the family of desire and myth" (1982, 28). Indeed, the thrust of many a feminist critique of the family comes down to the demand that we abandon the labelling of such alternative arrangements as immoral, evil, or unhealthy, and accept the reality of many forms instead of just one. But as scholars are coming to see, the image of a single "normal" family form cannot simply be argued away. Such core cultural images demonstrate a remarkable resilience, and their moral authority is enforced in a range of formal and informal mechanisms that make them extremely difficult to dislodge (see Richardson 1996, Introduction, esp. 2–10).

The second part of the chapter develops the insights of feminist scholars more directly. As I have just noted, one of the consequences of the rise of the domestic ideal was to focus attention upon families that failed to measure up. A second important consequence was the protective cloak of secrecy that enclosed modern family life. It is one of the ironies of social history that as the institution of the modern domestic family has risen to a central place in Western society around the figure of the wife/mother, whole areas within it—especially the contributions of women—have dropped from view. And as feminists have documented, the norm of privacy characteristic of the modern family obscured not only women's contributions, but also the inequalities and abuses they and their children suffered (see, e.g., Chalmers and Smith 1988). The point I shall be emphasizing in this part is that these long-hidden aspects of family life represent forms of conduct that are now *in the process of being problematized*. Such family realities as the unrecognized and unpaid labour of housewives, the "normal" violence of routine family life, and the structural impoverishment of women are being targeted by various groups wanting to raise their visibility and thus society's recognition of them as urgent social problems. These campaigns propose to turn these ordinary practices into occasions for intervention and social change. In this part, I shall take up some of these not-yet-problematized or newly problematized aspects of family life, as well as the sociocultural factors that have kept them invisible for so long.

Problem Families Then and Now

The Rise of the "Cult of Domesticity"

For readers unfamiliar with the recent renaissance in the social history of the family, I sketch below the emergence of the ideal that has so powerfully influenced our thinking about the way our life in families goes (and ought to go) round. Social historians are agreed that over the eighteenth and nineteenth centuries in Northern Europe, there arose in the burgeoning middle class not only a novel form of household organization,[1] but also a novel ethos of family life, a cult of domesticity that made the new form an object of veneration.[2] The most influential of these scholars, Philippe Ariès, describes the emergence of the modern family as "a revolution in sentiment." His ground-breaking book, *Centuries of Childhood* (1962), deals with the changes in family life from the late Middle Ages until the end of the nineteenth century and focusses mainly on France. Ariès claims that until the late eighteenth century, the family existed as a political and public body, a lineage or "house," with little or no private character. Gradually there emerged toward the middle of the eighteenth century a recognizably modern form of family, termed "intimate" or "domestic." This newly domestic family is characterized as a little nest of natural sentiment forged as a bulwark against the impersonal public arena.[3]

In general, the vast body of data assembled by the early writers, including Ariès, documented a new anxiety over "public immorality"—rowdy public festivals and drunkenness, celebratory public torture and executions, and wandering bands of youths. It found, as well, a new sense of the vulnerability of the child, the spread of the "little school" and of discipline, and a changed conjugal relation marked by a new emphasis on the importance of sentiment, manners, and hygiene. The outcome was a clear distinction for the first time between public and private spheres of life. With the concern for the protection of the child from the rough-and-tumble of the street and a growing intimacy between spouses, the domestic family had seemingly emerged from a sea of brutality and had become the standard of normal family life.

The nature and progress of the "domestic revolution" is still a topic of scholarly debate. For our purposes, however, it is sufficient to note that its rise parallels the rise of the modern state. And for the officials of the new state, the *premodern* family was "the problem"—an outmoded or "parasitic" institutional form whose members were thought to be making an insufficient contribution to the welfare of the larger society. The result was a host of attempts to reform the family so as to organize this flotsam within the "productive" fold. Most of the state's reform policies were not intended to replace the family, but to improve it. The baby bonus, for example, which began as a state payment to any mother willing to raise illegitimate children in her own family, became a mechanism which allowed the state to oversee the physical and moral hygiene of the bourgeois, and later the poor, family by measuring it against the standard of the new domestic ideal (Donzelot 1979). (For a similar interpretation of mothers' allowances as an instrument of social control in early twentieth-century Canada, see Strong-Boag 1982, 173, 220 n.55.) I shall return again to the thesis of state "tyranny." Whether or not one accepts it in its entirety, however, the outcome of the emergence of the domestic ethos seems beyond dispute: the standard of bourgeois family life—at least in its idealized form—was invested with moral and legal weight, and imposed[4] upon the other strata of society.

Though the ethos of domesticity is of European origin, the force of its influence elsewhere—in the United Kingdom (Barrett and McIntosh 1982; Gittins 1986; Lewis 1986), in the United States (Demos 1970; Bremmer et al. 1970–74; Finkelstein 1985), and to a lesser extent in Canada (Baker 1996; Iacovetta 1992; Houston 1982; Strong-Boag 1982; Nett 1981)—is well documented. In these societies, as in Europe, the increasing privilege accorded to the new ideal worked to produce a moral distinction between the "respectable" middle-class family, seen to approximate the model most closely, and the working-class family, which appeared to be unable to measure up. Such "deficient" families came to be defined as social problems—as threats to public order. In Europe, the working-class family took the brunt of these reforms; in North America, immigrant and First Nations families became the favoured targets, especially when it came to the cruder forms of intervention (for example, the "apprehension" or removal of children from homes deemed unfit). In Toronto in the late 1950s, for example, immigrant aid agencies promoted the reshaping of immigrant families along the lines of the bourgeois domestic ideal, and viewed such changes as a sign of successful Canadianization (Iacovetta 1992, 263).

Rearing the Vulnerable Child

What was it, in particular, that was deemed problematic about the "problem family"? The new rhetoric of domesticity encompassed a whole complex of beliefs about the ideal "feminine" woman (passive, refined, and maternal); the ideal conjugal relationship (intimate or compassionate); the value of the privacy of the home; and the place of the family in the larger milieu (a "haven in a heartless world"). And at its centre was the belief in the nature of childhood (innocent and vulnerable). In contrast to the premodern family, often a large and diverse household encompassing servants, lodgers, and kin, in which the community played a central role, the modern or domestic family is described as *child-centred*. This term refers to the new way of understanding childhood as a distinct social category defined by innocence and vulnerability, a view that stood in sharp contrast to the medieval one that tended "to ignore childhood as a transitional period soon finished and of no importance"[5] (Ariès 1962, 109–10).

This new understanding meant that the child and "society" must be segregated, for the child was seen to be vulnerable to society's corrupting influences.

The modern view of the child and of the child-centred family resulted in a revision in expectations about parenthood, and its effect was to produce an evaluation of immigrant, First Nations, and working-class families as quagmires of parental neglect rather than havens of care and responsibility. At the heart of the matter was the new demand that the "fit" parent carefully segregate the child from the street ("society")—that is, from the world of adults (meaning men) where bad influences were felt to lie. The child's proper sphere was to be the bourgeois home, now reformulated as a nursery of refinement and civility under the exclusive care of the mother ("the angel of the hearth").[6] In the bourgeois home, the mother's role was crucial: while her husband was engaged in the pursuit of a family wage, her responsibility was to maintain a respectable home and devote herself to her "natural" maternal calling.

Thus did the social rhetoric of domesticity map the world into separate spheres: the safe (purified) home, dominated by the child and the now infantilized mother, and the street, the unregulated realm of strangers, work, and war. The demand that these two spheres be kept apart, and that the child be kept on one side of the boundary (excepting carefully monitored excursions into the world beyond) is a relatively recent view of home and parenting. This approach has specific, traceable historical origins, and constitutes the most powerful criterion used by family reformers for identifying the unfit family and the negligent parent. Failure to meet this criterion, it was assumed, would produce an unruly child, a delinquent youth, and a criminal adult. The unfit family (in effect, the unfit mother) was thus labelled a social problem not only in its own right, but also because it was thought to spawn a host of other problems down the road. As Ehrenreich and English (1979) observe, the mother's "mission" was depicted as the moulding of the future society, and so the unfit mother would place that future in jeopardy.

I am proposing, then, that the roster of "urgent" family problems—the "slum" and immigrant families of the late nineteenth and early twentieth centuries; the alternative family forms of recent decades (divorced and "blended," gay/lesbian, and lone-parent families); and the "problem" that spans the entire period, the employed mother—all have this in common: they are defined as inadequate environments for the upbringing of the child. It is this judgement that will provide the rationale for state or informal intervention against them. Those families deemed to be reformable will be taught; the policing of others will be accomplished by different means, principally by denying them the status of "real" families. In the following section, I take up the "problem" of such families, and the array of efforts mounted to remedy them.

Policing the "Unfit" Family

The "Slum" Family

Ehrenreich and English have remarked that the American home itself—even the middle-class home—was a topic of anxious discussion in the years of rapid immigration and industrialization between 1860 and the First World War, being portrayed as an anchor in a world of instability. Despite this, they agree that all critics reserved their greatest concern for the urban slum, where lay the greatest threat to the child, to the family, and hence to social order ("civilization") (1979, 170).

The middle-class definition of the slum family as an unfit child-rearing milieu focussed on the most visible aspect of the problem: the "idle youth" who were marginally employed as bootblacks and newsboys, or those who were neither at school nor at work and simply roamed the streets (some 55 percent of children between 13 and 16 years of age, according to Katz's study of Hamilton in the 1850s; see Katz, in Nett 1981, 252). Solutions to what would become "the problem of juvenile delinquency" included "surrogate institutions for the lower classes approximately analogous to middle-class family life" (Glazebrook, in Nett 1981, 252)—orphanages, training schools, and the like—programs that installed the child in a "better" home, and later, attempts to teach the working-class mother modern methods of child rearing in situ. Programs of this sort began in the 1850s with the New York Children's Aid Society plan to send city children to upstate rural homes (Zelizer 1989, 381) where they were expected to grow into useful citizens. And in Canada, farm families in Ontario and the Maritimes—families that were enshrined in the ideology of the day as arcadian sanctuaries of all the old virtues—were the destination for children from the "slums" of Glasgow and other industrial cities in Britain.

The child's relation to work has played a highly visible role in the effort to regulate the working-class family in this century. During the last half of the nineteenth century, when school was not yet regarded as the only proper milieu for every child, children's wages provided an important part of family income and the working-class child could still choose earning over learning (Coulter 1982, 156; Bradbury 1982; 1996). But as the fully modern image of innocent childhood took hold and the demand for youth labour decreased, good parenting increasingly came to imply the complete segregation of the child from the "adult" world of paid labour. By the 1930s, parents who allowed or encouraged their children to work more than part-time were in danger of being labelled negligent, for school had become installed as "the dominant experience of growing up" (Gaffield 1982, 69).

The point at which the child is seen to overstep the boundary of innocence into the work-world of the adult is still an issue of moral and legal significance. But work (or failure to attend school) is only one of the many threats that were seen to endanger the vulnerable child. In general, families where the parents failed to observe the proper distinction between home life and street life, between the realm of the child and that of the (male) adult, were labelled as social problems (Miller 1990a). Any familial arrangement that embodied the old sociability—the mixing of young and old, the too-numerous children who stayed up too late and spilled off their porches into the city streets, and thus were exposed to the sights and sounds of adult talk and conduct (especially sexuality)—such a mixing of family and "world" increasingly symbolized danger to the modern spirit. Working-class girls should be at home, said disapproving turn-of-the-century middle-class reformers, rather than at dance halls or theatres where they were sure to fall prey to the temptations of the street (Valverde 1991). And in the homes of the poor, as a settlement house worker complained in 1900, "there is no meal hour and no bedtime, the children retiring late with the parents and eating where and when they please" (quoted in Ehrenreich and English 1979, 206). By appearing to invite too close a connection between the corrupting society

A Nineteenth-Century Expert Warns Girls about the Vices of Gambling

The most pernicious and scandalous practice which the female world have fallen into is gaming.... Who can consider, without a secret indignation, that all those affections of the mind, which should be consecrated to their children, husband, and parents, are thus vilely prostituted and lavished away, upon a game at loo, while the husband, and all the family, are neglected and made unhappy.... There are no greater enemies to a beautiful face, than the vigils of the card-table, and those cutting passions which naturally attend them. Hollow eyes, haggard looks, and pale complexions, are the unbecoming indications of those female worthies. Many a woman have I seen glide by me in her chair, at three o'clock in the morning, half dead, appearing like a spectre, surrounded by a glare of flambeaux. There is no chance for a thorough-paced gamester to preserve her natural beauty two winters successively.... The man who plays beyond his income, pawns his estate; [the woman]... yields up to dishonour; she entails an everlasting disgrace upon herself and all her family.

Source: Quoted in Thomas Kelly, *The New Female Instructor or Young Woman's Guide to Domestic Happiness* (London: Rosters, 1988), pp. 42–44.

and the innocent child, French Canadian, immigrant, and First Nations families were defined in professional and lay opinion as demoralized and unregulated. This feature, rather than their class background, their ethnicity, or their poverty per se, was the rationale that made social control campaigns against them credible. Several recent accusations of child neglect against immigrant parents show that this issue has not gone away.

Excursus: The Tyranny of the Experts

The social history of attempts to regulate family life is a complex and fascinating topic in its own right, but there is space enough here only to touch on it briefly. Prior to the rise of the modern state, the local community, including the local church, was the major agent of social control. When historians tell us that the family was embedded within the local community to a far greater extent than it is today, they mean in part that members of the community were involved in important family events— births, marriages, deaths—most of which we tend today to confine to "family and close friends." In the premodern world, the community participated in and validated these important turning points in people's lives, and so it is no surprise that the community, too, played a pivotal role in the control of family life. The mechanisms were local and informal, and included noisy public demonstrations called "shivarees," which were designed to humiliate the wrong-doer into right conduct. Such intervention worked because a person's good reputation was of real material and moral consequence in a small world.

But the rise of the modern state signalled the weakening of community authority, and the social control of the family became increasingly standardized, formal, and remote. The "slum" family can be seen as a kind of battleground for the whole range

Culture Clash: Foreign Parents, American Child Rearing

Sophisticated New Yorkers don't slow down at the sight of a headless chicken on the steps of the Bronx courthouse. They pretend not to notice when a taxi driver crosses himself passing a church. And they have learned to live with dense accents, impolite shopkeepers, loud music and the strong smell of curry.

But there are limits to how far New Yorkers are willing to go in the name of cultural sensitivity. That limit was recently tested in three cases involving children and their foreign parents.

In April a Russian couple left their 4-year-old daughter home alone and went out dancing. Last May a Danish tourist left her 14-month-old daughter outside a restaurant while she ate inside. This month a Russian émigré left her 7-year-old son to play in a park while she went to work.

The parents all told the police they were only doing what is the norm back home. Their lawyers claimed theirs were not criminal cases but incidents of cultural differences and that understanding, not punishment, was required. New Yorkers were unmoved. Here, they answered, we call that kind of behavior child endangerment. And it's illegal. In each of the three New York cases the parents were arrested and their children placed in foster care.

Social workers are trained to be sensitive to [cultural] idiosyncracies, but not permissive.... "Cultural differences are beautiful, but they have nothing to do with the law," [a social worker said]. "We can't possibly have a set of laws for Americans, a set of laws for immigrants and then a set of laws for tourists."

Julia Wrigley, a professor of Sociology ... and the author of *Other People's Children* (Basic Books, 1995) found that foreigners are often surprised at how sheltered American children are. "Our children dominate the household, the dinner table chatter," Mrs. Wrigley said. "But people from other cultures don't encourage high-demand children. Their children tend to be much more independent."

Social workers agree that education, not punishment, is the best way to adapt to America's attitudes. But if a child's life is at stake, emergency measures are required, [a social worker said]. The parents will have to learn the hard way.

Source: Mirta Ojito, "Culture Clash: Foreign Parents, American Child Rearing," *The New York Times,* June 29, 1997, p. E3. Copyright © 1997 by *The New York Times.* Reprinted by permission.

of social control strategies employed since the rise of the modern state. Sometimes the target of direct attack, it became the object of the civilizing mission undertaken by women at the turn of the century. Historians have documented the effort to improve the working-class mother in her own home—the stream of school and health "visitors" who exerted subtle forms of pressure upon mothers in an effort to improve the cleanliness and order of their homes, or to ensure their children's attendance at school. The visitors themselves were often well-to-do wives who saw the project of reforming the poor as a natural extension of their role as guardians of manners and morals. Visitors were instructed to give advice and encouragement, but never money; their interventions were couched in the language of friendship (Ehrenreich and English 1979, 172).

By the 1920s, however, that project had come to look like amateurish and unscientific tinkering, and the "problem" of the "slum" family became in its entirety the property of the new (male) child-care professionals. A poignant example of the "tyranny of the experts" can be found in the history of the famous Dionne quintuplets of Callander, Ontario. Elzire and Oliva Dionne had raised several other children in the rural French-Catholic tradition until the birth of their five daughters in 1934. Though poor and uneducated, M. Dionne had never failed to provide a family wage—the measure of a successful husband and father. But their lifestyle and parenting customs (calculated to rear useful rather than innocent children) proved a scandal to the child-care professionals whose attention they drew.

In her study of the reconstruction of child care by professional expertise, aptly titled "Intruders in the Nursery," Strong-Boag records the experts' dismay with the Dionnes' family environment:

> [The Dionnes] had met the requirements for exemplary parenthood according to their faith and culture: five living children, all nourished and housed without recourse to public assistance…. [But] their farmhouse, without indoor plumbing or electricity, and their time-honoured familial customs were hardly calculated to win the approval of the experts who flocked to attend Canada's greatest tourist attraction. A press largely sympathetic to the professionals helped mobilize sentiment against the seemingly backward, obstinate, greedy, and irresponsible Dionne parents. (1982, 174)

The author goes on to describe the loss of traditional parental authority suffered by the Dionnes, who were defined as unfit parents soon after the birth of their five daughters. They surrendered the girls to the state, who were then taken to a hospital and raised there in an appropriately scientific environment under the supervision of Toronto psychologist Dr. William Blatz, then guru of the child-study movement. There "the Quints" drew crowds of curious and admiring onlookers, many of whom would follow in the press the stories of their lives into adolescence and adulthood.

The tale of heavy-handed attempts to ensure the best upbringing for the quintuplets reminds us that efforts to enforce the ideal of bourgeois domesticity by influencing child-rearing practices have taken more than one form. By the 1930s, professional child-care experts in general held the view that families should be kept together and that parenting practices should be improved through lessons, manuals of advice, indirect government subsidies, and visitors of various stripes, although the apprehension of children from "unfit" parents—especially First Nations families—has not even today been eradicated. But for the Dionnes, the unique value of their very existence made them the target of an act of state intervention more brutal than was currently in vogue. The sisters have paid for the uninvited scientific and popular celebrity of their early lives with adulthoods marked by suicide, poverty, and depression. In the spring of 1998, the Ontario government finally settled a long-standing dispute with the three surviving sisters, now in their mid-60s, who charged that the province had mishandled the trust fund it set up for them back in the 1930s and 1940s. Earlier in February, a CTV public affairs program estimated the amount owed by the province to the Dionnes at between $2 million and $3 million. A spokesperson for the attorney-general said that although the government does not believe there is a legal obligation to support the Dionnes, "a decision has been made that the government wants to help the Dionnes to ensure that they can live in comfort and security" (*The Globe and Mail,* February 5, 1998, A5).

While recognizing some notorious exceptions such as the removal of the Dionne sisters, scholars have generally emphasized the shift from the direct regulation of child-rearing practices to benevolent "improvement," and rightly so; today, says one observer, children "are not supposed to be removed from their homes unless parental care poses a significant threat." Still, this scholar goes on to note that a disproportionate number of child "apprehensions" involve black and aboriginal children (Baker 1996, 291). The issue here is, of course, whose definition of "significant threat" is operative, as a group of Native leaders in a British Columbia town of Quesnel clearly recognized, after 71 children were seized by social workers early in 1998. Social workers who find themselves in the media limelight after incidents like this complain that they are just as frequently criticized for *failing* to act to remove an endangered child, and that they inevitably end up "damned if they do, and damned if they don't." Nevertheless, the longer sociological view reveals clearly that from the era when the Dionne Quints were young until today, such unilateral acts of state intervention continue almost always to be directed at society's most **marginalized** communities—and are conducted in a way that provokes humiliation, confusion, and sometimes violence.

Children First

Little Matthew Vaudreuil was abused to death by his mother in 1992. The case shocked British Columbians, provoked a judicial inquiry, and led to the ripping apart of the Ministry of Social Services and the creation of a new Ministry of Children and Families. The fallout from that case is still hot—and it explains the abrupt roundup of at-risk children by social workers in the town of Quesnel. Over the past few weeks, 71 children—1 percent of the town's kids—have been taken from their parents. The new bureaucracy is determined not to have another Matthew case on its hands.

Matthew's mother was a clearly unfit mother, a dangerous woman who abused drugs, lived in transient squalor, and sometimes supported herself as a prostitute. Although he was not yet 6 years old when he died, at least 60 reports about his safety and well-being had been made to authorities. He had been taken to the doctor 75 times and had seen 24 different physicians. Twenty-one different social workers had provided him with services.... Despite the mounting evidence, he was not ordered removed from the care of his biological mother. Keeping families together seems to have been a paramount concern.

Source: Editorial, *The Globe and Mail,* February 10, 1998, p. A20. Reprinted with permission from *The Globe and Mail.*

Native Leaders Angered by Seizures of Children

Native leaders will meet Children and Family Ministries staff to seek answers about why a record number of children have been seized in the last two months.

Also, five more social workers vowed over the weekend to stop child apprehensions after at least 23 native children were removed from their homes since December. Altogether, 71 Quesnel-area children have been apprehended by the ministry.

The apprehensions—without the involvement of native social workers, band members, or band elders—have strained relations between the ministry and the native community.

"They're going about things all wrong," said Chief Frank Boucher of the Lhtako band. "We want jurisdiction over the children to make our own decisions."

[Children and Families Minister] Priddy has defended the apprehensions as necessary. She cited one case where a child was suffering from dehydration and pneumonia and had a contagious skin infection when social workers intervened.

In other cases parents say they were told they didn't have enough toys or were accused of abuse for spanking their children.

Maureen Trotter of the Quesnel Women's Resource Centre said it is mostly families in poverty that were affected. A report from the University of Northern British Columbia indicates 25 percent of children in the area live in poverty, with an annual income of less than $22,000 for a family of three.

Source: The Canadian Press, as printed in *The Calgary Herald*, February 10, 1998, p. A19.

The Employed Mother: Whose Problem?

It should be clear by now that at the heart of the ethos of domesticity is the figure of the vulnerable child, together with the mother who is expected to make that child her first concern, even above herself. Some scholars argue, in fact, that a roster of claims about the nature and needs of the child, as set out in the cult of domesticity, is the cover for unjustified attacks upon legitimate and workable alternative familial arrangements. Nobody would object to employed mothers, or even to lesbian ones (the argument goes)—after all, what people choose to do is their own business—unless the welfare of the child were threatened; and that is a different story. Read this way, the bourgeois concept of the child, and of the child-centred family, becomes the key to understanding several important "family problems" of this century.

Demographers and historians assure us that mothers have always worked in and around the household for the family economy, and often in the paid labour force as well. But the "problem" of working mothers—by which is meant the view that mothers who should be minding their children are instead "out working"—does not arise until the emergence of the ethos of domesticity, which decreed that the role of mother, of nurturer, should become the central mission in a woman's life. This made paid work a man's activity, permissible for women only as secondary "help" (for "luxuries" or "pin money") or in an emergency.

The variety of attempts mounted by "experts" since the late nineteenth century to enjoin women to mother, especially by discouraging their efforts to encroach on the "proper" sphere of men, are described by Ehrenreich and English in *For Their Own Good*. They range from the threat of illness, to the promise of a new, socially useful evolutionary mission, to an attempt in the 1940s and 1950s to professionalize the "job" of mother in an effort to make its status the equal of the husband's. The perennial theme is the damage she would do if she "worked"—damage to *herself* (only a century ago women were warned that their reproductive organs would atrophy under the stress of "real" work, and that the home was the only medically safe focus for a woman's energies: see Ehrenreich and English 1979, 149), and to her *spouse* (whose emotional needs would go unfulfilled—or else he must satisfy them elsewhere). But all observers agreed that the greatest damage would be done to the *child*.

Despite the warnings of professional child-care experts, the overwhelming fact is that mothers, especially those with small children, have been steadily drawn into the work force since the turn of the century. Female participation in the work force was a mere 16.1 percent in 1901 (Statistics Canada 1974, 113); by 1951 it had increased marginally to 24 percent. The biggest jump came between 1961 and 1981: in these two decades women's participation nearly doubled, from 29.5 percent to 51.8 percent (Armstrong and Armstrong 1988, 276). In their overview of Canadian women at work, Lupri and Mills conclude that the increase in the proportion of married women who work for pay is "the single most dramatic and pervasive trend in the status of Canadian women since World War II" (1983, 44).

The trend described by these two researchers continues unabated: by 1983 the proportion of women in the labour force with children under 6 was 51.5 percent, and by 1991 it was 64 percent (Baker 1996, 22). To be sure, professional concern has abated somewhat since its height in the 1950s. Then, deprivation theories were in vogue, like Bowlby's, which argued that parental (i.e., maternal) rejection accounted for most cases of intractable juvenile delinquency (Pfohl 1985, 99). More recent reviews of the research fail to locate evidence of adverse effects of employed mothers on their children's well-being. Nevertheless, the psychiatric profession continues to trace adult deviance to "the psychic scars of childhood," and such an approach routinely points to the mother behind the child (Ambert 1996; Pfohl 1985, 100). The working mother is *still* a focus of anxiety, as recent debates in connection with the push for more day-care funding show.

Even now—despite their march into the work force—mothers themselves continue to show considerable ambivalence about the appropriateness of their own paid work: they work, or plan to, and all the while insist that their proper place is at home, "at least while the children are young" (Gaskell 1988, 157). Gaskell reminds us that the unsureness she witnessed in the girls she interviewed in Vancouver is a reflection of the way Canadians as a whole react: on the one hand they endorse equal opportunities for women "overwhelmingly," but on the other they strongly believe in mother-centred patterns of childrearing (Gibbins et al., quoted in Gaskell 1988, 156). Gaskell's study of girls was done in the 1980s, but the ambivalence remains: a survey published by Statistics Canada in late 1997 reports most Canadians as saying that "women have a duty to contribute to the household income, but paradoxically most also believe children suffer if both parents work" (reported in *The Globe and Mail,* February 7, 1998, D1).

This conflicting pair of demands is the real problem girls must come to terms with. And if the solution in other eras was to hide the paid work a woman did,[7] or to delegate it to someone more acceptable according to the rhetoric of domesticity, then the contemporary solution seems to be to define it as secondary work (that is, work that "helps out" the main breadwinner and provides "extras"), even though such work may well represent the largest financial contribution to the household (Brannen and Moss 1987, and see also McKee 1987). This discursive strategy allows women to work in the labour force at the same time that it allows them to define mothering as their *first* commitment (their primary or "real" work).[8] At another level, however, it is important to recognize that through such strategies women reiterate and reproduce the very social rhetoric that subordinates them (here, the ethos of mother-centred child care). In addition to the material factors that enforce the domestic ideal—the gender-segregated work force and continually inadequate day-care funding (Gaskell 1988)—we must recognize the part that women's own sense-making strategies play in shoring it up.

A New "Problem": The Lesbian Family

At the outset of this chapter, I contended that those family forms that deviated from the domestic ideal would be labelled as problems and were likely to become targets of social-control campaigns. Perhaps the most obvious challenges to the bourgeois ideal of the nuclear, heterosexual, male-dominated family are the communal families of the 1960s and the alternative family forms of the 1980s and 1990s, including gay and lesbian families, and single women who have chosen to have and rear children without a live-in man. For those in the society who see in these arrangements the "decline" or "decay" of the family, they are not alternative families but non-families, whose claims to "real" family status are entirely without legitimacy.[9]

It is the opinion of some sociologists that such a hard-line commitment to a single "normal" family form has been gradually replaced since the 1950s with a genuine pluralism. Speaking about ethnic diversity, for example, Hareven contends that, until very recently, alternatives to the ideal of the private nuclear family were "misinterpreted as 'family disorganization' simply because they did not conform to the official stereotype"; now, however, diversity is "being valued as a source of strength and continuity." Even more radical alternatives, states Hareven, are at least tolerated if not actually valued:

> Much anxiety has [also] been expressed over the increase in the proportion of couples living together unmarried, over homosexual partners or parents, and over a whole variety of alternative family forms and lifestyles.... [These] have now become part of the official fiber of the society, because they are now being tolerated much more than in the past. In short, what we are witnessing is not a fragmentation of traditional family patterns, but rather, the emergence of a pluralism in family ways. (1989, 54–55; and see also Ram and Romaniuc 1996)

Most feminists accept Hareven's construction of the issue, but reject her sunny conclusion. Notwithstanding the state's recognition of increased diversity in actual household arrangements, they would argue that the official view continues to define alternatives to the ideal as deviant and engages in direct and indirect policing of these numerous and often workable arrangements by denying them legal, economic, and social support (Gavigan 1997; Chunn 1992).

An examination of the state's treatment of one of these alternatives reveals a reality more complex, and more sociologically interesting, than either of the two positions taken above. I refer here to an interesting study of the five court cases specifically dealing with lesbian custody to appear in Canadian law reports prior to 1984 (Arnup 1988). This study showed that court decisions neither repressed nor tolerated lesbian families as such, but instead distinguished between "good" and "bad" lesbian families. Custody of children was awarded to those mothers who were prepared to support the ideal of (heterosexual) domesticity by maintaining a discreet public appearance and suppressing their involvement in lesbian proselytizing and political activities, but was denied to those who "flaunted" their lesbianism. The lifestyle of the latter, the judges argued, was found to have adverse effects on the welfare of the child.

Arnup's study has important implications for the question of the state's role in controlling at least this alternative family form. The first point concerns the form social control takes. Here we should note that the court avoids a direct attack on lesbians or lesbian mothers, preferring to use the child as the rhetorical mechanism of intervention. As in the case of employed mothers, the child becomes the crucial legitimate point of entry into the otherwise private doings of the family. The legal discrediting of the "bad" lesbian mothers takes indirect rather than direct form; that is, the court's decision is framed not as the repression of the lesbian parent per se (indeed, this argument is explicitly rejected) but in terms of a benevolent concern for the child's "best interests." This bears out Foucault's thesis about characteristically modern forms of disciplinary power (Foucault 1979). Moreover, the protective stance seems only a cover for the indirect policing of "bad" lesbian families, as there is a total lack of judicial interest in assessing the negative effects of consigning a child to a family whose members are bound over, as it were, to live a lesbian social reality in private and to proclaim a heterosexual one in public.

A second point concerns the goal of the state's efforts. It is clear from Arnup's study that the state's concern is not with the existence of lesbian families per se, but with the way such families represent themselves publicly with regard to the domestic standard or ideal.[10] As Arnup observes, the determining factor in a judge's decision is not the mother's sexual orientation but rather what she "does" with it (1988, 249). For our purposes, this means that the "problem" in a problem family does not lie in the domestic arrangement itself, but in the degree of public challenge it is seen to pose for the rhetoric of domesticity. Here the courts appear to be saying that what will jeopardize a child's "best interests" is not living in a lesbian family, but living in one that publicly declares lesbian family life to be *good*. In short, it is family rhetoric, not family structure, that the state is interested in policing.

The charge that the state will repress all alternative family *forms* thus seems misguided. Arnup's study suggests that the liberal state is more likely to tolerate the existence of many of these forms, so long as those involved agree to conduct themselves as reasonable facsimiles of the nuclear family (1988, 254). This strategy allows the state to preserve the appearance of tolerance while neutralizing rhetorical public challenges to the heterosexual ideal.[11]

TABLE 6.1 Lesbian and Gay Rights across Canada, 1998

	Discrimination against gays and lesbians prohibited in human rights legislation	Equal workplace benefits available to same-sex partners of government employees	Equal pension benefits available to lesbian and gay employees	Medical decisions on behalf of same-sex partner who is incapacitated	Adoption by same-sex couples allowed	Child and spousal support provisions extended to same-sex couples
Federal	✓	✓	✗[a]	n/a	n/a	n/a
Alberta	✓	✗	✗	✗	✗	✗
British Columbia	✓	✓	✓[b]	✓	✓	✓
Manitoba	✓	✓	✗	✗	✗	✗
New Brunswick	✓	✓	✗	✗	✗	✗
Newfoundland	✓	✗	✗	✗	✗	✗
Nova Scotia	✓	✓	✓	✗	✗	✗
Ontario	✓	✓	✓	✓	✓	✓[c]
Prince Edward Island	✓	✗	✗	✗	✗	✗
Quebec	✓	✗	✗	✗	✗	✗
Saskatchewan	✓	✓	✗	✗	✗	✗
Yukon Territory	✓	✓	✓	✗	✗	✗
Northwest Territories	✗	✓	✗	✗	✗	✗

[a] The Federal Government has accepted an Ontario Court ruling requiring it to accept for registration pension plans that offer equal pension benefits, but has not yet extended equal pension benefits to federal employees.

[b] British Columbia has introduced, but not yet enacted, legislation to extend equal pension benefits to those in same-sex relationships.

[c] Support rights extended by the Ontario Court of Appeal; decision currently under appeal to the Supreme Court of Canada.

Source: "Lesbian and Gay Rights across Canada," Equality for Gays and Lesbians Everywhere (Egale), September 1998.

In the last decade, gay and lesbian activists have begun to ask themselves what they have to gain or lose by representing themselves as families "just like any other" (Cossman 1997). Some argue that adopting such pro-familistic rhetoric only muffles the very real challenge that gay/lesbian families pose to an oppressive, patriarchal mainstream institution. Others argue that only by espousing pro-familistic rhetoric (i.e., "We are family") will gays and lesbians gain mainstream recognition of their relationships and entitlement to family benefits (Arnup 1997). In these debates, gay and lesbian activists are beginning to give new attention to the ways families are represented and the political consequences of those representations. Researchers, for their part, must balance their focus on domestic arrangements and behaviour with greater attention to the management of appearances, in particular to the social rhetorics family members fashion for themselves and for public consumption.[12]

Problematizing the Hidden Injustices of "Normal" Family Life

Because of the challenges they appear to pose to the ideal of bourgeois domesticity, the problems discussed in the first part of this chapter have all been hot topics in their day. Each has had (or is currently having) its moment of glory as the alleged cause of society's collapse or decline. In short, their high social visibility and their status as problems have been taken for granted by laypersons and professionals alike, who have focussed their energies on solutions.

The long view, however, reveals that social problems wax and wane, and that collective anxiety about any one may intensify or subside quite independently of any clear remedy. Scholars attuned to the historical aspect of the construction of social problems have attempted to capture it in the concept of the *career*. By inviting us to think of a problem as having a birth, a peak, and a decline, such a formulation reminds us of the *process* of problematization that any issue undergoes. As an issue of public concern, the problem of the "slum" family is, for the moment, in decline; the problem of homosexual families on the rise. "Working mothers" is a problem that makes a comeback whenever unemployment rates go up, or the subject of alternative child-care arrangements is re-opened.

I turn now to categories that have only recently become visible, and whose status as social problems is far from secure. These are *in the process of being problematized* and, in contrast to the problems already discussed, are at the beginning of their careers. Perceived by many in the society as more-or-less normal—"no big deal"— they are the focus of anxious concern to others, who cry, "Look at that! Here is a problem that *must* be fixed." The two nascent social problems I consider here are *domestic violence* and the **feminization of poverty**. Both issues are the object of determined efforts by women's groups and others, who propose to heighten their visibility in the hope of achieving a remedy. Part of the problem then, for these groups, is that issues like these are not yet seen as problem *enough*.

The invisibility of women's poverty and abuse is part of the more general invisibility of the bourgeois family itself. Social historians have shown that as customs like the shivaree faded away, and the social control of the family shifted out of the surrounding community to the state, the family was subjected to a generally lower degree of over-all scrutiny (Shorter 1975). At the same time, it became increasingly privatized, so that what went on in the family became for the first time "one's own business," and interested neighbours were redefined as nosy busybodies. The value that modern society places on privacy is a double-edged sword where families are concerned. As Laslett (1973) has remarked, privacy permits variability in conduct—while it gives some cover for our harmless eccentricities, it also permits excesses of patriarchal authority to go unseen.

Only over the last three decades have feminist scholars come to recognize the degree to which the dynamics of family life are *terra incognita*. Intimately familiar to all, but containing experiences too private or too mundane to be made the topic of deliberate study, the black box of the household has only recently been opened (Brannen and Wilson 1987, 1; and for the same point in connection with ethnic studies see Iacovetta 1992, esp. 264–66). The problems that have been exposed all have their roots in the gendered inequities of power embedded in the patriarchally organized domestic family.

The Feminization of Poverty

The feminization of poverty—meaning that women face a higher risk of poverty than men, and comprise a growing percentage of the poor—is a "significant long-term trend" (Battle 1988, 117). Figures for 1986 showed that lone women in Canada are more likely to be poor than are lone men (38.5 percent versus 29.2 percent), and that families headed by women are more likely to be poor than are those headed by men (40 percent versus 10 percent). There are many more women-led, single-parent families and this situation has become steadily more common: the number of poor women-led families tripled between 1961 and 1986 (Battle 1988, 2). Moreover, the overall reduction in poverty among the lone elderly in the 1980s and 1990s continued to favour older men, who remain less likely to be poor than are older women (Abu-Laban and McDaniel 1995, 101).

Why are women still more likely to be poor? As one might expect, the chance that *any* person will be poor is directly linked to that person's attachment to the labour force. Women who remained housewives all their adult years were disadvantaged materially by their total economic dependence on a husband whose support might suddenly disappear through divorce, desertion, or death, or who might fail to provide for them in pensions or wills (McDaniel 1996, 203).

The lot of the employed woman is not vastly different. All evidence points to the fact that while the level of women's entry into the work force is unprecedented, the jobs for which they are hired continue to be in overall terms the worst: they offer the lowest pay and the fewest benefits. Feminist scholars have noted that women's paid work is a kind of extension of the jobs they do at home: cooking, tending and cleaning, paperwork of various kinds; in short, the care and feeding of the social rather than the private household. Viewed historically, the picture is not much better; as particular skills or occupations become "feminized"—the job of secretary, for example, formerly male—their wages fall and they lose prestige (Lipman-Blumen 1984, 39). In sum, ever greater numbers of women are in paid work, and a growing percentage have considerable economic security, but the gendered segregation of the labour force, and the profile of women's participation in it (often marked by frequent "times out" for child rearing) means that women continue to be poorer, as workers and retirees, than men.

As policy-makers who advocate "rational" economic solutions to the problem of poor women discover, cultural assumptions about the nature of femininity play a crucial role both in the causes of women's poverty and in its invisibility as a social problem. In this connection, I would argue that women's poverty is seen as an extension of the normal role of dependence, as this is laid out according to the ethos of domesticity. If dependence on a husband is seen to be women's "normal" state, then the dependence of a single mother on the state will not "stick out" as a problem.[13] As Schur (1984) has observed, certain forms of deviance are commonsensically regarded as more appropriate for women than for men; being poor is one of these.

This assumption is compounded by the general devaluation of all the activities in the domestic sphere since the domestic revolution. The ideal of the home as a sanctuary has meant that "work" was reassigned to the public sphere, and hence mothering and child care were denied the status of "real" (i.e., paid) work. The dualism imposed by the radical separation of public and private spheres can be seen in the conviction that what women properly do in the home is the opposite of what goes on outside it. Rational arguments mounted by feminists in support of wages for housework continue to fail in the face of the resilient cultural assumption that "home" is precisely the place where work is absent.

Employed women who work the "double day" suffer the disadvantages of the invisibility of home and housework, but the heaviest burden of poverty falls to the women who never enter the labour force at all. These women are disadvantaged by a second, but related, assumption defining women as having "no head for figures." Accepted by wives and husbands alike to a considerable decree (the math phobia of female high-school students is the contemporary equivalent), some wives have no knowledge or understanding of their husband's financial situation until his death.

Wills themselves are a clue to the embeddedness of cultural assumptions about women as "property" or "naturally" dependent. In her historical study of bequests to women in turn-of-the-century Ontario, Cohen discovered that the vast majority of fathers with assets (mainly land and livestock) left only a tiny portion of those assets (an animal, some furniture) to their daughters, despite the life-long labour they contributed to the family economy (1988). These fathers stipulated, or simply assumed, that a woman's grown brothers or her spouse would see to her keep. By 1979, some 90 percent of Canadian married working men having survivor-benefit options in their pension plans chose not to take up these options for their wives (Novak 1985, 15); and as recently as the mid-1980s, 78 percent of private pensions in Canada still had no survivor provisions, though according to McDaniel, this figure is now somewhat reduced (1996, 101).

Here we see some of the ways in which cultural assumptions deriving from the ethos of domesticity legitimate the impoverishment of women. Moreover, these same beliefs are likely to shape state policy toward poor women. Unless the state is free of the cultural assumptions characteristic of the society around it—and there is every reason to doubt this possibility—then its perception of poor women's needs, and hence of a problem to be rectified as well as the resources that can be mobilized to offset it, will continue to flow through channels carved out by the cultural assumptions of the bourgeois family. In blunt terms, this means that "society" (and this includes impoverished women themselves) will continue to attach primary financial responsibility for the woman to "her" man. Structural changes in the labour force or in pension legislation will alleviate this situation marginally, but in the final analysis it must be dealt with in a way that challenges, rather than reiterates, the old cultural assumptions.

The Problem of Family Violence

Once thought of as a monolithic phenomenon, "family violence" is now seen as violence of several different kinds—against women, against children, against the old, and among children (that is, sibling violence). Not all of these forms of violent behaviour are equally problematized: greater visibility is currently attached to the abuse of women and children than to sibling abuse and the abuse of older family members. In what follows, I mention only three of these types, omitting a discussion of elder abuse. My purpose is not to summarize the research on all types of domestic violence (for this the reader should consult DeKeseredy 1996), but rather to highlight the cultural factors that work to keep so much violent family conduct *un*problematized, thus leaving the image of the family as a harmonious and peaceful place relatively undamaged.

Domestic violence is sometimes "woman-to-man" (Lupri 1990a),[14] but more often women and children are men's victims. Although it has addressed the problems of definition and perception to a degree, the scholarly literature on this subject has focussed largely on the matter of cause (or predisposing factors). Several early studies (Gelles 1977; Straus et al. 1980) revealed the degree to which violent conduct between members was a routine occurrence. They documented the existence of a gap between the image of the bourgeois family as a haven of harmony and safety, and the reality of family life, which proved to be awash in the punches, slaps, bites, and kicks of "routine" as well as severe violence (shootings, knifings, burnings). More recently, Lupri's national survey of spousal violence in Canada reported a roughly similar picture: members of six out of every hundred couples admitted to having slapped their partners within the past year, and 2.5 percent of the men, as well as 6.2 percent of the women, had beaten up their spouses. In addition, one person in every two hundred couples had taken a knife or gun to his or her partner, according to individuals' own reports (1990b, 8). Nor were these incidents one-time occurrences (1990b, 9–10). A recent Canadian survey indicates that 29 percent of women have experienced violence at the hands of their current or previous marital partner (Statistics Canada, 1993).

The Canadian study makes it clear that no group in the society is entirely free of violent family behaviour. But as many texts on the family now point out, violence against women and children was virtually ignored until the 1970s. Now so widely discussed and studied that it has become a vulgar cliché in the popular media, the high visibility of these types of violence would suggest that they are regarded as a more pressing social problem than, say, the impoverishment of women. Indeed, scholarly reports tend to give the impression that even if violent *family conduct* has not abated, then at least the *myth* of the harmonious family has been successfully debunked. Confronted by vast quantities of data, one would think that individuals have at last come to recognize the reality of the family for what it is: a violent place.

But this conclusion is unfounded. Though sociologists of the family warn that parental homicide is the most common killer of children, parents continue to fear the maniac in the schoolyard and the Halloween sadist (Best and Horiuchi 1985), and "streetproof" their children in defence against the largely ephemeral threat of the violent stranger. While the ChildFind organization assures us that fully 95 percent of child disappearances are at the hands of family members, we continue to fear the child stealer in the park. Although studies report that women are more likely to be attacked by people they know than by people they don't, front door peepholes (to let you know "who it is" before opening up) are still standard equipment for self-protection. And high-school students, young men and women alike, continue to believe that they are most likely to be raped by a stranger. These beliefs and products all rest on one assumption, and it is a keystone of the ethos of bourgeois domesticity: *the stranger is danger, but the familiar is safe*.[15]

What are we to make of such findings? The problem of the violent family is by no means a self-evident one for social scientists; even less is it so for ordinary members of society. The few studies that attempt to address the problem of *meaning* in violent families—how members involved in violent events interpret their own activities—suggest that violent conduct is defined in ways that strengthen, rather than challenge, the dominant imagery of family harmony. Some violent acts are **normalized**, that is, reinterpreted as acceptable: fights between siblings, for example, are defined as culturally acceptable "roughhousing" or "horseplay," and the degree of acceptability conferred on such conduct—"it's a healthy part of growing up"—is clearly at the root of the low degree of social concern this most common form of family violence elicits. Wife-slapping may be similarly normalized as an act of quasi-parental concern ("It's like when your kids do something wrong—you have to do something; you do it because you love them"; National Film Board of Canada 1979). Through the strategy of normalizing, violent conduct is made to fade back into the woodwork of ordinary family life (Stebbins 1988; Denzin 1984).

Family members employ another strategy that has the effect of protecting the image of family harmony. This strategy works by symbolically withdrawing family status from the perpetrator, and reassigning the event to the street and the stranger, that is, to the culturally appropriate site of danger according to the ethos of bourgeois domesticity. Thus, interviews with victims of severe family violence are filled with comments that redefine the intimate as "strange" or "other": "This wasn't the man I married!", "I just don't recognize her when she's like that," and so forth. By discursively reassigning the violent act(or) to a sphere (the street) and a category of others (strangers/non-family) that, since the emergence of the domestic family, has been the culturally appropriate site of violence, the violent act is remade in understandable form (Miller 1990b).

It is important to remember that these strategies are not dreamed up by the perpetrators of violent acts, nor by the victims. Instead, they rely on standard cultural assumptions or scripts provided by the patriarchal rhetoric of the bourgeois domestic family. They reveal both the strength of our continued loyalty to the image of family harmony, as well as the creative ways we rely on commonsense knowledge to bolster it. Instead of giving the lie to the rhetoric of family harmony, strategies like the ones mentioned here end up bolstering it. The study of such practices takes us to the heart of the contradictions and enigmas surrounding family violence.

Social Control

Interpretive studies of family violence help to show why it is so persistently regarded as a rare or pathological phenomenon (Lupri 1990a, 2) despite evidence to the contrary. For by reassigning severe or "deviant" violence to "others," we evade the recognition that our intimates can also do us harm. Our culturally structured inability to accept the deeply dialectical nature of intimate relationships (Lupri 1990b, 29) has important implications for the visibility, and hence for the social control, of family violence. Despite attempts to demonstrate "scientifically" that violence is distributed throughout the ambit of human experience, the violent person who is also an intimate is not yet a culturally credible category of deviant. We have no such trouble with the idea of a dangerous stranger, for strangers remain members of a systematically devalued category (Schur 1984). We feel we can justifiably act against the intruding axe-murderer, the pervert at the schoolyard gate, the con artist; but to act against an assailant who is also our spouse, parent, or child[16] calls up in us deep feelings of ambivalence. Only by *externalizing* the discrepant aspect of our intimate relationships as other, strange, perverse, or not quite ours are we able to deal unambivalently with domestic violence—to make it the object of some policy of social control. This is the legacy of the rhetoric of family harmony.

The tendency to **medicalize** family violence by attributing it to physical or mental illness worsens the problem. Quite apart from its lack of empirical support, this approach blinds us to the cultural roots of the way we understand the family and violence within it. By denying that normal (healthy) family members may *also* be violent and dangerous—without taking leave of their senses—this rationalization reaffirms the rhetoric that normal families are harmonious, and violent ones aberrations. Thus the immediate problem of violent conduct and what to do about it gives way to the deeper problem: the persistence of the myth of family harmony. If not more painful, this problem is more insidious, because the long-term effect of the sense-making techniques I have described here, both lay and professional, is to shift problems out of the family onto others. It is through these kinds of mechanisms that the "invisibility" of family violence is sustained.

Conclusions

The increased attention paid to social control and its historical evolution, especially since the publication of Foucault's *Discipline and Punish* (1979), has led to a re-evaluation of the linkage between family and state. Much of this literature reflects a growing distaste with what are perceived as the ever subtler and more insidious attempts by state agencies, especially by the "psy" professionals, to "besiege" the family in the name of solving its problems. Some of these writers (e.g., Lasch 1977) note the contradiction embedded in ever stronger efforts to shore up the family by expanding the state's role in it—in short, by undermining it still further as a source of autonomy. For these observers, the direction of state intervention is not the problem: the problem is intervention *itself*.

But the feminist scholarship of the 1980s and 1990s has revealed the difficulty in adopting a position uniformly for or against state intervention in the family. To be sure, feminist scholars have come to recognize the various ways in which the state's attempts to suppress or improve "problem" families has gone against women's own interests. As I have argued, state enforcement of the domestic family ideal has sometimes meant the direct or indirect repression of other evidently workable domestic arrangements, including those that women have worked out to make their lives easier (for example, the mother who puts herself or her child into the work force to make ends meet). Furthermore, historians have documented how a whole array of local institutions tying women in with their neighbours and kinsfolk were slowly eroded as they ran afoul of the domestic ideal, which advocated women's dependence on their husbands alone, and encouraged a relatively isolated family existence (Gittins 1986). And from the nineteenth century to the present, the gradual replacement of local forms of skill and knowledge by state-regulated professional expertise (for instance, the supplanting of midwifery by professional medicine or working-class methods of child rearing by "scientific" ones) has further depleted the authority of family members and of women in particular (Ehrenreich and English 1979; Donzelot 1979). In all of these instances, the very *solutions* that women have evolved to solve their family problems are themselves regarded as problems by the state. For these reasons and others, feminists stand alongside non-feminist conservative scholars in their opposition to further intervention in the family.

On the other hand, feminists have come to see that women now and in the past have welcomed, and even actively sought, the intervention of state agencies into their homelives. The first family scholars to open the black box of the household shed light on the taken-for-granted worlds of childhood, marriage, mothering, and the family economy, and immediately confronted "invisible" inequities between husbands and wives (such as wife abuse) that the state was soon pressured to recognize, then to redress. In sum, while the state has worsened—if not actually created—some family problems, it is regularly asked to remedy others.

The question is often raised whether the state, given its subservience to the interests of capital and hence its patriarchal bias, can ever be expected to act *against* those interests by taking the side of women in the family.[17] But recent studies have begun to rethink the view that the state is a monolith implacably opposed to the interests of women. Some of these studies show how bourgeois women have used alliances with the state to their collective political advantage. Others show how working-class women sought help from state agencies in matters of child rearing, or in order to escape domestic violence, and upon becoming clients, aggressively attempted to influence agency policy, sometimes successfully (Gordon 1989). And a third group of studies, which focus on the sense-making strategies of women living their lives in the interstices of a dominant patriarchal order (e.g., Brannen and Wilson 1987; Gaskell 1988; Smith 1987), suggest that the state cannot be adequately conceptualized as an external force controlling the lives of its passive victims.

In sum, all of these studies point to a more complex view of the relationships between family, women, and the state than was previously assumed. Instead of debating whether state intervention into family life is good or bad, family theorists have begun to reconceptualize the state as an environment within which family members are seen to be the agents of their own lives.

Summary

- No society is equally accepting of all forms of family and household life. Even in tolerant times, some family arrangements are thought of as right and natural, while others are seen as problems about which "something must be done."
- The family ideal that has predominated since the last century has been the nuclear, bourgeois, patriarchal family; alternative domestic arrangements that differ from the ideal type were and are still discredited and controlled.
- The study of family problems is the study of historical and political process whereby one community tries to impose its version of the good family upon other less powerful communities; family forms designated as problems (for example, the "slum" family or the lesbian/gay family) are usually the losers in the contest.
- Only if we ask *for whom* they are a problem will we be able to see why relatively harmless forms of domestic life have been attacked, while other blatant injustices, such as the abuse of women, were perceived as unproblematic for so long.

Questions to Consider

1. Make a list of the family problems you see mentioned in today's newspaper (not forgetting letters to the editor). Which interest groups are promoting the visibility of these issues? What techniques are they using to accomplish this? What obstacles stand in their way?

2. Compare your own family to the bourgeois domestic ideal. If you live in an "alternative" family, assess the social forces, if any, that pressure the members of your family to conform to the ideal. Consider both formal and informal mechanisms of social control in your answer. What strategies does your family employ to cope with these pressures?

3. Ask your grandparents to recall the urgent family problems of their day. How are they different from today's? Do they see these problems as having been resolved? In their view, what measures must be (or have been) taken to reach a solution?

4. Assemble a list of the entire range of behaviours your own family members would classify as "family violence." Would the very same behaviours be seen in the same light if they occurred between strangers? What might account for such a difference?

Suggested Readings

Ariès, Philipe. *Centuries of Childhood: A Social History of Family Life.* New York: Alfred A. Knopf, 1962.

Donzelot, Jacques. *The Policing of Families.* New York: Oxford University Press, 1979.

Ehrenreich, Barbara, and Dierdre English. *For Their Own Good: 150 Years of the Experts' Advice to Women.* Garden City, NY: Anchor Press/Doubleday, 1979.

Gordon, Linda. *Heroes of Their Own Lives.* New York: Viking/Penguin, 1988.

Zelizer, Viviana A. *Pricing the Priceless Child: The Changing Social Value of Children.* New York: Basic Books, 1985.

Glossary

cult or ethos of domesticity The dominant image of family life that emerged in the middle class in eighteenth- and nineteenth-century Europe: sentimental, child-centred, privatized, and patriarchal.

feminization of poverty The tendency for females to be economically poorer than males, especially as a result of their reliance on male providers.

marginalized To be seen as unusual and undesirable by mainstream social groups; applied to social arrangements or types of social conduct.

medicalization (of deviance) The redefinition of a deviant act by attributing it to illness rather than to immorality.

normalizing An interpretive strategy that minimizes the objectionable quality of a deviant act by stressing its similarity to culturally acceptable forms of conduct.

social control Formal and informal means of regulating deviant social conduct.

social problem A social condition or form of conduct labelled as problematic by a powerful group.

Notes

1. Scholars have generally rejected the once widely held view that associated modernization with a shift from extended to nuclear households. Contemporary studies now suggest that while the premodern household was never filled with kin, it did include an assortment of *others* we would now define as strangers (lodgers, apprentices, clients, and servants). The presence of these others signifies the sociability of the premodern family and its embeddedness in the local community, and this is the point contemporary scholars wish to emphasize. For a summary of this issue, see Hareven (1989, 41–42).

2. This statement is accurate so long as it is restricted to those historians who make an important place in their theoretical approaches for commonsense belief. For a brief introduction to other schools of thought on the origins of the modern family, see Anderson (1980). In this essay I am mainly concerned with what Anderson calls the "sentiments school," whose most influential figure is Ariès.

3. Though some of Ariès's claims have been severely criticized (in particular his famous thesis that childhood was not recognized as a distinctive phase of social life in the premodern world), his overall account of the emergence of a split between public and private spheres of social life and the new tenor of sentimentality that came to characterize the latter continue to be accepted.

4. More recent sociological studies tend to reject the idea that such standards are foisted upon a passive working class. These later studies illuminate the ways actors actively construct their worlds so as to reproduce or resist dominant social orders. I return to this issue later in this essay.

5. For a review of the debate over Ariès's thesis about the "discovery of childhood," see Howe and Bukowski (1996).

6. The North American suburb of the 1950s—a thoroughly feminized world—is a vivid expression of this view. On the same issue, Ambert (1996) has recently pointed out that the mother-centred model of parenting based on the domestic ideal is being exported to other non-industrial societies by influential North American journals and aid programs.

7. Working-class women developed an array of strategies that allowed them to bring in money while simultaneously appearing to conform to the middle-class family ideal, which called for a homebound wife. Some of these strategies included taking in lodgers, preparing meals for others for a fee, and even selling wood on the other side of town, thereby upholding their husband's status as sole breadwinner. See for example Ayers and Lambertz's (1986) discussion of such strategies in working-class Liverpool.

8. It appears that the relatively recent emergence of the concept of "quality time" performs the same function for women in the work force; that is, it manages or eases this dilemma by diminishing the significance of time spent away from young children and exaggerating the smaller portion of time spent at home.

9. For an excellent account of the difficulties lesbian parents encounter in their efforts to gain social recognition as a family as they deal with neighbours, educators, and others, see Nelson (1992).

10. For a somewhat similar argument that also emphasizes the connection between the visibility of a social problem and the importance of public challenges to mainstream family forms, see Bloul (1997). Here the author argues that the wearing of the Islamic headscarf is highly problematized in French society, in contrast to the relatively unproblematized issue of female genital mutilation (or excision), because the former, unlike the latter, is regarded as an "unbearable invasion of ethnic difference in [French] institutional spaces."

11. American president Bill Clinton appears to have arrived at just this sort of solution to the "problem" of homosexuals in the military: "Don't ask: don't tell."

12. Arnup's paper clearly demonstrates the greater political acceptability of some constructions or interpretations of family life over others. For a discussion of the way linguistic realities and metaphors structure our understanding of birth contracts (surrogate motherhood), see Vandelac (1988).

13. Cultural assumptions about femininity—specifically the view that women are natural caregivers—also explain the invisibility of a pressing but barely problematized issue. I refer here to the increasing demands placed on a generation of middle-aged women who are giving unpaid care to elderly relatives as well as holding down paid jobs in the labour force. The pressure on these women is increasing as governments shift the burden of caregiving to families (which often means women). See McDaniel (1996).

14. One of Lupri's most surprising findings was the high incidence and severity of woman-to-man violence. See his discussion of the problems of interpretation posed by such data (1990b, 8–9).

15. For an account of the remapping of social reality around the spheres of safe home and dangerous street and the discrediting of the latter assumptions, see Miller (1990a).

16. In connection with the invisibility of elder abuse, DeKeseredy mentions that the aged parent's sense of responsibility and commitment to a child may outweigh their willingness or ability to see that child as an abuser (and to act on that recognition) (DeKeseredy 1996, 268–71).

17. For a summary of this issue, see Pupo (1988).

References

Abu-Laban, S.A., and S.A. McDaniel. 1995. "Aging Women and Standards of Beauty." In *Feminist Issues: Race, Class and Sexuality*, ed. N. Mandell. Scarborough: Prentice-Hall Canada.

Ambert, A.-M. 1996. "An International Perspective on Parenting." In *Family Life: Patterns and Perspectives*, ed. C.J. Richardson. Toronto: McGraw-Hill Ryerson.

Anderson, M. 1980. *Approaches to the History of the Western Family, 1500–1914*. London: Macmillan.

Ariès, P. 1962. *Centuries of Childhood: A Social History of Family Life*. New York: Alfred A. Knopf.

Armstrong P., and H. Armstrong. 1988. "Women's Work in the Labour Force." In *Gender and Society*, ed. A.T. McLaren. Toronto: Copp Clark Pitman.

Arnup, K. 1988. "Lesbian Mothers and Child Custody." In *Gender and Society*, ed. A.T. McLaren. Toronto: Copp Clark Pitman.

———. 1997. "In the Family Way: Lesbian Mothers in Canada." In *Feminism and Families*, ed. M. Luxton. Halifax: Fernwood Publishing.

Ayers, P., and J. Lambertz. 1986. "Marriage Relations, Money, and Domestic Violence in Working-Class Liverpool, 1919–39." In *Labour and Love: Women's Experience of Home and Family 1850–1940*, ed. J. Lewis. Don Mills: Oxford University Press.

Baker, M., ed. 1996. *Families: Changing Trends in Canada*. 3d ed. Toronto: McGraw-Hill Ryerson.

Barrett, M., and M. McIntosh. 1982. *The Anti-Social Family*. London: Verso.

Battle, K. 1988. *Poverty Profile 1988: A Report by the National Council of Welfare*. Ottawa: Minister of Supply and Services.

Berger, P.L., and B. Berger. 1984. *The War Over the Family: Capturing the Middle Ground*. Garden City, NY: Anchor Press/Doubleday.

Best, J., and G.T. Horiuchi. 1985. "The Razor Blade in the Apple: The Social Construction of Urban Legends." *Social Problems* 32: 488–99.

Bloul, R.A. 1997. "Victims or Offenders: 'Other' Women in French Sexual Politics." In *Embodied Practices: Feminist Perspectives on the Body*, ed. K. Davis. London: Sage Publications.

Bradbury, B. 1982. "The Fragmented Family: Family Strategies in the Face of Death, Illness, and Poverty, Montreal, 1860–1885." In *Childhood and Family in Canadian History*, ed. J. Parr. Toronto: McClelland and Stewart.

———. 1996. "The Social and Economic Origins of Contemporary Families." In *Families: Changing Trends in Canada*, ed. M. Baker, Toronto: McGraw-Hill Ryerson.

Brannen, J., and P. Moss. 1987. "Dual Earner Households: Women's Financial Contributions after the Birth of the First Child." In *Give and Take in Families: Studies in Resource Distribution*, ed. J. Brannen and G. Wilson. London: George Allen and Unwin.

Brannen, J., and G. Wilson, eds. 1987. *Give and Take in Families: Studies in Resource Distribution*. London: George Allen and Unwin.

Bremmer, R.H., J. Barnard, T.K. Hareven, and R.M. Mennel, eds. 1970–74. *Childhood and Youth in America*. 3 vols. Cambridge: Harvard University Press.

Chalmers, L., and P. Smith. 1988. "Wife Battering: Psychological, Social, and Physical Isolation and Counteracting Strategies." In *Gender and Society*, ed. A.T. McLaren. Toronto: Copp Clark Pitman.

Chunn, D. 1992. *From Punishment to Doing Good: Family Courts and Socialized Justice in Ontario, 1880–1940*. Toronto: University of Toronto Press.

Cossman, B. 1997. "Family Inside/Out." In *Feminism and Families*, ed. M. Luxton. Halifax: Fernwood Publishing.

Cohen, M. 1988. *Women's Work, Markets and Economic Development in Nineteenth-Century Ontario*. Toronto: University of Toronto Press.

Coulter, R. 1982. "The Working Young of Edmonton, 1921–1931." In Parr, *Childhood and Family in Canadian History*.

DeKeseredy, W. 1996. "Patterns of Family Violence." In Baker, *Families: Changing Trends in Canada*.

Demos, J. 1970. *A Little Commonwealth: Family Life in Plymouth Colony*. New York: Oxford University Press.

Denzin, N.K. 1984. "Toward a Phenomenology of Domestic, Family Violence." *American Journal of Sociology* 90, no. 3: 483–513.

Donzelot, J. 1979. *The Policing of Families*. New York: Oxford University Press.

Ehrenreich, B., and D. English. 1979. *For Their Own Good: 150 Years of the Experts' Advice to Women*. Garden City, NY: Anchor Press/Doubleday.

Elias, N. 1978 [1939]. *The History of Manners*. New York: Urizen Books.

Finkelstein, B. 1985. "Casting Networks of Good Influence: The Reconstruction of Childhood in the United States, 1790–1870." In *American Childhood*, ed. J.M. Hawes and N.R. Hiner. Westport, CT, and London: Greenwood Press. 111–52.

Foucault, M. 1979. *Discipline and Punish*. New York: Vintage Books.

Gaffield, C. 1982. "Schooling, the Economy, and Rural Society in Nineteenth-Century Ontario." In Parr, *Childhood and Family in Canadian History*.

Gaskell, J. 1988. "The Reproduction of Family Life: Perspectives of Male and Female Adolescents." In McLaren, *Gender and Society*. 146–68.

Gavigan, S.A.M. 1997. "Feminism, Familial Ideology and Family Law." In *Feminism and Families*, ed. M. Luxton. Halifax: Fernwood Publishing.

Gelles, R.J. 1977. "Demythologizing Child Abuse." In *Families in Transition*, 2d ed., ed. A.S. Skolnick and J.H. Skolnick. Boston and Toronto: Little, Brown.

Gelles, R.J., and M. Straus. 1979. "Determinants of Aggression in the Family: Toward a Theoretical Integration." In *Contemporary Theories About the Family*, vol. 1, ed. W. Barr et al. New York: The Free Press.

Gittins, D. 1986. *The Family in Question: Changing Households and Familiar Ideologies.* New York: Humanities Press.

Gordon, L. 1989. "The Politics and History of Family Violence." In *Family in Transition,* 6th ed., ed. A.S. Skolnick and J.H. Skolnick. Glenview, IL: Scott, Foresman.

Hareven, T.K. 1989. "American Families in Transition: Historical Perspectives on Change." In Skolnick and Skolnick, *Family in Transition*, 6th ed.

Houston, S.E. 1982. "The 'Waifs and Strays' of a Late Victorian City: Juvenile Delinquents in Toronto." In Parr, *Childhood and Family.*

Howe, N., and W.A. Bukowski. 1996. "What Are Children and How Do They Become Adults." In Baker, *Families: Changing Trends in Canada.*

Iacovetta, F. 1992. "Making 'New Canadians': Social Workers, Women and the Reshaping of Immigrant Families." In *Gender Conflicts: New Essays in Women's History,* ed. F. Iacovetta and M. Valverde. Toronto: University of Toronto Press.

Lasch, C. 1977. *Haven in a Heartless World.* New York: Basic Books.

Laslett, B. 1973. "The Family as a Public and Private Institution: A Historical Perspective." *Journal of Marriage and the Family* 35: 480–92.

Lewis, J. ed. 1986. *Labour and Love: Women's Experience of Home and Family 1850–1940.* Don Mills: Oxford University Press.

Lipman-Blumen, J. 1984. *Gender Roles and Power.* Englewood Cliffs, NJ: Prentice-Hall.

Lupri, E. 1990a. "The Dialectics of Conjugal Violence." *Familiendynamik-Interdisziplinare Zeitschrift fur Praxis und Forschung* 15.

———. 1990b. "Harmonie und Aggression: Über die Dialektik ehelicher Gewalt." *Kölne Zeitschrift fur Soziologie und Socialpsychologie* 42, no. 3: 199. (Page references cited in the text are from the English version of this paper, which is available from the author.)

Lupri, E., and D.L. Mills. 1983. "The Changing Roles of Canadian Women in Family and Work: An Overview." In *The Changing Position of Women in Family and Society: A Cross-National Comparison,* ed. E. Lupri. Leiden: E.J. Brill.

McDaniel, S. 1996. "The Family Lives of the Middle-Aged and Elderly in Canada." In Baker, *Families: Changing Trends in Canada.*

McKee, L. 1987. "Households During Unemployment: The Resourcefulness of the Unemployed." In Brannen and Wilson, *Give and Take in Families.*

Miller, L.J. 1987. "Uneasy Alliance: Women as Agents of Social Control." *Canadian Journal of Sociology* 12, no. 4: 345–61.

———. 1990a. "Safe Home, Dangerous Street: Remapping Social Reality in the Early Modern Era." In *Perspectives on Social Problems*, vol. 2, ed. G. Miller and A. Holstein. Greenwich, CT: JAI Press.

———. 1990b. "Violent Families and the Rhetoric of Harmony." *British Journal of Sociology* 41, no. 2: 261–86.

National Film Board of Canada. 1979. *Loved, Honoured and Bruised.*

Nelson, F. 1992. "Lesbian Motherhood." Unpublished Master's Thesis, Department of Sociology, University of Calgary, Calgary, Alberta.

Nett, E. 1981. "Canadian Families in Social-Historical Perspective." *Canadian Journal of Sociology* 6, no. 3: 239–60.

Novak, M. 1985. *Successful Aging.* Toronto: Penguin Books.

Pfohl, S.J. 1985. *Images of Deviance and Social Control: A Sociological History.* New York: McGraw-Hill.

Pupo, N. 1988. "Preserving Patriarchy: Women, the Family, and the State." In *Reconstructing the Family: Feminist Perspectives*, ed. N. Mandell and A. Duffy. Toronto and Vancouver: Butterworths.

Ram, B., and A. Romaniuc. 1996. "New Trends in the Family." In *Family Life: Patterns and Perspectives,* ed. C.J. Richardson.

Richardson, C.J. 1996. *Family Life: Patterns and Perspectives.* Toronto: McGraw-Hill Ryerson.

Rubington, E., and M.S. Weinberg, eds. 1987. *Deviance: The Interactionist Perspective.* 5th ed. New York: Macmillan.

Schur, E. 1984. *Labeling Women Deviant: Gender, Stigma, and Social Control.* Philadelphia: Temple University Press.

Shorter, E. 1975. *The Making of the Modern Family.* New York: Basic Books.

Statistics Canada. 1974. *Perspective Canada 1.* Ottawa: Information Canada.

———. 1993. "The Violence Against Women Survey." *The Daily*, Nov. 18.

Statistics Canada, Canadian Centre for Justice Statistics. 1994. *Family Violence in Canada.* Ottawa: Ministry of Industry, Science and Technology.

Straus, M.A., R.J. Gelles, and S.K. Steinmetz. 1980. *Behind Closed Doors.* Garden City, NY: Anchor Books.

Stebbins, R. 1988. *Deviance: Tolerable Differences.* Toronto: McGraw-Hill Ryerson.

Strong-Boag, V. 1982. "Intruders in the Nursery: Childcare Professionals Reshape the Years One to Five, 1920–1940." In Parr, *Childhood and Family.*

Valverde, M. 1991. *The Age of Light, Soap and Water: Moral Reform in English Canada, 1885–1925.* Toronto: McClelland and Stewart.

Vandelac, L. 1988. "Mothergate: Surrogate Mothers, Linguistics and Androcentric Engineering." In McLaren, *Gender and Society.*

Zelizer, V.A. 1989. "Pricing the Priceless Child: From Baby Farms to Black-Market Babies." In *Family in Transition,* 6th ed., ed. A.S. Skolnick and J.H. Skolnick. Glenview. IL: Scott, Foresman.

PART III

Race and Ethnicity

INTRODUCTION

Racial and ethnic inequality is a basic feature of the Canadian mosaic. Racial privileges, like class privileges, reach far back into the Canadian past. The colonialization of the Native population, racist immigration policies directed against South Asians and Chinese, the internment of the Japanese—all of these attest to the racist policies and practices of the Canadian state. Racist policies and practices are present as well in the other institutions in this society, and continue to affect the current status of racial minorities in this country. Recent studies have exposed the myth that we have seen the end of racial inequality and that racism is a thing of the past. Instead, they show that racial minorities continue to occupy disadvantaged positions in Canadian society in spite of state policies to promote the cultural heritage and identity of various social groups, as well as educational programs to promote better understanding and tolerance. While patterns and practices of discrimination have changed over time, racial domination and racial inequality remain as permanent features.

The first two readings in this section address the issues of racism and racial inequality, and the institutional structures and arrangements that continue to sustain racial inequalities. The third reading provides an overview of the development and implementation of multiculturalism as a state policy.

The chapter by Vic Satzewich, entitled "Social Stratification: Class and Racial Inequality," examines the dimensions, meaning, and consequences of racism and racial inequality in Canada. Satzewich reviews various theoretical explanations of racial inequality and presents a critique of psychological, cultural, and human capital approaches. Racism, he argues, is not simply articulated and significant at the level of interpersonal relations; rather, racism and racial inequality are structural aspects of both the past and the present operations of Canada as a capitalist country. They have been central to the formation and reproduction of capitalist relations of production via the regulation of labour procurement.

Despite the fact that Canada was initially viewed as a white dominion, capitalism in this country has been unable to function without the presence of non-European workers. Still, people defined as non-European have occupied a precarious position in social, political, and economic relations. Their experiences in Canada have been affected in no small degree by institutional racism. This chapter identifies various forms of institutional racism to which non-European groups have been subject, and traces the continuities and variations in its meaning. It is manifested in various forms of exclusionary practices, in the allocation of people to specific sites in production relations, and in the social and political marginalization of groups of people. In conclusion, Satzewich argues the continuing relevance of racism in this country, to the extent that there are costs and benefits in the job market associated with ethnic origin. To be sure, racism no longer has the same economic impact in Canada that it had earlier in this century, and many of the blatant forms of racial discrimination have been eliminated. Current debate focusses on the continued impact of more subtle forms of racism and discrimination on the economic performance of and earnings disadvantages faced by some racial minority groups.

Of all its racial minority groups, Canada's First Nations population has faced the worst racism and racial exploitation. They live in an impoverished and subjugated position because of past colonization, in its various manifestations, as well as the current political, economic, and social oppression that they face. Their maintenance in a state of underdevelopment is manifested both economically and socially. In economic terms, they suffer poverty, unemployment, and welfare dependency; socially, they are plagued by conditions that include family breakdown and suicide. James Frideres, in his chapter entitled "First Nations: Walking the Path of Social Change," addresses many of the issues facing the First Nations. His thesis is that these problems must be discussed in the historical context of the First Nations' political, economic, and social subordination.

Frideres provides health, education, and economic data to demonstrate the conditions of inequality in which the aboriginal people live. They suffer high infant mortality, low life expectancy, and an abnormal rate of infectious diseases associated with, among other things, poor sanitation and housing. Their level of participation in education is low, and their dropout rate is high. Unemployment and welfare dependency affect their personal lives and undermine their communities. Frideres argues that these inequalities are the result of institutional structures and institutional discrimination against the Native people.

The chapter also provides a brief discussion of two other crucial issues: Native land claims and self-government. New structural arrangements are being negotiated to enhance Native control over the political, economic, cultural, and social spheres of their lives. While Frideres sees developments here in a favourable light, he is less optimistic about a rapid transformation of the situation of Canada's First Nations as a whole.

One of the federal policies that has received considerable attention in recent years is the policy on multiculturalism. Victor Ujimoto, in the chapter entitled "Multiculturalism, Ethnic Identity, and Inequality," discusses some of the salient aspects of this policy since its original announcement in 1971 and its ultimate proclamation in the Canadian Multiculturalism Act of 1988.

Multiculturalism is the most visible program designed by the state to promote the cultural heritage of minorities and to "assist all members of all cultural groups to overcome cultural barriers to full participation in Canadian society." The purpose of the policy, according to prime minister Trudeau, was "to break down discriminatory attitudes and cultural jealousies ... [and] form the basis of a society which is based upon fair play for all." Despite this intention, there is little indication, as the other two readings in this section show, that racial prejudice, discrimination, and inequality have become any less evident. This is because, as many critics have noted, this policy aims to solve non-cultural problems with cultural solutions. As is evident in Trudeau's statement, the government has considered "cultural barriers," and not racism or structured inequality, to be the "barriers to full participation."

Racism and racial inequality have political and economic roots in the history and social institutions of Canada, and their solutions lie beyond the removal of "cultural barriers." With its emphasis on culture, multiculturalism is quite rightly criticized as a policy of depolarization of minority issues, one that deflects their political and economic demands into linguistic and cultural alleys. Ujimoto points out that much has indeed been accomplished in the form of linguistic and cultural programs. However, he argues, structural changes are required to enable all Canadians to achieve equal access to and participation in Canadian society.

CHAPTER 7

Social Stratification: Class and Racial Inequality

Vic Satzewich

Learning Objectives

After studying this chapter, you should be able to
- Understand the dimensions, meaning, and consequences of racial inequality in Canada.
- Outline various theoretical explanations used to explain **racism** and racial inequality.
- Understand the dimensions and meaning of **institutional racism**.
- Understand how racism and racial inequality have been central to the formation and reproduction of capitalist relations of production.

Introduction

Canadians of European origin have, at best, a checkered history when it comes to dealing with groups of people defined as being ethnically or racially different from themselves. The idea that Canada is a tolerant, peaceful, and welcoming society is still drawn upon from time to time, particularly when the Canadian government wants to occupy the high ground in international politics. This image of Canada does have some basis in reality, particularly when compared with the situation in Germany, where neo-fascists harass, abuse, and even murder Turkish, eastern European, and Asian refugees and immigrants. Over the years, Canada has indeed become home to hundreds of thousands of refugees and immigrants from around the world. While not a myth, the image of Canada and Canadians as tolerant is not entirely accurate. The reception that various immigrant and refugee groups have received following their arrival has tended to fall somewhat short of the ideal. While racism and discrimination are arguably not as prevalent in Canada as in some other countries that come to mind, racism and discrimination do indeed constitute important parts of our social, political, and economic structures. While some of the more pernicious aspects of racist ideology and practice are now rejected by many Canadians, a sense still prevails whereby groups defined as "non-white" continue to be seen as "other" and as problem populations largely responsible for their own circumstances.

Even though most academics will acknowledge that racism and discrimination continue to be present within Canadian society, few agree as to its social significance and meaning. The first purpose of this chapter is to examine some of the theories of "race" and ethnic relations that have been used to try to explain the nature of social inequality between different groups of people. Second, this paper presents a historical discussion of the meaning of "race," and how racism was linked to the wider system of capitalism with its attendant structure of unequal class relationships. Finally, the chapter provides some contemporary evidence of the social significance of ethnic origin in the current operation of the Canadian labour market.

Racism and Capitalism

When the social sciences in North America were dominated by the structural-functional school of thought in the 1950s and 1960s, the literature on "race" and ethnic relations was dominated by sociologists constructing theories to either play down or explicitly deny the impact of racism and discrimination on the social position and experiences of groups of people. Since inequalities between groups of people were too obvious for even structural-functionalists to ignore, they tried to deflect attention away from the possibility that racism and discrimination were structural components of modern industrial societies. They also denied the possibility that the largely "white" majority was doing anything to subordinate, marginalize, or exclude groups defined as "non-white." As an alternative to explanations of social inequality that focussed on racism and discrimination, and sometimes after some very interesting mental gymnastics, sociologists tried to place the source of the "problem" on the people who were poor and who suffered the consequences of poverty, racism, and discrimination.

One strategy used by sociologists in their analysis of ethnic relations was an attempt to *a priori* explain away the possibility that racism and discrimination might be a "problem." For some analysts, racism is regarded as an irrational attribute in an otherwise fair, equal, and achievement-oriented society. Racism is either an anomaly that will eventually vanish because of the universalizing and levelling tendencies associated with "post-industrialism," or an otherwise secondary feature of social, economic, and political relations. Edward Herberg, in his book, *Ethnic Groups in Canada: Adaptations and Transitions*, presents the former position rather succinctly when he optimistically tells the reader that

> the maintenance of Canada's existing post-industrial society, and especially its economy, requires an absolutely unrestrained integration of workers in the society and economy, based on individual merit and potential for productive contribution. This kind of essential egalitarianism is absolutely incompatible with any kind of legal or geographic constraints on either free movement or the rights of all ethnic peoples and communities to participate voluntarily. (1989, 299–300)

The implication of his argument is clear. It suggests that racism, which involves both the delineation of group boundaries on the basis of physical or genetic criteria (such as skin colour, eye shape, head shape, or gene frequencies), as well as the development of ideas that involve evaluations of superiority or inferiority based on group differences, is a dysfunctional, irrational feature of social relations in the country (Miles 1982, 32–34; 1989). Furthermore, social practices based on racially or ethnically defined criteria that inhibit individual freedom and initiative are regarded not only as unconscionable, but also as unnecessary for present-day capitalist social and economic development. Thus, practices like job segregation or discrimination in employment that are based on race, ethnicity, or gender are seen to be remnants of a long-distant past.

Others, however, have taken a different tack. A theme running through the literature on ethnic relations is the individualization, or personalization, of the explanation of ethnic and racial inequality. As with the analysis of racism, these explanations tend to emphasize the anomalous nature of social inequality within a largely fair and equal society: there is an assumption of equality of opportunity within a framework of inequality of condition. The problem of inequality is not located in the structural operation of capitalist societies but rather tends to be located in the particular cultural or psychological characteristics of groups of people.

Many years ago, Rosen (1956; 1959), for example, suggested that ethnic groups differ with respect to their psychological make-up. He argued that groups differ in their levels of **achievement motivation**; their value orientations, which define and implement achievement-oriented behaviour; and their educational and vocational aspirations. That is, they differ with respect to their "psychological need to excel, [the] ... initial possession of or willingness to adopt the high valuation placed upon achievement and success" (Rosen 1959, 48). He studied six groups in the United States and concluded that Jews, Greeks, and white Protestants possess a higher level of achievement motivation than do Italians, Africans, and French Canadians. These differences in achievement syndrome, he argued, help explain the greater degree of upward mobility and economic success of the former groups in relation to the latter groups.

A similar line of argument has been pursued by psychologists interested in IQ differences among both ethnic groups and social classes. In the United States, Herrnstein and Murray have rekindled the debate about the relationship between genetically inherited intelligence and social class in their book *The Bell Curve*. They argue that "success and failure in the American economy, and all that goes with it, are increasingly a matter of the genes that people inherit" (1994, 91). In their view, intelligence is largely inherited from one's ancestors, and one's level of intelligence (measured through what they see as standardized and objective IQ tests), is largely responsible for poverty, wealth, welfare dependence, crime, and school performance. They argue that socio-economic background, which is the favoured explanatory variable of sociologists, is far less influential in explaining these conditions than is inherited intelligence. In Canada, Vernon (1984) has argued that Natives and "orientals" differed with respect to their scores on intelligence tests. These apparent psychological differences in IQ are then used by Vernon to explain why the latter achieve higher levels of formal education and occupy higher-status occupations than do Native people. More recently, Phillipe Rushton, a psychologist from the University of

Western Ontario, has suggested that the "white," "Oriental," and "Negro" "races" differ fundamentally in terms of personality and culture. These differences, according to Rushton (1987; 1988), are rooted largely in the biological make-up of the groups. He argues that, on average, "Orientals" possess larger brains and smaller genitalia than "whites" and "Negroes," and that "Negroes" possess smaller brains and larger genitalia than the other two groups. In both cases, "whites" fall between the other two groups in terms of brain size and genitalia. According to Rushton and his colleagues, these supposed genetic differences "explain" numerous personality and social differences between the groups, including what they see as a propensity to crime and poverty by "Negroes" and a propensity to lower criminality and licentiousness and "higher" culture for "Orientals" (see Rushton 1987; 1988).

Cultural explanations of inequality share a focus with psychological explanations in that the root of the problem is seen to lie either in the apparent failure of groups to assimilate into mainstream social relations (Gordon 1964), or in the existence of a **culture of poverty**, which precludes the possibility of social and economic mobility for certain groups of people (Lewis 1966). Within the assimilationist school, groups are seen to be held back from economic advancement by their unwillingness to relinquish "old world" values, attitudes, and beliefs, which are incongruent with the demands of industrialized, competitive, and achievement-oriented societies.

Within the "culture of poverty" school, Oscar Lewis (1966), an anthropologist, argues that living in a state of poverty creates a certain culture, which is characterized by, among other things, a low level of social organization; a deep-rooted hostility toward representatives of the larger society; and feelings of hopelessness, dependence, and inferiority. For Lewis, living within a culture of poverty sets into motion a self-fulfilling prophecy and creates internal, cultural barriers to social mobility and economic advancement.

In the United States, cultural arguments have been applied especially often to the situation of African-Americans in northern urban "ghettos." The Moynihan report, for example, argued that, during the course of the 1960s, the American government had increasingly removed structural barriers to the advancement of African-Americans by implementing various pieces of anti-discrimination legislation. However, formal, legal equality would not be enough to bring about substantive equality between "black" and "white" Americans. The past treatment of African-Americans meant that they could not take advantage of the new opportunities afforded to them through such legislation. The root of the problem, Moynihan argued, lay in the "deterioration" of the African-American family. This deterioration was initially the result of slavery, the particular patterns of Reconstruction, and the position of the African-American man, who, because of poverty, discrimination, and unemployment, could not earn a wage that would be sufficient to support his family. The emasculation of these men resulted in the rise of matriarchy within the community, which was then equated by Moynihan with a "tangle of social pathology." The latter included low levels of educational achievement among "ghetto" youth, high rates of crime, and an overall sense of alienation. Thus, the lack of a stable family structure resulted in the improper socialization of these youths and created the conditions whereby African-Americans could not take advantage of the ever-increasing opportunities in America.

Interestingly, this view of family structure as the root of the problem of "race relations" was also incorporated into the strange mix of political discourse and popular

Testing for Race and Intelligence

American whites have long harboured racist sentiments toward African-Americans. This racism was manifest in a variety of ways during the pre–Civil War era: in the exclusion of blacks from the freedom and equality provisions within the American constitution, to the often brutal treatment of slaves on plantations. After emancipation, racism continued to flourish both in the North and the South. In the North this racism became increasingly focussed in urban areas where blacks competed with white immigrants over jobs and housing. Blacks were resented for moving into neighbourhoods; they also were disliked even more for engaging in strikebreaking activities at the expense of the European immigrants (van den Berghe 1967). Given such anti-black sentiments, American whites were ready to accept any scientific proof for putting blacks back into place.

The growing popularity of ideologies based on scientific racism provided racists with the proof they required. Scientific racism was built on the premise that racial capacities between populations could be measured and evaluated by statistical means. Eventually, the doctrine of scientific racism latched on to the comparative measurement of intelligence between blacks and whites by way of IQ exams. The IQ test itself was designed by Stanford Binet for the discovery of deficiencies in the cognitive skills of French pupils. It was never really intended to measure the amount of intelligence a person possessed. Stanford Binet himself believed intelligence could not be correlated with precise mathematical certainty. Nevertheless, American interests applied the test indiscriminately during the latter stages of the First World War as a means of sorting raw recruits into two categories: officer rank or cannon fodder. Since blacks for a variety of reasons were more likely to perform poorly on these tests, the IQ exam quickly established itself as an instrument for proving racial inferiority.

Repeated testings revealed that blacks on the average scored about 15 percentage points less than whites on the IQ exam. This gap was taken as proof that blacks were intellectually inferior "stock" because of hereditary factors. With few exceptions, many believed this bio-genetic gap could never be bridged, even with the environmental improvements or enrichment programs. That being the case the implications were obvious. Blacks were destined for menial occupations. They did not require a sophisticated education system, since there was little hope for substantial improvement even with increased exposure or expenditure. In light of related theories such as Social Darwinism and eugenics, the biological deficit model of blacks was widely endorsed.

The IQ exam legitimized this popular conception of black inferiority. It invoked a set of statistics whose "halo effect" proved what many had secretly harbored. But in their hurry to promote white intellectual supremacy at the expense of blacks, the advocates of the IQ exam took some unwarranted liberties with the results. For example, while blacks scored consistently less than whites as a group, the range of variation between black and white scores was comparable. The highest and the lowest score within each category was approximately the same. Also relevant but widely ignored were variations in group averages. While blacks on the average scored about 15 percent lower than whites, 15 percent of the blacks scored higher than the average score for whites, suggesting by inference that some blacks were intellectually superior to whites.

(continued)

(continued)

Recent testing continues to confirm a discrepancy between white and black scores. Then as now, several reasons can account for black failure to score as high as whites on these exams. First, many believe that the IQ exam is culture bound (Dewdney 1994). It has been produced by Eurocentric experts and geared toward white middle-class children who are properly equipped to succeed because of in-school and out-of-class experience. Second, the IQ exam may not even measure intelligence. After all, what is intelligence? Does it consist of creativity, analytical skills, the ability to memorize and recall, the capacity to do well in school, or the ability to perform adequately in a non-educational environment? Put simply, IQ tests do not measure intelligence; rather, they measure a person's ability to perform well in comparison with others in intensively competitive contexts. Third, blacks bring a series of environmentally imposed disadvantages with them to the testing experience that go beyond the stigma of slavery or trauma of oppression. Many continue to experience discrimination, racism, slurs, and violence, on a daily basis. Malnutritional deficiencies resulting from poverty or poor prenatal care also interfere with high performance levels. Put another way, the whole experience of blacks has been warped and strained by historical and social circumstances making it impossible to validate comparative results—even when family background and educational levels are held constant. Fourth, part of the environmentally imposed disadvantages that blacks bring with them to the IQ situation are deficiencies within the education system. Many blacks must cope with poor and unequipped schools, are taught by insensitive teachers, labelled as losers or failures (and streamed accordingly), and are forced to study curricula that are denigrating, alienating, and confusing. A self-fulfilling prophecy is set into motion: Not only do many begin to doubt their abilities, but often conform to the stereotypes, thereby confirming them (Cose 1994).

In short, the IQ exam should not be employed as a basis for comparing blacks and whites in the United States—even if such tests can enhance meritocracy by overcoming conventional means of distributing rewards based on inherited wealth, connections, and "old-boys" networks, and ascriptive qualities related to race (Wooldridge 1994). Differences in scores do not necessarily correlate with innate capacities. Sociologically speaking, differences in scores can be explained not as a result of genes, nature, or heredity, but primarily because of opportunity structures, social conditions, and cultural values. In addition grave concern is raised about the political implications of the IQ exam. Such negativity can only breed a negative public climate toward black achievements, and the responsibility of white America to do something about it.

Source: A. Fleras and J.L. Elliott, *Unequal Relations: An Introduction to Race, Ethnic and Aboriginal Dynamics in Canada*, 2d ed. (Scarborough, ON: Prentice Hall Canada, 1996), pp. 55–56.

culture that characterized the thinking of Dan Quayle, the former vice-president of the United States. Former vice-president Quayle's remarks about the "glorification" of single motherhood on the television program *Murphy Brown* was only part of a wider neoconservative discourse in the United States in the late 1980s and early

1990s about the negative impact on society of single-parent families. Coming from a very different perspective, the Hollywood movie *Boyz in the 'Hood* reinforced Quayle's ideas. While the social and political messages contained in the movie are complex, it implies, nonetheless, that young African-American males need proper adult male role models in order to escape the cycle of poverty, crime, and gang violence in which many are caught. Conversely, this message suggests that female single parents are partially responsible for the many problems young children in urban American communities are experiencing.

Assimilationist and cultural arguments have also been applied to Canada's aboriginal people (Nagler 1972; Herberg 1989; but see Wien 1986, 89–90, for a critique). Nagler, for example, argues that Natives in Canada are not assimilated. The institutionalization of the reserve system in the late nineteenth and early twentieth centuries allowed Native people to retain many aspects of their traditional cultures. Coupled with a century of enforced idleness on the reserves, this created a culture of poverty inconsistent with the demands of urban living. He says that the lack of **assimilation** reflected in aboriginal peoples' different value structure has prevented their full participation in Canadian society. Thus, in Nagler's terms, "their basic values are at variance with the value system possessed by North American society. As such, the value of punctuality, saving, future orientation and the work ethic serve to maintain a vast separation between Indians and the rest of North American society" (1972, 134).

Within this context, some have used the presumed existence of cultural differences between groups as a basis for opposing the federal government's policy of multiculturalism. John Porter (1965) was one of the first Canadian sociologists to systematically study the link between social class and ethnicity, and he identified racism as an important variable in explaining the socio-economic differences between various ethnic groups in Canada. He was nevertheless opposed to the idea of a multicultural policy, in part, because it would permit groups to retain aspects of their cultures, which he felt would inhibit their mobility within modern, industrial societies (1986). Similarly, Canadian novelist Neil Bissoondath, in *Selling Illusions: The Cult of Multiculturalism in Canada* (1994), argues that the downside to state-funded multiculturalism is that it promotes outdated attachment to ethnic cultures, which in turn helps to ghettoize and marginalize groups from the "mainstream."

These explanations of inequality have been criticized on a number of grounds. First, the concept of assimilation is ill-defined. Assimilation implies that there are certain objective, widely accepted standards of behaviour that are indicative of social and structural integration (Li 1987, 215). Yet researchers rarely define which social practices are both necessary and sufficient conditions of being "assimilated." The central question that remains, then, is which behaviours indicate that a person is assimilated, and which behaviours indicate that a person is not assimilated.

Second, psychological tests of IQ tend to be culturally biased. What counts as knowledge differs from one group to another, and therefore intergroup differences in IQ probably measure the defects inherent in the measuring instruments rather than reflect actual differences in intelligence between groups (Bowles and Gintis 1977).

Third, these explanations tend to **blame the victim** (Ryan 1976). Ryan suggests that blaming the victim is an ideology that either intentionally or unintentionally mystifies social reality in order to justify the status quo. It is a mode of thinking in which poor people are seen to be entirely responsible for their own fate. Their personal "social maladjustment" or "social defects" structure and limit their economic opportunities. The victims of poverty are seen to be responsible for the lowliness of the positions in which they find themselves. Thus, it is a mode of thinking that individualizes the problem by attributing causal priority to factors within the victims themselves.

Fourth, these explanations confuse cause and effect in the explanation of inequality (Valentine 1968; Horan 1978). Values, attitudes, and orientations are assumed to be key causal variables in the stratification process. Still others assume that these values exist in relative isolation from the material circumstances in which poor people find themselves. This issue is especially noticeable in the Moynihan report, where the problems of the African-American family are seen to be rooted in history, not in current social and economic arrangements (Rainwater and Yancey 1967).

And, finally, these arguments do not recognize the impact that racism and discrimination have on social inequality. The remainder of this chapter suggests that,

---

Racism in Polls and Surveys

One of the first surveys of racist attitudes in Canada contained 57 attitudinal items pertaining to racial prejudice (Henry 1978). The findings revealed that 16 percent of the white mainstream population was extremely intolerant and 35 percent somewhat racist. At least 18 percent had very liberal views about race, and a further 30 percent were somewhat liberal.

The attitudinal survey literature has been remarkably consistent over the 15 years since that first survey was done. Most of the surveys show that between 10 percent and 20 percent of Canadians are extremely intolerant of racial minorities. Another 20 percent to 35 percent are somewhat racist. Combining these two findings suggests that a majority of the population could be characterized as racist.

A decade after the Henry study, another survey found that between 7 percent and 20 percent of Canadians could be described as strongly racist in their views (Environics 1988). Evidence of "hard core" racism included the following findings: 19 percent of Canadians agreed with "research findings" that "Orientals" were superior to whites who were, in turn, superior to blacks. Moreover, 13 percent of Canadians would exclude non-white groups from immigrating to Canada, 7 percent would not vote for a black political candidate, and 9 percent would not vote for a Chinese candidate.

A 1989 survey, conducted by researchers at the University of Toronto and York University, was designed to determine whether there was a significant difference between the racial attitudes of decision-makers—legislators, lawyers, administrators, and police officers—and those of the general population. The survey found that 23 percent of the "elite" Canadians thought minority groups needed to get rid of "harmful and irritating faults," compared with 39 percent of the general population who held the same view. Half of the decision-makers and 70 percent of the general population felt that immigrants often bring discrimination upon themselves; 16 percent of the "elites" and almost one-third of the general citizenry believed that "races are naturally unequal" (Gould 1990).

A 1989 poll in British Columbia, which receives most racial-minority immigrants settling in the West, indicated that many residents believed that immigra-

(continued)

(continued)

tion does not bring economic advantages to the province. These perceptions were held despite the fact that shortly before, a highly publicized report by Employment and Immigration Canada found exactly the opposite to be the case. The report demonstrated that after ten years in Canada, Third World immigrants paid more taxes per capita than did Western European immigrants. These perceptions were also not shaken by the well-reported findings of the province's central statistics bureau, which showed that Asian entrepreneurial immigrants contributed $122.9 million into the B.C. economy and $5.4 million into the Alberta economy in 1988. Although entrepreneurial immigrants from Asia created 15 000 jobs in Canada in 1988, nearly half of British Columbia's population thought there were too many immigrants of colour moving into the province.

In a Toronto survey in 1992, when asked how well their racial or cultural group was accepted, 80 percent of those surveyed in the black Canadian community, 63 percent in the Chinese Canadian community, and 62 percent of the East Indian–Pakistani Canadian community felt there was some prejudice toward them in Toronto. 73 percent of blacks, 48 percent of Chinese, and 47 percent of East Indians–Pakistanis felt discriminated against in obtaining work, compared with 31 percent of Jews, 16 percent of Portuguese, and 15 percent of Italians. In terms of discrimination in the legal or court system, the survey found that 49 percent of blacks felt they were discriminated against. Twenty-one percent of East Indian–Pakistanis felt this way and 9 percent of Chinese (*The Toronto Star* 1992).

A report by the Economic Council of Canada (1991) attempted to measure the changing attitudes toward prejudice over time by analyzing the results of 62 surveys taken from 1975 to 1990 by Gallup, Decima, Environics, and other polling organizations. The report found that respondents from communities with greater proportions of visible-minority immigrants were "likely to be more tolerant of racial and ethnic differences." The report also concluded that over time there were "diminishing levels of prejudice." However, the results should be approached with some caution, considering the unreliability and [questionable] validity of the many data sources as well as the kind of statistical analysis performed, which tends to obscure important variables, such as the unit of analysis, the nature of the questions, age distribution of the sample, socio-economic status of the respondents, age, educational background, gender, and the like.

A survey by the federal immigration department of 1800 adults and fourteen focus groups showed a "growing acceptance" of attitudes and practices that show a dislike for "foreigners." One-third of the respondents agreed it was important to "keep out people who are different from most Canadians," while more than half were "really worried that they may become a minority if immigration is unchecked." Almost half admitted there were too many immigrants, even though most actually underestimated how many people were admitted (*The Globe and Mail* 1992).

Given the extent of ethnocentrism in Canadian society, it is not surprising that these concerns are expressed. However, the number of people who hold these negative attitudes but are not expressing them far exceed those who do, for "fear of being stamped racists" (Samuel 1988; Wellman 1978).

(continued)

(continued)

In a national survey undertaken by Decima Research in October 1993 for the Canadian Council of Christians and Jews, many of the myths identified in Chapter 1 of this book [Henry et al. 1995] are reflected in the responses of 1200 respondents. Nearly three-quarters of respondents rejected the concept of Canada as a multicultural mosaic, and 72 percent believed that different racial and ethnic groups should try to adapt to Canadian society rather than preserve their original cultures. The survey found that 41 percent of respondents thought that Canada's immigration policy "allows too many people of different cultures and races to come to Canada," and 53 percent agreed with the statement that "some racial and ethnic groups don't make enough of an effort to fit into Canada." Half agreed with the statement: "I am sick and tired of some groups complaining about racism being directed at them," and 41 percent agreed they are "tired of ethnic minorities being given special treatment."

The findings demonstrated some of the paradoxes of racism in Canadian society. For example, while Canadians generally saw themselves as tolerant of other cultures and races, three-quarters believed that racism was a serious problem in Canada. These findings correspond with the central premise of this book [Henry et al. 1995]: although many white people profess to be liberal, fair minded, and unbiased, they have two opposing and contradictory sets of racial attitudes—one expressed in positive terms, the other reflecting negative perceptions, attitudes, and assumptions.

Source: Frances Henry et al., *The Colour of Democracy: Racism in Canadian Society* (Toronto: Harcourt Brace, 1995), pp. 87–89.

contrary to popular conception, racism has had and continues to have an important meaning within Canadian society. It argues that the negative evaluations of groups of people made on the basis of socially selected physical or genetic criteria have been central to the formation of Canadian capitalism. Racism is therefore centrally linked with racial inequality.

Population and Labour-Force Participation

Since the "discovery" by Europeans of what is now Canada, there has been de facto diversity, albeit existing under a set of ideological, political, cultural, and economic conditions that emphasized and gave priority to anglo-conformity. Over the years, this diversity has increased, in part because of the increasing demand for labour by Canadian employers and the inability of the traditional sources—Britain, Western Europe, and the United States—to fill this demand (Hawkins 1974).

Table 7.1 gives an indication of the changing ethnic composition of Canadian society between the 1901 and 1981 censuses. It shows that during the early years of the twentieth century, people of Asian, African, and Native ancestry accounted for 3.1 percent of the total population. Their proportion of the total population declined to 1.8 percent in 1951. Since the mid-1960s there has been a progressive increase in the size of the non-European population in the country. In 1961, the three groups made

TABLE 7.1   Ethnic and Racial Composition of Canada (Percent of Total Population), 1901–1981

Ethnicity	1901	1911	1921	1931	1941	1951	1961	1971	1981
Asian	0.4	0.6	0.7	0.7	0.6	0.5	0.7	1.4	2.2
Chinese	0.3	0.4	0.5	0.4	0.3	0.2	0.3	0.6	1.2
South Asian	—	0.1	0.1	0.1	0.1	0.1	0.2	0.6	0.8
Japanese	0.1	0.1	0.2	0.2	0.2	0.2	0.2	0.2	0.2
African	0.3	0.2	0.2	0.2	0.2	0.1	0.2	0.2	0.6
Natives	2.4	1.5	1.3	1.2	1.4	1.2	1.4	1.4	2.0
British	57.0	54.1	55.4	51.9	49.7	47.9	43.5	44.4	43.6
French	30.7	28.5	27.8	28.2	30.3	30.8	30.4	28.5	27.2
East European	0.6	2.3	3.1	5.6	5.7	5.9	7.6	6.0	4.8
West European	7.0	7.9	6.6	8.2	7.8	8.4	10.3	9.5	7.7
South European	0.2	0.7	0.9	1.0	1.1	1.2	2.6	4.5	4.7
Jewish	0.3	1.1	1.4	1.5	1.5	1.3	1.0	1.4	1.2
Other	1.1	3.1	2.6	1.5	1.7	2.7	2.3	2.7	6.0
Total[a]	100.0	100.0	100.0	100.0	100.0	100.0	100.0	100.0	100.0

[a] Figures were rounded to add to 100.

Source: Edward N. Herberg, *Ethnic Groups in Canada: Adaptations and Transitions* (Scarborough, ON: Nelson, 1989), pp. 40–43. © 1989 Nelson Canada, a Division of International Thomson Publishing.

up 2.3 percent of the population; in 1971 this figure increased to 3.0 percent and by 1981, 4.8 percent. The British and French proportion of the total population has correspondingly declined from 87.7 percent in 1901 to 70.8 percent in 1981.

Table 7.2 presents data on ethnic origins collected during the 1991 Census. The question on ethnic origin was changed in the 1986 Census to allow for people to identify their "roots" rather than their paternal line of descent. The change from "line of descent" to "roots" meant that Canadians could identify more than one ethnic origin in the 1986 and 1991 censuses. As indicated in Table 7.2, 71.1 percent of the Canadian population identified a single ethnic origin while 28.9 percent identified two or more ethnic origins. Using the new census categories, 20.8 percent of the population identified themselves as having British origins only, while 22.8 percent identified themselves as having French origins only. The addition of multiple response categories in the 1986 and 1991 censuses makes it difficult to compare the relative size of ethnic groups using previous census data.

Table 7.3 shows that non-Europeans are becoming increasingly important in the Canadian economy. It gives an indication of the labour force participation rates, the percentage of the labour force that is in part-time work, and the percentage of the labour force that holds low-skill occupations for select groups of men and women who live in Toronto, Montreal, and Vancouver. It shows that the overall labour force participation rates in the three cities was 77 percent for women and 90 percent for men. As a whole, **visible minority** men and women had lower rates of labour force participation than people who were not visible minorities; however, black and

TABLE 7.2   **Ethnic Origins of Canadian Population, 1991**

Origins	Males	Males %	Females	Females %	Total	Total %
Single origin						
British	2 793 060	20.9	2 817 990	20.6	5 611 050	20.8
French	3 016 400	22.6	3 130 205	22.9	6 146 605	22.8
West Europe	686 350	5.1	669 130	4.9	1 355 480	5.0
North Europe	106 610	0.8	106 995	0.8	213 605	0.8
East Europe	473 010	3.5	473 800	3.5	946 810	3.5
South Europe	711 295	5.3	667 735	4.9	1 379 030	5.1
Other Europe	125 755	0.9	125 385	0.9	251 140	0.9
Arab	85 995	0.6	66 995	0.5	152 990	0.6
West Asian	45 450	0.3	36 200	0.3	81 650	0.3
South Asian	217 215	1.6	203 080	1.5	420 295	1.6
E. & S.E. Asian	464 440	3.5	496 780	3.6	961 220	3.6
African	14 740	0.1	11 695	0.1	26 435	0.1
Pacific Islands	3 500	0.0	3 720	0.0	7 220	0.0
L.C.S. America	43 325	0.3	42 205	0.3	85 530	0.3
Caribbean	43 625	0.3	50 765	0.4	94 390	0.3
Black	107 195	0.8	117 420	0.9	224 615	0.8
Aboriginal	230 865	1.7	239 750	1.8	470 615	1.7
Other	403 960	3.0	376 080	2.8	780 040	2.9
Total single origin	9 572 790	71.7	9 635 930	70.5	19 208 720	71.1
Multiple origins	3 770 460	28.3	4 023 790	29.5	7 794 250	28.9
Total	13 343 250	100.0	13 659 720	100.0	27 002 970	100.0

Source: Adapted from Statistics Canada, *Ethnic Origins of Canadian Population, 1991*, Cat. no. 93-315.

Filipino women, and Filipino and Chinese men had rates of labour force participation that were equal to or higher than those for the work force as a whole. Taking into consideration the percentage of the labour force that is in part-time work, it can be seen that with the exception of Vietnamese, South Asian, and Filipino men and women, all of the visible minority groups were overrepresented in part-time work compared with the labour force as a whole. In addition, Table 7.3 demonstrates that with the exception of aboriginal, Arab, and West Asian men and women, and Chinese men, all of the visible minority groups were more likely to be in low-skill occupations than the labour force as a whole.

Figure 7.1 provides information on the age-standardized unemployment rates for visible minority groups in 1991. It shows that the overall rate of unemployment for

TABLE 7.3 Socio-Economic Characteristics of Canadian-Born, Foreign-Born, Select Visible-Minority Groups, and Aboriginal Groups for Females (and Males in Parentheses), Age 25–55, Living in Montreal, Toronto, or Vancouver Census Metropolitan Areas, 1991[a]

		Percentage of labour force			
	Percentage in labour force[b]		That is part-time		That holds low-skill[c] occupations
Females (Males)	77	(90)	11	(5)	9	(9)
Birthplace					
Canadian-born	78	(91)	20	(5)	6	(8)
Foreign-born	75	(89)	17	(5)	13	(11)
Member of a visible-minority group[d]					
No	78	(91)	20	(5)	8	(9)
Yes	74	(86)	14	(5)	14	(11)
Minority group[e]					
Aboriginal	71	(85)	21	(7)	7	(9)
Arab	58	(80)	19	(6)	9	(8)
Black[f]	78	(86)	15	(7)	15	(12)
Chinese	76	(88)	13	(5)	10	(7)
Filipino	89	(92)	11	(4)	11	(13)
Latin American[g]	65	(78)	20	(7)	18	(19)
South Asian	73	(90)	11	(4)	18	(11)
Vietnamese	67	(83)	10	(4)	16	(14)
West Asian[h]	60	(76)	25	(9)	9	(8)

[a] Excludes persons who are not permanent residents of Canada.

[b] Refers to the labour-market activity of the noninstitutionalized population during the week prior to enumeration (June 4, 1991).

[c] "Low-skill" refers to the lowest of four categories of skill used by Statistics Canada to classify occupational information on the basis of the following occupational characteristics: education, training or skill level required to enter the job, and the kind of work performed as determined by the tasks, duties, and responsibilities of the occupation.

[d] All persons categorized as "visible-minority" members according to Statistics Canada are included in this category even if they indicated other nonvisible ethnic origins.

[e] Includes persons who indicate membership in a single minority group; persons who indicate multiple memberships in one or more minority groups; and those who indicate membership in two groups or in one or more minority groups and one or more nonminority groups.

[f] Includes persons who reported Caribbean ethnic origins such as Ghanaian, Barbadian, Cuban, Guyanese, Haitian, Jamaican, or Trinidadian and Tobagonian.

[g] Includes persons who reported Latin American origins or Central and South American ethnic origins.

[h] Includes persons who reported Afghan, Armenian, Iranian, Israeli, Kurdish, Turk, and other West Asian ethnic origins.

Source: Monica Boyd, "Gender Inequality: Economic and Political Aspects," in *New Society: Sociology for the Twenty-First Century,* 2d ed., ed. Robert J. Brym (Toronto: Harcourt Brace, 1998), p. 201.

FIGURE 7.1   Age-Standard Unemployment Rates of Visible Minority Groups, Canada, 1991

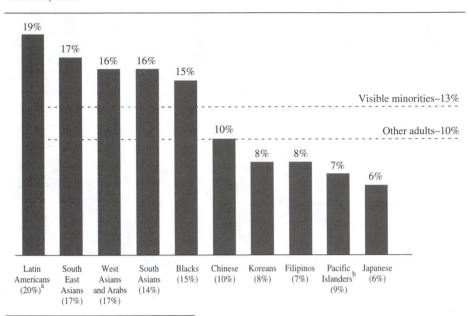

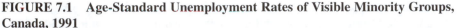

[a] Figures in brackets are the unemployment rates before age standardization.
[b] The Pacific Islander population does not include Filipinos.
Source: Karen Kelly, "Visible Minorities: A Diverse Group," *Canadian Social Trends*, Cat. no. 11-008E (Summer 1995): 3–7.

Canadians who are not of visible minority status was 10 percent. This is compared with an unemployment rate of 13 percent for visible minorities as a whole. Latin Americans, blacks, South and South East Asians, and West Asians and Arabs had unemployment rates that were between 15 percent and 19 percent, while Koreans, Filipinos, Pacific Islanders, and Japanese had unemployment rates that were below the average for both visible minorities and other adults.

Finally, Figure 7.2 shows the age-standardized proportion of visible minorities groups in selected occupations in Canada in 1991 and compares these with the labour force's as a whole. Figure 7.2 shows that various visible minority groups were more likely than others to be in service and manual labour occupations. In the case of other groups, 13 percent could be found in manual labour occupations whereas 32 percent of South East Asians, 29 percent of Latin Americans, 19 percent of South Asians, and 16 percent of blacks could be found in similar occupations. Ten percent of other groups were in service occupations, while 25 percent of Filipinos, 15 percent of Chinese, 14 percent of Pacific Islanders, and 13 percent of blacks and Latin Americans were in similar occupations. Figure 7.2 also shows that 10 percent of other groups were in managerial occupations, while only Koreans, Japanese, and West Asians and Arabs were above this level. Other visible minority groups were less

FIGURE 7.2   Age-Standardized Proportion[a] of Visible Minority Groups in Selected Occupations, Canada, 1991

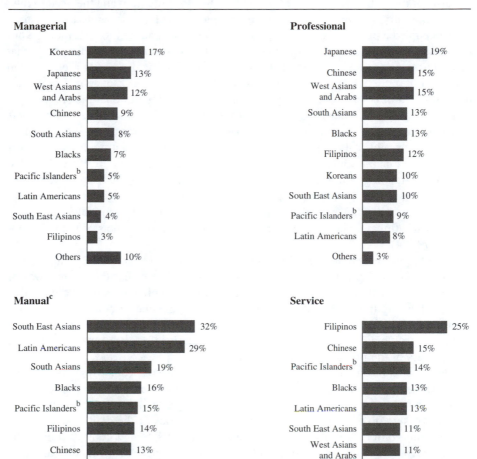

Managerial

Koreans	17%
Japanese	13%
West Asians and Arabs	12%
Chinese	9%
South Asians	8%
Blacks	7%
Pacific Islanders[b]	5%
Latin Americans	5%
South East Asians	4%
Filipinos	3%
Others	10%

Professional

Japanese	19%
Chinese	15%
West Asians and Arabs	15%
South Asians	13%
Blacks	13%
Filipinos	12%
Koreans	10%
South East Asians	10%
Pacific Islanders[b]	9%
Latin Americans	8%
Others	3%

Manual[c]

South East Asians	32%
Latin Americans	29%
South Asians	19%
Blacks	16%
Pacific Islanders[b]	15%
Filipinos	14%
Chinese	13%
West Asians and Arabs	10%
Japanese	8%
Koreans	8%
Others	13%

Service

Filipinos	25%
Chinese	15%
Pacific Islanders[b]	14%
Blacks	13%
Latin Americans	13%
South East Asians	11%
West Asians and Arabs	11%
South Asians	9%
Japanese	9%
Koreans	8%
Others	10%

[a] Only age-standardized proportions are shown because they are almost the same as those before standardization.
[b] The Pacific Islander population does not include Filipinos.
[c] Excludes skilled crafts and trades workers, as well as semi-skilled manual workers.
Source: Karen Kelly, "Visible Minorities: A Diverse Group," *Canadian Social Trends*, Cat. no. 11-008E (Summer 1995): 3–7.

likely to be in managerial occupations than those who were not members of visible minority groups. Visible minorities were, on average, as likely as others to be in professional occupations (Kelly 1995).

Institutional Racism: Canadian Dimensions

Because of the initial definition of Canada as a "white" dominion and the need to rely, at least partially, on non-European labour, people defined as non-white have historically occupied a precarious position in social, economic, and political relations. Non-Europeans were denied the same rights and privileges associated with citizenship that their counterparts took for granted. They have, both historically and at present, been defined as a particular type of problematic population. Their existence in Canada has been affected in no small degree by racism, particularly institutional racism.

In contrast to individual expressions of racism, institutional racism refers to sets of social practices that are institutionally based, make reference to invidious distinctions based on physical or genetic criteria, and have the effect of structuring what certain groups of people can and cannot do (Bolaria and Li 1985, 21). In Wilson's terms, "when the ideology of racial exploitation gives rise to normative prescriptions designed to prevent the subordinate racial group from equal participation in associations or procedures that are stable, organized and systematized ... institutional racism exists. Institutional racism therefore represents the structural aspects of racist ideology" (1973, 34).

Institutional racism has taken on a number of dimensions and has had a range of meanings within Canadian society. But this does not mean that the expressions of institutional racism have been haphazard and without implications for the operation of Canadian capitalism. Nor does it mean that it is unrelated to other developments within Canadian society. As Bolaria and Li (1985, 1) suggest, "race problems begin as labour problems." As such, the analysis of institutional racism must be linked to the analysis of the process of capital accumulation.

Institutional racism has acted to exclude certain groups of people from entering the country. This has been especially evident in the realm of state immigration controls, which in part are a means to regulate the labour supply so that large pockets of unemployed workers do not form within the spatial boundaries of the nation-state (Petras 1980). Immigration controls have acted to regulate the size and composition of the "reserve army of labour" to ensure that employers have access to required amounts and kinds of labour power, and that this army of unemployed does not get sufficiently large to cause a legitimation problem (through excessive unemployment), which the state would then have to resolve (Nikolinakos 1975; Castles and Kosack 1973).

The Chinese were one of the first groups subject to racially motivated immigration controls. Chinese labourers began to immigrate to Canada in the 1860s, and were drawn in on a large scale in the early 1880s by Andrew Onderdonk in order to complete the construction of the Canadian Pacific Railway (CPR). Once their labour power was no longer needed for the construction of the CPR, the Canadian state imposed, in 1885, a $50 head tax on Chinese labour migration. Any person of Chinese origin who intended to sell his or her labour power for a wage in this country had to pay a tax of $50 upon arrival in Canada. This initial tax did not deter Chinese migration. As a result, the head tax was increased to $100 in 1900 and $500 in 1903. In 1923, Chinese migration was essentially outlawed when the state implemented the Chinese Immigration Act. The act barred from entry to Canada all persons of Chinese descent, with the exception of merchants, diplomats, and students (Li 1979; Satzewich 1989c).

Other groups have also been subject to exclusionary racist immigration controls. South Asians were subject, by virtue of an order-in-council, to the "continuous journey" rule. Implemented in 1908, the order-in-council was directed specifically at curtailing South Asian migration to Canada. A small number of South Asians had arrived in Canada in 1905, and by 1908 a total of 5079 had entered Canada. Their entry sparked a hostile reaction on the part of government officials and the working class, which resulted in the passage of the regulation. According to this measure, immigrants who came to Canada "otherwise than by continuous journey from the countries of which they were natives or citizens, and upon through tickets purchased in that country may be refused entry" (Bolaria and Li 1985, 145). The only company that provided one continuous journey from India to Canada was the Canadian Pacific Railway steamship service, and the government issued directives that prohibited the company from selling South Asians a through ticket to Canada (Bolaria and Li 1985, 146). Other companies broke up the journey in Hawaii, so they could not carry any of these potential immigrants (Hawkins 1989, 17).

Furthermore, the South Asians who managed to enter the country before the passage of the continuous-journey regulations were "encouraged" by Canadian officials to leave because they, like the Chinese, were seen as unable to assimilate and as unwanted competition in the labour market (Ward 1978, 87; Satzewich 1989c). In 1908, the Department of the Interior attempted to organize an indentured labour scheme in which it would pay for the transportation of South Asian labourers who were resident in Canada to British Honduras. The plan never came to fruition because the department could not enlist the support of South Asian community leaders (Ward 1978, 87).

Various exclusionary mechanisms were also directed at those Chinese and other non-European workers who gained entry to Canada and remained in the country. In British Columbia, employers used Chinese workers primarily as cheap labour. They were also used to break strikes in mining or other resource-extraction industries (Ward 1978; Sampat-Mehta 1972). This resulted in an intense degree of working-class agitation directed against the Chinese. Many anti-Asian associations were formed, and much trade-union activity took the form of anti-Chinese agitation. While there were calls for the total elimination of Chinese immigration to Canada (which, as already noted, became a reality in 1923), much of the agitation was also directed at limiting the choices of employment of Chinese workers.

For instance, the Chinese were barred from working underground in coal mines, they could not hold a hand-logger's licence, they could not settle on crown land, they could not take up the professions of the law or pharmacy, and in the Prairie provinces, those Chinese who managed to start up a business of their own could not hire "white" women to work for them in restaurants or laundries (Li 1979). As Bolaria and Li (1985, 27) suggest, such forms of exclusion are an effective barrier that prevents non-European workers from moving away from undesirable jobs.

Institutional racism has also been used as an allocative mechanism: a means to allocate groups of people to certain sites in production relations. Capitalist production is such that some sectors require the existence of large pools of cheap and relatively docile workers that can be drawn upon when they are needed and displaced when not needed.

During the postwar period, one of the sectors of employment that was consistently short of labour was domestic service. Employers in search of domestics faced a recurring set of recruitment and retention problems. Because of the low pay and poor working conditions, Canadian women tended, if at all possible, to avoid this type of employment. With a dwindling supply of European women resident in refugee camps in Germany, Italy, and Austria who were willing to fill these jobs for even a short period of time, Canadian officials had to turn to non-traditional sources to fill this demand. That is, Canada had to turn to groups who were otherwise barred from entry into the country by virtue of the application of racist immigration practices (Satzewich 1989b).

In 1955, Canada agreed to allow women from the Caribbean to enter the country on a contractual basis to fill positions as domestic servants for middle-class Canadians. A quota of 200 women per year was initially established, but by the mid-1960s, the annual number of entrants increased to over 1000. They were initially granted entry on a migrant-labour basis in that their stay in the country was conditional upon their remaining in domestic employment for one year after their arrival (Bolaria and Li 1985, 178).

While these women were recruited to fill a genuine demand for domestic labour, it appears that Caribbean women were allowed in because of a process of racialization. Racialization refers to the attachment of social significance to patterns of physical differences like skin colour. In this case, incorporating these women as migrant labour was more desirable than as immigrant labour to the extent that the costs of the reproduction of labour power were to be borne in the Caribbean rather than in Canada. This made female Caribbean labour relatively inexpensive from the Canadian state's point of view. But, while the state officials wanted Canada's middle class to have access to these women's labour power, they also rather consistently expressed a concern over the possibility that Caribbean women might form families, give birth to Canadian-born offspring, and thus increase the resident black population. They feared the growth of such a population because it was felt that it would be the cause of "race relations" problems and hence disrupt the comparatively peaceful process whereby capital was accumulated in the country (Satzewich 1989b). This concern was in turn rooted in racist and sexist stereotypes about the sexuality of black women, which have their origins in eighteenth- and nineteenth-century justifications of slavery (Walvin 1987). Canadian state officials tended to regard black women from the Caribbean as promiscuous.

This concern was made manifest in several ways. The women were subject to compulsory medical examination. Ian Mackenzie, in his research into the recruitment of domestic workers, states:

> women arriving under the scheme were not only subjected to extensive medical tests in their home countries—including x-rays and tests for tropical diseases—but were subjected to extensive gynecological examinations (testing for syphilis) when they arrived in Canada. The governments of Jamaica and Barbados were expressly not informed of the tests. (quoted in Stasiulis 1987, 6)

Domestic servants who were of European origin were not subject to gynecological examinations.

Furthermore, in 1966, when the Canadian state was attempting to terminate the agreement by which Caribbean women came to Canada as domestic servants, the director of the Immigration Branch of the Department of Citizenship and Immigration argued that "West Indian mores are quite different from ours. Illegitimacy is pretty well accepted as a fact of life. It is not uncommon for a single girl to have children by two, three, or four different men" (quoted in Satzewich 1989b, 92).

These expressions of concern over black female sexuality were structured in turn by a concern over the growth of the resident black population in the country. Very generally, black people were defined by state officials as troublesome, to the extent that they were said to be the cause of social and racial problems in the country. As such, they were identified as a potential "enemy within," an enemy that would disrupt the relatively smooth processes of capital accumulation and social reproduction. Their incorporation as migrant labour was an attempt to solve a labour problem without disrupting the social order within which capitalist production took place.

Institutional racism has also been involved in the civil and political marginalization of groups of people. Status Indians (those people defined as an Indian by virtue of the Indian Act) could not vote in federal elections until the early 1960s. The Chinese were barred from voting in British Columbia elections from 1875 until the late 1940s, and the Japanese were disenfranchised in 1895. In 1896, the latter two groups were barred from voting in municipal elections in the province (Ujimoto 1985, 106).

Trade unions in British Columbia during the early years of the twentieth century generally excluded non-Europeans from joining and participating (Bolaria and Li 1985, 95). At the turn of the century, Chinese children were informally discouraged from attending public schools with European children (Ward 1978, 49). During the Second World War the Canadian government believed that the population of Japanese origin would constitute a "fifth column" that would help the Axis powers organize an attack on North America. As such, all Japanese in British Columbia were rounded up and placed in camps in the interior of the province or in work camps across the country. Their property was confiscated and then sold at bargain prices to their European neighbours (Ujimoto 1985, 133). After the war, some Japanese were deported at the same time that Canadian government officials were giving serious and thoughtful consideration to a proposal put forward by farmers that German prisoners of war held in camps in Ontario be allowed to stay and settle permanently in Canada if they took farm jobs (Satzewich 1989a). This suggests quite clearly that the Japanese Canadians, as non-Europeans, were seen as a greater threat to Canada than the possible admittance of a few thousand veterans of Hitler's army.

In general, non-Europeans were regarded by state officials as "racially" incapable of participation in bourgeois democratic political traditions. That is, they were regarded as incapable of taking on the responsibilities and duties of citizenship, which involved voting, getting an education, and participating in community life. The denial of the franchise and the inability to participate in mainstream union activities had the effect of further marginalizing these groups of people and of undercutting part of the political basis upon which they could resist their exploitation by capitalist employers.

Institutional racism has also contributed to the formation of social inequalities, particularly in the area of the denial of family life. Because non-Europeans have historically been defined as a problematic presence in the country, as already noted, state policies have been structured by a desire to preclude the emergence of Canadian-born generations of non-Europeans. Under the terms of the Chinese Immigration Act of

1923, even those married Chinese males who had already migrated to Canada, leaving their families in China, could not bring their wives and children with them to Canada. The law remained in force until after the Second World War (Li 1980). This prevented the formation of a second generation. It also led to a heavy reliance on ethnic associations for emotional and other support for Chinese men. In addition it "provided the conditions for certain vice industries, such as gambling and prostitution, to thrive among Chinatowns in North America, especially when the Chinese were generally denied acceptance into Canadian social life" (Bolaria and Li 1985, 95). The Canadian government's efforts to continually narrow the definition of a family member under family class immigration regulations is arguably a current covert attempt to use non-racial criteria to curtail family reunification among Asian immigrants in Canada.

Similarly, female workers from the Caribbean and male Caribbean farm workers have been admitted to the country on a migrant basis, in part because the state does not want these people to form family units and create a Canadian-born black population. It fears that they cause social and racial problems.

From the above it should be clear that racism has not been a secondary, anomalous feature in an otherwise free, equal, and universalistic Canadian society. Institutional racism has had important effects on particular groups of people, and the expressions of institutional racism have had strong, although not entirely determinate, links to the process of production.

In short, institutional racism can be seen as a set of social practices stemming from an ideology of racism. Ideas of inferiority and superiority, based on socially selected physical characteristics, are thus particular ideological mechanisms that contribute to the process of social reproduction—the reproduction of labour power and the social relations of production.

Ethnic and Racial Inequality

The various forms of institutional racism described above have both direct and indirect relationships to the economy and the dynamics of the Canadian labour market. Another specific area of concern within Canadian sociology has been the study of what Abella (1984) refers to as "systemic discrimination." According to Abella (1984, 10), **systemic discrimination** consists of

> the institutionalized systems and practices [that] result in arbitrary and extensive exclusions for persons who, by reason of their group affiliation, are systematically denied a full opportunity to demonstrate their individual abilities.

As noted earlier, the analysis of systemic discrimination in Canadian society was largely initiated by the late John Porter (1965). Porter, in *The Vertical Mosaic*, made extensive use of census data to argue that there was a reciprocal relationship between ethnicity and social class in Canada. For Porter, this **vertical mosaic** meant that a person's ethnic background had a significant impact on where he or she ended up in the larger system of class relations and social inequality within Canada. Since people of British and northern European origins controlled many of the political and economic resources in Canada, and since they regarded themselves as superior to groups from eastern Europe, Asia, and Africa, they tended to allocate the latter to subordinate positions in the labour market. That is, for Porter, racism and discrimination played an important role in the historical operation of the labour market in Canada.

Since the publication of *The Vertical Mosaic*, numerous Canadian sociologists have sought to further test the validity of Porter's arguments (Clement 1975; Lautard and Loree 1984; Satzewich and Li 1987; Beaujot, Basavarajappa, and Verma 1988; Darroch 1979; Boyd 1992). While the methods used to test the hypothesis of continued discrimination in the labour market have become more complex since the time that Porter wrote, many of the studies provide at least partial support for the suggestion that continued systemic discrimination still affects the Canadian labour market. Indeed, the entire premise of federal employment equity legislation introduced in 1986 is that women, visible minorities, aboriginal people, and the physically challenged face systemic discrimination in the labour market, and that this discrimination needs to be corrected, in part, through state intervention (Abella 1984).

Tables 7.4 and 7.5 present data from the 1991 Census of Canada that are analyzed by Pendakur and Pendakur (1995). In their analysis, Pendakur and Pendakur seek, in part, to test one of the central premises of employment equity legislation; namely, that there is systemic discrimination in the Canadian labour market. Pendakur and Pendakur examine the earnings of 25 ethnic groups in Canada in order to test whether a systematic pattern of disadvantage faced by visible minorities can be established.

Table 7.4 provides information on the average earnings of Canadian men and women who are between the ages of 20 and 64, who are not in school full-time, and who live in Montreal, Toronto, Hamilton, Edmonton, Calgary, and Vancouver. Earnings are listed for men and women, immigrants, and Canadian-born. Both the immigrant and Canadian-born categories are divided by white, aboriginal, or visible minority status. The table shows that the average earnings of white men born in Canada were $36 563. Visible minority men and aboriginal men born in Canada, on the other hand, had earnings that were respectively 13.4 percent ($31 653) and 21.4 percent ($28 725) below the average of white, Canadian-born men. White immigrants, on the other hand, earned 5.2 percent ($38 456) more, and visible minority immigrants earned 22.6 percent ($28 285) less than white, Canadian-born men.

For women, the overall pattern of earnings differentials is similar, but their magnitude is less. For example, white women born in Canada earned $23 173, whereas visible minority and aboriginal women born in Canada earned 0.1 percent ($23 149) and 14.2 percent ($19 887) less, and white immigrant and visible minority immigrant women earned 2.9 percent ($22 498) and 13.1 percent ($20 132) less than white women born in Canada.

On their own, these data provide a telling but nevertheless incomplete picture of the nature of earnings inequality in Canada. After all, the wages and salaries that people earn are conditioned by many factors, which need to be statistically controlled for in order to assess whether labour market discrimination is responsible for the discrepancies between groups. Using regression techniques, Pendakur and Pendakur (1995) introduce a number of other variables that help to explain the earnings levels of Canadians. These variables include occupation, industry of employment, household

TABLE 7.4   Mean Earnings by Visible Minority Status, Selected Canadian Cities, 1991

Immigrant status	Visible status	Earnings		Cases
		Mean	**Percent difference**	
Males				
Canadian by birth	white	$36 563	comparison	44 662
	visible	$31 653	−13.4%	923
	aboriginal	$28 725	−21.4%	1 055
Immigrant	white	$38 456	5.2%	12 088
	visible	$28 285	−22.6%	9 295
Females				
Canadian by birth	white	$23 173	comparison	42 305
	visible	$23 149	−0.1%	963
	aboriginal	$19 887	−14.2%	1 120
Immigrant	white	$22 498	−2.9%	10 049
	visible	$20 132	−13.1%	8 490

Note: Population includes permanent residents age 20–64 not in school full-time living in Montreal, Toronto, Hamilton, Edmonton, Calgary, and Vancouver. Does not include persons not reporting an education level, a household type, occupation or industry, or immigrants arriving after 1989.
Source: Krishna Pendakur and Ravi Pendakur, "Earnings Differentials among Ethnic Groups in Canada," Ref. no. SRA-34 (Social Research Group, 1995), p. 5.

type, census metropolitan area of residence, number of weeks worked, full- or part-time work status, knowledge of French and English, and level of education. All of these variables have an impact on earnings, so it is necessary to filter out their influence before any conclusions regarding discrimination in the labour market can be arrived at.

The data in Table 7.5 present the extent to which the earnings of 25 ethnic groups differ from the earnings of Canadian-born, British-origin men and women after all of the above sources of variation in earnings have been statistically controlled-for in a regression equation. It shows that Canadian-born men of European ethnic origin earned approximately the same as their Canadian-born British counterparts. While some groups earned slightly more and other groups earned slightly less than Canadian-born British men, in most cases these differences were not statistically significant. The exceptions to this pattern were Canadian-born French men, who received a small earnings premium (2.4 percent), while Canadian-born Greek and Portuguese men faced fairly large and statistically significant earnings penalties in the magnitude of 16.2 percent and 14.7 percent respectively.

When comparisons are made between Canadian-born British men and Canadian-born visible minorities, however, the results are somewhat more inconclusive because of the small number of cases in some of the cells (particularly for Canadian-born

TABLE 7.5   Selected Co-efficients from Log Earnings Regressions: Detailed Ethnic Groups,[a] Canada, 1991

			Men		Women	
			Regression 6.1		Regression 6.2	
Visible minority status	Ethnic response type	Ethnic group	Canadian by birth %	Immigrants %	Canadian by birth %	Immigrants %
White ethnic origins	Single ethnic responses only	British	comparison	0.6	comparison	−0.7
		French	2.4[c]	3.0	2.7[c]	10.0[c]
		Canadian	−1.9	−10.3[d]	−1.5	6.4
		Dutch	−2.3	−6.7[d]	−3.9	−7.2[d]
		German	0.5	−0.4	0.4	0.0
		Polish	−5.3	1.7	0.9	−1.8
		Hungarian	3.6	2.5	−0.7	−5.9
		Jewish	3.3	−3.3	4.5	−5.6
		Spanish	−9.3[b]	−7.2[d]	−12.8[b]	−12.9[c]
		Greek	−16.2[c]	−17.0[c]	−16.4[c]	−2.1
		Italian	−2.6	−5.2[c]	2.3	−2.7
		Portuguese	−14.7[c]	0.6	2.4	0.9
		Balkan	−7.0	−4.7	1.1	−1.9
		Ukrainian	1.4	0.8	3.6	12.4[d]
		Other	−0.7	2.1	17.0[c]	10.4[d]
	Multiple ethnic responses	British with white	−0.9	2.7	0.0	−9.6
		French with white	−2.1	10.9	0.8	12.5
		Southern European with white	1.7	−7.8	−4.3	12.3
		Central European with white	0.5	−0.2	2.9	8.2
		Other European with white	0.6	5.4	4.1	−10.7
Visible ethnic origins	Single ethnic responses only	Arab	−12.3[b]	−16.6[c]	9.0[b]	−10.6[c]
		Black	−16.3[c]	−21.0[c]	1.9	−11.7[c]
		Chinese	−12.7[c]	−12.0[c]	0.5	0.6
		Filipino	32.2[b]	−20.2[c]	−31.2[b]	−7.1[c]
		Latin	−0.1[b]	−19.1[c]	−13.5[b]	−7.3
		South Asian	4.5[b]	−14.4[c]	1.2	−0.8[c]
		Vietnamese	26.2[b]	−15.7[c]	−2.6[b]	−16.6[c]
		West Asian	−30.0[b]	−14.6[c]	24.5[b]	−8.1
		Other visible	−13.2[c]	−15.1[c]	2.5	−0.6

(continued)

TABLE 7.5   *(continued)*

			Men		Women	
			Regression 6.1		Regression 6.2	
Visible minority status	Ethnic response type	Ethnic group	Canadian by birth %	Immigrants %	Canadian by birth %	Immigrants %
Visible ethnic origins	Multiple ethnic responses	Visible minority with white	1.7[b]	−13.9[b,c]	−3.6	−10.0[b,c]
		British with visible	−1.2	−25.2[c]	−23.8	−6.6
		French with visible	−2.0	10.6[b]	5.8	21.0
		Southern European with visible	−14.3	7.5	39.6[b]	−15.0
		Central European with visible	−34.9	21.9[b]	6.7	5.1
		Other European with visible	−19.7	−21.1	27.1	−57.1[b,c]
		Visible minority with visible	9.5	−14.0[b,c]	−25.3[b]	−5.3[b]
Aboriginal origins	Single	Aboriginal	−18.6[c]	−47.6[b]	−2.2	−166.7[b,c]
	Multiple	Aboriginal with white	−14.8[c]	−45.1[b]	−13.6[c]	−78.6[b,c]
		Aboriginal with visible	−83.4[b,d]	−1.5[b]	30.6[b]	−40.7[b]
Place of schooling		USA, UK		10.9[c]		−2.3
		Southern Europe		−7.3[d]		−5.7
		Central Europe		−8.3		−7.8[a]
		Other Europe		−3.1		−1.2
		Asia, Africa		−1.3		−7.6[c]
		Other (includes Australia)		7.4[c]		2.2

$$R^2 = 0.428, n = 67\ 247 \qquad R^2 = 0.471, n = 62\ 926$$

[a] Controls are occupation, industry, household type, city, weeks worked, full/part-time, language, education, and political experience; [b] denotes less than 50 observations in the cell; [c] denotes significance at the 5% level, and [d] at the 10% level.

Source: Krishna Pendakur and Ravi Pendakur, "Earnings Differentials among Ethnic Groups in Canada," Ref. no. SRA-34 (Social Research Group, 1995), p. 15.

Arab, Filipino, Latin, South Asian, Vietnamese, and West Asian men). It is not, therefore, clear whether the values in the cells reflect real differences or whether they are due to the small number of cases. Table 7.5 does show, however, that there are statistically significant earnings differences between Canadian-born British men and black, Chinese, and other visible minority men in the magnitude of between 12.7 percent and 16.3 percent.

Considering the case of women, Table 7.5 shows that Canadian-born French and other European women earned 2.7 percent and 17 percent more, and Canadian-born Greek women earned 16.4 percent less than their Canadian-born British counterparts. In the case of other Canadian-born European groups, the earnings differences with Canadian-born British women were not statistically significant. As in the case of men, comparisons of Canadian-born visible minority women with Canadian-born British women are difficult to make because of the small number of cases in Canadian-born Arab, Latin, Filipino, Vietnamese, and West Asian categories. Additionally, the differences that do exist are not statistically significant, which suggests that there is no clear-cut pattern of economic disadvantage faced by Canadian-born visible minority women.

When looking at how immigrants compare with the Canadian-born of British origin, a somewhat more certain pattern of earnings inequalities can be observed. While some European immigrants, such as the Dutch, Spanish, and Greek, earn less than the comparison group, all of the male visible minority immigrant groups earned between 12 percent and 21 percent less than Canadian-born British males. Similarly, in the cases where there are statistically significant earnings differences between women, we see that French, Ukrainian, and other European immigrants earned more than their British counterparts, whereas Dutch, Spanish, Arab, black, Filipino, South Asian, and Vietnamese groups earned between 7.1 percent and 16.6 percent less than the comparison group.

Finally, with the exception of single-origin aboriginal women born in Canada, the differences in earnings between aboriginal people and Canadian-born British men and women tend to be large and statistically significant. Single-origin aboriginal men born in Canada earned 18.6 percent less, and multiple-origin aboriginal men earned 14.8 percent and 83.4 percent less than the comparison group, for aboriginal with white and aboriginal with visible origins, respectively.

While the data do not support the conclusion that all visible minorities in Canada face earnings penalties, Pendakur and Pendakur (1995) nevertheless feel that there is cause for concern that some visible minorities face systemic discrimination in the Canadian labour market. For instance, black men born and schooled in Canada may expect to earn 16 percent less than similarly educated and aged Canadian-born men of British origin (Pendakur and Pendakur 1995, 17). Visible minority immigrant men seem to face some form of systemic discrimination in the Canadian labour market that cannot be easily explained away by apparent differences in the qualifications that they bring to Canadian society.

While care needs to be taken in the interpretation of this data, other studies using different measures, different sample populations, and different techniques tend to confirm these findings (see Li 1988; 1992; 1996). What they suggest, but do not necessarily prove, is that groups of people with the same qualifications, gender, experience, and occupation face discrimination in the labour market.

This discrimination can take the form of a submerged split labour market (Bonacich 1976; 1979) whereby entrenched European workers have been able to impose differential pay scales for the employment of recent immigrants and non-Europeans (see Calliste 1987; Li 1979). It can also take the form of employers' refusal to accept foreign-earned employment credentials, hence causing employer-based discrimination. This is a theme that emerged out of the hearings held by the government's task force on multiculturalism in the preparation of its report, *Equality Now!* (Special Committee on Visible Minorities 1984), and that was echoed in the royal commission report, *Equality in Employment* (1984). According to the latter, non-European immigrants have reported that "they were people with recognized qualifications and proven job skills who found, nonetheless, that they were simply not promoted or given the same opportunities as whites with similar qualifications" (Royal Commission 1984, 47). Thus, individuals with the same qualifications and experience are unequally rewarded because of the belief of some employers that such experience is less relevant to Canadian conditions, or not comparable to Canadian training. The economic savings that employers stand to gain from these practices would not be inconsiderable. Given the increasing importance of non-European labour in the labour market, these earnings differentials could become the object of increasing concern, if not hostility, on the part of the non-European factions of the working class.

Conclusions

Racism and racial inequality have been central to the formation and reproduction of capitalist relations of production in Canada. Racism is not an anomalous feature of social and economic relations that will eventually disappear of its own accord. Rather, racism is intrinsically linked with the process of capitalist production via the regulation of the labour supply, the allocation of groups of people to particular sites in production relations, and the political marginalization of groups of people, which makes them less able to resist exploitation by employers by political means.

This conception of institutional racism does not bode well for state-funded efforts to improve "race relations" (Bolaria and Li 1985, 29–31). Given a structural analysis of institutional racism, efforts to reduce racism that focus on multicultural education and increasing intercultural contacts are doomed to be of limited value and success. The assumption underlying such efforts is that racism is the result of ignorance or malevolence on the part of individuals, and that education is all that is required for amelioration. The analysis of racism that is inherent in these efforts and practices simply contributes to the further mystification of institutional racism, and hence is nothing more than an attempt to "give the appearance of change without changing the status quo" (Bolaria and Li 1985, 29).

Summary

- A variety of social-psychological approaches have been developed in order to explore the link between ethnicity/race and economic achievement. Early sociologists argued that groups differed in terms of their level of achievement motivation and that these differences accounted for variations in economic performance. Others argued that some groups were characterized by a "culture of poverty" that was responsible for poor socio-economic conditions. More recently, there has been a rekindling of interest in the supposed links between race, IQ, and economic achievement. These explanations have been criticized on a variety of grounds. One of the main problems with these explanations is that they under-emphasize the link between racism and capitalism.

- Canada is an ethnic and racially diverse society. Changes in Canadian immigration policy in the 1960s made it possible for people from a wide variety of countries to enter Canada.
- Canada has a history of institutional racism. That history entailed the denial of various civil, political, and economic rights. Racism affected immigration control, the jobs that people could work in, where people lived, and even where people sent their children to school.
- It is clear that racism no longer has the same economic impact in Canada that it had earlier this century. Many of the blatant and obvious forms of racial discrimination have been eliminated. However, there are debates about the continued importance of more subtle forms of racism and discrimination on the economic performance of groups. While data suggest that visible minorities do not face across-the-board economic discrimination, some groups do face earnings disadvantages and these may be due, in part, to racism.

Questions to Consider

1. What is the major focus of the psychological and cultural explanations of ethnic and racial inequality? What are the criticisms that have been made against these explanations of inequality?

2. What are the dimensions of institutional racism in Canada? How can they be linked to the operation of the capitalist system?

3. What evidence is there for racially based earnings inequalities in Canada? Do costs and benefits associated with ethnic origin exist in the job market? How are these inequalities rooted in the operation of the capitalist system?

4. To what extent are efforts to eliminate institutional racism likely to be successful if they focus attention on education and cross-cultural misunderstanding? Why?

Suggested Readings

Bolaria, B. Singh, and Peter Li. *Racial Oppression in Canada*. 2d ed. Toronto: Garamond Press, 1988.

Bonacich, Edna. "The Past, Present, and Future of Split Labour Market Research." In *Research in Race and Ethnic Relations*, ed. C. Marrett and C. Leggon. Greenwich, CT: JAI Press, 1979, 17–64.

Herrnstein, Richard, and Charles Murray. *The Bell Curve: Intelligence and Class Structure in American Life*. New York: Free Press, 1994.

Li, Peter, ed. *Race and Ethnic Relations in Canada.* 2d ed. Toronto: Oxford University Press, 1998.

Rainwater, L., and W. Yancey. *The Moynihan Report and Politics of Controversy.* Cambridge, MA: MIT Press, 1967.

Ryan, William. *Blaming the Victim.* New York: Vintage Books, 1976.

Satzewich, Vic, ed. *Racism and Social Inequality in Canada.* Toronto: Thompson Educational Publishers, 1998.

Glossary

achievement motivation A concept that focusses on the supposed differences in psychological makeup (the need to excel, a high value placed on achievement and success) of groups in order to explain why some groups do better in the labour market than others.

assimilation The process whereby ethnic groups take on the culture and values of the dominant group.

blaming the victim A tendency to blame poor people for their own poverty. It is usually used as an ideology to justify the status quo.

culture of poverty A cultural pattern characterized by a low level of organization, hostility to representatives of the larger society, and feelings of hopelessness, dependence, and inferiority.

institutional racism Normative prescriptions derived from racist ideas that subordinate groups and deny equal participation in societal institutions.

racism A set of ideas that suggests that groups can be arranged in a hierarchy of biological superiority and inferiority.

systemic discrimination Institutionalized systems and practices that result in arbitrary and extensive exclusions for persons who, by reason of their group affiliation, are systematically denied a full opportunity to demonstrate their individual abilities.

vertical mosaic A term developed by John Porter to describe the reciprocal relationship between ethnicity and social class in Canadian society.

visible minority A term that came into widespread use in the 1980s in Canada as a synonym for race.

References

Abella, R.S. 1984. *Equality in Employment: A Royal Commission Report.* Ottawa: Minister of Supply and Services.

Beaujot, R. 1992. "The Socio-Demographic Impact on Immigration." In *The Immigration Dilemma,* ed. S. Globerman. Vancouver: The Fraser Institute.

Beaujot, R., K. Basavarajappa, and R. Verma. 1988. *Current Demographic Analysis: Income of Immigrants in Canada.* Ottawa: Statistics Canada.

Bissoondath, N. 1994. *Selling Illusions: The Cult of Multiculturalism in Canada.* Toronto: Stoddart.

Bolaria, B.S., and P. Li. 1985. *Racial Oppression in Canada.* Toronto: Garamond Press.

Bonacich, E. 1976. "Advanced Capitalism and Black–White Race Relations in the United States: A Split Labour Market Analysis." *American Sociological Review* 41: 34–51.

———. 1979. "The Past, Present and Future of Split Labor Market Research." In *Research in Race and Ethnic Relations*, ed. C. Marrett and C. Leggon. Greenwich, CT: JAI Press. 17–64.

Bowles, S., and H. Gintis. 1977. "I.Q. in the U.S. Class Structure." In *Power and Ideology in Education*, ed. J. Karabel and A. Halsey. New York: Oxford University Press. 215–31.

Boyd, M. 1992. "Gender Visible Minority and Immigrant Earnings Inequality: Reassessing an Employment Equity Premix." In *Deconstructing A Nation: Immigration, Multiculturalism and Racism in 1990s Canada*, ed. V. Satzewich. Halifax: Fernwood.

–––––. 1998. "Gender Inequality: Economic and Political Aspects." In *New Society*, 2d ed., ed. R.J. Brym. Toronto: Harcourt Brace.

Calliste, A. 1987. "Sleeping Car Porters in Canada: An Ethnically Submerged Split Labour Market." *Canadian Ethnic Studies* 19: 1–36.

Castles, S., and G. Kosack. 1973. *Immigrant Workers and Class Structure in Western Europe.* London: Oxford University Press.

Clement, W. 1975. *The Canadian Corporation Elite.* Toronto: McClelland and Stewart.

Cose, E. 1994. "Color-Coded 'Truths.'" *Newsweek,* October 24.

Darroch, G. 1979. "Another Look at Ethnicity, Stratification, and Social Mobility in Canada." *Canadian Journal of Sociology* 4: 1–25.

Economic Council of Canada. 1991. *Report.* Ottawa.

Environics. 1998. *Focus Canada Survey.*

The Globe and Mail. 1992. October 14.

Gordon, M. 1964. *Assimilation in American Life.* New York: Oxford University Press.

Gould, T. 1990. "Who Do You Hate?" *Toronto Life* (October).

Hawkins, F. 1974. "Canadian Immigration Policy and Management." *International Migration Review* 7: 141–53.

–––––. 1989. *Critical Years in Immigration: Canada and Australia Compared.* Montreal and Kingston: McGill-Queen's University Press.

Henry, F. 1978. *Dynamics of Racism.* North York, ON: York University.

Herberg, E. 1989. *Ethnic Groups in Canada: Adaptations and Transitions.* Scarborough, ON: Nelson.

Herrnstein, R., and C. Murray. 1994. *The Bell Curve: Intelligence and Class Structure in American Life.* New York: Free Press.

Horan, P. 1978. "Is Status Attainment Research Atheoretical?" *American Sociological Review* 43: 534–41.

Kelly, K. 1995. "Visible Minorities: A Diverse Group." *Canadian Social Trends.* Ottawa: Statistics Canada. Cat. no. 11-008E.

Lautard, H., and D. Loree. 1984. "Ethnic Stratification in Canada, 1931–1971." *Canadian Journal of Sociology* 9: 333–43.

Lewis, O. 1966. *La Vida: A Puerto Rican Family in the Culture of Poverty.* New York: Random House.

Li, P. 1979. "A Historical Approach to Ethnic Stratification: The Case of the Chinese in Canada." *Canadian Review of Sociology and Anthropology* 16: 320–32.

–––––. 1980. "Immigration Laws and Family Patterns: Some Demographic Changes Among Chinese Families in Canada, 1885–1971." *Canadian Ethnic Studies* 12: 58–73.

–––––. 1987. "Race and Ethnic Relations." In *An Introduction to the Social World*, ed. R. Richardson and L. Tepperman. Toronto: McGraw-Hill Ryerson. 211–35.

–––––. 1988. *Ethnic Inequality in a Class Society.* Toronto: Wall and Thompson.

–––––. 1992. "Race and Gender as Basis of Class Fractions and Their Effects on Earnings." *Canadian Review of Sociology and Anthropology* 29: 488–510.

–––––. 1996. *The Making of Post-War Canada.* Toronto: Oxford University Press.

Mackenzie, I. 1986. "The Canadian State and Domestic Workers from the Caribbean: The Domestic Scheme." Paper. Carleton University.

Miles, R. 1982. *Racism and Migrant Labour.* London: Routledge and Kegan Paul.

–––––. 1989. *Racism.* London: Tavistock.

Nagler, M. 1972. "Minority Values and Economic Achievement: The Case of the North American Indian." In *Perspectives on the North American Indian*, ed. M. Nagler. Toronto: McClelland and Stewart. 131–41.

Nikolinakos, M. 1975. "Notes Towards and General Theory of Migration in Late Capitalism." *Race and Class* 17: 5–18.

Pendakur, K., and R. Pendakur. 1995. *Earnings Differentials among Ethnic Groups in Canada.* Ottawa: Heritage Canada.

Petras, E. 1980. "The Role of National Boundaries in a Cross-National Labour Market." *International Journal of Urban and Regional Research* 4: 157–95.

Porter, J. 1965. *The Vertical Mosaic.* Toronto: University of Toronto Press.

–––––. 1986. *The Measure of Canadian Society.* Ottawa: Carleton University Press.

Rainwater, L., and W. Yancey. 1967. *The Moynihan Report and the Politics of Controversy.* Cambridge: MIT Press.

Rosen, B. 1956. "The Achievement Syndrome: A Psychocultural Dimension of Social Stratification." *American Sociological Review* 21: 203–11.

———. 1959. "Race, Ethnicity, and the Achievement Syndrome." *American Sociological Review* 24: 47–60.

Royal Commission on Equality in Employment. 1984. *Report.* Ottawa: Minister of Supply and Services.

Rushton, P., and A. Bogaart. 1987. "Race Differences in Sexual Behaviour: Testing an Evolutionary Hypothesis." *Journal of Research in Personality* 21: 529–51.

———. 1988. "Race Versus Social Class Differences in Sexual Behavior: A Follow-up Test of the r/k Dimension." *Journal of Research in Personality* 22: 259–72.

Ryan, W. 1976. *Blaming the Victim.* New York: Vintage Books.

Sampat-Mehta, R. 1972. *International Barriers.* Ottawa: Harpell's Press.

Samual, J. 1988. *Immigration and Visible Minorities in the Year 2001: A Projection.* Ottawa: Centre for Immigration and Ethnocultural Studies.

Satzewich, V. 1989a. "Canadian Capitalism and Unfree Labour: The Incorporation of Polish War Veterans." *Studies in Political Economy* 26: 98–123.

———. 1989b. "Racism and Canadian Immigration Policy: The Government's View of Caribbean Migration, 1962–1966." *Canadian Ethnic Studies* 21: 77–97.

———. 1989c. "Racisms: The Reactions to Chinese Migrants in Canada at the Turn of the Century." *International Sociology* 4: 311–27.

Satzewich, V., and P. Li. 1987. "Immigrant Labour in Canada: The Cost and Benefit of Ethnic Origin in the Job Market." *Canadian Journal of Sociology* 12: 229–41.

Special Committee on Visible Minorities in Canadian Society. 1984. *Equality Now!* Ottawa: Minister of Supply and Services.

Stasiulis, D. 1987. "Rainbow Feminism: Perspectives on Minority Women in Canada." *Resources for Feminist Research* 16: 5–9.

Toronto Star. 1992. "Minority community Survey."

Ujimoto, V. 1985. "The Japanese." In Bolaria and Li, *Racial Oppression.* 105–36.

Valentine, C. 1968. *Culture and Poverty.* Chicago: University of Chicago Press.

Van der Berghe, P. 1967. *Race and Racism.* New York: John Wiley and Sons.

Vernon, P. 1984. "Abilities and Achievements of Ethnic Groups in Canada with Special Reference to Canadian Natives and Orientals." In *Multiculturalism in Canada*, ed. R. Samuda et al. Boston: Allyn and Bacon. 382–95.

Walvin, J. 1987. "Black Caricature: The Roots of Racism." In *"Race" in Britain*, ed. C. Husbands. London: Hutchinson. 59–72.

Ward, W.P. 1978. *White Canada Forever.* Montreal and Kingston: McGill-Queen's University Press.

Wellman, D. 1977. *Portraits of White Racism.* Cambridge, UK: Cambridge University Press.

Wien, F. 1986. *Rebuilding the Base of Indian Communities: The Micmac in Nova Scotia.* Montreal: Institute for Research on Public Policy.

Wilson, W. 1973. *Power, Racism, and Privilege.* London: Collier Macmillan.

CHAPTER 8

First Nations: Walking the Path of Social Change

James S. Frideres

Learning Objectives

After studying this chapter, you should be able to

- Give a socio-demographic profile of **aboriginal** Canadians.
- Understand the issues of land rights and self-determination.
- Assess the economic and social consequences of institutional racism and racial exploitation as directed toward First Nations.
- Outline the historical background of colonial exploitation and the establishment of a political and economic structure that continues to mitigate against the integration of aboriginal people into Canadian society.

Introduction

Recent studies of income distribution in Canada reveal that the gap between rich and poor is increasing. The rich are controlling greater resources, while the poor have less access to Canada's increasing wealth. Aboriginals have, in absolute terms, increased their earning power over the past half century, but relative to the earning power of mainstream society, this increase is much less. And, while their involvement in mainstream society has increased, it has been marginal and episodic. As a result, relatively speaking, aboriginals have a diminished access to the resources available to other Canadians. This plight facing aboriginal Canadians is not new—it has been recognized for many years (Mallea 1994). However, little has been done to change the social and economic conditions of aboriginals. It is important to understand that the current situation cannot be fully explained without being placed within a historical context. For example, in the nineteenth century, many aboriginals were becoming successful farmers. However, strong lobbying efforts by the farmer's associations resulted in the federal government's withdrawing any financial or technical help to aboriginal people. As a result, they were not able to enter the economic sphere through farming. As technology for farming continued to develop, it became impossible for aboriginals to develop their land for agricultural purposes. Today, most aboriginal land remains in pasture, undeveloped, and/or leased to non-aboriginal farmers.

Two factors seem to have mitigated against any real meaningful change. First, Canadians have seen the "problem" as being the aboriginals', not mainstream society's. Embodied in this belief is the assumption by the majority that Indians do not know what is best for themselves, that there is something unique about aboriginal society that prevents them from entering the mainstream. Second, structural changes have been introduced to ensure that the wealthy of our society are not disadvantaged. Only sectoral changes have been introduced when dealing with aboriginals, for example, changes that are made in the educational institutional order but without concurrent changes in other institutions such as the economy.

As we shall discover, the state is *not* a neutral agent of the people, but is biassed in favour of those with wealth—large national and international corporations as well as wealthy individuals. As we analyze the bias of the system, we shall also see that, contrary to popular belief, the social system does not produce a society that is democratic, just, and equal for all (Henry et al. 1995). In the case of aboriginal people, Dyck (1997b) points out that the administration of Indian Affairs by the state has taken a form of coercive tutelage, resulting in the current social and economic status of aboriginal peoples. This has produced an "upside-down" society, with a few benefiting at the expense of the many. In short, the structure of our institutional arrangements and the laws supporting them are the source of the "aboriginal problem." This institutional order and its linkages will be the focus of this chapter as we attempt to unravel the causes that have marginalized, and continue to marginalize, aboriginal Canadians at the bottom position of our hierarchical society.

Aboriginal Canadians

Aboriginal people are just one of the many minority groups that make up Canadian society. While they may have a special legal position within the Canadian Constitution, they have not benefited from such a "citizen plus" status. On the contrary, because of the stereotypes that are attached to "Indians" and the negative prejudicial attitudes that are directed toward aboriginal people, they find themselves victims, and have been forced to remain in a subordinate status since the eighteenth century. Because of the visibility of aboriginal people and of their current social position in society, it has been impossible for them to escape the niche set aside for them by those Canadians who make up the dominant group. While Canadians have implemented laws outlawing individual discrimination (e.g., human rights codes) and have supported the underlying philosophy of multiculturalism, aboriginal people still find themselves subject to prejudice and discrimination. Overt individual prejudice and discrimination are less evident than they were 50 years ago, but today we find systemic discrimination and covert prejudice being practised on a day-to-day basis.

This chapter will provide a brief historical review of aboriginal–European contact, and go on to discuss selected attributes of aboriginal people. Before proceeding to further discuss these matters, we will present a socio-demographic profile of Canada's aboriginal population—their numbers, location, achievements in the field of education, occupation, and income. We will conclude with an explanation of how their marginal social position has come about and has been sustained for well over two centuries.

Defining an Aboriginal

Under the Canadian Constitution of 1982, aboriginal Canadians are defined as status (or legal) **Indians**, Inuit, and Métis. The reader should be aware that the definition of an aboriginal person has changed many times over the past hundred years and continues to change today.[1] In addition to the three categories identified above, there are many other individuals who are not, for legal purposes, aboriginal even though they might look like aboriginals, live like aboriginals, and speak an indigenous language. For example, legal Indian women who married non-legal Indian men lost their Indian status. A similar fate awaited their children. Under recent federal changes (Bill C-31), some of those people who lost their Indian status have now been reinstated as Indians. Others are defined as Indians until they reach a certain age, after which they will no longer be considered an Indian.[2] The term "Indian" is a legal term employed by the federal government that places individuals with this label in a special category, subject to the rules and regulations of the **Indian Act**. Moreover, they are considered wards of the federal government and subject to the Department of Indian Affairs. The term Métis has a legal definition only in Alberta, even though it represents the offspring of Indian–European marriages, evident all over Canada. Today, the federal government uses a "self-definition" to determine the number of Métis in Canada. Until recently, they have been considered, for the most part, as Canadians without any special status and fall under provincial legislation (see Kennedy 1997 for a discussion of the process of ethnogenesis). Inuit and Inuvialuit usually reside in the Northwest Territories, northern Quebec, or Labrador. While they are dealt with through the provisions of the federal Indian Act, they are not considered Indians.

The development of numerous categories with shifting boundaries to define aboriginal peoples has not been a historical accident. It is, rather, an example of how minor cultural and physiological differences can be accentuated over time when it is in the interest of the dominant group. Eventually groups begin to accept these labels, the attributes associated with those labels, and the boundaries of their group. These boundaries may become the basis for conflict, such as among the different groups of aboriginal peoples. Under these conditions, the dominant group will define groups and then treat them as either homogeneous or heterogeneous, depending upon the dominant group's best interest. Thus it should come as no surprise that the definition of who is Indian, Métis, and Inuit has changed over time, as have the rights attached to each group.

The total aboriginal population of Canada is just over 800 000, making up about 3 percent of the total Canadian population. Table 8.1 provides the specific details. If one adds to these numbers the individuals who are not legal aboriginals, it is estimated that approximately two million Canadians hold aboriginal ancestry.

In the past half century, the number of aboriginals has more than doubled. This dramatic increase has three sources. First, there has been an extremely high natural growth rate, reaching nearly 3 percent at times. The fertility rate for aboriginal

TABLE 8.1   Categories of Aboriginal People in Canada by Population, 1996

Status Indians[a]		554 200	
	Treaty reserve		74%
	Treaty non-reserve		4%
	Non-treaty reserve		20%
	Non-treaty non-reserve		2%
Métis		210 190	
	On colony		2%
	Off colony		98%
Inuit		41 080	
	With disc number		57%
	Without disc number		43%

[a] Status Indians are sometimes referred to as registered or legal Indians.

Sources: Department of Indian Affairs and Native Development, *Indian Register, 1961–87* (Ottawa: Minister of Supply and Services, 1987); DIAND, Basic Departmental Data—1991 (Ottawa: Minister of Supply and Services, 1992); Census Canada, 1996.

women is nearly twice as high as the Canadian rate of 1.63 births per 1000 women aged 15–44 years. Second, the death rate has decreased substantially over the past half century due to increased health care, especially neonatal health care. For example, in the period from 1960 to 1990, the deaths per 100 000 population for aboriginals decreased from 387 to 174.3. Aboriginal infant mortality rates (infant deaths per 1000 live births) decreased from 54 in 1963 to around 15 in 1996; a figure similar to that of the total Canadian population. Finally, there has been a substantial addition to the number of aboriginals due to legislative changes. Specifically, since Bill C-31 (1985) brought about a redefinition of aboriginal, over 200 000 names have been added to the list of individuals who can claim to be aboriginal. As a result of this bill, the average annual growth rate during the 1980s ranged from 5 percent to 7 percent. This growth rate has decreased over the past few years but still remains near double the general Canadian growth rate. Where do aboriginal people reside? As Table 8.2 indicates, approximately 18 percent reside in each of Ontario and British Columbia, an additional 16 percent in Manitoba, 15 percent in Alberta, 14 percent in Saskatchewan, less than 10 percent in Quebec, and about 5 percent in the Atlantic provinces.

Using Statistics Canada data, the percentage of **North American Indians** residing on reserves or settlements was calculated. The data are surprising. They show that in the North, almost all live off-reserve.[3] In almost all provinces, nearly half of the Indian population no longer live on reserves, with the exceptions of the Atlantic provinces and Manitoba, where only 39 percent and 38 percent, respectively, live off-reserve. Clearly the data reveal a continuing urbanization of the aboriginal population of Canada. Aboriginal people not living in urban centres live on nearly 3000 reserves or settlements distributed throughout the country. The size of each of these reserves varies from a few hectares in British Columbia to thousands of hectares in Alberta. And, as Table 8.2 shows, a little over 70 percent of all the reserves in Canada are in

TABLE 8.2   Aboriginal Population and Lands, by Region, 1996

	Atlantic Provinces	Quebec	Ontario	Manitoba	Saskatchewan	Alberta	British Columbia	Northwest Territories	Yukon	Canada
Total aboriginal population, 1996	33 785	71 415	141 525	128 685	111 245	122 840	139 655	39 690	6 175	799 010
% of total aboriginal population, 1996	4.7	8.9	17.7	16.1	13.9	15.4	17.5	5.0	0.8	100
% of total population/territorial population, 1984	6.1	1.0	1.3	11.7	11.4	4.6	3.8	61.9	20.1	2.8
% living off-reserve, 1991[a]	39	59	42	38	46	53	50	98	94	28.7
% of Indian bands, 1985	5.2	6.6	21.3	10.1	11.5	6.9	33.1	2.4	2.9	100 (N=594)
% of reserves and settlements, 1985	2.9	1.4	8.1	4.5	6.2	3.9	70.5	1.3	1.1	100 (N=2285)

[a] North American Indian only. Statistics Canada, *Age and Sex*, Aboriginal Data, Cat. no. 94-327, Table 4, pp. 16–17.

Source: Adapted from Statistics Canada, "The Socio-Demographic Conditions of Registered Indians," *Canadian Social Trends*, Cat. no. 11-008E (Winter 1986): 3.

British Columbia. These reserves are entrusted to political structures referred to as bands. Currently there are nearly 600 different bands, which means that in many cases there is more than one reserve per band.

Historical Relations between Aboriginals and Non-Aboriginals

To understand the "aboriginal problem" fully, we must place it in a historical perspective. At the time of contact with Europeans, it is estimated that there were about 250 000 aboriginal people living in what is now called Canada. By Confederation (1867), this number had been reduced to slightly more than 100 000. Epidemics, poor health, European-inspired wars, and acts of genocide by the Canadian government led to this dramatic reduction in population (Siggner 1986). For the first half of the twentieth century, the aboriginal population remained relatively constant. It was only after World War Two that a small increase in the aboriginal population began to be noticed. Other groups such as the Métis were defined out of existence by the government, and it would not be until the passage of the Canadian Constitution (1982) that they would be considered a legal ethnocultural group in Canada (Kennedy 1997).

In the early nineteenth century, when Native–European contact became sustained, the Canadian government enacted a policy of "civilizing" aboriginals, a policy it has continued to implement as we enter the twenty-first century. Early contacts were generally symbiotic, but it was not long before the pressure of European settlement changed the nature of the relationship. At first, European colonists were interested in creating and maintaining positive relations with aboriginal people; contractual relationships such as military alliances predominated. In the early nineteenth century, aboriginals played a prominent role in the development of Canada and were treated respectfully,[4] since they were allies of the government and important to the Canadian economy. After the War of 1812, however, the usefulness of aboriginals as military allies became minimal. By the 1830s their military role was obsolete, and they were no longer considered a valued group in Canadian society. As time went on, they became, rather, an obstacle to European settlers attempting to cultivate the land. As Trigger (1986) points out, from the mid-1800s aboriginals ceased to be a living presence in the lives of most Canadians.

As a tentative solution to dealing with aboriginals, Peace and Friendship treaties were established in the Maritime provinces from quite early on. The **Royal Proclamation of 1763** was one such attempt simultaneously to maintain the peace, allow settlement of the country, and pacify the aboriginals.[5] Nevertheless, as more and more immigrants entered the country, greater pressure for land and settlement emerged. Immigrants began to settle in the countryside and develop an extensive agricultural economy. This influx began to put pressure on the aboriginal people's traditional lifestyle. Their nomadic way of life was disrupted and they had to share the natural food supply with the settlers. Ecological changes began to have an effect on the flora and fauna, and aboriginal people struggled for survival against diseases and epidemics.

Disease did more than decimate the aboriginal population; it prepared the way for subsequent phases of European contact by breaking the aboriginal's morale and by cracking their spiritual edifice (Buckley 1992). Some commentators have observed that epidemics made aboriginal people believe that their cultural system had lost its influence over the supernatural realm. In short, the epidemics subverted the aboriginal cultural system and opened the way to a corruption of the aboriginal's relationship with the land.

By the mid-1880s, the government's responsibility toward aboriginals shifted to that of caretaker, particularly of their land. The government passed statutes exempting aboriginals from taxation and sought to ban the selling of liquor to aboriginals as well. The protection being offered aboriginals was only to continue until they became "civilized." This **civilizing policy** is most explicitly stated in the Civilization of Indian Tribes Act (1857). Paternalism would dominate relations with aboriginals for the next century. As Bartlett (1988) points out, federal government interference in the daily lives of aboriginals reached its zenith during the Depression.

In the middle of the nineteenth century, it was the Saulteaux who first insisted on a specific **treaty**. Fear of violence motivated the government to respond (Morris 1880). The government had assumed, at the outset, that they could simply take over the land occupied by aboriginals, but aboriginal resistance forced them to reconsider their strategy of developing the West and to implement a policy of land acquisition. Therefore, the federal government embarked upon a policy of "negotiating" treaties with the aboriginal population as part of the larger strategy of "taking care" of them. The Robinson Huron Treaties (1850) were quickly followed by the numbered treaties, which were still being drafted in the early twentieth century.

Figure 8.1 identifies the land area encompassed in the treaties, which created reserves for aboriginals and extinguished all aboriginal land rights for the people taking treaty. This period in Canadian history was pivotal in the social placement of aboriginals in Canada.

The Canadian government, despite having established reserves in order to allow for European settlement and agricultural development of the land, did not develop a coherent or consistent policy for dealing with the aboriginal population. There was agreement by the colonizers that aboriginals needed to assimilate into the dominant society and that integration was inevitable. Many felt that aboriginals would become extinct within a few years.[6] As a result, the government's notion of itself as the aboriginal's caretaker changed and it began to consider how the process of assimilation could be facilitated. Some felt that isolation of aboriginals on reserves would render them harmless and that within a few years they would either die out or lose their identity through the proselytizing efforts of various religious groups. Others felt that social and residential integration of aboriginals was the solution to the "Indian problem." Over time, both strategies were employed, and each had both positive and negative effects upon aboriginal communities and their residents. In the end, it was decided to continue the policy of isolation (maintenance of reserves), to be aided by the efforts of various religious and public agencies to assimilate aboriginals. It became clear, however, that aboriginals were no longer defined as an important segment of our society. As Trelease (1960) and Carter (1990) point out, as aboriginal people grew economically subordinate to Europeans, their ability to contribute to their own culture and their confidence in their own value system were undermined. As a result, they became increasingly susceptible to Christian proselytizing, and by the 1920s they had been relegated to the periphery of our modern industrial society.

FIGURE 8.1   Indian Land Surrendered for Treaties

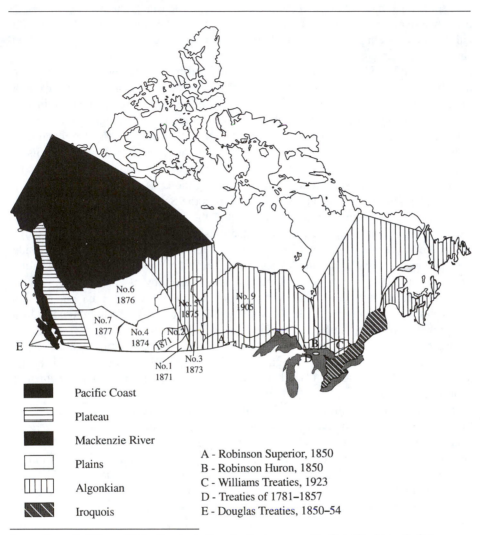

Pacific Coast

Plateau

Mackenzie River

Plains

Algonkian

Iroquois

A - Robinson Superior, 1850
B - Robinson Huron, 1850
C - Williams Treaties, 1923
D - Treaties of 1781–1857
E - Douglas Treaties, 1850–54

Source: James S. Frideres, *Native Peoples in Canada: Contemporary Conflicts* (Scarborough, ON: Prentice-Hall, 1988), p. 10.

Nevertheless, aboriginal people still constituted a visible segment of the Canadian population, and the government continued to develop policies and programs to handle this "problematic" group. Early policies were piecemeal and independent; they dealt with aboriginal issues only as they emerged. The Indian Act, implemented in 1876, was simply a compilation of previous acts and an attempt to sort out their contradictions. Nevertheless, once it was consolidated, the Indian Act became, and continues to be, the most pervasive piece of federal legislation in regulating and controlling the lives of status Indians as well as in influencing how other aboriginal people are treated.

One hundred years after the Indian Act of 1876 was implemented, legal authority over the management and control of Indian lands and property remained with the

Superintendent of Indian Affairs. The subsequent amendments of the Indian Act (it is estimated that there have been over 500) have ranged from prohibiting Indians from engaging in certain cultural activities (e.g., the Potlatch and the Tamanawas) to defining Indians as non-Indians if they voted in a federal election. Barsh (1994) concludes that this policy of "civilization" adopted by the federal government has included, as its control thesis, the cultural destruction of aboriginals.

After the Second World War, the Canadian government gave up its "caretaking" role and embarked upon a "democratization" policy. Federal policies were implemented that produced the illusion that status Indians had decision-making powers. This process continues to evolve, as status Indians today attempt to implement strategies for **self-government**. Nevertheless, assimilation of aboriginals remains the pre-eminent goal of the government. As recently as 1969, the federal government developed a policy in a White Paper that declared as its aim the total assimilation of the aboriginal population.

Because most aboriginals lived in rural areas until after 1950, their presence and their contribution to the building of Canada were ignored or minimized (Trigger 1986). Repressive legislation kept them from organizing and building social movements to promote their interests, and isolation on reserves restricted their participation to the margins of the larger society. As cities expanded their economic influence in the 1950s and 1960s, more jobs became available and aboriginal migration to urban areas accelerated. By 1990, nearly two-thirds of the aboriginal population lived in urban areas.[7] However, they quickly found that, in a segregated society such as Canada, life in an urban area did not easily open the door to economic opportunity or prosperity.

In summary, the interest of the Canadian state in dealing with aboriginal peoples was, and continues to be, linked to acquiring and using land (and its resources) for the benefit of the state. Adopting an approach of "coercive tutelage," the federal government has treated, and continues to treat, aboriginal people as being incapable of making informed decisions. The creation of the Department of Indian Affairs and the Indian Act are the most lasting edifices that embrace such a philosophy (Dyck 1997a).

Control of Institutional Orders

Until recently, aboriginal people have not been able to exert any real power. Most of the day-to-day decisions that influenced them were made, in secret, by Indian Affairs officials. Any decisions made by local band councils were subject to approval by the Department of Indian Affairs and Northern Development (DIAND), whose officials were the major political and economic force on the reserve. Aboriginals were not allowed to handle their own affairs because of an administrative structure that denied them the opportunity to learn new ways of doing things while at the same time rendering traditional culture ineffective (Thomas 1966–67).

The land policy adopted by the federal government (in agreement with the provincial governments), had an immediate and lasting impact upon aboriginal people. Land set aside for aboriginal peoples was selected because it was away from the main routes of travel, unsuitable for agricultural development, and lacking in natural resources identified or required at the time (Wax 1971). The result has been that most reserves have not had an adequate ecological basis for their existence as self-sufficient communities. Thus, from their inception, the reserves have required extensive subsidization; in turn, this has legitimized Indian Affairs' involvement in aboriginal communities.

We will look at three different institutional orders that directly impact upon aboriginal peoples' way of life and quality of life. How organizations focussed on health, education, and economics have affected aboriginal people over the past century will be analyzed. As noted earlier, the Canadian state has used several different models of control to deal with aboriginal peoples (Taylor-Henley and Hudson 1992). The first and most pervasive model was that of assimilation. The second model, the integrated model, involved creating a local advisory structure that included some aboriginal people but was controlled by external agents (e.g., provincial authorities, Indian Affairs) through funding and defining acceptable projects. Today, an attempt is being made to develop further models of delegated authority or autonomy. While these latter models are being discussed, the federal and provincial governments still retain control linkages. State funding, for example, continues to promote state interference with the standards and types of services provided by and for aboriginal people.

Since the turn of the century, the major policy trend in Canadian society has been the development of the welfare state, which has resulted in the transformation of previously private relationships into public ones. The state has entered into almost all social and economic aspects of Canadian life in an attempt to increase equality by redistributing income, and aboriginals are just one group that have come under its influence. As Brooks (1989) points out, however, the welfare state as it exists today has been constructed without any significant success in reducing the unequal distribution of income. This is particularly notable in the case of Canada's aboriginal people. Since the end of the Second World War, aboriginal people have not enhanced their economic status or relative position in the Canadian class system.

Health

It should be stated at the outset that the federal government believes that, with certain exceptions, it does not have any legal or fiduciary obligations with regard to health care for aboriginal people. Nevertheless, it has accepted some responsibility and nearly $500 million is spent annually by the federal government on aboriginal health. At the same time, it has refused to support non-legal aboriginals as well as Indians who do not live on reserves. In 1986, the federal government began transferring health-care services from the Medical Services Branch to aboriginal communities. This transfer is just part of the overall "devolution" policy of the government and supports the general movement toward aboriginal self-government.

As noted earlier, the mortality rate for aboriginal people has decreased dramatically over the past half century. Since the 1960s, aboriginal people have been able to participate in the same health-care programs available to other Canadians (Barsh 1994). However, *access* to health facilities for most aboriginal people remains problematic. For example, Health Canada (1991a) notes that almost one-tenth of aboriginal communities are nearly 100 kilometres from the closest health practitioner, or lack public transport to the closest town to obtain medical care. Available data show that the mortality rate—11 per 1000 population in 1950—has been reduced to 3.5 in 1996. Nevertheless, the current rate is still twice the national rate for all Canadians.

Table 8.3 reveals that the aboriginal infant mortality rate is nearly twice that of the general Canadian population. For specific age groups, such as those aged 5 to 19, the mortality rate of registered Indians is four times the national rate. And since 1988, a disturbing trend in infant mortality for aboriginal people has emerged: perinatal deaths (still births and deaths of infants under one week old) are on the increase and nearly twice as high as the total Canadian rate (Frideres 1998). This may reflect the diet and lifestyle of aboriginals.

The data in Table 8.4 reveal the extent of chronic illness among aboriginal people. In the first half of the twentieth century, infectious and parasitic digestive and respiratory diseases were the main cause of death of aboriginal people. Since then, some of these diseases have sharply declined in importance. Since the 1960s, however, injury and poisoning, circulatory system diseases, and neoplasms (malignant tumours) have become the main cause of death within Indian communities. Moreover, the pattern of mortality for aboriginals is different from that of other Canadians. Aboriginal deaths are much more likely to be caused by accidents and much less likely to result from cancer. As Barsh (1994) points out, although deaths from gastrointestinal and respiratory disease are only slightly higher for aboriginal people than non-aboriginal Canadians, *chronic illness* from these causes is much higher, indicating nutritional and water-quality problems. A study in Manitoba (Health and Welfare, 1991b) revealed that aboriginals were four times more likely to be hospitalized for respiratory disease or for infectious or parasitic disease and three times more likely to be hospitalized with perinatal complications. Information from Indian Affairs and from Medical Services shows that nearly 60 percent of Indian illnesses and deaths are alcohol-related. Bienvenue (1985) points out that general living conditions and feelings of uselessness and estrangement from the larger society are important factors underlying the nature and circumstances of aboriginal illness and death.

TABLE 8.3   Infant Mortality Rate (per 1000) for Aboriginal and Total Canadian Population, 1960–1995, Selected Years

	Aboriginal	All Canadian
1960	82.4	28.4
1975	39.0	14.3
1980	27.2	10.4
1985	18.1	8.0
1990	12.2	6.8
1995	12.0	6.5

Source: Adapted from Statistics Canada, *Deaths*, Cat. no. 84-211.

TABLE 8.4 Number of Deaths and Mortality Rates by Cause among Registered Indian Population in Canada (Rate per 100 000), Selected Years

	1955	1978	1986	1990
Infectious and parasitic	74.7	14.3	N/A	4.2
Neoplasms	48.0	61.3	51.8	52.1
Endocrine, nutritional and metabolic diseases, and immunity disorders; diseases of the blood and blood-forming organs	9.3	15.0	N/A	10.7
Mental disorders	N/A	12.3	N/A	3.9
Diseases of the nervous system and sense organs	5.3	10.8	N/A	4.5
Diseases of the circulatory system	166.7	176.8	124.9	105.0
Diseases of the respiratory system	231.3	57.8	39.7	30.8
Diseases of the digestive system	69.3	30.8	25.1	16.8
Diseases of the genito-urinary system	16.0	13.1		10.6
Complications of pregnancy, childbirth, and the puerperium	6.0	0.0	N/A	0.3
Diseases of the skin and subcutaneous tissue; diseases of the musculoskeletal system and connective tissue	8.7	3.9	N/A	1.6
Congenital anomalies	24.7	16.6	N/A	10.1
Certain conditions originating in the perinatal period	99.3	22.7	N/A	5.3
Symptoms, signs, and ill-defined conditions	100.0	29.3	N/A	16.8
Injury and poisoning	122.0	276.6	161.1	107.2
Others	70.7	11.2	N/A	N/A

Sources: **1955–1960**: Health and Welfare Canada, Medical Services Branch, *Annual Report, 1962*; **1978–1982**: Health and Welfare Canada, *Indian and Inuit Health Status Indicators, 1974–1983* (Ottawa: Demographics and Statistics Division, 1988); DIAND, *Basic Departmental Data* (Ottawa: Minister of Supply and Services, 1993).

Barsh (1994) points out that the hospital separation rate of all cardiovascular diseases has remained constant over the past two decades at seventeen per thousand. As the reader can see in Table 8.4 diseases of circulatory, respiratory, and digestive systems are the major causes of mortality among the registered Indian population.

Tuberculosis has long been considered a problem of epidemic importance for aboriginals. Thousands of aboriginals died from tuberculosis in the first half of this century and its toll on the integrity of aboriginal families, their productivity, and their mental health has been devastating. While the rate of TB infections decreased after the 1950s, it is once again on the upswing. The rate of tuberculosis is 43 times as high among status Indians as among non-aboriginal Canadians. In 1992, the rate for registered Indians stood at 81.3 per 100 000 population, higher than rates of infection in some of the poorest countries in the world (in Africa the rate is about 80 per 100 000). For all aboriginals, the rate was lower, at 60.8 per 100 000. These figures indicate a relationship of TB prevalence with poverty, poor nutrition, and poor housing conditions. Barsh (1991) found that dietary intake is related to resistance to respiratory and gastrointestinal infections as well as to diabetes mellitus. He also noted that cardio-vascular problems such as lung disease and diabetes can come about as dietary intake changes due to high intake of store-bought starch, fat, and processed sugar; foods that are cheap and purchased by people living in poverty.

In the end, all these factors have relevance to the average life span. Table 8.5 shows that average life expectancy for Indians and the total Canadian population. The data show that while the average life expectancy for Indians has increased by over ten years in the past quarter century, it still lags behind the average Canadian life expectancy by more than five years.

Housing can be considered another dimension of health. Governmental assistance in providing housing is necessary because of the legal framework of the Indian Act. Until recently, the Department of Indian Affairs administered and delivered all aspects of housing for registered Indians. As a result, aboriginal people have had little say about the type and location of their housing, and the services linked to it. Although the aboriginal population has steadily increased over the past quarter century, the number of dwellings on reserves has not kept up with this increase, so over-crowding is endemic for most aboriginal communities.

The lack of new houses and the aging of existing houses has meant that housing standards have decreased over the years. For example, 33 percent of the on-reserve houses are in good enough condition to require regular maintenance only, compared with 53 percent of off-reserve housing and 67 percent of the total Canadian housing stock. Nearly 40 percent of on-reserve housing requires major repairs, compared with only 16 percent of off-reserve housing and only 8 percent of the total Canadian

TABLE 8.5 Life Expectancy for Indian and Total Canadian Population by Sex, 1975–2000 (Projected)

| | Men | | Women | |
	Indian	Total Canadian population	Indian	Total Canadian population
1975	59.2	70.0	65.9	77.3
1980	60.9	71.8	68.0	78.7
1985	63.9	72.8	71.0	79.6
1990	66.9	73.9	74.0	80.7
1995	69.1	74.9	76.2	81.9
2000 (projected)	70.2	75.7	77.3	82.7

Source: Statistics Canada, *Age and Sex*, Aboriginal Data, 1993. Cat. no. 94-327, p. 25.

housing stock. In addition, because of the substandard construction materials used in aboriginal housing, the life span of these houses is less than half that of the average Canadian house (Canada 1997). Recently, it was estimated that over 10 percent of the existing housing stock on reserves required complete replacement (Barsh 1994). However, because new houses are not being built, these houses continue to be lived in by an increasing number of aboriginal families.

The extent to which a people are dependent upon social assistance represents a third dimension of health. The data show that aboriginal people rely upon social assistance more than any other ethno-cultural group in Canada does. In the early 1970s, fewer than 25 000 aboriginals were recipients of social assistance. By 1980, this number had increased to nearly 40 000 and by 1995, to over 60 000. Expenditures for aboriginal social assistance have increased from $53 million in 1973 to over $400 million in 1994. The extent to which the state is involved in child care is also indicative of the future of that people. Over 4 percent of aboriginal children under age 16 are now under state care, and that number is increasing.

In summary, social assistance is a major problem for aboriginal people. Structural factors created by government policies have forced aboriginal people to become dependent upon government social assistance; yet many Canadians engage in a form of personal attacks, implying that aboriginals themselves are the cause of their need for social assistance. Despite our commitment to a social welfare state, most Canadians feel that aboriginals are not trying hard enough to integrate into the economic sphere of Canadian society. We grudgingly, and not without comment, give social assistance to aboriginals, while failing to solve the underlying social and economic conditions aboriginals live in.

Education

The legal basis of the federal government's special relationship with Aboriginals stems from the Constitution Act, 1867. Different sections of the Indian Act allow the minister of Indian Affairs to operate schools and enter into agreements with provincial and municipal governments, school boards, and religious or charitable organizations with regard to the education of aboriginal children. Over the years, the Department of Indian Affairs has exercised these legal rights many times. In addition, under various cabinet decisions and Treasury Board authority, the government has extended its educational support services to include pre-kindergarten and post-secondary programs. However, at no time in the past were aboriginals consulted or allowed to participate in the formal education of their children.

Educational services provided to aboriginals at the turn of the century were provided by various religious organizations subcontracted by the federal government. After the Second World War, however, the state intervened and substituted a secular education for the missionary efforts. At this time the federal government began to sign agreements with the provinces to provide aboriginal students with an education in provincial schools alongside non-aboriginal students, in order to ensure assimilation and reduce costs. Over the past two decades this plan of action has changed and band schools (schools operated and controlled by aboriginal people on the reserve) have become the most common type of school attended by aboriginal students. Today

Natives and Quality of Life

The population surge among aboriginals (estimated to double by 2015) is coming two decades after the rest of the country and is happening as Canadians grow increasingly intolerant. A report by senior federal bureaucrats claims that the high levels of social stress and conflict found in aboriginal communities is morally, ethically, and politically unacceptable.

While there have been improvements since the 1970s in living conditions such as education and economic opportunities, the treatment of aboriginal people is frequently referred to in international circles as a "black mark" on Canada's otherwise good reputation. Attempts to improve the quality of life for aboriginals is running into a wall of resistance from aging Canadian baby boomers.

The report claims that the aboriginal population is out of sync with the general Canadian population, noting that the Canadian social safety net is now being cut by the baby boomers who benefited from it. They go on to note that aboriginal people need the services and supports at a time when those supports are under attack and when the attitude and willingness of Canadians to provide support has been fundamentally altered.

Other findings in the report show that Canadians are extremely sensitive to special treatment for aboriginal people. It refers to the recent Insight Poll that found nearly half of Canadians believe the standard of living of Natives was the same or better than that of the average Canadian. They also found that 40 percent of Canadians believe that aboriginals have themselves to blame for their problems. A majority of Canadians feel that aboriginal people are being unreasonable in pursuing their land claims.

The study makes it clear that the problems faced by aboriginal communities are real. The rate of incarceration of aboriginals is five to six times higher than the national average. Illiteracy is double. Income is one-half to one-third that of non-aboriginals, and unemployment in some communities is beyond 80 percent. Life expectancy is ten years less than the Canadian average and many infectious diseases are reaching epidemic proportions.

there are nearly 300 band schools operating across the country. In addition, several post-secondary aboriginal schools are providing additional educational services to students.

With the increase in aboriginal schools, there has been a concomitant increase in aboriginal student enrollment. Over the past quarter century, the number of status Indian students has steadily increased. In 1960, enrollment was 42 000, which represented about three-quarters of the aboriginal population between 4 and 18. Today there are nearly 100 000 students, representing over 95 percent of the school-aged children. In 1960, about 4 percent of aboriginal students graduated from high school. Today that figure has increased to about 15 percent. While the *increase* has been dramatic, the total figure is disappointing when compared with the over 70 percent of the Canadian school-aged population that graduates from high school.[8]

National data show that aboriginal students are staying in school longer and attending more post-secondary educational institutions than in the past. In the 1950s, the enrollment of an aboriginal student in university was a newsworthy event. In 1960, fewer than 400 aboriginal students were attending any kind of post-secondary educational institution. Today we find that over 6000 aboriginal students are enrolled in university and another 21 000 are attending other post-secondary educational institutions. While these figures represent significant increases, they still only include 5 percent of the aboriginal population over 20 years of age, compared with the nearly 30 percent of the national population who are attending post-secondary educational institutions. As the number of aboriginal students increases, government policy (Bill C-91) and funding allocations have changed to make it more difficult for them to obtain funding. The impact of such changes will take some time to assess, although the total number of aboriginals attending post-secondary educational institutions has remained constant since the passage of the bill. Census data show that 59 percent of on-reserve aboriginals (aged 15 to 24) are not attending school, compared with 47 percent of off-reserve aboriginals and 38 percent of the general population. Of those attending school, 39 percent of on-reserve aboriginals, 47 percent of off-reserve aboriginals, and 55 percent of the general population attend full-time. The remainder of the population in each category attend part-time.

Table 8.6 reveals the level of education currently held by aboriginal people 15 years of age and older. It shows that well over one-third have less than a Grade 9 education. Almost three-quarters have not progressed past high school. These figures need to be compared with the total Canadian population's, which shows that only 14 percent have less than a Grade 9 education and less than two-thirds have not progressed past high school. As for higher education, only 1 percent of aboriginal peoples have a university degree, compared with almost 12 percent of the general Canadian population. Off-reserve aboriginals, however, have similar educational profiles to those of the general Canadian population.

The reader should remember that education is not a neutral activity; it is profoundly political (Haig-Brown 1995). This is reflected in the curriculum and the

TABLE 8.6 Highest Level of Education for Aboriginals and Total Canadian Population by Residence (15 Years and Older), 1995

	Aboriginal		Total Canadian population
	On-reserve	Off-reserve	
Less than grade 9	36.5%	14.4%	13.9%
Grades 9–13	37.3	44.0	48.5
Trade certificate	3.1	3.5	4.0
Other non-university	9.2	24.3	22.3
Some university	4.2	8.2	9.4
University degree	1.2	5.5	11.4

Source: Adapted from Statistics Canada, *Profile of Canada's Aboriginal Population, 1995,* Cat. no. 94-325, pp. 16–17.

teachers, as well as in the function of the state. For years, the federal government, under the Indian Act, assumed total control of aboriginal education. In doing so, it politicized the educational process. As Battiste and Barman (1995) point out, it defined education as transforming the mind of the aboriginal youth rather than educating it. In carrying out such a policy, aboriginals were soon deprived of their world view, language, and cultural values.

Until the 1960s, Aboriginal education was dominated by "residential schools" operated by religious organizations under contract to the federal government. The year 1969 is viewed as a watershed in aboriginal education. When the White Paper policy tried to transfer federal responsibility to the provinces, aboriginal people "drew a line in the sand." They began to see white educators as racists and oppressors. Aboriginal people began to argue that they had the right to administer and deliver educational programs for their children. By 1973, the federal government agreed to implement the policy of Indian control of Indian education. As a corollary, provincial intrusions to Indian education were stopped and aboriginal leaders were given jurisdictional control and responsibility for Indian education.

To implement this policy, regional Indian cultural and educational centres were established throughout Canada, educational programs at various universities were created,[9] and aboriginal teacher-training programs were developed. As the federal government allowed aboriginal communities to develop their own education models and gain jurisdiction over their children's education, more and more communities began to take control of their schools. In 1975 only 53 communities had taken control of their schools. Twenty years later, a majority of bands were operating aboriginal schools. Nevertheless, even though a majority of aboriginals complete their primary grades in band schools, if they wish to continue their education, they must enroll in integrated schools, which are controlled by non-aboriginal school boards.

While the early days of aboriginal control focussed on aboriginal student success in the educational context, today the goals and objectives of aboriginal education are focussed on salvaging aboriginal languages, culture, and society, as well as ensuring that these values and culture are transmitted to the next generation (Battiste and Barman, 1995). Aboriginal education must build upon the strong foundations of ancestral heritage and culture and incorporate the wisdom and knowledge of elders (Assembly of First Nations 1988). Questions about educational jurisdiction, management, and control are no longer debated. Rather, issues such as delivery and evaluation programs of aboriginal education are on the discussion table (Assembly of First Nations 1990). Recently, aboriginal communities are claiming the federal government has failed to implement the 1973 policy as intended. A parliamentary Standing Committee on Aboriginal Affairs (Canada 1990) also noted that the intended consequences of the early policy have not come to fruition, as nearly half of the aboriginal population in Canada are functionally illiterate.

Today, aboriginal schools are not only confronted with funding problems, they are also plagued by questions of what the school curriculum will be. Questions such as what processes must accompany cultural and linguistic development and inclusion, what the meaning of renewal and revision is in the contemporary educational context, and whether contemporary Eurocentric or traditional aboriginal models of education should be employed need to be answered. As Battiste and Barman (1995) point out, these questions have caused considerable confusion for aboriginal educators and the schools as they try to implement programs consistent with their philosophy. As we enter the twenty-first century, these issues will need to be sorted out.

The Economy

Aboriginal people living on reserves have differential access to and participation in the economy from those who live off-reserve. Reserves are generally isolated from the mainstream economy, have inadequate infrastructure to support any local economy, and have a concentration of power in the hands of a few families. On the other hand, they have access to support structures (e.g., family and kin), are linked to the welfare economy, have access to federal services, and allow for considerable unfettered social mobility. Aboriginals living in urban settings find their social support networks limited and have difficulty accessing a variety of services. Their involvement in the economy is limited to certain marginal sectors, and they find their social mobility limited (Chiste 1996). Moreover, they do not have access to land-based resources, such as oil, gas, and gravel. Therefore, two economic profiles can be constructed, reflecting aboriginal residence on- or off-reserve.

The data in Table 8.7 reveal the occupational distribution of aboriginal people by residence, compared with that of the general Canadian population. The data show significant occupational differences between the on-reserve population and the general Canadian population. Over 17 percent of on-reserve aboriginal females work in manual or semi-skilled jobs, while only about 11 percent of the Canadian population occupy such jobs. For males the difference is even greater. Nearly half of the aboriginal males, compared with less than one-third of the total Canadian population, hold manual or semi-skilled jobs. When we look at the upper end of occupational status, we find a reversal. For female aboriginals, less than 6 percent work in upper and middle management jobs. On the other hand, over 16 percent of the total Canadians population work in such jobs. For males a similar disparity occurs. Overall, the data show an overrepresentation of aboriginals in low-status jobs and an underrepresentation in high-status jobs.[10]

The occupational distribution of aboriginal people has an effect on their income levels. Data on the income distribution for aboriginal people are revealed in Table 8.8. These data show the income disparity between aboriginal people and the general Canadian population. Again, the discrepancy is less for the off-reserve population. Aboriginals on reserves are four times more likely to earn less than $1000 income than are non-aboriginals. At the higher end of the income scale, ten times the percentage of the total population than of on-reserve aboriginals make more than $50 000 (George and Kuhn 1994).

Aboriginal income is influenced by factors in addition to educational attainment and occupational distribution. Less than 10 percent of the on-reserve aboriginal population worked full-time, while the rate was 90.5 percent for the off-reserve population. However, if we compare those individuals who worked full-time, we still find income differentials. For aboriginals on-reserve who worked full-time, the average annual salary was $21 787. For off-reserve aboriginals, the average salary was $29 485; for the average Canadian, it was $33 714.[11] Unemployment rates also varied among groups, averaging nearly 35 percent to 50 percent for on-reserve aboriginals,

TABLE 8.7   Distribution of Aboriginal and Total Canadian Population for Selected Occupations, by Sex, 1991

Occupation	Female			Male		
	On-reserve	Off-reserve	Total Canadian population	On-reserve	Off-reserve	Total Canadian population
Upper and middle management	5.9%	6.7%	16.1%	7.0%	6.8%	11.5%
Professional and semi-professional	21.0	35.5	20.8	7.0	10.3	15.1
Clerical	17.5	26.5	28.9	2.5	33.5	6.4
Service	17.1	20.3	13.8	5.7	8.8	7.0
Manual and semi-skilled	17.4	12.6	10.9	47.4	41.3	30.7

Source: Adapted from Statistics Canada, *Profile of Canada's Aboriginal Population, 1995*, Cat. no. 94-325, p. 22.

and less than 20 percent for off-reserve aboriginals. Overall, the Canadian public experienced a 10 percent unemployment rate (Statistics Canada 1994).

The socio-economic profile of aboriginal people reveals low educational achievement, low-status jobs, part-time employment, and low income. Moreover, there is little opportunity for them to upgrade their educational qualifications or enter high-status jobs. While, as noted earlier, the number of young aboriginal people is increasing, their potential for labour force involvement is discouraging. Furthermore, the

TABLE 8.8   Income for Aboriginals and/or Registered Indians Compared with Income for Total Canadian Population (15 Years and Older, with an Income), 1995

Total income	On-reserve	Off-reserve	Total Canadian population
<$1000	13.9%	5.6%	3.5%
$1000–$4999	23.7	14.8	9.8
$5000–$9999	21.9	17.5	14.5
$10 000–$19 999	24.4	25.2	24.4
$20 000–$29 999	9.8	16.1	18.2
$30 000–$49 999	6.3	15.9	20.4
$50 000+	<1.0	4.8	9.8

Note: On-reserve includes those living on designated reserve or other officially designated area (e.g., Métis colony).

Source: Adapted from Statistics Canada, *Profile of Canada's Aboriginal Population, 1995*, Cat. no. 94-325, p. 28.

percentage of "dependent" aboriginal people (those under 15 and over 64 years of age) is on the increase and there is little evidence to suggest that it will level off or decrease in the near future. Barsh (1994) found that the average Canadian of working age must now support 1.1 individuals too young or old to work, while for aboriginals this ratio is 1.5 and will continue to grow.

Pendakur and Pendakur (1995) compared aboriginal incomes with those of the white, Canadian-born population, with controls for such social factors as level of education and occupation (i.e., individuals having similar levels of education and occupational status were compared). The results showed that individuals claiming to be aboriginals received about 19 percent less income than white, Canadian-born individuals. When respondents gave multiple responses the picture changed. For those who claimed aboriginal status and another "white" ethnic origin, their average yearly earnings were about 15 percent less than those of white, Canadian-born individuals. However, if individuals claimed a multiple response (both aboriginal and visible minority status), their average income was 84 percent less than that of white, Canadian-born individuals.

Most aboriginal people are marginal participants in the country's economy. The on-reserve population face additional structural disadvantages, such as an inability to obtain bank loans, or the lack of development capital from Indian Affairs. Moreover, their inability to accumulate savings makes it difficult to generate new businesses on the reserve. This lack of economic participation has been characteristic of aboriginals for the past half century. It means that Aboriginals serve as a secondary labour pool, providing cheap labour when the supply is scarce and being quickly laid off when it increases. In short, this suggests that aboriginal workers are useful to the dominant society because their presence ensures that the labour supply consistently meets industry's needs, keeping labour costs down and profits up. This dual labour market allows the private sector to ignore the secondary labour pool during periods of unemployment, relying on the state to transfer funds to it in the form of social assistance.

Land Claims

As Figure 8.2 reveals, a significant portion of the land in Canada is currently under dispute as to ownership. The extent of these claims can be better appreciated when it is understood that ownership of nearly three-quarters of British Columbia is being contested by aboriginal people. The **land claims** made by aboriginal people encompass both comprehensive and specific claims.

Comprehensive claims are based upon aboriginal peoples' traditional use and occupancy of the land. *Specific claims* are based on allegations that the government did not fulfil specific obligations to aboriginals under the treaties, the Indian Act, or some other agreement (Cassidy and Dale, 1988b). Comprehensive claims have arisen in Yukon, Labrador, most of British Columbia, northern Quebec, and most of the Northwest Territories. They include such issues as land title; specified hunting, fishing, and trapping rights; financial compensation; and other rights and benefits. Nearly 300 specific claims also have been submitted for negotiation, with another 1500 to 2000 expected to be submitted in the next decade. To fully appreciate the rate of resolution, it should be noted that today only 30 have been settled.

FIGURE 8.2 Lands Contested and/or Settled under the Comprehensive Claims Process

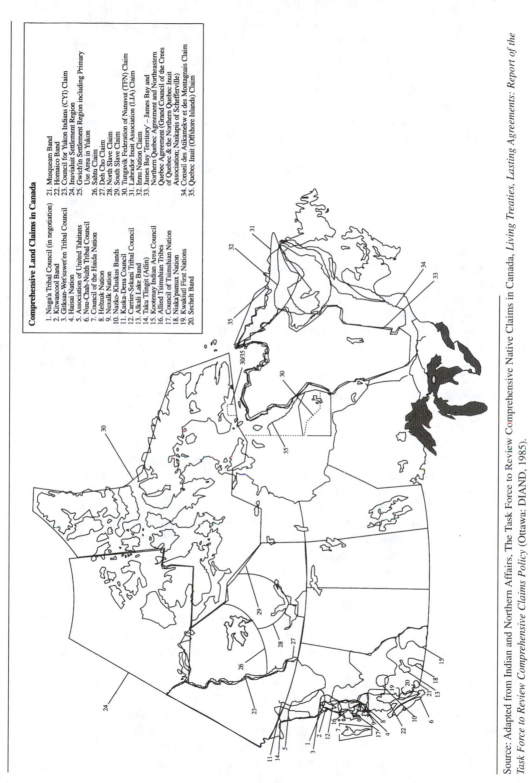

Comprehensive Land Claims in Canada

1. Nisga'a Tribal Council (in negotiation)
2. Kitwancool Band
3. Gitksan-Wet'suwet'en Tribal Council
4. Haisla Nation
5. Association of United Tahltans
6. Nuu-Chah-Nulth Tribal Council
7. Council of the Haida Nation
8. Heltsuk Nation
9. Nuxalk Nation
10. Nazko-Kluskus Bands
11. Kaska-Dena Council
12. Carrier-Sekani Tribal Council
13. Alkali Lake Band
14. Taku Tlingit (Atlin)
15. Kootenay Indian Area Council
16. Allied Tsimshian Tribes
17. Council of Tsimshian Nation
18. Niaka'pamux Nation
19. Kwakiutl First Nations
20. Sechelt Band
21. Musqueam Band
22. Homalco Band
23. Council for Yukon Indians (CYI) Claim
24. Inuvialuit Settlement Region
25. Gwich'in Settlement Region including Primary
    Use Area in Yukon
26. Sahtu Claim
27. Deh Cho Claim
28. North Slave Claim
29. South Slave Claim
30. Tungavik Federation of Nunavut (TFN) Claim
31. Labrador Inuit Association (LIA) Claim
32. Innu Nation Claim
33. James Bay Territory – James Bay and
    Northern Quebec Agreement and Northeastern
    Quebec Agreement (Grand Council of the Crees
    of Quebec & the Northern Quebec Inuit
    Association; Naskapis of Schefferville)
34. Conseil des Atikamekw et des Montagnais Claim
35. Quebec Inuit (Offshore Islands) Claim

Source: Adapted from Indian and Northern Affairs, The Task Force to Review Comprehensive Native Claims in Canada, *Living Treaties, Lasting Agreements: Report of the Task Force to Review Comprehensive Claims Policy* (Ottawa: DIAND, 1985).

The issue of land claims may seem to be a recent phenomenon. However, land claims have been a major issue with aboriginal people for well over two centuries. For aboriginal people early Peace and Friendship treaties were attempts to resolve the land ownership issue; however, these "treaties" were not meant, at least by the colonists, as negotiations over land ownership (Task Force 1985). Later, more specific treaties were drafted and presented to aboriginals across the country. By the 1930s, when sufficient land had been acquired from aboriginals for agricultural, residential, and industrial development, the treaty process was ended. However, few of the treaties signed were acceptable to aboriginal people, who objected to their content. Nevertheless, the Government of Canada refused to take their concerns or objections seriously and, in some cases, passed legislation making it difficult for aboriginals to pursue legal avenues for compensation. For example, in 1927, section 141 of the Indian Act was passed to prohibit status Indians from raising money or retaining a lawyer in order to pursue a land claim. The federal government also took the position that it had met all of its legal obligations regarding land compensation for aboriginals, and that where land had not been "treatied out," there were no aboriginal land rights.

This position on aboriginal land rights would come crashing down with the *Calder* decision by the Supreme Court in 1973. In this decision, the Court agreed that aboriginal land rights existed and that a process of extinguishment had to be established. It also was at this time that the federal government divided aboriginal claims into comprehensive and specific (Isaac 1995). Subsequent court decisions (*Guerin* 1984; *Sparrow* 1990) have supported the 1973 decision and have forced the government to review more closely both comprehensive and specific claims presented by aboriginals. However, in 1991, the *Delgamuukw* case, in which the judge ruled that aboriginal title in parts of British Columbia had been extinguished, placed the earlier decisions in question.

On December 11, 1997, the Supreme Court of Canada ruled that aboriginal people have a constitutional right to own their ancestral lands and to use them as they wish, overturning the *Delgamuukw* decision. The Court ruled that the then chief justice, Allan McEachern of the B.C. Supreme Court, erred in his decision by not allowing aboriginal oral histories to be part of the court documents. For those Aboriginals who have not signed away their lands by taking treaty, the Court ruled that title to the land has not been extinguished. Moreover, their land use rights are not limited to traditional customs such as hunting and fishing and First Nations have exclusive right to occupy the land. Finally, the Court provided a new test for proving aboriginal title. The Court specified that aboriginals need only prove they had occupied a disputed piece of land when Canadian title was established. The decision has direct implications for all aboriginal lands not under treaty, in British Columbia, portions of Quebec, Ontario, Prince Edward Island, Newfoundland, and the Northwest Territories.

The Court ruled that aboriginal right to title is inalienable—it cannot be sold, except to the Crown. In addition, the land is communally owned by aboriginals and they have the exclusive right to use the lands. Moreover, the land can be used for all modern purposes, including setting up casinos or establishing mining operations. However, the land may not be used for purposes directly opposed to the original use (e.g., paving over a religious area to create a parking lot). The ruling overrides the decision of the B.C. court, which had dismissed claims from the Gitksan and Wet'suwet'en tribes over a 60 000 square kilometre area of British Columbia. The Supreme Court also recommended that settlement of aboriginal land claims be pursued through negotiations rather than through the courts.[12] The ruling means that aboriginal title must be taken into account when any form of development takes place in British Columbia.

Today Canadians have settled several major comprehensive land claims: The James Bay and Northern Quebec Agreement (1975), the Northeastern Quebec Agreement (1978), the Inuvialuit of Western Arctic Agreement (1984), the Gwich'in Agreement (1992), and more recently the Nunavut Agreement (1997). However, many more await resolution as the government has limited to ten the number of claims that can be negotiated at one time.

In 1991, the Indian Claims Commission was created[13] to carry out three activities with regard to Indian land claims: (1) to examine claims rejected by the federal government, (2) to review compensation awards, and (3) to help mediate disputes

---

Supreme Court Will Hear Land Claims

B.C. chiefs are taking their fight for aboriginal rights to the Supreme Court of Canada in what has been called the most important land claims case in Canada. The case involves two bands, the Gitksan and Wet'suwet'en.

This case emerges out of the infamous *Delgamuukw* case, which was brought to the courts in 1984. The Gitksan and Wet'suwet'en claimed ownership and jurisdiction over 57 000 square kilometres of northwestern British Columbia, about the size of Nova Scotia. An earlier court decision (a decision made by Chief Justice Allan McEachern of the B.C. Supreme Court in 1991) ruled against their claim and this was appealed. In 1993, the B.C. Court of Appeal overturned some of the original judgment and aboriginals viewed the decision as a partial victory. The court ruled that Native rights were never extinguished by the colonial government before Confederation, and thus aboriginal rights are protected in the Constitution. However, the appeal court rejected the aboriginal claim to jurisdiction and self-government on traditional territories. If the Supreme Court upholds the first part of their decision and overturns the second part, it would give aboriginals a strong bargaining position in future land negotiations.

Aboriginal leaders were outraged by the original decision (*Delgamuukw* case) and wanted to pursue an appeal immediately. However, the B.C. government intervened and began negotiations with the Gitksan and Wet'suwet'en in an attempt to move the case out of the court room and onto the bargaining table. When the B.C. government decided to suspend the talks with the two bands, the case was sent back to the court. It has taken fourteen years to find its way to the Supreme Court of Canada.

At stake is more than just salmon-rich rivers, minerals, forestry, and a number of river systems. This case will force the top court to grapple directly with the profound issues of self-government and land ownership. As one Chief, Ed John, noted, this case will determine the legal and ultimately the political foundation of the existence of First Nations in British Columbia.

between the government and aboriginals.[14] However, the federal government was not bound by its recommendations and in 1996, all five members of the Commission resigned to protest government inaction on their decisions and recommendations.

Recent court decisions have rekindled aboriginal rights beyond those of simple land ownership. In late 1997, the New Brunswick Queen's Bench ruled that aboriginals have the right to cut trees on Crown land with no restrictions.[15] A week later the British Columbia Appeal Court ruled that the province did not have exclusive control over its forests as long as aboriginal claims were not resolved. In short, aboriginal people were defined as having "vested" rights in the land and its property that need to be taken into account when the Crown is deciding what to do with the land. These decisions have added a new dimension to the ongoing aboriginal rights debate.

In 1990, a trilateral structure (federal, provincial, First Nations) was put in place to oversee and co-ordinate treaty negotiations. It was to involve a six-stage process, ending with the implementation of a treaty. For example, in British Columbia there are over 50 First Nations (making up 75 percent of all aboriginals in the province) involved in the process. Whether or not the remaining aboriginal groups will participate remains to be seen. Nevertheless, this new strategy is attempting to circumvent the existing legal and financial roadblocks to resolving aboriginal claims. It is different from previous strategies in that until recently, the federal government has approached all aboriginal claims with the aim of securing title to the land and extinguishing all claims. Aboriginal people, however, want the comprehensive claims agreements to affirm their aboriginal rights. In addition, they want the agreements to encourage economic development and help aboriginal communities achieve self-sufficiency. They also hope that the new process will enable them to establish political, social, and economic institutions that will allow their communities to become self-governing.

Self-Government

Until recently, the federal government's response to aboriginal demands for self-determination has been negative. The government has argued that aboriginal sovereignty could not exist because the only sovereignty that existed in Canada was vested in the Crown. Moreover, all existing legislation has been placed within the jurisdiction of federal or provincial governments. However, in 1985, the *Musqueim* case persuaded the government to rethink its position. This came on the heels of the patriation of the Constitution (1982), a series of first ministers' conferences, and the failure of the federal government's Optional Indian Government legislation.

As a result of these events, the issue of aboriginal self-government has taken on a force not experienced before. Nevertheless, without the endorsement of the provincial premiers, no constitutional procedures can be undertaken to implement it. Instead, the federal government has embarked on a number of non-constitutional initiatives to achieve aboriginal self-government, and has taken the position that each community should be able to tailor its form of government to its own needs and aspirations. The Sechelt Indian Band Self-Government Act (1986) was the first example of such provisions and it was hoped that it would become the template for future negotiations. However, the provinces' reluctance to endorse self-government and the currently existing legislation (e.g., the Indian Act) remain formidable obstacles to aboriginals' obtaining self-government.[16]

Aboriginals have been asking for constitutional recognition and protection of their rights in terms of broad, undefined structures, with the details to be worked out later. On the other hand, neither the federal government nor provincial governments are willing to acknowledge self-government without knowing what the concept entails. This impasse is referred to as the "empty" versus the "full" medicine chest dilemma. Factors such as aboriginal suspicion of government, the urbanization of aboriginals, and the role of the provincial governments pose additional impediments to the discussion (Peters 1994). Finally, the financial implications of moving to self-government have drawn out the negotiations. In the end, negotiations continue between the parties in an attempt to resolve the issues and entrench self-government within the aboriginal community.[17]

A Sociological Analysis

A group's position in society is a result of many different structural factors, all of which have operated over a long time period. As well, members of the dominant society have readily accepted and promoted social structures that operate in their favour. Through socialization and control of the institutional spheres that make up our society, we accept and defend the current structures that reinforce the existing social arrangements among different ethnic groups.

Our explanation of aboriginal–white relations focusses on the structure of institutionalized **discrimination**, both direct and indirect. This concept identifies those actions, whether prescribed by an organization or by the community, that have a negative impact on members of a minority group (Feagin and Feagin 1986; Henry et al. 1995). These actions may have been established and carried out with no intent to harm members of a minority group. However, this does not mean that members of a minority group never experience the hostility of a bigot. It simply means that a more complete explanation must take into account the structure of institutions in our society, their linkages, and the norms that support the institutions. It is the pattern these institutional structures create that has a cumulative impact on certain groups and places them in a disadvantageous position. For example, the federal government's refusal to support aboriginal peoples' request for agricultural development at the turn of the century was based upon an economic rationale. Because aboriginals did not have access to other forms of capital, it permanently created a marginal population. This historical decision, which is no longer visible to people today, has had long-lasting impacts upon aboriginal people.

Until recently, overt, direct discrimination was common in many institutions within Canadian society. For example, many employers routinely refused to hire aboriginals. By the 1970s, however, human rights and antidiscrimination legislation brought about a substantial decrease in direct, individual discrimination against ethnic minorities. However, a commensurate increase in the social position of aboriginals had not been evidenced. Individual discrimination is not the sole explanation for the disadvantageous position in which aboriginals find themselves; other structural factors need to be investigated (Fleras and Elliott 1992).

Discrimination takes place in a variety of contexts, for example, employment, housing, or dating. Many people may not be in a position to carry out specific acts of discrimination; however, the existing structures allow for covert, indirect systematic (institutionalized) discrimination. In the arena of employment, recruitment practices, screening practices, terms and conditions of employment, and layoff practices are all areas in which institutional discrimination may take place. For example, aboriginals have not been able to move into blue and white collar jobs because of their lack of education, a condition brought about by the educational policies of the federal government. They have not been able to move into administrative positions because of seniority or tenure practices that were established years ago. Since employment procedures usually begin by world of mouth, and most employees are non-aboriginal, aboriginals do not fit into the existing network, and thus are excluded from even knowing about the potential pool of prospective jobs (McMillan 1988).

The mechanisms of discrimination in such areas as employment and housing are interlinked. When we add other institutional spheres in which discrimination can occur (e.g., education), we begin to see a seamless web that determines the life chances of all people. Going to the "right" school will link you to certain people and institutions. Having a particular job will structure your social relationships and link to further occupational choices. Put another way, living on a reserve will limit your mate selection, occupation, educational achievements, and life chances. Being able to "break out" of this web is difficult, as social structures continually impose limits to the boundaries of what people can and cannot do. Institutional structures in other areas of our lives—for example, courts, health systems, and the political process—are interrelated with education, employment, and housing. In the end, all the institutions of society are interconnected and have an impact on every individual's life chances. Aboriginals are part of this structure and are subject to the forces exerted by these institutional spheres.

The Normative Basis for Discrimination

Most Canadians agree that people in poverty need help to integrate into Canadian society. Most also would agree that a variety of social services need to be directed toward those in need. At the same time, however, instead of offering sympathy, being concerned, or offering help to aboriginals, we define the situation in such a way that they become responsible for their poverty, as though they deserve to be poor because of some individual defect. In short, we blame the victims. We are convinced that aboriginal people are poor, marginal members of society through their own fault. In the end, this ideology allows those who are not poor to relieve themselves of responsibility. It supports their inaction when it comes to helping poor people such as aboriginals. As Henry et al. (1995) point out, stereotypes are attached to visible minority groups, such as aboriginals, and they are then labelled as disreputable, deviant, lazy people.

There is also a tendency to blame social problems on individuals rather than on the social system. Most people define a social problem as behaviour that deviates from the norms and standards of society. Because we do not critically examine the way things are carried out in society, we tend to question the exceptions. The normative system that is taken for granted has, for most people, an aura of sacredness about it. Traditions and customs associated with the social system are generally evaluated ethnocentrically and then defined as the "right way." Logically, then, those who deviate from these norms are the source of trouble. The obvious question is, why do these people deviate from the norms? Because most people view themselves as law abiding, they feel those who deviate do so because of some kind of personal character defect or individual maladjustment.

Interpreting social problems solely within an individual framework has serious implications. First, it frees government, the business world, the justice system, and the educational system from any blame. This protection of the established social order against criticism makes it more difficult to change the dominant economic, social, and political institutions (Eitzen and Zinn 1989, 12–13). The approach of blaming the victim also enables the authorities to control deviants under the guise of being helpful. A social control mechanism of this approach is that it allows deviant individuals and groups to be controlled in a publicly acceptable manner. Deviants—whether they are criminals or social protesters—are dealt with by social control agents (e.g., police, educators) who are able to administer a number of "therapies" or sanctions to deal with the deviant. In the end, a victim-blame approach requires the individual to change, not the structure of society; it focusses attention on the individual, not on the institutional arrangements of organizations in society.

The victim-blame approach finds support in a certain logical fallacy. When we overgeneralize, using one or two striking examples to illustrate a general principle, we commit the *fallacy of dramatic instance*. The tendency to do so may be difficult to overcome because of the limited number of cases that make up an individual's personal experience. Thus, when people comment on the attributes of aboriginal people, it generally reflects their limited and biased personal experience, for example, of being accosted by an aboriginal outside a liquor store, or of seeing aboriginals intoxicated and near a pub. On the other hand, individuals will also note that a particular aboriginal person "made good" in the dominant society as an indication that it is possible for all aboriginals to become part of the larger society. If it is objected that this is an exception to the rule, it will be claimed that if one aboriginal person can make it, they all can!

Recently, however, the **Royal Commission on Aboriginal Peoples** has suggested actions that they feel will begin to untie the Gordian knot and allow aboriginal people to achieve self-determination.

Royal Commission on Aboriginal Peoples

In 1990, out of the embers of the Oka crisis, the federal government established a Royal Commission to investigate the position of aboriginal people in Canadian society and to make recommendations on how they could best integrate into mainstream society. Co-chaired by an Indian (George Erasmus), the commission completed its report seven years later. The report is comprehensive in nature, focussing on aboriginal health, land claims, self-government, economic development, housing, justice, and education. It recommends that federal spending on aboriginal people be increased from the current $7.5 billion to just over $11 billion per year, arguing that if additional expenditures are not made now, the resultant costs in twenty years will be more than double. For example, addressing the $3 billion housing crisis now will result in long-term savings after fifteen years. The Commission claims that expenditures in economic development and self-government will lead to long-term savings in welfare, while, at the same time, creating healthier communities.

The report is a pragmatic assessment and presents solutions to current problems facing aboriginal people. However, it was published at a time when both federal and provincial governments were enacting fiscal austerity programs, and the suggestion to spend more on aboriginal peoples did not resonate with current government spending restrictions. One year after the report was published, few of the recommendations presented by the Royal Commission have been enacted. The federal government argues that it is "way ahead" of the report in addressing the problems faced by aboriginal communities, and that many of its recommendations have already been addressed.

However, in early 1998 the federal government announced that it would contribute $700 million in new funding for aboriginal people and issue an apology for their treatment of aboriginal people. The specific allocation of the funds will range from compensation for abuse at residential schools (the healing fund)[18] to improving living conditions (e.g., education, training) on reserves. Half of the new funding will be directed toward improving aboriginal housing, health, and employment opportunities. These monies will accompany a four-part strategy put forth by the federal government (*Gathering Strength*), which will include building stronger communities and economies, strengthening aboriginal governance, and multi-year and core funding for aboriginal groups.

In addition, the federal government and the Assembly of First Nations agreed, in early 1998, to establish a new "nation-to-nation" relationship between the government and Indians on reserves. This agreement has angered other aboriginal groups (e.g., Inuit, Métis, off-reserve aboriginals) who were excluded from the negotiations. Given that nearly 60 percent of the aboriginal population is off-reserve, it is surprising that they were not included in the discussions. This agreement—which includes commitments to establish mechanisms for joint decision making, and a possible national tripartite process that would include the provinces—is the first time the federal government has accepted a "government-to-government" relationship with aboriginals.

Conclusions

The exposure of aboriginal people to both individual and systemic discrimination for an extended period has excluded them from full participation in Canadian society. The networks and linkages of institutions have formed a seamless web that has prevented aboriginals from benefiting from the improved quality of life that most Canadians have experienced over the past half century. While some of this discrimination has been dealt with by human rights legislation, forms of systemic discrimination still remain. As a result, aboriginals remain in the marginal sectors of our society and have had their culture systematically devalued. At the same time, the federal government has consistently advocated, under various guises, an assimilationist policy. The central policy implement, the Indian Act, reflects this ideology and continues to play an important role in the life of aboriginal people.

Many different programs have been implemented to deal with the "Indian problem," but they have not been successful. The government's inability to substantially alter the position of aboriginal people in Canadian society is indicative of the strength of institutional barriers and of their interconnectedness. Today government officials continue to develop policies that will maintain the marginal position of aboriginals in our society. Their focus on the individual and lack of concern over the institutions and their linkages suggest that any program developed to enhance the position of aboriginals will fail. On the other hand, innovative policies focussing on structural factors such as self-government and the transfer of power to band councils may bring about some changes for aboriginal peoples.

Nevertheless, as Sampson (1992) points out, the failure of the federal government to develop a policy to provide for the general enhancement of aboriginals and create a framework for self-government reflects a hidden agenda. This unspoken agenda includes the attenuation of aboriginal rights, particularly in the area of self-government. Overall, Canadian law has acted as a vehicle of **totalization**—juridical doctrine ordering all aspects of aboriginal peoples' lives (Kulchyski 1994)—emphasizing the principle of "delegated authority" that can unilaterally be withdrawn by the Crown.

Summary

- Recent Canadian polls suggest that Canadians view aboriginal people as being "just like themselves." They do not see this group of people as underskilled, impoverished, or having a quality of life less than their own.
- For those aboriginal people who are seen as part of the underside of Canadian society, most Canadians see their position as a result of their own fault.
- This chapter has shown that aboriginal people occupy the lowest rungs in almost every dimension of social life.
- As a consequence of their poor education and peripheral labour force participation, the income of aboriginal people is the lowest of all ethnic groups in the country.
- Historical decisions by the dominant groups have created an environment and structure that has kept aboriginal people from achieving success.
- Steps are being taken by aboriginal people to develop their land, enhance their self-worth, and take control of their lives. New structural arrangements are being negotiated, and aboriginal people are trying to establish some modicum of control.

Questions to Consider

1. How would you define an aboriginal? An Indian?

2. How would you characterize the relations between aboriginals and non-aboriginals historically? What about today?

3. Provide some evidence to show that aboriginal people do not have the same standard of living as most Canadians. Has this changed over time?

4. Why do aboriginals view land claims as important? How are they related to self-government?

5. What did the Royal Commission on Aboriginal Peoples have to say about Canadian society?

Suggested Readings

Frideres, J. *Aboriginal Peoples in Canada.* Scarborough: Prentice Hall Allyn and Bacon Canada, 1998.

Haig-Brown, C. *Taking Control: Power and Contradiction in First Nations Adult Education.* Vancouver: University of British Columbia Press, 1995.

Mallea, R. *Aboriginal Law: Apartheid in Canada.* Brandon, MB: Bearpaw Publishing, 1994.

Peters, E. *Aboriginal Self-Government in Urban Areas.* Kingston, ON: Queen's University, Institute of Intergovernmental Relations, 1994.

Morris, A. *The Treaties of Canada with the Indians of Manitoba and the Northwest Territories.* Toronto: Public Archives of Manitoba, 1880.

Glossary

aboriginal Refers to a category of people who define themselves as North American Indian, Métis, or Inuit.

civilizing policy A historic policy developed by the federal government with respect to aboriginal peoples in order to carry out assimilation.

discrimination Actions carried out by the dominant group that have a negative impact on members of a subordinate group.

Indian (North American Indian) A legal definition that includes any individual who meets the criteria to be registered by Indian Affairs.

Indian Act A legal statute that has been established by the Government of Canada and determines the legal rights, responsibilities, and obligations of Indians and the federal government.

land claims Aboriginal claims to land ownership. It also refers to the policy developed by the Canadian government regarding how disputes over land ownership will be settled.

Royal Commission on Aboriginal Peoples An ad hoc committee established by the federal government in 1991 to investigate aboriginal issues. It collected data, engaged in public discussion, and made recommendations to the Canadian government.

Royal Proclamation of 1763 When New France was ceded to the British Crown, the British issued a document confirming aboriginal land rights and outlining the procedures by which lands could be taken from Indians.

self-government Aboriginal claims to the right to develop governmental structures that will allow them to achieve the goal of greater autonomy and control over their lives.

totalization According to Kulchyski (1994), totalization is "the process by which objects, people, spaces, times, ways of thinking, and ways of seeing are ordered in accordance with a set of principles conducive to the accumulation of capital and the logic of the commodity form."

treaty Written documents identifying negotiated agreements between Indians and the Government of Canada.

Notes

1. It is important that the reader appreciate these changes in definitions. This is especially so when data are being compared over time or between different federal or provincial agencies. It is almost impossible to accurately compare statistics between agencies because of these changing definitions. In this chapter, statistics will be taken from Census Canada and Indian Affairs.
2. Indians are also referred to as status or registered Indians. Non-status Indians are not subject to the Indian Act nor do they have the same rights as Indians.
3. In these areas, while treaties have been signed, reserves have not been established. Land settlements have been resolved (partially) through comprehensive land claim settlements.
4. An excellent historical analysis of aboriginal–European relations, focussing on the Mikmaw, is presented in Henderson (1997).
5. This document has become an important component in the legal action aboriginals have taken against the federal government as they try to settle their land claims.
6. By the mid-1880s, the Beothuk of the Atlantic region had indeed been annihilated.
7. If the focus is on registered Indians, today nearly 40 percent live off-reserve.
8. It is estimated that about an additional 5 to 7 percent of non-aboriginal youth obtain their high-school equivalency by the time they reach 25.
9. Later, aboriginal centres at Canadian universities would be phased out or reduced in scope and content.
10. It should be noted that nearly 40 percent of aboriginals (on-reserve) work in government service industries, while only 7.7 percent of the total Canadian population work in this industry. Thus, the existing profile is substantially influenced by such an external force.
11. It should also be noted that only 60 percent of income to on-reserve aboriginals is from employment, while nearly 80 percent of the income for the general public is from employment.
12. This court case began more than 20 years ago and cost an estimated $20 million. Aboriginals argue that their rights are based upon the 1763 Royal Proclamation, which acknowledged that aboriginals own the lands they use and occupy until they are ceded to or purchased by the Crown.
13. The Commission was to be phased out in early 1999.
14. It costs $2.6 million to process an average land claim, with settlements averaging about $2.5 million.
15. In late February 1998, the province filed an appeal.
16. In fact, the Province of British Columbia is currently trying to force the Sechelt to relinquish powers given to them under the Sechelt Self-Government Act.
17. Recently the Province of Manitoba, the federal government, and the Indians of Manitoba negotiated an agreement that will see aboriginal communities carry out the activities previously enacted by the two level of governments.
18. Individuals will not receive compensation from this fund. They must launch individual lawsuits against the government in order to obtain individual compensation. To date, over 100 individual lawsuits have been settled, some for as much as $400 000.

References

Assembly of First Nations. 1988. *Tradition and Education: Towards a Vision of our Future. A Declaration of First Nations Jurisdiction of Education.* Ottawa: Assembly of First Nations.
———. 1990. *Towards Linguistic Justice for First Nations.* Ottawa: Assembly of First Nations.
Barsh, R. 1991. "Ecocide, Nutrition, and the 'Vanishing Indian.'" In *State Violence and Ethnicity,* ed. Pierre van den Berghe. Boulder, Colorado: University Press of Colorado. 221–51.

———. 1994. "Canada's Aboriginal Peoples: Social Integration or Disintegration?" *The Canadian Journal of Native Studies* 14, no. 1: 1–46.

Bartlett, R. 1988. *The Indian Act of Canada.* Saskatoon: Native Law Centre, University of Saskatchewan.

Battiste, M., and J. Barman. 1995. *First Nations Education in Canada: The Circle Unfolds.* Vancouver: University of British Columbia Press.

Bienvenue, R. 1985. "Colonial Status: The Case of Canadian Indians." In *Ethnicity and Ethnic Relations in Canada*, 2d ed., ed. R. Bienvenue and J. Goldstein. Toronto: Butterworths. 199–216.

Brooks, S. 1989. *Public Policy in Canada.* Toronto: McClelland and Stewart.

Buckley, H. 1992. *From Wooden Ploughs to Welfare: Why Indian Policy Failed in the Prairie Provinces.* Montreal and Kingston: McGill-Queens University Press.

Canada, Government of. 1990. *You Took My Talk.* House of Commons Standing Committee on Aboriginal Affairs, 4th Report. Ottawa: Queen's Printer.

———. 1994. *Profile of Canada's Aboriginal Population.* Ottawa: Statistics Canada. Cat. no. 94-325.

———. 1997. *Housing Need Among Off-Reserve Status Indian Households in Canada, 1991.* Research and Development Highlights, Socio-Economic Series, Issue #37. Ottawa.

Carter, S. 1990. *Lost Harvests.* Montreal and Kingston: McGill-Queen's University Press.

Cassidy, F., and N. Dale. 1988a. *After Native Claims?* Victoria, BC: Morriss Printing Company.

———. 1988b. *Alternative Claims? The Implications of Comprehensive Claims Settlements for Natural Resources in British Columbia.* Lantzvill, BC: Oolichan Books; Halifax, NS: Institute for Research on Public Policy.

Chiste, K., ed. 1996. *Aboriginal Small Business and Entrepreneurship in Canada.* Ottawa: Captus Press.

Dyck, N. 1997a. *Differing Visions.* Halifax: Fernwood Publishing.

———. 1997b. "Tutelage, Resistance and Co-optation in Canadian Indian Administration." *Canadian Review of Sociology and Anthropology* 34, no. 3: 333–48.

Eitzen, S., and M. Zinn. 1989. *Social Problems*, 4th ed. Boston: Allyn and Bacon.

Feagin, J., and C. Feagin. 1986. *Discrimination American Style,* 2d ed. Malabar, FL: Kriege Publishing.

Fleras, A., and J. Elliott. 1992. *The 'Nations Within': Aboriginal–State Relations in Canada, the United States, and New Zealand.* Toronto: Oxford University Press.

Frideres, J. 1998. *Aboriginal Peoples in Canada.* Scarborough: Prentice Hall Allyn and Bacon Canada.

George, P., and P. Kuhn. 1994. "The Size and Structure of Native–White Wage Differentials in Canada." *Canadian Journal of Economics* 27: 20–42.

Haig-Brown, C. 1995. *Taking Control: Power and Contradiction in First Nations Adult Education.* Vancouver: University of British Columbia Press.

Health and Welfare Canada. 1991a. *Health Status of Canadian Indians and Inuit, 1990.* Ottawa: Medical Services Branch, Minister of National Health and Welfare.

———. 1991b. *Statistical Profile of Native Mental Health.* Ottawa: Minister of National Health and Welfare.

Henderson, James. 1997. *The Mikmaw Concordat.* Halifax: Fernwood Publishing.

Henry, F., C. Tator, W. Mattis, and T. Rees. 1995. *The Colour of Democracy: Racism in Canadian Society.* Toronto: Harcourt Brace.

Isaac, T. 1995. *Aboriginal Law: Cases, Materials, and Commentary.* Saskatoon: Purich Publishing.

Kennedy, J. 1997. "Labrador Metis Ethnogenesis." *Ethnos* 62: 3–4, 5–24.

Kulchyski, P. 1994. *Unjust Relations: Aboriginal Rights in Canadian Courts.* Toronto: Oxford University Press.

Mallea, R. 1994. *Aboriginal Law: Apartheid in Canada.* Brandon, MB: Bearpaw Publishing.

McMillan, A. 1988. *Native Peoples and Cultures of Canada.* Vancouver: Douglas and McIntyre.

Morris, A. 1880. *The Treaties of Canada with the Indians of Manitoba and the Northwest Territories.* Toronto: Public Archives of Manitoba.

Pendakur, K., and R. Pendakur. 1995. *Earnings Differentials among Ethnic Groups in Canada.* Ottawa: Strategic Research and Analysis, Social Research Group, Department of Canadian Heritage.

Peters, E. 1994. *Aboriginal Self-Government in Urban Areas.* Kingston, ON: Queen's University, Institute of Intergovernmental Relations.

Royal Commission on Aboriginal Peoples. 1996. *People to People, Nation to Nation: Highlights from the Report of the Royal Commission on Aboriginal Peoples.* Ottawa: Minister of Supply and Services.

Sampson, F. 1992. "An Historical Consideration of Ontario Aboriginal Policy." In *Co-Existence? Studies in Ontario First Nations Relations,* ed. B. Hodgins, S. Heard, and J. Milloy. Peterborough, ON: Trent University, First Centre for Canadian Heritage and Development Studies.

Siggner, A. 1986. "The Sociodemographic Conditions of Registered Indians." *Canadian Social Trends* (Winter): 2–9.

Statistics Canada. 1994. *Profile of Canada's Aboriginal Population.* Cat. 94-325. Ottawa: Government of Canada.

Task Force to Review Comprehensive Claims Policy. 1985. *Living Treaties: Lasting Agreements.* Report of the Task Force to Review Comprehensive Claims Policy. Ottawa: Department of Indian Affairs and Northern Development.

Taylor-Henley, S., and P. Hudson. 1992. "Aboriginal Self-Government and Social Services: First Nations–Provincial Relationships." *Canadian Public Policy* 18, no. 1: 13–26.

Thomas, R. 1966–67. "Powerless Politics." *New University Thought* 4: 44–53.

Trelease, A. 1960. *Indian Affairs in Colonial New York: The Seventeenth Century.* New York: Random House.

Trigger, B. 1986. "The Historians' Indian: Native Americans in Canada in Canadian Historical Writing from Charlevoix to the Present." *Canadian Historical Review* 67, no. 3: 315–42.

Wax, M. 1971. *Indian Americans.* Englewood Cliffs, NJ: Prentice-Hall.

CHAPTER 9

Multiculturalism, Ethnic Identity, and Inequality

K. Victor Ujimoto

Learning Objectives

After studying this chapter, you should be able to
- Outline the most significant aspects of the policy of **multiculturalism**, from its inception in 1971 to its proclamation in the Canadian **Multiculturalism Act** in 1988.
- Understand the different ways in which the concept of multiculturalism has been interpreted.
- Assess the positive contributions of the policy of multiculturalism in promoting linguistic and cultural problems, and its limitations in solving problems of **racism** and racial **inequality**, which require the removal of structural and institutional barriers.
- Assess how the policy of multiculturalism is adjusting to the changing realities of global economics.
- Appraise the changing demographic profile of urban Canada and its implications for cultural pluralism.
- Assess the key variables that may impact on Canadian **citizenship** and perceived divided loyalties.

Introduction

An examination of recent immigration trends in Canada reveals that more and more immigrants are coming from Asia, Africa, and South America than from the traditional immigrant source countries in Europe. Residents of centres such as Montreal, Toronto, and Vancouver do not have to consult government statistics to recognize the changing demographic composition of Canadian society. Along with this demographic change go cultural and social changes as well. The heterogeneous nature of Canadian society was recognized by the Canadian government in 1971 when it announced its policy on multiculturalism. How did this policy come about and what was its impact on the various ethnic groups in Canada? In this chapter we shall examine some of the salient aspects of multiculturalism as a state policy from the time of its original announcement through to its ultimate proclamation in the Canadian Multiculturalism Act in 1988.

In announcing the government policy on multiculturalism on October 8, 1971, prime minister Pierre Elliott Trudeau stated the following in the House of Commons:

> National unity, if it is to mean anything in the deeply personal sense, must be founded on confidence in one's own individual identity; out of this can grow respect for that of others and a willingness to share ideas, attitudes and assumptions. A vigorous policy of multiculturalism will help create this initial confidence. It can form the base of a society which is based on fair play for all.

This recognition of the diversity of Canadian society occurred after many decades of debate over the question of relations between English and French, culminating in the appointment of the Royal Commission on Bilingualism and Biculturalism. Burnet (1987, 67) has observed that ethnic independence movements were active throughout the world and Quebec was already caught up in the growing nationalism. The federal government's response was to establish the royal commission, which was asked to make recommendations on "what steps should be taken to develop the Canadian Confederation on the basis of an equal partnership between the two founding races." At the same time, the terms of reference of the royal commission referred to "the contribution made by other ethnic groups to the cultural enrichment of Canada, and the measures that should be taken to safeguard that contribution."

The Royal Commission on Bilingualism and Biculturalism was "to deal with other ethnic groups only as they affected English–French relations" (Burnet 1987, 68). Although only eight ethnic groups made written submissions on the cultural contributions of their respective ethnic groups, it soon became evident that many more ethnic groups wanted to be recognized. The resulting Book 4 of the report of the commission was therefore devoted to the history, economic structure, social patterns, and the maintenance of language and culture of many other ethnic groups. The final report, which was released in March 1970, recommended that "the teaching of languages other than English and French, and cultural subjects related to them, be incorporated as options in the public elementary school programme, where there is sufficient demand for such classes." One of the many difficulties to be encountered later in taking action on this recommendation was that educational matters were within the jurisdiction of the provinces; consequently, the introduction of new curriculum material varied from province to province.

On October 8, 1971, the federal government's response to Book 4 was to accept all of the recommendations and to proclaim a policy of multiculturalism. Burnet (1987, 68) has summarized the essential aspects of the government response as follows, in a passage taken from the debate held in the House of Commons:

> First, resources permitting, the government will seek to assist all Canadian cultural groups that have demonstrated a desire and effort to continue to develop a capacity to grow and contribute to Canada, and a clear

need for assistance, the small and weak groups no less than the strong and highly organized.

Second, the government will assist members of all cultural groups to overcome cultural barriers to full participation in Canadian society.

Third, the government will promote creative encounters and inter-change among all Canadian cultural groups in the interests of national unity.

Fourth, the government will continue to assist immigrants to acquire at least one of Canada's official languages in order to become full partici-pants in Canadian society.

In order to implement the policy of multiculturalism, the government established six programs: programs for the federal cultural agencies—for example, the National Museum of Man, National Library, Public Archives, and National Film Board; pro-grams for the teaching of official languages; programs for Canadian ethnic studies and ethnic histories, and the culture development program; and other multicultural grants to support the development of various cultures and languages. Initially, these programs were targeted to the "other ethnic groups" (other than anglophones and francophones); however, the policy of multiculturalism applies to all groups today. Individuals "drawn from forty-seven ethnocultural backgrounds" constituted the first Canadian Consultative Council on Multiculturalism, whose specific mandate was to advise the minister responsible for multiculturalism. Since then, several other com-mittees have emerged to establish both short-term and long-term priorities for multi-cultural policy and research. Short-term priorities dealt with the establishment of local community cultural centres or multicultural centres, and facilitating the arts, ethnic press, and media in a multicultural society. Long-term issues that have been addressed concern federal–provincial policy on language and cultural retention.

Since the introduction of the policy on multiculturalism in 1971, much has been accomplished at various levels. At the community level, there has been active partic-ipation in various ethnocultural activities. Multicultural centres have been established in many locations, including some communities that are quite small. At the provin-cial level, formal organizations have been established to co-ordinate diverse multi-cultural activities. The Ontario Multicultural Association/Association Multiculturelle de l'Ontario (OMAMO), the Multicultural Council of Saskatchewan, and the Affiliation of Multicultural Societies and Service Agencies (AMSSA) of British Columbia are specific examples. At the national level, the Multiculturalism Directorate of the Department of the Secretary of State has initiated several research and publication projects, such as the non-official languages study by O'Bryan, Reitz, and Kuplowska (1976) and the studies on attitudes toward multiculturalism conduct-ed by Berry, Kalin, and Taylor (1977). Recent publications by Fleras and Elliott (1992; 1996), Hryniuk (1992), Satzewich (1992), Kymlicka (1995; 1997), and Henry et al. (1995) have made significant contributions to our understanding of multicul-turalism. More recently, the inclusion of multiculturalism as an important component in developing health policies and programs has been advanced by Masi, Mensah, and McLeod (1993), Ujimoto (1994), Yeo and Gallagher-Thompson (1996), Helman (1997), and Markides and Miranda (1997). These publications and others enabled members of the ethnocultural communities to examine their place in Canadian society and to strengthen their own **ethnic identity**.

The Concept of Multiculturalism and Ethnic Identity

Multiculturalism as a concept has been viewed in several different ways since its introduction. First, as Kallen (1982, 51) has observed, the term *multiculturalism* has been used "to refer to the 'social reality' of ethnic diversity." As a reflection of the cultural diversity of Canadian society, multiculturalism as a state policy has legitimized the values, norms, beliefs, and identity of ethnic groups. A development concomitant with cultural pluralism has been the questioning of the meaning of assimilation. In a pluralistic society, what are the dominant values to which people are expected to assimilate or acculturate? Kallen observes that "people are coming to the realization that their own personal dignity is bound up with the collective dignity of their ethnic community." In contemporary Canadian society, then, multiculturalism has served to facilitate the individual's identity as well as that of the ethnic community.

A second way in which multiculturalism has been used, as described by Kallen (1982, 51), is "to refer to the federal government policy designed to create national unity in ethnic diversity." She notes that several assumptions are rooted in this model of multiculturalism. The first assumption is that "members of all ethnocultural collectivities are both able and willing to maintain their ethnocultural distinctiveness." The second is that "levels of **prejudice** and **discrimination** between ethnic collectivities are low enough to allow mutual tolerance." The third assumption is that there is a "rough equivalence in the distribution of power among the various ethnic collectivities, so that no one population can assume dominance and control over others." Finally, the model assumes that "members of the different ethnic collectivities in society will mutually agree to limit and control the extent, spheres and nature of interaction between them." Given all of these assumptions, Kallen argues that interethnic relations would take the form of ethnic segmentation and that every citizen's identity would "become hyphenated, i.e., ethnic-national, with equal weights on both sides of the hyphen."

A third way in which multiculturalism has been used, according to Kallen (1982, 51), is "to refer to the ideology of cultural pluralism (the Canadian mosaic) underlying the federal policy." She observes that "unlike the ideal model of cultural pluralism which assumes that every individual and group desires to maintain a distinctive ethnic identity and heritage," the Canadian policy of multiculturalism recognizes the freedom of individuals to choose their own affiliations either within or outside their own ethnic collectivities. In addressing those ethnocultural groups that have the desire or possess the organizational abilities to develop their own traditional cultures, the Multiculturalism Directorate of the Secretary of State will facilitate or assist them to meet their objectives. As noted earlier, the government will also assist members of the various ethnic groups to participate fully in the social, economic, cultural, and political spheres of Canadian society. Some ethnic groups, however, must still overcome barriers before they can become fully integrated members of Canadian society.

Multiculturalism: Myth or Reality

Since its proclamation in 1971, multiculturalism as a state policy has been examined and debated by the public and by members of the academic community. The complexities of the issues surrounding multiculturalism will become obvious when we consider some of the arguments advanced by Canadian scholars. At a conference held at the University of Alberta in 1975, Burnet (1981, 44) noted that although the

---

Interpreting Multiculturalism

The concept of multiculturalism is still not very well understood by Canadians today, some 25 years since the adoption of the multiculturalism policy. Fleras and Elliott (1996, 324) note that the essence of multiculturalism cannot be captured by any simple definition. They suggest that distinctions must be made "between multiculturalism as a 'thing' or as a 'process' or as a 'condition.'" Thus, multiculturalism can be interpreted at different levels as illustrated in the table below.

Levels of Interpretation of Multiculturalism

Multiculturalism as fact	Multiculturalism as ideology	Multiculturalism as policy	Multiculturalism as process
Empirical description of ethnic reality in Canada	Prescriptive statement of what ought to be—a set of ideas and ideals that extol the virtues of tolerance and diversity	Accommodation of diversity through explicit state initiatives: (a) celebrating differences, (b) managing diversity, and (c) citizenship and belonging	Manipulation by political sectors (multiculturalism means business) and minority sectors (culture + equality)

Source: A. Fleras and J.L. Elliott, *Unequal Relations: An Introduction to Race, Ethnic and Aboriginal Dynamics in Canada*, 2d ed. (Scarborough: Prentice Hall Canada, 1996), p. 326. Reprinted with permission of Prentice Hall Canada, Inc.

Multiculturalism as Fact

Multiculturalism as fact essentially reflects, like the first of Kallen's three models (1982, 51), the social reality of ethnic diversity. This reality is based on official Statistics Canada census data. For example, the ethnic diversity of Canadian society according to the 1996 Census of Canada, as reported by Mitchell (1998, A1), is illustrated in the charts on the next page. These data simply illustrate the proportion of Canadians who indicated their ethnic heritage; they do not inform us about the various characteristics of the ethnic groups except to note that their presence can no longer be ignored.

(continued)

(continued)

Visible Minorities in Canada, 1996

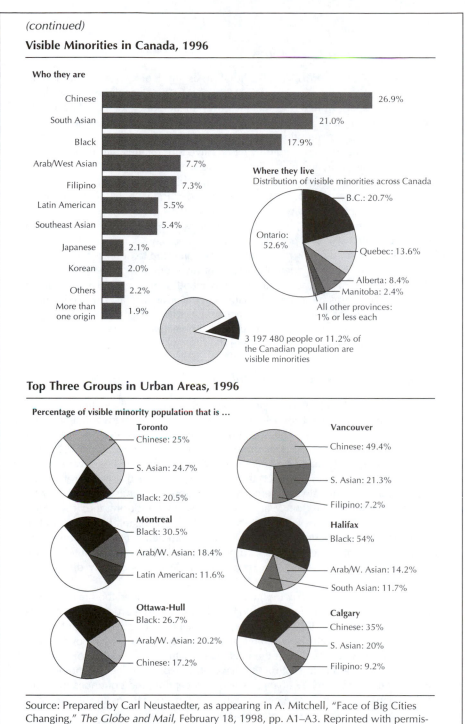

Who they are

Chinese	26.9%
South Asian	21.0%
Black	17.9%
Arab/West Asian	7.7%
Filipino	7.3%
Latin American	5.5%
Southeast Asian	5.4%
Japanese	2.1%
Korean	2.0%
Others	2.2%
More than one origin	1.9%

Where they live
Distribution of visible minorities across Canada

- B.C.: 20.7%
- Ontario: 52.6%
- Quebec: 13.6%
- Alberta: 8.4%
- Manitoba: 2.4%
- All other provinces: 1% or less each

3 197 480 people or 11.2% of the Canadian population are visible minorities

Top Three Groups in Urban Areas, 1996

Percentage of visible minority population that is ...

Toronto
- Chinese: 25%
- S. Asian: 24.7%
- Black: 20.5%

Vancouver
- Chinese: 49.4%
- S. Asian: 21.3%
- Filipino: 7.2%

Montreal
- Black: 30.5%
- Arab/W. Asian: 18.4%
- Latin American: 11.6%

Halifax
- Black: 54%
- Arab/W. Asian: 14.2%
- South Asian: 11.7%

Ottawa-Hull
- Black: 26.7%
- Arab/W. Asian: 20.2%
- Chinese: 17.2%

Calgary
- Chinese: 35%
- S. Asian: 20%
- Filipino: 9.2%

Source: Prepared by Carl Neustaedter, as appearing in A. Mitchell, "Face of Big Cities Changing," *The Globe and Mail*, February 18, 1998, pp. A1–A3. Reprinted with permission from *The Globe and Mail*.

(continued)

(continued)

Multiculturalism as Ideology

In Fleras and Elliott's terms, "multiculturalism as an ideology refers to a norma-tive statement of 'what ought to be'" (1996, 326). This is analogous to Kallen's second model, in which "the federal government policy designed to create national unity in ethnic diversity" (1982, 251). However, Fleras and Elliott add several additional assumptions to those of Kallen. First, it is assumed that "minority cultures can constitute living and lived-in realities that impart mean-ing and security to adherents at times of stress or social change" (1996, 326). Cultural differences, in other words, are compatible with national goals.

The second assumption noted by Fleras and Elliott is that "multiculturalism does not downgrade diversity as contrary to the goals of national unity or socio-economic progress" (1996, 326). That is, cultural diversity should be accepted as an equal and integral aspect of the national ideology.

The third, and perhaps most important, assumption to address today and in the future is "the open minded philosophy firmly grounded on the principles of tolerance and mutual respect" (Fleras and Elliott 1996, 327). This statement should be treated as a worthwhile national educational goal. It would further enhance individual self-esteem by facilitating ethnic identity as an integral aspect of Canadian culture. As an educational objective, mutual respect can be enhanced while reducing prejudice and discrimination.

Multiculturalism as Federal Policy

Although multiculturalism as a federal policy has received much attention since the promulgation of the 1988 Multiculturalism Act, various government initia-tives on ethnic relations can be traced back to the 1940s. A report prepared for the Corporate Review Board, Department of Canadian Heritage (1996, 12) notes that the federal government sought ethnic support for the Canadian war effort in 1942. It must be noted, however, that such support over the years from some ethnic groups was not always welcome. For example, Japanese Canadians who had volunteered for the Boer War were rejected. Again, during the First World War, Japanese Canadians were not able to enlist in the Canadian army, but in 1916, they received permission from Ottawa to commence military training and to organize the Japanese Volunteer Corps (Ujimoto 1983, 133). Volunteering for army service at the outset of the Second World War was equally difficult for Japanese Canadians.

The federal initiatives on multiculturalism as it was understood in the 1950s and 1960s emphasized naturalization and citizenship participation, and as Canadian Heritage (1996, 12) reports, government policies were meant to fur-ther recognize cultural diversity and national unity issues. The recognition of cultural diversity was based on the inadequate nature of the policy of assimila-tion. As Fleras and Elliott (1996, 330) have observed, the policy of multicultur-alism has undergone many changes since its inception and continues to adjust to the changing realities of globalization. The transformations in the policy of multiculturalism can best be assessed as a social change process.

(continued)

(continued)

Multiculturalism as Process

The changes in multiculturalism policies can be observed through the various programs administered by the Department of Multiculturalism and Citizenship over the years. In the 1970s, the major thrust of the multicultural programs was to celebrate cultural diversity. This was most appropriate for the period as many new immigrants still retained their own cultural language, customs, and ethnic identity. These government initiatives facilitated various ethnic groups in retaining their cultural heritage, while assisting immigrants to adjust to and overcome cultural barriers in Canadian society. The celebration of multicultural festivals enabled ethnocultural groups to participate together and to create new meanings for Canadian citizenship through cultural diversity. A decade later, federal multiculturalism policy encouraged ethnocultural communities to articulate their own goals. The major task for the multiculturalism directorate was to create and manage the new institutions and changing social structures of Canadian society. The principle of equality naturally meant addressing issues of prejudice, discrimination, and racism. Various objectives were established to manage cultural diversity through race relations programs.

Canada became the first country to endow multiculturalism with legal authority through the interpretation of the 1982 Charter of Rights (Fleras and Elliott 1996, 333). The Canadian Multiculturalism Act of July 12, 1988, officially recognized the principles of institutional accommodation, and the promotion of the cultural and racial diversity of Canadian society.

The enhancement of multiculturalism is now an integral component of federal legislation such as the Constitution of Canada, the Canadian Charter of Rights and Freedoms, the Citizenship Act, as well as the Canadian Race Relations Foundation, which was established in 1996. Gradual institutional accommodation of ethnocultural members is occurring in many government departments such as Agriculture Canada, Environment Canada, Industry Canada, and Statistics Canada. The degree of institutional accommodation across Canada is yet to be established [at the time this article was written] with the 1996 Census of Canada.

use of the term *multiculturalism* was "less dangerous than the use of multiracialism," there were problems with the term. It is a very imprecise term, Burnet observed, one that is used in several different ways even among social scientists; in addition, this term "emphasizes the past." Burnet argued that the ambiguity in the word *multiculturalism* was created by "the ambiguity between culture as separateness and culture as distinctiveness." In general, Burnet recognizes the very essence of culture as "a reference to the recurrent, to tradition, to heritage," but pointed out that in the modern world even complete and living cultures undergo change. Since much of multiculturalism has to do with the retention or preservation of traditional culture, Burnet noted, we do not have a clear understanding of whether it is the collective heritage or the particular heritage of individuals that has to be maintained.

Concerning this issue, it should be noted that for some ethnic groups in Canada, such as the Japanese Canadians, there are other complications in that there are distinct intergenerational differences. Only the *issei*, or immigrant generation, was socialized in the living traditional culture of Japan. For the *nisei*, or second-generation Japanese Canadians, only a small proportion of those who were born before the Second World War possessed any knowledge of the folk customs and traditions of their parents. Because of political and historical circumstances, such as their internment, there were interruptions in the educational and socialization processes of the *nisei*; this necessitated a relearning of, or reintroduction to, traditional Japanese culture at a later time, when it became fashionable to re-examine one's **cultural heritage** and ethnic identity.

Over the years, a number of studies have used the concepts of **ethnicity** and multiculturalism in a similar vein. Peter (1981, 56) notes that both of these terms have been characterized by emphasizing such concepts as "ethnic identity, emerging ethnic boundaries, ethnic boundary markers, ethnic recognition," and he takes issue with Burnet's interpretation of multiculturalism. According to Peter, Burnet holds that

> multiculturalism within a bilingual framework can work if it is interpreted as is intended—that is, as encouraging those members of ethnic groups who want to do so to maintain a proud sense of the contribution of their own group to Canadian society. Interpreted in this way, it becomes something very North American: voluntary marginal differentiation among peoples who are equal participants in the society. If it is interpreted in the second way—as enabling various peoples to transfer foreign cultures and languages as living wholes into a new place and time—multiculturalism is doomed.

Concerning the above quotation, what is at issue for Peter is the assumption that "there is such a thing as a Canadian society which exists more or less independently of ethnic groups and toward whose development ethnic groups are encouraged to make their various contributions," Peter argues that it is "perhaps more justifiable to claim that the interaction of various ethnic groups, including the multiethnic English and French speakers, in fact does constitute Canadian society." Peter asks: "Why is there always the assumption that ethnic groups are somehow outside the mainstream of Canadian society; that they need to make selected contributions, etc.?" He answers his own questions by noting the distribution of political power among various groups in Canadian society today. Peter (1981, 57) argues that multiculturalism presented as a liberal policy is essentially a policy of "ethnic group containment" and that ethnic groups are "steered away from any contact with political and economic powers and are neutralized in their role as providers of individual satisfaction."

The relationship between ethnicity and power has been examined by Isajiw (1978, 33), who draws our attention to the fact that social mobility and occupational competition may lead to a greater awareness of one's ascriptive characteristics, or ethnicity. This awareness may eventually transcend the private sphere and move into the much broader political environment. Before this can occur, however, there must be a restructuring of institutional arrangements within both the ethnic community and Canadian society at large, as institutional arrangements define the position of ethnic groups in the hierarchy of power relationships. Peter (1981, 59) faults Isajiw and other sociologists for not taking their analysis of ethnicity in terms of power and politics any farther. This reluctance of theirs to deal with ethnicity in terms of power and politics, Peter argues, is "proportionate to their commitment to the policies of bilingualism and multiculturalism, and ultimately to the concept of Canadian unity as proposed by the Liberal government."

He advances several good reasons why this should be so. One reason stems from the fact that Quebec was actively seeking independence, and thus the possibility of providing additional fuel to an already simmering issue was avoided at all costs. What this situation really indicated was the very fragile nature of Canadian Confederation at this time. The gravity of the situation appears to have been weighed subsequently in typical Canadian fashion by the creation of the Task Force on Canadian Unity. Peter argues that the task force "felt it necessary to deal with those factors which the B. and B. report desperately tried to avoid—the nature and distribution of political powers in Canada" and questions why "neither French Canada nor Canada's diverse ethnic groups could be pacified by the bilingual-multicultural policy."

Peter lists two main purposes that the Canadian government policy of multiculturalism within a bilingual framework was intended to serve:

1. The policy of bilingualism was at once an appeasement policy toward a revitalised Quebec and a containment policy regarding its claim to political power.
2. The policy of multiculturalism served as a device to legitimize the continued dominance of the ruling English-speaking elite and secure its position in society at a time when its position was threatened by Quebec's claim to political power on the one hand and by the economic and cultural vitality of ethnic groups on the other hand.

He argues that the very essence of the Bilingualism and Biculturalism report was "to obscure the French Canadian challenge to political power and deflect it into linguistic and cultural directions." The reference to the development of "the Canadian Confederation on the basis of an equal partnership" could be construed as referring to "a redistribution of political powers on the basis of equality between French and English Canadians" (Peter 1981, 60). It appears, however, that this interpretation of the term "equal partnership" was diverted to cover only the linguistic and cultural dimensions of equality. Similarly, in the matter of ethnic politics, Peter argues that multiculturalism was "mainly intended to buy off the compliance of ethnic groups and thereby legitimize and justify the B. and B. policy." This was neatly achieved by "modernizing the traditional conception of ethnicity as an element standing somewhat outside the mainstream of Canadian society, from which individuals were expected to graduate in order to become full-fledged Canadians." This expectation on the part of the dominant groups meant they never seriously considered ethnic groups as competition for power, status, and resources. As Peter has cogently argued, "bilingualism, biculturalism and multiculturalism were based on a model of ethnic acquiescence to the rule of the dominant groups, forestalling all ethnic self-assertion in the form of ethnic interest groups." Although it is beyond the scope of the present chapter, there are similarities to be observed in the political dimensions of the Bilingualism and Biculturalism Commission, the Task Force on Canadian Unity, and the deliberations on the Meech Lake Accord. While the accord took into account the "distinct society" aspects of Quebec, it did not recognize multiculturalism, aboriginal rights, the equality of all Canadians (for example, the equality of men and women), and the commitment of Canadian society to fundamental rights and freedoms.

Globalization and Multiculturalism: Their Impact on Citizenship

The influence of global economics as well as international politics on Canadian society has not only altered our traditional immigration pattern, but it has also elevated our general awareness and knowledge of events outside of Canadian society. As Samuel and Schachhuber (1995, 23) have observed, new patterns of communications and intercultural relations have also taken place. Social change is a gradual and extremely slow process and it can occur only if the appropriate framework for change is already established. The Multiculturalism Act of 1988 provided the basic foundations that facilitated subsequent social change to be accommodated. This fact is not understood or appreciated by many critics of multiculturalism.

Criticisms that multiculturalism did not provide adequate social and political accommodations for ethnic minorities are important to note. It must be understood, however, that social and cultural change and subsequent political change cannot be achieved overnight. At best, such social change is an inter-generational process that takes at least several decades. Japanese Canadians, for example, were once categorized as "enemy aliens" and deprived of their civil rights but can now claim that their second- and third-generation Canadians have an interethnic marriage rate approximating 80 percent.

Globalization and the role of information technology are also important factors to consider. Today, Canadians are finally waking up to the reality of global business, and thus the "Team Canada" approach to foreign markets has been developed by the federal and provincial governments in co-operation with the corporate business sector. Many recent entrepreneurial-class immigrants to Canada are now serving an important facilitator role to bridge the cultural, social, and political gaps between Canada and various Pacific Rim countries. This "Team Canada" approach was also employed to establish economic links with the newly emerging Eastern European countries. It is too early to judge its success or failure, but it has served as a stimulus for many Canadians to request more courses in our educational system to reflect the new reality of global human resources development and intercultural communication.

While the globalization of our economy has led Canadian educators to introduce international content in social science courses, the lack of concurrent emphasis on Canadian citizenship has become readily apparent. The balance between the appreciation of one's cultural heritage and of Canadian citizenship must be restored if multiculturalism is not to become a divisive factor in Canadian society. Information technology that once greatly facilitated business transactions between Canada and the new immigrant's homeland has also enabled new immigrants to remain in constant touch with their homeland. Since international communications today can be accomplished instantaneously, new immigrants to Canada have been able to maintain their previous cultural, social,

(continued)

(continued)

and political ties. To what extent are the civic responsibilities of new Canadians with Canada? This very important question cannot be answered at this present juncture; however, there are specific examples in recent years in which the issue of divided loyalties has been manifested in Canada. Bissoondath quotes a CBC news report that "stated that an estimated 250 sons of Croatian immigrants, young men of able body and (presumably) sound mind, had left this country to take up arms in defence of Croatia" (1993, 375). This is, of course, a great contrast to the situation over half a century ago when Japanese Canadians were prevented from volunteering their services in the Canadian army.

There are several variables to consider when examining situations that may lead to perceived divided loyalties. First, from a sociological perspective, the age of the individual at the time of emigration will have a considerable influence on the extent, content, and commitment of loyalties formed. Second, the degree to which individuals were socialized in the values, beliefs, and customs of their ethnic homeland may also contribute to divided loyalties. Third, the lack of emphasis on the obligations of Canadian citizenship will also tend to dilute a sense of loyalty or commitment to Canada. This latter situation is compounded by the fact that in some cases, individuals may be holding dual citizenship rights and their degree of commitment to one country may depend on the economic or political situations of the other country in which they hold their citizenship rights.

Another issue that centres on divided loyalties concerns recent refugees to Canada. Often, refugees to Canada appear to be more interested in the politics of their homelands than in becoming Canadian citizens. Perhaps this is to be expected, as many have left their close relatives behind. Their appreciation of Canadian society will come with time, as they become resocialized through Canadian citizenship education and achieve a sense of belonging in their new Canadian environment.

Multiculturalism and Inequality

It has been noted above that when the Royal Commission on Bilingualism and Biculturalism was established, there was already a political movement in Quebec seeking independence. A concomitant development based on social changes that were occurring within the Native Canadian communities was the "Red Power" movement. The government at the time did not view Native Canadian issues to be as important as those of French Canada. As Burnet (1987, 67) has noted, the government did not establish a royal commission to address Native Canadian demands, but instead appointed a committee of anthropologists to report on selected Native issues. The extent to which Native Canadian issues were viewed as being peripheral to central Canadian issues was reflected in the failure to address aboriginal rights in the Meech Lake Accord. Furthermore, it is noted by Burnet that the Hawthorn–Tremblay report dealt with only about a quarter of the Indian, Inuit, and Métis people.

The words "equal partnership" that were included in the mandate of the Bilingualism and Biculturalism Commission obviously referred to the two founding peoples. However, the extent to which the concept of equality can be generalized to other ethnic groups remains unclear. It can be argued that some ethnic groups, particularly those belonging to the visible minorities, are particularly disadvantaged. Perhaps an example will illustrate this. While it is true that the policy of multiculturalism attempts to facilitate the retention and development of one's culture and language, not all ethnic groups are capable of applying for the available government support. Some groups have many members who are well educated and possess the necessary skills and organizational abilities to take advantage of government programs, while other groups, such as the more recent refugee arrivals in Canada, are not very well equipped to do so. Furthermore, not all groups have access to the information required for applying for government support in the first place. In those instances where ethnic minorities do manage to apply for grants, these grant applications will very likely be rejected because the evaluation criteria often do not coincide with the needs of the ethnic community that made the grant application. As Peter (1981, 58) has noted, it is the classic case of a relationship in which one group defines the rules of the game to which the other group, in this case the ethnic minority, must comply.

Another inequality stems from the fact that not all ethnic groups are equally represented in Canadian society. Thus, although the government may provide financial support to some ethnic groups, that support is based essentially on the strength of the community, which in turn is based on its membership size. This implies that small ethnocultural groups will not be able to maintain their language and culture to the same extent as the larger ethnic groups. This differential ability of ethnocultural groups to maintain their language and culture will thus have an impact on the maintenance of their ethnic identity as well.

A crucial variable to examine in our analysis of the relationship between multiculturalism and inequality is the degree to which multicultural education is available in our schools. As noted previously, educational matters fall within the jurisdiction of the provincial governments and thus the development of multicultural curricula varies across the country. Through the federal government policy of multiculturalism, funds have been made available to relevant provincial departments for the teaching of languages other than English and French. However, Mazurek (1983, 27) has observed that not all ethnic groups are represented in the curriculum. Those immigrant groups that are numerous and well organized and who are able to exert some political leverage on the provincial departments of education have been the most successful in securing a place in the curriculum for their languages, courses in their history, and other subjects. At present, Ontario, Manitoba, Saskatchewan, and Alberta have taken the lead in providing multicultural education; however, all provinces have now taken some initiatives in multicultural education. Because educational matters remain a provincial responsibility, a universal curriculum is not foreseen. However, there is a considerable amount of information exchange on curricula between provinces. It must be noted in passing that while the federal government has provided support for non-official languages, Rocher (1984, 45) has observed that no federal support has been given in establishing French education outside of Quebec. Rocher is concerned that, in Montreal, the policy of multiculturalism within a bilingual framework has already resulted in a bilingualism that is English–Greek, English–Italian, and English–German rather than the English–French bilingualism desired by the Montreal school boards.

Multiculturalism: Continuing Challenges

The present debate in Canada on language, cultural pluralism, and education will continue into the future (Hryniuk 1992). The divisive issues may be further exacerbated if our political leaders do not comprehend the main principles of earlier pieces of legislation such as the Canadian Constitution of 1982, the Charter of Rights and Freedoms, the controversial Quebec language legislation in Bill 101, and the implications of the failure of the Meech Lake Accord. Many of our current problems stem from the fact that we have addressed each of the issues concerning language, cultural pluralism, and education as separate entities rather than as interrelated aspects of Canadian society. How else can one explain that the separate institutional arrangements at various government levels—federal, provincial, and municipal or county—often work to the disadvantage of one another? We have now arrived at a point in our nation building that we should think more systemically, that is, in terms of interdependencies and reciprocal relationships between various levels of government and other institutions in this society. This would help avoid duplication of programs, eliminate contradictory policies, and provide a framework for addressing, in a comprehensive manner, linguistic, cultural, educational, and constitutional issues, and contributing to national unity and nation building.

Mallea (1984, 1) informs us that in our public schools very little progress has been made in adopting a more positive stance toward other languages and cultures; rather, the public schools have gone out of their way to eradicate them. There seems to be far greater appreciation of the assimilation and conformity models than the multicultural model of Canadian society. There must be a far greater emphasis on the desirability of cross-cultural understanding and harmony as an integral aspect of the "capacity to grow and contribute to Canada," one of the key statements in the original policy on multiculturalism (Ujimoto 1982, 111). Instead, the leaders of the ethnocultural communities have taken to political action to seek better representation for their particular groups. This works only for those able to mount a political lobby and to mobilize community resources. This mobilization is often at the expense of individual interests and also risks the possible segmentation of ethnic communities.

An important intervening factor affecting cultural pluralism in Canada today is the economic trend toward globalization. The economic dimension of multiculturalism is a new force yet to be reckoned with in the global information society. Today, business transactions occur worldwide quite instantaneously, and the federal government has been quick to realize the advantages of the linguistic skills and cross-cultural business expertise possessed by members of the ethnocultural communities. While these potential ethnocultural resources are just beginning to be felt, counter-productive forces are also developing that threaten to erode the vital progress achieved thus far.

One such development is the immigration criteria recently proposed in the report *Not Just Numbers: A Canadian Framework for Future Immigration*, the release of which has created considerable furor across the country. One of its recommendations is that "the core standard for official language ability should be proficiency (meaning a level of fluency sufficient to enter the Canadian labour force) in at least one of the two official languages" (Immigration Legislative Review 1997, 20). Members of several ethnic minority communities have perceived this recommendation to be quite similar to the sinister legislation passed in British Columbia in an earlier era to stem immigration from China, Japan, and India.

That legislation, passed in British Columbia between 1897 and 1906, was based on the Natal Act of 1897, which Australia adopted at the urging of Joseph Chamberlain, Britain's colonial secretary (Adachi 1976, 9). On August 31, 1900, British Columbia passed an act that authorized a language test to be administered to persons entering the province. As Adachi (1976, 43) has noted, "little attempt was made to obscure the fact that it was a measure aimed at the Chinese and the Japanese." In 1903 and 1905, the British Columbia legislature again passed bills to administer educational tests to Oriental immigrants (Adachi 1976, 45). Memories from this period of Canadian history still remain and the emotions it invokes can be rekindled quite easily.

The issues noted here require a much more careful analysis than is possible in one chapter. Only two important factors of contemporary society will be noted briefly. First, it must be recognized that the demographic composition of Canadian society has changed. Not only is our population rapidly aging, the ethnic composition of our population is rapidly changing. These two characteristics of our demography have necessitated changes in our educational curricula through the introduction of gerontology courses and transcultural nursing and medicine courses in a few of our universities. The first national conference on health care and multiculturalism was held in Toronto from March 30 to April 1, 1989. Second, we are now well into the postindustrial or the information age. We are able to communicate globally in seconds, not days, and the global society we are creating requires further break down of international, national, and regional barriers. Although these factors may appear to be outside the scope of our immediate concerns with regard to multiculturalism, the recognition and appreciation of emerging demographic transition and information technology would contribute not only to *nation* building at home, but also to a global society and a future role and position for Canada in the community of nations (Ujimoto 1992, 352).

Conclusions

In this very brief essay, we have examined some of the key aspects of the policy of multiculturalism. Academics will continue to debate the issues in the years to come as we grapple with the demographic changes in our society and the need to reflect these changes in our educational curricula, but we need more than debate. Structural changes are required in our society if we wish to develop more creative approaches to enable all Canadians to achieve equality of access and equality of participation in various Canadian institutions. With the passage of the Canadian Multiculturalism Act, Bill C-93, on July 12, 1988, we were all very optimistic. However, events since the failure of the Meech Lake Accord do not bode well for multiculturalism in Canada. There is no longer a separate House of Commons Standing Committee on Multiculturalism, an effective all-party group that dealt with multicultural policy issues. Furthermore, like many other programs and services, multiculturalism has not escaped the budget cuts limiting program funding. Regardless of these setbacks, the

Multiculturalism: The Demographic Fact

A major challenge facing Canadian society is the changing demographic profile of many of our cities. The 1996 Census of Canada reveals that "about one in ten Canadians—or 11.2 percent—are neither white nor aboriginal" (Mitchell 1998, A1). If specific cities are considered, 32 percent of the total population in Toronto are categorized as visible minorities. This profile is followed by Vancouver and Calgary with 31 percent and 16 percent respectively.

According to the Statistics Canada classification of visible minorities, as reported by *The Globe and Mail* (Mitchell 1998, A3), they consist of Chinese (26.7 percent), South Asian (21.0 percent), black (17.9 percent), Arab/West Asian (7.7 percent), Filipino (7.3 percent), Latin American (5.5 percent), Southeast Asian (5.4 percent), Japanese (2.1 percent), Korean (2.0 percent), other (2.2 percent), and more than one origin (1.9 percent). Note, however, that several of the categories are not homogeneous cultural groups. For example, the South Asian category consists of East Indian, Pakistani, Punjabi, and Sri Lankan ethnic groups. Similarly, the Southeast Asian category includes Cambodian, Indonesian, Laotian, and Vietnamese.

Although the percentage composition of each visible minority ethnic group is important in terms of establishing their relative size in Canadian society, it is equally important to note that about one in three—or 29 percent—of the visible minority population was born in Canada (Mitchell 1998, A3). *The Globe and Mail* further reports that "In fact, 42 percent of the blacks in Canada were born in Canada. And because Canada has had immigrants from Japan for so long, fully 65 percent of the Japanese population in this country was born here." The implication of this data is that generational differences must be considered when establishing, for example, multicultural health-care policies for our aging population. Demographic data from the census are crucial in dispelling beliefs that visible minorities are recent arrivals to Canada.

policy framework and foundation for multiculturalism in Canada have been firmly established to enable it to continue and to flourish, and perhaps to serve as a model for other nations.

Summary

- The main objectives of the policy of multiculturalism are to promote the cultural heritage of minorities and to break down discriminatory attitudes and cultural barriers to minorities' full participation in society.
- The policy of multiculturalism is no longer confined to a single government department, but it encompasses other departments such as Foreign Affairs and International Trade in order to reflect the realities of globalization.
- This policy is criticized because of its focus on "cultural barriers" to equality and its failure to recognize the historical and structural roots of racism and racial and ethnic inequality.

• The relationship between cultural pluralism and its role in strengthening Canadian citizenship must be evaluated in terms of intervening conditions such as the globalization of economics and politics.

Questions to Consider

1. What were some of the social and political factors taking place in Canadian society that resulted in the formation of the Royal Commission on Bilingualism and Biculturalism?

2. What aspects of the policy of multiculturalism have been criticized?

3. What aspects of multiculturalism as a state policy do you think have enhanced Canadian society?

4. Given the recent changes in the demographic composition of Canadian society, how important is the Multiculturalism Act of 1988?

5. Do you agree or disagree with Karl Peter that the policy of multiculturalism is essentially a policy of "ethnic group containment"?

6. Why do you think that the Meech Lake Accord did not recognize multiculturalism, aboriginal rights, and equality between men and women when it was first formulated?

Suggested Readings

Fleras, Augie, and Jean Leonard Elliott. *Multiculturalism in Canada: The Challenge of Diversity.* Scarborough: Nelson Canada, 1992.
———. *Unequal Relations: An Introduction to Race, Ethnic and Aboriginal Dynamics in Canada,* 2d ed. Scarborough: Prentice Hall Canada, 1996.
Hryniuk, Stella. *20 Years of Multiculturalism: Successes and Failures.* Winnipeg: St. John's College Press, 1992.
Kallen, Evelyn. "Multiculturalism: Ideology, Policy, and Reality." *Journal of Canadian Studies* 17, no. 1 (1982): 51–63.
Kymlicka, W. *Multicultural Citizenship.* New York: Oxford University Press, 1995.
Lewycky, Laverne. "Multiculturalism in the 1990s and into the 21st Century: Beyond Ideology and Utopia." In *Deconstructing a Nation: Immigration, Multiculturalism, and Racism in 90s Canada*, ed. Vic Satzewich. Halifax: Fernwood Publishing, 1992.
Multiculturalism: The First Decade. Special issue of *Journal of Canadian Studies* 17, no. 1.
Ujimoto, K.V. "Multiculturalism and the Global Information Society." In *Deconstructing a Nation: Immigration, Multiculturalism, and Racism in 90s Canada*, ed. Vic Satzewich. Halifax: Fernwood Publishing, 1992, 351–57.

Glossary

citizenship A status of rights, privileges, and responsibilities conferred on a person who owes allegiance to a country.

cultural heritage A system of rules, meanings, knowledge, artifacts, and symbols that is transmitted from generation to generation.

discrimination A reflection of the behavioural aspects of prejudice. It denies equal treatment or equal opportunity to members of society because of race, gender, ethnicity, religion, or disability.

ethnic identity The distinguishing characteristic or personality of an individual that identifies a person to a particular ethnic group.

ethnicity Both the subjective sense of belonging to a particular ethnic group based on one's origins or parentage, traditional values, and beliefs, and the objective aspects as manifested in attitudes and behaviour that reflects those values and beliefs.

inequality A condition or quality of being unequal or uneven; a condition of disparity in opportunity, power, pay, prestige, and privilege.

multiculturalism The cultural and racial diversity of Canadian society, as reflected in empirical fact, ideology, policy, or dynamic process.

Multiculturalism Act An act passed by the Federal government in 1988 to recognize and to promote the understanding that multiculturalism reflects the cultural and racial diversity of Canadian society.

prejudice A set of prejudgements that are derived from generalizations about others and that are often inaccurate and misleading.

racism An organized set of beliefs based on the superiority of one racial group over another. The notion of superiority is based on a combination of prejudice, discrimination, and the perception of social power and privilege in society.

References

Adachi, K. 1976. *The Enemy That Never Was: A History of Japanese Canadians.* Toronto: McClelland and Stewart.

Berry, J.W., R. Kalin, and D.M. Taylor. 1977. *Multiculturalism and Ethnic Attitudes in Canada.* Ottawa: Ministry of Supply and Services.

Bissoondath, N. 1993. "A Question of Belonging: Multiculturalism and Citizenship." In *Belonging: The Meaning and Future of Canadian Citizenship,* ed. W. Kaplan. Montreal and Kingston: McGill-Queens University Press. 368–87.

Burnet, J. 1981. "The Definition of Multiculturalism in a Bilingual Framework." *Multiculturalism in Canada.* Edmonton: University of Alberta. 43–57.

———. 1987. "Multiculturalism in Canada." In *Ethnic Canada: Identities and Inequalities*, ed. L. Driedger. Toronto: Copp Clark Pitman. 65–79.

Canadian Heritage. 1996. *Strategic Evaluation of Multicultural Programs.* Ottawa: Department of Canadian Heritage, Corporate Review Branch.

Fleras, A., and J.L. Elliott. 1992. *Multiculturalism in Canada: The Challenge of Diversity.* Scarborough: Nelson Canada.

———. 1996. *Unequal Relations: An Introduction to Race, Ethnic and Aboriginal Dynamics in Canada.* 2d ed. Scarborough: Prentice Hall Canada.

Henry, F., C. Tator, W. Mattis, and T. Rees. 1995. *The Colour of Democracy.* Toronto: Harcourt Brace.

Helman, C.G. 1997. *Culture, Health and Illness. An Introduction for Health Professionals,* 3d ed. Oxford: Butterworth-Heinemann.

Hryniuk, S. 1992. *20 Years of Multiculturalism: Successes and Failures.* Winnipeg: St. John's College Press.

Immigration Legislative Review. 1997. *Not Just Numbers: A Canadian Framework for Future Immigration.* Ottawa: Citizenship and Immigration Canada.

Isajiw, W.W. 1978. "Olga in Wonderland: Ethnicity in a Technological Society." In *The Canadian Ethnic Mosaic*, ed. L. Driedger. Toronto: McClelland and Stewart. 29–39.

Kallen, E. 1982. "Multiculturalism: Ideology, Policy, and Reality." *Journal of Canadian Studies* 17, no. 1: 51–63.

Kymlicka, W. 1995. *Multicultural Citizenship.* New York: Oxford University Press.

———. 1997. "Immigrants, Multiculturalism and Canadian Citizenship." Paper prepared for the panel on "Cultural Diversity and Canadian Citizenship," 50th Anniversary of the Canadian Citizenship Conference. Ottawa, February 15.

Lewycky, L. 1992. "Multiculturalism in the 1990s and into the 21st Century: Beyond Ideology and Utopia." In Satzewich, *Deconstructing a Nation.* 259–401.

Mallea, J.R. 1984. "Cultural Diversity and Canadian Education." Introduction to *Cultural Diversity and Canadian Education*, ed. J.R. Mallea and J.C. Young. Ottawa: Carleton University Press. 1.

Markides, K.S., and M.R. Miranda. 1997. *Minorities, Aging, and Health.* Thousand Oaks, CA: Sage Publications.

Masi, R., L. Mensah, and K.A. McLeod, eds. 1993. *Health and Cultures: Exploring the Relationships.* vols. 1 and 2. Oakville, ON: Mosaic Press Publishers.

Mazurek, K. 1983. "Multiculturalism and Schools: A Critical Analysis." In *Racial Minorities in Multicultural Canada*, ed. P.S. Li and B.S. Bolaria. Toronto: Garamond Press. 26–30.

Mitchell, A. 1998. "Face of Big Cities Changing." *The Globe and Mail*, February 18: A1–A3.

O'Bryan, K.D., J.G. Reitz, and O.M. Kuplowska. 1976. *Non-official Languages: A Study in Canadian Multiculturalism.* Ottawa: Minister Responsible for Multiculturalism.

Peter, K. 1981. "The Myth of Multiculturalism and Other Political Fables." In *Ethnicity, Power and Politics in Canada*, ed. J. Dahlie and T. Fernando. Toronto: Methuen. 59–60.

Rocher, G. 1984. "The Ambiguities of a Bilingual and Multicultural Canada." In Mallea and Young, *Cultural Diversity.* 41–47.

Samuel, T.J., and D. Schachhuber. 1995. "A Portrait of Canadian Diversity." In *Canadian Diversity: 2000 and Beyond*, ed. S.E. Nancoo and S. Ramcharan. Mississauga: Canadian Educator's Press. 7–33.

Satzewich, V. 1992. *Deconstructing a Nation: Immigration, Multiculturalism, and Racism in 90s Canada.* Halifax: Fernwood Publishing.

Taylor, C., K.A. Appiah, J.Habermas, S.C. Rockefeller, M. Walzer, and S. Wolf. 1994. *Multiculturalism: Examining the Politics of Recognition.* Princeton, NJ: Princeton University Press.

Trudeau, P.E. 1975. Speech, House of Commons, October 8, 1971. Ottawa: Canadian Consultative Council on Multiculturalism.

Ujimoto, K.V. 1982. "Visible Minorities and Multiculturalism: Planned Social Change Strategies for the Next Decade." *Journal of Canadian Studies* 17, no. 1: 111–21.

———. 1983. "Institutional Controls and Their Impact on Japanese Canadian Social Relations." In *Racial Minorities in Multicultural Canada*, ed. P.S. Li and B.S. Bolaria. Toronto: Garamond Press. 121–47.

———. 1992. "Multiculturalism and the Global Information Society." In Satzewich, *Deconstructing a Nation.* 351–57.

———. 1994. "Racial and Ethnic Dimensions of Aging: Implications for Health Care Services." In *Racial Minorities, Medicine and Health*, ed. B.S. Bolaria and R. Bolaria. 201–24.

Yeo, G., and D. Gallagher-Thompson. 1996. *Ethnicity and the Dementias.* Washington, D.C.: Taylor and Francis.

PART IV

Institutional Structures and Inequality

INTRODUCTION

Although Canada is one of the richest countries in the world, these riches are unevenly distributed in the society. Inequalities of income produce differential opportunity structures and different life chances (material and social rewards) for individuals and social groups. These life chances are reflected in such measures as education, health, nutrition, and treatment by the justice system.

The first reading in this section, entitled "Transforming Canada's Education System: The Impact on Educational Inequalities, Opportunities, and Benefits," examines the nature and purpose of formal education in Canada, differential accesses to educational opportunities and their impact on employment, income, and other life chances. Terry Wotherspoon discusses inequalities in educational opportunities and benefits by race, class, and gender. Wotherspoon examines recent attacks on Canada's education system, which are posed in the form of concern over educational excellence and proposals for "lifelong learning." Although the concerns and proposals are defined in a way that presents them as being in the national interest, he argues that they serve to advance specific business and political interests seeking profitable investment and a highly productive work force.

These debates have emerged at a time when the notion of equality of educational opportunity is being challenged as an organizing principle in Canadian education. The chapter shows that while the expansion of the education system since the middle of the twentieth century has allowed greater opportunities for participation in formal education programs, different class, gender, and racial groups have experienced persistent inequalities in educational opportunities and benefits. In conclusion, Wotherspoon argues that the impact of recent attacks on the education system is likely to increase educational selectivity and inequality to the detriment of disadvantaged persons.

In his chapter, "The Canadian Criminal Justice System: Inequalities of Class, Race, and Gender," Leslie Samuelson discusses the unequal involvement and treatment of individuals in the justice system based upon their class, race, and gender. He shows that the political–economic elite is able to influence the political–legal process so that corporate crimes (social, economic, and physical harms inflicted on society in the process of capital accumulation) are not treated very seriously, under either criminal or regulatory law, while the lower class is prosecuted quite severely for ordinary street crime. This is illustrated with data on the flouting of occupational health and safety laws, on price fixing, and on other illegal corporate activities. The evidence also strongly suggests class bias in policing and arrests, and in differential prosecution, sentencing, and granting of parole. Access to legal services follows the same pattern: low income individuals are less likely to retain private legal counsel to safeguard their legal rights.

Racial inequalities are evident in the overrepresentation of Native peoples in the criminal justice system. Samuelson argues that Native overrepresentation is but one manifestation of the destruction and dislocation of indigenous peoples that has taken place under colonialism, and of their continued disadvantaged position. They are subject to racial bias in policing, prosecution, sentencing, and incarceration. The problem of racism in policing is also manifest in the excessive use of force and the relatively high number of killings by police of racial minorities.

The treatment of women in the justice system has received considerable attention. The main issues in this area have been the biases, injustices, and ineffectiveness of the criminal justice system in dealing with women who have been the victims of domestic violence and sexual assault, and injustices and problems faced by incarcerated women.

In conclusion, Samuelson argues that liberal–critical initiatives aimed at the reform of laws and programs to suit the needs of Native and female offenders are desirable, and may have some success. But to reduce significantly the inequalities of class, race, and gender, the focus needs to be put on change in the structural and cultural conditions and inequalities of power that lie at the centre of the problems.

CHAPTER 10

Transforming Canada's Education System: The Impact on Educational Inequalities, Opportunities, and Benefits

Terry Wotherspoon

Learning Objectives

After studying this chapter, you should be able to
- Critically examine recent demands for educational reform.
- Examine the nature and purposes of formal **education** in Canada.
- Distinguish between different views of **equality of educational opportunity**.
- Assess the varied contributions that education is expected to make to **social mobility** and advancement.
- Determine crucial dimensions of educational inequality on employment, income, and other life chances.
- Understand the relationship between educational change and transformations in other aspects of society.

Introduction

Recent social and economic changes have raised serious questions about the relevance of formal education, or schooling, to contemporary life. The question, "What's wrong at school?" posed in the headline of a feature story in *Maclean's* magazine in 1993 (July 11) was replaced three years later by a new question—"Who needs schools?" (Dwyer 1996, 40). The growing importance of global markets and international linkages, new information technologies, demands for highly skilled labour, and significant lifestyle changes have given new importance to educational programs and credentials at the same time as the viability of existing educational institutions and processes is being challenged by critics on several fronts. From the high-profile report of the U.S. National Commission on Excellence in Education (1983), which stressed the urgent need to attack an apparent crisis of educational "mediocrity" in America, to repeated calls for "lifelong learning," "flexible" educational programs, and "core curricula" throughout Canada and elsewhere, there is a sense that something is amiss in school systems, and that it requires immediate and extensive replacement or repair. David Crombie, Canada's secretary of state in 1988, declared that "we must begin rebuilding our system of post-secondary education today if we are to give succeeding generations their 'fighting chance' tomorrow.... Certainly in the future, even more than today, education will be a life-long process and repeated retraining will be a routine matter for everyone" (Secretary of State 1988, 13–14). Investment in the learner is a "key to economic advancement" in an "increasingly tough world economy," according to the former Ontario premier, David Peterson, while a "loose and tight" school system "in which freedom exists within structure, in which the system's need for conformity and standardization is balanced by no less important needs for diversity and individualization" was advocated in a 1988 royal commission report on education in British Columbia (British Columbia 1988, 220; *Star-Phoenix* [Saskatoon], April 25, 1989, A14). New Brunswick's Commission on Excellence in Education (1993, 65) emphasized the importance of a "learning society" in which educational experiences are integrated throughout an individual's lifetime, while Ontario's Royal Commission on Learning (1994b, 27) stressed that "information technology is one of the engines needed to drive the necessary transformation of the education system." The federal government's Green Paper in 1994 highlighted the central role of education and training in order to overcome the nation's "skills deficit" so as to produce "the best-educated, best-trained workforce in the world" (Canada 1994, 10).

The Case for Educational Reform

The case for educational reform is a persistent theme in reports, discussion papers, and statements presented by governments, business groups, community organizations, and media. A report by Ontario's Royal Commission on Learning illustrates the sense of crisis surrounding demands for education systems to cope within a context of massive social transformations.

It may be that ours is the era of the educational crises that so many generations before us feared they were facing: it is impossible to envision a time when huge new resources will be available to deal with the maladies the system faces, but there is a very real sense that social problems will not decline, putting even greater strains on schools. This Commission celebrates the rainbow that Canada has become, but we acknowledge that this increasing diversity adds new dimensions to the work of the school system.

Fears of permanent unemployment or, at best, underemployment, will continue to create anxiety for parents and students alike. Many people will continue to look to schools for vocational salvation, while the incessant pressure to be "competitive" will add to the tensions that afflict every part of the learning process. Technological change comes hurtling at us with such speed that it

(continued)

(continued)

seems impossible to guess what tomorrow will demand and—more specifically for the Commission's purposes—how to prepare young people, and many not-so-young people, to cope with whatever it is that lies ahead.

Characterized by bureaucratic structures right out of the automobile assembly lines—with the same kinds of mass production techniques, work specialization, fragmented programs, standardized procedures, hierarchical authority, and compliant workers—our schools, miraculously and with remarkable effectiveness, have taken us through this century. But it seems unrealistic to believe that, without change, they can handle the challenges of the next. What has been acceptable, if not always outstanding, is now in real danger of failing unless it is dramatically reshaped.

It is clear to us that neither now nor in the past have schools been the disasters some critics claim, or the triumphs some defenders insist they are. And we acknowledge that even if every one of our recommendations were scrupulously implemented, the same might well be true 25 years from now.

There are, in fact, many good reasons why schools will always disappoint to some degree or other. The fact is that there are no scientific solutions to the education crisis as, we confess frankly, some of us innocently believed when we began this assignment.

First and foremost, schools are human enterprises attempting to develop and shape human minds and spirits, with all the imperfections and imprecisions that implies. While we agree that this is an era of scientific miracles and that the growth in knowledge is exponential, to this very moment, the world's leading experts—using all their passionate, erudite convictions—disagree on the way the human personality develops and how the mind learns. Nor should we disregard the diverse personal and collective value systems within which this process takes place.

Any school child who watched last night's television news can attest that, too often, there is little relationship between knowledge and wisdom. Given the fallibility of all human-made institutions, it is hard to fathom why schools, of all the precarious and fragile enterprises possible, are expected to be flawless, superior to all our other frail undertakings.

As society transfers ever-greater burdens and responsibilities to the education system, should we be particularly disappointed or surprised when it doesn't succeed where families, or communities, or social agencies, or religious organizations have failed?

Yet, in the name of realism, even as the Commission urges modest expectations, we find ourselves, at the end of our task, filled with a surprising but gratifying optimism about the enormous possibilities the future can offer—not will, but can—because success is by no means inevitable.

Source: Excerpt from *For the Love of Learning: Report of the Royal Commission on Learning, Volume 1: Mandate, Context, Issues* (Publications Ontario, 1994), pp. 4–5. © Queen's Printer for Ontario, 1994. Reproduced with permission.

Surely most of us would readily agree with the sentiment that formal education should be made relevant to the changing needs of both the learner and society, since a stagnant education system offers few advantages to anyone. But what is the connection between the rhetoric and realities of educational transformation? Why has there been a resurgence of interest in the politics of education? Who is defining the issues, and what are the implications of educational structures and transformations for learners and other social groups? This chapter addresses these questions by considering the ways in which formal education contributes to social inequalities of class, gender, and race. The chapter contends that formal education operates in contradictory ways. While general trends to increase the provision of formal educational services have tended to expand opportunities for minority groups, education has also contributed to the subordination of these minorities. In this context, current debates around education are linked to the agendas of political and economic interests that seek to make education and its consequent inequalities more directly responsive to priorities determined by capitalist labour markets and the aggressive quest for new avenues of profitable investment.

The Politics of Educational Reform

From its inception, mass public schooling has been employed to integrate children into the fabric of social life. It is important to recognize, though, that the social "mainstream" is not a natural or given entity but rather is subject to different definitions and organizational forms advanced by persons who occupy distinct places within the social structure. The various perspectives that people employ to make sense of social reality affect not only where they stand on particular social or political issues, but also what phenomena they consider to be debatable issues. Our ability to understand the world always involves, of necessity, some selectivity. Not all positions, however, are considered valid in the context of politics, media, and other public discourse. In fact, one of the major consequences of modern education systems is to offer legitimacy to particular views of the world that correspond to dominant patterns of activity and belief, serving in the process to undermine or ignore alternatives (Apple 1988; Wotherspoon 1987).

For example, few people would disagree that high illiteracy rates pose a disturbing dilemma in an era in which nearly all individuals have access to at least ten years of free public schooling. Over the past few years, an extensive media blitz and a series of government-funded programs served to remind us how pressing a problem illiteracy was. They focussed on a 1987 national newspaper survey, which claimed that more than one in five Canadians lacked necessary skills in reading, writing, or computing to the extent that their ability to perform everyday work tasks was impaired. Yet, despite the high profile given the issue, few commentators challenged the timing of the sudden elevation to public consciousness of a phenomenon that had existed for decades. Even fewer sought to explain why something that was commonly seen as a social problem had been transformed into an economic matter that "cost" business "at least $4 billion a year in accidents, errors and lost productivity," with an estimated additional $6 billion lost annually in earnings, training, and other costs (Maynard 1989, 88). Individuals and schools were blamed for their failure to produce a literate population. Meanwhile, the possibility was ignored that illiteracy was in fact the product of a complex set of economic and social relationships that had for decades proven beneficial to groups such as employers of low-cost, poorly qualified labour power. At a more general level, the search for educational "excellence" and "quality" that characterized the war against illiteracy had a broad appeal that masked the real intentions of business interests to promote a type of "excellence" and "quality" that served their own particular purposes (Shor 1986).

Until the recent attacks on education systems, the most common way in which participation in education has been viewed in our society has been through a liberal orientation that addresses the rights and opportunities of individuals. The liberal perspective portrays formal education as a **meritocracy**, or a vehicle for nurturing the talents and capacities of each individual in harmony with his or her ability to contribute productively to social development. Such a view contends that to deny opportunity to individuals or groups of people is both morally unjust and counterproductive to the advancement of society, since industrial societies cannot afford to allow talent and brainpower to go to waste. The liberal orientation is often supported with reference to notions of a meritocracy in which social and economic rewards, such as prestige and wealth, are allocated to individuals as an incentive to maintain skilled and industrious performance in order to fulfil the most crucial social tasks (see Mazurek 1987).

Conceptions of equality of opportunity emphasize the need for fairness in social organization. Even the most ardent advocates of the liberal view acknowledge that there are several meanings to "equality of opportunity," ranging from simple assurances that all persons are allowed exposure to schooling and other common services to more active measures that attempt to equalize people's life chances (see Coleman 1968). Still, each of the liberal variants is premised on the assumption that individual differences are translated into unequal distributions of social rewards and outcomes without which society would be unable to function effectively and efficiently.

Despite the appeal for fairness and justice in liberal conceptions of equality of opportunity, and widespread public support for the sentiment that equality of opportunity should be a guiding principle in the organization of Canadian schools (Livingstone and Hart 1987, 21–22), several challenges to the notion have been mounted in recent years. As John Porter observed in 1977, "If the question were asked which of the major social innovations of the twentieth century had most failed in its mission a likely answer would be public education" (Porter 1987, 242). Both the political right and left have questioned the usefulness of equality of opportunity as an organizing principle in capitalist societies, the former because government efforts to maintain the rights of minority groups are seen as too costly to maintain and contrary to the principles of market-driven economies, and the latter because the promised opportunities have not been delivered for many persons in the form of substantial social advancement. This dissatisfaction is in part responsible for the emergence of contemporary debates over the future of education. On one side are proponents of a conservative view that schools are failing to teach the fundamental knowledge and skills required in a core area of academic subjects, while on the other are parents and employers who demand that schooling be made more directly responsive to labour-force requirements (Livingstone 1985). Regardless of the different positions on what schools should be doing, schooling is subject to the critique that whatever it is doing now is inadequate.

Unfortunately, most critics of public education's apparent failure tend to substitute a general discontent with formal educational institutions for a more sustained analysis of what schools do and why they operate as they do. An excessive faith in the ability of formal education systems either to overcome social and economic disparities or to match labour-force requirements is based on a misrepresentation of the history and practice of education. Education systems are not and cannot be an effective panacea for social and labour-market problems. In practice, as Carnoy and Levin (1985, 5) emphasize, formal systems of education in capitalist societies are driven by two contradictory dynamics. One is the thrust in liberal democracies toward greater equality of opportunity and participation in economic and political life for all members of society; the other is the fundamental conflict and **structured inequality** upon which a capitalist economy is based. In other words, while educational institutions are important mechanisms whereby persons are channelled into various positions within social divisions of labour governed by relations of domination, subordination, and exploitation, schools remain part of a public sphere of social life that is open to scrutiny and participation by a diverse, often conflicting, array of social groups.

The Dimensions of Educational Expansion in Canada

One of the major consequences of educational conflict and contradictions has been the massive expansion of the education sector within the welfare state. As the data in Table 10.1 indicate, annual educational expenditures in Canada have increased steadily since the Second World War, rising by a factor of more than 135 between 1950–51 and 1995–96. The strongest growth has been at the university, community college, and trade/vocational training levels. The figures suggest a strong national commitment to educational expansion, especially as educational expenditures climbed to reach nearly one-tenth of Canada's gross national product (GNP) in 1970. Despite slower rates of growth in educational expenditures and their decreased proportion of the GNP from the late 1970s through the 1980s, the continuing high levels of fiscal support for education have opened opportunities for greater segments of the population to benefit from participation in educational programs.

Evidence of increased postwar educational enrollment is shown in Table 10.2, although it is clear that the rates of enrollment increase have been substantially lower than the rates of cost increase. At the non-university post-secondary (community college) level, for example, expenditures between 1950–51 and 1995–96 rose by a factor of 374 while enrollment increased 14 times; at the university level, costs over the same period increased by more than 200 times while enrollment increased 9 times. It is clear that educational expansion and massive investment in education programs have made it increasingly possible for more people to attain both longer exposure to and higher levels of formal education. The rapid expansion of universities and the opening of community colleges in the 1960s allowed many to attain post-secondary credentials that previously had been limited to small sectors of the population. Between 1961 and 1996, the proportion of the population 15 years of age and over who had less than Grade 9 declined from 44 percent to 12.6 percent, while the proportion who had received at least some post-secondary education rose from 13 percent to 47.6 percent (Mori and Burke 1989, 13; Statistics Canada 1997c, 198). Educational attainment rose for all age cohorts, with an overall increase in the median

TABLE 10.1 Expenditures on Education in Canada, by Level, 1950–1996, $ Millions (% Increase over Preceding Period in Parentheses)

Year	Elementary/secondary		Trade/vocational		Non-university post-secondary		University		Total		Total education expenditures as % of GDP[a]
1950–51	359.1		12.8		11.6		55.2		438.8		2.4
1955–56	674.4	(87.8)	19.2	(50.0)	31.0	(167.2)	104.4	(89.1)	829.1	(88.9)	2.9
1960–61	1 328.3	(97.0)	47.2	(145.8)	57.6	(85.8)	272.9	(161.4)	1 706.0	(105.8)	4.4
1965–66	2 410.8	(81.5)	153.4	(225.0)	98.8	(71.5)	736.6	(169.9)	3 399.6	(99.3)	6.1
1970–71	4 880.4	(102.4)	574.8	(274.7)	430.0	(335.2)	1 790.8	(143.1)	7 676.0	(125.8)	9.0
1975–76	8 433.8	(72.8)	841.8	(46.5)	975.7	(126.9)	2 760.5	(54.1)	13 011.7	(69.5)	7.8
1980–81	14 730.4	74.7)	1 309.3	(55.5)	1 822.8	(86.8)	4 437.7	(60.8)	22 300.2	(71.4)	7.2
1985–86	21 946.6	(49.0)	2 832.9	(116.4)	2 783.9	(52.7)	7 000.6	(57.8)	34 564.1	(55.0)	7.2
1990–91	30 681.2	(39.8)	4 019.6	(41.9)	3 566.6	(28.1)	10 410.4	(48.7)	48 677.9	(40.8)	7.3
1995–96	36 348.0	(18.5)	6 686.8	(66.4)	4 339.2	(21.7)	11 761.0	(13.0)	59 135.0	(21.5)	7.6

[a] Figures from 1950–51 to 1975–76 are for gross national product, producing rates that tend to be slightly higher than for gross domestic product.

Sources: **1950–51 to 1970–71:** Compiled from Statistics Canada, *Historical Compendium of Education Statistics*, Cat. no. 81-568 (Ottawa: Minister of Supply and Services, 1978); **1974–75 to 1990–91:** Compiled from Statistics Canada, *Education in Canada* (Annual series), Cat. no. 81-229 (Ottawa: Minister of Supply and Services); **1995–96:** Compiled from Statistics Canada, *Education Quarterly Review* 4, 3, Cat. no. 81-003 (Ottawa: Minister of Industry, 1997).

TABLE 10.2   Full-Time Enrollment in Canada, by Level of Study, Selected Years, 1950–1996 (000s) (% Increase over Previous Period in Parentheses)

Year	Elementary/ secondary		Non-university post-secondary		University		Total	
1950–51	2 625		28		64		2 717	
1955–56	3 291	(25.4)	33	(17.9)	73	(14.1)	3 397	(25.0)
1960–61	4 204	(27.7)	49	(48.5)	114	(56.2)	4 368	(28.6)
1965–66	5 201	(23.7)	69	(40.8)	204	(78.9)	5 475	(25.3)
1970–71	5 888	(13.2)	166	(140.6)	310	(52.0)	6 364	(16.2)
1975–76	5 595	(–5.0)	222	(33.7)	371	(19.7)	6 188	(–2.8)
1980–81	5 106	(–8.7)	261	(17.6)	383	(3.2)	5 750	(–7.1)
1985–86	4 928	(–3.5)	322	(23.4)	467	(21.9)	5 717	(–0.6)
1990–91	5 141	(4.3)	325	(0.9)	532	(13.9)	5 998	(4.9)
1995–96	5 459	(6.2)	390	(20.0)	573	(7.7)	6 422	(7.1)

Sources: **1950–51 to 1970–71**: Compiled from Statistics Canada, *Historical Compendium of Education Statistics,* Cat. no. 81-568 (Ottawa: Minister of Supply and Services, 1978); **1975–76 to 1990–91**: Compiled from Statistics Canada, *Education in Canada* (Annual series), Cat. no. 81-229 (Ottawa: Minister of Supply and Services); **1995–96**: Compiled from Statistics Canada, *Education Quarterly Review* 4, 3, Cat. no. 81-003 (Ottawa: Minister of Industry, 1997).

years of schooling among the population 15 years and over, nationally, from 11.3 years in 1976 to 12.5 years in 1991 (Statistics Canada 1997c, 197).

Nonetheless, despite the general upgrading of educational credentials, it is important to recognize that considerable segments of the population continue to be excluded from post-secondary educational programs and other formal training opportunities beyond elementary and secondary school. In 1994–95, for example, 31 percent of men and 36 percent of women in the 18 to 24 age group were enrolled in full-time post-secondary studies in Canada while 52.4 percent of the nation's adult population (51.1 percent of men and 53.7 percent of women) had no post-secondary education (Statistics Canada 1997c, 95, 198). Part of the continuing debate over education concerns the extent to which these proportions should be altered to emphasize either greater accessibility or increasing selectivity with respect to opportunities for advanced education (see, e.g., Accessibility Task Force 1989; Bercuson, Bothwell, and Granatstein 1984).

A sense of urgency in determining educational priorities is heightened by the politics of educational finance. The rapid growth in educational expenditures has made education a visible target for governments preoccupied with deficit reduction and fiscal restraint. As the figures in Table 10.1 show, Canada has experienced declining rates of increase in expenditures on education and a reduction in the level of education spending in relation to other national expenditures since the 1970s. Schools, colleges, universities, and other educational institutions that had benefited from educational expansion in the 1960s and early 1970s have had to assess their priorities as they adopt cost-containment strategies and seek out new sources of revenue. The symptoms of educational reorganization are visible in a wide range of activities, including program cuts, curricular reorganization, teacher and faculty militancy, restrictions on student loans and bursaries, and closer working relationships between corporate and educational sectors (Livingstone 1987; Newson and Buchbinder 1988). In the process, education is being promoted by economic, political, and even educational leaders as a "commodity" that must be managed rationally in order to advance the national interest in increasingly competitive world markets driven by innovation, managerial flexibility, and high technology. Individuals who do not hold educational credentials are warned that they are at risk of losing out on the most lucrative and desirable labour market opportunities (Arnoti 1987, 31–32). We are left to conclude both that the education system cannot be maintained in its existing costly state and that an undereducated populace constitutes a barrier to the advancement of national productivity.

Ironically, exhortations that people must become educated in order to have labour-market success are emerging at a time when it is becoming increasingly difficult for many to continue into advanced education. Educational funding by sources other than provincial, territorial, municipal, and federal governments has increased from 7.6 percent of educational costs in 1975–76 to 12.2 percent in 1997–98 (Statistics Canada 1997a, 74). While the overall change does not seem to be that large, it becomes more significant when one considers that much of the additional burden of financing education has been placed on individuals. A 1983–84 National Post-Secondary Student Survey, for example, revealed that for full-time post-secondary students aged 30 years and under, contributions from parents increased from 47 percent of non-repayable funding of education in 1974–75 to 55 percent in 1983–84, while parents accounted for 20 percent of student-loan funding in 1983–84, up from 15 percent in 1974–75 (Porter and Jasmin 1987, 32). There have been steady increases in the numbers of students who have had to borrow funds from student loans programs or other sources and in the amounts they borrowed. Among students who graduated from post-secondary programs in 1990, 54 percent of career technical graduates (compared with 41 percent of those who graduated in 1982) and 61 percent of university graduates (compared with 50 percent of those who graduated in 1982) had to borrow funds to finance their education. The amounts students borrowed also rose. Comparing those who graduated in 1986 with 1990 graduates, the debt loads of career-technical program graduates increased by 14 percent in real terms, to $7300, while debt loads for university graduates increased by 26 percent, to $11 150 (Little and Lapierre 1996, 44–45). This means that access to formal education is increasingly subject to limitation based on the individual's or family's ability to pay, thereby contributing to educational inequalities. Before we consider the implications of challenges to the principle of equality of educational opportunity, however, it is important to examine the extent to which equal opportunity prevails in access to and attainment in education programs in Canada.

Inequalities of Educational Opportunities

While increasing numbers have benefited from exposure to formal educational programs since the Second World War, there are strong, persistent disparities in enrollment and attainment (years of schooling completed) patterns. This section examines inequalities along dimensions of class, gender, and ethnicity.

Data collected in a 1983–84 National Post-Secondary Student Survey, reproduced in Table 10.3, indicate that the incomes and occupations of students' parents have a strong impact on enrollment in post-secondary programs. One-half of students in graduate studies and just under one-half of undergraduates, compared with about one-quarter of college career students (registered in job-specific vocational or technical programs) and just over one-third of students in college programs where credit is obtained toward university standing, have fathers in managerial, semi-professional, and professional occupational categories. These proportions are nearly reversed for students with fathers in skilled and semi-skilled crafts and trades, who make up just under one-half of students in college career programs and about a quarter of university students. It is noteworthy that students whose fathers are in managerial, semi-professional, and professional occupations are overrepresented at all levels compared with the total proportion of the male work force in those occupations, while students whose fathers are in other occupational categories are underrepresented relative to the general male work force. Overall, based on the relationship between students' enrollment in post-secondary educational programs and their fathers' occupations, there is a strong likelihood that the occupational distribution will be reproduced from generation to generation. The same trends hold true with respect to the combined income of students' parents. While there are substantial numbers of students with parents in each income category represented in each type of educational program, there are some evident disparities. The greatest proportion of college career students are from lower-income families, while the highest income level ($45 000 and over) is the predominant category for students in university programs.

Several other studies have reported similar trends. Porter, Porter, and Blishen (1982) demonstrate in a survey of Ontario students that a student's socio-economic background is positively correlated with his or her educational aspirations and enrollment in educational programs, and influences even more strongly the student's eventual level of **educational attainment**. Social class has a higher impact on the likelihood of high-school completion than does mental ability (Porter, Porter, and Blishen 1982, 288–89). Anisef and Okihiro (1982, 128), employing Ontario data from the 1970s, also show the strong influence of social class on educational attainment, particularly in universities, which tended to draw heavily from upper socio-economic strata; non-university post-secondary programs, by contrast, were attended by high numbers of students from both advantaged and disadvantaged groups. Similarly, Guppy, Mikicich, and Pendakur (1984) observe throughout the twentieth century a gradual decline in educational inequalities based on parental background, but they conclude that social origin continues to exert a strong influence on students' educational attainment, particularly for those students who attain a university education (see also Guppy and Arai 1993). Data from a 1988 national survey of persons who graduated from trade/vocational, college, and university programs in 1986 also reveal that an individual's likelihood of continuing to higher levels of post-secondary education increases with the amount of education attained by his or her parents (Clark 1991, 11). Curtis, Livingstone, and Smaller (1992, 10), observe with respect to data from Ontario that young people whose parents are employers or professionals are between two-and-a-half to four times more likely to go to university, and between

TABLE 10.3 Full-Time Students in Canada, 1983–1984: Type of Occupation of Father and Combined Income of Parents, by Type of Student

Type of student	Type of occupation of father (percent)						
	Managerial, semi-professional, professional	Clerical, sales, service	Skilled, semi-skilled, crafts and trades	Labourer	Other	Total[b]	Number of students
College career	26	21	46	3	4	100	130 049
College transfer	36	23	33	2[a]	6	100	50 657
Undergraduates	45	21	27	2	5	100	267 481
Graduate students	50	19	23	—[a]	6[a]	98	21 191
Total male labour force	25	27	48		—[a]	100	6 896 000

Type of student	Combined income of parents (in $000)					
	0–22	23–33	34–44	45+	Total[b]	Number of students
College career	33	27	21	19	100	122 657
College transfer	28	25	19	29	100	48 809
Undergraduates	26	21	18	35	100	253 905
Graduate students	31	20	16	33	100	22 726

[a] Numbers are too low or too unreliable to estimate.
[b] Totals may not sum to 100 because of rounding.
Source: Adapted from Statistics Canada, *The Labour Force*, Cat. no. 71-001 (January 1987): 22–23.

three to five times less likely to drop out of high school, than the sons and daughters of industrial workers and unskilled workers.

Class and family background are not the only factors that influence educational opportunities and achievement. One of the most pervasive bases of social and educational inequality is gender. At first glance, it would appear that the importance of gender differences for education is diminishing. In the 1950–51 academic year, for example, female students constituted less than one-quarter (21.7 percent) of full-time university undergraduate students in Canada, while by 1994–95, that proportion had risen to more than one-half (54.2 percent); female students also accounted for over half (52.9 percent) of full-time community college enrollment in 1994–95, including 66.7 percent of those in career programs (Statistics Canada 1983, W341-2; Statistics Canada 1997c, 52–54). The proportions of female students are even higher when part-time students are taken into account. In 1994–95, for example, women constituted 62.5 percent of part-time university undergraduate students, 52.8 percent of part-time graduate students, and 61.5 percent of part-time community college students (Statistics Canada 1997c, 52–58). Moreover, female students have moved into several non-traditional areas of study, particularly in the professions. Between 1970–71 and 1994–95, the proportion of women in full-time undergraduate studies in medicine increased from 18.1 to 49.6 percent; in law, the proportion rose from 12.7 to 51.8 percent; in dentistry and dental studies, from 5.6 to 44.1 percent; in commerce and business administration, from 10.2 to 46.1 percent; and in agriculture, from 10.5 to 48.8 percent (calculated from Statistics Canada 1977, 138–39; Statistics Canada 1997c, 62–66).

Despite these signs of greater gender equality in enrollment in post-secondary programs, gender segregation prevails throughout education programs at nearly all levels. As Gaskell (1981) emphasizes, women on the whole have at least as much formal education as men, but men and women tend to participate in different kinds of educational programs and receive different educational credentials. The data in the previous paragraph show that the proportion of women in full-time studies is greater than that of men enrolled at all levels of post-secondary education, except graduate studies, where women constitute 43.7 percent of full-time students (Statistics Canada 1997c, 52–58). However, most disciplines of study have remained highly gender-segmented. In 1994–95, women predominated in areas such as nursing (91.0 percent), household science (90.1 percent), and education (94.6 percent) in universities, and in secretarial sciences (94.9 percent), health sciences (81.8 percent), and social services (84.0 percent) in community colleges, while men prevailed in such areas as physical sciences (69.9 percent) and engineering (80.9 percent) in universities, and in engineering technology (87.8 percent) and electronics and electrical technology programs (94.9 percent) in community colleges (Statistics Canada 1997c, 60–67). Gender segregation has also remained high in trades training programs outside of post-secondary institutions. The overall proportion of women in occupational, institutional, and apprenticeship training programs is very low, ranging from 4 to 30 percent; within these programs, women are concentrated in training for traditionally female occupations in the clerical and service sectors such as food and beverage services, hairdressing, and secretarial work, while men are concentrated in training for blue-collar occupations such as machining, work in construction trades, and product assembly or repair (Boothby 1986, 17–19).

Formal educational credentials at the highest level are held mostly by men. In 1994, 51.2 percent of the 21 292 master's degrees and 69.1 percent of the 3552 earned doctorates awarded in Canada went to men (Statistics Canada 1997c). Men are also concentrated in programs that offer credentials oriented to specific careers, providing opportunities for direct access into labour-force positions that tend to offer relative job and wage security. The ratio of graduating males to females, for example, is 150 to 1 in construction electrician courses, 137 to 1 in courses in plumbing and pipe trades, and 40 to 1 in mechanical engineering degree programs (Mori and Burke 1989, 40). Although women, historically, have tended to predominate in programs that offer general certificates or degrees, such as general arts programs or broad vocational training programs that provide fewer job-specific work skills, there is some evidence that this trend is reversing (Boothby 1986, 17; Clark 1991, 60–61). Nonetheless, the general pattern is in some ways a reversal of what happens in high school, where girls are commonly prepared for specific vocational careers and boys are given more general training, which is later supplemented by paid training or apprenticeship for particular careers (Gaskell 1981). In short, there seems little likelihood that greater participation rates in formal education will automatically reverse women's traditional socio-economic disadvantages relative to men given pronounced differences in the patterns revealed by males' and females' programs of study and entry into labour markets.

Distinctions among ethnic groups constitute a further dimension of educational inequality. Based on an analysis of 1981 census data for Canadian labour force participants 15 years and older, Li (1988, 76–79) identifies patterns of clearly differentiated educational attainment. Persons of Jewish and Chinese origin hold the strongest likelihood of having completed university education, while persons of southern European origin have the lowest attainment of university degrees and the highest likelihood of having less than secondary education. Overall, only a few groups, including persons of Jewish, British, northern and central European, African, and Chinese origin have attained more than the national average of 11.56 years of schooling. Some of the variability can be explained by such factors as age and immigration patterns. For example, according to the 1991 census, for persons aged 15 years and over, Canada's immigrant population had 12.8 median years of schooling compared with 12.5 for the non-immigrant population; the gap was widest for older-age cohorts and among immigrants who arrived prior to the 1960s. Immigrants were also more likely than persons born in Canada to have university degrees (14 percent of immigrants compared with 11 percent of adults born in Canada had university degrees in 1991) and to have less than Grade 9 (with rates of 19 percent for immigrants, and 21 percent of immigrant women, as opposed to 13 percent of the Canadian-born) (Badets and Chui 1994, 41–44). A major reason for this variability lies in Canada's selective immigration policies, which since the 1960s have placed high value on formal education and skill training (Li 1988, 81).

It is more difficult to assess the direct impact of educational processes and institutions on opportunities and attainment for various ethnic groups. Nonetheless, it is clear that notable disparities do exist. The experience of Canada's aboriginal peoples, who have been consistently underrepresented in educational opportunities and achievement for several decades, strongly illustrates the nature of educational inequality in Canada.

Data from the 1991 census show that, for the population 15 to 49 years not attending school full-time, 16.8 percent of the aboriginal population and 28.1 percent of Natives living on-reserve had less than Grade 9 education, compared with 4.9 percent of the total population. Of the aboriginal population, 32.2 percent had at least some post-secondary education, compared with 52.5 percent of the general population (Statistics Canada 1993c). Trends associated with the educational attainment of younger cohorts appear to be more favourable. In 1995–96, 82 percent of Native children aged 4 to 18 living on-reserve were enrolled in schools; also that year, 75 percent of on-reserve students, compared with 19.6 percent in 1980–81 and 3.4 percent in 1960–61, remained in school continuously to Grade 12 (Department of Indian Affairs and Northern Development 1997, 32, 34). Among persons in the 17- to 34-year age cohort, in 1994–95, 6.5 percent of registered Indians participated in some form of post-secondary education, compared with a national rate of 10.4 percent (Department of Indian Affairs and Northern Development 1997, 37), although aboriginal people continue to be relatively more disadvantaged with regard to the kinds and levels of programs they are enrolled in. While recent First Nations initiatives such as band-controlled education and vocational programs have offered grounds for optimism that aboriginal peoples' educational status is likely to improve, there continue to be disturbing signs that such improvement may be limited (Frideres 1998, 165–68; Satzewich and Wotherspoon 1993, 144–46). The federal government decision in the late 1980s to revoke the "E-12 guidelines" and restrict funding support for Native post-secondary education is an example of how a policy shift toward self-government may be more a manifestation of government cost-restraint than a show of true concern for the welfare of Canada's aboriginal peoples (Lanceley 1991).

In summary, this section has examined several examples of inequality in educational opportunity and attainment according to the dimensions of class and socio-economic background, gender, and ethnicity. General historical trends reveal that the expansion of Canada's education system, in terms of both overall enrollment and increasing participation in post-secondary programs and vocational training, has allowed for extensive participation and achievement in formal education programs by groups such as women and Native people who previously had limited educational opportunities. Nonetheless, there is considerable evidence that persistent inequalities are deeply ingrained into the structure of Canada's education system. The next section discusses the major consequences of these disparities by examining inequalities in the distribution of benefits from education.

Inequality of Benefits from Formal Education

The importance of formal education as a mechanism for granting credentials in Canadian society, as in other industrialized democratic societies, relies upon a strong relationship between educational achievement and general economic and occupational opportunities. Overall, a person's likelihood of being employed and having a higher income increases with the level and amount of their formal educational credentials. In 1996, labour force participation rates were 27.3 percent among adults with less than Grade 9, compared with 51.6 percent of high-school graduates and 82.1

Educational Solutions for Aboriginal Peoples

Improved educational access and attainment are recognized by aboriginal people as central to their aspirations for self-government and fuller participation in all areas of social and economic life. A report by the Royal Commission on Aboriginal Peoples summarizes some of the key areas in which educational solutions are required as part of a wider strategy of economic development.

First, while there is strong reason to believe that further investments in education and training will improve labour force outcomes, the potential benefits should not be exaggerated. They will help, but they will reduce inequalities by only 10 to 25 percent, even if equality in levels of education and training is achieved. Even when other observable characteristics are taken into account, there remain gaps in labour market outcomes for single-origin aboriginal and non-aboriginal Canadians on the order of 50 percent.

Second, high school completion rates must continue to improve. Youth who fail to complete high school face a labour market that increasingly demands completion or better. Future generations must have at least the minimum required for success in employment and for entry into higher education.

Third, we have the drawbacks of obtaining some post-secondary education or training but not acquiring a degree or certificate. This does not apply to university education or to all subgroups uniformly. For example, the results differ somewhat by sex, age and on- or off-reserve location. Nevertheless, this finding warrants further investigation. The picture might change if it were possible to separate out those who completed non-university post-secondary studies from those who enrolled but did not complete their studies. The result may also hinge on the kinds of occupations that predominate in the non-university post-secondary field and their vulnerability to fluctuations in the demand for labour.

Fourth, in addition to increased enrollment in and completion of university education, more graduates in scientific technology and economic development are particularly needed. A very low number of aboriginal students are enrolled in, or have graduated from, scientific and technical programs.

Finally, lack of completion of elementary school among older aboriginal people must be addressed. As we discuss in Volume 3, Chapter 5 [of *Report of the Royal Commission on Aboriginal Peoples*], the most pertinent policy direction for this portion of the population is adult education and literacy programming, including encouragement to return to school to complete studies. Educational solutions may not always be appropriate, however, and a number of recommendations would go some distance to improving the economic situation of those with low levels of education (for example, expanding the land and resource base, supporting the traditional economy, making innovative use of income support programs).

Source: Excerpt from Privy Council Office, *Report of the Royal Commission on Aboriginal Peoples, Volume 2: Restructuring the Relationship* (Ottawa: Minister of Supply and Services, 1996), pp. 969–70. Reproduced with the permission of the Minister of Public Works and Government Services Canada, 1998.

percent of those with a university degree (Statistics Canada 1997e, B11). Although age and other factors account for some of these differences, education's relationship to employment prospects is nonetheless clear. That same year, the unemployment rate for men with less than Grade 9 education was 15.3 percent, compared with 9.9 percent for high-school graduates, 8.2 percent with a post-secondary certificate or diploma, and only 4.7 percent with a university degree, while for women the corresponding unemployment rates were 14.0 percent for those with less than Grade 9, 9.4 percent for high-school graduates, 8.1 percent with a post-secondary certificate or diploma, and 5.7 percent with a university degree (Statistics Canada 1997e, B11). In 1996, the median income of families headed by a person with less than Grade 9 education was \$31 811, well below comparable figures of \$48 542 for families headed by a high-school graduate, and \$73 793 for families headed by a university graduate (Statistics Canada 1997d, 81).

National surveys of persons who graduated from educational programs reveal that differences in benefits from education tend to be both immediate and compounded over time. Graduates from 1982 experienced an overall average increase in income of one-third between 1984 and 1987, compared with an average of 13 percent for all workers employed full-time on a full-year basis (Statistics Canada 1989, 51). Similarly, while 1990 graduates from post-secondary programs received comparable returns on their education two years later, their real earnings had increased by a further 10 percent or more by 1995 (Little and Lapierre 1996, 36; Paju 1997, 11–13). Table 10.4 illustrates the general tendency for average earnings to increase with higher levels of educational credentials with persons who held postgraduate university degrees making on average more than twice the earnings of persons with trade and vocational training.

It is important to note also the perpetuation of strong gender disparities. The figures in Table 10.4 reveal that women earned less than men at all levels except for university graduates who received a doctorate in 1990 (a very small proportion of the total population). The highest gender gaps in average earnings, historically, have been among those with the lowest levels of educational credentials. Data suggest that the wage gap is narrowing slowly, shifting in accordance with changes in work and labour markets that favour those with the highest educational attainments. Among people who worked full-time on a full-year basis, women earned on average 73.1 percent of men's average earnings in 1995 compared with 63.7 percent in 1981. Among those with a university degree, the ratio of women's to men's average earnings in 1995 was 76.1 percent, while among those with some high school, the comparable figure was 65.1 percent; for those with less than a Grade 9 education, the ratio was 69.6 percent, suggesting the relatively poor occupational conditions for both men and women with low educational attainment (Statistics Canada 1997b, 20–21).

These wage differentials can be explained, in part, by differences in the educational programs and career options available to or followed by men and women. For example, data collected on 1982 university bachelor's and first professional degree graduates working full-time in 1984 revealed that 32 percent of women compared with 13 percent of men were employed in teaching and related occupations. Women graduates had gone into such areas as health care (about 15 percent) and clerical work

TABLE 10.4 Median Earnings (in Constant 1992 Dollars) of Graduates Working Full-Time Two Years after Graduation

		1982 graduates in 1984		1986 graduates in 1988		1990 graduates in 1992	
		Median earnings ($000)	Gender gap[a] (%)	Median earnings ($000)	Gender gap[a] (%)	Median earnings ($000)	Gender gap[a] (%)
No degree		23.9	64.1	23.5	62.1	22.6	72.4
Certificates/ diplomas:	Trade/ vocational	20.8	81.1	22.4	76.5	23	84
	Career/ technical	25	80.1	26	87.1	26	89.3
University degrees:	Bachelor's	31.9	91.6	31.9	93	32	96.9
	Master's	44.4	85.8	44.8	90	44	93.3
	Doctorate	47.1	88.7	46	94.9	46	104

[a] Women graduates' median earnings as a percentage of men's. For those with no degree, a gender gap is included for comparison purposes only based on estimate from persons who had some or completed high school in 1984, 1988, and 1992, respectively.

Source: Adapted from Statistics Canada, *Labour Force Annual Averages*, Cat. no. 71-220 (February 1997).

(10 percent), where numbers of men were low, and the male graduates had concentrated in areas such as engineering, natural sciences, and mathematics (23 percent), where there were few women employed (Picot, Wannell, and Lynd 1987, 41–42).

Even in occupations where men and women are employed with equivalent educational credentials, wage gaps are apparent. Data on full-time full-year workers from the 1991 census reveal that, for example, in health diagnosing and treating occupations requiring university degrees (such as medicine, dentistry, and veterinary occupations), men earned on average $99 626 whereas women earned $61 606; male kindergarten and elementary school teachers earned on average $45 971 compared with $37 699 for female kindergarten and elementary teachers; for bookkeepers and accounting clerks with trades certification, diplomas, or some post-secondary education, males earned on average $31 389 whereas females averaged $23 880; and for workers in food and beverage serving occupations, men earned on average $17 822 compared with $13 037 for women (Statistics Canada 1993a).

Results from national surveys of graduates reveal in more detail how unemployment rates are closely related to educational credentials. According to the survey of 1982 graduates, initially conducted during a major recession, 15 percent of graduates from trades and vocational programs were unemployed in 1987 compared with 24 percent in 1984; the proportion of college graduates who were unemployed in 1987 was 5 percent, half of the figure for 1984; and only 4 percent of university graduates were unemployed in 1987 compared with 9 percent in 1984 (Statistics Canada 1989,

2). There is, however, evidence to indicate that shifting labour-force patterns are affecting different categories of graduates in particular ways. Among 1986 graduates surveyed, 16 percent of persons who graduated from trade/vocational programs were unemployed in 1988 compared with 7 percent of community college graduates and 9 percent of university graduates (Clark 1991, 20). Moreover, of those graduates who were unemployed, the duration of unemployment was associated with levels of education. In 1992, students who had graduated two years earlier from trades and vocational programs who experienced unemployment were out of work for an average of 7.7 months compared with an average of 5.8 months for unemployed career/technical college graduates and 5.4 months for university graduates (Little and Lapierre 1996, 32–33).

There continues to be a strong connection between educational opportunities and wider socio-economic opportunities amid important structural changes in labour markets. In the rise of the "service economy," new job creation is centred, on the one hand, around several higher-level jobs (characterized by relatively high wages, good working conditions, and requirements for advanced, specialized credentials) and massive growth, on the other hand, in the number of lower-level jobs (characterized by low wages, poorer working conditions, and little job-specific training). A corresponding decline in the proportion of jobs in intermediate categories (see, e.g., Economic Council of Canada 1991; Myles, Picot, and Wannell 1988) indicates that educational selectivity remains at the core of economic adjustment processes.

Education has implications for several forms of social opportunities in addition to employment and income. Such problems as poverty, criminality, illness, malnutrition, and racism have been linked by governments and researchers to low levels of educational attainment (Ghosh 1995, 10–11; National Council of Welfare 1997). In short, education plays a major role in either shaping or reinforcing a person's social opportunities.

Conclusions

There are different ways in which we can interpret the trends presented in this chapter. With some exceptions, Canadian data reflect a general tendency for increased access to educational opportunities and a correlation between level of educational attainment and socio-economic benefits. On the basis of these trends, it is commonly concluded that the Canadian education system is essentially successful as a mechanism for ensuring fair and open competition for available life opportunities. It seems reasonable to make the conclusion that social success depends on a person's ability to gain strong educational credentials. Success or lack of success follows, apparently, as a consequence of individual capabilities and initiative. In other words, if a person is highly motivated to succeed, the educational opportunities are there to enable him or her to advance out of a cycle of poverty and low standard of living. From this viewpoint, which is represented in the quotations that were presented at the beginning of this chapter, the education system is judged to be a failure only when it reduces individuals' motivations to succeed. When students drop out of school before graduation or achieve low levels of formal certification, the losers are the individual, who does not reap the benefits that education offers, as well as society as a whole, which suffers from the waste of talent. In a society characterized by rapid technolog- ical change and faced with the requisite to develop an increasingly productive work force under the challenge of strong international competition, it is, apparently, imper- ative that all individuals be driven to their highest levels of achievement for the common good. Within this context, critics of Canada's education system look envi- ously at nations such as Japan where a streamlined, highly competitive education system is assumed to be a fundamental engine of efficient productivity and massive economic growth (see, e.g., Maynard 1989).

It is instructive, however, to examine the trends using different sets of assumptions and points of emphasis. The data reveal that there are significant inequalities in edu- cational enrollment and achievement that transcend individual differences and reflect instead the continuing importance of factors such as class, gender, and race. In other words, a person's prior place in the social structure influences both the opportunities for and benefits from education. Consequently, it is necessary to look at social, eco- nomic, and political structures rather than individual characteristics in order to explain social and educational failure and success.

There are several specific reasons why different persons and groups may fail or succeed in and out of school systems, constituting a complex equation that involves such factors as language, race, and gender stereotyping; parental background; stu- dent–teacher interaction; curriculum options; mental and verbal ability; and even "luck" (see, e.g., Martin and Macdonell 1982, and Wotherspoon 1998 for reviews of the literature). While it is important to look at the relative impact each of these vari- ables has on people's life chances, it is also necessary to see these features as part of a totality that both reinforces and is produced by a social structure based on relations of inequality and of domination and subordination. Viewed in such terms, inequali- ties in educational opportunities and benefits are not merely unfortunate by-products of a formal education system, which requires some minor readjustments or repairs to stay in tune with social and technological change. To the contrary, the production of unequal social opportunities has been a systematic, regular feature of Canada's edu- cation system that has served to perpetuate the inequalities embedded within capital- ist society. What is at issue in contemporary demands for "quality education," "lifelong learning," "flexibility," "accountability," and "competitiveness" is not altru- istic concern for the learner, but rather a direct response to capital's demands for an affordable, productive, and compliant work force. The shift has not been complete, but the terrain has clearly shifted away from an emphasis on participation, which did afford minority groups some opportunity for social advancement, to a more restric- tive ethos defined by a small number of business and political leaders and driven by market competitiveness.

Summary

- Recent demands for educational reform in Canada highlight the need for account- ability and responsiveness to market forces.
- Formal education is organized around diverse, often competing, goals.

- Education remains important because it provides credentials and opportunities for social advancement, but it also maintains and legitimizes existing social inequalities.
- Since the Second World War, more Canadians have received increasing amounts of formal education.
- This educational expansion has meant that several groups—especially women, the poor, and visible minorities—have gained access to socio-economic and educational opportunities that were previously limited.
- Nonetheless, there continue to be profound inequalities in access to education and especially in the kinds of education received by different groups.
- These inequalities are likely to be translated into differential benefits and opportunities in employment, income, and other areas beyond education.

Questions to Consider

1. How has the concept of equality of opportunity been defined by different groups in Canada? Compare these definitions with the application of the principle to the organization of educational institutions.

2. Compare and contrast the major explanations of class, gender, and racial inequalities in educational opportunity and attainment.

3. Discuss how the concept of "educational excellence" is employed as an ideology. How is the concept related to contemporary changes in work and education?

4. To what extent can education be effective as a tool to reduce levels of social and economic inequality? Why?

5. Discuss the relationship between the trends in educational inequality emphasized in this chapter and significant developments in the history of Canadian education.

Suggested Readings

Anisef, Paul, and Paul Axelrod. *Transitions: Schooling and Employment in Canada.* Toronto: Thompson Educational Publishing, 1993.

Carnoy, Martin, and Henry S. Levin. *Schooling and Work in the Democratic State.* Stanford: Stanford University Press, 1985.

Erwin, Lorna, and David MacLennan. *Sociology of Education in Canada: Critical Perspectives on Theory, Research and Practice.* Toronto: Copp Clark Longman, 1994.

Gaskell, Jane. *Gender Matters from School to Work.* Toronto: OISE Press, 1992.

Wotherspoon, Terry. *The Sociology of Education in Canada: Critical Perspectives.* Toronto: Oxford University Press, 1998.

Glossary

education The social process in which knowledge, skills, and values are transmitted among individuals. Education encompasses both formal education (or schooling), in which teaching and learning are systematically organized through particular institutions, and informal education, which includes forms of learning that occur in everyday or community contexts.

educational attainment The highest level or number of years of education that a person has achieved, normally at the completion of his or her studies.

equality of educational opportunity The extent to which individuals or groups have similar chances to participate in formal education.

meritocracy A social system in which position is determined according to achievement or merit.

social mobility Chances of movement, either between generations or over the course of a person's lifetime, through different levels of social or economic hierarchies.

structured inequality An arrangement of social positions whereby different individuals or groups have unequal access to valued social resources.

References

Accessibility Task Force. 1989. *Issues and Options Open to the Future: Accessibility, Equity, and Higher Learning for the People of Saskatchewan.* Saskatoon: University of Saskatchewan Accessibility Task Force.

Anisef, P., and N. Okihiro. 1982. *Losers and Winners: The Pursuit of Equality and Social Justice in Higher Education.* Toronto: Butterworths.

Apple, M.W. 1986. *Teachers and Texts: A Political Economy of Class and Gender Relations in Education.* New York: Routledge and Kegan Paul.

Arnoti, B. 1987. "Low Educational Attainment in Canada, 1975–1985." *Canadian Social Trends* (Spring): 28–32. Cat. no. 11-008E.

Badets, J., and T.W.L. Chui. 1994. *Canada's Changing Immigration Population.* Ottawa and Scarborough: Statistics Canada and Prentice-Hall Canada. Cat. no. 96-311.

Bercuson, D., R. Bothwell, and J. Granatstein. 1984. *The Great Brain Robbery: Canada's Universities on the Road to Ruin.* Toronto: McClelland and Stewart.

Boothby, D. 1986. *Women Re-entering the Labour Force and Training Programs: Evidence From Canada.* Study prepared for the Economic Council of Canada. Ottawa: Supply and Services Canada.

British Columbia. 1988. *A Legacy Learners: The Report of the Royal Commission on Education.* Victoria: Province of British Columbia.

Canada. 1994. *Agenda: Jobs and Growth. Improving Social Security in Canada: A Discussion Paper.* Ottawa: Human Resources Development Canada.

Carnoy, M., and H.M. Levin, 1985. *Schooling and Work in the Democratic State.* Stanford: Stanford University Press.

Clark, W. 1991. *The Class of 1986: A Compendium of Findings of the 1988 National Graduates Survey of 1986 Graduates with Comparisons to the 1984 National Graduates Survey.* Ottawa: Employment and Immigration Canada. (LM 198E/1/92).

Coleman, J. 1968. "The Concept of Equality of Educational Opportunity." *Harvard Educational Review* 38, no. 1 (Winter, Special issue): 7–22.

Curtis, B., D.W. Livingstone, and H. Smaller. 1992. *Stacking the Deck: The Streaming of Working-Class Kids in Ontario Schools.* Toronto: Our Schools/Our Selves Education Foundation.

Department of Indian Affairs and Northern Development. 1997. *Basic Departmental Data, 1996.* Ottawa: Supply and Services Canada.

Devereaux, M.S., and D.J. Higgins. 1988. "Part-Time Adult Training." *Canadian Social Trends* 11 (Winter): 28–30. Cat. no. 11-008E.

Dwyer, V. 1996. "Surfing Back to School," *Maclean's,* August 26: 40–46.

Economic Council of Canada. 1991. *Employment in the Service Economy.* Ottawa: Supply and Services Canada.

Frideres, J.S. 1998. *Native Peoples in Canada: Contemporary Conflicts,* 5th ed. Scarborough, ON: Prentice-Hall Allyn and Bacon Canada.

Gaskell, J.S. 1981. "Equal Educational Opportunity for Women." In *Canadian Education in the 1980's,* ed. J.D. Wilson. Calgary: Detselig Enterprises. 173–93.

Ghosh, R. 1995. "Social Change and Education in Canada." In *Social Change and Education in Canada,* 3d ed., ed. R. Ghosh and D. Ray. Toronto: Harcourt Brace. 3–15.

Guppy, N., and A.B. Arai. 1993. "Who Benefits from Higher Education? Differences by Sex, Social Class, and Ethnic Background." In *Social Inequality in Canada: Patterns, Problems, Policies,* 2d ed., ed. J. Curtis, E. Grabb, and N. Guppy. Scarborough, ON: Prentice-Hall. 214–32.

Guppy, N., P.D. Mikicich, and R. Pendakur. 1984. "Changing Patterns of Educational Inequality in Canada." *Canadian Journal of Sociology* 9, no. 3 (Summer): 319–31.

Lanceley, D. 1991. "The Post-Secondary Education Assistance Program for Indian Students: The Vehicle for the Voice of Opposition." In *Hitting the Books: The Politics of Educational Retrenchment,* ed. T. Wotherspoon. Toronto: Garamond Press and Social Research Unit. 235–48.

Li, P.S. 1988. *Ethnic Inequality in a Class Society.* Toronto: Wall and Thompson.

Little, D., and L. Lapierre. 1996. *The Class of '90: A Compendium of Findings from the 1992 National Graduates Survey of 1990 Graduates.* Ottawa: Minister of Public Works and Government Services Canada. Cat. no. MP43-366/1996E.

Livingstone, D. 1985. *Social Crisis and Schooling.* Toronto: Garamond Press.

———. 1987. "Crisis, Classes, and Educational Reform in Advanced Capitalism." In *The Political Economy of Canadian Schooling,* ed. T. Wotherspoon. Toronto: Methuen. 57–67.

Livingstone, D.W., and D. Hart. 1987. "The People Speak: Public Attitudes toward Schooling in Canada." In *Social Change and Education in Canada,* ed. R. Ghosh and D. Ray. Toronto: Harcourt Brace Jovanovich. 3–27.

Martin, W.B.W., and A.J. Macdonell. 1982. *Canadian Education: A Sociological Analysis,* 2d ed. Scarborough, ON: Prentice-Hall.

Maynard, R. 1989. "Look, Jane, Dick Can't Read," *Report on Business Magazine* (May): 87–96.

Mazurek, K. 1987. "Multiculturalism, Education, and the Ideology of the Meritocracy." In *The Political Economy of Canadian Schooling,* ed. T. Wotherspoon. Toronto: Methuen. 141–63.

Mori, G.A., and B. Burke. 1989. *Educational Attainment of Canadians.* Ottawa: Supply and Services Canada. Cat. no. 98-134.

Myles, J., G. Picot, and T. Wannell. 1988. "The Changing Wage Distribution of Jobs, 1981–1986." *The Labour Force, October 1988.* Ottawa: Statistics Canada and Supply and Services Canada. 85–129.

National Commission on Excellence in Education. 1983. "A Nation at Risk: An Imperative for Educational Reform." *Education Week* April 27: 12–16.

National Council of Welfare. 1997. *Poverty Profile 1995.* Ottawa: Supply and Services Canada.

New Brunswick. 1993. *To Live and Learn: The Challenge of Education and Training. Report of the Royal Commission on Excellence in Education.* Fredericton: Commission on Excellence in Education.

Newson, J., and H. Buchbinder. 1988. *The University Means Business: Universities, Corporations, and Academic Work.* Toronto: Garamond Press.

Ontario. 1994a. *For the Love of Learning. Report of the Royal Commission on Learning, Volume 1: Mandate, Context, Issues.* Toronto: Queen's Printer for Ontario.

———. 1994b. *For the Love of Learning. Report of the Royal Commission on Learning, Volume IV: Making It Happen.* Toronto: Queen's Printer for Ontario.

Paju, Michael. 1997. *The Class of '90 Revisited: Report of the 1995 Follow-Up Survey of 1990 Graduates.* Ottawa: Minister of Public Works and Government Services Canada. Cat no. MP43-366/1-1997.

Parliament, J.-A. 1986. "Education in Canada: Selected Highlights." *Canadian Social Trends* (Autumn): 15–20. Cat. no. 11-008E.

Picot, W.G., T. Wannell, and D. Lynd. 1987. "1976 and 1982 Postsecondary Graduates: Selected Highlights of their Labour Force Experience." *Canadian Social Trends* (Autumn): 38–42. Cat. no. 11-008E.

Porter, J. 1987. "Education, Equality, and the Just Society." In *The Measure of Canadian Society: Education, Equality and Opportunity,* ed. J. Porter. Ottawa: Carleton University Press. 242–80.

Porter, J., M. Porter, and B.R. Blishen. 1982. *Stations and Callings: Making it Through the School System.* Toronto: Methuen.

Porter, M., and G. Jasmin. 1987. *A Profile of Post-Secondary Students in Canada: The 1983–1984 National Post-Secondary Student Survey: Summary National Data.* Ottawa: Secretary of State and Statistics Canada.

Royal Commission on Aboriginal Peoples. 1996. *Report of the Royal Commission on Aboriginal Peoples, Volume 2: Restructuring the Relationship, Part Two*. Ottawa: Minister of Supply and Services Canada.

Satzewich, V., and T. Wotherspoon. 1993. *First Nations: Race, Class, and Gender Relations*. Scarborough, ON: Nelson.

Secretary of State. 1988. *Access to Excellence: Being Canadian ... Working Together for Post-Secondary Education: Federal–Provincial Initiatives*. Ottawa: Secretary of State of Canada.

Shor, I. 1986. *Culture Wars: School and Society in the Conservative Restoration, 1969–1984*. Boston: Routledge and Kegan Paul.

Statistics Canada. 1977. *Education in Canada 1976*. Ottawa: Supply and Services Canada. Cat. no. 81-229.

———. 1978. *Historical Compendium of Education Statistics from Confederation to 1975*. Ottawa: Minister of Industry, Trade and Commerce.

———. 1983. *Historical Statistics of Canada*, 2d ed. Ottawa: Supply and Services Canada.

———. 1989. "The Class of '82 Revisited." *Education Statistics: Service Bulletin* 11, no. 1 (February). Cat. no. 81-002.

———. 1993a. *Employment Income by Occupation, The Nation*. Ottawa: Minister of Industry, Science and Technology. Cat. no. 93-332.

———. 1993b. *Educational Attainment and School Attendance, The Nation*. Ottawa: Minister of Industry, Science and Technology. Cat. no. 93-328.

———. 1993c. *Schooling, Work and Related Activities, Income, Expenses and Mobility: 1991 Aboriginal Peoples' Survey*. Ottawa: Minister of Industry, Science and Technology. Cat. no. 89-534.

———. 1997a. "Advance Statistics; Education at a Glance," *Education Quarterly Review* 4, 3 (Fall): 70–88. Cat. no. 81-003.

———. 1997b. *Earnings of Men and Women 1995*. Ottawa: Minister of Industry. Cat. no. 13-217.

———. 1997c. *Education in Canada 1996*. Ottawa: Minister of Industry. Cat. no. 81-229.

———. 1997d. *Income Distributions by Size in Canada 1996*. Ottawa: Minister of Industry. Cat. no. 13-207.

———. 1997e. *Labour Force Annual Averages 1996*. Ottawa: Minister of Industry. Cat. no. 71-220.

Wotherspoon, T. 1987. "Conflict and Crisis in Canadian Education." In *The Political Economy of Canadian Schooling*, ed. T. Wotherspoon. Toronto: Methuen. 1–15.

Wotherspoon, Terry. 1998. *The Sociology of Education in Canada: Critical Perspectives*. Toronto: Oxford University Press.

CHAPTER 11

The Canadian Criminal Justice System: Inequalities of Class, Race, and Gender

*Leslie Samuelson**

Learning Objectives

After studying this chapter, you should be able to
- Think critically about the Canadian justice system.
- Understand the difference between the rule of law and the reality of the justice system in terms of formal equality.
- Understand the nature and the extent of unequal involvement and treatment in the criminal justice system based on class, race, and gender.
- Contemplate the likelihood of, and best venues for, progressive criminal justice.

Introduction

In this chapter we provide a critical criminological analysis of the Canadian criminal justice system. We focus on three related issues, which we have separated for analytical purposes. These concern inequalities of race, class, and gender, in terms both of individuals' involvement in the justice system and of their treatment in it. We first outline the core of a critical criminological analysis of law and society, as well as some important developments within it.

The critical, or conflict, perspective in criminology emerged largely in the 1970s, and challenged conservative neoclassical and liberal pluralist conceptions of law and society (cf. Taylor, Walton, and Young 1973). The central focus for the emerging critical criminology was on how class-based inequality was enforced and legitimated by legal codes and state agencies of control. As Ratner and McMullan (1987, 10) note,

* This chapter is adapted from Leslie Samuelson, "Crime as a Social Problem: From Definition to Reality," in *Power and Resistance: Critical Thinking About Canadian Social Issues*, 2d ed., ed. L. Samuelson and W. Anthony (Halifax: Fernwood Press, 1998). Used with permission.

conservative and liberal criminologists more or less tacitly accepted the bourgeois legal ideology that had evolved over the past 200 years.

Here law is treated as relatively unproblematic. Citizens are expected to obey the law on the assumption that the legal system and the state are neutral institutions seeking to advance the common good (the conservative point of view) or the interests of successful competitors (the pluralist position) by rational and efficient means (Ratner and McMullan 1987, 10). As these and other critical criminologists point out, however, this ideology perpetuates an uncritical acceptance of the legal system and of the political–economic order that is both supportive of, and supported by, the legal system.

Early critical analyses of law, crime, and the state were, however, criticized on several fronts. First, it was noted, they ignored gender. A range of analyses are emerging that focus on how criminal and civil law, and the treatment of women in the justice system, reinforce not only capitalist society with its inequalities, but also the patriarchal subjugation of women (Chesney-Lind and Bloom 1997).

Early critical criminology can also be criticized for its analysis of "race." In most early critical criminological research, such as that by Quinney (1970) and Chambliss and Seidman (1971), race is largely ignored as an issue in its own right; it appears mainly as a proxy indicator of social class status—the central concern of critical criminology (cf. Hawkins 1987).

Finally, Ratner and McMullan (1987) note that current conflict analyses of society must attempt to integrate substantive investigations into a general political economy of state control of social relations through law. As they point out, none of the conservative, liberal pluralist, or early orthodox Marxist analyses of society offered any cohesive statement of the role of the state in the functioning of law and social control in capitalist society. The perspective advocated by Ratner and McMullan is particularly appropriate when analyzing state-sponsored legal reforms, such as victim–offender mediation programs and sentencing reforms.

The developments in critical criminological studies of society that address these criticisms have led us to organize this chapter as follows. We first present an analysis of inequalities of involvement and treatment of individuals in the justice system based upon class, race, and gender. Then we consider whether current and developing criminal justice policies are likely to produce any meaningful change in the structural–cultural conditions that are largely responsible for crime and inequalities of treatment within the justice system. This question is crucial. One of the central concerns confronting critical legal scholars is the extent to which laws and legal systems can be used to alter radically the current status quo.

Class

There are two basic dimensions in the critical criminological analyses of the class-biased nature of law. One is what gets defined in legislation as crime and what is controlled through regulatory law. The second is the differential processing of working-class and professional-class individuals and corporations in the criminal justice system for "criminal acts."

Critical criminologists, who follow a **political economy** approach to the analysis of crime, hold that a relatively small group of individuals control a very large proportion of the wealth and political power in our society. While not necessarily acting in unison, this elite is able to influence the political–legal process so that the social, economic, and physical harms they inflict upon society in the process of capital accumulation are not treated seriously under either criminal or regulatory law. By contrast, the crimes committed by working-class people, which are very frequently a result of their marginalized life circumstances, are prosecuted more severely under the law, with incarceration frequently being the result. As Engels (1892, 95) had long ago noted:

> When one individual inflicts bodily injury upon another, such injury that death results, we call the deed manslaughter; when the assailant knew in advance that the injury would be fatal, we call his deed murder. But when society places hundreds of proletarians in such a position that they inevitably meet a too early and an unnatural death, one which is quite as much a death by violence as that by the sword or bullet; when it deprives thousands of the necessaries of life, places them under conditions in which they *cannot* live—forces them, through the strong arm of the law, to remain in such conditions until that death ensues which is the inevitable consequence—knows that these thousands of victims must perish, and yet permits these conditions to remain, its deed is murder just as surely as the deed of the single individual.

The pioneering Canadian research in this area (Goff and Reasons 1978) has established the state's failure to define as **corporate crime** behaviours whose economic and physical costs, both to individuals and the environment, far exceed those of street crime (Gordon and Coneybeer 1995; Snider 1994). Corporate crime, or "suite crime," is defined as "crime" committed by a corporate official in the pursuit of organizational goals, usually profit. These acts are illegal under either criminal or regulatory law—or would be if we applied the criterion of economic and physical harm to society, which is ostensibly the core criterion of prohibitions and punishments in the Canadian Criminal Code.

Critical criminologists essentially agree that the cost to society of corporate crime far exceeds that of street crime. Exact Canadian data are hard to come by. However, Snider (1994, 276) puts the issue into focus with U.S. data: "Corporate crime costs far more than street crime—all the street crime in the U.S. in a given year is estimated to cost around $4 billion, much less than 5 percent of the average take from corporate crime." U.S. junk bond king Michael Milken alone, she notes, was indicted on 98 racketeering and securities fraud charges and assorted offences. This theft was given an initial very conservative estimate of $325 billion. His company, Drexel Burnham, pleaded guilty to some charges and was fined a small fraction of the losses. The massive Bre-X swindle in Canada constitutes another notable recent similar case of fraud. Or consider the crime of homicide: virtually no one disputes the fact that killing someone is a serious criminal act, and there are continuing flurries and at times much debate over whether or not we should have the death penalty for first-degree murder. In Canada there is one homicide roughly every twelve hours, but even conservative estimates indicate that a worker dies from a preventable employment condition almost every six hours. From 1985 through 1987, actual on-the-job fatalities averaged approximately 907 per year in Canada (Reasons, Ross, and Patterson 1991). In comparison, there were 335 first-degree murder cases in Canada in 1987 (Statistics Canada, 1988). Not so long ago, as Reasons, Ross, and Patterson (1986) show, occupational hazards were the third leading cause of death in Canada, preceded only by heart disease and cancer.

In considering "assault," Desmond Ellis (1986, 94–95) states: "If official statistics on work-related injuries are compared with statistics on criminal code assaults in Canada, then the corporate assault rates are conservatively estimated to be 25 times greater than the conventional street assault rate." Unfortunately, this statistic is much less publicized.

In the 1991 update to their article, Charles Reasons, Lois Ross, and Craig Patterson note, using U.S. data, that only about one-third of all deaths and job injuries can be related to worker carelessness. About 40 percent of job injuries are due to illegal working conditions, while legal but unsafe working conditions account for about another 25 percent of injuries on the job. Snider (1994, 276) notes that the United States has the highest rate of homicide for the developed world, with 20 000 murders in an average year. By contrast, there are 14 000 deaths per annum from industrial accidents, frequently due to safety code violations, and 30 000 deaths from unsafe and usually illegal consumer products.

This issue can be vividly, and sadly, illustrated by recent multiple death industrial events in Canada. To classify these industrial deaths as "accidents," as they generally are, completely obscures the context within which they occur. McMullan and Smith's analysis of the 1982 Ocean Ranger oil rig tragedy, in which 84 lives were lost, puts the case more clearly. According to the conclusions of the official investigation itself, "intervention could have offset design flaws and overcome lax shipping classifications, inadequate seaworthy standards, and poor marine training of staff and prevented the disaster" (cited in McMullan and Smith 1997, 62). I grew up in St. John's, the supply depot for this rig. Local people working on the rig had nicknamed the rig the "Ocean Danger" because of its poor safety standards and operation. But jobs are in short supply on the East Coast; for some of these local people whom I knew it was their last job. More recently, in 1992 the (Nova Scotia) Westray mine explosion claimed 26 lives and also was no accident. "Initial investigations suggest the existence of careless management, unsafe working conditions that included explosively high levels of methane and coal dust, outdated equipment, and a remarkably lax and inept regulations and enforcement system" (McMullan and Smith 1997, 62). They then add, "Sadly, further evidence shows that both federal and provincial governments overruled their own officials who had warned them against opening the mine for health and safety reasons, and then covered up their roles in the disaster."

Governmental complicity of this type is not unique. The Dalkon intrauterine device had severe problems reported by women right from the start of its marketing in North America in 1971. These problems were largely ignored, and by 1974 the Dalkon shield had killed 17 women and infected and injured another 200 000 (McMullan et al. 1992, 15). But the shield was not removed from the so-called marketplace. Instead, corporate executives of A.H. Robins dumped several million unsterilized units in bulk packages onto foreign Third World markets—distributed by the U.S. Agency for International Development's Office of Population. Costing only 25 cents to produce (Sherrill 1987, 51) these several million IUDs were sold for $4.35, a good profit still for A.H. Robins, with the justification "that any contraceptive device was better than none, especially since birth rates were so high in Third World countries" (McMullan 1992, 15). An example of a rationally calculated and even budgeted corporate crime is the Ford Motor Company's Pinto design-flaw consumer deaths. McMullan (1992, 10) notes that "crash tests prior to marketing had shown the gas tank would rupture if hit from behind, even by cars moving at 21 miles per hour." To further quote McMullan (1992, 10):

> Corporate executives had full knowledge of these [Pinto] faults but deliberately decided not to correct them. They had calculated that they would save more than $85 million by delaying lifesaving correctives but would lose no more than $200,000 per death in legal suits. As a result, they chose to put profits before people. Here is how a company memorandum put it:

Benefits

Savings: 180 burn deaths, 180 burn injuries, 2,100 burned vehicles
Unit Cost: $200,000 per death, $67,000 per injury, $700 per vehicle
Total Benefit: $(180 \times \$200,000) + (180 \times \$67,000) + (2,100 \times \$700) =$ $49.5 million

Costs

Sales: 11 million cars, 1.5 million light trucks
Unit Cost: $11 per car, $11 per truck
Total Cost: $(11 \text{ million} \times \$11) + (1.5 \text{ million} \times \$11) = \$137$ million

> This cold calculus suggested that delaying action on car improvement and safety was cost-effective and therefore desirable, even if such safety standards and correctives would result in fewer auto fires and fewer burn deaths and injuries.

Corporate disregard for the health and safety of workers and consumers—coupled with extremely lax governmental control and sanctioning of corporate lawlessness—has been well documented as the basic cause of these injuries and deaths (McMullan 1992; Snider 1988; Reasons, Ross, and Patterson 1986; 1991; Hagan 1985; Brannigan 1984). While there has since been a move to harsher penalties, even when charges are forthcoming, most corporate officials and corporations generally experience few economic, social, or legal penalties. Why is this so? Many analysts see the answer in the class bias of criminal law.

In the first place, the corporate lawlessness documented above is often not even defined as criminal. Most often these costly and harmful behaviours are illegal, but within regulatory law rather than in the Criminal Code where most street crime is placed. This distinction is often made on the basis of legal notions of culpability that were established to prosecute individual offenders for street crime, but not corporations or corporate officials for industry-related killings. In Canada prior to 1941, corporations were immune to any criminal liability because they were deemed to have no mind of their own (McMullan 1992, 80). There was little progress in this area until the late 1970s and early 1980s. Cases heard before the Supreme Court of Canada, such as *Sault Ste. Marie* (1978), *The Canadian Dredge and Dock Co. Ltd* (1985), and *Southam Inc. v. Hunter* (1983), have made some progress toward fitting corporate offenders into an individualist model of liability, evidence, procedure, and sanction (McMullan 1992).

But McMullan (1992) also notes the dispute and confusion existing over whether the **Canadian Charter of Rights and Freedoms** under section 7 and section 1(d) is meant to enforce relatively rigid *mens rea* (guilty mind) requirements for the prosecution of corporate offenders. Decisions at the provincial appeal court level have generally muted the penalty in corporate prosecutions by eliminating incarceration.

McMullan (1992) also states that in the *Irwin Toy Ltd.* case, the Supreme Court of Canada ruled that a corporation's economic rights were not protected by section 7 of the Charter, as are the "life, liberty, or security of the person." While the matter is still up in the air, Canadian judicial history suggests that Canadian courts have not been inclined to extend the scope of corporate criminal proceedings to include the illegal acts or omissions of a corporation's agents or employees. In addition to the problem of *mens rea*, corporations have almost exclusively been prosecuted only for regulatory violations—such as those governing health and safety—and not for the consequences of those violations (Reasons, Ross, and Patterson 1986; McMullan 1992). For example, a company would be fined for not installing safety bolts in a construction crane, but not prosecuted for the death of several workers who were below the crane when it collapsed (as in a recent case in Western Canada). Corporations have frequent and vociferous input into the regulations governing them, generally under the guise of being enlisted to co-operate in creating "workable laws." The result is a lax system of regulation.

One of the most notable examples of this co-optation of law by corporations is the matter of workers' compensation schemes. While the programs have improved the lot of workers in some ways, injured workers lost all rights of prosecution of or compensation from corporations covered by the schemes. The only sources of redress and appeal are the compensation boards (Reasons, Ross, and Patterson 1986, 124).

Two further dimensions of legal regulation—or more specifically the lack thereof—are responsible for the high cost to society of corporate crime. First, corporations are often able to avoid prosecution for illegal activity. Second, even when they are prosecuted, the penalty is usually an inconsequential fine levied against the corporation, while individual corporate decision-makers are usually not singled out, legally or publicly. Even when individual corporate offenders are named, the penalties, both legal and social, are usually only nominal.

In the early 1970s the Ford Motor Company was fined a total of $7 million. The next year the salaries of all the chief executives—to whom apparently no very great amount of opprobrium was attached—were increased. Moreover, Clinard and Yeager (1980) found that if corporate executives do resign or get fired, they frequently get rehired very shortly afterwards, often as "consultants." Finally, it appears that corporations as a whole also do not suffer greatly from opprobrium. An international study failed to find evidence that a company's "stock prices, reputations, sales, or anything else suffered more than temporary embarrassment as result of involvement in corporate crime" (cited in Snider 1988, 261).

Snider (1993) documents the extremely low rate of prosecution and nominal penalties under the Canadian Combines Investigation Act, which was instituted in 1889 and replaced by the Competition Act in 1986. The act has been one of four major forms of regulatory law ostensibly governing corporations. Over a recent 22-year period there were 89 prosecutions under the act, with 57 offences deemed founded. The fines levied in these cases were small, averaging from $7000 to $8000 per company. Snider also notes that the infrequent recommendations for prosecution coming from the conservative Restricted Trade Practices Commission could still be turned down by the Department of Justice, and were in over 10 percent of the cases. It appears that in the period Snider was studying the legal–political system had little interest in prosecuting corporate crime, and things since then have not improved. The Competition Act focusses on the provision of a stable and predictable climate for business, and meaningful punishment for offenders has been virtually removed (Snider 1993, 110).

These examples indicate a significant class bias in the application of criminal, regulatory, and social justice. It should not be hard to understand why Edwin Sutherland (1977) found, in his pioneering work on corporate crime, that 90 percent of the 70 largest corporations in the United States were habitual offenders, with an average of fourteen convictions per corporation (see also Clinard and Yeager 1980). John Hagan (1992, 465) reports that more than half of Canada's largest corporations have been recidivists (convicted more than once), with an average of 3.2 decisions against them.

Perhaps we need punitive corporate "three strikes and you're out" legislation. Canada has seen fit to get tough on street crime in the past decade, with amendments to the Criminal Code and sentencing practices. As a result, federal inmates, most notably, will likely increase by about 100 percent (8938 to 18 000) between 1982 and 2000 (*The Globe and Mail* 1995, A6). At least the lenient attitude toward corporate crime and white-collar criminals is hardening, socially and judicially, as power confronts resistance. First, opinion polls reveal that popular thinking and sentiment are in favour of much tougher laws, regulations, and sanctions regarding corporate misconduct than the state has been delivering. Second, in some instances judicial decisions have emphasized corporate responsibility for harmful acts. For example, the Alberta Court of Appeal recently held that a bankrupt oil company had to spend money to clean up hazardous well sites before creditors received money (McMullan 1992, 116). Finally, there have been proposals to break down the individual and organizational inducements to corporate crime, and traditional defences for it, through the creation of a culture that does not tolerate corporate crime. The proposed solutions include "shaming and positive repentance, new legal tools and controls, corporate accountability and restructuring, new forms of penalty and criminal sanctioning, and the application of countervailing force against corporate crime" (McMullan 1992, 118).

In Canada one of the strongest indicators of this hardening is the 1987 replacement of the **Environmental Contaminants Act** with new legislation providing for fines of up to $1 million per day and up to five years' imprisonment for guilty executives. Consistent with the global concern over the environment, legislation is apparently beginning to get tougher in Canada, both provincially and federally. For example, the federal environment department prosecuted 22 corporate polluters in 1991, compared with only one in 1987. As well, in the early 1990s, the former president of Varnicolor Chemical Ltd. was sentenced to eight months in jail for contaminating soil and ground water on company property in a southwestern Ontario town—perhaps the longest sentence ever for an environmental offence in Canada (*Calgary Herald* 1992, B14).

A final, but very important dimension of class bias in the criminal justice system is the differential conviction and sentencing for street crime involving poor and working-class offenders as compared with middle-class or wealthier offenders. Griffiths and Verdun-Jones (1994, 290) review the literature on this concern. They note that the question is somewhat complex, depending on the charge, previous record, whether individuals are found guilty on all or some charges, and the sentence given. However, a couple of things stand out fairly clearly. Research found that privately represented defendants were found guilty in 54 percent of their trials, while the equivalent figure for poor defendants with legal aid lawyers was 72 percent. As Michael Mandel's (1983) study of the relatively lenient sentencing practices for middle-class and upper-class offenders showed, even when found guilty the judicial myth that the "social opprobrium of trial" punishes upper-class offenders sufficiently was pervasive.

There is some hope, Snider (1994) notes, that at least in some respects the rich won't always get richer, often at great physical and economic cost to society, while the poor get prison. Snider states, "pro-regulatory pressure groups (for example, environmental activities, 'green' politicians trying to eliminate chemicals from farmers' fields, unionists working to secure stronger health and safety laws in the workplace, and feminists working to control the pharmaceutical industry) are absolutely central to the regulatory process" (1994, 278). It is the pressure they exert, she adds, that provides the crucial leverage that forces the state to direct at least some attention to the area of corporate crime.

Race

Canada is not alone in the **overrepresentation of aboriginal peoples** in its criminal justice system. Australia and the United States, for example, have similar experiences (Samuelson 1995). This is not some accident of history, nor the result of a pathology of "lawlessness" among some non-white people. The overrepresentation of aboriginal people in the Canadian justice system is but one legacy of the destruction and dislocation of indigenous peoples that took place under **European colonialism**.

The European colonial political and economic subjugation of territories around the world has been rapidly diminishing. However, it is largely the white colonial population of European origin—and not the original inhabitants of these relatively new nations—who are enjoying freedom from colonialism and its concomitant exploitation and oppression. Essentially, indigenous peoples are still treated as a colonial population, and Canada has been no exception. As Mikel (1979/80, 35) noted, Canada has kept its "Indians" in concentration camps, known as reserves, for about 125 years and has regulated their behaviour in all aspects. Getting this colonialist fact recognized and changed in our ostensibly postcolonialist era is apparently much harder to do in Canada than in the international arena.

Mary Ellen Turpel/Aki-kwe (1992) notes that Canadians like to think of themselves as strong supporters of international rights, ready to contribute troops under the United Nations banner if need be to places like Bosnia and Kuwait. However, she also states that Canada has become increasingly marginalized when the subject of indigenous rights is raised in international political circles. For example, the Director of the Canadian Institute for Human Rights and Democratic Development, Ed Broadbent, recently remarked that he would be in a particularly difficult position when he raises questions about human rights abuses in other countries because "these countries will be saying to me: 'What about aboriginal rights in Canada?' " Canada, Turpel points out, "has been found in violation of international human rights standards on two separate occasions by the United Nations Human Rights Committee because of its treatment of aboriginal peoples, and further indigenous complaints [especially by Labrador Innu] are pending" (1992, 80). As Waldram (1994, 53) has aptly noted, in 1990 the Canadian government sent 1500 armed troops to the Gulf War in Kuwait. But it also sent 3000 troops to Mohawk lands in Quebec after armed Mohawks blocked a gravel road to protest the expansion of a golf course by the neighbouring non-aboriginal town of Oka.

The overinvolvement of Canadian aboriginal peoples with the justice system and their resistance to it can be fully understood only within this political, social, and economic context. An overinvolvement in crime is but one of the social problems that have been generated by the relatively "passive genocide" perpetrated against aboriginal peoples, largely under the rhetoric and guise of "assimilation." As the recent Royal Commission on Aboriginal Peoples (1996, 5–7) final report on justice clearly recognized, the involvement of aboriginal peoples with the justice system tends to indicate the existence of "social" rather than "criminal" problems. Thus, the most central social problems in the area of crime and its treatment are the ones that society creates for aboriginal individuals—not those created by any individual criminal pathology. Put simply, the problem is racism.

The frequent public perception of aboriginal people as "drunks," "lazy," and "criminal" has long confused symptoms with the underlying causes of these social problems (Hylton 1982, 125). Confusing symptom with cause is convenient, because it allows for a one-way street of criminal justice policies and programs that address the "problem of crime" without seriously challenging the status quo of the Canadian political economy. Like most systems of domination from Roman slavery onward, this one depends on those in power developing strong ideologies and typifications that justify their control over subject populations. This was certainly true historically in Canada; unfortunately, it has re-emerged in modern form recently. A recent poll of Canadians confirms a general backlash of attitudes toward Indian, Inuit, and Métis people in the past couple of years. Conveniently and blindly ignoring historical and current realities, almost half of Canadians believe aboriginals have an equal or better standard of living than the average citizen. And 40 percent believe that Natives "have only themselves to blame for their problems" (*Star-Phoenix* 1997). The reality for many aboriginal people, however, is very harsh.

As Satzewich and Wotherspoon (1993) note, the overrepresentation of aboriginal people in the justice system holds for nearly all categories of offenders, all types of

Seeking the Power to Change

The houses are pocked with bullet holes.

The graveyards are full of children.

This is not Sarajevo, but the war here is 20 years old and no one can say who's winning.

"As long as I can remember we've had a solvent-abuse crisis here at Shamattawa," said a tired Liberty Redhead, 25. "I look back on my childhood days and I used to do it when I was younger, it's part of the lifestyle on the reserve."

The latest figures make the solvent-abuse situation at Shamattawa crystal clear.

At least 80 percent of young people living in this moribund community 650 kilometres northeast of Winnipeg are known to habitually sniff gasoline, nail polish remover, paint thinner, varnish, airplane glue—anything they can get their hands on.

The solvent-abuse epidemic is beyond critical. There are about 700 people living here. Of those, 418 between the ages of 3 and 18 have been identified as chronic substance abusers. The habit has reached its third generation: parents and grandparents who have suffered brain damage 10 and 20 years ago have produced a new generation of sniffers.

"We did a count in January," said Philip Johnson of British Columbia's Round Lake Treatment Centre, who has been working with a team of crisis workers at Shamattawa since December. "There is a high rate of abuse in this community. We found 418 chronic sniffers—but that number has decreased since then."

Despite its tragic litany of self-abuse, people say life is slowly turning around for the better at Shamattawa. Although "better" is a difficult concept to reconcile with the picture the settlement presents: half the dishevelled houses have no running water, unemployment is at 90 percent, the 15-amperage hydro power is unpredictable, and one in ten young people has tried to commit suicide in the past eighteen months.

Trouble at Shamattawa reached a zenith in July of 1992 when there was one slaying and seven attempted murders on the reserve, which has a documented history of abuse dating from 1974. RCMP reinforcements were called in to relieve the bedraggled detachment when the chief was suddenly killed by his wife in a domestic dispute nearly two years ago.

The troubles continued as Shamattawa then entered into another cycle of mass suicide attempts. "I think people here have suffered more than other communities," said the current Chief, William Miles. "I don't know about Davis Inlet or Pikangikum but there are a lot of sick people here."

At Pikangikum, just over the provincial boundary from Shamattawa in Northern Ontario, the chief there, Gordon Peters, quit last week in despair over a rash of suicide attempts by young people. But at Shamattawa, the situation is equally desperate, if not worse. "We've had a problem in the past of high suicide rates," said Mr. Miles. "In the last year and a half we've had five suicides and 60 attempted suicides.

"We're trying to tackle the problem," said the chief. "We're trying to put pressure on to try to stop it. A lot of our kids are addicted to sniffing and we have no treatment centre. Our kids are getting a lot of brain damage."

(continued)

(continued)

It was only a few years ago that law and order broke down to the point where the school principal and seven teachers fled Shamattawa fearing for their lives. Eighteen months ago the four RCMP officers stationed here were ducking bullets fired at their homes at night. As recently as last April, it was reported that there were 264 cases on the Shamattawa court docket, in a community where there is no justice of the peace to expedite the caseload.

But Chief Miles isn't alone in offering some cautious optimism.

"The bad news is past," said Shamattawa band elder Allan Redhead. "The previous chief and council wasn't really enforcing their authority to stop the alcoholism and sniff problem. They didn't try to do anything to stop it. Now we're starting to see some successes."

Liberty Redhead is one such story. Although he is just 25, he has beaten his addiction to solvents. He is being trained by the Round Lake volunteers to help other young people in Shamattawa win their war against chemical dependency. When the Round Lake staff leave next month, Liberty Redhead and a handful of others will be left to take on the sniff battle themselves.

Mr. Johnson of the Round Lake centre said changes at Shamattawa must come from within. "It's been a very moving experience coming here to an isolated community and working with the people," he said. "The community very much wants to change. I've seen a lot of changes here in a very short period of time. A lot of people are coming forward now to look for answers."

Source: David Roberts, *The Globe and Mail*, March 14, 1994.

institutions, and all regions of the country, albeit not equally. Overall, 17 percent of persons incarcerated in Canada were aboriginal, while only 3.7 percent of the population reported aboriginal origins in the 1991 census. In the Western provinces, however, this overrepresentation is by far greatest. Averages for the past few years for sentenced admissions to custody show that aboriginal inmates made up 17 percent in B.C. institutions, 31 percent in Alberta, 73 percent in Saskatchewan, and 57 percent in Manitoba. The average drops off dramatically to 7 percent in Ontario (LaPrairie 1996, 33). To spotlight the worst-case scenario, she notes that the aboriginal:non-aboriginal ratio of sentenced admissions is nearly 25:1 in Saskatchewan. How can anyone see these aboriginal peoples as having "an equal or better standard of living than the average Canadian"?

These data present a bleak picture. But recent studies indicate that the overrepresentation of aboriginal peoples in the justice system will only continue to increase rapidly, especially in Western Canada, in tandem with the recovery of their population from near devastation in the early part of this century.

The Alberta report (1991, 8–17) provides a worst-case scenario of what could happen in Western Canada if the trends of the criminal justice system continue to be based on colonialism:

Projections indicate that by the year 2011, aboriginal offenders will account for 18,552 (38.5 percent) of all admissions to federal and provincial correctional centres in Alberta, compared to 29.5 percent of all such offenders in 1989. The aboriginal offender admission population is expected to increase by 69.1 percent from 10,968 in 1989 to 18,552 in 2011, compared to a 13.3 percent increase for the non-aboriginal population.

Lest these data be insufficient to generate concern and change in the criminal justice system and society, the report adds the following: "A rough estimate, using an average length of time in custody of 30 days and an average cost per day of $100.00, indicates that the increase in aboriginal offender admissions alone would cost an extra $22,752,000. This figure does not include inflation. These costs—the financial costs to society as a whole and *the human cost to the aboriginal community in particular*—are extremely high" (1991, sec. 8, 17).

While women in general constitute a pronounced minority in the justice system, aboriginal women are the most disproportionately represented group in both provincial and federal institutions. Although they made up less than 3 percent of the population of women in Canada, in 1991 aboriginal women formed almost 50 percent of the female inmate population in provincial and territorial correctional institutions (LaPrairie 1996, 34). This figure goes down to 17 percent for the more serious federal admissions (sentences of 2 years and over) to penitentiary. This overrepresentation had its greatest concentration in Western Canada. Daubney (1988) found that about 83 percent of the inmates of the Pine Grove Provincial Prison for women in northern Saskatchewan were aboriginal, a figure that has apparently now gone up to about 95 percent (Deputy Director, Pine Grove Institution).

Aboriginal women do not only enter the justice system with more frequency than both non-aboriginal women and aboriginal men, they also enter it quite early in life. A study by the Ontario Native Women's Association (cited in LaPrairie 1987, 104) found that 37 percent of the aboriginal women interviewed in Ontario provincial correctional institutions were 20 years of age or younger, 52 percent were first arrested between the ages of 14 to 17, and 18 percent were even younger when first arrested. In addition, 55 percent had been incarcerated one to three times previously, 40 percent had been arrested fifteen times or more, and 21 percent had seventeen prior incarcerations. Aboriginal females are thus driven up the one-way street of criminal justice early in life and often very frequently, although usually for less than 30 days (Daubney 1988, 221).

To fully understand aboriginal female overinvolvement in the justice system, we must consider the kinds of lives that aboriginal women often experience. LaPrairie (1996, 36) notes Ontario research that found alcohol abuse, unemployment, and poor living conditions associated with arrest and incarceration of aboriginal women. The vast majority had dependents but no steady employment. The report of the Task Force on Federally Sentenced Women, she adds, found 69 percent of individuals interviewed reported experiences of childhood violence, rape, regular sexual abuse, witnessing a murder, or watching their mothers repeatedly being beaten. Nearly 90 percent have alcohol and drug problems (LaPrairie 1996, 37). These data match up fairly well with those in Western Canada (Daubney 1988).

To make matters worse, Sugar and Fox (1989–90) and Satzewich and Wotherspoon (1993) argue that aboriginal women are one of the most oppressed groups in Canadian society generally, but that when they are incarcerated they face several additional factors that impede "healing instead of rage." As Satzewich and Wotherspoon (1993, 198) point out, these factors "include severely inadequate prison facilities and programs, cultural and gender-biased assessment standards, failure to acknowledge and treat the realities of aboriginal women's abusive life histories, and unsympathetic prison regimes." The recently opened Healing Lodge for federally sentenced aboriginal women, in Maple Creek, Saskatchewan, is one very important example of an attempt by Corrections Canada and aboriginal peoples to change these dismal judicial and social realities.

An important issue that must be confronted here is the extent to which the treatment of aboriginal peoples is the result of prejudice and discrimination among Canadians generally and criminal justice personnel in particular. Geoffrey York's book *The Dispossessed: Life and Death in Native Canada* provides a sad historical, and telling modern, picture of the racist treatment of aboriginal peoples. York reports on a study of capital murder cases from 1926 to 1957 (capital punishment by hanging ended in 1962 in Canada). The study found that the risk of execution for an English Canadian who killed a white person was 21 percent, whereas an "Indian" who killed a white person in the same circumstances had a 96 percent risk of execution. Research discovered memos from Indian Affairs bureaucrats recommending that "Indian" offenders be executed because Native peoples needed "special deterrence" (1990, 157). In our day, York notes the differential charging of aboriginal people by police for relatively minor public order offences. Research done in Regina "found that 30 percent of the Indians arrested for drunkenness were charged and sent to court. By contrast only 11 percent of non-Natives were charged and sent to court" (1990, 149). York's overcharging concerns were vociferously repeated by the Aboriginal Justice Inquiry of Manitoba. A large part of the overpolicing of aboriginal peoples, it stated, must be blamed on persisting stereotypical racist attitudes and actions directed against them (1991, 595).

The discussion of how to develop more appropriate criminal and social justice programs, which would be reflective of both the past and present cultural and structural conditions of aboriginal peoples, began to receive attention in the justice system in the mid-1970s (Ekstedt and Griffiths 1988), but has exploded in the 1990s.

These reports have come to emphasize the need for aboriginal self-determination, the resolution of land claims, and the reconstruction of a viable modern aboriginal society within Canada as the most fundamental "justice" concerns. Piecemeal reforms that are not part of this larger initiative, however well-meaning they may be, achieve little substantial success. Unfortunately, the lack of implementation of recommendations from the National Conference on Native Peoples and the Criminal Justice System in the mid-1970s (Ekstedt and Griffiths 1988, 32) continues in the 1990s. The Royal Commission on Aboriginal Peoples (RCAP) roundtable (1993) and final (1996) justice reports noted that some modest reforms have occurred. However, it was well documented in an opening chapter to the roundtable report (1993, 37) that most of the recommendations made in the 1990s justice inquiries (for a summary see 1993, 15–38) had not been addressed, especially those that required substantial restructuring and transfer of control to aboriginal peoples. In important respects, **postcolonial justice** is only slowly being rationed out to aboriginal peoples.

Let us look at these hard-won initiatives. The RCAP (1996, 82–128) final justice report lays out seven basic areas of aboriginal initiatives and steps by non-aboriginal governments and justice agencies to be more responsive to aboriginal people's experiences and needs:

1. **Aboriginal policing:** Until the early 1970s, policing services to aboriginal communities were largely run by the RCMP as part of their role in enforcing the Indian Act. The early 1970s saw the beginning of band policing, expanded in 1978 substantially in Quebec (Amerindian Police Council) and Manitoba (Dakota Ojibway Tribal Council). In 1992 the federal government announced a policy of transferring all on-reserve policing to bands by about the year 2000.

2. **Indigenization:** Attempts to make the current system less alienating without substantially changing the structure and control of the criminal justice system, and/or aboriginal overinvolvement, at least directly. A favoured government response in terms of money spent on aboriginal justice initiatives, up to 90 percent (RCAP 1996, 93). Three main venues: aboriginal justices of the peace and judges, aboriginal court workers, and cultural awareness programs/training for justice personnel.

3. **Indian Act provisions for on-reserve justice initiatives:** Sections of the Indian Act (sec. 81 and sec. 83) provide for band by-laws, though requiring minister of Indian Affairs approval. Section 107 of the Indian Act was used to replace the Indian agent with on-reserve courts, which are especially active in Mohawk communities at Kahnawake and Akwesasne.

4. **Diversion programs and related activities:** Alternatives for justice system processing. Guilt/innocence generally replaced with admit responsibility. Diversion can be pre-charge or post-charge pre-plead. With diversion no criminal record. Diversion active at different times across country from Nova Scotia (at Shubenacadie) to Toronto (Aboriginal Legal Services of Toronto) to Yukon (Kwanlin Dun Justice Project, Whitehorse).

5. **Elders panels and sentencing circles:** These alternative measures sprang originally from the far North, especially the seminal case *R. v. Moses*, to replace "fly-in suitcase" punitive justice. In elders panels, elders or community leaders sit with the judge and advise on sentencing openly or privately. In a sentencing circle, the accused, the victim, family, and community members sit in a circle to discuss the case and the sentence, with the judge retaining final say. Criteria for sentencing circles were set out in *R. v. Alaku*.

6. **Young offender initiatives:** The Young Offenders Act (YOA) passed in 1982 to replace the Juvenile Delinquents Act (1908). Contrary to popular myth, the YOA is very punitive in terms of incarceration for youth, especially for aboriginal youth. Canada is considering emulating New Zealand family group conferencing (FGC), which is based on Maori restorative justice. In New Zealand, FGC has produced a decline of about 50 percent in youth custody, and, notably, 90 percent of police are satisfied with the FGC process.

7. **Aboriginal initiatives in prison:** Increasingly, aboriginal prisoners maintain their right to participation in spiritual and healing ceremonies, as an existing right under section 35 of the Constitution Act, 1982, and under the Charter of Rights and Freedoms. In response, 1992 legislation by Parliament obliges Correctional Services Canada (CSC) to provide programs designed to meet aboriginal offender needs. Changing the CSC is very difficult, but recently a new

holistic healing facility opened near Edmonton for some federally sentenced aboriginal men, in addition to one in Maple Creek for federally sentenced aboriginal women (see also LaPrairie 1996).

Gender

Early critical criminological analyses of social inequalities, justice, and social change virtually ignored women. Gregory (1986) notes, for example, that Taylor, Walton, and Young's groundbreaking 1973 book, *The New Criminology*, did not contain a single word about women. A recent analysis of Canadian criminal justice (Griffiths and Verdun-Jones 1994) still only devotes about seven out of 660 pages to discussing women and justice. Still, gender is beginning to emerge as a rapidly growing component of criminology and socio-legal studies (see Faith 1993; Chesney-Lind and Bloom 1997; Dobash, Dobash, and Noaks 1995).

What concern there has been with gender and justice has been variously grounded in mainstream criminology, liberal feminism, and radical feminism, each with its own central focus, which has resulted in a set of relatively disparate debates. Fortunately, a more promising comprehensive, theoretical, analytical, and policy-based **socialist feminist perspective** is emerging. As Elizabeth Comack (1992, 156) states, "Socialist feminists focus on the interconnection between capitalism (class) and patriarchy (gender) and the manner in which class and gender relations are manifested in the productive and reproductive spheres of society." In addition, Comack (1992) notes, as do other writers, that the structure of inequality in Canadian society includes racism as well.

Within criminology, the starting point for empirical analyses of the involvement of women in crime has generally been grounded in a mainstream criminological concern with the causes of crime. This approach usually emphasizes the generally low rate of female involvement in crime (Hagan 1985; Hartnagel 1996). For example, in 1995 women accounted for only 12.2 percent of all adults charged with violent crimes in Canada; even their property crime involvement rate—about 23 percent of all offenders—still indicated a reasonably large gender gap (Statistics Canada 1996). It is the increases in female criminality in the past decade-and-a-half, however, that have caused the greatest stir.

Recent data show that from 1968 to 1992 the rate for all Criminal Code offences increased by 99 percent for males and 303 percent for females (Hartnagel 1996). As early as the mid-1970s, Canada was said to be witnessing the rise of the "new female criminal," apparently a result of the encroachment of liberated women on a traditional male preserve (Adler 1975). Social roles for women were said to be changing, with women achieving greater equality of involvement not only in society generally, but also in the criminal justice system. This has been dubbed the "converging role thesis." In summarizing this literature, Hartnagel (1992) points out that a 1969 report by the Canadian Committee on Corrections found that 80 percent of the increase in the female crime rate from 1960 to 1966 was primarily due to convictions of women for simple theft. In a major review of studies on gender differences in crime, Smith and Visher (1980) came to a similar conclusion. Hartnagel states that 82 percent of the increase in women charged with Criminal Code offences was for non-violent crime. He notes that from 1968 to 1992 the proportion of all women charged for violent crime increased by only 7 percent, from 10 percent to 17 percent (1996, 104).

It would seem safe to conclude that "female experiences are not moving beyond traditional roles, either legitimate or illegitimate" (Steffensmeier cited in Hartnagel 1996, 110). As Johnson and Rodgers note (1993, 98), women's involvement in crime "is consistent with their traditional roles as consumers, and increasingly, as low income, semi-skilled, sole support providers for their families. In keeping with the rapid increase in female-headed households and the stresses associated with poverty, greater numbers of women are being charged with shoplifting, cheque forging and welfare fraud." Elizabeth Comack's (1996a; 1996b) analyses of women in conflict with the law have found very similar relationships between the everyday conflicts and dilemmas of women and their troubles with the law.

While role convergence and a less "chivalrous" or "paternalistic" (see Chunn and Gavigan 1995) judicial system cannot totally be ruled out as factors in women's involvement in crime, a more fruitful explanation would lie elsewhere. Continuing extensive female job ghettoization, the feminization of poverty (Johnson and Rodgers 1993; in the U.S. see Gimenez 1991), and the development of a youth consumer market frequently directed at teenage females (Greenberg 1977) are more basic to the understanding of female patterns and rates of involvement in crime.

The justice system's treatment of women who have been the victims of crime has also been the object of considerable critical scrutiny in the past two decades. The main areas of concern have been the system's biases, injustices, and ineffectiveness-es in dealing with women who have been the victims of **domestic violence** and sexual assault (Gregory 1986, 326). Domestic violence is a central concern of radical feminists, and in the last decade or so academic research and writing on the subject have mushroomed, along very fractioned lines (Currie and MacLean 1992; Ursel 1991).

Domestic violence, almost always against women, occurs in a large number of Canadian families. The early research in this area by Linda MacLeod (1980) estimated, for example, that at least 10 percent of women in Canada were battered by their partners each year. Unlike street crime, where victim and offender are overconcentrated in the lower socio-economic level of society, this violence is spread across all social classes. Recent data from the Violence Against Women Survey found that 25 percent of Canadian women over the age of 16 experienced violence from a current or post-marital partner (Comack 1996a, 155). Moreover, in 1995 a woman was six times more likely to be killed by a spouse than by a stranger (Statistics Canada 1996).

Past police policy in Canada frequently emphasized minimal intervention on the part of police, according to Burris and Jaffe (1983). In an earlier study the same two authors found that police laid assault charges in only 3 percent of all family violence cases, even though 20 percent of the victims were advised to seek medical treatment and 60 percent were told to lay their own charges (Jaffe and Burris 1981).

In the early 1980s, criminal justice and especially police policy in this area underwent a significant change (Burris and Jaffe 1983). The police force in London, Ontario, was one of the first in Canada to correct the judicial neglect of violence against women. In May 1981 it instituted a policy encouraging officers to lay assault charges in cases of domestic violence. Officers were told that they did not have to witness the assault—they only needed to have reasonable and probable grounds to believe that an assault had occurred (for example, injury serious enough for them to advise the women to seek medical attention). This was followed by a similar initiative in Manitoba, where the changes in police practice have not only led to a dramatic increase in charges laid but also to an equally dramatic increase in convictions for spousal abuse and in the development of treatment programs for batterers; and to a change in the attitudes of crown prosecutors to abuse cases (see Ursel 1998).

The problem of the victims' reluctance to press charges is frequently cited as a reason for police non-intervention in domestic violence. Under the new Ontario policy, the number of private informations—where the victims had to press charges themselves—dropped substantially, from 46 to 13. This fact was all the more important given that police-laid charges were more likely to go to criminal court and end in guilty verdicts than charges pressed through family courts, and the police charges took only about three-quarters of the time to reach their final disposition (Burris and Jaffe 1983). Feminists had philosophical problems with this in that it was tantamount to taking power out of the women's hands to decide their own future and handing it over to the state.

In line with this initiative—and the data from the controversial 1981–82 Minneapolis policing experiment that found a recidivism rate of 19 percent for arrested abusers compared with a rate of 35 percent for cases dealt with by mediation only—a 1983 national directive encouraged police to lay charges in wife-battering cases.[1] Canada was the first country to adopt such a nationwide directive. As Comack (1992) notes, police training was upgraded to stress sensitive intervention in wife assault cases, and several provinces—such as Manitoba—have established specialized courts to deal with domestic violence (Ursel 1998; Prairie Research Associates, Inc. 1994).

As a result of these initiatives, the courts began to deal with increasing numbers of abusive men. "In the province of Manitoba alone, for example, the number of individuals (approximately 96 percent of whom were men) charged with spousal assault increased from 1136 in 1983 to 2779 in 1990" (Comack 1996a, 156). Moreover, as MacLeod (1987) stated in her second report for the Canadian Advisory Council on the Status of Women, the number of transition houses providing shelter for battered women more than tripled, from 85 in 1982 to 264 in 1987.

However, much criticism and controversy exist over the "success" of these initiatives. Currie (1990) and Currie, MacLean, and Milovanovic (1992) point out that there are serious concerns about how the current focus on violence against women can feed into a reactionary law and order lobby (see also MacLeod 1987). Interwoven here is the concern that this "institutionalization" of women's issues fails to deal with the unequal distribution of societal resources and power. Currie and her co-authors frame the problem well: "Within a discourse that concerns legal rights, police protection, and criminal justice, this issue is transformed into a technical matter that can be safely met within the current system without any significant changes in relations of power [between men and women]" (1992, 29).

However, as Jane Ursel (1998) argues about the experiences of the battered women's movement and the Winnipeg Family Violence Court, the positive dimensions of state-sponsored approaches to domestic violence must be recognized. She acknowledges elsewhere that "not all actors and agencies in the field will share the analysis of patriarchy common to the founders of the battered women's movement" (Ursel 1991, 285; see also Rock 1986, 218). Nonetheless, she does find an element of encouragement: "It has been demonstrated that, as a result of state involvement, the number of services for wife abuse victims increased ten fold from 1982 to 1990" (1991, 283). Still, Comack (1996a, 158) directs us to the continued importance of radical transformation in our society, when she writes of the Montreal massacre at the École Polytéchnique:

> While the murder of fourteen women in Montreal has understandably received the attention and publicity it deserves, it is also noteworthy that the violence that women encounter at the hands of men has become "routine." In August 1990 alone, eleven women in Montreal were killed by their male partners, many of them estranged. Yet, two of every three women going to a shelter in Montreal are turned away because of lack of space.

Not surprisingly, patterns of and responses to sexual assault mirror those regarding domestic violence.[2] It is estimated that one in four Canadian women will be sexually assaulted, yet what is most noteworthy is that only 38 percent of an estimated 17 300 sexual assaults, overwhelmingly against females, were reported to police. While a third of the victims of sexual assault cited fear of revenge by the offender, 43 percent cited the attitude of the police or courts as the reason for not reporting the incident (Solicitor General of Canada 1985). Sexually assaulted women were generally more afraid of the additional suffering and humiliation that the justice system would be likely to inflict on them than they were of reprisals by the offender. The fact that only a small fraction of rapists were actually convicted also did little to reassure victims of sexual assault (Snider 1991, 252).

In recent years there have been efforts made in Canada to reduce the trauma visited upon sexually assaulted women. The legal charge of rape was abolished in a 1983 reform to the Criminal Code, as well as the separate charges of indecent assault male and indecent assault female. Contrary to much public concern and fear over girls being sexually molested, before 1983 indecent assault on a female only had half of the maximum penalty that indecent assault on a male had (five versus ten years). In a male-dominated criminal justice system, it was apparently much less deviant for offenders (generally males) to sexually molest girls than boys.

As I have already noted, in place of the rape law, the federal government created three levels of sexual assault based upon the degree of violence. The intent was to reduce the stigma of rape (and, hence, increase reporting by victims) and to emphasize, as many academics and feminists had strenuously contended, that rape was primarily a violent act of male domination in sexual form. The old rape prohibition was, moreover, primarily a paternalistic form of social control against females, not protective legislation, in that it reinforced the idea of women as the property of men (husbands, for example, were immune from criminal sanction under the old law). Not surprisingly, the charge of rape was not even in the "Offences Against the Person" section of the pre-1983 Criminal Code. Rape was in section four of the Canadian Code under "Sexual Offences, Public Morals, and Disorderly Conduct."

There have also been changes in the procedural law governing the examination of persons alleging sexual assault, and the rules of evidence in such cases. Before 1983 the testimony of the victim alleging rape had to be corroborated by other evidence. If it was not, the judge had to instruct the jury on the danger of convicting the accused based upon uncorroborated testimony (Brannigan 1984, 27–28). However, no such warning had to be issued in criminal trials generally—for example, if the victim was identifying an individual who had stolen her purse. As well, the "doctrine of recent complaint" was abolished. This doctrine implied that if a woman reported an offence on the first reasonable opportunity, she was supposedly more "trustworthy" or "believable" in her claim than if she waited until later. The law also formally limited, in 1983, the extent to which the victim could be questioned about her previous sexual activity in a sexual assault trial—the so-called "rape shield provision" (Task Force on the Status of Women 1985, 109–13). The aim of this provision was to prevent a victim's sexual conduct from being used to discredit her.

Still, much scepticism existed over the extent to which these changes would produce any meaningful increase in the reporting of sexual assault by females, or ameliorate judicial stereotyping and traumatization of sexually assaulted women. Despite the legal reforms, many feminists maintained that "justice" would still be elusive for many victims of sexual violence, because "changing the content of law does not ensure that implementation of the changes will reflect the objectives of the legislature" (Allison 1991, 2). This scepticism was apparently warranted. In August 1991 the Supreme Court of Canada, in a 7–2 decision, struck down section 246.6 of the Criminal Code, the "rape shield provision." The 1991 ruling was justified on the basis that section 246.6 could deny the accused the right to a fair trial, as enshrined in sections 7 and 11(d) of the Charter. The Canadian Parliament responded quickly with new legislation, Bill C-49, which amended the Criminal Code to clarify when "No means No" and to restrict the obtaining and admissibility of evidence on the victim's sexual conduct.

However, several analysts have argued that Bill C-127 (the 1983 rape law change) offered little hope that rape would diminish (Boyle 1984: Heald 1985; Snider 1985; Ruebsaat 1985; Hinch 1985). Although the new legislation attempted to address some of the inequities in the original law, the present law—especially in relation to its application—remains decidedly sexist and unjust.

This view received substantial support in the Department of Justice's evaluation of the 1983 sexual assault legislative changes. The study noted that the most substantial change came from the part of the victims. From 1982 to 1990, the number of women coming forward to report a sexual assault climbed from 12 848 to 32 861. Regarding other areas of the criminal justice system the report concluded: "It is apparent that the situation has not changed since the introduction of the new legislation. In particular, unfounded rates, rates of cases cleared by charge, and conviction rates have remained more or less constant" (Canada, Department of Justice 1990, 55). A more recent study echoes this conclusion:

> While Bill C-127 was heralded as the beginning of a new age of gender neutral jurisprudence, this study's analysis suggests that it had little or no impact on the willingness of the state to redress historical gender inequity

through law ... law reforms, although struck in good faith, may be futile
when created and administered in class-biased, gender-biased, socio-economic systems. (Schissel 1996, 126)

It is important that women come forward to report sexual assault. However, as the
data show, the 1983 law did not create substantive legal reform. Whether the new Bill
C-49 provisions will help remains to be seen. As Comack (1996a, 157) noted appre-
hensively about Bill C-49, an important distinction must be made between law as legislation and law as practice.

Another major concern in the area of gender is the injustices and problems faced by
incarcerated women. The issues here exemplify the ideologies and social practices that
are often central in the subjugation of females in patriarchal and capitalist society.

As Berzins and Cooper note in their forceful liberal feminist critique of incarcerated females: "A historical review of the treatment of the federal female offender in
Canada reveals a mixture of neglect, outright barbarism, and well-meaning paternalism" (1982, 401; see also Faith 1993 and Carey 1996). Female offenders have been
contradictorily portrayed as "poor and unfortunate" women in need of protection and
as "scheming temptresses who are lazy and worthless" (Cooper 1993, 33). Currie
(1986) would probably challenge the "well-meaning" dimension of paternalism; at
most, it reflects a "helping" attitude that masks the social control and subjugation of
women. More accurate is a statement by Ekstedt and Griffiths: "Prison, as a micro-
cosm of society, reflects all those inequalities which discriminate against women, be
their source historical, social, or administrative convenience" (1988, 337).

The truth of this statement, past and present, can easily be documented.
Imprisoned women have expressed feelings of frustration, pain, anger, anxiety, and
grief overwhelmingly associated with their everyday experiences of living inside
prison. On this issue, Kendall notes that women "stressed that their incarceration

---

The Violence Affects Us All

The violence affects us all. We all know family members, neighbours, friends, or
co-workers hurt by violence against women. As women, we know the fear of this
violence: our hearts speed up, we plan where we will walk or park our cars,
what we will or will not wear, we defy or ignore our fears, we deny the dangers
and stay inside, and within those walls too often we live with the terror and with
the violence. It gets mixed up with our families, our dreams, our unbearable
memories.... There are no easy answers to ending violence against women. But
one thing is clear—violence against women will not be eliminated until the
social climate is changed, until *all* women are honoured as full and equal members of society, until *all* our lives matter, and our futures and our bodies belong
to us.

Source: Words spoken by Keith Louise Fulton at the opening of the December 6th
Women's Grove Memorial, Winnipeg, Manitoba, September 24, 1995. As quoted in E.
Comack, *Women in Trouble: Connecting Women's Law Violations to Their History of
Abuse* (Halifax: Fernwood Press, 1996). Reprinted with permission.

stripped them of control over their own lives including their schedules, activities, and space" (1993, 4), a situation reminiscent of many women's experiences of abuse prior to incarceration. In the face of all this, and in spite of the inhibited possibilities for independence and the punitive sanctions for displays of their autonomy on the inside, women are still expected by the correctional staff and the parole board to take self-determined action in "making responsible choices" to become "law-abiding citizens." As Kendall (1993) clearly points out, "women are caught in a paradox between what they are allowed to do and what they are told or expected to do." A similar picture has been painted for female "delinquents."

Looking at the old Juvenile Delinquents Act, West (1984) found that three-quarters of young women incarcerated were deemed by the court to be neglected or dependent, and were not considered to be delinquent. These are women whose "offences" consisted primarily of apparent early sexual activity, truancy, disobedience, swearing, and running away (so called "status offences"). West concurs with Geller (1987) that the youth court was more concerned, under the rhetoric of paternalism, with policing the boundaries of traditional gender stereotypes—the double sexual standard—than it was with the protection of young women per se.

The old Juvenile Delinquents Act of 1908 was replaced by the Young Offenders Act (YOA), which was phased in during the early 1980s. This new act was supposed to end the evils of the previous juvenile legislation. For example, juveniles can now no longer be formally prosecuted or incarcerated for "status offences" such as truancy and incorrigibility. Still, the YOA is being used to bring more youth into court. Manitoba has seen increases of 150 percent in incarceration rates for youth since the introduction of the YOA, and youth are being held in custody much longer (Geller 1987, 121; see also Markwart 1992, 246). Unfortunately, the general public now believes that the YOA and youth court are far too lenient on young people in conflict with the law, both male and female. This view is especially inflamed because of the infrequent, but highly publicized, cases of youth homicide. However, as Bernard Schissel concludes in his study of youth crime, "most ... kids ... are in trouble for violations of the formal bureaucratic rules of the Young Offenders Act, and are not the gun-toting kids pictured in *MacLean's* and *Alberta Report*." He adds, "To those who argue that the Young Offenders Act is allowing youths to 'get away with murder,' I would say that nothing can be further from the truth" (1997, 99).

Finally, on the issue of incarcerated adult females, Cooper analyzes the evolution of the **Federal Prison for Women (P4W)** in Kingston, Ontario. P4W opened its doors in 1934, just across the road from the Kingston Penitentiary for Men, which had previously housed federally sentenced women. All federally sentenced women from across Canada were now to be gathered into a centralized institution, modelled generally after federal male penitentiaries. The management of P4W continued to be the responsibility of the male penitentiary warden. However, at P4W there were no gun towers and, unfortunately, no outside windows, no enclosed recreation grounds, no provision for outdoor exercise of any kind, nor educational facilities for the female prisoners (Cooper 1987, 13).

It is thus not surprising that virtually every major commission investigating Canada's penal system, from the 1938 Archambault Report onward, severely criticized conditions at P4W and generally recommended its closure, agreeing that the relatively small number of female prisoners should be housed in their home provinces. Indeed, as Cooper (1987) notes, since 1968 no fewer than thirteen government studies, investigations, and private sector reports have been produced that reiterate this basic conclusion. The recalcitrance of the Canadian justice system to change is well indicated by the fact that Berzins and Cooper, the two women whose task it was to improve services and programs at P4W and who were instrumental in producing a meaningful review of the existing programs, were fired in 1979 by Correctional Services of Canada. Their report did not meet with the approval of the commissioner of corrections, although it did become public by accident.

Most seriously, the group Women for Justice, distressed by the lack of change that had accompanied report after report, finally achieved a landmark 1981 Human Rights of Canada Commission decision. The Commission ruled that Correctional Services of Canada was discriminating against female prisoners at P4W. Berzins and Cooper (1982) noted that there were major deficiencies in facilities and programs compared to those available to federally incarcerated men.

Federal penitentiaries for men were spread across the country, but although some federally sentenced women were able to do time in provincial institutions (through a federal–provincial agreement), only the Kingston facility existed for women until recently. Correctional Services saw the use of one centralized federal facility for the relatively small number of women as being the most cost-effective system. Within this one facility, all federally sentenced women were housed as maximum security prisoners, which also provided a justification for limiting the quantity and quality of programs offered to them.

P4W had a high suicide rate, especially for aboriginal women, who were often incarcerated far from home. A 1990 coroner's inquest into the death of Sandra Sayer connected the suicide rate to the institution's systemic discrimination. Sayer, a 24-year-old Saulteaux, was found hanging from the bars of her cell less than two months before her expected release date—which was not an unusual incident at P4W. In early February 1991, a group of female prisoners had barricaded themselves in the prison recreation room to protest the fourth aboriginal inmate suicide in sixteen months. The prison's response was to quell the protest by use of an assault team, dogs, and tear gas (*Star-Phoenix* 1991a). Rather than being placed in specialized psychiatric facilities, traumatized female inmates were confined to segregation facilities—spartan cells locked 23 hours a day. They lost the comforts of their home cells—the family photographs on their walls, their television, their books—at a critical time. They were stripped of their clothing and left wearing a paper gown *(Star-Phoenix* 1991b, D1). These conditions were reportedly worse than those in any male institution (Berzins and Cooper 1982, 406).

The programs offered at P4W constituted another form of blatant discrimination. Ekstedt and Griffiths (1988) discuss in detail the inadequacies and biases of programs at P4W and in provincial institutions, and provide a history of the criticism that has been levelled at them. Prison programs for women repeat, and attempt to reinforce, the stereotypical social and occupational roles of women in society. The 1978 Proudfoot Commission inquiry cited working in the prison laundry, working in a beauty parlour, doing kitchen work, and learning sewing as typical correctional programs for women. Berzins and Hayes note that the epitome of education in P4W, introduced as a result of the 1981 Human Rights Commission decision, was the introduction of word processors. But women were taught keyboarding only, not programming, reinforcing their chances of experiencing poverty on their release and hence possibly starting the criminal cycle again (1987, 173).

Importantly, 1990 saw the release of the report by the Task Force on Federally Sentenced Women, *Creating Choices*. The 1990 report established five fundamental principles:

1. empowering women (programs to raise their self-esteem)
2. providing more meaningful choices in programs and community facilities (a wider range of options)
3. treating women with respect and dignity (to enhance self-respect)
4. providing a physically and emotionally supportive environment
5. sharing responsibility for prisoners' welfare among correctional workers and members of the community (co-operation among government, correctional workers, and voluntary organizations)

The plan called for regional facilities, a healing lodge, and a community release strategy. Moreover, each of these were to differ from traditional "male-oriented" corrections.

After the publication of the Task Force Report the announcement was finally made that P4W would be closed and that five new regional facilities, and a "healing centre" for aboriginal women at Maple Creek, Saskatchewan, would be built. Change did not come easily at P4W, however. In April 1994 the male Institutional Emergency Response Team from Kingston penitentiary was sent to P4W to "quell a violent incident." The public release of the horrific, brutal institutional response to an inmate–staff confrontation, which was videotaped, resulted in a 1996 Commission of Inquiry. Its final report was very critical of the substantial abuse of these inmates and the violation of numerous Correctional Service formal procedures. To cite one example:

> Mace was used to subdue three of the inmates involved in the April 22nd incident. Although Correctional Service policy contains elaborate provisions with respect to decontamination following the use of mace, in this case, decontamination was limited to pouring some glasses of water over the inmates' eyes. (Canada 1996, 31)

It concluded that, overall, "Nearly every step that was taken in response to this incident was at odds with the intent of the new [*Creating Choices*] initiatives" (Canada 1996, 24).

Summary

- To move beyond piecemeal and partial socio-legal reforms in the area of gender and social justice, it is necessary to develop a more comprehensive theoretical, analytical, and policy-based socialist feminist critique of our society.
- Currie states: "What is necessary is a distinctly 'feminist' criminology which can explain crime in general while studying women in particular. The goal of such an investigation should be not only to understand the involvement of women in officially recorded crime, but to understand the oppression of women, without this becoming a tool of oppression itself" (1986, 237).

- Feminist criminologists such as Gregory (1986) and Chesney-Lind and Bloom (1997) argue that what is needed is a dynamic and integrated analysis of the inter-relationships between patriarchy, capitalist society, and state control of women.
- Critical criminologists have come to see locating racism in such an analysis as a critical part of this project as well.

Questions to Consider

1. Critically evaluate the truth of the statement that "criminal law and the justice system protect us from serious economic and physical harm."

2. To what extent are upper-class individuals treated more favourably than lower-class people by the Canadian justice system?

3. Explain the nature of the overinvolvement of aboriginal peoples in the justice system, and the signs of positive change in this area.

4. Are women treated better by the justice system than men? Explain.

5. How likely is it that inequalities of involvement and treatment in the justice system based upon class, ethnicity, and gender will disappear in the near future?

Suggested Readings

Aboriginal Justice Inquiry of Manitoba. *The Justice System and Aboriginal People*. Report. Winnipeg: Supply and Services Canada, 1991.

Adelberg, Ellen, and Claudia Currie. *In Conflict with the Law: Women and the Canadian Justice System*. Vancouver: Press Gang, 1993.

Chesney-Lind, Meda, and Barbara Bloom. "Feminist Criminology: Thinking about Women and Crime." In *Thinking Critically about Crime*, ed. B. MacLean and D. Milovanovic. Vancouver: Collective Press, 1997.

DeKeseredy, Walter, and Martin Schwartz. *Contemporary Criminology*. Toronto: Wadsworth, 1996.

McMullan, John. *Beyond the Limits of the Law: Corporate Crime and Law and Order*. Halifax: Fernwood, 1992.

Royal Commission on Aboriginal Peoples (RCAP). *Bridging the Cultural Divide*. Ottawa: Minister of Supply and Services Canada, 1996.

Glossary

Charter of Rights and Freedoms, section 7 and section 1(d) Prior to 1941, corporations were immune to any criminal liability because *mens rea*, "guilty mind," could not corporately exist. Section 7 and section 1(d) of the Charter have been used to argue against this rigid *mens rea* requirement in prosecution of corporate crime.

corporate crime Harmful economic, human, and environmental acts committed by corporate officials in the pursuit of organizational goals, usually profit, and generally unpunished by the state.

domestic violence Usually violence against women by their partners. The Violence Against Women Survey found that 25 percent of women over 16 years of age experience violence from a current or post-marital partner.

Environmental Contaminants Act New legislation after 1987, which substantially increased the penalty for environmental pollution to up to $1 million per day and up to five years in prison for guilty corporate executives.

European colonialism The takeover by white settlers of land belonging to aboriginal peoples, resulting in their near genocidal destruction, both physically and culturally.

Federal Prison for Women (P4W) P4W opened in 1934 to house federally sentenced women. Conditions were very harsh, paternalistic, and far inferior to prisons for men. Inmate despair and suicide were thus a major problem.

overrepresentation of aboriginal peoples in the justice system In the 1991 census, aboriginal peoples accounted for 3.7 percent of the Canadian population, and yet, 17 percent of incarcerated Canadians are aboriginal. In the West this percentage is especially high (73 percent in Saskatchewan).

political economy Wealth and political power concentrated in a few individuals and corporations, giving them substantial political, legal, and economic control over our ostensibly democratic society.

postcolonial justice An alternative system of justice for aboriginals that includes aboriginal self-determination and resolution of land claims in conjunction with traditional healing and harmony restoration.

socialist feminist perspective A focus on the relationship between class and gender and how it is manifested, especially in the subjugation of women in the productive and reproductive spheres of society.

Notes

1. See Currie and MacLean (1992) for a critique of the Minneapolis research.
2. One of the most criticized cases has been the well-known ruling in *Pappajohn v. the Queen* (1980), in which the controversial decision given in *Morgan* (1975) was upheld. In *Pappajohn*, the Supreme Court of Canada held that an honest mistake of belief to consent were grounds for a defence to the charge of rape, whether there were reasonable grounds for that belief or not. This "honest-mistake-of-fact" defence was allowed in *Pappajohn*, even though in the latter part of the alleged repeated raping the victim was bound to the bedposts and gagged.

References

Aboriginal Justice Inquiry of Manitoba. 1991. *The Justice System and Aboriginal People*. Vol. 1. Winnipeg: Queen's Printer.

Adler, F. 1975. *Sisters in Crime*. New York: McGraw-Hill.

Alberta. 1991. *Justice on Trial*. Edmonton: Task Force on the Criminal Justice System and Its Impact on the Indian and Métis People of Alberta.

Allison, M. 1991. "Judicious Judgements? Examining the Impact of Sexual Assault Legislation on Judicial Definitions of Sexual Violence." In *Criminal Justice: Sentencing Issues and Reforms*, ed. L. Samuelson and B. Schissel. Toronto: Garamond Press. 279–97.

Berzins, L., and S. Cooper. 1982. "The Political Economy of Correctional Planning for Women: The Case of the Bankrupt Bureaucracy." *Canadian Journal of Criminology* 24: 399–417.

Berzins, L., and B. Hayes. 1987. "The Diaries of Two Change Agents." In *Too Few to Count: Canadian Women in Conflict with the Law,* ed. E. Adelberg and C. Currie. Vancouver: Press Gang. 163–79.

Boyle, C. 1984. *Sexual Assault.* Toronto: Carswell.

Brannigan, A. 1984. *Crimes, Courts, and Corrections.* Toronto: Holt, Rinehart and Winston.

Brodeur, J.P., C. LaPrairie, and R. McDonnell. 1991. *Justice for the Cree: Final Report.* Cree Regional Authority: Grand Council of Crees (of Quebec).

Burris, C., and P. Jaffe. 1983. "Wife Abuse as a Crime: The Impact of Police Laying Charges." *Canadian Journal of Criminology* 25: 309–18.

Calgary Herald. 1992. "Tough Laws Catch Up with Corporate Polluters." September 10.

Canada, Department of Justice. 1990. *Sexual Assault Legislation in Canada: An Evaluation–Overview.* Ottawa: Supply and Services Canada.

Canada. 1991. *Aboriginal Peoples and Criminal Justice.* Ottawa: Law Reform Commission of Canada.

———. 1996. *Commission of Inquiry into Certain Events at the Prison for Women in Kingston.* Ottawa: Public Works and Government Services.

Canadian Committee on Corrections. 1969. *Toward Unity: Criminal Justice and Corrections.* Ottawa: Queen's Printer.

Carey, Carolyn. 1996. "Punishment and Control of Women in Prison: The Punishment of Privation." In *Social Control in Canada: A Reader in the Social Construction of Deviance,* ed. B. Schissel and L. Mahood. Toronto: Oxford University Press.

Chambliss, W., and R. Seidman. 1971. *Law, Order, and Power.* Reading, MA: Addison-Wesley.

Chesney-Lind, M., and B. Bloom. 1997. "Feminist Criminology: Thinking about Women and Crime." In *Thinking Critically about Crime,* ed. B. MacLean and D. Milovanovic. Vancouver: Collective Press.

Chunn, D., and S. Gavigan. 1995. "Women, Crime and Criminal Justice in Canada." In *Canadian Criminology,* ed. M. Jackson and C. Griffiths. Toronto: Harcourt Brace.

Clinard, M., and P. Yeager. 1980. *Corporate Crime.* New York: The Free Press.

Comack, E. 1992. "Women and Crime." In *Criminology: A Canadian Perspective,* 2d ed., ed. R. Linden. Toronto: Harcourt Brace Jovanovich. 127–62.

———. 1996a. "Women and Crime." In *Criminology: A Canadian Perspective,* 3d ed., ed. R. Linden. Toronto: Harcourt Brace.

———. 1996b. *Women in Trouble.* Halifax: Fernwood Publishing.

Cooper, S. 1987. "The Evolution of the Federal Women's Prison." In Adelberg and Currie, *Too Few.* 127–44.

———. 1993. "The Evolution of the Federal Women's Prison." In *In Conflict with the Law: Women and the Canadian Justice System,* ed. E. Adelberg and C. Currie. Vancouver: Press Gang.

Currie, D. 1986. "Female Criminality: A Crisis in Feminist Theory," In *The Political Economy of Crime,* ed. B. MacLean. Scarborough, ON: Prentice-Hall.

———. 1990. "Battered Women and the State: From a Failure of Theory to a Theory of Failure." *Journal of Human Justice* 1: 77–96.

Currie, D., and B. MacLean, eds. 1992. *Rethinking the Administration of Justice.* Halifax: Fernwood Publishing.

Currie, D., B. MacLean, and D. Milovanovic. 1992. "Three Traditions of Critical Justice Inquiry: Class, Gender, and Discourse." In *Rethinking the Administration of Justice,* ed. D. Currie and B. MacLean. Halifax: Fernwood Publishing.

Daubney, D., chairman. 1988. *Taking Responsibility: Report of the Standing Committee on Justice and Solicitor General on Aspects of Corrections.* Ottawa: Supply and Services Canada.

DeKeseredy, W., and M. Schwartz. 1996. *Contemporary Criminology.* Toronto: Wadsworth.

Dobash, R.E., R.P. Dobash, and L. Noaks, eds. 1995. *Gender and Crime.* Cardiff: University of Wales Press.

Ekstedt, J., and C. Griffiths. 1988. *Corrections in Canada.* Toronto: Butterworths.

Ellis, D. 1986. *The Wrong Stuff.* Toronto: Collier McMillan.

Engels, F. 1892. *The Condition of the Working Class in England in 1844.* London: George Allen and Unwin.

Faith, K. 1993. *Unruly Women: The Politics of Confinement and Resistance.* Vancouver: Press Gang.

Forcese, D. 1992. *Policing Canadian Society.* Scarborough, ON: Prentice-Hall.

Geller, G. 1987. "Young Women in Conflict with the Law." In Adelberg and Currie, *Too Few.* 113–26.

Gimenez, M.E. 1991. "The Feminisation of Poverty: Myth or Reality?" *Social Justice* 17, no. 3: 43–67.

The Globe and Mail. 1995. "Penitentiaries Close to Overcrowding Crisis." February 6.

Goff, C., and C. Reasons. 1978. *Corporate Crime in Canada*. Scarborough, ON: Prentice-Hall.

Gordon, R., and I. Coneybeer. 1995. "Corporate Crime." In *Canadian Criminology*, ed. M. Jackson and C. Griffiths. Toronto: Harcourt Brace.

Greenberg, D. 1977. "Delinquency and the Age-Structure of Society." *Contemporary Crises* 1: 189–223.

Gregory, J. 1986. "Sex, Class, and Crime: Towards a Non-sexist Criminology." In *The Political Economy of Crime,* ed. B. MacLean. Scarborough, ON: Prentice-Hall.

Griffiths, C., and S. Verdun-Jones. 1994. *Canadian Criminal Justice,* 2d ed. Toronto: Harcourt Brace.

Hagan, J. 1985. *Modern Criminology*. Toronto: McGraw-Hill Ryerson.

———. 1992. "White Collar and Corporate Crime." In *Criminology: A Canadian Perspective*, 2d ed., ed. R. Linden. Toronto: Harcourt Brace Jovanovich. 451–73.

Hartnagel, T. 1992. "Correlates of Criminal Behaviour." In *Criminology: A Canadian Perspective*, 2d ed., ed. R. Linden. Toronto: Harcourt Brace Jovanovich.

———. 1996. "Correlates of Criminal Behaviour." In *Criminology: A Canadian Perspective*, 3d ed., ed. R. Linden. Toronto: Harcourt Brace.

Hawkins, D. 1987. "Beyond Anomalies: Rethinking the Conflict Perspective on Race and Criminal Punishment." *Social Forces* 65, no. 3: 719–45.

Heald, S. 1985. "Social Change and Legal Ideology: A Critique of the New Sexual Assault Legislation." *Canadian Criminology Forum* 7.

Hinch, R. 1985. "Canada's New Sexual Assault Law: A Step Forward for Women?" *Contemporary Crises* 9: 1.

Hylton, J. 1982. "The Native Offender in Saskatchewan: Some Implications for Crime Prevention Programming." *Canadian Journal of Criminology* 24: 121–31.

Jackson, M., and C. Griffiths. 1995. *Canadian Criminology*. Toronto: Harcourt Brace.

Jaffe, P., and C. Burris. 1981. *An Integrated Response to Wife Assault: A Community Model*. Ottawa: Solicitor General of Canada.

Johnson, H., and K. Rodgers. 1993. "A Statistical Overview of Women and Crime in Canada." In *In Conflict with the Law: Women and the Canadian Justice System*, ed. E. Adelberg and C. Currie. Vancouver: Press Gang.

Kendall, K. 1993. "Creating Safe Places: Reclaiming Sacred Spaces." Paper prepared for the 7th National Roundtable for Women in Prison Family Violence Programming in Jail and Prisons Workshop. Washington, DC.

LaPrairie, C. 1994. "Native Women and Crime in Canada: A Theoretical Model." In Adelberg and Currie, *Too Few*.

———. 1996. *Examining Aboriginal Corrections in Canada*. Ottawa: Supply and Services Canada.

Linden, R., ed. 1996. *Criminology: A Canadian Perspective*, 3d ed. Toronto: Harcourt Brace.

MacLean, B., and D. Milovanovic. 1997. *Thinking Critically about Crime*. Vancouver: Collective Press.

MacLeod, L. 1980. *Wife Battering in Canada: The Vicious Circle*. Ottawa: Canadian Advisory Council on the Status of Women, Minister of Supply and Services.

———. 1987. *Battered But Not Beaten ... Preventing Battering in Canada*. Ottawa: Canadian Advisory Council on the Status of Women.

Mandel, M. 1983. "Imprisonment, Class, and Democracy in Contemporary Canadian Capitalism." Mimeograph. Toronto: Osgoode Hall Law School.

Markwart, A. 1992. "Custodial Sanctions under the Young Offenders Act." In *Juvenile Justice in Canada*, ed. R. Corrado, N. Bala, R. Linden, and M. Leblanc. Toronto: Butterworths.

McMullan, J. 1992. *Beyond the Limits of the Law: Corporate Crime and Law and Order*. Halifax: Fernwood Publishing.

McMullan, J., D. Perrier, S. Smith, and P. Swan. 1997. *Crimes, Laws and Communities*. Halifax: Fernwood Publishing.

McMullan, J., and S. Smith. 1997. "Toxic Steel: State-Corporate Crime and the Contamination of the Environment." In McMullan et al., *Crimes, Laws and Communities*.

Mikel, D. 1979/80. "Native Society in Crisis." *Crime and Justice* 617: 32–41.

Pappajohn v. The Queen. 1980. *52 Canadian Criminal Cases*, 2d ed. 481–515.

Prairie Research Associates, Inc. 1994. *Manitoba Spouse Abuse Tracking Project Final Report Vol. 1*. Winnipeg: Manitoba Research and Statistics Directorate.

Quinney, R. 1970. *The Social Reality of Crime*. Boston: Little, Brown and Company.

Ratner, R., and J. McMullan. 1987. *State Control: Criminal Justice Politics in Canada*. Vancouver: University of British Columbia Press.

Reasons, C., L. Ross, and C. Patterson. 1991. "Your Money and Your Life: Workers Health in Canada." In *The Social Basis of Law*, 2d ed., ed. S. Brickey and E. Comack. Toronto: Garamond Press. 131–41.

Reiman, J. 1994. *The Rich Get Richer and the Poor Get Prison: Ideology, Crime and Criminal Justice*, 4th ed. Toronto: Allyn and Bacon.

Rock, P. 1986. *A View from the Shadows*. Oxford: Clarendon Press.

Royal Commission on Aboriginal Peoples (RCAP). 1996. *Bridging the Cultural Divide*. Ottawa: Minister of Supply and Services Canada.

———. 1993. *Aboriginal Peoples and the Justice System: Report of the National Roundtable on Aboriginal Justice Issues*. Ottawa: Minister of Supply and Services Canada.

Ruebsaat, G. 1985. *The New Sexual Assault Offences: Emerging Legal Issues*. Ottawa: Supply and Services Canada.

Samuelson, L. 1995. "Canadian Aboriginal Justice Commissions and Australia's 'Anunga Rules: Barking Up the Wrong Tree.'" *Canadian Public Policy* 21, no. 2: 187–211.

Star-Phoenix [Saskatoon]. 1991a. "21 Female Prisoners Charged After Riot." February 13: A15.

———. 1991b. "Dying to Get Out of PHW." March 23: D1.

———. 1997. "Half of Canadians Polled Believe Natives Well Off." June 21.

Satzewich, V., and T. Wotherspoon. 1993. *First Nations: Race, Class, and Gender Relations*. Toronto: Nelson.

Schissel, B. 1996. "Law Reform and Social Change: A Time-Series Analysis of Sexual Assault in Canada." *Journal of Criminal Justice* 24, no. 2: 123–38.

———. 1997. *Blaming Children: Youth Crime, Moral Panics and the Politics of Hate*. Halifax: Fernwood Publishing.

Sherrill, R. 1987. "Murder Inc.: What Happens to Corporate Criminals?" *Utne Reader* (March/April). As cited in *Beyond the Limits of the Law*, R. McMullan. Halifax: Fernwood Publishing.

Smith, D., and C. Visher. 1980. "Sex and Involvement in Deviance/Crime." *American Sociological Review* 45: 691–701.

Snider, L. 1985. "Legal Reform and the Law: The Dangers of Abolishing Rape." *International Journal of the Sociology of Law* 4.

———. 1988. "Commercial Crime." In *Deviance: Conformity and Control in Canadian Society*, ed. V. Sacco. Scarborough, ON: Prentice-Hall. 231–83.

———. 1991. "The Potential of the Criminal Justice System to Promote Feminist Concerns." In *The Social Basis of Law*, 2d ed., ed. E. Comack and S. Brickey. Toronto: Garamond Press.

———. 1993. *Bad Business: Corporate Crime in Canada*. Toronto: Nelson.

———. 1994. "The Regulatory Dance: Understanding Reform Processes in Corporate Crime." In *Readings in Critical Criminology*, ed. R. Hinch. Scarborough, ON: Prentice-Hall.

Solicitor General of Canada. 1985. "Female Victims of Crimes." *Canadian Urban Victimization Survey*. Ottawa: Supply and Services Canada.

Statistics Canada. 1988. *Canadian Crime Statistics*. Ottawa: Supply and Services Canada.

———. 1996. *Canadian Crime Statistics*. Ottawa: Supply and Services Canada.

Sugar, F., and L. Fox. 1989/90. "Nistum peyako sht'wawin iskwewak: Breakin Chains." *Canadian Journal of Women's Law* 3: 465–82.

Sutherland, E.H. 1977. "Crimes of Corporations." In *White-Collar Crime: Offences in Business, Politics, and the Professions*, ed. G. Geis and R. Meier. New York: Free Press. 71–84.

Task Force on Federally Sentenced Women. 1990. *Creating Choices*. Ottawa: Correctional Service of Canada.

Task Force on the Status of Women. 1985. *A Feminist Review of Criminal Law*. Ottawa: Supply and Services Canada.

Taylor, I., P. Walton, and J. Young. 1973. *The New Criminology: For a Social Theory of Deviance*. London: Routledge and Kegan Paul.

Turpel, M. (Aki-Kwe). 1992. "Further Travails of Canada's Human Rights Record: The Marshall Case." In *Elusive Justice: Beyond the Marshall Inquiry*, ed. J. Mannette. Halifax: Fernwood Publishing.

Ursel, J. 1991. "Considering the Impact of the Battered Women's Movement on the State: The Example of Manitoba." In *The Social Basis of Law*, 2d ed., ed. E. Comack and S. Brickey. Toronto: Garamond Press. 261–88.

———. 1998. "Eliminating Violence Against Women: Reform or Cooptation in State Institutions." In *Power and Resistance*, 2d ed., ed. L. Samuelson and W. Anthony. Halifax: Fernwood Publishing.

Waldram, J. 1994. "Canada's 'Indian Problem' and the Indian's Canada Problem." In *Power and Resistance*, ed. L. Samuelson. Halifax: Fernwood Publishing.

West, G. 1984. *Young Offenders and the State*. Toronto: Butterworths.

York, G. 1990. *The Disposed: Life and Death in Native Canada*. Toronto: Little, Brown.

P A R T V

Environment and Urbanization

INTRODUCTION

There is growing awareness in this country of environmental degradation and its negative consequences to human existence and survival. These concerns are not only about chemicals and air pollution, but also about the social environment, such as population density, violence and crimes, and social conflicts. Two articles in this section address these issues.

Michael Clow and Lawrence Felt, in the chapter entitled "Industrial Development and Environmental Integrity: Contradiction or Co-existence," focus on the magnitude and seriousness of damage to the ecosystem and discuss the framework for evaluating competing assessments of this damage.

Evidence presented in this chapter shows that extensive environmental degradation exists even now. Deadly pollutants in the waterways, ozone thinning, air pollution, and damage to forests are all too apparent. The human cost of environmental degradation is substantive and increasing in the form of illness and deaths arising from extensive and prolonged exposure to various pollutants. The rise of global corporations and the increased scale of economic integration have meant the globalization of environmental degradation.

Clow and Felt argue that the twin themes of insatiable human needs and never-ending economic growth, which have simultaneously driven and justified economic activity in the past, are no longer sustainable. The reality of ecological constraint requires us to shape future activities in ways that prevent further environmental damage. The protection of the ecosystem, Clow and Felt argue, will require fundamental changes in human cultural values, human ethical standards, and the organization of human society.

Alison Hayford, in her chapter, "Urbanization: Issues and Problems," discusses the problems that have come to be identified with urban centres. Canada has one of the most urbanized populations in the world; more than two-thirds of the Canadian population live in metropolitan areas. In 1996, Canada's four largest cities—Toronto, Montreal, Vancouver, and Ottawa-Hull—contained nearly four out of every ten Canadians.

Urbanization is the result of the development of productive forces in agriculture that promote migration from rural to urban areas and the settlement of immigrant populations in cities. In recent years, overseas immigration has contributed to the ethnic and racial diversity of cities such as Toronto and Vancouver.

Hayford discusses crime, policing, racial conflict, and problems of the social order, the urban environment, traffic, housing, and the quality of life. Many urban problems, Hayford argues, are not the product of "abnormality" or "deviance," but result from urban structures themselves, including population density, the heterogeneous and diverse nature of urban populations, and the differential power relationships within cities. Other problems—for example, those in the area of housing—are the result of contradictions between private profit and the needs of the population. These contradictions lead to high land values, unaffordable rents, and ghettoization of the poor and racial minorities in cities. Traffic congestion is the result of a combination of factors, namely, inadequate public transportation, the necessity of commuting to work, and cultural attitudes toward "independence" that express themselves in the cult of the private automobile.

Hayford argues that inequality of power and differential power relationships are the major source of urban problems. Solutions, therefore, would require structural transformation of power relations and a shift of production and development to meet human needs rather than the desire for profit.

CHAPTER 12

Industrial Development and Environmental Integrity: Contradiction or Co-existence

Michael Clow and Lawrence Felt

Learning Objectives

After studying this chapter, you should be able to
*   Understand the scale and extent of current environmental damage worldwide.
*   Understand why the twin themes of insatiable human wants and never-ending economic growth are no longer relevant guides for the future.
*   More fully appreciate the extent to which the earth's **ecosystem** poses constraints upon human activity.
*   Consider the contradictions between unbridled **economic growth** and human survival in light of current knowledge.
*   Assess alternative perspectives on how human societies might be organized if environmental damage is to be contained.
*   Consider fundamental changes that might be needed in cultural values and ethical standards in light of current knowledge of environmental damage.

Introduction

Increasingly persuasive evidence suggests that humans may well be on the way to making the earth unfit for their continued existence (Mungall and McLaren 1991). Despite unparalleled industrial expansion, the most palpable lesson of the late twentieth century is that humans are but *one* among *many* living species that must co-exist within the natural boundaries of a complex life-support system composed of air, water, and a thin layer of soil (Wagner 1974). The combination of this life-support system and the complexes of living organisms living in some degree of interdependence is termed an *ecosystem*.

The failure to properly consider this ecosystem has led to a scale and rate of environmental damage unprecedented in human history (Gould 1993). Does this mean that continued pursuit of industrial development and our survival are incompatible? If fundamental changes are required in the ways human societies are organized, what are they? Are new cultural values and ethical standards needed? We shall attempt to answer these questions by focussing upon four issues: (1) the magnitude of environmental damage; (2) various assessments concerning its seriousness and ease of repair; (3) strategies for evaluating competing assessments; and (4) some implications should we need to redirect human activity to avoid unimpeded industrial expansion and economic growth.

The Extent of Environmental Damage

For most of our fifty-odd thousand years on this planet, humans have shaped and reshaped their physical environment to meet real or perceived needs. Earliest humans set fires to clear land, built weirs to harvest fish, and diverted waterways for irrigation. While most, if not all, such actions inflicted damage upon the environment, effects tended to be localized because of the relatively small numbers of humans living in dispersed settlements, the primitive technology utilized, and the frequent presence of cultural values emphasizing interdependence between humans and their environment.

In the past 200 years, and most importantly during the past 60 years, the situation has changed dramatically. The harnessing of science and technology in the name of industrial development has brought hitherto unimaginable material prosperity to a minority of the world's population. Increasingly, however, we have come to recognize the horrendous price being extracted in environmental and human terms for this prosperity. Deadly pollutants in our waterways, the thinning of the ozone layer, cities choked with smog, the ravaging of non-renewable resources to fuel an apparently insatiable demand, the plundering of other living creatures without regard to consequences—these are all increasingly characteristic of human life on earth (Arnason and Felt 1995; Allen 1994). The rise of global corporations and the drastically increased scale of economic integration has meant that no place or creature remains immune to environmental damage[1] or plunder. Indeed, some informed commentators, such as Dr. David Suzuki, have warned that humans have only a limited time to save the earth from becoming unfit for themselves and their offspring.

The magnitude of degradation is truly staggering. Consider the thin layer of atmosphere surrounding the earth. It consists of oxygen, a protective layer of ozone, as well as major concentrations of carbon dioxide and water vapour. The atmosphere plays a critical role in sustaining life by promoting photosynthesis and maintaining temperature so that water remains liquid. Natural changes have occurred within the atmosphere over the centuries, but nonetheless, this delicate life-maintaining balance has remained within limits that allow life to thrive.[2]

That humans pollute the air they breathe is certainly not news. Intensive burning to clear or replenish agricultural land, smelting operations to create metals, and the use of hydrocarbon-based materials (wood, coal, and petrochemicals) all emit potentially damaging by-products into the air. Incidents of localized air pollution go back at least to the first cities (World Meteorological Association 1989).

Increasingly, however, the damage is global, as population increases dramatically and industrialized activities penetrate to the more-remote regions. Clearly, the atmosphere is not a limitless ocean of gas into which we can endlessly spew our refuse. An increased abundance of carbon is one example of deleterious change. A by-product of combustion and a critical component in the gas carbon dioxide, carbon is appearing in the atmosphere in excessive amounts, contributing to the "greenhouse effect" of increased global warming.[3] In the past 90 years, amounts of carbon as well as carbon dioxide have risen to levels above 300 parts per million volume (see Figure 12.1). Such amounts are unprecedented in scientific data going back 100 000 years.

FIGURE 12.1 Concentration of Carbon Dioxide

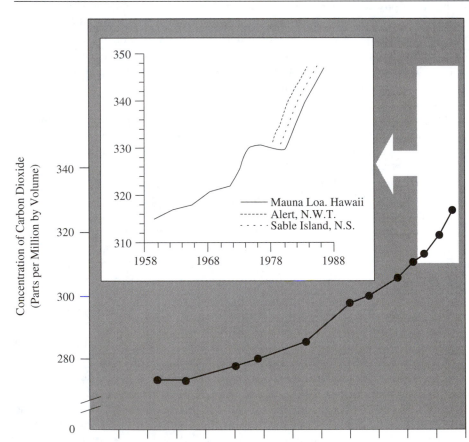

Source: Atmospheric Environment Services Canada, Canadian Baseline Program and National Oceanic and Atmospheric Administration/Climate Monitoring and Diagnostics Laboratory, Boulder, Colorado.

These increases have largely resulted from cutting down forests, which absorb carbon dioxide and release oxygen; tilling lands; and burning fossil (hydrocarbon-based) fuels. Other harmful by-products have also resulted from these activities, including acid rain, airborne toxic chemicals, and artificially produced chlorofluoro-carbons (CFCs).

Damage to our water and land has been equally dramatic. Vast as the earth's oceans appear, their use as a dump for sewage and toxins has now come to have significant effects. As a result their capacity to neutralize toxins as well as produce living organisms—from the smallest phytoplankton necessary for photosynthesis to larger animals harvested for human consumption—is diminishing. A tragic example of the latter are the Beluga whales of the lower St. Lawrence estuary. Once abundant, these animals are now ailing—both individually and as a species—as a result of chemical toxins escaping from plants far upriver. Recently, they were added to Canada's list of endangered species.

Fresh water fares no better. Many, if not most, of the largest lakes and rivers suffer from various forms of damage. In many parts of the world, supplies of unpolluted fresh water are becoming increasingly scarce (Keating 1986). In some instances, fresh water is present but is too polluted for human consumption. In other situations, overuse has lowered the water table, resulting in drought. Even supplies of water deep in the earth, termed aquifers, are becoming contaminated. Nor is this a phenomenon only of Western industrial, urban societies. Even in remote Northern Thailand, water is becoming a scarce commodity. Water supplies there have decreased by 50 percent in the past 30 years (*The Globe and Mail*, February 15, 1994, A11). The flow of the Ping River, the major river in northern Thailand, has decreased by over 40 percent as a result of forestry activities. Forest cover is necessary for retaining rainfall and releasing it slowly throughout the year. Foreign demand for lumber has meant that nearly half of the Thai forests have been chopped down in the past 30 years.

Terrestrial damage has also accelerated substantially. In the past 10 000 years, approximately one-third of the earth's forests have been removed, most during the past 80 years. As you read this, large portions of the tropical rain forests of South America and Southeast Asia are being removed to promote highly mechanized, large-scale farming or livestock grazing. Given the shallowness and generally low nutrient levels associated with rain-forest soil, subsequent agricultural use is typically of fairly short duration and the possibility of rain-forest regeneration negligible. If current rates of deforestation continue, much of the Amazonian rain forests will be gone by the year 2000. This conflict between preservation and cutting of forests is occurring throughout the world. In Canada, pitched confrontations have recently occurred in British Columbia over the removal of old-growth forests that are hundreds of years old.

Why are forests so important? Forests might be termed the "lungs of the world" because the trees and plants take in carbon dioxide and release oxygen through photosynthesis. Forests are the world's greatest engine for storing the sun's energy, which they do by converting carbon dioxide and water into living tissue. In a single day, a lone deciduous tree can pump and transpire as much as 20 000 litres of water, converting carbon dioxide at the same time. By doing this, trees play an important role in regulating the global carbon dioxide balance. In addition, trees filter various pollutants from the air. Finally, dense forests, particularly in the tropics, play an important part in maintaining global genetic diversity. Without the dense green forest mantle, much of the animal life we know cannot survive and would not have evolved (Mungall and McLaren 1991, 171).

Our damage to the earth's environment is not just physical. Some creatures are depleted inadvertently as **habitat** is destroyed, while others feel the effects of intentional pursuit. Humans, the ultimate predators, secure much of their food through various forms of hunting. Increasingly, we have turned to the oceans as our last hunting frontier. Despite the oceans' vastness, the effects of human predation are abundantly clear there as well. The populations, and hence the harvests, of many marine animals, particularly fish, have begun to decline. In Eastern Canada, two recent scientific assessments (International Committee on Northwest Atlantic Fisheries 1992; Alverson 1991) indicate that stocks of northern codfish (*Gadus atlantica*) have plummeted to their lowest levels in history, necessitating a complete fishery closure and displacing about 30 000 fishers and plant workers (see Figure 12.2). So low is the

FIGURE 12.2   Northern Cod Spawning Biomass, 1962–1992, Age 7 and Over

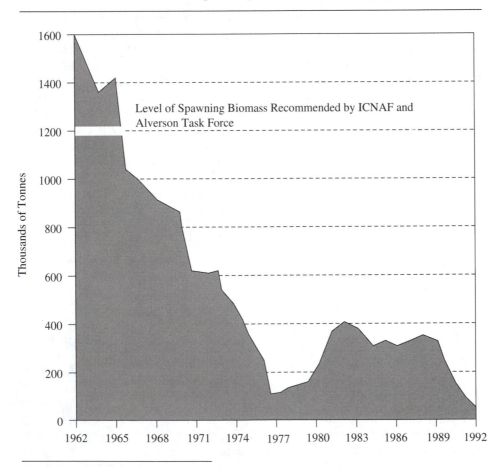

Source: Fisheries and Oceans Canada.

spawning biomass (the number of fish of spawning age) that some doubt whether recovery is even possible. Even in 1998, six years after the fishery's closure, there is little scientific evidence that populations of this fish have substantially rebuilt themselves (FRCC 1998). Similar stories can be told of other times and places. So efficient have modern, technologically sophisticated fishing boats become that fish no longer have any sanctuary (McGoodwin 1990).

Human health has not escaped the effects of environmental degradation. Whether through the air we breathe, the water we drink, the food we eat, or the job at which we work, the human cost of environmental damage is substantial and increasing. Be it Minimata disease from ingesting mercury-contaminated fish or radiation contamination from drinking milk produced by cows downwind of airborne radioactive pollution, illness and death represent an increasingly serious problem. For large numbers of workers, the effects of various pollutants routinely produced in the workplace is more direct (Bolaria 1991). Asbestos, coal, and uranium, as well as hundreds of chemicals, are known to cause serious, often life-threatening illness with new linkages occurring continuously as the period of exposure increases. In light of such a litany of damage to humans and the environment, one is well advised to consider the future course of industrial development.

Is Global Industrialization Sustainable?

This question is largely rhetorical, since little persuasive evidence *doesn't* suggest that we must change current economic activities to reduce, if not eliminate, environmental damage. The more germane questions are what amount of reduction is required and how it might be accomplished. Three alternative perspectives attempt to answer these questions. They vary considerably in their assessment of the seriousness of environmental damage and the social reorganization necessary to deal with it. The three are popularly known as the **classical liberal**, **limits to growth**, and **environmental management perspectives**.

Classical Liberal Perspective

The classical liberal view minimizes the seriousness of environmental damage and suggests that technological "fixes" are possible to remedy the worst manifestations of damage. In this view, the natural environment is both passive and forgiving; it provides a cornucopia of resources for human advancement[4] (Evernden 1985; 1992). This perspective provided the ideological justification for industrialization in the early nineteenth century, and is still very much in vogue. It considers damage to habitat, atmosphere, oceans, and soil to be localized and therefore of no general concern to human society at large. Nature is an external storehouse of resources, natural forces, and "lower" living organisms to be channelled and reshaped by science and technology for humankind's continuous and unlimited economic growth. The pursuit of economic growth is equated with moral progress, and elements of the environment are considered as merely cheap factors of production or repositories of waste products.

Within this perspective, modernization and development are central concepts of social change both in the developed West and in the developing world. Modern industrial societies represent the apex of human potential and offer the highest quality of life for their citizens. They represent the culmination of human social development, providing a beacon for less-developed societies to follow. Modern societies are marked by the institutional capacity to overcome any technological or organizational limitations to economic expansion and increasing affluence. Educational institutions, the division of labour in society, and the very organization of firms, government policy, city planning, and indeed all our societal arrangements are seen as the means to material progress.

Although best known for his biting criticism of the contradictions within capitalist economic development, **Karl Marx** shared much of this classical liberal view insofar as the environment and environmental damage were concerned. He was in wholehearted agreement with capitalist thinkers on the central importance of human progress. Marx openly identified both increasing abundance and power to appropriate the natural environment as the natural goal of humanity and the key to continuing general human improvement (Marx 1973, 409).

Marx viewed the process of capitalist industrialization as a special breakthrough in the history of human development because it created unprecedented expansion of the productive capacity of mankind and transformed our relationship with the natural world. The great civilizing influence of capital was its capacity to end material scarcity and make abundance possible. Marx predicted that, following the socialist revolution and the elimination of class conflict, the resulting society would be able to speed up technological innovation and economic expansion for the benefit of all.

Limits to Growth Perspective

The classical liberal view of human dominance and its general optimism about the future has been severely challenged in recent years. The most radical challenge has been labelled the Limits to Growth perspective after the famous study at the Massachusetts Institute of Technology that gave currency to its basic premise (Meadows et al. 1972). This perspective argues the existence of clear ecological limits to the scale and kinds of economic activities in which humans can engage. The argument is predicated on an analysis of the consequences of human activity on the earth's **biosphere**.

To understand the complex relationship between human activity (particularly industrial activity) and the natural environment, we must move beyond the isolated, necessarily fragmented understanding embodied in the theories of physics, chemistry, biology, or geology. We must aim, instead, for a more holistic understanding of life based on a complex network of living plant and animal communities, called habitats, and on the non-living cycles of the air, water, and land that connect and sustain them. Together, earth's habitats and its ocean, air, and soil cycles constitute the biosphere (Chant 1972; Commoner 1971, 11–14).

Our dependence upon the biosphere for economic activity is twofold. First, materials, energy sources, and life processes produced and reproduced by the biosphere are what humans appropriate as renewable resources. Second, we rely on the biosphere to absorb our wastes by recycling biodegradable wastes back into the elements of the biosphere, and by harmlessly and invisibly disposing of non-biodegradable materials, including highly toxic by-products created in our factories. As the scale and complexity of economic activity increases, the greater becomes the demand on the biosphere.

Central to the limits to growth perspective is the idea that it is the biosphere as a whole that produces plants, animals, water, and air—which we term "renewable resources." The plants and animals of each community, or habitat, can survive only because the habitats are connected and supported by the air, water, and soil cycles of the earth. This interdependence is critical. While we may talk as if we depend upon the recovery of a particular fishery resource, such as northern cod, or for a certain amount of rainfall to ensure bountiful wheat harvests, our dependency is more complex. We do not depend solely on a particular piece of the biosphere; we depend on the operation of the whole system.

Environmental problems are human disruptions of the natural operation of the biosphere (Raskin and Bernow 1991, 87; Benton 1989, 74). They potentially imperil the very basis of human life, let alone economic activity. Renewable resources can only be renewed if the habitats of the planet operate; only if the ocean, atmosphere, and other physical and chemical cycles operate; and only if the wastes of our production don't poison its habitats. The limits to growth perspective argues that, since we need to maintain the integrity of the biosphere to sustain life, there are necessarily limits both to the capacity of the biosphere to provide renewable resources for human use, as well as to the kind and volume of wastes that the biosphere can absorb without impairing its capacity to reproduce renewable resources and handle new waste.

Partisans of this approach argue that commitments to merely *minimize* the environmental impact of particular new development projects, or even of economic expansion in general, will be insufficient to prevent us from moving beyond the biosphere's capacity. Thus, minimizing the negative effects of new ore smelters, making nuclear generation plants safer, controlling urban expansion into the countryside, and preserving a small amount of special habitat to maintain biodiversity will be insufficient to deflect humankind from a path of ecological exhaustion. Inevitably, ecological constraints will limit the size of the economy as well as the kinds of technologies that we can utilize.

Proponents of the limits to growth view have long been aware that their position directly challenges the environment–society relationship upon which the prevalent classical liberal view of progress and human betterment is based. In magazines such as *The Ecologist*, the liberal view has been criticized and ultimately dismissed as being naïvely optimistic and dangerous for the future of the earth. In the same breath, advocates have dismissed most Marxian-based critiques of contemporary society, since as we have seen, that orientation shares many of the core assumptions of the classical liberal view.

The Environmental Management Perspective

By the late 1960s, it had become clear that developed societies were running out of clean air and water, trees, ores, fish, and virtually every natural resource (Marchak

1983; Marchak et al. 1987). Denial was no longer possible. If economic growth was to continue, it was necessary to take action to curb the most damaging excesses of environmental destruction (Woodrow 1977). The result was the emergence of a new conventional wisdom, one recognizing pollution and the exhaustion of renewable resources. It embraced the view that ecological problems result largely from human disruption of the biosphere. It rejected, however, what was perceived as the extremism of the limits to growth conclusion. Rather, this view argued that a technological solution exists for every ecological constraint if caution and prudence are employed.

The resulting new orthodoxy has come to be known as **sustainable development**. Coined in the popular Brundtland Report, *Our Common Future* (WCED 1987), it articulates a middle path between the traditional liberal view and the limits to growth positions, in which environmental management can be practised to ensure sustainable development. Sustainable development is a process of economic growth in which industrial expansion can occur without jeopardizing the opportunities of future generations. Such a path can preserve, not degrade, the ecological basis of economic activity without the pessimism and radical reorganization required by the limits to growth view.

The Brundtland Report assumed that reckless exploitation of renewable resources and dirty technology are primarily responsible for the disruption of the biosphere. Significantly, the report argues against the existence of a *necessarily absolute constraint* on economic growth per se (WCED 1987, 8). Instead, better management of the world's environment will produce more renewable resources from the land and the sea. Technological innovation will improve efficiency in the use and reuse of energy and materials, and will also reduce pollution. Confidently assuming the absence of any present or future resource shortages or pollution buildups, the report claimed that infinite economic expansion was possible and desirable if business and governments co-operated to take the necessary measures to sustain development.

The attraction of such an environmental management perspective is obvious. It does not fundamentally challenge current societal practices nor the ideological foundation of classical liberalism upon which they rest. Material progress remains both the goal and the driving force of social development. Environmental problems are uninformed by-products of economic expansion subject to technical fixes.

Environmental management has come to fit very nicely within contemporary environmental rhetoric. Brundtland refrains from laying the blame for environmental problems at the feet of any particular actors, instead seeing environmental damage as a common problem for which we all share blame. This politically correct report did not even inflame divisions over the proper roles and responsibilities of government and private enterprise. Free-market enthusiasts and those who wished for greater government intervention could each devise hypothetical schemes for business–government partnerships to achieve sustainable growth. Since environmental damage was a common problem, individual efforts could also assume importance. Thus, the movement for responsible environmental behaviour took off, with everyone from kindergarten students to senior citizens being cajoled to practice the three "Rs": reduce, reuse, and recycle.

Evaluating Competing Perspectives

The question now arises as to which perspective has the greatest weight of evidence behind it. The serious contenders are clearly the environmental management and limits to growth perspectives. Documented evidence of environmental damage is far too extensive to deny the problem, as is done in the classical view. Therefore, we will direct our evaluation to the remaining two perspectives.

Both views agree that environmental problems arise from the disruption of biospheric processes and that an intact biosphere is necessary for continued large-scale economic activity. Both agree that we have erroneously presumed our economic activity would not undermine the biosphere's ability to produce renewable resources and process waste. Both also concur that the contemporary scale and variety of economic activities simultaneously create greater dependence upon the biosphere as well as greater capacity to interfere, intentionally and unintentionally, in the natural processes operating within it. In our opinion, the debate between them can be reduced to one point of fundamental disagreement: whether or not technological innovation and resource management can prevent ecological exhaustion and ultimately reduce, perhaps even eliminate, the biosphere's capacity to support human life (Clow 1990).

We will use Figure 12.3 in order to assess the adequacy of each perspective. As indicated in our earlier discussion, both perspectives share a great deal in their understanding of the relationship between human economic activity and the environment. It is therefore possible to determine the kinds of efforts required to sustain increasing economic activity over some reasonable period of time. It appears that six critical sets of activities must be undertaken in a properly balanced combination if sustained growth is to be achieved.

These six are as follows:

1. Somehow get more materials and energy from the biosphere (such as materials extracted from the earth's crust, and energy from the sun or from geothermal sources) without in so doing increasing the disruption of the biosphere.
2. Somehow get more useful work from a given flow of energy and similarly waste less material in the production process.
3. Somehow produce more durable products, which therefore need to be replaced less often, and make them easier to reuse, rebuild, and recycle.
4. Somehow produce products with less wastes, with no more wastes than can be recycled or returned safely to the biosphere, and with wastes that are easier to reuse or recycle.
5. Somehow reuse more waste energy, recycle more industrial waste, and recycle thrown away or junked products without increasing energy and material used in the process.
6. Somehow dispose of wastes in the biosphere in forms, locations, and quantities that can be returned to the natural flow of such materials and energy without further disruption of the habitats and cycles of the biosphere.

The magnitude of such efforts to maintain sustainable growth without continuing to damage the environment is seldom appreciated. Technological innovations increase

FIGURE 12.3 The Economy–Nature Relationship and the Requirements for Sustaining Economic Growth

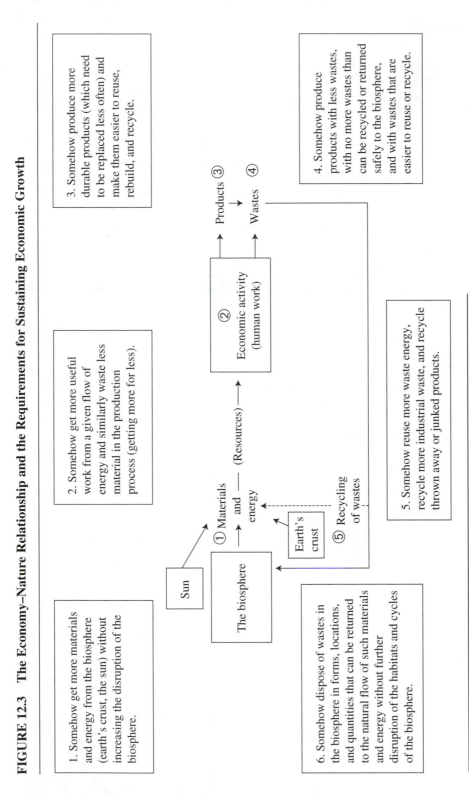

1. Somehow get more materials and energy from the biosphere (earth's crust, the sun) without increasing the disruption of the biosphere.

2. Somehow get more useful work from a given flow of energy and similarly waste less material in the production process (getting more for less).

3. Somehow produce more durable products (which need to be replaced less often) and make them easier to reuse, rebuild, and recycle.

4. Somehow produce products with less wastes, with no more wastes than can be recycled or returned safely to the biosphere, and with wastes that are easier to reuse or recycle.

5. Somehow reuse more waste energy, recycle more industrial waste, and recycle thrown away or junked products.

6. Somehow dispose of wastes in the biosphere in forms, locations, and quantities that can be returned to the natural flow of such materials and energy without further disruption of the habitats and cycles of the biosphere.

① Materials and energy (Resources) →
② Economic activity (human work)
Products ③
Wastes ④
⑤ Recycling of wastes
Sun
The biosphere
Earth's crust

Note: In order to sustain economic growth indefinitely, all these measures must be continually and indefinitely refined and improved.

efficiencies in the use of energy and materials in industrial processes, the production of more durable products with less waste, and the more efficient recycling of what reduced waste remains. Similarly, they stimulate both natural habitats and artificial ocean, forest, and field "agricultures" to produce more of the plants and animals we want without increasing the disruption of natural and humanly created agricultural habitats. Such technological innovation would have to be ongoing, synchronized, and co-ordinated to keep the ecological demands of a growing economy within the envelope of the biosphere's capacity to sustain. Big leaps forward in one area, energy production for example, would be of no help if matching gains were not made in other areas of technological innovation. For sustainable growth, this range of improvements would have to continue on an indefinite basis. Otherwise, limitations on production would quickly arise from the inability of the earth to supply the increasing ecological demands of an expanding economy.

In light of such a presentation, it is difficult to believe that technological innovation and wise resource management will be able to indefinitely sustain economic growth while containing environmental degradation. Technological innovation and resource management are not magical, yet an act of magic seems necessary. Greater and greater amounts of product must be conjured up from the same amount of materials; greater effort from the same amount of energy. Ever more renewable resources must be conjured up from the earth. Less wastes, and wastes ever more integrated into the natural flows of energy and materials in the biosphere, must result from industrial processes. Technology merely taps into natural processes and directs them for human ends. Technological manipulations of natural processes are doubly constrained—first by the limited efficiency of our processes and devices and second by the characteristics of the natural processes with which we are interfering.

Tasks 2 to 5 in Figure 12.3 represent efforts to "get more from less": increased efficiencies in the use and reuse of materials and energy, and reduction in the volume and toxicity of wastes in all areas of production. But the efficiency of our devices and processes are not indefinitely improvable. The efficiency of all our devices and processes is restricted, in the last analysis, by the laws of thermodynamics (Georgescu-Roegen 1980). These scientific principles establish a limit to the flow of energy that can be tapped and turned into useful effort for human purposes. Similarly, there are limits to the efficiency of our use of materials. At some point, all technologies exhaust their possibilities for improvement. Our machines, devices, and industrial practices seldom approach anything like their theoretical limits of efficiency because of the exponentially increasing cost of developing and utilizing what are only marginally more efficient improvements.

The exponential increase in our production over the past two centuries has relied on the intensified exploitation of known natural forces augmented by the rapid discovery of new ones. As is all too well known, the process has also led to exponential increases in ecological disruption. For individuals inclined to trust in the emergence of technologies based on mysteries of nature not yet uncovered, it is important to remember that even if new forces of nature are discovered, there will be ecological consequences to harnessing them for human production. The 1950s belief that nuclear fission would provide clean, unlimited new electrical energy comes uncomfortably to mind.

Tasks 1 and 6 focus on constraints arising from those characteristics of the biosphere with which our ecological demands interfere. Task 1 concerns the provision of an expanding supply of renewable and non-renewable resources, while Task 6 concerns the effects of pollution.

Unfortunately, wise management cannot induce the biosphere to produce more and more renewable resources. Economic activities of society are essentially parasitic upon the natural processes of the biosphere. Plants and animals consumed by the economy, and all the materials and energy in the air, water, and soil cycles appropriated by economic activity, are pulled out of their role in the normal operation of the biosphere. As in any parasitic relationship, too much appropriation from the host interferes with its ability to reproduce. With regard to non-renewable resources from the earth's crust, the extraction of materials often destroys overlying habitats and, as in the example of mining, can contribute massive pollution to the biosphere. In short, it seems hopelessly naive to expect an endlessly growing supply of either renewable or non-renewable resources will come without a corresponding increase in environmental damage.

It is also impossible to guarantee that wastes from our economic activities will become increasingly compatible in volume, location, and composition with the natural flows of energy and materials to which they are added. It would appear to be a task of exponentially increasing difficulty to more and more closely match biodegradable wastes with natural biospheric flows and cycles. More difficult still, considering that wastes produced by many modern industries—notably nuclear power, petrochemicals, and mining—are simply incompatible with the health of living things. In some cases it may be possible to utilize hazardous technologies on a small scale by effective closed-cycle production systems, recycling, and toxic waste destruction measures in combination. There appears, however, to be no way to operate such hazardous processes to allow an ever-greater scale of use.

Despite the current popularity of sustainable development as a solution to our ecological woes, the above review suggests that it would be difficult, if not impossible, to achieve. Technical measures to reduce the ecological demands of production on the biosphere—such as pollution controls; improved energy efficiency; extensive recycling of resources; the production of more durable, long-lasting products; and the aggressive restoration of renewable resources—can reduce the degradation of the biosphere to some degree. Production may even be increased for a time with fixed volumes of materials, energy, and waste disposal capacity. Ultimately, however, ecological constraints will indeed limit the scale of economic activity and the constitution of productive forces, in spite of our best efforts to innovate. The underlying assumption that material progress can be a permanent feature of human society is manifestly in error.

Implications of Limited Growth for Industrial Society

The twin themes of insatiable human need and never-ending economic growth, which have simultaneously driven and justified economic activity in the industrial world for over 200 years, are no longer sustainable in industrialized countries, let alone exportable to less industrialized ones. The reality of ecological constraints requires that we understand the environmental consequences of human activity and shape future activities in ways that prevent environmental damage. This strategy is clearest for so-called renewable resources but can be generalized to other areas as well.

Renewable resource industries are distinct from other areas of economic activity because they directly depend on exploiting the productive power of the biosphere. We harvest natural habitats and expect them to regrow more of the plants and animals we want. We extract energy and materials from the non-living cycles of the biosphere and expect them to be renewed as well. We also set up artificially constructed habitats of agriculture, silviculture, and aquaculture within the biosphere and expect it to support them.

In harvesting natural habitats, we are extracting wild plants and animals from communities of interdependent species (see the box on the next page). If one wishes to harvest over an indefinite period of time, that is, practise sustainability, resource practices must not damage the whole habitat and, simultaneously, must not over-harvest the particular species pursued. To discern the level of what is usually termed a **sustainable yield** requires a substantive knowledge of the particular ecosystem. Similarly, extraction of renewable materials and energy from their natural cycles in the air, water, or earth's crust must not upset the physical cycles of the biosphere. As we have already seen in countless places, where natural flows of energy are diverted from their normal cycles on a large scale, for example by damming large watersheds, broad and deleterious effects on dependent habitats result.

In farming, silviculture, and aquaculture, we do not actually grow the crops or animals, rather we *appropriate* the bio-physical processes of the biosphere to grow them for us (Kelly and Sandersen 1990). We create habitats for those plant and animal species that we desire, with little regard to consequences to the larger ecosystem. Salmon aquaculture is a good example: as a result of massive salmon farming, new diseases have been introduced to wild fish. Disease has been spread by escaped individuals, bays and fiords have been polluted with excess artificial food pellets that sink to the bottom and decay, and the genetic integrity of many stocks has been threatened as domesticated fish escape to interbreed with wild fish. The more intensive the pursuit of such activities, the greater the damage to natural ecosystems. The process can be stated as a validated proposition: The more intensive the production process, the greater the input required per unit of production (fertilizer, etc.), the less the stability of the farmed or artificial habitat, and the greater the destruction to local, possibly even remote, ecosystems. It is increasingly being recognized by biologists, ecologists, silviculturalists, and other related professionals that stable, sustainable farming of the land and sea can only emerge by limiting the intensity of production and building more diverse, better-balanced habitats (Jacobs 1993).

In manufacturing and service industries, the dependence on resource inputs from the biosphere is often less visible. Unlike food products, pulp and paper and extractive industries, aircraft manufacturing, banking, or the computer industry are seen as being relatively free from ecological constraints. Of course any reflection will reveal this is not so. Aluminum manufacturing for aircraft production is one of the largest users of energy. Banking, hospitals, and other service industries require large volumes of energy, paper products, and water—all inputs from the biosphere. Even computer components require large amounts of energy for the manufacturing of silicon chips. They also emit radiation into the biosphere as they hum on a desktop or on someone's lap.

Fishing Down the Ocean's Food Web

Humans, along with countless other creatures, have long used the world's oceans for food. Dependable and seemingly inexhaustible, various fish species have sustained humans from the earliest recorded times. Unfortunately, experiences of the last 30 years have dramatically demonstrated that even the oceans have their limits. Recent studies by the United Nations suggest over half of all known ocean fish species are being caught at or beyond their sustainable levels. Several species, such as the cod of the North Atlantic, a staple for European and northeastern peoples for 500 years, may be on the verge of extinction. In light of this new awareness of the oceans' limits, it is instructive to see how fishing nations are responding. Quite simply, are nations adopting more sustainable fishing practices? Several examples suggest, regrettably, that the answer is negative. A telling example can be found in Canadian and other national responses to the dramatic overfishing and resulting depletion of northern cod.

Ocean scientists typically think of the ocean's fish and other living creatures as composing a complex, hierarchical food web or chain (the technical term is trophic system). At each level in this chain, certain organisms are found that feed on organisms at lower levels and in turn provide food themselves (become prey) for those at higher ones. At the bottom of the chain are phytoplankton—microscopic, free floating, photosynthetic organisms residing in the upper layers of water where light is abundant. In a fundamental sense they are the foundation of all ocean life. Zooplankton and other small organisms feed on these, and in turn provide food and energy to more complex marine animals such as shrimp and crab. Larger, more complex animals in turn prey on shrimp, crab, and other species. For any given ocean, it is possible to designate which level in the food chain a certain species occupies. At the highest level, of course, are the largest fish and mammals, including humans. Humans have typically sought species fairly high in the trophic system because of their greater economic importance. Whaling is the most obvious example, although "high-value" fish such as salmon, tuna, cod, and bluefish also tend to be found at the upper end of the oceans' food webs. These species higher in the food chain have borne the brunt of human exploitation.

One of the more dramatic examples of overfishing is the northern cod, a firm-fleshed, bottom-dwelling fish of the North Atlantic pursued for hundreds of years by Europeans and later by North Americans. Due to a variety of factors, of which overfishing was likely the most important, the population of this fish has been reduced to less than 5 percent of its former level. The initial response to this population collapse was to declare a moratorium on fishing in Canada, throwing as many as 40 000 people on Canada's East Coast out of work, in the hope that the population would rebuild. A secondary response was to redirect fishing effort further down the food chain to other high-value species such as shrimp, lobster, and crab. As a result, landings of these formerly "secondary" species have come to dominate catches and income. The accompanying four charts convey this example of "prey switching" in graphic detail.

The upper left chart chronicles the decline in cod and other bottom-dwelling species (groundfish) since 1985 as well as the corresponding rise in shellfish, primarily crab and shrimp. The two charts on the right summarize the

(continued)

(continued)

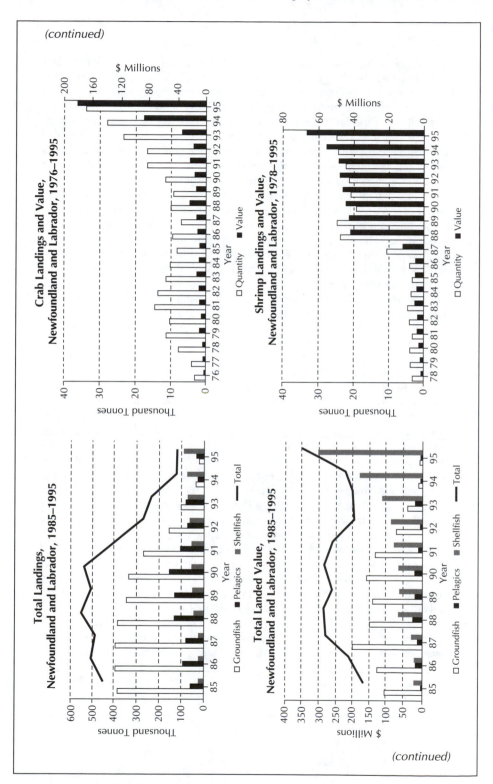

(continued)

(continued)

amount and value of landings for crab and shrimp respectively from the late 1970s to 1995. Note in particular the dramatic increases beginning in 1987. Finally, the lower left chart summarizes the transition that has occurred in the Newfoundland and Labrador fishery. Not only have crab and shrimp replaced the traditional fisheries based primarily upon bottom-dwelling fish such as cod, flounder, and sole, the total value of the provincial fishery has soared to record values since 1992. This transformation raises a number of important issues about the future. Are these new fisheries sustainable? What are the implications of moving down the food web in response to overfishing?

While definitive answers await further investigation, several concerns have been raised. Many fishermen and some ocean scientists feel that the level of current populations of shrimp and crab is due at least in part to the removal of cod from the food chain. It is therefore uncertain what will happen to current numbers should groundfish populations recover. It is also unclear what role ever-increasing fisheries for these species might have on the ability of groundfish stocks to recover.

A more general cautionary note concerning fishing down the food web has been raised by several ocean scientists, notably Daniel Pauly. In a recent article in the journal *Science* (February 14, 1998), he notes a worldwide tendency for fishing nations to deplete valuable species, typically at or near the top of the oceans food webs, and then to simply relocate their fishing effort to lower trophic levels. In many cases, the population dynamics of newly targeted species are not fully understood. Of even greater concern is the lack of understanding of the food webs themselves and the roles various species assume within them. Experimental evidence has documented, in both fresh and salt water, that removing certain species in a food web can profoundly affect the nature of the web itself. Moreover, some scientists believe that the lower in the food chain the species that are targeted are, the more widespread and potentially disruptive the effects might be. In other words, the lower in the food web commercial exploitation goes, the greater the possibility for widespread alteration in the oceans' capacity to produce food may be. In light of several nations' plans to harvest phytoplankton and zooplankton in substantial amounts, these concerns may very well amount to more than alarmist cries.

The worldwide trend to concentrate the commercial fishing effort lower and lower down the food chain as a response to excessive exploitation of higher level species is not likely to be sustainable over several generations, based on the partial information known at this time. Most benignly, such strategies most likely displace and delay the next fishery crisis until such a time as the newly targeted species are overfished. At their worst, they may create fundamental alterations in the oceans' life-generating food production system, with unknown consequences. It would be difficult to call either consequence sustainable.

Source: Government of Newfoundland and Labrador, Ministry of Fisheries, Food and Aquaculture.

Manufacturing and service industries, with the obvious exceptions of chemical, steel, and other heavy manufacturing, are not as obviously linked to ecological damage as resource industries are. Their damage usually undermines the biosphere in ways that do not directly undermine the ability of the offending industry to continue operating. Damage is more general, affecting human health and the biosphere's capacity to support other human activities. For example, acid rain produced by burning coal does not damage the supply of coal or the immediate capability to run a coal-fired plant. The damage is done to human lungs, plants, soil, and buildings. Agriculture and forestry are directly affected. Acid rain will only indirectly effect the ability to burn coal by eventually reducing the ability of green plants to produce free molecular oxygen.

It goes without saying that non-renewable resources must be conserved rather than recklessly pursued. As much as possible, alternative, renewable products—either naturally or artificially produced—must be found as well. Where toxic waste products remain (the nuclear power industry is a good example), their effects upon the biosphere must also be considered and contained.

Above all, an integrative procedure is required that traces the full chain of environmental dependencies of each stage of any production process. By tracing these direct and indirect effects on the environment, it is possible to determine the scale and character of an industry's ecological demands. Such an analysis requires some knowledge of the physical, chemical, and biological character of the production process and its consequences.

Service sector activities need not be treated differently from goods production in our argument. While they may consume less energy and material and produce only information, medical assistance, amusement, or intangible products, they also involve the conversion of material and energy into wastes.

To examine the entire economy, one must add up the entire ecological demand of all economic activities. In fixing the sustainable scale of any specific activity, the competition of different industries for the same limited carrying capacity must be factored into the assessment. Proponents of managed or sustainable development would set the scale of economic activity at the level of maximum sustainable yield. In other words, economic activity could expand to some level of maximum sustainable ecological demand. This is very risky. Our ability to accurately predict maximum levels of resource extraction and waste absorption is dubious, as Canadians have recently learned with the collapse of the East Coast fisheries.

Conclusions

Spiralling environmental degradation challenges our current understanding of how society operates, the nature of human wants, and the likely path of future development. Most social analysis inadequately addresses the ecological consequences of human activity. As well, unbridled growth is assumed to be both desirable and possible. Yet ecological consequences are critical and unconstrained growth unlikely. All is not lost! If we can change society before we undermine the ecological basis for a reasonable standard of living, it may be possible to maintain much of the economic achievement of the past 200 years and share these material benefits with others. The more we hesitate to move toward an ecologically sustainable economy, the less will be the planet's productive capacity when we finally do.[5]

We have a reasonably good picture of the biophysical constraints within which we will have to operate during the next century. The implications for present and future society are quite clear. They include three imperatives:

1. **Reduce** the scale of economic activity. We must not only innovate to use fewer resources and produce less waste, we must also limit economic activity to a scale that can be supported by the environment.
2. **Refrain** from economic activities whose technological basis cannot be safely tolerated and supported by the biosphere. Many old and new technologies that we would once have hailed as the progressive fruit of industrial progress must be seen as overutilized. Some are likely to be simply unsustainable. This may very well involve a shedding of nuclear power as well as of much of the petrochemical and automobile industries, and an increased wariness of bio-engineering. Technological innovation must be redirected from increasing productive forces to reducing total ecological demand.
3. **Restore** the earth's habitats and physical cycles in order to strengthen the biosphere's damaged productive capacity.

These will not be accomplished easily. Industrial societies are highly complex social entities. While there is an increasing awareness of the scale of environmental damage and of the need for fundamental change (Tindall 1993), economic transformations will be difficult. Powerful economic and political interests will likely balk when the magnitude of required change is more fully understood (Clow 1992). So too may many individuals and groups in the more developed societies as they face the day-to-day consequences of such change. Yet fundamental change is essential. The human being is an animal that has moved out of ecological balance with its environment. It is imperative that we recognize this humbling lesson and reorganize human life to redress the imbalance. Implementation represents the foremost challenge for twenty-first–century society.

Summary

- Human life exists as an integrated part of a larger physical and biological environment termed a biosphere.
- Past and present human activity has dramatically disrupted and damaged parts of this biosphere.
- Damage to the biosphere ultimately damages the capacity of human life, directly through increased disease and illness and indirectly by making the biosphere less capable of supporting human activity.
- Insatiable human wants and uncontrolled growth over the last 200 years are the underlying causes for the present situation.
- Near universal agreement now exists that substantial changes need to be made in cultural values and human organization.

- Contemporary debate focusses on whether we need to severely limit further economic growth or whether we can have more balanced "sustainable development."
- Sustainable development is likely to be problematic, even contradictory, despite its reassuring tone and ideologically comforting language.
- Dramatic reorganization emphasizing *reducing* economic scale, *refraining* from unsafe technologies, and *restoring* natural habitats and physical cycles must be achieved.

Questions to Consider

1. Environmental damage used to be considered a local problem. Why is this view inadequate?

2. Why do you think sociology has not incorporated a wider sense of the biosphere into its analysis and understanding of human life?

3. It has been argued that, if present trends continue, the world will become polluted to the point where modern industrial societies cannot be sustained. What solutions would you propose to avert such a situation?

4. If economic growth cannot continue at anything near historic levels, what effects might this have on you personally?

5. According to the chapter, why does the limits to growth perspective seem a more accurate reflection of the future than one stressing managed, sustainable development?

6. If the limits to growth perspective is an accurate prediction of the future, what specific changes would you expect to see in your own community?

Suggested Readings

Arnason, R., and L. Felt. *The North Atlantic Fishery*. Charlottetown: Institute of Island Studies, University of Prince Edward Island, 1995.

Chant, D.A. *Pollution Probe*. Toronto: New Press, 1972.

Daly, H.E., and J. Cobb. *For the Common Good: Redirecting the Economy towards Community, the Environment and a Sustainable Future*. Boston: Beacon Press, 1989.

Evernden, N. *The Social Creation of Nature*. Baltimore: Johns Hopkins University Press, 1992.

Gould, S. *The Flamingo's Smile*. New York: W.W. Norton, 1985.

Keating, M. *To the Last Drop: Canada and the World's Water Crisis*. Toronto: Macmillan, 1986.

Jacobs, M. *The Green Economy: Environment, Sustainable Development and the Politics of the Future*. Vancouver: University of British Columbia Press, 1993.

Owens, S. *Energy, Urban Form and Planning*. London: Pion Press, 1986.
Wilson, E., ed. *Biodiversity*. Washington, DC: National Academy Press, 1988.

Glossary

biosphere The total, complex network of living plants and animals and their physical surroundings, the oceans, and air and soil cycles operating as an interdependent system necessary for life at a world system level. An ecosystem at the level of the entire planet.

classical liberal perspective Until recently, the dominant view of humans and their relations to their living and physical environment. The natural environment is passive and forgiving and provides the natural resources to meet human needs and wants. Nature is best seen as a "natural storehouse" of resources, natural forces, and "lower" living organisms. Pursuit of economic growth is equated with moral progress and the environment is considered an inexhaustible supply of resources.

economic growth The use of labour, capital, and natural resources to increase the production of goods and services for a given community, region, or state.

ecosystem The combination of a life support system composed of air, water, and a thin layer of soil, and the complexes of living species in some degree of interdependence.

environmental management perspective See **sustainable development**.

habitat A complex network of living plant and animal communities and their physical surroundings. One of the building blocks of the biosphere.

limits to growth perspective This perspective argues that reckless economic growth threatens the earth's biosphere and hence our future existence. Advocates call for a shift away from a growth-driven, increasingly sophisticated technological approach to strategies that actively attempt to dramatically reduce economic growth.

Karl Marx Political theorist of the last half of the nineteenth century. A primary critic of capitalistic development, Marx emphasized the enslaving power of capitalist forces and called for their overthrow. Ironically, his view of the environment was similar to that of advocates of the classical liberal perspective.

sustainable development A major view of how to respond to the problems of environmental damage resulting from uncontrolled industrial development, sometimes termed the "environmental management" perspective. It suggests that wise planning and innovative technology can allow for continued growth without jeopardizing the opportunities of future generations. The popular report *Our Common Future* (also referred to as the Brundtland Report) advocates better management and greater sensitivity toward environmental effects. It also suggests that innovative technology can allow continued economic growth.

sustainable yield A level of harvest of a renewable natural resource that allows the resource to reproduce; a yield sustained at a level that is not threatening to the resource. For example, a sustainable yield of fish would be a catch level that does not threaten the capacity of the species to maintain a healthy population. An important term associated with the sustainable development orientation.

Notes

1. For a very good overview of the pervasiveness of ecological damage, see Mungall and McLaren (1991). This volume is the result of a project by the Royal Society of Canada to assemble disciplinary specialists to summarize and document environmental damage and explore the implications for the planet. Written for a wide audience, it represents one of the best summaries on global damage and its implication for human life.

2. It is true that climates and relative proportions of ingredients in the atmosphere have changed slightly, but only slightly. For example, mean surface temperatures of the whole planet have remained within a range of only 7 degrees celsius, including the ice ages. Concentrations of carbon dioxide, so necessary for photosynthesis, have varied from 200 parts per million in glacial periods to 300 parts in interglacial times. Methane, another important gas necessary for maintaining the earth's capacity to retain heat, has remained relatively constant over the past 10 000 years at least. See World Meteorological Association (1989).

3. Fluctuations in climate have been documented in considerable detail over the course of the past several thousand years. Increasingly, we are being forced to recognize that human influences can produce changes in the natural climate system that are greater and faster than anything previously documented. Industrialization and economic growth can significantly alter the energy exchanges of the atmosphere by altering its chemistry. These effects threaten not only climate but also the productive capacity of the earth as well as human health.

   How does this occur? Within the atmosphere are small amounts of a number of gases, popularly called "greenhouse gases" because they alter the flow of heat and energy through the atmosphere much as the glass shell of a greenhouse does. Such gases include nitrous oxide, methane, and carbon dioxide. In historical concentrations, they play a critical role in the earth's capacity to retain heat and energy. Unfortunately, human population growth and accelerated industrial activity at a global level are increasing the concentrations of these gases at alarming rates. The effect is that greater heat is trapped near the earth's surface along with higher levels of water vapour (clouds). Massive climatic changes can result from the melting of polar ice caps (and therefore increased sea levels) to the creation of expanded desert areas from what used to be agricultural lands.

4. For a thorough philosophical and historical analysis of how post-Enlightenment society has "socially created" a sense of nature as an object external to us whose purpose is to benefit humankind see Evernden (1985 and 1992). It is particularly important to note that the sense of nature that informs contemporary society has been socially constructed out of specific historical circumstances and should not be considered as part of any inherent human characteristic. According to Evernden, this is also true of ideologically based ideas such as unlimited growth and the insatiability of human needs. Many non-Western societies have had, and continue to have, conceptions of nature in which the integration and interdependency of human life with the larger ecosystem are much more pronounced.

5. It is essential that the unbridled pursuit of growth to satisfy allegedly insatiable human needs be understood as a social construction and not as the reflection of some inevitable, fixed genetic characteristic of the species. Human behaviour and organization appear too diverse to be explained by the narrow dictates of genetic determination. Had we dominating, universal instincts, such as insatiable material needs, we would likely be trapped by them in a few fixed habitats, in a particular ecological niche, and with a singular social organization set by our genetic programming like all other animals. As such, we would pose no more threat to the rest of the biosphere than wolves, lions, deer, horses, or the other great apes. Instead, we have invented ways of life and spread out of whatever habitat we evolved in to adapt ourselves to living virtually anywhere on the planet. In the course of this expansion, we have devised a vast and highly diversified array of human societies, the vast majority of which have *not* been committed to the ever greater accumulation of material wealth. See Gould (1993) for a review of some of the relevant literature.

References

Allen, J. 1994. *Environment 94/95*. Guilford, CT: Dushkin Publishing Group.

Alverson, L. 1991. *The Status of Stocks of Gadus Atlantica in NAFO Areas 2J, 3K, L*. St. John's: Northwest Atlantic Fisheries Centre.

Arnason, R., and L. Felt. 1995. *The North Atlantic Fishery*. Charlottetown: Institute of Island Studies, University of Prince Edward Island.

Benton, T. 1989. "Marxism and Natural Limits: An Ecological Critique and Reconstruction." *New Left Review*, no. 178: 51–86.

Bolaria, B.S. 1991. "Environment, Work and Illness." *Social Issues and Contradictions in Canadian Society*. Toronto: Harcourt Brace Jovanovich. 222–46.

Boreham, G., and R. Leftwich. 1971. *Economic Thinking in a Canadian Context*. Toronto: Holt, Rinehart and Winston of Canada.

Chant, D.A. 1972. *Pollution Probe*. Toronto: New Press.

Clow, M. 1990. "Sustainable Development Won't Be Enough." *Policy Options/Options Politiques* 11, no. 9: 6–9.

———. 1992. "Ecological Exhaustion and the Crisis of Global Capitalism." *Our Generation* 23, no. 1: 1–25.

Commoner, B. 1971. *The Closing Circle: Nature, Man and Technology*. New York: Bantam Books.

Daly, H.E., and J. Cobb. 1989. *For the Common Good: Redirecting the Economy towards Community, the Environment and a Sustainable Future*. Boston: Beacon Press.

Evernden, N. 1985. *The Natural Alien*. Toronto: University of Toronto Press.

———. 1992. *The Social Creation of Nature*. Baltimore: Johns Hopkins University Press.

Fisheries Resource Conservation Council (FRCC). 1998. *1998 Annual Report on the Status of Northern Cod*. Ottawa: FRCC.

Georgescu-Roegen, N. 1980. "The Entropy Law and the Economic Problem." In *Economics, Ecology, Ethics: Essays towards a Steady-State Economy*, ed. H. Daly. New York: Anchor Books. 49–60.

Gould, S. 1993. *Eight Little Piggies: Reflections in Natural History*. New York: W.W. Norton.

International Committee on Northwest Atlantic Fisheries (ICNAF). 1992. *Report on the Status of Gadus Atlantica in the Northwestern Atlantic*. Halifax: ICNAF.

Jacobs, M. 1993. *The Green Economy: Environment, Sustainable Development and the Politics of the Future*. Vancouver: University of British Columbia Press.

Keating, M. 1986. *To the Last Drop: Canada and the World's Water Crisis*. Toronto: MacMillan.

Kelly, M., and K. Sandersen. 1990. "Sea Changes, Sustainability and Strategies." *Alternatives* 17, no. 1: 30–36.

Marchak, P. 1983. *Green Gold: The Forest Industry in British Columbia*. Vancouver: University of British Columbia Press.

Marchak, P., N. Guppy, and J. Macmillan. 1987. *Uncommon Property: The Fishing and Fish Processing Industries in British Columbia*. Vancouver: University of British Columbia Press.

Marx, K. 1973. *Grundrisse: Foundation of the Critique of Political Economy*. Trans. M. Nicholas. New York: Vintage Books.

McGoodwin, J. 1990. *Crisis in the World's Fisheries*. Stanford: Stanford University Press.

Meadows, D.H., D.L. Meadows, J. Randers, and W.W. Behrens. 1972. *The Limits to Growth*. New York: New American Library.

Mungall, C., and D. McLaren. 1991. *Planet Under Stress: The Challenge of Global Change*. Toronto: Oxford University Press.

Raskin, P.D., and S.S. Bernow. 1991. "Ecology and Marxism: Are Red and Green Complementary?" *Rethinking Marxism* 4, no. 1 (Spring 1991): 87–103.

Tindall, D. 1993. "The New Class Theorists: Participation in the BC Environmental Movement." Paper given at the Annual Meeting of the Canadian Sociology and Anthropology Association. Ottawa. June.

World Commission on Environment and Development (WCED). 1987. *Our Common Future*. Report of the Brundtland Commission. Oxford: Oxford University Press.

Wagner, R. 1974. *Environment and Man*, 2d ed. New York: W.W. Norton.

Woodrow, R.B. 1977. "The Development and Implementation of Pollution Control Programs in Canada 1966–1974." Unpublished Doctoral dissertation. Guelph: University of Guelph.

World Meteorological Association. 1989. *Proceedings, World Conference on the Changing Atmosphere: Implications for Global Security*. Brussels: World Meteorological Association.

CHAPTER 13

Urbanization: Issues and Problems

Alison Hayford

Learning Objectives

After studying this chapter, you should be able to
- Describe the major issues of Canadian **urbanism**, including those that arise from the ordinary practices of daily life.
- Outline some of the major theoretical approaches to the study of cities.
- Understand the roots of urban issues and the ways in which our society might deal with them.

Introduction

A **city** is, quite simply, a relatively dense, large settlement with a non-agricultural economic base. And yet there is nothing simple about cities: there is a long tradition in Western society of seeing cities as sources of social problems. Even if as Canadians, we like to think we've avoided the kinds of problems that exist in U.S. cities—drugs, crime, racial conflict, economic decay—we're still a bit uneasy about our own cities, and we're still concerned about the quality of urban life (Central Mortgage and Housing [CMHC] 1979). Many of the major social concerns of Canadians—such problems as unemployment and national unity—are not specifically urban, but there are many issues that we do associate, rightly or wrongly, with cities. For example, we tend to see problems such as crime and drug use and social issues such as the impact of immigration on Canadian society as part of urbanism— the concentration of people in cities and the social patterns that emerge in such settlements. Many people see cities as causes of serious social problems such as youth crime and drug use; alternatively, we assume that more general social problems such as racism become worse in cities than in other places. In either case, we identify these issues and problems as specifically urban—as problems that have a particular association with cities and city life.

Canadians tend to regard cities with mixed feelings. We see them as places of great social and economic opportunities—but we often believe that the danger of cities outweighs the opportunities they offer. Many people see the urban environment as a threat in itself to the well-being of urban dwellers; for example, it is common to blame urban problems on the simple fact that cities contain large numbers of people. We often think that problems arise because too many people live too close together, because many people will have many social differences, and because most city dwellers are strangers to one another. While it is possible that these things are factors in creating some of the problems we associate with urbanism, they don't explain all of the problems of cities or the differences among cities. It's important to realize that cities reflect the structures and values of the societies that create and sustain them. To understand urban issues and problems, we need to understand the social forces that create cities.

Canadian Urbanism

Most Canadians live in cities. More than a third of the population lives in or near our three largest cities alone, while over three-quarters of Canadians live in urban areas. This means that most Canadians live in environments that mix social classes, races, and cultures. It means that most of us live among strangers, in places that use formal regulation to achieve order—from traffic lights and noxious weed ordinances to laws governing public morality. Yet while cities are a central fact of life for Canadians, we see them as creating problems.

An unexpected kind of problem—the most basic problem, perhaps, for scholars and policy-makers—is to define what a city is. We may know instinctively, but social scientists and politicians find it more difficult to develop meaningful definitions. How big is a city in area and population? Who governs cities? Is a low-density suburban area whose residents work in a city part of that city, or is it a separate social and political unit? Where dozens of cities have grown together, is there one city, or many?

In Canada, provincial governments have the power to define the boundaries, types of government, and legal responsibilities of municipalities, including the largest cities (Tindal and Tindal 1979, 1–18; Garber and Imbroscio 1996, 605–606). This is a significant power; municipal governments often have responsibility for maintaining such things as sanitation services, education, and social housing, but they do not have full power over their own revenue bases, their systems of management, or even their geographic areas. The actions of provincial government can have profound consequences for residents of cities, yet city dwellers may find that they have little direct say in decisions that affect their lives. This can happen even where a city is a major financial and political power, as we have seen in the case of the Government of Ontario's decision to amalgamate a number of Ontario urban municipal governments, including that of Toronto (Government of Ontario 1996; KMPG Canada 1997). The provincial government encountered widespread opposition to this plan in Metro Toronto (e.g., Jacobs 1997; Ruppert 1997; Sewell 1997), and its six municipalities held a referendum in which those who voted decisively rejected the proposed changes (Citizens for Local Democracy 1997a; No Megacity Coalition 1997). Despite this, the Government of Ontario proceeded with its legislation, and the new City of Toronto (often called the Megacity) came into being on January 1, 1998 (Government of Ontario 1996; Government of Ontario 1997b; Milroy 1997). Urban amalgamation in Ontario also involved significant changes to the funding of local services such as social assistance, housing, and education. Again, these decisions were made largely at the provincial level, although it is municipal governments and urban dwellers who will have responsibility for implementing them, including making up lost provincial funding (Government of Ontario 1997a; 1997b; Milroy 1997; Women Plan Toronto 1997; Citizens for Local Democracy 1997b; United Way 1997).

Part of provincial power over municipalities is the right to define what they are. Ordinary words like "city" or "town" may mean different things in different provinces, and there is little comparability; Melville, Saskatchewan, with about 5000 people, and Toronto, with over 4 million, are both legally designated as cities, yet they are clearly different kinds of places. If we want to compare cities across Canada, we need common terms and definitions other than those established by provinces. For this reason, Statistics Canada has developed a set of definitions that distinguish among different levels of urban centres. These definitions are concerned with functional relationships and practices; thus they identify populations as urban on the basis of their involvement in an urban system rather than on the basis of legal designations. Statistics Canada's basic concept is that of the **urban area**, an area with 1000 or more people and a density of 400 or more people per square kilometre (Statistics Canada 1992). In some parts of the world, agricultural villages might fit such a definition, but urban centres reflect the characteristics of specific societies, and since Canada as a whole is sparsely populated, this definition of "urban" makes sense for Canadian society. An urban area is a **Census Metropolitan Area (CMA)** if the core urban area is very large (a population of at least 100 000) and geographically adjacent areas (rural as well as urban) are socially and economically integrated with the core (Statistics Canada 1997a, 181). **Census Agglomerations (CAs)** are urban areas where the urban core has a population of at least 10 000 but less than 100 000; again, as with CMAs, adjacent areas are included in CAs if they are functionally integrated (Statistics Canada 1997a, 181–82). Integration is measured by such factors as where people work; for example, if a substantial proportion (40 percent) of people in a town or rural area adjacent to a large urban core work in the core, the smaller place is part of the CMA or CA (Statistics Canada 1997a, 193). Thus, these categories reflect the fact that cities involve more than co-occupancy of a given region—they also involve economic and social interactions that are spatially concentrated and non-agricultural.

Cities are formed in social systems that allow the geographic concentration of wealth and people (Harvey 1976, 195–284). The economies, political systems, and social organization of urban societies all support this concentration. Before the nineteenth century, in all parts of the world, even those that supported cities, most people lived in rural areas and were involved primarily in agriculture or related activities; it was only with the Industrial Revolution two hundred years ago that the massive **urbanization** of human populations began. Even before the rise of industrial urban society, however, much of what rural people produced went to support cities, whether through the workings of the market or through taxation and other forms of appropriation. Furthermore, even in societies where urban populations were only a small percentage of the total population, rural people were usually subject to city-based political power, though this was often mediated through local leaders such as a land-based nobility or religious leaders.

Canada, though its relatively small population occupies a huge territory, has one of the most urbanized populations in the world. Canada became predominantly urban (with more than half its population in urban centres) by the 1930s (Burke 1987b, 14). The rate of urbanization has varied greatly among provinces, however; a majority of people in British Columbia and Ontario lived in cities by 1911, while Prince Edward Island was still predominantly rural in 1986 (Burke 1987b, 14). In 1951, the first year the concept of the CMA was used, there were 15 CMAs in Canada, containing about 42 percent of Canada's population. By 1991, there were 25 CMAs; by 1996, nearly 64 percent of Canada's population lived in these centres (Statistics Canada 1998d; 1998e). In 1996, Canada had four urban areas of over a million people—Toronto, Montreal, Vancouver, and Ottawa-Hull; nearly four out of every ten Canadians (37 percent) live in these four cities (Statistics Canada 1998d; 1998e) (see Table 13.1).

Canada's cities, and in particular Canada's larger cities, have long been the destinations of migrants and immigrants. Only about a quarter of people moving within Canada move from urban to rural areas. Most people move from cities to other cities, often from smaller to larger centres. Of the people moving from rural areas, most end up in cities rather than smaller centres—70 percent of rural migrants by the end of the 1970s (Burke 1987b, 14–15). Immigrants from other countries are also attracted primarily to Canada's larger centres. Of all immigrants to Canada between 1981 and 1991, 66 percent went to the three largest cities. Of the immigrants who came to Canada between 1991 and 1996, 93 percent chose to live in a CMA, and most (nearly 75 percent) of these immigrants live in Toronto, Montreal, or Vancouver (Statistics Canada 1997c, 5). In 1996, immigrants made up 42 percent of the population of Toronto (Statistics Canada 1997c). About 42 percent of all new arrivals to Canada in the 1991–96 period settled in the Toronto CMA, while 18 percent went to Vancouver and 13 percent to Montreal (Statistics Canada 1997c, 5).

These numbers alone don't express the full significance of immigration and its impact on Canada's cities. Before 1961, most immigrants to Canada came from Europe. In the 1990s, however, the majority of immigrants come from other parts of the world, in particular Asia (though substantial numbers come from the Caribbean, Africa, Latin America, and the Middle East). Because immigration has been concentrated so heavily in a few cities, the cultural and ethnic composition of the population in most of Canada has not been much affected by this shift. The three largest CMAs, however—Toronto, Vancouver, and Montreal—have been profoundly changed by immigration, and in their suburban areas as well as urban cores, institutions such as public schools and health-care facilities have had to adjust to new demands created by a changing population (Ray, Halseth, and Johnson 1997). While many Canadians may see these changes and the new demands they create as a social problem, many others see immigration as a source of cultural and economic richness and opportunity.

The processes of urban concentration in Canada have varied over time. Sometimes the largest centres have attracted the greatest growth, sometimes middle-sized cities and suburban or bedroom communities have been the focus of growth (Statistics Canada 1987). The general trend, however, has been for most Canadians—those born here as well as immigrants—to live in or near the larger urban centres.

TABLE 13.1   Population of Canada's Census Metropolitan Areas, 1991 and 1996

CMA	Rank in 1996/1991	1996 population	1991 population	% change
Toronto	1/1	4 263 757	3 989 933	9.4
Montreal	2/2	3 326 510	3 208 970	3.7
Vancouver	3/3	1 831 665	1 602 590	14.3
Ottawa-Hull	4/4	1 010 498	941 814	7.3
Edmonton	5/5	862 597	841 132	2.6
Calgary	6/6	821 628	754 033	9.0
Quebec	7/8	671 889	645 550	4.1
Winnipeg	8/7	667 209	660 450	1.0
Hamilton	9/9	624 360	599 760	4.1
London	10/10	398 616	381 522	4.5
Kitchener	11/12	382 940	356 421	7.4
St. Catharines-Niagara	12/11	372 406	364 552	2.2
Halifax	13/13	332 518	320 501	3.7
Victoria	14/14	304 287	287 897	5.7
Windsor	15/15	278 685	262 075	6.3
Oshawa	16/16	268 773	240 104	11.9
Saskatoon	17/17	219 056	210 949	3.8
Regina	18/18	193 652	191 692	1.0
St. John's	19/19	174 051	171 848	1.3
Sudbury	20/21	160 488	171 848	1.8
Chicoutimi-Jonquière	21/20	160 454	160 928	−0.3
Sherbrooke	22/22	147 384	140 718	4.7
Trois-Rivières	23/23	139 956	136 303	2.7
Saint John	24/24	125 705	125 838	−0.1
Thunder Bay	25/25	125 562	124 925	0.5

Note: Notice the great variability of growth rates in the five-year period; it is clear that some cities and regions of the country are growing while others are barely holding their own. Pay attention to the size of the population base—while Toronto's rate of growth was less than that of Vancouver, it had 134 000 more new inhabitants than Vancouver did—its rate of growth is lower because it is bigger to begin with. Another point to note is the stability of relative rankings of cities in this period—the only changes are in 7/8, 11/12, and 20/21; there has been no major shift in rankings since Montreal went from first to second place in the 1976 census (after begin Canada's largest city since before Confederation in 1867). Note that Ottawa-Hull became Canada's fourth million-person CMA in the 1991–96 period.

Source: Adapted from Statistics Canada, *A National Overview—Population and Dwelling Counts*, Cat. no. 92-357.

Issues of Urbanism

Urban societies are inevitably heterogeneous in important ways. In addition to divisions between cities and countryside, there are almost always significant ethnic, class, and other differences within the populations of cities. Most often, when we talk about urban problems we are referring to those within cities. Modern industrial and postindustrial societies such as Canada have become so thoroughly urbanized that few people know or think about conflicts between city and countryside. Only occasionally do rural–urban issues come to public consciousness—as when farm communities are disrupted by the demands of urban-based banks, for example, or when provincial legislatures dominated by rural representatives impose particular forms of government on unwilling cities.

Often we define urban problems as those that seem to rise out of urbanism itself. Violence, crime, racial and cultural conflict, housing shortages, and other forms of social dislocation are all associated with the dense, mixed populations of large urban centres. Although such problems also exist in rural areas, we still perceive them to be worse in cities. But if we want to explain all the problems of cities, we must add to these demographic factors an understanding of cities' social organization, which invariably reflects that of the whole society.

Some social theorists argue that urban societies are inherently unequal (Badcock 1984; Childe 1950; Davis 1990; Harvey 1976; Shurmer-Smith and Hannam 1994; Zukin 1991), since the social processes that allow the geographic concentration of people also involve the social concentration of wealth and power. These economic and political inequalities are matched by divisions of age and gender, which seem so natural that we rarely see them as issues. They are, nonetheless, important aspects of city life that have the potential to create problems. The specific forms urban divisions take may vary, but social inequality remains a characteristic of urban society.

Defining Urban Problems

The definition of social problems depends on the extent to which they are recognized, and even if problematic conditions are present by some objective measure, they are not necessarily recognized as being worthy of public concern. Crime is perhaps the one issue that has been a fairly consistent concern of urban dwellers and urban media. Other urban conditions emerge as public issues for certain periods of time. For example, homelessness is not a new phenomenon, but it did not became an important social issue in Canada until the 1980s—it wasn't even included in the 1970 survey of urban issues (CMHC 1979). While homelessness still concerns many people, particularly in the larger cities, (Toronto Coalition against Homelessness 1996), in some ways it has become so much a part of urban life that even where the homeless are both numerous and visible, homelessness is sometimes seen as more of a nuisance than a tragedy. Similarly, urban environmental issues became important in the 1970s and 1980s, but in the 1990s these issues have receded somewhat from public view; housing gets only occasional attention, even though it is one of the most basic elements of city environments and the one with the most immediate impact on the lives of city dwellers. The issue that has emerged in Canada in the 1990s is immigration, perhaps because an increasing proportion of newcomers to Canada have non-European origins; while this is not a specifically urban issue, most immigrants settle in the three largest CMAs, and immigration issues are often associated with quality-of-urban-life issues.

In addition to issues we choose to recognize as urban problems, cities must deal with other conditions that have important consequences for urban life. Unemployment and poverty, for example, are by no means restricted to cities, but their effects can be particularly visible and dramatic in urban settings. Whether or not we choose to see the issues that arise in cities as problems, they often have roots in larger issues, and to understand what goes on in cities we must look at these larger issues as well.

Problems We Recognize

Crime

Perhaps the one problem that almost everyone would name if asked to make a list of urban problems is crime (Canadian Centre for Justice Statistics 1995; CMHC 1979; Hartnagel 1978; Kennedy and Krahn 1983; Merry 1981; Sacco 1981). While we fear such things as pollution and isolation, we tend to fear our fellow humans even more—especially if they are young, male, and from racial or cultural minorities (Merry 1981, 4–10). This may be one reason that many people perceive the changing ethnic composition of the largest cities and their suburbs as threatening. Perceptions of crime are difficult to measure, but they do seem to change over time. While a 1981 survey showed that 40 percent of urban Canadians indicated they felt unsafe in their own neighbourhoods at night (Johnson 1988, 24), a 1993 survey showed that 86 percent of Canadians were "very or somewhat satisfied" with their general level of safety, and that about 25 percent felt "very unsafe" in their area after dark (Canadian Centre for Justice Statistics 1995). (These two surveys are not completely comparable, since the second was not restricted to urban Canadians.) The 1993 survey also showed that there are generational and sex differences in attitudes towards safety; both older men and women of all ages felt less safe in their own neighbourhoods after dark than did younger men. People who live in inner-city neighbourhoods may feel particularly at risk, especially people who are vulnerable for other reasons such as poverty and racism (LaPrairie 1994, 188–89). Surveys of crime show that when we talk about urban crime, we do not mean all kinds of crime; few crime surveys indicate much fear that hackers will break into our bank accounts or medical records. Instead, we fear being assaulted by strangers or having our houses broken into. When we talk about urban crime, then, we usually mean physical attacks on ourselves or our property by strangers.

To some extent our association of cities and crime is warranted. While there is no simple correlation between city size and violent crime rates, overall the larger cities tend to have higher rates. In 1987, the violent crime rate was highest in the largest cities (250 000 or more people)—933 per 100 000 population; cities with 10 000 to 50 000 people had a rate of 769 per 100 000 (Johnson 1988, 29). Some large cities, however, have violent crime rates lower than those in smaller centres; Calgary, for example, whose population was undergoing the kind of growth and social dislocation that is often supposed to give rise to crime, had a violent crime rate of 571 per 100 000 in 1987, while small, relatively homogeneous Charlottetown had a rate of 892 (Statistics Canada 1988, 3-1, 3-11). These differences may reflect variations in reporting; in a small centre like Charlottetown, people may be more prone to report crime than they are in larger and more impersonal cities, where many people may perceive police as unfriendly and unco-operative. There are still anomalies, however; Calgary had the lowest violent crime rate of any of the larger cities, but Edmonton, similar to Calgary in many ways, had one of the highest (Johnson 1988, 28).

If we look at overall crime statistics, the picture is even less clear. The largest cities had an overall crime rate of 11 597 per 100 000 people in 1987 (Statistics Canada 1988, 3-1), but smaller cities (those with populations of 25 000 to 249 000) had higher overall crime rates than larger cities, with populations of 250 000 and over (Statistics Canada 1988, 3-7).

Part of this difference arises from property crimes, which have higher rates in smaller cities of 50 000 to 249 000 people than in the largest cities of 500 000 and over (Statistics Canada 1988, 3-1 to 3-3). All three of the smaller-sized groups of cities also have higher rates of other crimes, which range from infractions of municipal by-laws to federal drug statutes (Statistics Canada 1988, 3-1 to 3-62). But even the smallest centres included in the crime statistics, those with populations of 100 to 2499, had violent crime rates of 784 per 100 000 in 1987 (Statistics Canada 1988, 3-1 to 3-62).

Whatever factors contribute to crime, such typically urban conditions as mixed populations, social dislocation, and the presence of strangers can provide only partial explanations. Crime statistics show that the intense, emotionally fraught relationships of family and friendship can be as dangerous as city streets (Merry 1981, 6–7). For women in particular, the family home can be more dangerous than public places. In general, the people most likely to fear street crime—women and the elderly—are the least likely to be its victims; it is young males who both commit crime and fall victim to it (Johnson 1988, 27; Kennedy and Krahn 1983, 12). Such distorted perceptions might arise in part from media coverage of crime news, which can exaggerate the dangers of crime (Graber 1980); they also arise from social values that condone and even encourage violence in some situations.

Racial Conflict

Images of urban problems are often linked with images of racial conflict. A number of factors combine to make us associate racial issues with urbanism. Immigrant and migrant groups, many of whom are now of non-European origin (Statistics Canada 1998b; 1998f) are concentrated in cities; Canada's Native population has also been undergoing rural-to-urban migration, with more than a third of status Indians now living in cities (Clatworthy and Hull 1983, 4–5; Frideres 1983, 187). Migrant groups may be more likely than the rest of the population to be poor, to have cultural values that differ from dominant ones, and to have visible social and environmental difficulties (Parrish 1986; Winn 1988).

While larger urban centres tend to have more diverse populations than smaller places do, we can see from Table 13.2 that there is a great variation in the levels of diversity of Canada's CMAs. The proportion of visible minorities (defined by

TABLE 13.2   Aboriginal and Visible Minority Populations in Canada's CMAs, 1996

CMA	Total aboriginal population	% of CMA	Total visible minority population	% of CMA
Calgary	15 195	1.9	127 555	15.6
Chicoutimi-Jonquière	1 255	0.8	700	0.4
Edmonton	32 825	3.8	115 430	13.5
Halifax	2 115	0.6	22 320	6.8
Hamilton	5 460	0.9	48 910	7.9
Kitchener	2 260	0.6	33 815	8.9
London	4 385	1.1	30 325	7.7
Montreal	9 965	0.3	401 425	12.2
Oshawa	2 160	0.8	16 035	6.0
Ottawa-Hull	11 605	1.2	115 460	11.5
Quebec	2 605	0.4	9 815	1.5
Regina	13 605	7.1	10 355	5.4
St. Catharines-Niagara	3 960	1.2	13 445	3.7
Saint John	665	0.6	2 555	2.1
St. John's	700	0.4	2 370	1.4
Saskatoon	16 160	7.5	11 250	5.2
Sherbrooke	400	0.3	3 015	2.1
Sudbury	4 625	2.9	2 840	1.8
Thunder Bay	6 070	5.9	2 685	2.2
Toronto	16 095	0.4	1 338 095	31.6
Trois-Rivières	750	0.5	1 240	0.9
Vancouver	31 140	1.7	564 600	31.1
Victoria	6 570	2.2	22 915	7.6
Windsor	2 255	0.8	27 615	10.0
Winnipeg	45 750	6.9	73 310	11.1

Source: Adapted from Statistics Canada, <www.statcan.ca:80/english/pgdb/people/population/demopn40f.htm>.

Statistics Canada as "persons, other than aboriginal peoples, who are non-Caucasian in race or non-white in colour") ranges from less than half a percent of the population in Chicoutimi-Jonquière to over 30 percent in Toronto. Size is only one factor—apart from Montreal, Quebec's CMAs are less diverse than those in other parts of Canada, which suggests that non-European immigrants are not moving into these cities. While a substantial proportion of aboriginal (North American Indian, Métis, and Inuit) people now live in cities, particularly in Western Canada, they do not form a large part of the population of any given CMA.

At all levels of government, Canada has multicultural policies whose aim is to provide some kind of recognition to minority groups (Kallen 1988). What this means in practice, however, is unresolved. Governments may be happy to provide funding for ethnic dance groups and once-a-year multicultural festivals, but they may be less happy about having minority groups in city hall. Visible minorities are underrepresented in official organs of government; whether this is the result of differences in education and culture or of discrimination is a much-debated issue. In any case, visible minority groups, increasingly, see having a voice in managing the community as an important social issue.

The different cultural values and practices of some minority groups may also be seen as threatening to **social order**, especially when the groups form coherent communities. This is one reason we associate racial problems with the large, spatially concentrated minority populations of cities. Urban life can cause problems for those migrants who have not been prepared for it (Clatworthy and Hull 1983, 67–70; Frideres 1983, 199; LaPrairie 1994, 16–19; Parrish 1986). Furthermore, resistance to assimilation can create social conflicts, which are increasingly focussed in cities.

Urban minority populations can be relatively large and sometimes, as in the case of Native people, highly mobile (Clatworthy and Hull 1983, 47–50; Frideres 1983, 195–96). Both of these factors make it less likely that informal community structures will be adequate to deal with community difficulties (Frideres 1983, 197–207), though migrants to urban centres often have ties to family or friends who help them adjust (LaPrairie 1994, 188–89). In addition, changing political beliefs make it less likely than in earlier eras that minority groups will accept assimilation as the primary solution to social and economic difficulties (Elliott 1979, 1–6). Thus, one aspect of contemporary Canadian urban life is the need for government-funded social support structures to meet the cultural needs and demands of particular groups. Medical and social services are one area where cultural issues can arise. To help respond to the needs of a multicultural society, hospitals and courts in many Canadian cities now train staff to deal with cultural differences, and many of these institutions also provide translation services for immigrants. The particular problems that minority people face in the justice system have been recognized as important issues, and in some cities there are special programs to help aboriginal people deal with the justice system. In most of Canada's larger cities, various cultural and ethnic groups sponsor education programs for their children, including, in some cases, in schools receiving public funding. Programs for immigrants and migrants can be politically problematic, however, since they may cause resentment among groups that do not have such special programs. Conflict also arises within groups using social services, because community groups sometimes have internal divisions (Nagata 1979; Parrish 1986) and because control of these services may represent control over significant resources.

Urban Environments

We see urban environments in two somewhat conflicting ways: as the product of natural forces, and as human creations that we can control and through which we can affect social behaviour. In Canadian cities, these conflicting attitudes toward the urban environment have had important effects. We often assume that the natural forces of the marketplace will result in a livable urban environment and that government intervention should therefore be minimal, and be regulatory rather than direct (Weaver 1984). When these forces fail to create livable urban environments, we often have few resources with which to respond.

Through the 1960s, concepts of urban issues in both Canada and the United States reflected assumptions about the impact of city environments on the social and moral characters of their residents (Jacobs 1961; Rutherford 1984, 437–38; Weaver 1977, 31). It was often assumed that crowded housing and congested streets could lead to the breakdown of social order. The establishment of housing codes, zoning ordinances, and great parks in the larger cities reflected the desire of urban reformers to control the quality of urban life and create better citizens; the spatial segregation of functions was supposed to protect families from exposure to the amoral world of industry and commerce. We still live with the consequences of these values, in cities whose commercial districts are dead outside of business hours and whose residential neighbourhoods offer few opportunities for employment and little convenience in the management of everyday life.

With very few exceptions (e.g., Old Quebec), Canadian cities are typical North American cities in their basic forms. Canadian cities are somewhat more densely developed than are cities in the United States (Goldberg and Mercer 1986), though this is changing as governments have become less involved in regulating land development (Filion 1996, 1652–54; Garber and Imbroscio 1996). In both countries, the single most important element of the urban landscape is residential housing, and of this, the single most important element is detached, owner-occupied houses in relatively low density developments where other land uses (such as commercial areas) are severely restricted or lacking altogether. The preference for this kind of housing is strong (Bourne 1993a; 1993b; Harris and Pratt 1993), even though high housing costs can be a serious problem for many Canadian households (Filion and Bunting 1990). Nearly 69 percent of the 6.2 million households in Canada's CMAs are one-family households (Statistics Canada 1993, 16–31), and the rate of growth for private dwellings is greater than that of the population in general (Statistics Canada 1997b, 8). Although this kind of housing and the low-density, single-use neighbourhoods associated with it create conditions that can be problematic in the management of daily life, preference for this kind of urban environment is both wide-spread and deep, and apart from a few urban critics, most people do not see it as an issue.

While today we rarely assume that simplistic causes and effects relate the physical environment to behaviour, we still assume some kind of relationship. We talk about design as a solution to some of the social problems of cities (Jacobs 1961, 143–221), especially crime (City of Regina 1983); we have fresh air funds to send poor children to the purity of the countryside; and there is still strong resistance to allowing mixed-use land development.

In recent years, concerns about urban environments have changed (Miller and Newman 1988). Scandals raised about the damage to health that results from mismanagement of the environment have made ordinary citizens aware that they are at risk. One of these followed the burning of a warehouse in which PCBs were stored in a residential area in Quebec, contaminating hundreds of houses and forcing the evacuation of hundreds of people for several weeks. A public that has come to perceive such dangers as important has often come into conflict with private industry and public agencies who deny or minimize them.

Environmental problems also arise because urban areas concentrate the production of waste; city air may contain up to 25 times the contaminants found in rural areas (Spirn 1984, 42). A large city can produce hundreds of tonnes a day of carbon monoxide, smoke, toxic chemicals, and everyday household garbage. The air, soil, and water of cities contain a great variety of pollutants (Taylor 1993, 309, 317–21), and in places these reach high enough levels that they have serious consequences for the health of city dwellers. Children can be particularly vulnerable; for example, one common urban pollutant is lead, which is known to affect the mental abilities and physical growth of children. In one Toronto neighbourhood in 1984, 20 percent of the children tested were found to have toxic levels of lead, even though the lead problem had been identified more than ten years earlier and steps had supposedly been taken to correct it (Saskatchewan Council for International Development 1987). The management of waste has become a major problem for municipalities and for senior governments. In the mid-1980s, Ontario had 11 000 industrial plants dumping wastes into municipal sewage systems, many of which in turn dumped these wastes into water systems that are sources of drinking water downstream (Keating 1986). At the same time, a quarter of Ontario's municipal sewage-treatment plants were breaking three of the province's antipollution guidelines, while 64 percent failed to meet guidelines for phosphorus levels (Keating 1986).

Pollution, like crime, is not just a city problem. Rural and small-town people have problems with water quality that are often worse than those of people in cities, as well as problems with garbage and air pollution. In cities, however, the scale and concentration of these problems is much greater. The built environment of cities can also aggravate pollution problems, since they tend to be more humid, hot, and cloudy than surrounding rural areas, and this can worsen the effects of pollutants (Spirn 1984, 44). Because many of these problems arise from the way we organize our cities, however, it will be difficult to control pollution without making fundamental changes to the physical, economic, and political structures of cities.

Smog Pushes Death Rates Up in Canada's Cities

Breathing the heavily polluted air in Canadian cities is deadly, a study conducted by three federal scientists suggests.

Polluted air is having a noticeable effect on the rate at which people die: Mortality climbs measurably when smog is at its worst. Residents of Quebec City were most affected. The death rate there surged 11 percent, from an average of 7.7 deaths a day to 8.6, during periods of high air pollution.

The study also found higher mortality levels associated with dirty air in the other ten cities investigated, which covered most of Canada's major urban areas and a total population of 10.8 million. London at 10.6 percent and Hamilton at 10.3 percent had the next-largest increases in smog-induced mortality levels, while the smallest increases, 3.6 percent, were found in Windsor and Edmonton.

Air-pollution levels varied among the cities studied. No region had uniformly higher or lower levels of contaminants. The study, described as one of the most extensive undertaken in the world, reviewed more than 800 000 deaths that occurred over an eleven-year period and found that levels of common air pollutants, such as ozone and sulphur dioxide, are playing a role in when people die.

This study looked at the effects of the broad soup of pollutants contained in city air. "What people have found in cities all over North America, Europe, and South America is that when air pollution is high more people die, and when air pollution is low fewer people die," said Richard Burnett, a scientist with the environmental health directorate of the federal Health Department and one of the authors of the study.

The study follows data released by the Ontario Medical Association that said smog kills up to 1800 people in Ontario each year.

Although there have been some improvements in air quality in Canada because of pollution-control measures adopted in the 1980s, there are concerns that increased gasoline use and deregulation of the electric-power industry, a heavy fossil-fuel user, will erode these gains. For the other cities covered by the study, the increased risk of death during high-pollution episodes was: Montreal 8.4 percent, Ottawa 4.8 percent, Toronto 6.5 percent, Winnipeg 6.4 percent, Calgary 9.7 percent, and Vancouver 8.3 percent.

Source: Martin Mittelstaedt, "Smog Pushes Death Rates Up in Canada's Cities," *The Canadian Press*, May 30, 1998.

Traffic and Quality of Life

One major problem that complicates dealing with urban air pollution is the multitude of unidentifiable sources. Almost the whole population helps create the 50 percent of urban air pollution caused by motor vehicle exhaust in our automobile-dependent cities (Goodall 1992; Spirn 1984, 44). By 1989 there were 16.7 million registered vehicles in Canada, an increase of 26 percent over 1979, and 77 percent of these were passenger cars (Goodall 1992, 22). While Canadian cities are somewhat less decentralized than U.S. cities (Goldberg and Mercer 1986, 151–53), they have undergone similar processes of suburbanization and spatial segregation. The low-density city has effects that go beyond those of air pollution. Most Canadians live in low-density neighbourhoods where public transportation is uneconomic and where it is difficult or impossible to walk to many of the services that people need, such as shopping areas, schools, and places of employment (Filion 1996, 1644–48).

By the late 1980s, 80 percent of travel in Canadian cities was by private automobile (CMHC 1987b, 29), and as low-density residential areas have grown, the need to use private automobiles has grown as well. Even Toronto's well-developed public transit system has seen a major decline in ridership (Filion 1996, 1645). Reliance on private transportation is a matter of necessity as much as choice. By 1980, only about one-third of Canadians surveyed lived within about three kilometres or less of work, and less than half of the people surveyed felt that public transportation was a real option (Statistics Canada 1982). The average commuting time in Canadian cities was 19 minutes in 1980, but it was 29 minutes for people using public transportation and only 11 minutes for those using private automobiles (Statistics Canada 1982); the extra time is a strong incentive to use private cars. In 1980, 90 percent of people with a choice used private cars rather than public transportation for commuting, a figure that was only slightly lower in the larger cities such as Toronto that have well-developed public transit systems (Statistics Canada 1982).

Table 13.3 shows 1996 data on people commuting to work in Canada's CMAs. There are some surprises: for example, in 13 of the 25 CMAs, more people walk to work than take public transportation. Some statistics are less surprising: two-thirds or more of commuters drive private vehicles; a larger proportion of people use public transportation in the bigger cities, where it tends to be more available and convenient. Large numbers of Canadians get to work by driving private vehicles over distances of several kilometres: the 65.3 percent of Toronto commuters who drive private vehicles equal more than 1.1 million people and cars! Both the social costs of commuting (e.g., in time spent behind the wheel of a car rather than in more interesting activities) and the economic costs (e.g., in road maintenance, snow removal, and air pollution) are major aspects of urbanism in Canada.

Where public transit is unavailable or slow and inadequate, individuals have little choice but to use private vehicles for commuting and errands. Yet where large numbers of people commute, public transit can also result in high levels of pollution; the only real solution to the problems of pollution and congestion is to lessen the need to travel. In most cities, however, affordable housing is available primarily in neighbourhoods and suburbs that are distant from places of employment; where inner-city neighbourhoods are improved through gentrification, housing often becomes too expensive for most wage-earners. Although decreasing the need for travel within cities may be the only real solution to the traffic and pollution problems that arise from reliance on motor vehicles, the high cost of physically restructuring our cities puts this kind of solution largely out of reach.

TABLE 13.3   City Life: Commuting to Work, 1996

CMA	Number of commuters	Median distance commuted in kms	% commuting 10 km or more	% commuting as drivers of cars, vans, or trucks	% taking public transport- ation	% walking to work
CANADA	7 389 885	7.4	38.2	70.5	14.8	5.0
Calgary	367 315	7.5	33.9	72.8	12.6	5.4
Chicoutimi- Jonquière	58 095	4.3	26.0	83.3	2.2	6.5
Edmonton	363 515	7.6	37.4	76.9	9.0	5.0
Halifax	141 760	6.3	23.6	66.6	10.0	9.9
Hamilton	256 835	7.4	40.2	78.1	8.0	5.2
Kitchener	168 815	5.3	27.0	79.8	3.9	5.7
London	163 490	5.4	24.1	77.3	6.1	6.6
Montreal	1 336 975	8.2	42.4	66.6	20.3	5.9
Oshawa	111 745	9.4	48.5	81.2	5.6	4.1
Ottawa-Hull	436 450	7.8	39.4	64.3	17.1	6.9
Quebec	281 380	6.8	31.6	76.2	9.2	7.2
Regina	83 300	4.4	10.4	79.2	5.0	5.8
St. Catharines- Niagara	143 005	5.3	33.7	83.0	2.0	5.4
Saint John	46 270	7.5	42.4	75.4	4.6	6.8
St. John's	66 620	5.2	26.4	76.5	2.4	6.7
Saskatoon	90 320	4.8	15.0	77.8	5.1	6.4
Sherbrooke	59 185	4.6	24.1	80.2	5.3	7.5
Sudbury	62 085	6.5	36.8	77.8	5.0	6.4
Thunder Bay	50 780	4.4	17.6	81.0	3.4	5.8
Toronto	1 785 435	9.3	47.4	65.3	22.0	4.6
Trois-Rivières	52 550	4.6	24.0	84.1	2.3	7.0
Vancouver	742 330	7.7	39.9	70.6	14.3	5.8
Victoria	121 725	4.7	22.3	67.1	9.9	9.8
Windsor	115 725	5.9	25.9	82.5	3.4	5.1
Winnipeg	284 180	6.1	23.0	68.1	14.4	6.2

Note: People who commute as passengers in private vehicles not included in this table.

Source: Statistics Canada, *Employed Labour Force 15 Years of Age and Over by Sex, Showing Mode of Transportation, for Canada, Provinces, Territories, and Census Metropolitan Areas, 1996 Census*, Cat. no. 93F0027XDB96019.

The forms of Canadian cities can also exacerbate the problems faced by low-income people (Bourne 1993b, 1313). People who cannot afford private cars, for example, may be unable to travel to jobs, since public transportation may be inadequate or lacking altogether. Facilities such as good schools, child care, shopping, and such amenities as parks may be particularly limited in poorer neighbourhoods, yet it is the people in those neighbourhoods who are most in need of such facilities, since they are least able of all urban dwellers to provide such things for themselves (Mackenzie and Truelove, 1993). Poor neighbourhoods are also likely to be unhealthy neighbourhoods, with higher rates of illness and lower life expectancies than in other parts of urban areas; while some of this is undoubtedly a consequence of poverty itself, some is a result of the relatively high levels of outdoor and indoor pollution that characterize poor neighbourhoods (Taylor 1993, 311–21).

Housing

While much poor-quality housing in Canada is rural, we often think of housing problems as urban. There are several reasons for this. Housing prices are high in most Canadian cities, particularly in Toronto and Vancouver, and it is often difficult for urban working people to buy houses (Sewell 1994, 17–26). In addition, a substantial number of Canadians have difficulty affording rental housing (Sewell 1994, 23–26, 117–31), even if it is available; vacancy rates for rental housing are often low.

One important reason that we sometimes see housing as an urban crisis is the visibility of homeless people in cities. While we do not know how many people are in this situation, we do know that demand for space in hostels and other shelters is high. In Toronto alone, several thousand people may seek shelter each night, while as many as 100 000 are at risk of becoming homeless (O'Connor 1987; Fine 1989b; Toronto Coalition against Homelessness 1996). It is not just the numbers of people without regular places to live that make homelessness emerge as an urban issue. In the past, most homeless people were men whose lack of places to live was seen as their personal problem (Dear and Wolch 1987, 30–31). In the 1980s, however, more and more families with children began to appear in shelters, and we began to see the homeless as victims rather than as deviants. It is now common to argue that the primary cause of homelessness is lack of affordable housing rather than the personal failures of the homeless (McLaughlin 1987; Halpern 1989, 25–26).

Whatever the levels of homelessness, a lack of affordable housing is a problem in Canadian cities (CMHC 1987b, 23–25), especially Toronto, where in 1990 the average price of a new house was more than $459 509 (CMHC 1990, 33). Scarcity can also be a problem. In 1990, rental vacancy rates in Vancouver and in Toronto and some other Ontario cities were under 1 percent (CMHC 1990, 34). This means that employed young adults in Toronto may be unable to afford housing and still must live with their parents at an age when they would normally expect to be independent (Fine 1989a).

Many of the homeless, however, are people who might have difficulty coping even if a good stock of affordable housing were available. Twenty percent of Canadian shelter users are current or former psychiatric patients, and one-third have problems with alcohol abuse (McLaughlin 1987, 5). Studies in the United States also show that large numbers of the homeless are people with mental disabilities or problems with substance abuse (Dear and Wolch 1987, 175–79; Halpern 1989, 26–27; Kolata 1989). Simply increasing the quantity of housing would not solve the problems these people face.

Problems of Normal Life

Even social practices that seem normal to us can create social problems, and this is as true of life in cities as of any other area of social practice. Responses to urban issues can create problems of their own, as can be seen in the phenomenon of **NIMBY**, or "**Not in my back yard.**" Canadians want solutions to problems of waste management, housing, and other conditions of urban life, but they also want to insulate their own neighbourhoods and their own lives from these solutions. People want good, human housing for the poor, the mentally disabled, and others—but not next door. People want well-managed systems for the disposal of wastes—but not down the street. People want to clean up air pollution—but not if it means they can't drive their own cars.

We still hold to the "ideal" of the private city in which different functions are spatially segregated, in which neighbourhoods are as homogeneous as possible, and in which the poor and the miserable are out of sight. What Dear and Wolch call "landscapes of despair" are acceptable only at the other end of town.

One of the most important aspects of urbanism is that many urban problems are not the product of abnormality or deviance, but result instead from aspects of life that we take for granted as natural and even healthy. Urban populations are divided by ethnicity and culture, age and gender. These divisions can create differing needs and interests, which can result in social and spatial conflicts (Andrew and Milroy 1988). There are many examples of these conflicts in everyday life. The need for adults to travel to and from work on city streets can conflict with the needs of children for safe outdoor space to play in. The concentration of retail outlets in strip developments and malls means that people who can't drive have no independent access to shops and that parents can't send children to the store on errands. These issues may seem trivial, but they affect the patterns of our daily lives by imposing such needs as private cars, shopping trips, and the constant supervision of children, which might not otherwise exist and which can be a source of stress, vulnerability, and conflict. Some of these problems of normality are outlined here.

Family, Gender, and Age

Cities are not one-size-fits-all environments. Women and men, younger and older adults, adults and children, those who are able in body and mind and those who are

City Life: Gender Differences

Cities are diverse, and in some ways each population group occupies a different city from the others. One important social difference that affects urban life is gender. Men and women have different relationships to the labour force and different responsibilities for household work and child care. While it's not always easy to find measures of these differences, we can see them in some statistics. For example, in every CMA in Canada,

- more females than males take public transportation when they commute—60 percent (70 196) of those who take public transit are women;

- more males than females drive private vehicles to get to work—58.6 percent (3.3 million) of drivers are men;

- more females than males commute as passengers in cars driven by others; and

- males commute longer median distances than females (differences range from 0.4 km to 4.1 km).

These statistics show several aspects of gender relationships as they affect urbanism. As Pratt and Hanson's research shows, women are more likely than men to choose workplaces close to home in order to balance work and domestic responsibilities. Women are also likely to earn less than men and to be less able to buy vehicles and more likely to depend on other sources of transportation. Finally, where husbands and wives share a car, the husband is more likely to drive—which is not necessarily a privilege, given the stresses of rush-hour traffic!

Sources: Adapted from Statistics Canada, *Employed Labour Force 15 Years of Age and Over by Sex, Showing Mode of Transportation, for Canada, Provinces, Territories, and Census Metropolitan Areas, 1996 Census,* Cat. no. 93F0027XDB96019.

not—all have different patterns to their lives and different social and spatial needs. This reality might seem obvious, yet it is one that few theorists, planners, and politicians have paid attention to. One of the fundamental problems that Canadian city dwellers must deal with is that even normal, unproblematic urban and suburban areas are sources of conflicts and inconveniences in our everyday lives. Cities are not built to accommodate the needs of people who must juggle the demands of workplace and home, who must care for dependents, or whose condition means they cannot drive; indeed, city environments can be inhospitable even to something as basic as the family. Canadian cities reflect assumptions about family life and gender roles that were never true for everyone, and that now apply to only a small part of the population, yet our urban environments cannot be changed as quickly as social practices and cultural values have changed over the past 30 years.

Canadian cities are characterized by the geographical separation of residential areas from the places where people work, shop, and run other errands. We take this for granted, and most Canadians would probably agree that this is an appropriate form of urban development. Yet while this urban form might work reasonably well for families in which one adult does nothing but manage the household while another is responsible for earning the household's income, it is a problematic form for many families and individuals. People who cannot drive, including children and people with certain disabilities, may find themselves isolated and dependent in the middle of cities (Blomley 1994); many old people whose reflexes and eyesight are no longer good resist giving up their cars because the loss of mobility would be too great a sacrifice. In addition, this typical urban form creates problems for families with multiple wage earners, which are now typical; by the mid-1980s, over 60 percent of families relied on the incomes of both spouses (*The Globe and Mail*, May 13, 1989, D2). The geographic separation of the different destinations that family members must travel to as part of daily or weekly routines imposes real costs in time and effort. Adults in the labour force may not only have to travel to work, but also have to go to several different parts of a city to take children to and from school or child care, shop for groceries, visit and run errands for elderly parents, and perform the other activities that are necessary parts of daily life. Because women still have the primary responsibility for household management, including child care, they can be particularly strongly affected by the spatial arrangements of urban areas; women develop a number of strategies for dealing with their different needs, including taking part-time rather than full-time work and choosing proximity to home rather than levels of pay in deciding on which jobs they take (Pratt and Hanson 1991).

The form of Canadian cities can cause particular problems for the poor. A little over 12 percent of families were living below the poverty line in 1986 (National Council of Welfare 1988, 7), and the numbers of poor urban dwellers remain high (Bourne 1993b, United Way 1997). As individuals, we have little control over the costs of the necessities of life—housing, food, transportation, and clothing—and many poor and low-income families spend over 50 percent of their incomes on food and shelter alone (Burke 1987a, 21). Middle-class families may encounter difficulties in their ordinary urban environments, but similar difficulties become worse for the poor, who cannot, for example, opt out of bad schools and who may not be able to find work because they have no transportation to places where there are jobs.

The changing nature of the family has led to more and smaller households, creating an increased demand for housing (CMHC 1987b, 11; Fine 1989b; Skaburski 1997, 276–78). The existing private housing market and government programs have not met these expanded needs, particularly those of lower and lower-middle income groups and of households with special needs, such as those headed by single parents or with physically disabled members (Hulchanski 1996; Sewell 1994, passim). In some cases, government responses to housing problems have made them worse (CMHC 1987b, 49). For example, zoning regulations that restrict neighbourhoods to households composed of related people can keep housing costs higher for individuals by making it difficult for groups of unrelated people to share a home (Fine 1989b), while public housing has often created seriously problematic environments for families (Sewell 1994, 149–57). Typical suburban houses do not have space for extra adults such as grandparents, and zoning regulations often make it illegal to build "granny flats" for older relatives; thus families dealing with increasingly dependent older relatives often cannot resolve problems by bringing their relatives to live with them.

Theories of Urban Life

In general, we take everyday life for granted, and see its problems as personal rather than social in nature. We see social actions as problematic not when they are expected of a given group or situation, but when they seem to threaten the social order. Drug use, for example, is often tolerated as long as it seems largely restricted to marginal and deviant populations. When drug use extends to the middle class, however, it is seen to threaten social stability; when it arises even in smaller communities that are supposed to be free of urban problems, it becomes a crisis (Mayer 1989).

The issue of social order in cities has been a traditional concern of social theory. The classic formulations of the Chicago School dealt with the question of whether a breakdown of order is inherent in cities (Park 1967). Social researchers of the Chicago School argued that cities developed through natural ecological processes that sorted out the various parts of the population, thus minimizing the stress that is assumed to arise when different groups come into contact (Saunders 1981, 48–79). According to this perspective, while urbanism does break down the kind of order that might characterize traditional rural communities, cities develop their own, more formal, means of social regulation, which replace the more organic order of smaller communities (Wirth 1957). These theories have provided justification for many typical planning and development practices in North American cities, such as the development of specialized neighbourhoods and the use of zoning regulations.

Unlike the theories of the Chicago School, many of the urban theories that have developed since the 1970s stress concepts of power and conflict in urban communities. Theorists see cities as contested terrains in which various groups have different claims upon resources such as space, and in which great inequalities among groups are evident in the extent to which they succeed in claiming resources (Castells 1979; Davis 1990; Filion 1996; Harvey 1976; Wilson 1987; Zukin 1991). While earlier versions of these theories tended to stress abstract social relations, urban theories of the 1990s show an increasing awareness of urban space and urban environments as important issues. The restructuring of urban economies has often meant increasing geographic and social isolation of the poor (Bourne 1993b; Wilson 1987; 1996), and despite a degree of gentrification of inner cities which has kept some higher income earners in those areas, in general income disparities between inner cities and suburban areas in Canadian cities continue to be significant (Bourne 1993b).

In general, recent urban theories tend to be more concerned with justice, social control, and the inequalities of the marketplace than with social order. These theories reveal urban contradictions and conflicts in ways that earlier theories did not. For example, while Chicago School theorists argued that minority groups had the ability to create orderly communities, they did not deal with the threat such minority communities posed to existing social and political power structures. Thus theorists in this tradition were not able to explain why urban renewal projects were often aimed at relatively stable ethnic and working-class neighbourhoods rather than at the poorest areas of cities. Theorists who focus on issues of power and inequality can provide some explanation for this, by recognizing the ways in which stable, well-organized neighbourhoods threaten the power of city hall (Caro 1974; Lorimer 1970).

Property and Conflict

Canadian cities are based on private property; about two-thirds of Canada's housing units are privately owned (McLaughlin 1987). Most commercial and industrial land is also privately owned. While private property may be subject to some degree of government control, such control is limited. With the rise of the shopping mall, even the kind of space that was once public—street space—has become private property— mall space—whose owners can restrict access and impose control through the use of private police forces that are often poorly trained and unrestricted.

Although private property is rarely seen as an urban problem, it can be a major source of social conflict. Public control over the quality of housing is difficult to enforce, and property rights may exceed individual political rights. Homeless people have no right to occupy vacant housing, and if they do occupy and improve it, they have no claim on it if the legal owner decides to take it back. In general, Canadian governments support the rights and interests of private property owners; in some cities, property owners still have more voting rights than people who have no property. Both public and personal conflicts can arise over the use of property, especially if the decisions of owners conflict with the needs of the larger community. When communities develop to the point where they can act in their own interests, they may come into conflict with property owners and the governments that support them.

The private housing market has had an important impact on the social structure of Canadian cities. The processes of sorting and segregation of populations may not be natural, as suggested by the Chicago School, but they do exist. Canadian cities are divided economically, with different socio-economic groups occupying different areas (Bourne 1993b; Goldberg and Mercer 1986, 154–61; McGahan 1986, 154–72); sometimes geographical mobility is so limited that certain neighbourhoods function as ghettos (Clatworthy and Hull 1983, 57–59; Wilson 1987). Socio-economic status is often associated with other social factors, such as age, sex, and race, and cities are divided along these lines as well. Factors of socio-economic condition such as life expectancy, employment, and educational attainment are expressed spatially through, among other things, the forces of the private housing market.

The housing market creates geographic divisions within cities because groups differ greatly in their ability to pay for housing. The poor are restricted in their choices, and often can find housing only in limited areas, where it is affordable though often of poor quality. Low-income people can rarely buy housing—they must rely on rental housing and private landlords. While every province has some regulations against discrimination, single mothers, visible minorities, and other groups still encounter overt and covert restrictions on the housing to which they have access. Social housing may overcome some of these spatial divisions; while the big public housing projects of the major cities testify to earlier ghettoizing of the poor (McMillan 1987), in the 1980s infill projects that scatter social housing through various neighbourhoods became more accepted. Social housing is limited, however. Of the units built between 1965 and 1986, 52 percent were intended for the elderly; most of the rest were for families, with virtually none for unattached individuals (McLaughlin 1987, 3).

Finding Solutions

As governments and city dwellers know all too well, there are no easy solutions to urban problems. We have invested billions of dollars in the construction of low-density cities that make it almost impossible to find alternatives to the private automobile; we have over 40 years of housing policies that encourage people to speculate in real estate and the housing market and thus undermine the stability of neighbourhoods; we have a political commitment to the rights of property owners that makes it difficult for governments to intervene on behalf of the social good. In addition, there is no general agreement that any of these problems are in fact problems.

Solutions to urban problems must ultimately be social rather than individual because the problems themselves so often result from structural factors in our society rather than from individual failings. It is also true, however, that urban problems cannot disappear without the active participation of city dwellers in identifying and implementing solutions.

Conclusions

Urban problems are real; they are more than just a matter of cultural perception or social definition. How we respond to problems, however, is very much a matter of perception and definition—we tolerate many inconveniences and even conflicts if they arise from conditions that we see as normal. Our definitions of both normality and problems have a profound impact on responses to urbanism. When we define "normal" life as taking place in communities in which social interactions are predictable and stable, then city life, with its anonymity and unpredictability, seems abnormal. Yet we can also define normality as a high level of centralized services and economies of scale, which makes cities the measure of normality. Our attitudes toward cities, their benefits, and their problems are ambivalent.

Cities in Canada, like cities everywhere, reflect the social structures and practices of the society to which they belong. Canada contains a great deal of social diversity and inequality. Men and women fill different social roles and have different social needs, as do adults and children. The population varies greatly by race and ethnic background; values and social structures also reflect regional differences. Canadians are divided as well by the kinds of work they do and by their economic and social power. Needs differ because of the different social roles and cultural practices that characterize the population and the ability of individuals and groups to meet their needs differs with their social power.

Because different groups have different degrees of decision-making power, Canada's cities do not always reflect the diversity of their populations. Usually, a relatively small number of people have the power to make the decisions that affect cities, and many city dwellers find themselves coping with problems that they do not have the power to resolve. The major decisions that shape cities tend to reflect the values and needs of the most powerful members of the community, such as large businesses and property owners, while minority groups, children, small businesses, and other less-powerful members of society find that there are few means of meeting their particular needs.

This inequality of power is a major source of urban problems; our cities reflect this in both their physical environments and their social structures. Traditional urban theories tended to see differences in power as natural rather than as problematic, defining the social processes of city life in ecological terms. While these theories contain important insights, particularly in their argument that urban populations have the capacity to create meaningful communities, they tend to downplay the importance of social inequality and conflict and the extent to which urban development reflects the decisions of powerful groups.

The large, dense, varied populations that characterize Canadian cities do create problems. Not all people in these cities have the same needs or can benefit equally from given conditions, and population size can be a problem. The wastes produced by millions of people occupying a relatively small area are not easy to handle; getting tens of thousands of people to and from work, school, and leisure activities is difficult; providing adequate housing and social institutions for populations whose family structures, values, and languages vary is more of a problem than providing these things to small, stable, homogeneous populations. Population alone, however, does not create problems. What matters is how we organize our daily lives.

In one sense, urban problems are insoluble: there is no perfect means of creating livable cities. We shall be much closer to solutions, however, if we recognize and respect the capacity of urban communities to create social order, if we move away from economic definitions of efficiency in which property has more rights than people, and if we recognize that while the interests of various groups can differ— even conflict—we must try to manage the urban community to meet those differing needs rather than to deny them. Solutions to urban problems depend on our recognition that problems are real and on our willingness to give people the power and means to find solutions.

Summary

- More than two-thirds of Canadians live in metropolitan areas—cities and their suburbs; nearly 9.5 million live in the four largest metropolitan areas alone (those with more than a million people). Thus the everyday lives of most Canadians are urban lives. Indeed, cities are such important social, political, and economic forces that even those people who live in small towns and rural areas are strongly affected by them.
- While most Canadians are urban, living in or near large metropolitan areas, we tend to have mixed feelings about cities. Many people see cities as sources of serious

social and environmental problems such as crime and pollution. At the same time, however, we see cities as places of opportunity. We see this in the fact that people continue to move from smaller centres to larger ones to find work, to get educations, and to have opportunities for artistic expression and other forms of individual freedom. While many people choose to live in suburbs rather than cities, most Canadians continue to live in large metropolitan areas.

- It is hard to define "city" in a way that works in different societies. Cities exist where social systems produce a surplus, allowing the concentration of wealth and people. One reason for our mixed feelings about cities is that they seem to absorb a disproportionate amount of our resources. Yet cities are also places where wealth is produced and opportunities are expanded.

- "Urbanism"—the way of life in cities and the process of becoming urban—raises many issues. Some of these are problems are often associated with urbanism in some way, even if they are not directly caused by city life; these include crime, ethnic heterogeneity and racial conflict, and pollution. Others are problems we might not recognize as such because they seem normal, but in fact they create issues we must deal with; these include the separation of where we live from where we work and run errands, high levels of mobility that undermine community, and the ways in which private property shapes development.

- While we often blame the large size and the heterogeneity of city populations for urban problems, we need to recognize that other factors are more important. Canada's cities, like all cities, reflect the particular processes and values of Canadian society. One important reality of Canadian society is that not all people have equal voices in making decisions about cities—about what gets built or torn down, about what services are offered, and about the many other aspects of urban life. Thus Canada's cities, like all cities, reflect social inequalities.

Questions to Consider

1. What are the basic kinds of urban centres that are recognized by Statistics Canada? How and why are these different from common uses of words such as "city" and "town"?

2. What urban problems are of most concern to Canadians? What urban problems that you consider important are not discussed in this chapter?

3. What kinds of social differences exist within urban populations? Do these differences become social divisions and sources of conflict?

4. What typical forms are taken by Canadian cities? How do these physical environments affect the lives of the people who live within them? What social values and practices shape these cities?

5. What is the relationship between Canadian cities and senior (provincial and federal) governments? What are some of the consequences of this relationship for cities?

Suggested Readings

Andrew, Caroline, and Beth Moore Milroy, eds. *Life Spaces: Gender, Household, and Employment*. Vancouver: University of British Columbia Press, 1988.

Sewell, John. *Houses and Homes: Housing for Canadians*. Toronto: James Lorimer and Company, 1994.

Wilson, William Julius. *When Work Disappears: The World of the New Urban Poor*. New York: Knopf (Random House), 1996.

Zukin, Sharon. *Landscapes of Power: From Detroit to Disney World*. Berkeley: University of California Press, 1991.

Glossary

Census Agglomeration (CA) An urban area (defined in terms of density of population and labour force characteristics) with a core population of 10 000 to 99 999, along with adjacent rural and urban areas that are integrated with the urban core. This definition has changed as Canada's population has become urbanized; before the 1981 census, the core population for CAs was 2000 (Statistics Canada 1997a, 181).

Census Metropolitan Area (CMA) An "urban core" of at least 100 000 people and the adjacent urban and rural areas ("urban and rural fringes") that are socially and economically integrated with the urban core. Integration is defined in terms of labour markets and commuting areas. This definition has changed as Canada's population has changed; the category of the CMA first appeared in the 1951 census, when the urban core was set at 50 000, and the whole CMA had to have a minimum population of 100 000. The urban core was defined as 100 000 in the 1981 census (Statistics Canada 1997a, 181).

city A relatively large, relatively dense, relatively permanent settlement whose occupants are primarily involved in non-agricultural economic activities. Legal definitions of cities can vary widely among countries and even within countries such as Canada, where these definitions are part of provincial legislation. This means that Statistics Canada cannot rely on legal definitions, and has developed its own definition: an area is urban if it is continuously built up and has at least 400 people per square kilometre.

NIMBY ("Not in my back yard") The attitude of urban dwellers who might agree that particular services and functions such as group homes might have a place in cities, but not in their neighbourhoods. Many people who are not involved in urban government on a regular basis may become involved over NIMBY issues that they see as threatening the safety and property values of their neighbourhoods.

social order The extent to which social relationships and practices are organized in ways that are shared by groups of people and thus are relatively predictable. Urbanization, particularly rapid urbanization, has led many political and cultural leaders and social theorists to fear that orderly social relations will be replaced by disorder—by a loss of common understanding, goals, and practices; thus much urban planning and regulation has been aimed at creating "orderly" environments.

urban area The general concept underlying the more specific definitions of CMAs and CAs: the idea that urbanism is not restricted to or defined by the legal political boundaries of cities, but instead is a matter of the characteristics of the population and of the environment they live in. Regardless of its legal definition, an area is urban if it contains a lot of people who live close together in a largely built environment, and who are involved in non-agricultural activities (Statistics Canada 1997a, 193).

urbanism There are two basic meanings for this term: (a) The way of life of people in cities—the social, economic, psychological, and other characteristics that are particular to people living in urban areas; (b) The kind of society that supports cities—the particular economic, political, and social arrangements that enable a society to concentrate people and resources in urban areas.

urbanization The process by which a population comes to live in cities (urban areas) and develops the particular characteristics of urban dwellers. It usually involves three demographic changes: an increasing number of cities, the increasing size of those cities, and an increasing proportion of the total population that lives in urban areas. By implication, urbanization also involves changes in the nature of social relationships and perhaps of psychological qualities of individuals.

References

Amit-Talai, V., and H. Lustiger-Thaler, eds. 1994. *Urban Lives: Fragmentation and Resistance*. Toronto: McClelland and Stewart.

Andrew, C., and B.M. Milroy, eds. 1988. *Life Space: Gender, Household, and Employment*. Vancouver: University of British Columbia Press.

Badcock, B. 1984. *Unfairly Secured Cities*. Oxford: Basil Blackwell.

Badets, J. 1993. "Canada's Immigrants: Recent Trends." *Canadian Social Trends* 29 (Summer): 8–11.

Bish, R.L. 1996. "Amalgamation: Is It the Solution?" <http://www.hsd.uvic.ca/PADM/research/lgi/reports/amsol.htm>.

Blomley, N. 1994. "Representing the Canadian City: Space, Power, and Mobility Rights." In *Urban Lives: Fragmentation and Resistance*, ed. V. Amit-Talai and H. Lustiger-Thaler. Toronto: McClelland and Stewart. 45–70.

Bourne, L.S. 1993a. "The Myth and Reality of Gentrification: A Commentary on Emerging Urban Forms." *Urban Studies* 30, no. 1: 183–89.

———. 1993b. "Close Together and Worlds Apart: An Analysis of Changes in the Ecology of Income in Canadian Cities." *Urban Studies* 30, no. 8: 1293–1317.

Bourne, L.S., and D.F. Ley. 1993. *The Changing Social Geography of Canadian Cities*. Montreal and Kingston: McGill-Queen's University Press.

Burke, M.A. 1987a. "Average Expenditure of Urban Canadians." *Canadian Social Trends* (Summer): 20–21.

———. 1987b. "Urban Canada." *Canadian Social Trends* (Winter).

Canadian Centre for Justice Statistics. 1995. "Fear and Personal Safety." <http://www.mala.bc.ca/~anderson.fear.htm>.

Caro, R. 1974. *The Power Broker: Robert Moses and the Fall of New York*. New York: Knopf.

Castells, M. 1979. *The Urban Question: A Marxist Approach*. Cambridge: MIT Press.

Central Mortgage and Housing Corporation (CMHC). 1979. *Public Priorities in Urban Canada: A Survey of Community Concerns*. Ottawa: CMHC.

———. 1987a. *Canadian Housing Statistics 1987*. Ottawa: CMHC.

———. 1987b. *Human Settlements in Canada: Trends and Policies, 1981–1986*. Prepared by Rostum. Ottawa: CMHC.

Childe, V.G. 1950. "The Urban Revolution." *Town Planning Review* 21, no. 1 (April): 3–17.

Citizens for Local Democracy Web Site. 1997a. "Detailed Referendum Results." <http://www.web.net/
~citizens/103Black /refresults.html#eastyork>.

———. 1997b. "Understanding the Megacity: What Does Amalgamation Mean?" <http://www.
community.web.net/citizens/103Black/megaunderstand.html>.

City of Regina Planning Department. 1983. *Designing Crime out of Downtown*. Regina: City of
Regina.

Clatworthy, S.J., and J. Hull. 1983. *Native Economic Conditions in Regina and Saskatoon*. Winnipeg: Institute of Urban Studies, University of Winnipeg.

Davis, M. 1990. *City of Quartz: Excavating the Future in Los Angeles*. London/New York: Verso.

Dear, M.J., and J. Wolch. 1987. *Landscapes of Despair: From Deinstitutionalization to
Homelessness*. Princeton: Princeton University Press.

Dyck, I. 1989. "Integrating Home and Wage Workplace: Women's Daily Lives in a Canadian
Suburb." *The Canadian Geographer* 33, no. 4: 329–41.

Elliott, J.L. 1979. *Two Nations, Many Cultures: Ethnic Groups in Canada*. Scarborough, ON:
Prentice-Hall.

Filion, P. 1996. "Metropolitan Planning Objectives and Implementation Constraints: Planning in a
Post-Fordist and Postmodern Age." *Environment and Planning A* 28: 1637–60.

Filion, P., and T.E. Bunting. 1990. *Affordability of Housing in Canada*. Ottawa: Minister of Supply
and Services Canada.

Fine, S. 1989a. "Empty Nest? It's Crowded for Parents in Toronto," *The Globe and Mail*, June 8: A1,
A2.

———. 1989b. "Fractured Families are Forced to Live 'Underground.'" *The Globe and Mail*,
February 4: D2.

Frideres, J.S. 1983. *Native People in Canada: Contemporary Conflicts*, 2d ed. Scarborough, ON:
Prentice-Hall.

Garber, J.A., and D.L. Imbroscio. 1996. "The Myth of the North American City Reconsidered: Local
Constitutional Regimes in Canada and the United States." *Urban Affairs Review* 31, no. 5:
595–624.

Goldberg, M.A., and J. Mercer. 1986. *The Myth of the North American City: Continentalism
Challenged*. Vancouver: University of British Columbia Press.

Goodall, A. 1992. "Motor Vehicles and Air Pollution." *Canadian Social Trends* 24 (Spring): 21–26.

Government of Ontario. 1996. *Bill 103: City of Toronto Act*.

Government of Ontario, Ministry of Municipal Affairs and Housing. 1997a. "Developing the
Framework for the Greater Toronto Services Board." <http://nrserv.mmah.gov.on.ca/inthnews/
backgrnd/970213e.htm>.

Government of Ontario, Ministry of Municipal Affairs and Housing. 1997b. "Ontario Government
Business Plans 1997–98." <http://www.gov.on.ca/MBS/english/press/plans/mah.html>.

Graber, D.A. 1980. *Crime News and the Public*. New York: Praeger.

Halpern, S. 1989. "The Rise of the Homeless." *New York Review of Books*, February 16: 24–27.

Harris, R., and G.J. Pratt. 1993. "The Meaning of Home, Homeownership, and Public Policy." In
The Changing Social Geography of Canadian Cities, ed. L.S. Bourne and D.F. Ley. Montreal
and Kingston: McGill-Queen's University Press. 281–97.

Hartnagel, T.F. 1978. "The Perception and Fear of Crime: Implications for Neighbourhood
Cohesion, Social Activity and Community Affect." *Edmonton Area Series Report No. 5*
(February).

Harvey, D. 1976. *Social Justice and the City*. London: Edwin Arnold.

Hulchanski, J.D. 1996. "On Market Failure: Rental Housing Demand and Supply in Metro Toronto."
Speaking Notes: Metro Toronto Planning and Transportation Committee, June 12. <http://
www.community.web.net.citizens/96Black/hulchAppendix.html>.

Jacobs, J. 1961. *The Death and Life of the Great American Cities*. New York: Vintage Books.

———. 1997. "Deputation Given to the Standing Committee on General Government Conducting
Hearings on the City of Toronto Act—Bill 103." February 3. <http://www.community.web.net/
citizens/103Dep/jjacobs.html>.

Johnson, H. 1988. "Violent Crime." *Canadian Social Trends* (Summer): 24–29.

Kallen, E. 1988. "Multiculturalism as Ideology, Policy, and Reality." In *Social Inequality in Canada:
Patterns, Problems, Policies,* ed. J. Curtis, E. Gable, N. Guppy, and S. Gilbert. Scarborough,
ON: Prentice-Hall. 235–47.

Keating, M. 1986. "97 Ontario Firms Violate Guidelines for Water Pollution." *The Globe and Mail*,
December 24: A9.

Kennedy, L.W., and H. Krahn. 1983. "Rural–Urban Origins and Fear of Crime: The Case for 'Rural
Baggage.'" *Edmonton Area Series Report No. 28* (July).

Kolata, G. 1989. "Twins of the Street: Homelessness and Addiction." *New York Times*, May 22: A1, 10.

KPMG Centre for Government. 1997. "Fresh Start: An Estimate of Potential Savings and Costs from the Creation of a Single-Tier Local Government for Toronto." <http://www.kpmg.ca/centre/vl/cg_gta.htm>.

LaPrairie, C. 1994. *Seen But Not Heard: Native People in the Inner City*. Ottawa: Department of Justice of Canada.

Lorimer, J. 1970. *The Real World of City Politics*. Toronto: James Lewis and Samuel.

Mackenzie, S., and M. Truelove. 1993. "Changing Access to Public and Private Services: Non-Family Childcare." In *The Changing Social Geography of Canadian Cities*, ed. L.S. Bourne and D.F. Ley. Montreal and Kingston: McGill-Queen's University Press. 326–42.

Mayer, J. 1989. "Spreading Plague: Seaford, Del., Shows How Crack Can Savage Small-Town America." *The Wall Street Journal*, May 4: A1, 10.

McGahan. P. 1986. *Urban Sociology in Canada*. Toronto: Butterworths.

McLaughlin, M. 1987. *Homelessness in Canada: The Report of the National Inquiry*. Ottawa: Canadian Council on Social Development.

McMillan, S. 1987. "Forty Years of Social Housing in Toronto." *Canadian Social Trends* (Winter).

Merry, S.E. 1981. *Urban Danger: Life in a Neighbourhood of Strangers*. Philadelphia: Temple University Press.

Miller, D., and K. Newman. 1988. "How Much Do Canadians Care? Lots!" *The Globe and Mail*, April 23: D4.

Milroy, B.M. 1997. "Urban Government in the Toronto Area." January 12. <http://www.community.web.net.citizens/103Black/milroy_study.html>.

Nagata, J.A. 1979. "One Vine, Many Branches: Internal Differentiation in Canadian Ethnic Groups." In Elliott, *Two Nations*. 173–81.

National Council of Welfare. 1988. *Poverty Profile 1988*. Ottawa: Supply and Services Canada.

No Megacity Coalition. 1997. "Vote No Megacity." <http://www.pathcom/~tprjohn/nmc.htm>.

O'Connor, K. 1987. "Massive Home-Building Program Said Solution to Housing Crisis." *Leader-Post* (Regina), June 5: A3.

Ontario Waste Management Corporation. 1982. *Waste Quantities Study*. August. Don Mills, ON: Proctor and Redfern Group.

Park, R. 1967. *The City*. Chicago: University of Chicago Press.

Parrish, C. 1986. "Between Two Worlds." *Inside Canada and the World* 52, no. 4: 26–28.

Pratt, G., and S. Hanson. 1991. "On the Links Between Home and Work: Family-Household Strategies in a Buoyant Labour Market." *International Journal of Urban and Regional Research* 15, no. 1: 55–74.

Ray, B.K., G. Halseth, and B. Johnson. 1997. "The Changing 'Face' of the Suburbs: Issues of Ethnicity and Residential Change in Suburban Vancouver." *International Journal of Urban and Regional Research* 21: 75–99.

Rose, A. 1980. *Canadian Housing Policies, 1935–1980*. Toronto: Butterworths.

Ruppert, E.L. 1997. "Provincial Downloading: Still Wrong in Principle." Citizens for Local Democracy. May 5. <http://www.web.net/~citizens/DLBlack/ruppert.html>.

Rutherford, P. 1984. "Tomorrow's Metropolis: The Urban Reform Movement in Canada, 1880–1920." In *The Canadian City: Essays in Urban and Social History*. Ottawa: Carleton University Press. 435–55.

Sacco, V.F. 1981. "Perceptions of Crime and Anemic Adaptations." *Edmonton Area Series Report No. 34* (October).

Saskatchewan Council for International Development. 1987. *Our Land, Our Cities, Our Future*. Regina.

Saunders, P. 1981. *Social Theory and the Urban Question*. London: Hutchinson.

Sewell, J. 1994. *Houses and Homes: Housing for Canadians*. Toronto: James Lorimer and Company.

———. 1997. "Presentation to the Committee on General Governance." February 13. <http://www.community.web.net/citizens/103Dep/jsewell.html>.

Shurmer-Smith, P., and K. Hannam. 1994. *Worlds of Desire, Realms of Power: A Cultural Geography*. London: Edward Arnold.

Skaburski, A. 1997. "Gender Differences in Housing Demand." *Urban Studies* 34, no. 2: 275–320.

Social Planning Council of Winnipeg. 1997. "Acceptable Living Level." (September). <http://www.ccsd.ca/cspn/all.htm>.

Spirn, A.W. 1984. *The Granite Garden: Urban Nature and Human Design*. New York: Basic Books.

Statistics Canada. 1982. *Travel to Work, 1976–1980*. Ottawa: Minister of Supply and Services.

———. 1987. *Urban Growth in Canada*. Ottawa: Supply and Services Canada.

———. 1988. *Canadian Crime Statistics 1987*. Ottawa: Canadian Centre for Justice Studies.

———. 1992. *Urban Areas: Population and Dwelling Counts*. Ottawa: Supply and Services Canada.

———. 1993. *Housing Costs and Other Characteristics of Canadian Households. The Nation— 1991 Census*. Ottawa: Minister of Industry, Science, and Technology.

———. 1997a. *1996 Census Dictionary*. Ottawa: Minister of Industry. Cat. no. 92-351.

———. 1997b. "1996 Census of Canada—Population and Dwelling Counts." *The Daily* (April 15). <http://www.statcan.ca/Daily/English/970415/d970415.htm>.

———. 1997c. "1996 Census of Canada: Immigration and Citizenship." *The Daily* (November 4). <http://www.statcan.ca/Daily/English/971104/d971104.htm>.

———. 1998a. "Aboriginal Identity Population by Age Groups, 1996 Census." <http://www.statcan. ca:80/english/Pgdb/People/Population/demo38d.htm>.

———. 1998b. "Census Metropolitan Areas—Aboriginal Population." <http://www.statcan.ca/ english/Pgdb/People/Population/demo39b.htm>.

———. 1998c. "Persons Registered Under the Indian Act, Living On and Off Reserve, 1996 Census." <http://www.statcan.ca:80/english/Pgdb/People/Population/demo37.htm>.

———. 1998d. "Population of Census Metropolitan Areas." <http://www.statcan.ca/english/Pgdb/ People/Population/demo05.htm>.

———. 1998e. "Population by Selected Age Groups and Sex for Census Metropolitan Areas, 1996 Census—100% Data." <http://www.statcan.ca/english/census96/cma.html>.

———. 1998f. "Visible Minority Population, 1996 Census." <http://www.statcan.ca/english/Pgdb/ People/Population/demo40d.htm>.

Taylor, S.M. 1993. "Geography of Urban Health." In *The Changing Social Geography of Canadian Cities*, ed. L.S. Bourne and D.F. Ley. Montreal and Kingston: McGill-Queen's University Press.

Tindal, C.R., and S.N. Tindal. 1979. *Local Government in Canada*. Toronto: McGraw-Hill Ryerson.

Toronto Coalition against Homelessness. 1996. <http://www.competitor.net/electric/homeless/inquiry>.

United Way. 1997. "The United Way on Downloading." March 1. <http://www.web.net/~citizens/ DLBlack/united.html>.

Weaver, J. 1977. *Shaping the Canadian City: Essays on Urban Politics and Policy, 1890–1920*. Toronto: Institute of Public Administration of Canada Monograph No. 1.

———. 1984. "'Tomorrow's Metropolis' Revisited: A Critical Assessment of Urban Reform in Canada, 1890–1920." In Stelter and Artibise, *The Canadian City*. 456–77.

White, C.A. 1986. *Inside Canada and the World* 52, no. 4.

Wilson, W.J. 1987. *The Truly Disadvantaged: The Inner City, the Underclass, and Public Policy*. Chicago: University of Chicago Press.

———. 1996. *When Work Disappears: The World of the New Urban Poor*. New York: Knopf (Random House).

Winn, C. 1988. "The Socio-Economic Attainment of Visible Minorities: Facts and Policy Implications." In Curtis et al., *Social Inequality*. 195–213.

Wirth, L. 1957. "Urbanism as a Way of Life" *American Journal of Sociology* 44 (July 1938). Reprinted in *Cities and Society*, ed. P.K. Hatt and A.J. Reiss. New York: The Free Press.

Women Plan Toronto. 1997. "The Effects of Megacity Proposals on Women in Metro." <http:// web.community.web.net/citizens/103Black/women_and_megacity.html>.

Zukin, S. 1991. *Landscapes of Power: From Detroit to Disney World*. Berkeley: University of California Press.

PART VI

Health and Illness

INTRODUCTION

A number of issues and contradictions regarding health, illness, and the health-care system are currently being debated in Canada. The perceived rapid rise of health-care costs has contributed to a critical examination of the organization and structure of health-care delivery. The relationship of population characteristics to health is being questioned in light of evidence that different socio-economic groups are unequal in their health status. Meanwhile, we have also come to associate inadequate working conditions and environmental degradation with injury and illness.

Broader demographic issues also make their impact on health and health care. The "demographic transition"—commonly spoken of as the aging of Canada's population—is expected to have vast implications. Some of them are already visible in changing Canadian patterns of morbidity and mortality.

Faced with this range of pressing issues, Canadians have come to re-examine the general principles on which their health insurance program was founded. Readings in this section examine two specific health-related issues: aging, and health and mental illness.

Karen R. Grant, in the chapter entitled "Health Care in an Aging Society: Issues, Controversies, and Challenges for the Future," discusses the relationship between demographic and epidemiological transitions and the demand on health services, with particular focus on the aged population.

The demographic profile of Canadian society is rapidly changing. It is projected that, by the year 2011, persons 65 years or older will constitute nearly one-quarter of the Canadian population. Another demographic factor worth noting is that women are disproportionately represented among the elderly.

The elderly population is by no means homogeneous. It is diversified and stratified by socio-economic status, gender, and ethnicity. Regardless of this diversification and stratification, all elderly people face some common health problems. Advancing age is accompanied by a normal decline in physical and mental ability, and by increasing difficulty in functioning in society. This raises the issue of how well the health sector and other institutions will respond to the health and other needs of the aged population.

Grant provides a review of the demographic characteristics of the Canadian population and the socio-economic characteristics of the aged. She also gives an overview of the development of Canada's health insurance system and the five principles on which it was initiated: accessibility, comprehensiveness, universality, portability, and public administration. It is evident that medicare has not met all its objectives. For example, different groups experience differential access to and utilization of services. Urban–rural inequalities in Canada are reflected in the regional maldistribution of services.

The morbidity patterns of the aged are different from those of the rest of the population. Epidemiological evidence indicates a much greater likelihood of chronic conditions and various functional limitations in the later stages of life. While health seems to diminish with age, there is much variability among the aged in incidence and type of sickness by income, gender, and other social variables.

As would be expected, the elderly have been found to make disproportionate use of acute- and chronic-care hospital beds and long-term facilities. Data also confirm the observation that some segments of the elderly are more likely to be hospitalized and for a longer period of time and that some seniors make more extensive use of health services. All health facilities and services are expensive. Because of aged patients' presence in these facilities, the aged population is being blamed for escalating health costs and the related fiscal crisis. Grant argues, however, that, rather than blaming the elderly for the fiscal crisis, we should look at the demands for services generated by the providers of care (specifically, medical doctors), and at existing treatment orientations, patterns of medical practice, and generally, at the organization of the health-care system. The increasing "medicalization" of conditions and their treatment, the extensive use of pharmaceuticals, and the trend to hospital-based care and technology-intensive treatment need to be scrutinized. Likewise, modern medicine's curative rather than preventative orientation, and its individualist and reductionist diagnoses and intervention, all require careful analysis in any reasoned discussion of the current contradictions of the health-care system, and its reform and transformation.

Grant argues that many of the problems of the elderly are not amenable to the traditional forms of medical treatment and that health and social care are needed to respond to many of these problems. The increasing recognition of the social determinants of health requires a shift toward preventive health education and health promotion, and community-based alternatives to curative and institutional care.

In the next chapter, "Social Dimensions of Mental Illness," James Stolzman discusses a number of issues involved in the definition, diagnosis, and treatment of mental disorders. He also examines the rationale and implications of divergent perspectives brought to the study of mental illness by sociologists, psychologists, and psychiatrists. He particularly focusses on the difference between sociological and psychological analyses of mental illness, medical and sociological conceptions of mental illness, and the importance of extra-scientific factors such as politics, cultural norms, social standards of normalcy, and structural and contextual factors involved in the diagnoses and social patterning of mental illness.

Stolzman points out that there is no consensus among scholars and clinicians about the nature and causes of mental disorders. This lack of agreement over the very nature of mental disorders hampers efforts to define the concept. This is largely because there is no one property shared by all types of mental disorders, nor is there any single trait that distinguishes the mentally disturbed from the mentally sound. He outlines the three-part definition of mental disorder by the American Psychiatric Association, and points out its limitations, primarily its lack of consideration of cultural, social, and other contextual factors that are crucial in categorizing specific kinds of behaviour as normal or abnormal and acceptable or unacceptable. Stolzman states that it is precisely this dimension of socially defined "strangeness" that is missing in the psychiatric definition of mental disorder. Mental illness is not only a "biophysical state" but also a "social state."

Although it is customarily viewed as a psychological and/or biological phenomenon, mental illness also has many social dimensions. Psychiatric diagnoses of mental disorders depend on cultural norms, social standards of normalcy, and contextual factors. Social analysis of mental disorder puts the focus on the social environment that affects the patterning of psychological distress. The biomedical conception of madness as a disease, he argues, is a socially constructed interpretation whose hegemony may be attributable more to its consonance with certain cultural beliefs than to its scientific utility. Stolzman discusses the social and historical circumstances that fostered the "medical model," and suggests that the acceptance of the view of madness as a disease has been aided by the progressive encroachment of medicine into more and more areas of modern life—the "medicalization" of life. Psychiatric diagnoses, he points out, are social judgements subject to bias. Rosenhan's study of "normal" people who sought and gained admission to mental hospitals illustrates the contextual nature of psychiatric assessments.

Many social scientists, as well as foes of psychiatry, have criticized the medical model. It is contended that the medical terminology and the myth of value-free science disguise the social control function of modern psychiatry. Similarly, as Stolzman points out, the aura and trappings of medicine that surround mental illness designations may hide their intimate connection with prevailing societal values. Psychiatric assessments are not independent of political, social, and cultural contexts. A notable demonstration of this thesis was the debate within the American Psychiatric Association that led to its vote to remove homosexuality from its official list of mental illnesses, following challenges by gay rights activists.

Many of the ideas that inform this critique of psychiatric enterprise are derived from the sociological perspective called societal reaction or labelling theory. Stolzman discusses both the contributions and the limitations of this perspective in the study of mental illness.

The medical model's exclusive concentration on the individual ignores the role of social factors in the origin of mental disorder. The source of psychological distress may reside in, for example, the family environment of the people identified as mental patients. Other features of the social environment are known to contribute to differential rates of mental disorders among the population—for example, unemployment, social class, gender, and marital status.

Stolzman points out that the relevance of social factors in analyzing mental disorders has been seriously underestimated by both the mental health community and the public at large. He argues that social factors are thoroughly involved in both the assessment and the causation of mental disorders. Our cultural assumptions that equate mental health with normality, conformity, and adjustment serve to conceal disturbances that stem from collectivities and social relationships. It is perhaps our persistent fear of madness that accounts for much of the public appeal of the medical model.

Sociological analysis seeks to explain variations in the rates or social patterning of mental illness. Psychological analysis, in contrast, addresses the question of why some individuals are mentally ill and others are not. Social patterns of mental disorders appear to be related to socially structured inequality and ambiguity. In conclusion, Stolzman suggests that the challenge of identifying the salient conditions and factors linking social systems, stress, mental anguish, and psychiatric impairment is to bridge the differences between biomedical and social perspectives on mental disorders.

CHAPTER 14

Health Care in an Aging Society: Issues, Controversies, and Challenges for the Future

Karen R. Grant

Learning Objectives

After studying this chapter, you should be able to
- Understand the issue of **population aging** in Canada, including how this trend varies by social factors such as class and gender.
- Outline the history of Canadian medicare since its inception in the 1950s through to the present era of cost cutting.
- Assess the relationship between health and aging, taking into account life expectancy, mortality, morbidity, and health-care utilization.
- Understand the health and social problems associated with drug utilization among seniors.
- Assess the concept of population aging as a *public issue* that is treated as a *private trouble* of individuals.

Introduction

This chapter examines several issues and controversies related to health care and aging in Canadian society, and explores the relationship between demographic and epidemiological transitions and the demand on health services by seniors. Although being old and being sick are not equivalent, there is a general impression that older Canadians suffer inordinately from declining health, and consequently utilize health services more than other segments of the population. To many, the crisis in medicare is associated with a growing aged population. In this chapter, we explore trends in population aging, as well as the factors that contribute to the greying of Canadian society. In additions, students will learn about the relationship between health and aging, with a particular emphasis on the health services implications of chronic disease and declining health among Canadian seniors. For example, inasmuch as declining health is associated with aging (particularly for very elderly seniors), we must ask about how well the medical care and social systems will be able to deal with an increasingly aged population.

> I am not mad, only old. I make this statement to give me courage ... I am in a concentration camp for the old, a place where people dump their parents or relatives exactly as though it were an ash can ... I have to hang on to every scrap of information I have to keep my sanity, and it is for that purpose that I am keeping a journal. Then if I forget things later, I can always go back and read them here.
>
> I call it *The Book of the Dead*. By the time I finish it I shall be dead. I want to be ready, to have gathered everything together and sorted it out, as if I were preparing for a great final journey. I intend to make myself whole here in this Hell. It is the thing that is set before me to do. So, in a way, this path inward and back into the past is like a map, a map of my world. If I can draw it accurately, I shall know where I am. (Sarton 1973, 3–4)

So begins the journal of 76-year-old Caro Spencer who, following a heart attack, finds herself sent off by her family to a home for the aged. Her journal reveals the despair and degradation, the loneliness and helplessness of an elderly woman. Her experience is not uncommon in our contemporary society.

Although there has been a progressive aging of the Canadian population over the past century, it is only in the last few decades that this phenomenon has attracted much attention from academics and the popular press. A voluminous research literature has been amassed and it is now commonplace to see headlines decrying the problems of a growing elderly population. We hear of "geriatric bed blockers" inappropriately occupying acute-care hospital beds as they await transfer to long-term care institutions. This practice contributes to lengthy queues for people in need of acute care in Canadian hospitals. We hear of elders making extensive use of health-care and social services, thus placing undue economic (and other) burdens on our welfare state institutions. Expressed in terms of an **old age dependency ratio**, we are left with the impression that elders are not making a "real" contribution to society, but instead are exacting a burden on the rest of society. We hear of drug dependency and **iatrogenesis** experienced by elders because of the numerous prescription medications they receive. And so on.

To a considerable degree, aging has become a social problem (Macintyre 1977), or what C. Wright Mills called a public issue (1959). For Mills, using a "sociological imagination" involves the ability to transcend a problem's personal, individual qualities, so that a particular phenomenon can be understood within the larger social and historical milieux. In this way, private troubles (such as growing old) are no longer private matters at all, but rather public issues that involve the entire array of social institutions and values of a society.

This chapter is devoted to a consideration of the very public and social nature of population aging, and the response of the health-care system to a changing demographic profile in this country. Throughout, the objective is to reinforce the point that population aging highlights many of the contradictions and conflicts within the health-care system and within society at large. Consequently, it is argued that to see aging as the private trouble of individuals is misguided and problematic. This chapter examines several issues and controversies related to health care and aging in Canadian society, and asks whether the elderly have become a scapegoat for the failures of Canadian medicine and medicare.

In the first section of the paper, a demographic profile of Canada's aging population is offered. This is followed by a brief look at Canada's medicare program, a description of the health of Canada's elderly population, and a discussion of some of the relevant empirical work done by sociologists and gerontologists on the health-care utilization patterns of seniors. This latter discussion is intended to address the question of whether the elderly, as a group, make disproportionately greater use of the health-care system than other age groups do. Finally, a glimpse at the elderly's use of prescription drugs is used for illustrative purposes, to highlight the problems and challenges associated with population aging in contemporary Canadian medicine and society. The discussion closes with a consideration of how Canada will deal with its aging population as it moves into the twenty-first century.

A Demographic Profile of Canada's Elderly

In recent years, a good deal has been written about the aging of the Canadian population. Demographers and gerontologists have described what amounts to a "seniors boom" (Stone and Fletcher 1986), which is having a profound effect on the cultural and economic institutions of Canadian society. The best-selling book *Boom, Bust and Echo* (Foot 1996) warns of the economic and social consequences of the aging "baby boom" generation. It is not too much of an exaggeration to say that Canada is "greying." According to the United Nations, a population is considered "aged" when persons 65 years and older constitute more than 7 percent of the population (McDaniel 1986). With about 12 percent of our population over the age of 65, Canada qualifies as an aged nation.

Canada's population is in a state of transition. Just a century ago, Canada's **population pyramid** was heavily weighted toward the younger ages, with elders constituting only a relatively small fraction of the total population. More recently, however, the pyramid's shape has changed. Younger people (sometimes called Generation X) are fewer in number, and there is an increase in older age groups, most notably persons in their middle years (i.e., baby boomers). As shown in Table 14.1, the number of seniors in Canada has increased steadily over the past century. Whereas in 1891 elders accounted for only 4.5 percent of the total Canadian population, in 1991 nearly 12 percent of the population was 65 years or older (Statistics Canada 1992). Based on current projections, it is estimated that persons 65 years or older will constitute nearly one-quarter of the population by 2011. By 2031, 9.2 million Canadians will be 65 years or older, compared with the current 3.7 million Canadians in the same age group (Denton and Spencer 1996).

A similar characterization can be made for other industrialized nations, such as the United States, where more than 11 percent of the population was 65 or older in 1981

TABLE 14.1   Number and Percentage of Population Aged 65 and Older, Canada, 1891–1991

Year	Number of persons aged 65+	Percentage of population
1891	218 790	4.5
1901	271 201	5.0
1911	335 315	4.7
1921	420 244	4.8
1931	576 076	5.6
1941	767 815	6.7
1951	1 086 237	7.8
1961	1 391 154	7.6
1971	1 744 405	8.1
1981	2 360 975	9.7
1986	2 697 580	10.7
1991	3 200 000	12.0

Sources: N.L. Chappell, L.A. Strain, and A.A. Blandford, *Aging and Health Care: A Social Perspective* (Toronto: Holt, Rinehart and Winston, 1986), p. 19; Statisitics Canada, *Age, Sex and Marital Status*, Cat. no. 93-310 (Ottawa: Minister of Supply and Services, 1992).

(Institute for Philosophy and Public Policy 1988; Brody, Brock, and Williams 1987; Dorney 1983; Stone and Fletcher 1988). Some European countries have somewhat larger elderly populations; for example, in 1981, approximately 15 percent of Britons and 16.5 percent of Swedes were 65 and older (McDaniel 1986). By contrast, countries in the developing world do not have large numbers of elders. To be sure, the differences in the demographic make-up of any society are tied very much to social and economic conditions; in the developing world, conditions are not always conducive to a long life.

What has just been described is something demographers call population or demographic aging. Demographic aging refers to the progressive aging of a population (as opposed to the aging of individuals). There are several reasons underlying the phenomenon of demographic aging in Canada and other industrialized nations (McDaniel 1986; Stone and Fletcher 1986). First of all, improvements in health care (a subject to which we will return later in this chapter) have led to significant declines in mortality over the past century, which has contributed to the aging of Canada's population. It is important to note, however, that reduced mortality and increased longevity owe much more to improvements in sanitation, personal hygiene, and living standards than to specific medical measures per se (McKeown 1979; McKinlay et al. 1983). This is not to suggest that doctors have made no contribution—only that public health measures have had a more significant impact on declines in mortality.

This having been said, the effects of improved health care on population aging really are limited, since it is the young and not the old who have benefited most (McDaniel 1986). Medicine has been most effective in dealing with acute conditions, which are more likely to affect younger members of society. In the past century, pro-phylactic measures have been developed to control or eliminate most infectious dis-eases. The same is not true for chronic conditions, which more commonly affect older members of the population. Though some medical measures allow for the extension of human life, McDaniel (1986) suggests that there is a ceiling to the biological life span that medicine has not appreciably altered. McKinlay et al. (1983) also indicate that where medical measures have lengthened life, they have often produced more years of disabled life, a very high cost indeed.

The second major factor contributing to population aging is immigration. Canada's relatively open immigration policy has brought a steady influx of mostly young immigrants from various parts of the world over the past century. In the first half of this century, the wave of immigration was from Eastern and Western European countries. More recently, a substantial proportion of immigrants are coming to Canada from countries in Southeast Asia, the Indian subcontinent, and Latin America. The earlier immigrants to Canada are now among the elderly, while the more recent immigrants "contribute to the relative youthfulness of the country and ... stave off aging of the population" (McDaniel 1986, 6).

The third, and most important, factor responsible for population aging is the decline in fertility. While the effects of declining fertility are obvious in terms of family size and composition (i.e., the average number of children per family is still less than two), its effects on population aging are not as readily apparent. Yet the reduced fertility of Canadians in the past century has meant that while the absolute number of elders in a population may not have increased, the fact that younger age groups are relatively smaller automatically increases the proportional size of the elderly segment of the population. Gee (cited in McDaniel 1986, 6) puts this rather succinctly: "Population aging is an unplanned byproduct of planned parenthood."

With the aging of Canada's population has come the realization that not all indi-viduals have an equal likelihood of surviving to advanced age. We have already noted the differences in life expectancy between developed and developing countries. A similar differential exists within Canada, as is shown in Table 14.2. Proportionally, the greatest numbers of elders are found in Saskatchewan, Manitoba, and Prince Edward Island, while in the Northwest and Yukon Territories, elders make up only a small fraction of the total population. Aboriginal persons, many of whom live in Canada's territories (as well as on reserves and in large cities), represent a much smaller proportion of persons aged 65 and over when compared with all other Canadians. In 1986, for example, approximately 10 percent of the Canadian popula-tion was 65 or older, while only 4 percent of aboriginal Canadians were 65 or older (National Advisory Council on Aging 1993). Poverty and deprivation, as well as living in rural and remote areas with limited access to health services, no doubt con-tribute to the poorer health and shorter life expectancy of aboriginal Canadians.

If we look at the age composition of the elderly population, here too, we find important variation. Elder Canadians are getting older. Recent evidence from Statistics Canada indicates that the proportion of seniors 65 years and older increased 17.5 percent between 1986 and 1991. Between 1981 and 1991, the number of Canadians 85 years and older jumped 31 percent, from 194 000 to 283 000 (National Advisory Council on Aging 1993). The growth rates of the aged have continued to

TABLE 14.2   Percentage of Persons Aged 65 and Over in Canada, by Province, 1971, 1981, 1986, 1991

Province/ territory	Percentage of persons aged 65 and over				75+ age group as a % of 65+ in 1991
	1971	1981	1986	1991	
Saskatchewan	10.2	12.0	12.7	14.1	44.7
Manitoba	9.6	11.9	12.6	13.4	43.6
Prince Edward Island	11.0	12.2	12.7	13.2	45.7
British Columbia	9.4	10.9	12.1	12.9	40.7
Nova Scotia	9.2	10.9	11.9	12.6	42.4
New Brunswick	8.6	10.1	11.1	12.2	41.8
Ontario	8.4	10.1	10.9	11.7	39.7
Quebec	6.9	8.8	10.0	11.2	38.6
Newfoundland	6.2	7.7	8.8	9.7	39.7
Alberta	7.3	7.3	8.1	9.1	40.4
Yukon	2.8	3.2	3.7	4.0	24.4
Northwest Territories	2.2	2.9	2.8	2.9	14.9
CANADA	8.1	9.7	10.7	11.6	n/a

Sources: Statistics Canada, *Age, Sex and Marital Status*, Cat. no. 93-310 (Ottawa: Minister of Supply and Services, 1992); Statistics Canada, *A Portrait of Seniors in Canada*, Cat. no. 89-519 (Ottawa: Minister of Supply and Services, 1990); National Advisory Council on Aging, *Aging Vignettes*, 1993.

increase over the past century, as is revealed in Table 14.3. Demographers project that the rate of population growth for all elders will decline somewhat at the start of the next century, but that this will be followed by an increase in the number of elders around 2030.

One of the more interesting sources of variation among Canada's elderly has to do with gender. Put rather succinctly, aging is a women's issue (Dulude 1978; Nett 1982; Estes, Gerard, and Clarke 1984; Reinharz 1986; Russell 1987; McDaniel 1988; 1989), since women are disproportionately represented among the elderly. This gender imbalance became most apparent in the 1950s (see Table 14.3). Currently, nearly 60 percent of seniors are women. The imbalance of the sexes owes much to the greater longevity of females and the higher rates of mortality among males, topics to be considered shortly.

The importance of gender differences in longevity is seen in terms of the sex ratio. In Canada in 1991, for every 100 men aged 65 years or older, there were 138 women. The ratio becomes even more lopsided among the old—for every 100 men aged 85 years or older, there were 200 women (National Advisory Council on Aging 1993). The consequences of this imbalance are profound in terms of health and social policy, as well as at a more personal level. For example, widowhood is "an expectable life event" for most women, particularly elderly women (Martin Matthews 1987) and it has been estimated that most women who marry can expect to live ten years as

TABLE 14.3   Population Growth Rates and Sex Ratios at Age 65 and 85, Canada, 1920–2030

Time period[a]	Average annual population growth rate				Men per 100 women	
	Total	65+	75+	85+	65+	85+
1920–30	1.79	3.72	3.18	1.76	104.9	81.2
1930–40	1.15	3.36	4.24	4.32	108.9	81.6
1940–50	2.05	4.12	3.99	5.33	104.1	77.5
1950–60	3.03	2.92	4.44	4.25	95.2	77.0
1960–70	1.95	2.49	3.54	6.96	82.0	67.2
1970–80	1.26	3.49	3.08	4.57	75.0	50.5
1980–90	1.13	3.49	4.58	3.94	73.2	39.9
1990–2000	1.20	2.36	3.84	5.76	75.2	40.0
2000–10	0.90	1.56	1.81	3.51	76.3	40.8
2010–20	0.82	2.94	1.34	1.03	77.7	43.0
2020–30	0.70	2.51	3.57	1.70	78.3	43.9

[a] Figures after 1980 are based on projections.

Source: L.O. Stone and S. Fletcher, "Demographic Variations in North America," *North American Elders* (Contribution to the Study of Aging, No. 8), ed. E. Rathbone-McCuan and B. Havens (Westport, CT: Greenwood Press, 1988), p. 13. Copyright 1988 by Eloise Rathbone-McCuan and Betty Havens. Reprinted with permission of the publisher.

widows. In 1991, 28 percent of women 65 years and older were widowed, while 82 percent of women aged 90 and older were widowed. Among seniors, 13 percent of men (as compared with 47 percent of women) were widowed in 1991 (National Advisory Council on Aging 1993). The potential adverse effects of widowhood have been well documented (see, for example, Lopata 1987). Beyond this, the large numbers of elderly women who may or may not have sources of support (because of a loss of spouse or peers) means that community and other institutional supports need to be found for this segment of the elderly population.

Another variable that is often considered when describing the elderly is their socio-economic situation. It is commonplace to hear of elders barely eking out a living on their pension monies. For many elders in Canada, the loss of financial security is a part of growing old. It has been estimated that most elders can expect their incomes to drop by about half at retirement. While the economic situation of elders has improved substantially as a result of government and private pension plans instituted in the post–Second World War era, a risk of poverty remains for large numbers of elderly persons, particularly women. Dulude has noted that "to be old and female is the best combination to ensure being poor in Canada ... to be old and a widow is an even better one" (1978, 38).

In 1990, approximately 60 percent of seniors had a total annual income of less than $15 000 (Ulysse 1997). Several studies over the past few decades indicate that elderly women's total annual incomes remain approximately 60 to 65 percent of those of their male counterparts. For example, Norland (1994) reported that in 1991, the average income for men 65 years and older was $24 500, while for women in the same age group it was only $15 300.

Public policy analysts note with some pleasure that the proportion of low-income seniors has declined somewhat in recent years. According to the National Advisory Council on Aging (1993), between 1980 and 1990 the proportion of elders living below the poverty line was reduced from 13 percent to 4 percent. The Council notes that "although not classified as having low incomes, many seniors still hover on the margins of poverty and would join the ranks of the official poor if the Low-income Cutoff [poverty line] were shifted slightly upwards" (1993, Vignette #4).

Elders' primary sources of income include Old Age Security, the Guaranteed Income Supplement, and the Canada (and Quebec) Pension Plans. In addition to these programs, various provinces have created programs and tax subsidies for elders. Together, all public programs account for about half of elders' incomes (National Council of Welfare 1984). For many elders, the public monies they receive are augmented by private pensions funded through payroll deductions. As noted by the National Council of Welfare, however, "the failings of private pension plans are glaring: most working Canadians are not covered by them (especially lower wage earners and workers in the private sector) and the minority who do belong typically receive meagre pensions that are not adequately protected against inflation" (1984, 68). And, it should be added, most private plans do not benefit women, since few of today's elderly women were employed outside the home; consequently, they stand a much greater chance of finding themselves in poverty in their "golden years."

The economic situation described above is, of course, not the lot of everyone. There are affluent persons among Canada's elderly—approximately 5 percent of seniors earn an annual income greater than $50 000, and of these 20 percent earn more than $100 000 annually (Ulysse 1997). The increasing economic vitality of a small but growing segment of the elderly population has led some to conclude that seniors don't all live in misery and despair, and that this segment of the population wields considerable economic (consumer) power. The primary thesis of *Boom, Bust and Echo* (Foot 1996) is just that—that entrepreneurs would do well to plan for the coming bulge in the generation of seniors who, as baby boomers, dictated consumer choices and lifestyles. Because this segment of the population is so large, how they age will have major consequences for our society.

Economic security among Canada's seniors very much depends on their gender, marital status, occupation history, and access to private pensions. More women than men rely on government transfers as the primary source of their income in old age. In the period between 1990 and 1994, elderly unattached men saw an increase in their annual average income of $2033. For elderly unattached women, annual average incomes declined during this same period by $1069 (Ulysse 1997). Fewer women have access to private pension benefits, and a smaller proportion of women set aside savings in pension plans or registered retirement savings plans (RRSPs). For seniors who rely on private investments, the recent decline in interest rates has seriously reduced their annual average incomes.

Demographic differences are among the most salient variables that influence health and well-being, but there are other variables among Canadian seniors, including urban or rural residence, education levels, marital status, and living arrangements (see Chappell, Strain, and Blandford 1986; Novak 1988; Centre on Aging 1996). It is important to note how heterogeneous the elderly are as a group. Indeed, the demographic make-up of elders often parallels the demographic make-up of the rest of society.

Typically, we tend to lump all persons with a particular attribute together, and make assumptions based upon various stereotypes. This tendency applies to elders just as it does to other identifiable social groups (e.g., women, aboriginal people, or people with disabilities). While stereotypes can tell us something about the attributes of such groups, more often than not, truths, half-truths, and outright lies are mixed into the stereotypes that we develop. When these stereotypes misinform, they have the potential to cause divisions and conflicts between people. On this basis, a growing number of researchers reject the stereotypes of deprivation, isolation, and loss that so commonly described seniors even a decade ago. In their most vile form, these stereotypes lead to a form of bigotry described by Robert Butler as **ageism** (1969; 1980). Ageism is a form of prejudice against elders that "reflects a deep-seated uneasiness on the part of the young and middle-aged—a revulsion to and distaste for growing old, disease, disability; and fear of powerlessness, 'uselessness,' and death" (Butler 1969, 243). Based on many unfounded myths,[1] ageism often has the result of making seniors feel stigmatized and devalued, and may exacerbate the difficult conditions that can be associated with growing old (Dorney 1983). As we shall almost surely all grow old some day, it is time to rid ourselves of these misconceptions. It is also time to enhance our understanding of the aging process and its implications for society and its institutions. Perhaps one of the institutions most affected by population aging is the health-care system, to which we will now turn.

A Brief Look at Canada's Health-Care Program

In recent years, Canada's health-care system has come under increasing scrutiny and criticism. Seldom a day goes by without a headline in one newspaper or another claiming that the health-care system is in a state of crisis. Long queues for surgery and specialist care, bed closures, shortages of nurses and doctors, and striking health-care workers are now commonplace. Yet despite these concerns, Canada's health-care system and medicare program are viewed around the world as exemplary. Indeed, few Canadians today can remember a time when medicare did not exist, and most Canadians could not imagine life without medicare.

Comprehensive, universal, government-funded health insurance, or medicare, has been in place for more than 25 years. Though the first hospital insurance plans were introduced in 1947 in Saskatchewan and in 1957 throughout Canada, it was not until 1972 that all Canadians had coverage for medical and hospital services through the Hospital Insurance and Diagnostic Services Act and the Medical Care Act. In recent years, these two pieces of legislation have been superseded by the Canada Health Act (1984).

The early government initiatives in health care came largely as a result of the 1964 Hall Royal Commission on Health Services, although the impetus underlying the program had its base in the government's post–Second World War reconstruction plan (which also included federal initiatives in the area of pensions). Guided by the knowledge that many Canadians did not have access to quality medical care, Justice Hall recommended that the provincial and federal governments introduce a program that would remove the economic barriers that prevented many Canadians from receiving necessary medical care (Hatcher 1981; Torrance 1981). Funding for the program came through taxation, and the government initially agreed to share the costs of health care on a fifty–fifty basis with the provinces, provided that each provincial plan met five requirements:

1. accessibility (reasonable access should be guaranteed to all Canadians);
2. comprehensiveness (all necessary medical services should be guaranteed, without dollar limit, and should be available solely on the basis of medical need);
3. universality (all Canadians should be eligible for coverage on uniform terms and conditions);
4. portability (benefits should be transferable from province to province); and
5. administration by a public non-profit agency or commission.

Beginning in 1977, as a result of the implementation of the Established Programs Financing Act (EPF), the formula for sharing costs was changed. In part, this change was introduced by the federal government as a cost-saving mechanism. Following the introduction of medicare, the governments of Canada (particularly the federal government) found the costs of this program difficult to bear. By the mid-1970s, approximately 7 to 7.5 percent of the Gross National Product (GNP) was being allocated to health care. In order to put a ceiling on this expense, the federal government introduced the EPF, which tied federal contributions to the size of the population and the growth in the GNP. Rather than providing dollar-for-dollar funding, the federal government provided each province with a block of funds (transfer payments) to be used by the provinces in support of health services, education, and social assistance. By the mid-1980s, it was estimated that the changes brought about by the EPF had reduced federal contributions to medicare from 50 percent to approximately 38 percent (Barber 1989).

The EPF, for all intents and purposes, ushered in the progressive erosion of medicare in Canada. Beginning in 1983, the Trudeau government began to reduce its transfers to the provinces. The Mulroney government, in 1986, changed the EPF formula to GNP growth minus 2 percent, and then in 1990 to GNP growth minus 3 percent. In 1991, with the passage of Bill C-20, the Mulroney government froze EPF growth for an additional two years. This bill also made it possible for the federal government to withhold transfers to the provinces if they allowed any breaches of the Canada Health Act, notably if hospitals charged user fees or doctors extra-billed their patients (Paul 1998).

The latest wrinkle in federal–provincial funding of health care has been the creation of the Canada Health and Social Transfer (CHST). The CHST was introduced by the Chrétien government in 1996–97 to replace the EPF and the Canadian Assistance Plan. The CHST provides federal funding as a combination of cash contributions and tax points. It is intended to reduce federal contributions to social spending in health, education, and social assistance—and that is exactly what is happening. According to Kent (1997), "all that is left of federal involvement ... is a relatively small block grant arbitrarily fixed by Ottawa without reference to the health and social costs incurred by the provinces." The current federal contribution toward health, education, and social assistance is $12.5 billion, which represents approximately 15 percent of the costs of these programs.[2] As a result, provincial treasuries bear a sizable proportion of the remaining costs (in 1994–95, the provinces spent $79 billion). In 1996, expenditures for health care alone in Canada amounted to $75.2 billion or $2510 per capita, representing 9.5 percent of the GNP.

There is understandable resentment on the part of the provincial governments about how the funding of medicare has evolved over time. Lured into the creation of a universal, comprehensive public health-care system, the provinces now find themselves bearing considerable costs for an increasingly expensive, technology-intensive health system. The federal government (beginning with Trudeau and continuing with Mulroney and Chrétien) has gradually and substantially reduced its contributions to medicare and other social spending, all the while insisting that "national standards" must be maintained by the provinces. The federal government threatens that departures from the founding principles of medicare—most notably, the prohibition against extra-billing and user fees that create barriers to accessibility—will result in even further reductions in the federal contributions to medicare. Court challenges to federal penalties have been waged in a number of provinces in recent years. According to some critics, the federal government has lost the moral authority to insist that the provinces steadfastly uphold the principles of medicare when its contribution has become so meagre. Health Canada (1997) reports that the actual federal contribution to health expenditures in 1996 was a mere 3.5 percent of the total, with the remainder paid for through provincial funding (64.4 percent), private expenditures (30.1 percent), municipal funding (1.0 percent), and workers' compensation (0.8 percent).

It is little wonder that critics of the CHST accuse the current government of a total abandonment of the values and principles that guided the Liberal Party of Canada in the formation of medicare in the 1950s and 1960s. It is also little wonder that the provincial governments have "cold feet" about embarking on any new initiatives in health care, such as a national home-care program or a national pharmacare program. Both of these were suggested by the National Forum on Health in its report to the government in 1997, but the provincial governments insist that they must have a larger say in health-care policy given that they are footing the lion's share of the bill. Co-operative federalism requires sharing this authority, and the provincial governments will not settle for less.

Most observers believe that the reduction in federal contributions to medicare has imperilled the system to a considerable degree. But it is also true that several provincial governments have opted to reduce their contributions to the health system. They have initiated major system restructuring, contending that there is too much fat in the system or that resources are being used inefficiently (Armstrong and Armstrong 1996). Under the rubric of "health reform," provincial governments have downsized the health-care system, reducing the number of hospital beds, laying off nursing and other health-care workers, limiting the number of services that are insured and restricting access to others.

Federal and provincial politicians know that it will not be easy to abandon medicare. Former prime minister Mulroney learned such a lesson when he attempted to de-index old-age pensions in this country in the mid-1980s. At the same time, in their quest to deal with the debt, governments have effectively put medicare under the knife. Some believe that the system has been so severely compromised that it is in need of life-support. There is little hope that this situation will be reversed so long as declining federal transfers and provincial downsizing continue.

The increasing costs of health care today, coupled with the changing disease (mostly chronic) and demographic (increasingly older) profiles of the country heighten concerns about medicare's future. This "sacred trust" is under attack. Efforts by the federal government to privatize Crown corporations raise the spectre that medicare may someday be privatized as well, returning Canada to a system not unlike that of the United States. The establishment of private clinics and hospitals in various provinces is the thin edge of a wedge. How government fiscal and free-trade policies like NAFTA and the Multilateral Agreement on Investment (MAI) will affect medicare and other social programs is not entirely clear at this time.

Canada's medicare program, though progressive in its intent to promote universal access to health services, is what Waitzkin (1983) calls a **reformist**, rather than revolutionary, **reform**. Medicare simply changed the way that people paid for health services, rather than reorganizing the way services were provided. As noted by Swartz:

> State hospital and medical insurance effected no change in the nature of the health-care system. Its control remained firmly in private hands, held by physicians and the drug and medical supply corporations. What health insurance amounted to was an unlimited subsidy to these fractions of the bourgeoisie in the form of a guarantee by the state of payment for any services and goods physicians mandate. (1987, 581)

Medicare left intact a private, fee-for-service medical practice, and ensured public payment to it (Evans 1984; Swartz 1987). This is not an unimportant point, as many of the problems that elders have with the health-care system can be traced to the nature of medical practice in this country.

Even the most ardent supporter of medicare would readily acknowledge that the system is not beyond criticism or the need for some types of reform. For example, services, facilities, and personnel continue to be maldistributed among urban, rural, and remote areas of the country. Physicians and hospitals are primarily found in urban centres, as are research and teaching facilities, because it is not feasible to locate facilities in all areas, particularly those that are sparsely populated. Even within cities, not everyone has equal access to the same quality medical care. Various groups, differentiated on the basis of age, sex, race, and socio-economic status, have different susceptibilities to disease and disability; they also experience differential access to quality health services. This problem is best summarized by what Julian Tudor Hart called "the inverse care law": "the availability of good medical care tends to vary inversely with the need for it in the population served" (1971, 412; cf. Grant 1988).

A second major problem noted in recent years concerns the alleged overuse of the health system by the public. It is claimed that because many Canadians have an almost insatiable appetite for medical services, do not pay for health services at the time they receive them, and have no knowledge of the actual costs of care, they inappropriately use the system. Frequenting emergency rooms for routine care is perhaps the most common illustration of this misuse.

Utilization studies have shown that Canadians began to use health services more extensively following the introduction of the national program (Evans 1984). To deal with the public's alleged overuse or misuse of the system, user fees have been implemented at various times in various jurisdictions. In 1968, for example, not long after the introduction of medicare in Saskatchewan, the provincial government instituted a system of modest co-payments for office, hospital, and outpatient visits. Initially these user fees resulted in a reduction in days spent in hospital, but those effects were only temporary. Beck (1973; 1974) observed that co-payments reduced the poor's use of physicians' services by approximately 18 percent, and the entire population's use by approximately 6 to 7 percent. In light of this evidence that co-payments resurrected economic barriers to care, the Saskatchewan government discontinued the program in 1971. More recently, the federal government has banned extra-billing—a practice started in many provinces in the 1970s and still evident in the 1990s—on the argument that it compromises medicare's principle of reasonable access. As already noted, there are forces at work eroding the accessibility requirement of medicare, and it will be difficult to prevent their continuation (and intensification) under conditions where government funding of the program continues to decline (Armstrong and Armstrong 1996).

Although patients may not always use the health-care system as efficiently as possible, some health economists have argued that the system is driven by the provider rather than by the user. That is, doctors determine how resources will be used—they determine who gets what, when, why, and how much. Doctors prescribe drugs and admit patients to hospitals, determining how long they will stay and what services they will receive. Hospital care is the most expensive component of health-care expenditures. According to Evans (1984), while physicians earn only about 20 percent of every dollar spent on health, they influence how the rest of that dollar is spent. In light of this statistic, reforms to individuals' utilization habits would be best directed toward physician, rather than patient, behaviour.

While medical care is a crucial component of the health delivery system, the needs of many Canadians, and of elders in particular, cannot be met by medical services alone. More medical care does not in itself lead to better health. That the formal system of health care must be augmented by informal and community-based care has been realized for a long time, but only now are governments looking to develop a social care infrastructure based in the community. The development of community-based alternatives to institutional care are highly desirable in that they allow people to be more independent by remaining in their homes and neighbourhoods where familiar social supports are more readily available. At the same time, the off-loading of caring work from professional health-care workers to unpaid caregivers in the home has fallen disproportionately on women, often at a cost to their own health and well-being. A recent study reported that most caregivers experienced some disruption in their lives, and 27 percent of women caregivers indicated that their health had been affected by their caring work (Cranswick 1997).

Programs providing social care have yet to receive the kind of funding that medicare has, or they have been considered add-ons with varying services, eligibility requirements, and user fees (Schwenger 1987). Furthermore, while federal legislation more or less guarantees that all Canadians shall have access to medical services, no such guarantees exist with respect to community services. The decentralized nature of health and social programs for the elderly makes assurances of equal access problematic (Chappell, Strain, and Blandford 1986; Chappell 1987; 1988; Statistics Canada 1986).

There is indeed a cost crisis in Canada's medicare program. On the one hand, more money is spent on health care today than ever before, but on the other hand, almost everywhere one turns, the system appears to be underfunded. This contradiction plagues the Canadian health-care system, but how we might effect a desirable solution to the cost crisis remains a matter of considerable debate.

This cursory look at Canada's health-care system reveals the complexity of challenges we face in this area of public policy. Several important points discussed here have a bearing on how health care is delivered and how the system responds to the demands made by consumers and providers. These, and various related issues, will be elaborated on and applied to elders in particular later on. First, however, we will look at the health of Canada's elderly.

A Health Profile of Canada's Elderly

As Canadian society has aged, much attention has focussed on the health consequences of this demographic shift. Inasmuch as declining health is often associated with aging (Longino and Soldo 1987), a great deal of attention is directed to the association between sickness and the aging process. Recent evidence suggests that the health and life expectancy of elders is improving, and at a quicker pace than for other age groups (Guralnik and Kaplan 1989; Brody 1989; Ulysse 1997). In this section, we look briefly at the health of Canadian seniors, and then turn to the question of how well the health and medical care systems deal with an increasingly aged population.

Health can be assessed in a number of ways, the most common of which use life expectancy, mortality, and morbidity statistics. In the past century, dramatic increases in life expectancy have been achieved in Canada and other industrialized countries. As noted in Table 14.4, a male born in 1986 could expect to live about 73 years, while a female could expect to live to the ripe old age of 80. In the period between 1931 and 1986, the net gains in expected years of life for males and females were, respectively, 13.04 and 17.63 years. Table 14.4 also shows the increases in life expectancy at age 60 and age 80. Longevity has increased for both sexes, although for women the increases have been more substantial.

The leading causes of death for Canadian seniors—heart disease, cancer, and stroke—mirror those for all Canadians. Diseases of the circulatory system are the number one killer of both men and women, with the rates elevated for persons 65 years and older (Centre on Aging 1996). There is an important difference, however, as to when the risk of heart disease becomes elevated—while men are more likely to be struck down by a heart attack in their mid-years (beginning around age 35), women are at greater risk in their post-menopausal years (beginning around 55). This difference is attributed to the protective effects of estrogen on women.

Based on 1986 data, the second leading cause of death for elderly men is lung cancer, while for elderly women, it is stroke. Prostate cancer ranks sixth as a leading

TABLE 14.4   Life Expectancy by Sex, at Birth, Age 60, and Age 80, Canada, 1931–1986, Selected Years

Year	At birth		At age 60		At age 80	
	Male	Female	Male	Female	Male	Female
1931	60.00	62.10	16.29	17.15	5.16	5.92
1941	62.96	66.30	16.06	17.62	5.54	6.03
1951	66.33	70.83	16.49	18.64	5.84	6.38
1956	67.61	72.92	16.54	19.34	5.89	6.75
1961	68.35	74.17	16.73	19.90	6.14	6.90
1966	68.75	75.18	16.81	20.58	6.36	7.26
1971	69.34	76.36	16.95	21.39	6.41	7.88
1976	70.19	77.48	17.23	21.96	n/a	n/a
1981	71.88	78.98	17.96	22.85	n/a	n/a
1986	73.04	79.73	18.41	23.17	n/a	n/a
Gains:						
1931–76	10.19	15.38	0.94	4.81	n/a	n/a
1931–86	13.04	17.63	2.12	6.02	n/a	n/a

Sources: Statistics Canada, *Canada Year Book, 1994*, Cat. no. 11-402E, Table 4.1, p. 148; *Historical Statistics of Canada*, 2d ed., Cat. no. 11-516E, pp. B59–74.

cause of death among elderly men, and breast cancer ranks fifth among women (Ulysse 1997). Cancer incidence has risen steadily in recent years, although for persons diagnosed with many forms of cancer, early detection and better treatment have meant improved survival rates. According to the National Advisory Council on Aging (1993), roughly two-thirds of all cancer deaths occur among individuals aged 65 and older.

The sex differences in death rates merit further consideration. With the exception of cerebrovascular disease (stroke), males have higher death rates than females. Health researchers suggest that the discrepancy in mortality experience between males and females owes much to how we live. For example, differences in lifestyles, socialization and social role behaviour, risk-taking behaviour (e.g., tobacco and alcohol consumption, physical fitness, preventive health behaviours), and experiences of stress and the ability to cope with it (e.g., the Type A or coronary-prone behaviour pattern) are all thought to contribute to the differential mortality experience of males and females (Kandrack, Grant, and Segall 1991). Biological factors may also operate here (Waldron 1976), although sociologists have long argued that social factors are more important.

It is commonly assumed that being old means being sick. Today, however, there is much evidence to suggest that many seniors are living longer healthier lives (Foot 1996; Ulysse 1997; Macleod and Associates 1997). Both men and women participating in the 1991 Manitoba Study of Health and Aging tended to rate their health as "pretty good" or "very good," although those over 85 became more likely to state that their health was "not too good" (Centre on Aging 1996).

At the same time, epidemiological evidence indicates that there is a much greater likelihood of chronic conditions and various forms of functional limitation occurring in the later stages of the life cycle. Data from the Canada Health Survey and the National Population Health Survey indicate a significantly higher prevalence of chronic health problems among elders than among younger persons. Acute illnesses are less common among elders than other age groups; however, they may be more debilitating for older persons (Verbrugge 1985).

While the mortality and life expectancy data clearly favour women, measures of morbidity do not. Put succinctly, the research evidence suggests that "women get sicker, but men die quicker" (Grant 1989). Women report a greater prevalence of most chronic health problems at all ages, including at age 65 and over (Statistics Canada 1981; Federal, Provincial and Territorial Advisory Committee on Population Health 1996). In the Manitoba Study of Health and Aging, women tended to report more chronic health problems than men, the only exceptions being hearing and memory loss. Common health problems reported by Manitoba seniors included arthritis/rheumatism, trouble with feet or ankles, high blood pressure, ear trouble/hearing loss, eye trouble not relieved by glasses, heart/circulation problems, stomach troubles, memory loss, trouble with nerves, and chest problems (Centre on Aging 1996, 84). American data based on self-reports and physical examinations show a similar pattern (Verbrugge 1985; 1986; Wingard 1984).

Verbrugge (1985) has pointed to the fact that there is no necessary correspondence between cause of death and illness experience (cf. Chappell, Strain, and Blandford 1986; Statistics Canada 1981). For example, in the U.S. Health Interview Survey, it was found that older women report a high rate of coronary and other circulatory symptoms, yet it is older men who are more likely to die of heart disease. It is possible that women's experience with various chronic conditions may be less severe and less lethal than men's. Some of the chronic conditions afflicting elderly women (e.g., arthritis) may be the source of diminished functioning, but they are unlikely to be the primary cause of death (Verbrugge 1985).

One problem that is more common among older women than men is osteoporosis (brittle bones), which is believed to affect approximately 25 percent of post-menopausal women (National Advisory Council on Aging 1993). According to Ulysse (1997), most cases of hospitalization related to osteoporosis involve women; in fact, osteoporosis—associated with hip fractures, fractures to the wrist and spine, and accidental falls—is the second leading cause of hospitalization for elderly women. The cost of hip replacement surgery is considerable ($400 million in 1990), and is expected to increase in the future. Yet, for those whose functional capacity is restored, the benefits to their quality of life are incalculable.

Another health problem affecting elders is Alzheimer's disease, which ranks as the tenth leading cause of death in Canada. The prevalence of dementias increases with age (Ulysse 1997), but while some forms of dementia may occur throughout life, Alzheimer's disease commonly occurs among elders. The 1991–92 Canadian Study of Health and Aging estimated an age-standardized rate of Alzheimer's disease of 51 per 1000 persons aged 65 years and over, and an age-standardized rate of all types of dementia of 80 per 1000 persons aged 65 years and older. Both the Canadian and Manitoba Studies of Health and Aging report higher rates of all dementias and Alzheimer's disease among women (Centre on Aging 1996). The National Advisory Council on Aging (1993) estimates that by the year 2006, 324 000 seniors will suffer some form of dementia, representing a 71 percent increase since 1991.

Based on data from the Canada Health Survey (Statistics Canada 1981), physical functioning declines with age. This study found that less than 10 percent of persons under 65 had any limitations on their usual activities, while almost 40 percent of those aged 65 and older were limited in their activity to some degree. Furthermore, approximately the same proportion of males as females experienced partial or total activity limitation at all ages, including the older age brackets. Women, however, reported more disability days—time taken off from their usual activities as a result of poor health. This latter finding was true at all ages, elders included. Table 14.5 provides data on total disability days in 1985, by gender and age. Overall, 14 percent of Canadians aged 15 and over reported at least one disability day during the two-week period prior to the survey. Reported disability days increased considerably after age 64, to 17 percent among those aged 65 to 74, and to 24 percent among those aged 75 years and over. A higher proportion of females reported disability in all age groups. The largest difference was in the age group of 75 years and over—28 percent for females and only 18 percent for males. Reporting on the Health and Activity Limitation Surveys in 1986 and 1991, Raina, Dukeshire, and Lindsay (1997) found that approximately 40 percent of seniors had at least one disability. Mobility and agility disabilities[3]—by far the most common types of disabilities—are more commonly experienced by elderly women, as are seeing disabilities. Hearing and speaking disabilities are more common among elderly men.

What can we conclude about the health of Canadian seniors? First, being old and being sick are *not* synonymous. While some elders may experience impairment with advancing years, this is not the lot of everyone. Health seems to diminish with age, but other variables—gender, class, and income level—also influence susceptibility to poorer health, and the degree of impairment one experiences (Ulysse 1997). Let us now consider how elders use health care and how well their needs are being met by the formal system of care.

TABLE 14.5   Percentage of Population 15 Years of Age and Over Reporting Disability Days, by Age Group and Sex, Canada, 1985 (Two-Week Period)

	Both sexes	Male	Female
All age groups	14	11	17
15–64	13	10	15
65–74	17	14	19
75 years and over	24	18	28

Note: Figures in this table combine bed disability days and major activity loss days to arrive at total disability days.

Source: Adapted from Statistics Canada, *Health and Social Support, 1985*, Cat. no. 11-612, No. 1, Table 39, p. 134.

Health Care and Aging in Canada

"The elderly who receive medical care receive more of it than the young" (Barer et al. 1987, 858). The jury is still out on how much seniors cost the Canadian health-care system. Still, it is widely believed that seniors do use health services more than individuals in other age groups, and that their use of health services intensifies as they get older and sicker. The proportion of health expenditures devoted to the care of seniors is variously estimated to be as low as 20 percent or as high as 50 percent of spending (National Advisory Council on Aging 1996).

According to an examination of late 1970s Manitoba health statistics by Roos, Shapiro, and Roos (1984), persons 65 years and older (9 percent of the total population in 1977) consumed 43 percent of all acute hospital days. In 1978, these researchers found that seniors consumed 36 percent of all short-stay hospital days. Persons 70 to 85 years of age consumed three times as many hospital days as those under 60; those 85 years or older consumed ten times as many as those under 60 (cf. Shapiro and Roos 1986; Shapiro and Tate 1985). On this basis, the study concluded that hospital use increases with age, and that a small segment of the elderly population (and of the population as a whole) accounts for a large proportion of utilization of the system.

But this evidence from the 1970s is a less than complete account of the relationship between age and health-care use. In 1994–95, Manitoba seniors (who constituted just over 13 percent of the population) received approximately 28 percent of all medical services provided and accounted for almost 32 percent of all hospitalizations (Centre on Aging 1996). Individuals in the under-45 age group (who constituted nearly 68 percent of the population), however, received 49 percent of medical services and accounted for 53 percent of all hospitalizations. The average length of a hospital stay for those under 45 was 4.2 days, while for seniors between 65 and 74 it was 12.6 days, and for seniors 75 years and older it was 20.1 days in hospital. These differences reflect the nature and severity of disease typically affecting different age groups—younger people are more likely to suffer from short-term acute conditions, whereas older people may require longer periods of hospital-based treatment for conditions such as coronary artery disease or cancer.

A recent Saskatchewan study by the National Advisory Council on Aging found that seniors also use doctors' services more than those in other age groups. "In 1987, a physician was consulted 21 times by men 65 and over and 23 times by women 65 and over; in comparison, men and women aged 45 to 64 used a doctor's services 11 times and 14 times, respectively" (1996, Vignette #31).

It has been estimated (based on 1981 census data) that 7.5 percent of persons aged 65 and older and 35.6 percent of persons aged 85 and older reside in long-term care institutions (residential treatment centres, nursing homes, personal care homes, etc.) (Forbes, Jackson, and Kraus 1987). Studies suggest that there has been a steady increase in long-term institutionalization over the past several decades, particularly for the very old.

These data confirm the observation that some segments of the elderly population are more likely to be hospitalized, and for longer periods of time, and that some seniors make more extensive use of health services than those in younger age groups.

These data also tell us that our health-care system has a very strong institutional focus. Chappell (1988) suggests that the very name *medi*care underscores the medical emphasis of Canada's health-care system. Although relatively few elders are institutionalized, this type of care is labour- and technology-intensive: the conditions inpatients may suffer are often chronic and may cause functional impairments. Hospital and other institutional care, whether for frail elders or others, is expensive, consuming approximately half of every health dollar in Canada (Chappell, Strain, and Blandford 1986; Evans 1984; Centre on Aging 1996).

Whether elders are best served by acute-care or long-term care facilities is a separate issue. Sociologists have long decried the adverse consequences of institutional life, which include fostering "learned helplessness," "institutionalism," and so on (cf. Goffman 1961; Gubrium 1975). Numerous critics have suggested that there are plenty of people in Canadian hospitals who don't belong there and that Canadians are kept in hospitals too long (Evans 1984). Can a system that stresses reactive acute care adequately deal with individuals who suffer from chronic conditions, which require a more holistic, social, and health (as opposed to medical) focus?

About a decade ago, researchers began turning their attention to the problems that occurred when acute-care beds in general hospitals were being blocked by elderly persons who were awaiting placement in long-term care facilities (Marshall 1987). These "geriatric bed blockers" were seen as difficult to place in long-term care facilities, and family members stood accused of being reluctant to provide supportive services to frail elders about to be discharged. Marshall (1987) suggested an alternative explanation for this phenomenon—that the reimbursement system in Canada's medicare program promotes delayed discharges because it does not consider the level or severity of care. Hospitals are reimbursed for acute-care beds even if they are occupied by a chronic-care patient. In a general hospital, a patient awaiting discharge is a relatively "cheap" patient, but in a long-term care facility, that same patient (who might require several hours of intensive nursing care) is an "expensive" patient. It requires no advanced degree in economics or managerial science to figure out why frail elders are occupying acute-care beds!

The reluctance of families to take their frail elderly relatives home probably has much to do with the negative connotations of nursing homes that have been cultivated over the past few decades. Forbes, Jackson, and Krause (1987), among others, have suggested that the manner in which Canada's medicare program evolved may also help to explain why an institutional focus remains and why families prefer hospital to nursing-home care. Hospital services, they point out, were insured first, only later to be followed by medical services and some community/home services.

The issue of "geriatric bed blockers" has not gone away. In the winter of 1998, journalists across the country reported on the swelling of hospital emergency rooms (and emergency-room hallways!) with sick people, many of whom were seniors. A particularly difficult flu season was blamed for this inundation. However, critics of provincial health ministries accused the governments of having made so many deep cuts to the system that it was hemorrhaging, leaving too few long-term care beds, too many people being discharged from hospital too soon, and too few nurses to take care of patients.

It is difficult to make broad generalizations about the relationship between age and the use of health services. Roos, Shapiro, and Roos (1984), McKinlay (1972), and

Grant (1984) suggest that utilization is influenced by numerous factors, including the attributes of patients and physicians, and the settings in which medicine is practised. Keeping this in mind, Roos, Shapiro, and Roos note that "although the elderly initiate most ambulatory physician visits, the physician largely determines whether an individual will be admitted to a hospital" (1984, 35). Charges, then, that elders make disproportionate use of the health system should be tempered by some understanding of the reasons for various types of utilization, and the sources of the decision making. Roos, Shapiro, and Roos suggest that "a preoccupation with the influence that increasing numbers of elderly will have on the health-care system should not mask the potentially even greater impact that the increasing physician supply in North America is likely to have on health expenditures during the next decade" (1984, 35).

This latter point is significant because, in many ways, it hints that the elderly have become the scapegoats for the funding crisis in medicare today. The prospect of population aging sends chills down the spines of health ministers! Branch, Sager, and Meyers (1987) describe long-term care policy in the United States as being "mired in trench warfare," and population aging as a "demographic time bomb." Elders' omnipresence in long-term facilities and in increasing numbers of beds in acute-care hospitals make them easy targets. More reasoned scrutiny of Canadian medicine and medicare would suggest that population aging is not so much the problem. In fact, according to the National Advisory Council on Aging:

> Population aging contributes to rising health-care costs, but less so than other factors. In the Organization of Economic Cooperation and Development (OECD) community, which includes Canada, population aging was estimated to account for 22 percent of the growth in health-care costs between 1960 and 1988. The remaining 78 percent of growth in health-care costs was attributed to factors such as inflation, the growth of the Gross National Product (GNP), and to political and professional choices. (1996, Vignette #25)

It should also be added that how health and illness (of the young and old alike) are currently dealt with by doctors and hospitals creates much of the crisis in health care. It is beyond the scope of this chapter to provide a detailed account of the failures of Canadian medicine and medicare, but a few examples that intimately touch the lives of many seniors will illustrate the basic argument.

The use of pharmaceuticals in medical practice today is extensive. Health Canada data estimates that the 12 percent of the population that is 65 years or older receives one-quarter of all prescription medication (National Advisory Council on Aging 1996). German and Burton (1989) have reported that 75.2 percent of elders in the United States who visit physicians are issued at least one prescription, if not more. Cooperstock's research in Canada (1971) indicates that the likelihood of receiving prescription medications increases with age and that elderly women receive a disproportionate number of prescriptions each year, many of these being mood-altering or psychotropic medications. Harding's Saskatchewan study (1986) found that the elderly received 43 percent of all central-nervous-system drug prescriptions, and that 19 percent of persons 60 years and older had at least one prescription, the most common drug being Valium (diazepam). The National Advisory Council on Aging

(1996) reported that in 1993, seniors in Ontario had an average of 27 prescriptions each, while Quebec seniors were issued 33 prescriptions each.

Though typically viewed as a blessing, drugs (like magic bullets) can be a curse as well, particularly for elderly persons. According to Hoppel (1985), adverse drug reactions are more common among elders than other age groups, and may be a factor contributing to mental impairment and behavioural imbalances that precipitate hospitalization. Many elders take multiple prescriptions, and often combine the use of prescription drugs with over-the-counter medications or alcohol (Pascarelli 1974). Such practices can lead to interactions that effectively neutralize the beneficial effects of some drugs, or worse yet, create adverse drug reactions that may lead to a number of adverse health consequences or even drug dependency (Harding 1986).

Drug surveillance programs have been instituted in a number of cities to aid and educate seniors about their use of medications. As important as these programs are, they are like "all the King's horses and all the King's men [who] couldn't put Humpty together again." There is no effort to stop the problem at its source (which is doctors' prescribing behaviour), revealing an undercurrent of "victim blaming." Moreover, these programs do not address why drugs have become so pervasive in medical practice.

Some research on the doctor–patient relationship suggests that the brevity of their encounter may be a factor (Grant 1984). The average medical encounter lasts only six to ten minutes (Balint and Norell 1973), and Keeler et al. (1982) found that the duration of medical encounters declined with the age of the patient. The problem of ageism, mentioned earlier, may also lead to inappropriate prescribing (Butler 1969; 1980; Carson 1977; Rodin and Langer 1980) or differential treatment of elders as compared with younger patients (Linn and Linn 1982). Although attitudes toward aging and the aged have changed, long-held stereotypes and avoidance behaviours on the part of younger physicians remain problematic (Haug and Ory 1987; Spence et al. 1968; Karasu, Stein, and Charles 1979; Cyrus-Lutz and Gaitz 1972; Ford and Sbordone 1980; Hickey et al. 1976; Ray, Raciti, and Ford 1985).

The prescription pad is often used by doctors to terminate the encounter with the patient. Anecdotal information from medical practitioners suggests that some prescribe drugs because they think that patients want them to (Grant 1984). The pharmaceutical companies, which aggressively market their products to doctors, cannot be ignored as a powerful influence on physicians' prescribing behaviour. It is estimated that approximately 20 percent of each company's manufacturing costs are spent on advertising of one sort or another, and approximately 45 percent of all promotional activities involve sales representatives (Lexchin 1988).

The widespread use of drugs in the doctor–patient relationship may also reflect the degree to which the medicalization of the human condition has taken hold in North American society (Zola 1986). Sandelowski offers this account:

> The presence of the prescription pad validates the physician's right and obligation to treat an ever-growing number of human concerns, and it also signifies that only he can give "health" to another person because only he can legally prescribe drugs ... Life itself is viewed as an illness requiring the skilful intervention of a physician ... It is the physician who has become the final arbiter as to when and how human beings will become

> well ... The physician has been instrumental in causing a "sickening" dependence upon drugs, especially among women. (1981, 236)

Old age has been medicalized (Arluke and Peterson 1981; Ulysse 1997), as have women's bodies (Reissman 1983). Being old and female, therefore, is a double whammy (Sontag 1972; Posner 1977; Chappell and Havens 1980; Dulude 1978). With a biomedical definition of a problem, it is not long before the technology of medicine will find an application!

Do the "magic bullets" of prescription drugs work? Or do they simply exacerbate existing health and social problems for elders? Do they create new iatrogenic problems? What role do pharmaceuticals play in promoting, rather than preventing, disease and disabling conditions? What proportion of cases seen by physicians or admitted to hospitals are in some measure the by-product of therapeutic processes? These are questions for which there are no hard and fast answers, but they underscore some of the controversies and contradictions of modern medical practice, and suggest the need for reforms to the system so that the health needs of patients (young and old) can be more readily accommodated.

Conclusions

At the outset of this chapter, it was noted that aging is best viewed as a public issue, rather than a private trouble. Routinely, the social nature of aging and the consequences of the aging process are forgotten or ignored. The experience of growing old can be seen either as a trial or as just another stage of life. In either case, living to a good old age has become a matter of personal responsibility in this society.

In this chapter, we have considered some aspects of the health-care system's response to the aging of Canadian society. It would seem that the medical profession and the institutions and policies that make up the Canadian health-care system have yet to evolve a correspondence between patient needs and service provision.

The medical profession's treatment (some would say, mistreatment) of elders must change. Medicine has a traditionally narrow scope and understanding of disease etiology. Consequently, diagnoses and interventions tend to be carried out at a highly reductionistic and individualistic (rather than social) level. Therapeutic practice continues to be heavily weighted toward hospital-based, technology-intensive medical care. Some believe that pharmaceuticals are prescribed too often to elders, and sometimes inappropriately. These drugs may simply mask symptoms, without addressing the underlying cause of disease.

Indeed, many of the problems of elders are not amenable to traditional forms of medical treatment. Studies of community care reveal that medical solutions are not necessarily indicated for problems that are social in origin (Chappell, Strain, and Blandford 1986). In other words, health and social services are increasingly needed where medicine has been used in the past. The recommendation by the National Forum on Health (1997) that the government introduce a national home-care program may signal a realization that both health and social care are needed to respond to many problems faced by Canadian seniors.

The changing epidemiological picture—from infectious to chronic diseases—demands a preventive, rather than reactive, approach to care. While there is some optimism that a more preventive focus is being integrated into medical training and practice, this development has yet to be seen in the forms of treatment used.

This chapter has shown that the current structure of health care in Canada is not yet fully prepared to meet the health needs of its aging population. Barer et al. (1987) accuse service providers of engaging in a "sham" policy debate with respect to the impact of seniors on the health-care system. Discussions have focussed primarily on the growing numbers of elders, their increasing levels of morbidity, and the utilization of health resources that accompanies this morbidity. Arguing that "hordes" of old people are about to descend upon us, and that they will be sicker and thus use more health services, may have worked in the past to garner more resources within the system. But that approach no longer works. Health ministers across the country listen unsympathetically to claims that population aging requires more resources in the system. In a climate in which governments are scaling back their public investment in health and social spending, it seems unlikely that health ministers will be convinced that more hospital beds, more doctors and nurses, and more medical care generally is the best way to produce health—whether the population is aging or not. Instead they insist that the current level (or less) of resources will have to be used better—that "health reform" will solve all of our problems. But most of what is now being promoted as health reform will do little to address the fundamental problems referred to in this chapter. Since the early 1970s, Canadian health ministers have been trying to shift the focus toward the *social* determinants of health. It is unlikely that they will revert back to a more biomedical orientation and reinvest in medical care. Instead, they will continue to promote preventive health care and community-based alternatives to institutional care. It will take some time to fix the health-care system for everyone, not just for seniors.

Summary

- The social nature of aging and the consequences of the aging process are routinely forgotten or ignored; in Canadian society, living to a good old age has become a matter of personal responsibility.
- The medical profession and the institutions and policies that make up Canada's health-care system have yet to evolve a correspondence between patient needs and service provision; the treatment of elders by the medical profession must change.
- Health and social services are increasingly needed where medicine has been used in the past. Both health and social care are needed to respond to many of the problems faced by Canadian seniors.
- It is clear that the current structure of health care in Canada is not yet fully prepared to meet the health needs of its aging population.

Questions to Consider

1. Why is Canada considered an aged nation? How does our experience compare with other countries?

2. What is population aging? How is it different from individual aging? What are the determinants of population aging? What are the determinants of individual aging?

3. Are the health needs of seniors being met by the current structure of health care in Canada? If not, why not?

4. Suppose that you were in an advisory position in Canada's Ministry of Health (or the provincial healthy ministry). What policy recommendations would you make to alleviate some of the challenges to the health-care system posed by population aging?

5. What are the reasons for the institutional focus of health care in Canada? What types of non-institutional alternatives are there, and how can these be integrated into the health delivery system?

Suggested Readings

Armstrong, P., and H. Armstrong. *Wasting Away: The Undermining of Canadian Health Care*. Toronto: Oxford University Press, 1996.

Chappell, N.L, L.A. Strain, and A.A. Blandford. *Aging and Health Care: A Social Perspective*. Toronto: Holt, Rinehart and Winston, 1986.

Foot, David K., with Daniel Stoffman. *Boom, Bust and Echo*. Toronto: Macfarlane Walter & Ross, 1996.

National Forum on Health. *Canada Health Action: Building on the Legacy*. 2 Vols. Ottawa: Minister of Works and Government Services, 1997.

Novak, M. *Aging and Society: A Canadian Perspective*, 2d ed. Toronto: Nelson, 1993.

Glossary

ageism A form of prejudice among the young against the elderly.

iatrogenesis The process in which treatment by doctors results in illness.

old age dependency ratio The ratio of persons 65 years and older to those in the labour force.

population aging The progressive aging of a population.

population pyramid A graphical depiction of the population of any country. It shows the age and sex structure of a population, with two sets of bar graphs laid back to back.

reformist reforms Reforms that provide small material improvements while leaving intact overall political and economic structures; in other words, reformist reforms help to preserve the system. They are contrasted with *non-reformist (revolutionary) reforms*, which do not merely modify material conditions, but achieve long-term changes in structures of power and finance, and expose and highlight structural inequities.

Notes

1. A few of the common myths about aging include (1) that elders are unhappy, lonely, and live in isolation; (2) that elders are, by definition, sick; (3) that elders are traumatized by retirement and the loss of economic, social, and familial roles; (4) that elders' interest in sexual activity passes with their age—indeed, that elders are sexless; (5) that elders are set in their ways; and (6) that elders are doomed to senility (Chappell, Strain, and Blandford 1986).
2. Although the federal government planned to use the CHST to reduce spending in the period between 1998 and 2000, its February 1998 budget indicates that funding levels will be maintained at the 1997–98 level, without further reductions.
3. Mobility disabilities include trouble walking 400 metres, trouble walking up and down stairs, trouble carrying a 5 kilogram object, trouble moving from room to room, and trouble standing for 20 minutes. Agility disabilities include trouble bending to pick up objects, trouble dressing and undressing, trouble getting in and out of bed, trouble cutting one's toenails, trouble grasping or handling things, and trouble cutting one's food (Raina, Dukeshire, and Lindsay 1997).

References

Arluke, A., and J. Peterson. 1981. "Accidental Medicalization of Old Age and its Social Control Implications." In *Dimensions: Aging, Culture and Health*, ed. C.L. Fry. New York: Praeger. 271–84.

Armstrong, P., and H. Armstrong. 1996. *Wasting Away*. Toronto: Oxford University Press.

Balint, E., and J.S. Norell. 1973. *Six Minutes for the Patient: Interactions in General Practice Consultation*. London: Tavistock.

Barber, J. 1989. "Sick to Death." *Maclean's*, February 13: 32–35.

Barer, M.L., R.G. Evans, C. Hertzman, and J. Lomas. 1987. "Aging and Health Care Utilization: New Evidence on Old Fallacies." *Social Science and Medicine* 24: 851–62.

Basen, M.A. 1977. "The Elderly and Drugs: Problem Overview and Program Strategy." *Public Health Reports* 92: 43–48.

Beck, R.G. 1973. "Economic Class and Access to Physician Services Under Public Medical Care Insurance." *International Journal of Health Services* 3: 341–55.

———. 1974. "The Effects of Co-payments on the Poor." *Journal of Human Resources* 9: 129–42.

Becker, M.H., ed. 1974. *The Health Belief Model and Personal Health Behavior*. Thorofare, NJ: Charles B. Slack.

Branch, L.G., A. Sager, and A.R. Meyers. 1987. "Long-Term Care in the United States: A Study in Trench Warfare." In *Health in Aging: Sociological Issues and Policy Directions*, ed. R.A. Ward and S.S. Tobin. New York: Springer. 215–32.

Brody, J.A. 1989. "Toward Quantifying the Health of the Elderly." *American Journal of Public Health* 79: 685–86.

Brody, J.A., D.B. Brock, and T.F. Williams. 1987. "Trends in the Health of the Elderly Population." *Annual Review of Public Health* 8: 211–34.

Butler, R.N. 1969. "Age-ism: Another Form of Bigotry." *The Gerontologist* 9: 243–46.

———. 1980. "Ageism: A Foreword." *Journal of Social Issues* 36: 8–11.

Carson, R.A. 1977. "Stereotyping, Segregating and Stigmatizing the Old." In *Social Issues in Health Care*, ed. D.J. Self. Norfolk, VA: Teagle and Little. 52–63.

Centre on Aging. 1996. *Manitoba Fact Book on Aging*. Winnipeg: University of Manitoba.

Chappell, N.L. 1987. "The Interface among Three Systems of Care: Self, Informal and Formal." In *Health in Aging: Sociological Issues and Policy Directions*, ed. R.A. Ward and S.S. Tobin. New York: Springer. 159–79.

———. 1988. "Long-Term Care in Canada." In *North American Elders: United States and Canadian Perspectives*, ed. E. Rathbone-McCuan and B. Havens. New York: Greenwood Press. 73–88.

Chappell, N.L., and B. Havens. 1980. "Old and Female: Testing the Double Jeopardy Hypothesis." *The Sociological Quarterly* 21: 157–71.

Chappell, N.L., L.A. Strain, and A.A. Blandford. 1986. *Aging and Health Care: A Social Perspective*. Toronto: Holt, Rinehart and Winston.

Cooperstock, R. 1971. "Sex Differences in the Use of Mood-Modifying Drugs: An Exploratory Model." *Journal of Health and Social Behavior* 12: 238.

Cranswick, K. 1997. "Canada's Caregivers." <http://www.hc-sc.gc.ca/datahpsb/seniors/seniors/pubs/survey.htm>.

Cyrus-Lutz, C., and C.M. Gaitz. 1972. "Psychiatrists' Attitudes toward the Aged and Aging." *The Gerontologist* 12: 163–67.

Denton, F.T., and B.G. Spencer. 1996. "Population Aging and the Maintenance of Social Support Systems." IESOP Research Paper No. 9, McMaster University.

Dorney, R.P. 1983. "Old Age and Long Term Care in the U.S.A." Unpublished manuscript, Department of Sociology, Boston University.

Dulude, L. 1978. *Women and Aging: A Report on the Rest of Our Lives*. Ottawa: Canadian Advisory on the Status of Women.

Estes, C.L., L.E. Gerard, and A. Clarke. 1984. "Women and the Economics of Aging." *International Journal of Health Services* 14: 55–68.

Evans, R.G. 1984. *Strained Mercy: The Economics of Canadian Health Care*. Toronto: Butterworths.

Federal, Provincial and Territorial Advisory Committee on Population Health. 1996. *Report on the Health of Canadians*. <http://www.hc-sc.gc.ca/hppb/nhrdp/healthofcanadians/cont-e.htm>.

Foot, D.K. with D. Stoffman. 1996. *Boom, Bust and Echo*. Toronto: Macfarlane Walter and Ross.

Forbes, W.F., J.A. Jackson, and A.S. Kraus. 1987. *Institutionalization of the Elderly in Canada*. Toronto: Butterworths.

Ford, C.V., and R.J. Sbordone. 1980. "Attitudes of Psychiatrists toward Elderly Patients." *American Journal of Psychiatry* 137: 571–75.

Garnick, D.W., and T. Short. 1985. *Utilization of Hospital Inpatient Services by Elderly Americans*. Hospital Studies Program, Hospital Cost Utilization Project Research Note 6. Washington, DC: U.S. Department of Health and Human Services (PHS Pub. No. 85-3351).

German, P.S., and L.C. Burton. 1989. "Medication and the Elderly: Issues of Prescription and Use." *Journal of Aging and Health* 1: 4–34.

Goffman, E. 1961. *Asylums*. New York: Anchor Books.

Grant, K.R. 1984. "Clinical Decision-Making as Social Triage: The Influence of Non-biomedical Factors on Physician Behavior." Unpublished manuscript, Department of Sociology, Boston University.

———. 1988. "The Inverse Care Law in Canada: Differential Access under Universal Free Health Insurance." In *Sociology of Health Care in Canada*, ed. B.S. Bolaria and H.D. Dickinson. Toronto: Harcourt Brace Jovanovich. 118–34.

———. 1989. *Lifestyle, Gender and Health: An Examination of the Canada Health Survey*. Unpublished Doctoral Dissertation, Department of Sociology, Boston University.

Gubrium, J. 1985. *Living and Dying and Murray Manor*. New York: St. Martin's Press.

Guralnik, J.M., and G.A. Kaplan. 1989. "Predictors of Healthy Aging: Prospective Evidence from the Alameda County Study." *American Journal of Public Health* 79: 703–708.

Harding, J. 1986. "Mood-Modifiers and Elderly Women in Canada: The Medicalization of Poverty." In *Adverse Effects: Women and the Pharmaceutical Industry*, ed. K. McDonnell. Toronto: Women's Press. 51–86.

Hatcher, G.H. 1981. *Universal Free Health Care in Canada, 1947–1977*. Washington, DC: U.S. Department of Health and Human Services (NIH Pub. No. 81-2052).

Haug, M.R., and M.G. Ory. 1987. "Issues in Elderly Patient–Provider Interactions." *Research on Aging* 9: 3–44.

Health Canada. 1997. *Canada's Health System*. <http://www.hc-sc.gc.ca/datapcb/datahesa/hlthsys/Ehlthsys.htm>.

Hickey, R., W. Rakowski, D.F. Hultsch, and B.J. Fatula. 1976. "Attitudes toward Aging as a Function of In-Service Training and Practitioner Age." *Journal of Gerontology* 31: 681–86.

Hoppel, C.L. "The Uses and Misuses of Pharmacology." In *The Physical and Mental Health of Aged Women*, ed. M.R. Haug, A.B. Ford, and M. Sheafor. New York: Springer. 207–16.

Institute for Philosophy and Public Policy. 1988. "The Graying of America." *Report of the Institute for Philosophy and Public Policy* 8: 1–5.

Kandrack, M-A., K.R. Grant, and A. Segall. 1991. "Gender Differences in Health Related Behaviour: Some Unanswered Questions." *Social Science and Medicine* 32: 579–90.

Karasu, T.B., S.P. Stein, and E.S. Charles. 1979. "Age Factors in Patient–Therapist Relationship." *Journal of Nervous and Mental Disease* 167: 100–104.

Keeler, E.B., D.H. Solomon, J.C. Beck, R.C. Mendenhall, and R.L. Kane. 1982. "Effect of Patient Age on Duration of Medical Encounters." *Medical Care* 20: 1101–1108.

Kent, T. 1997. "Medicare: How to Keep and Improve it, Especially for Children." <http://www.cyberplus.ca/~caledon/full83.htm>.

Lexchin, J. 1988. "Profits First: The Pharmaceutical Industry in Canada." In *Sociology of Health Care in Canada*, ed. B.S. Bolaria and H.D. Dickinson. Toronto: Harcourt Brace Jovanovich. 497–513.

Linn, B.S., and M.W. Linn. 1982. "Patient Symptoms and Physician Prescribing Patterns in the Elderly." *Social Science and Medicine* 16: 1531–38.

Longino, C.F. Jr., and B.J. Soldo. 1987. "The Graying of America: Implications of Life Extension for Quality of Life." In *Health in Aging: Sociological Issues and Policy Directions*, ed. R.A. Ward and S.S. Tobin. New York: Springer. 58–85.

Lopata, H.Z., ed. 1987. *Widows, Volume II: North America*. Durham, NC: Duke University Press.

Macintyre, S. 1977. "Old Age as a Social Problem: Historical Notes on the English Experience." In *Health Care and Health Knowledge*, ed. R. Dingwall, C. Heath, M. Reid, and M. Stacey. London: Croom Helm. 41–63.

Macleod, L., and Associates. 1997. *Toward Health—Aging Communities: A Population Health Approach*. Ottawa: Division of Aging and Seniors, Health Canada.

Marshall, V.M. 1987. "Older Patients in Acute-Care Hospital Setting." In *Health in Aging: Sociological Issues and Policy Directions*, ed. R.A. Ward and S.S. Tobin. New York: Springer. 194–208.

Martin Matthews, A. 1987. "Widowhood as an Expectable Life Event." In *Aging in Canada: Social Perspectives*, 2d ed., ed. V.M. Marshall. Toronto: Fitzhenry and Whiteside. 343–66.

McDaniel, S.A. 1986. *Canada's Aging Population*. Toronto: Butterworths.

———. 1988. "Getting Older and Better: Women and Gender Assumptions in Canada's Aging Society." *Feminist Perspectives* 11, Canadian Research Institute for the Advancement of Women.

———. 1989. "An Aging Canada: Sandwich and Caregiver Dilemmas." *Perspectives: Journal of Gerontological Nursing Association* 12, no. 2: 15–18.

McKeown, T. 1979. *The Role of Medicine: Dream, Mirage or Nemesis?* Oxford: Basil Blackwell.

McKinlay, J.B. 1972. "Some Approaches and Problems in the Study of the Use of Services: An Overview." *Journal of Health and Social Behavior* 13: 115.

McKinlay, J.B., S.M. McKinlay, S.E. Jennings, and K.R. Grant. 1983. "Mortality, Morbidity and the Inverse Care Law." In *Cities and Sickness: Health Care in Urban America*, ed. A.L. Greer and S. Greer. Beverly Hills, CA: Sage. 99–138.

Mills, C.W. 1959. *The Sociological Imagination*. New York: Oxford University Press.

National Advisory Council on Aging. 1993. *Aging Vignettes #1–#20*. Ottawa: National Advisory Council on Aging.

———. 1996. *Aging Vignettes #21–#33*. Ottawa: National Advisory Council on Aging.

National Council of Welfare. 1984. *Sixty-Five and Older: A Report of the National Council of Welfare on the Incomes of the Aged*. Ottawa: Minister of Supply and Services.

National Forum on Health. 1997. *Canada Health Action: Building on the Legacy*. 2 vols. Ottawa: Minister of Public Works and Government Services.

Nett, E.M., ed. 1982. "Women as Elders." *Resources for Feminist Research* 11 (Special Issue).

Norland, J.A. 1994. *Profil des personnes âgées au Canada*. Ottawa: Minister of Public Works and Government Services. Cat. No. 96-312F.

Novak, M. 1988. *Aging and Society: A Canadian Perspective*. Toronto: Nelson Canada.

Pascarelli, E.F. 1974. "Drug Dependence: An Age-Old Problem Compounded by Old Age." *Geriatrics* 29: 109–15.

Paul, A. 1998. "The Rise and Fall of Medicare." *Winnipeg Free Press*, April 12: A6.

Posner, J. 1977. "Old and Female: The Double Whammy." *Essence* 2: 41–48.

Raina, P., S. Dukeshire, and J. Lindsay. 1997. "Prevalence, Risk Factors, and Primary Causes of Disability among Canadian Seniors: An Analysis of the 1986 and 1991 Health and Activity Limitation Surveys." IESOP Research Paper No. 11, McMaster University.

Ray, D.C., M.A. Raciti, and C.V. Ford. 1985. "Ageism in Psychiatrists: Associations with Gender, Certification, and Theoretical Orientation." *The Gerontologist* 25: 496–500.

Reinharz, S. 1986. "Friends or Foes: Gerontological and Feminist Theory." *Women's Studies International Forum* 9: 503–14.

Reissman, C.K. 1983. "Women and Medicalization: A New Perspective." *Social Policy* 14: 3–18.

Rodin, J., and E. Langer. 1980. "Aging Labels: The Decline of Control and the Fall of Self-Esteem." *Journal of Social Issues* 36: 12–29.

Roos, N.P., E. Shapiro, and L.L. Roos. 1984. "Aging and the Demand for Health Services." *The Gerontologist* 24: 31–36.

Russell, C. 1987. "Ageing as a Feminist Issue." *Women's Studies International Forum* 10: 125–32.

Sandelowski, M. 1981. *Women, Health, and Choice*. Englewood Cliffs, NJ: Prentice-Hall.

Sarton, M. 1973. *As We Are Now*. New York: W.W. Norton.

Schwenger, C.W. 1987. "Formal Health Care for the Elderly in Canada." In *Aging in Canada: Social Perspectives*, 2d ed., ed., V.M. Marshall. Toronto: Fitzhenry and Whiteside. 505–19.

Shapiro, E., and N.P. Roos. 1986. "High Users of Hospital Days." *Canadian Journal on Aging* 5: 165–74.

Shapiro, E., and R.B. Tate. 1985. "Predictors of Long Term Care Facility Use among the Elderly." *Canadian Journal on Aging* 4: 11–19.

Sontag, S. 1972. "The Double Standard of Aging." *Saturday Review* 55: 29–38.

Spence, D.L., E.M. Feigenbaum, F. Fitzgerald, and J. Roth. 1968. "Medical Student Attitudes toward the Geriatric Patient." *Journal of the American Geriatrics Society* 16: 976–83.

Statistics Canada. 1981. *The Health of Canadians: Report of the Canada Health Survey*. Ottawa: Minister of Supply and Services.

———. 1986. *Age, Sex, and Marital Status*. Ottawa: Minister of Supply and Services. Cat. No. 93-101-1986. Table 1-13.

———. 1987. *Health and Social Support, 1985*. No. 1. Ottawa: Minister of Supply and Services. Cat. No. 11-612.

———. 1988. *Canada Year Book 1988*. Ottawa: Minister of Supply and Services.

———. 1990. *Canada Year Book 1990*. Ottawa: Minister of Supply and Services.

———. 1992. *Age, Sex, and Marital Status*. Ottawa: Minister of Supply and Services. Cat. No. 93-101-1992. Table 1-13.

Stone, L.O., and S. Fletcher. 1986. *The Seniors Boom: Dramatic Increases in Longevity and Prospects for Better Health*. Ottawa: Minister of Supply and Services.

———. 1988. "Demographic Variations in North America." In *North American Elders: United States and Canadian Perspectives*, ed. E. Rathbone-McCuan and B. Havens. New York: Greenwood Press. 9–36.

Swartz, D. 1987. "Conflict and Accommodation in Canadian Health Policy." In *Health and Canadian Society*, 2d ed., ed. D. Coburn, C. D'Arcy, G.M. Torrance, and P. New. Toronto: Fitzhenry and Whiteside. 568–89.

Torrance, G.M. 1981. "Socio-Historical Overview: The Development of the Canadian Health System." In *Health and Canadian Society*, ed. D. Coburn, C. D'Arcy, P. New, and G. Torrance. Toronto: Fitzhenry and Whiteside. 9–28.

Tudor Hart, J. 1971. "The Inverse Care Law." *The Lancet* 1: 405–12.

Ulysse, P.-J. 1997. "*Population Aging: An Overview of the Past Thirty Years*." Ottawa: Division of Aging and Seniors, Health Canada.

Urquhart, M.C., and K.A.H. Buckley, eds. 1983. *Historical Statistics of Canada*, 2d ed. Ottawa: Statistics Canada.

Verbrugge, L.M. 1985. "An Epidemiological Profile of Older Women." In *The Physical and Mental Health of Aged Women*, ed. M.R. Haug and A.B. Ford. New York: Springer. 41–64.

———. 1986. "From Sneezes to Adieux: Stages of Health for American Men and Women." *Social Science and Medicine* 22: 1195–1212.

Waitzkin, H. 1983. *The Second Sickness: Contradictions of Capitalist Health Care*. New York: Free Press.

Waldron, I. 1976. "Why Do Women Live Longer Than Men?" *Social Science and Medicine* 10: 349–62.

Wingard, D.L. 1984. "The Sex Differential in Morbidity, Mortality and Lifestyle." *Annual Review of Public Health* 5: 433–58.

Zola, I.K. 1986. "Medicine as an Institution of Social Control." In *Sociology of Health and Illness: Critical Perspectives*, 2d ed., ed. P. Conrad and R. Kern. New York: St. Martin's Press. 379–90.

CHAPTER 15

Social Dimensions of Mental Illness

James Stolzman

Learning Objectives

After studying this chapter, you should be able to
- Appreciate the difference between sociological and psychological analyses of mental disorder.
- Compare and contrast the medical conception of mental disorder as a biophysical state and the sociological conception of mental disorder as a social state.
- Understand how extra-scientific factors (e.g., politics and public relations) figured in the rise and consolidation of the medical model of mental illness.
- Explain how psychiatric diagnoses of mental disorders depend upon cultural norms, social standards of normality, and contextual factors.
- Identify both the contributions and the limitations of the **labelling perspective** on mental illness.
- Understand how culture and social structure are sources of social stress that help explain the social patterning of mental disorder.
- Explain the relationships between social stress, psychological distress, and mental disorder.

Introduction

It is widely acknowledged that mental illness is a serious social problem in contemporary society. Reliable figures on the number of people suffering from mental disorder are difficult to calculate for a number of reasons. Foremost among these is the fact that mental health statistics are based on treatments administered by psychologists and psychiatrists. However, we have learned from numerous community studies that many persons with psychological problems go undetected and unreported either because they receive no professional treatment or because they obtain help outside the mental health system—from friends, relatives, co-workers, members of the clergy, spiritual guides, and so on. Another factor confounding efforts to arrive at valid estimates of the **true prevalence** of mental disorder is the fact that many mental or emotional problems manifest themselves as physical ailments. Doctors in general practice report that approximately 20 percent or more of their patients present symptoms such as back pain, headaches, or difficulty in breathing for which they can find no organic cause. While they are typically not classified as such, it is probable that a substantial portion of these complaints would be diagnosed by psychiatrists as psychosomatic disorders.

There is, then, good reason to believe that the actual rate of persons having some kind of mental illness is considerably greater than is indicated by official statistics. Nevertheless, Statistics Canada (1981) estimates that one out of every eight Canadians can expect to be treated for a mental disorder at least once during his or her lifetime. According to the Canadian Mental Health Association, psychiatric problems affect more Canadians annually than all other health problems combined, including cancer and heart disease. The social costs of this problem are often expressed in terms of the large number of aggregate work days lost due to illness and the enormous expenditures required to treat and service the mentally ill. To be sure, these are valid indicators, but as William Cockerham has observed, any full accounting of the costs of mental illness needs to include what is arguably its most damaging consequence—namely, "its shattering effect upon the lives of its victims and their families" (1996, 2). These dimensions of the problem are not easily measured, but as anyone whose life has been touched by mental illness will readily attest, the torment, anguish, embarrassment, and despair attending mental disorders is indeed substantial.

Although it is commonly acknowledged to be a terrible and tragic problem in today's society, mental illness is seldom viewed as a social phenomenon. For most of this century accounts of mental illness have emphasized its psychological elements. Sigmund Freud and psychoanalysis helped make popular the image of mental illness as an expression of an impaired mind. In recent decades biological interpretations of mental illness have gained prominence. Modern psychiatry and neuroscience have pointed to evidence that genetic factors and/or chemical imbalances in the brain are the underlying cause of schizophrenia, manic depression, and other types of mental disorder.

I do not wish to dispute the reality or importance of either psychological or biological factors in mental illness. I take it as axiomatic that something is indeed wrong with the minds and/or bodies of individuals afflicted with mental disorders. However, acceptance of this proposition does not mean that factors falling outside the realm of biology and psychology are therefore insignificant. In this chapter I will attempt to advance the argument that social factors are also fundamental to any comprehensive understanding of mental disorder. I will contend that people do not become mentally ill in a vacuum; it is rather a profoundly social experience that is conditioned and shaped in myriad ways by features of the social context within which it occurs. In the sections that follow, I will begin by discussing how social factors figure in the very nature of what we mean by mental disorder. I will then examine the prevailing medical view of mental illness as a modern socio-cultural construct. Next I will consider the influence of social factors in psychiatric diagnosis and the labelling of mental illness in everyday life. The chapter will conclude with a discussion of the relationship between social stress and patterns of mental disorder.

Social Evaluations and the Nature of Mental Disorder

It may not surprise you to learn that there is no consensus among scholars and clinicians about the causes of mental disorder. If you suspected that there exist a number of competing explanations—each with its own champions, pet theories, and research studies that seem to confirm its view of mental disorder—you would be absolutely right. This situation is not especially unusual in the study of human behaviour, nor is it necessarily a deterrent to the advance of knowledge. Controversy and debate among proponents of rival ideas often motivate scholars to clarify issues and to devise studies that yield better answers to the questions that divide them. In the case of mental disorder, however, we are talking about a more fundamental kind of disagreement. As Morris Rosenberg (1992) has recently observed, an extraordinary fact about mental disorder is that, despite all the years of attention they have paid to it, experts are unable to agree about its essential features or defining characteristics. Perhaps this is because there is no single trait that distinguishes the sane from the insane, nor any one property that is common to all the various types of disorders. At any rate, scholarly opinion about the nature of mental disorder is not merely divided, it is in total disarray. In Rosenberg's words, "What is noteworthy about mental illness is the fact that there are so many different ideas about what it is" (1992, 1).

The Psychiatric Definition of Mental Disorder

The lack of agreement over the very nature of mental disorder has obviously hampered efforts to define the concept. For many years the psychiatric profession avoided this issue altogether. Significantly, before 1975 most of the standard textbooks and diagnostic manuals used to train psychiatrists did not define mental disorder (Cockerham 1996, 4). In the 1970s the American Psychiatric Association commissioned a task force to remedy this deficiency prior to publication of the third edition of its *Diagnostic and Statistical Manual of Mental Disorders* (DSM-III) in 1980. The following three-part definition of mental disorder resulted from this endeavour:

1. It is a condition that is primarily psychological and that alters behavior, including changes in physiological functioning if such changes can be explained by psychological concepts, such as personality, motivation, or conflict.
2. It is a condition that in its "full-blown" state is regularly and intrinsically associated with subjective stress, generalized impairment in social functioning, or behavior that one would like to stop voluntarily because it is associated with threats to physical health.
3. It is a condition that is distinct from other conditions and that responds to treatment. (Spitzer and Wilson 1975, 829, as quoted in Cockerham 1996, 4)

What can one say about this definition? First of all, its length and cumbersomeness are probably related to the fact that it is the creation of a committee that was attempting to find a way to incorporate the diverse, if not divergent, views of the association's members in a coherent, all-encompassing statement. While laudable, this mission may have been achieved at the price of sacrificing cogency.

But I believe there is another reason why this convoluted definition fails to register an impression with us, and it pertains more to what it omits than to what it includes. Specifically, the psychiatric definition makes no mention of the quality of mental disorder that sociologists and anthropologists—as well as ordinary people in everyday life—tend to regard as its hallmark. All cultures appear to make a distinction between persons whose thoughts, emotions, and behaviour are judged to fall within a socially accepted range of "normality" and persons who exhibit unusual thoughts, emotions, or behaviour that place them outside the prevailing standards of normality. To be sure, societies can and do differ dramatically in the specific kinds of behaviour they deem to be acceptable or unacceptable. There is also tremendous variation in the belief systems cultures utilize to explain why some people's behaviour is abnormal. The point here, however, is that whatever it is that strikes them as aberrant and however they explain it, people in all societies distinguish between the sane and the insane. Moreover, they make this differentiation by assessing the extent to which certain kinds of behaviour either fit with, or deviate from, what is commonly regarded as normal in a particular culture or subculture. Persons whose behaviour is perceived to be inexplicably odd or bizarre run a high risk of being identified as insane.

It is precisely this dimension of socially defined "strangeness" that is missing in the psychiatric definition of mental disorder. The centrality of this notion in our own culture is evident in the colloquial expressions we use to denote mental illness—"nuts," "demented," "loony," "deranged," "crazy," "bonkers," and so on. These terms all convey a definite sense that the mentally ill are very different from ostensibly normal members of society. Embedded within such terms is of course the unfortunate social stereotype of the mentally disordered person as someone whose behaviour is irrational, unpredictable, incomprehensible, out of control, or dangerous. Like all stereotyped thinking, the harsh prejudgements contained in these categorical assumptions frequently turn out to be unfounded and unwarranted when applied to specific individuals. However, their durability and popularity in the face of such repeated refutation is a measure of how deeply held such ideas are in our society.

Biophysical and Social Conceptions of Illness

What, you may ask, does all of this have to do with the issue of how to adequately conceptualize the nature of mental disorder? To answer this question it may be useful to introduce a distinction the sociologist Eliot Freidson (1973) makes between illness as a "biophysical state" and illness as a "social state." In the former meaning, illness is a pathological condition of the body that impedes its normal functioning. Viewed in this manner, the pathology is conceived as an objective, material reality that is independent of how or what anybody thinks about it. Brain damage is thus a biophysical state; it exists regardless of whether the individual who suffered the injury acknowledges it or not, or what he or she or anyone else thinks or feels about it.

But, says Freidson, illness is also a social state. Calling something an illness has meanings and consequences independent of the biological condition of the body.

People's beliefs and feelings about illness do not negate the reality that a person's body is diseased. But whether what ails the person is defined and treated as an "illness" (as opposed to some other kind of phenomenon), and what these different responses mean to the person afflicted and those with whom he or she interacts, can be extremely consequential for what happens to that person. To quote Freidson:

> Consider two men in different societies, both with the same debilitating infection: in one case, the man is said to be ill, put to bed, and taken care of by others; in the other case, he is said to be lazy, and he is abused by others. The course and outcome of the disease may be the same biologically in both cases, but the social interplay between the sick man and others is significantly different.... While disease may be "there," it is what we, as social beings, think and do about it that determines the content of our lives. (1973, 208)

Most psychiatrists regard mental disorder as a biophysical state. For them mental disorder is a pathological mental condition, something that exists entirely within the mind or body of an individual person. What other people or the person who has the disorder happen to believe about his or her mental state is considered totally irrelevant to the issue of whether someone is mentally ill. The primary, if not sole, basis for making such a determination is whether or not the psychiatrist has reason to believe the person's mental functioning is impaired.

This conception of mental disorder has its critics, including several who are practising psychiatrists (e.g., Breggin 1991). All but a few of these challengers accept that many mental illnesses involve objective biological or physiological abnormalities. What they object to is the proposition that mental illness is *solely* a biophysical condition. They contend that mental illness is also a social state because sociological criteria are integral to who and what gets identified as mentally ill, and because the designation of mental illness embodies social meanings that significantly affect the fate of those so identified. I will amplify these points later in the chapter. More immediately, I want to direct your attention to how the image of insanity as illness arose historically in Western society.

Images of Mental Disorder as Cultural Constructions

Mental Disorder as Illness

The terms "mental illness" and "mental disorder" are often used interchangeably. This would be fine except, as we have just seen, some more contentious issues about the nature of mental disorder revolve around the implications and connotations of understanding it as an "illness." In my teaching and writing on this subject I prefer to use mental disorder instead of the more familiar mental illness, because I consider the latter a "loaded" concept. By this, I mean that its uncritical adoption tacitly prejudges an issue about which there exists a division of opinion. More specifically, the issue of whether psychiatric problems are essentially the same as, or different from, physical diseases is in fact a subject of debate. In the circumstance, referring to such problems as mental illness tends to lend support to those who argue in favour of similarity. By contrast, the concept of mental disorder has the virtue of being neutral; it avoids the implications that accompany the concept of illness without precluding the possibility that some or even all of those implications may be valid.

I of course realize that this debate over nomenclature is unknown to most people. Neither do I have any illusions that greater awareness of the issue would create many converts to my position. I harangue the students in my Sociology of Mental Disorders class on this score every year, yet most of them continue to use the term mental illness in their speech and writings. The widespread usage of the latter concept in both our society and worldwide is a telling indicator of which side is winning the terminology debate in the court of public opinion. It is no contest; people have been voting with their vocabulary and the clear victor is the view that mental disorders qualify as illness.

It should also be appreciated that mental illness is not an isolated, stand-alone concept. It derives much of its currency from its connection to a constellation of terms that together comprise a coherent image of the phenomenon of mental disorder. The vocabulary both professionals and laypersons in our society use when they are referring to mental problems is replete with terms originally associated with physical illness—"diagnosis," "patient," "pathology," "therapy," "symptom," "cure," and so on. Clearly, this language as well as the whole conception of the causes, course, and treatment of mental disorder derives from a medical idiom (Grusky and Pollner 1981, 24). The ideas informing this conception are commonly known as the **medical model of mental disorder**. According to this conception, mental problems can be understood and treated like diseases of the body. Mental illness is regarded like any other illness except that its characteristic "symptoms" consist of unusual thoughts, feelings, or behaviour rather than physical abnormalities. As with physical illness, the patient's symptoms are attributed to an underlying pathology that requires accurate diagnosis in order to be properly treated by medical means.

In one form or another the medical model has become securely established in the social organization of our mental health care system.[1] Moreover, the imagery of mental problems associated with this model is thoroughly ingrained in Western culture. The medical model of mental disorder is hegemonic; its tenets and assumptions are taken for granted and accepted as virtually self-evident truths. In the minds of most people, the medical model is not just one way of understanding mental disorder, it is *the* way. All of this lends the medical model an aura of naturalness. However, this paradigm is in fact a social construction of reality devised by individuals and groups of people in particular historical circumstances. The ideas that comprise the model have been developed and disseminated through a process of cultural transmission. Various elements of the model have undergone modification and revision as it has evolved over several generations. But as its principles are passed on from one generation to next through various agencies of socialization, its credibility is continually enhanced. Other possible ways of construing mental disorder increasingly strike people as wrongheaded. Thus it is perfectly understandable that as this process unfolds, members of society become ever more oblivious to the fact that these collectively shared views about mental disorder are learned cultural constructs. For this reason it may be instructive at this juncture to offer a brief historical overview of the rise and consolidation of the medical model of mental illness.

Madness as Demonic Deviance

Western medicine's involvement as a profession in the treatment and care of persons suffering from insanity did not begin in earnest until sometime in the late eighteenth century. Prior to this era, and especially during the Middle Ages, a very different image of what we would today call mental disorder prevailed. The Catholic Church was at the centre of life in medieval Europe and questions about human conduct were interpreted according to religious precepts. Supernatural forces were seen as responsible for "madness." The minds and bodies of the mad were thought to be in the grip of evil spirits, such as the Devil or witches. Pfohl (1994, 22) refers to this view as the **demonic perspective**. The strange behaviour of the mad was equated with sinfulness. As wicked sinners who had transgressed God's will, the mad were objects of extreme ridicule and scorn. At best, they were tolerated as harmless "fools" or amusing "village idiots." At worst, they were persecuted, tortured, and put to death. The witch hunts of the late Middle Ages in Europe and of the seventeenth century in the New England colonies no doubt represent the most tragic expression of the demonic perspective. A collective mania, born of religious fervour, led to the arrest and execution of thousands of people, mostly females, suspected of being witches. Scholars who have studied this grim episode of history tend to agree that, judged by today's standards, many of the victims of the witch hunts were mentally ill and others were nonconformists of sound mind whose "deviant" beliefs or actions were perceived as a threat to the established order.

By the dawn of the eighteenth century, which has come to be called the Enlightenment or Age of Reason, demonology was gradually rejected in favour of a more secular, progressive, and humane view of mental abnormality. It was during this era that the mad along with various other types of people considered to be social problems—vagrants, invalids, criminals, the "feeble-minded"—were rounded up and incarcerated in institutions that segregated them from the mainstream of society. By all accounts, the conditions in these asylums were appalling. The mad and other inmates were physically shackled in cold, dark, rat-infested dungeons that were layered with their own excrement. These institutions were essentially punitive and coercive; if they alleviated any of the residents' misery, it was not necessarily by design.

Asylum Reform and the Medicalization of Madness

The good news is that this sorry state of affairs generated a movement for reform of these institutions among humanitarians and other concerned citizens. One of these reforms was to take the mentally disturbed out of the prisons and jails and place them in separate institutions, usually called "lunatic asylums." Enlightened reformers—men like Chiarugi in Italy, Pinel in France, Tuke in England, and Rush in the United States—insisted that society must acknowledge and respect the basic human rights of persons suffering from madness. As a result of these reform measures, the chains and other methods of physically restraining patients were removed. Inmates were accorded greater freedom including opportunities for exercise and recreation. Sanitation of the asylums was improved. The reformers opposed various cruel institutional practices that had been imposed on the mad against their will. They called instead for a regimen based on "moral treatment"—which, as the phrase implies, meant treating the insane with sympathy, respect, and kindness.

Although some of them were called "hospitals," these early mental asylums were not really medical institutions. Most doctors who practised medicine in this era claimed no special expertise or competence for treating madness. This changed dramatically over the course of the nineteenth century. By century's end the medical profession had installed itself as society's legitimate authority on madness and its representatives were in charge of the institutions dedicated to caring for the insane. How medicine managed to achieve this position of dominance is contrary to what most people today might imagine. It is often presumed that physicians earned this status by virtue of the scientific superiority of their explanatory theories and methods of treatment. Conrad and Schneider (1980) have examined this issue and they offer a significantly different interpretation. These authors contend that the authority of the physicians is more a tribute to their political leadership than to their scientific acumen. Beginning with the efforts of aforementioned pioneers (Chiarugi, Pinel, and Rush were all physicians), medical doctors were everywhere in the vanguard of the asylum reform movement. As a result of their energy, dedication, and skills as leaders, they commonly became the superintendents of the reformed institutions.

As physicians took up the task of administering the new asylums, one upshot was that the medical profession gradually annexed responsibility for treatment of mental disorder to its traditional jurisdiction of physical illness. Conrad and Schneider do not fault them for this. The point of their thesis is rather that there was nothing particularly "medical" about either the theoretical understanding of mental disorder or the methods and programs these doctors/reformers/asylum directors developed to treat it. It is true that these men genuinely believed that future scientific and medical research would ultimately demonstrate that the causes of insanity are organic. Their immediate concern, however, was what to do about the growing problem of madness in the emerging industrial societies of their time. Paradoxically, their analysis of this question was essentially sociological. According to Conrad and Schneider, these men tended to share a conservative ideological perspective that attributed the increased incidence of madness and many other human problems to the decline of the traditional social order. It was their conviction that the combined forces of industrialization, secularization, and urbanization had uprooted people both physically and spiritually. In their view the new social order lacked community, stability, and moral cohesion; these features made it a fertile environment for insanity. Conrad and Schneider point out that this ideology also informed the rationale of the insane asylums they administered. These forerunners of modern psychiatry envisioned these institutions as a refuge from the harsh realities of life in industrial society. The asylums were designed to provide their inhabitants with what the larger society denied them—namely, security, routine, and discipline.

In sum, medicine's authority as the "gatekeepers" responsible for mental disorder initially derived from the instrumental role these doctors played in championing moral treatment and asylum reform. But it would take several decades before the medical profession actively promoted the medical interpretation of mental illness. Why was this? I have already suggested that their own commitment to this perspective was, at this early stage of their involvement, abstract and half-hearted. Conrad and Schneider point out that, even if the medical profession had been more inclined to champion an alternative view of madness, it did not originally possess the wherewithal to shape public opinion. Throughout most of the nineteenth century medicine was certainly a respected profession, but it did not have anything like the enormous prestige it subsequently enjoyed in this century. Its later triumph fostered hopes that medical knowledge might be applied to solve a variety of other human problems, a process aptly referred to as the "medicalization of life." The medical profession, usually with enthusiastic public support, has cast an ever wider net in tackling a broad range of human maladies that supposedly can be effectively addressed as "illnesses" requiring medical intervention. For example, persons society formerly considered to be "drunks" or "problem drinkers" are today viewed as afflicted with the disease of alcoholism. The list of behaviours believed to be amenable to medical treatment continues to lengthen.

The Drug Revolution and Public Acceptance of the Medical Model

The general trend toward medicalization clearly helped psychiatry redefine madness as mental illness. Efforts to portray mental disorder as a form of "sickness" have had to overcome widespread public scepticism about this new imagery. Attitude surveys consistently reveal that people's perceptions of the mentally ill are in key respects closer to their perceptions of the criminal than of the physically ill. Such resistance notwithstanding, I believe one can identify a turning point in the relatively recent past when proponents of the medical model scored a major breakthrough in winning public support for their views. This moment can be dated to the discovery and use of psychoactive medications to treat mental disorders.

The "drug revolution" in mental health care began on a limited scale in the 1950s and has steadily expanded ever since. The routine and wholesale prescription of tranquilizers, antidepressants, and antipsychotic medications to alleviate the symptoms of various mental disorders has been highly controversial. But I wish to submit that one consequence of this pharmacological revolution in psychiatry is indisputable: it has made the profession's case for conceiving psychological problems as "illnesses" far more compelling.

It should be remembered that prior to the advent of these medications, Western psychiatry and psychology were heavily influenced by Freudian psychoanalysis and sundry other approaches to mental disorder, many of which emphasized its social and psychological dimensions. Various forms of "talk therapies" were in vogue. Popular culture seized upon the psychoanalyst's couch as the symbol of what psychotherapy was all about. None of this really jibed with conventional notions of either illness or medical practice. The impact of drug therapies on popular consciousness stands in sharp contrast to this reaction. Psychiatry's critics are fond of observing that medications only relieve the symptoms of mental disorder; they do not eliminate or "cure" its underlying causes. This may be true, but it does not discount the fact that these drugs appear to make most patients feel better and act more "normal." Indeed, it is hard to imagine anything that could be more persuasive in selling the medical model to the public than observing doctors prescribe pills to their sick patients who, after ingesting them, generally get better. This by itself is a powerful message.

Other results of the drug revolution have added to the lustre of the medical model. For example, the use of medications has substantially reduced the number of persons with mental disorders who are treated in hospitals or other institutional settings. Admittedly, **deinstitutionalization** has generated a number of new problems in caring for the mentally ill (see Isaac and Armat 1990). This trend has enabled politicians, public administrators, and pharmaceutical companies to argue, quite plausibly, that these "miracle drugs" have not only saved taxpayers millions of dollars by emptying overcrowded hospitals, but, in the bargain, they have also permitted thousands of would-be patients to lead relatively normal lives in the community. All in all, then, the pharmacological revolution in psychiatry has been a spectacular public relations coup for advocates of the medical model of mental disorder. This success helped offset some unflattering publicity the profession had attracted as a result of difficulties encountered in the area of diagnosis. The next section offers an overview of some of the trials and tribulations of psychiatric assessment.

Social Factors in Psychiatric Diagnosis

The Radical Critique of Psychiatry

The basic objectives of psychiatric diagnosis are to determine whether or not a person has a mental disorder and, if so, to ascertain what type of disorder it is. Diagnosis is obviously crucial to the whole mental health care enterprise. To be effective, a treatment plan generally needs to be based on a proper assessment of the type and extent of a person's problems. But making an accurate judgement about somebody's mental condition is not always a simple or straightforward task. On the contrary, psychiatric diagnosis is a complicated venture fraught with hazards.

The perils and pitfalls of psychiatric assessment came to public attention in the 1960s and 1970s when psychiatry was a favourite target of political and cultural radicals. "Shrinks" were castigated as agents of social control and apologists for the status quo. The radicals' polemics often centred on psychiatry's dubious diagnostic standards and procedures. A common allegation was that, wittingly or unwittingly, the consequences of psychiatric diagnosis invariably tended to endorse dominant societal values. Western psychiatrists were likened to their counterparts in the Soviet Union, where large numbers of political dissidents were medically certified as mentally ill and incarcerated in mental institutions. In the West, psychiatry's complicity in serving the interests of established power was deemed to be less blatant, but thereby more insidious, than the Soviet example. Radicals and other critics of psychiatry charged that the profession's claims of scientific objectivity and political neutrality were a sham. Psychiatric theory and practice were said to be guilty of serious racial, gender, and class bias. The errors and prejudices of its diagnoses were seen as an expressions of the privileged social standing of the profession's members, who were overwhelmingly white, male, and affluent.

I might have added that most were heterosexual, since "exhibit A" in the case against psychiatry was the profession's position on homosexuality. Up until the early 1970s the American Psychiatric Association considered homosexuality a mental illness, and it was "officially" listed as such in earlier editions of the DSM. After years of protracted lobbying by (and occasional confrontations with) gay rights activists, in

1973 the APA's membership voted, after much rancorous debate, to declassify homo-sexuality as a mental disorder (Bayer 1986). Critics of the medical model generally applauded this decision, but were quick to add that everything about this controver-sy gave lie to psychiatry's claim that it was "value-free" and "above politics." As I have noted, the APA's struggle over this issue involved lobbying, debates, and con-frontations and was ultimately resolved by means of a vote! If the profession was hoping to persuade its critics that politics were not involved in medical judgements about illness, then this episode was a disaster of titanic proportions.

In fact, this whole period was a terrible one for psychiatry. Some of the most inci-sive and damning critiques of the psychiatric enterprise came from within the pro-fession's own ranks. The two most prominent mavericks were Thomas Szasz and R.D. Laing. Each produced influential works debunking many of the fundamental aims and assumptions of psychiatry (Szasz 1961; 1970; Laing 1969; Laing and Esterson 1970). Many radical academics, journalists, and non-medical psychothera-pists added their voices to the critique of psychiatry. The highly publicized "Rosenhan study" is a prime example of a wide-ranging body of literature whose point of view was aptly called **anti-psychiatry**. Writings expressing ideas critical of psychiatry and the medical model found a sizable and receptive audience in the 1960s and 1970s, a time when a number of other established institutions, values, and cul-tural practices were also subjected to radical scrutiny.

The combined effect of all these criticisms dealt a serious blow to the morale and confidence of the once-proud psychiatric profession. Kirk and Kutchins point out that the attacks were particularly threatening to psychiatrists because "they questioned the conceptual integrity of the entire enterprise" (1992, 22). In so doing, they raised fun-damentally troubling questions such as the following: "Did mental illness exist? What was its conceptual definition? On what basis could diagnostic judgements be made? Could psychiatrists recognize mental illness when it exists?"

Because its practitioners are trained in medicine and pride themselves on the sci-entific basis of their clinical work, the doubt cast on psychiatrists' ability to properly assess the nature of people's problems occasioned some serious individual and col-lective soul-searching within the profession. What, they pondered, was responsible for psychiatry's seeming inability to accurately recognize, identify, and classify mental illness when it occurred? Before we discuss where efforts to answer this ques-tion led the profession, I first want to review how sociologists and other critics ana-lyzed psychiatry's less than stellar performance with respect to diagnosis.

Diagnostic Bias and the Illusion of Objectivity

Sociologists tended to concur with exponents of "anti-psychiatry" that it was the pro-fession's rigid adherence to the medical model of insanity that caused or contributed to many of its diagnostic failings and missteps. Psychiatrists' conviction that mental and physical illness are equivalent led them to believe, erroneously in my opinion, that they could arrive at adequate judgements about the mental state of individual patients with-out regard to social standards and cultural norms. Moreover, psychiatrists' medical training predisposes them to seriously underestimate how the social context within

The Rosenhan Study

In 1973, an article titled "On Being Sane in Insane Places" appeared in the respected journal *Science*. It was authored by an American psychologist named David Rosenhan. The article presents and discusses the results of a bold experiment Rosenhan designed to see what would happen if normal people sought to gain admission to mental hospitals. Would psychiatrists be able to distinguish between the sane and the insane? In this study, eight of Rosenhan's research associates, all of whom had no history of psychiatric problems, agreed to seek admission to twelve different mental hospitals by falsely reporting a single symptom—that they had heard a voice that seemed to be saying something like "empty," "hollow," or "thud." They did not use their real names and those who were mental health professionals claimed other occupations. Otherwise they answered the hospital staff's questions about their personal histories and circumstances truthfully. The eight "pseudopatients" were admitted to the twelve hospitals without exception. All were judged to be severely disordered; one was diagnosed as manic depressive, the other eleven as schizophrenic. Once admitted, their instructions were to stop pretending they heard voices and to fake no other symptoms. They were urged to "act normal" and to co-operate with the wishes of the staff, except for swallowing the medications. A stipulation for participating in the experiment was that Rosenhan's collaborators had to remain in hospital until they "earned" discharges by displaying behaviour that convinced the staff they were sane. All of them managed to eventually get released, after stays in the hospital ranging from 7 to 52 days, with a diagnosis of schizophrenia "in remission." None of the eight were detected as imposters by any of the psychiatrists or other hospital personnel, but in several instances some of the real patients voiced suspicions that they were "faking it."

The article also makes mention of a second, separate experiment conducted after the premise and general results of the first were known to members of the mental health community. In the "sequel," Rosenhan led the staff at a psychiatric hospital not included in the original study to believe that one or more pseudopatients would seek admission to their institution over the next few months. Afterward Rosenhan asked them to try to identify which of their patients were bogus. Judgements were obtained on 193 patients admitted during the intervening period. Each hospital staff member who had sustained contact with a patient was asked to rate the likelihood that he or she was in fact a pseudopatient. At least one staff member expressed a high degree of confidence that 41 of the 193 patients were planted by Rosenhan; 23 of these patients were strongly suspected by both a psychiatrist and one other staff member. In fact, the whole scenario was a ruse; none of the patients admitted were Rosenhan confederates.

Rosenhan's study created quite a stir. For the most part it was a hit with sociologists and critics of the medical model. The article has become a classic in these circles; indeed, it is one of the most reprinted, cited, and discussed scholarly articles of twentieth-century social science. The study is perhaps equally well known to psychiatrists and psychologists, but this is because many of them considered it outrageous. Their critiques of the study mostly centred on its ethics and research methodology. Some of these criticisms were, in my opinion, valid. One can find flaws in the design and execution of these experiments, although

(continued)

(continued)

this is true of most social science research. Moreover, Rosenhan's reliance on deception in the conduct of the study would likely contravene ethical guidelines for research that have since been adopted by most professional associations. But the excessively hostile tone and vitriolic language of his detractors suggests that their objections were really about something else. Rosenhan clearly touched a nerve with many psychiatrists and other mental-health professionals. My reading of their irate reaction to the study is that they felt its conclusions were an indictment of both their competence and their professionalism, even though Rosenhan explicitly stated that this was not his belief. Unfortunately, this interpretation caused many of the study's critics to completely miss Rosenhan's points regarding the importance of contextual factors in diagnosis.

Source: Based on a reading of David Rosenhan, "On Being Sane in Insane Places," in *Labeling Madness*, ed. T. Scheff (Englewood Cliffs, NJ: Prentice Hall, 1975), pp. 54–74.

which diagnosis takes place can significantly influence one's perception and judgement. Like physicians practising in other branches of medicine, psychiatrists approach diagnosis as a technical, science-based procedure. Medical education does not appear to sensitize physicians to the proposition that diagnosis is itself a social activity subject to many of the same constraints and influences as "ordinary" behaviour. Below I will try to indicate how these proclivities and blind spots made the profession vulnerable to the charges of bias and political partisanship.

Beginning with his classic treatise, *The Myth of Mental Illness*, first published in 1961, Szasz has argued that it is fallacious for psychiatrists to think that diagnosing mental disorders is purely a matter of assessing whether the patient's symptoms satisfy or fail to satisfy certain objective criteria. This is possible with symptoms of physical illness because physicians can refer to objective measures and benchmarks of what constitutes health. When a doctor suspects illness because a patient displays, say, a fever or high blood pressure, the judgement is not a subjective one, nor is the standard of health or normality against which these symptoms are measured arbitrary. According to Szasz, the same cannot be claimed for most psychiatric symptoms and clinical judgements about mental illness. Where disorders of the mind are concerned, what qualifies as a symptom and the criteria for establishing what is "normal" typically depend on knowledge of factors external to the "diagnosee"—namely, cultural norms and the evaluations of persons with whom he or she interacts. Deciding whether someone's behaviour is, for example, "irrational," "compulsive," or "manic" and whether or not such behaviour is symptomatic of a disorder or illness is partly a subjective undertaking that necessarily requires attention to factors whose locus is neither the mind nor the body of the person being examined. Szasz's writings contain many examples that underscore this point. One of these has been nicely summarized by Cockerham. In the passage below he describes how Szasz dissects the logic involved in ascertaining whether or not someone is "delusional."

> Szasz says that a man's belief that he is Napoleon or is being persecuted by the Communists cannot be explained by a defect or disease of the nervous

system. Statements such as these are considered to be mental symptoms only if the observer (the audience) believes that the patient is not Napoleon or is not being persecuted by the Communists. Thus the statement that X is a symptom of a mental disorder includes a social judgment. The observer must match the person's ideas and beliefs to those held by the observer and the rest of society. In other words, a person's behavior is judged by how well his or her actions "fit" a concept of normality held by a social audience. (Cockerham 1996, 86–87)

Conventional psychiatrists justify ignoring the "social audience" in making diagnoses on two grounds. The first, to reiterate, is that what others think about the behaviour of the person examined is extraneous, since the illness presumably resides entirely in his or her mind and/or body. The second justification follows from this and, curiously, is aimed at preventing exactly the kinds of biases and value judgements of which the profession has been repeatedly accused. To elaborate, psychiatrists appear to believe that restricting diagnosis to evaluation of the patient's mental and physical condition is a means of avoiding judgements based on the physician's personal values or society's dominant ideology. The task of assessing whether a patient is sick or well is thought to be strictly a clinical issue; it supposedly does not matter whether the physician or society approves or disapproves of how the patient thinks, acts, or feels. Excluding social evaluations and other social factors is said to be in keeping with the scientific character and mandate of psychiatry. It is simply assumed by medical practitioners that commitment to the methods of science facilitates objectivity and minimizes the possibility of bias, error, and distortion. Ironically, the profession's uncritical adoption of procedures that had been proven successful in diagnosing physical illness seem to have had the opposite, albeit unintended, effect when applied to the assessment of mental disorders.

Why has the conventional strategy backfired? If Szasz and other critics of the medical model are correct, examination of the extent to which a patient's thoughts, emotions, or behaviour correspond with culturally defined standards of normality is intrinsic to proper psychiatric assessment. Ruling consideration of such factors out of bounds because they are supposedly extraneous does not make them go away or diminish their importance. Instead I would argue that it creates a situation where unarticulated value assumptions enter the diagnostic process through the back door, uninvited.

Put another way, if it is true that mental illness is inherently defined in terms of some standard of normality, decreeing that society's standards are irrelevant does not make it possible to arrive at diagnoses that do without any conception of normality. It merely permits and fosters the illusion that social evaluations are not implicated in psychiatric assessment. In the absence of explicit standards, implicit notions of normality operate as the baseline from which the mental state of patients is evaluated. Not surprisingly, under the circumstances these implicit, unarticulated standards usually turn out, upon inspection, to reflect either the personal views of the psychiatrist and/or the prevailing values of the larger society. This is why I believe it is fair to conclude that adoption of the medical model has been more of an inducement than a deterrent to biased, value-laden diagnoses of psychological problems. On the other hand, the aura and trappings of science that surround mental illness designations effectively camouflage and legitimate the fiction that standards and procedures for judging psychiatric impairment are essentially the same as those involved in assessing physical ailments.

Contextual Factors and Psychiatric Assessment

The notorious Rosenhan study highlighted another reason why diagnosis has proven to be so vexing for the psychiatric profession. The medical orientation and training of psychiatrists incline them to believe that diagnosis is a passive technical process in which the goal is to accurately assess the patient's mental condition by determining whether or not impairment is present, and if it is, identifying the type of illness responsible for its particular presenting symptoms. It follows from this definition of the situation, wherein the pathology or illness is purportedly an objective property of the patient's mind/body, that, in Rosenhan's words, "the salient characteristics that lead to diagnoses reside in the patients themselves" (1975, 5). In other words, psychiatric diagnoses proceed on the assumption that what the psychiatrist sees are objective symptoms that, correctly interpreted, define and signify the patient's condition.

Given this understanding of diagnosis, it is little wonder that psychiatrists were embarrassed and outraged by Rosenhan's finding that they could not reliably distinguish between the sane and the insane. It also helps to explain why so many of them apparently missed the whole point of these experiments. Rosenhan challenged their supposition that there are only two salient variables governing diagnostic outcomes—namely, patients who either have or don't have a disordered mind and psychiatrists who either do or don't have the skills, training, and insight to adequately evaluate the patients' mental state. The burden of Rosenhan's own interpretation of the study's results is that this formulation of the diagnostic process completely omits a crucial set of factors that significantly impinge on psychiatric evaluations. He calls these "contextual factors" (Rosenhan 1981). Foremost among them is the social system of mental health care within which diagnosis occurs, meaning the set of relationships between people occupying different positions (patients, psychiatrists, nurses, orderlies, hospital administrators, and so on) each with its own role expectations, interests, and spheres of authority. Rosenhan's thesis is that these social arrangements exert a powerful influence over diagnosis because they affect and colour how patients and their behaviour are perceived by psychiatrists and other actors in the system. Though their role in constraining behaviour and shaping perceptions of persons operating in a social system can be profound, the impact of these contextual factors is often only dimly visible to those involved.

In view of their opaque quality, it might be worthwhile to spell out exactly how contextual factors coloured the perceptions and judgements of psychiatrists and other hospital staff in the settings Rosenhan investigated. Allow me to review the main elements in the scenario contrived by Rosenhan. A number of strangers presented themselves, apparently on their own volition, to the admissions desks of various mental hospitals and reported that they had been hearing voices. It is probable that in this environment that the hospital staff would share most or all of the following beliefs:

- Patients in mental hospitals are there because they have mental disorders.
- Normal people do not want to be mental patients.

- People who voluntarily seek psychiatric assessment do so out of genuine concern for their mental health.
- Hearing voices is a fairly common symptom of schizophrenia.
- It is better for the hospital to admit people who may or may not be mentally ill than to turn them away.

These beliefs were, of course, perfectly reasonable in the mental hospital setting. Taken together, they created a mindset among the staff that induced them to mistake Rosenhan's pseudopatients for real patients. The fact that the pseudopatients were actually sane individuals who acted "normally" did not really matter; the staff's assumptions predisposed them to construe the personal traits and behaviour of the pseudopatients as signs of their abnormality.

In this particular situation, Rosenhan was right: the characteristics of the social context influenced the diagnoses more strongly than the characteristics of the individuals who were diagnosed. In another kind of setting, it would almost certainly have been a different story. What if, Rosenhan queries, instead of a mental hospital, this same ruse had been tried at a private cocktail party where all the hospital staff happened to be in attendance? One cannot know for certain, but under these conditions I think it would be a safe bet that the psychiatrists and other hospital staff would not have perceived or judged the pseudopatients as schizophrenics who belonged in a mental institution. In Rosenhan's experiment the context and climate of belief in the hospital setting were so compelling that one could argue that it would have been a more astounding result if the staff had correctly diagnosed the pseudopatients as sane and refused to hospitalize them.

In most situations psychiatrists encounter, the impact of contextual factors on the diagnostic process is rarely so dramatic. But neither are such factors usually totally absent. Here are just a few examples of items commonly present in the social environment of medical practice that have been known to affect diagnoses:

- *Medical decision rules*: Scheff (1984) has discussed how psychiatrists, like other doctors, develop norms about what to do in cases of uncertainty—more specifically whether it is better to err in the direction of presuming illness or presuming health. Incidentally, Scheff found the operative rule in psychiatry to be, "When in doubt, diagnose illness" (1984, 80).
- *Fads and fashions*: The popularity of diagnostic categories fluctuates considerably over time and place. For many years rates of schizophrenia were far higher in the United States than in Great Britain. When researchers examined why this was so, they discovered that most of the difference resulted from the greater reluctance of British psychiatrists to employ schizophrenia as a "catch-all" category for ambiguous cases. More recently, in North America, the number of persons diagnosed with multiple personality disorder went from extremely few to many thousands in a relatively short period. This disorder, which has been surrounded by controversy throughout, is today reportedly being diagnosed far less frequently again.
- *Extra-scientific contingencies*: Diagnoses are important to medical practitioners for a host of reasons that extend beyond their scientific purpose. I will mention three that are sometimes of vital interest to mental health professionals. Insurance policies typically cover treatment for some types of disorders and not others. Government and other sources of funding for medical research, treatment facili-

ties, and so on are granted or withheld largely on the basis of trend data on the numbers and types of diagnosed cases. Psychiatrists are frequently called upon to provide expert testimony in legal proceedings; the gist of their diagnoses can usually be predicted if one knows whether the prosecution or the defence hired their services.

The foregoing examples are merely a sampling of the sorts of contextual factors that inevitably impinge on psychiatric diagnosis in the real world. Critics of the medical model believe that psychiatry's inattention to these factors has contributed substantially to its difficulties. For the most part, however, the psychiatric profession has rejected this interpretation of the problem. Instead, it has pointed the finger at psychiatry's humanistic and psychoanalytic legacy as being largely responsible for what was wrong with traditional diagnostic procedures (Preskorn 1995). Many psychiatrists and psychologists believed that the ideas of Freud and his disciples had systematically retarded progress in understanding and treating mental illness. They argued that the Freudians and exponents of other "psychodynamic" approaches to mental disorder paid only lip service to the methods of science and the medical model. A common criticism was that these perspectives were not grounded in laboratory research. Freud's trademark concepts—unconscious motivation, Oedipus complex, transference, penis envy, repression, and so on—increasingly came to be seen as unnecessary philosophical baggage whose time was past.

The advent of the "drug revolution" and the professional crises of the 1960s and 1970s gave a tremendous boost to the steadily growing number of psychiatrists who believed that the way forward for the profession was to redouble efforts to base clinical practice on scientific principles and research. Advocates of this position clearly dominate both psychiatry and psychology today. The priority of this new psychiatric establishment has been to thoroughly overhaul the profession's diagnostic procedures. The last two editions of the DSM clearly reflect the leadership's desire to improve the reliability and validity of psychiatric diagnosis by reconstructing it on a solid, science-based foundation. Have they succeeded in this mission? The new psychiatry certainly gives every appearance of being founded on scientifically validated knowledge and procedures. But appearances can sometimes be deceiving. Kirk and Kutchins (1992) have closely examined how the DSM was revised and they conclude that the science involved was more rhetoric than substance and that behind all the changes was a self-serving political agenda.

Societal Reaction to Mental Disorder: The Contributions and Limits of Labelling Theory

Many of the ideas that inform the critique of the psychiatric enterprise outlined above derive from a sociological perspective known as the societal reaction model, or more simply, labelling theory. The labelling perspective was initially developed by scholars interested in a new way of thinking about crime and other types of so-called deviant behaviour. Traditionally, studies in this field had concentrated on the issue of what motivates people to violate society's laws and social norms. Accordingly, theory and research attempted to explain how social and psychological characteristics of individuals led them to commit deviant acts. The chief innovation of the new approach was to shift the focus from the deviants themselves to society's response to deviance. Instead of confining inquiry to the standard question of what caused the deviant to behave as he or she did, this novel approach asked why society judged the behaviour to be deviant, and what the consequences were of this response. Note that from this perspective deviance is not a quality of the act a person performs; behaviours themselves are said to be neither inherently deviant nor inherently conforming. Whether or not behaviour is deviant depends on how others define and react to it in a particular social setting.

Scheff: Mental Illness as Residual Deviance

Thomas Scheff and other sociologists have applied the societal reaction model to the study of mental disorder. Scheff's groundbreaking work, *Being Mentally Ill* (1984 [1966]), was written as a counterweight to the individualistic approaches of psychiatry and psychology, both of which he believed had failed to appreciate the huge impact of social processes on the occurrence of mental disorder. This alternative model starts with the observation that many of the symptoms of mental illness (hallucinations, continual talking to oneself, compulsivity, and so on) can be seen as behaviours that do not conform to a special subset of society's agreed-upon rules and norms. Contravention of most social rules does not usually result in the offender being defined as deviant, let alone mentally ill. But, argues Scheff, there are some social rules that are so totally accepted by everyone, so much taken for granted, that breaking them is perceived as very bizarre, almost unnatural, behaviour. Scheff calls these "residual rules" and their violation **residual rule-breaking**. Examples might include wearing stockings on your hands, singing out loud while riding the bus, or standing in a crowded elevator facing the rear. While such behaviour would be regarded as highly peculiar, the initial response of many people would probably be to ignore it or to downplay its significance. In some instances, however, certain people may react to such odd behaviour by bringing it to the attention of authorities who, in turn, arrange for the person to undergo a psychiatric examination. If the latter results in the person being formally designated as mentally ill, the label may set him or her on a life trajectory driven by this selective, pejorative definition. The attitudes and behaviour of other people, including loved ones, toward the person are modified in light of the belief that he or she is mentally ill. They "rewrite the person's biography" in order to make his or her past and present behaviour consonant with the culture's stereotype of insanity. In the face of such a crisis, the person's original symptoms are apt to recur or even intensify. Scheff suggests that, once labelled, the person may be rewarded for accepting a definition of himself or herself as mentally ill and for complying with society's expectations of a mental patient. Where this happens the person's identity has likely been transformed and he or she may be said to have taken on the social role of mental illness.

Various commentators have stated that it is inappropriate and misleading to call this approach a theory because, strictly speaking, theories explain problems and labelling theory does not provide an explanation of mental disorder. Scheff (1975) has himself acknowledged that developing a formal scheme that might "explain" mental disorder was not one of his objectives. He states that his goals were more modest, and centred on two concerns. First of all, he wanted to describe "the way that society reacts to 'mental illness' and how this reaction contributes to the problem." A second objective of his writings was to formulate a critique, "a protest against the practices it describes" (Scheff 1975, 2). These are certainly legitimate aims, but it is true that description and criticism are not the same thing as explanation. Scheff might have avoided misunderstanding if he had called this approach a "model" or "perspective." Even though their purpose is not explanatory, models/perspectives nonetheless perform a valuable "sensitizing" function by supplying a conceptual "map" of complex empirical data. The approach to mental disorder, initiated by Scheff and extended by other social scientists, thus deserves to be judged by how helpful it has been as a guide to inquiry. I will attempt to identify what I see as the strengths as well as the limitations of this model.

I believe one of Scheff's most important contributions has been the conception of mental illness as "residual deviance." The insight informing this notion is that cultures have a series of categories for designating behaviour that is contrary to shared social expectations. These categories enable members of society to make sense of behaviour that is in some way unusual or that goes against the cultural grain. The nature of these categories varies from culture to culture, but whatever form they take, most deviant behaviour falls squarely into one of these pigeonholes. A dilemma cultures face is how to make sense of odd behaviour that doesn't clearly fit into any of the standard categories. Scheff describes such deviance as "residual" because it consists of various kinds of behaviour that remain unclassified after the others have been sorted. Such behaviours tend to elicit fear and loathing because they defy the regular categories by which people apprehend reality. A resolution of this dilemma is to create a special omnibus category for these miscellaneous types of strange and otherwise perplexing conduct. In medieval Europe and the New England colonies during the late seventeenth and early eighteenth centuries, witchcraft was the residual deviance category. I think Scheff is correct when he asserts that in our culture it is mental illness.

Stigma and the Negative Consequences of Psychiatric Labels

I am also of the opinion that the central tenet of this perspective—namely, the proposition that defining and labelling someone as mentally ill has real consequences for the person's fate and behaviour—is unassailable. Granted, advocates of this model are prone to overstate the seriousness and inevitability of these consequences. Likewise, they sometimes speak as if the torment and misery of the person defined as mentally ill is entirely an artifact of the label and the social **stigma** that goes with it. I will have more to say about this rather dubious implication in a moment, but these exaggerated claims should not blind us to the soundness of this basic tenet of the labelling perspective.

A finding of sociological research that was conducted many years before anyone had even heard of "labelling" or "societal reaction" models lends corroboration to this fundamental insight. I am referring to research on American soldiers during the

Second World War (Stouffer et al. 1949). Many soldiers who saw combat experienced what at the time was euphemistically called "battle fatigue." This was a polite term for what, in other circumstances, would have been called a mental breakdown (Busfield 1996). One of the issues the research team looked at was variations in soldiers' rates of recovery from these trauma-induced episodes. In the course of examining a variety of factors associated the speed and extent of recovery, the researchers happened upon an unexpected or "serendipitous" finding. It concerned the type of treatment soldiers received after suffering a breakdown. The military's policy was, if circumstances allowed, to hospitalize such soldiers. However, quite often this option was simply not feasible and victims of battle fatigue had to be cared for within their units. Common sense would of course suggest that, other things being equal, the hospitalized soldiers would have recovered faster and more fully than those who remained in the battle zones. The former obviously had many advantages to aid in their recovery—sanctuary from the rigours of combat, access to vastly superior medical facilities, better food and nutrition, more sanitary conditions, and so on. Yet, to the investigators' astonishment, the recovery rates of these men were significantly poorer.

This result was rather puzzling at the time, but viewed in hindsight, it is a textbook case for the labelling paradigm. This paradigm permits us to understand how, for these men, being hospitalized turned out to be a liability. The hospitalized soldiers were defined and treated as psychiatric cases, whereas the symptoms of the other men were "normalized." The differential response of others to these soldiers' problems clearly impacted on their lives and their well-being.

Why does labelling someone mentally ill have such negative consequences? It is surely neither the label itself nor the act of labelling per se that engenders deleterious effects. The labels rather derive their potency from the meaning they have for the people involved. Figuring out what "mental illness" means to people in our society is not easy. In recent decades the medical profession and mental health associations have trumpeted the message that mental problems are genuine illnesses and therefore the persons afflicted should not be blamed or condemned for having them. Despite these valiant efforts, it is not at all clear that the public is buying the message. I say this even though recent public opinion polls do seem to indicate the presence of generally more favourable attitudes toward the mentally ill than in the past. What is more, they reveal greater public acceptance, at least in the abstract, of the conception of psychological problems as illness. However, these same studies also contain findings that point in the opposite direction. For example, many respondents express agreement with statements that the mentally ill are dangerous, unpredictable, and responsible for their own misfortune.

I would go even further and state that many of the medieval notions of madness discussed earlier in the chapter have by no means been extinguished from our collective consciousness. For example, I doubt anyone would deny that demonology is alive and well in popular culture, especially in the "horror film" genre where the villain of the piece is typically a perverse, sadistic, menacing figure who, predictably, has just escaped from a mental asylum. I of course recognize that the movies, comic books, or Stephen King novels that convey these images are fictional, but their popularity and resonance with audiences suggests that they are tapping into deep-seated fears many of us harbour about mental illness. Indeed, the prospect of "going crazy" or "losing one's mind" remains one of the supreme terrors of human existence. Future educational campaigns may well foster positive public attitudes concerning mental illness, but I suspect that the changes are apt to be superficial. Beneath these socially acceptable beliefs lies a sediment of relatively unenlightened feelings and ideas that keeps mental illness shrouded in ignorance, fear, and shame. This is the wellspring of the awful stigma still associated with mental illness and there appears to be no reason to think that it is losing any of its force. It may be a fuzzy one, but people in our society still acknowledge the presence of a boundary line that divides the sane from the insane. Moreover, I think it is almost universally understood that the stakes involved in crossing that line are very high indeed. Regrettably, to be mentally ill continues to mean that a person's value and sense of self-worth as a human being are at risk. Beyond having to cope with the distress intrinsic to mental disorder, persons treated for mental illness still commonly report that they must also struggle with feelings that they are "freaks," "losers," or social outcasts. As long as this is the case, designating someone mentally ill is apt to have fateful consequences for the person so labelled.

One of the merits of the societal reaction perspective is that it demonstrates how labelling places a person in situations that render it extremely difficult for him or her to continue following the normal routines of everyday life, thereby inducing the person to behave "abnormally." I admit that some of the hideous connotations associated with mental illness in our society often make being labelled insane a hurtful and oppressive experience. However, one can concede that community response is critical, both in shaping how persons defined as mentally ill view themselves and in channelling their behaviour onto certain paths, without assuming that labelling is a self-fulfilling process that, once initiated, necessarily culminates with the labelled person capitulating to society's definition by altering his or her identity and adopting the role of mental illness. The implication that "labels are destiny" amounts to sociological determinism. Some of this model's exponents may need to be reminded that this whole approach to human behaviour emerged out of a sociological tradition known as "symbolic interactionism," which deliberately eschewed this way of thinking. Symbolic interactionists maintain that individual behaviour is not automatically determined by social situations and structures; rather, it emanates from how people define these situations and how they choose to respond to such structures. Applying this principle to the societal reaction model of mental disorder, we might say that while both "labellers" and "labellees" may find themselves in social contexts not of their own making, both parties still have the freedom to make choices that depart from the script. In short, labelling need not be an inexorable or irreversible process.

Labelling and the Causes of Mental Disorder

I will conclude this section by commenting on what many observers consider to be the chief deficiency of the societal reaction perspective—namely, its silence on the following fundamental questions:

- What causes mental disorder?
- Why, in the same social environment, do some individuals become mentally ill while others do not?
- If medical means are misguided, what should be done to treat mental illness?

These are all valid and important questions and it is quite true that the societal reaction model does not address them. Why not?

One reason is that these questions call for full-fledged theoretical explanations, but models or perspectives, as I noted earlier, are merely heuristic devices that serve as a general guide to a given domain of inquiry. However, I think the main reason why these questions have been neglected is because the labelling approach was created and developed by sociologists, not by psychologists and psychiatrists. The questions themselves reflect the agenda and mandate of these allied professions. Unlike sociology, psychology and psychiatry both have a clinical function, which is to say that its practitioners offer treatment to people who suffer from mental disorder. Sociology's concerns in the area of mental disorder tend to be intellectual rather than practical. As observers and critics standing outside the clinical arena, sociologists do not feel an obligation to devise new methods or strategies for treating mental illness. The labelling perspective's affiliation with sociology may also explain this approach's not addressing why some individuals become mentally ill while others do not. Again, this is a perfectly legitimate question, but explaining individual behaviour is the task of psychology, not sociology. Sociological analysis instead endeavours to explain the social patterning of behaviour. The psychologist and psychiatrist want to know why a person thinks, feels, or acts in a particular way. The sociologist, on the other hand, seeks to explain why the incidence of certain ways of thinking, feeling, or behaving is higher or lower among various social categories of people and under certain kinds of social conditions. The "psychological why" and the "sociological why" are directed at different aspects of mental disorder.

I have argued that the labelling perspective's avoidance of the questions listed above can largely be attributed to the simple fact that its proponents are sociologists addressing sociological issues and concerns. The very different aims of sociological analysis and clinical practice has no doubt muddled debate over the relative merits of the medical and societal reaction models of mental disorder. Once these differences are appreciated, the number of genuinely contentious issues still subject to debate is considerably diminished. I believe one of these remaining issues has to do with the causes of mental disorder.

Sociologists can justify ducking this issue by utilizing the same arguments outlined above. For the most part sociologists probably do not need to concern themselves with the causes of mental disorder, but the question of causation does have a significant bearing on the adequacy of the labelling perspective. Sociology's sidestepping of the issue fosters some unfortunate impressions. One such implication is that who gets labelled mentally ill and why is totally capricious and unrelated to whether or not persons so designated suffer from psychological impairment. It likewise seems to imply that persons defined and labelled as mentally ill would be able to behave normally and lead normal lives if only members of the community, especially mental health professionals, did not brand them with stigmatizing labels.

Defenders of the societal reaction model do not necessarily endorse these suggestions, but in the absence of any acknowledgement that psychiatric symptoms usually have a basis in the mind and/or body of the person who exhibits them, the labelling perspective leaves itself wide open to these implications. It is worth noting that the original formulation of the model did not evade the question of causation. As we have seen, Scheff's theoretical model centred on "residual rule-breaking" as a form of behaviour that, under some circumstances, can result in a definition of the offending individual as mentally ill. However, Scheff did not claim that such behaviour was baseless. On the contrary, he hypothesized that residual rule-breaking "arises from fundamentally diverse sources (that is, organic, psychological, situations of stress, volitional acts of innovation or defiance" (1975, 9). In other words, Scheff stipulated that the behaviours that trigger the whole labelling process have their origin in something that is both real and separate from the reaction of others. But of course this proviso is perpendicular to the main thrust of the perspective, which depicted the "labellee" as caught in a web of societal expectations that elicit and reward "crazy" behaviour.

What captured the imagination of those attracted to this model was its counterintuitive notion that insanity lies in the eyes of the beholder/labeller. This theme appealed to the sensibilities of both liberals and radicals inclined to side with underdogs pitted against "the system's" agents of social control. These sentiments echoed concerns expressed by followers of anti-psychiatry; in fact, the labelling perspective and anti-psychiatry were contemporaneous and mutually reinforcing schools of thought. More specifically, Szasz's thesis that "mental illness is a myth" has come to be joined, in many commentaries, with the societal reaction approach. While they have some commonalities, the linkage between the two is rather tenuous. Szasz's rejection of psychiatric orthodoxy arises from an analysis that bears little resemblance to the societal reaction viewpoint. Justified or not, the *perception* that the labelling perspective has incorporated Szasz's wholesale dismissal of the illness metaphor has helped to eclipse Scheff's initial qualifications regarding the "diverse sources" of bizarre behaviour and psychiatric symptoms.

What is certain is that the perceived connection to Szasz's critique of the medical model did not endear the labelling perspective to mainstream psychiatrists and psychologists. For them mental illness was anything but mythical; it was an objective disease state of the mind/body that exists independently of our awareness, reactions, and definitions of it. Illness is illness no matter what anybody calls it or thinks about it. Any suggestion to the effect that persons defined by mental health professionals as mentally ill are merely the hapless victims of labelling and other social contingencies was deemed both irresponsible and a denial of reality.

My own position leans in the direction of these critics, even though I do not subscribe to the biomedical view that mental disorders are illnesses. The term "mental disorders" encompasses a very broad spectrum of heterogeneous conditions. Some of these conditions, such as Alzheimer's disease, appear to be very similar to physical illness; others, like "borderline personality disorder" strike me as very dissimilar to bodily disease. Many mental disorders seem to fall somewhere in between these two poles, combining a mixture of traits, some akin to physical illness, some not. As I stated at the outset of this chapter, to my way of thinking it is eminently more sensible to call the general category of these diverse conditions "mental disorder" than "mental illness." Many of the arguments advanced by Szasz and others opposed to the illness metaphor are, in my judgement, quite sound.

However, it does not follow from these arguments that we should also scrap the concept of mental *disorder*. I believe the latter is a viable concept that helps to avoid some of the more dubious connotations of both the medical model and its antithesis, anti-psychiatry. To refer to a certain mental condition as a "disorder" leaves open to empirical examination the extent to which it possesses characteristics associated with physical ailments. In so doing, the concept does not make the mistake of presuming the extreme opposite conclusion—namely, that people seeking psychiatric help suffer from nothing more than what Szasz called "problems in living." Mental illness may or may not be a myth, but I submit that mental disorder decidedly is not. Disorder denotes that something about a person's mental or emotional state is awry, unbalanced, disturbed, or impaired. The locus of the trouble may be in the person's mind, body, or social environment—or some combination thereof. Whatever the source, mental disorders have a reality and existence that is at least partly, though not necessarily entirely, independent of how clinicians and other members of society define and respond to them. Labelling and the reaction of others to the behaviour of a person with a mental disorder may influence its course, for either better or worse, but I agree with those who contend that there is ordinarily much more to the disorder than the label and the response of labellers. From this standpoint it would be a reasonable working hypothesis that a disordered mental state may be present prior to the onset of the labelling process.

Unlike the biomedical perspective, with its presupposition that "pathology is everything," this conception of mental disorder leaves plenty of opportunity for applying the insights of the labelling perspective. To postulate that some degree of impairment is an inherent feature of mental disorder does not diminish the need for social analyses. The domain of mental disorder is now, and will continue to be, one where there are discrepant, often conflicting, judgements about whether particular individuals, mental conditions, or types of behaviour qualify as disordered. The views of the wider society, a person's significant others, various mental health professionals, and the individual under scrutiny all matter, as does the interplay among all these competing views. In such a situation the number of possible permutations is staggeringly complex. Psychiatrists and psychologists have expertise that bears on a few—admittedly vitally important—parts of this puzzle. But understanding how their definitions and judgements influence and are influenced by other parties or aspects involved in the situation is not part of their clinical training or orientation. Making sense of the larger picture, including the interrelationships and interaction between all the components, requires an imagination and expertise of a different sort. Sociologists and other social scientists familiar with the dynamics of the labelling process have a great deal to contribute to the analysis of such scenarios.

Social Sources of Stress and Patterns of Mental Disorder

I have argued throughout this chapter that social factors have a major impact on many aspects of mental disorder. Even "hard-line" biomedically oriented psychiatrists and psychologists would probably agree with this generalization. Disagreements between mental health professionals and sociologists more often occur when the issue turns to one of causation. Are there, in fact, grounds for claiming that mental disorder has social causes? It would be extremely presumptuous of me to suggest that I have the answer to a question of this magnitude and complexity, but I do think there is something to be gained from attempting to clarify what is and what is not involved in making such a claim. This will be one of the objectives in the discussion that follows.

Sociological versus Psychological Analysis

Much of the confusion surrounding the question of causation again stems from a failure to distinguish between the very different objectives of sociological and psychological analysis. By way of review, sociology does not even pretend to explain individual behaviour; this is the task of psychology. No amount of sociological knowledge will ever enable us to understand why a person acts one way rather than another. This does not mean that social factors are never among the causes of an individual's behaviour. They may or may not be, but determining this calls for a mode of inquiry that centres on the individual person as its unit of analysis. Sociological analysis takes a different tack. Sociology investigates patterned interactions among groups of people; its focus is on the social contexts in which human life occurs (Johnson 1991). Sociologists are interested in social patterns of behaviour, not the individual cases that make up those patterns. In studying suicide, for example, the sociologist tries to explain why suicide *rates* vary among different social groups and categories (e.g., by religion, level of education, marital status, gender) or under different social conditions (e.g., wartime vs. peacetime, periods of economic prosperity vs. periods of economic decline). Just as sociology is unable to account for why Mr. Smith but not Mr. Jones committed suicide, psychological analysis cannot tell us why, for example, Protestants have substantially higher rates of suicide than either Catholics or Jews. Questions about individual behaviour and questions about social patterns of behaviour are both eminently worthy of serious inquiry. Psychological analysis is well suited for addressing the former type of question and sociological analysis is indispensable for the latter. But both approaches are asking for trouble when, as they sometimes do, they cross over into the other's territory.

What does this distinction mean for the sociological study of mental disorder? First of all, it means that sociological analysis absolutely cannot account for why some individuals develop a mental disorder while others do not. It also underlines that the kinds of questions sociology is equipped to address are those concerning the ways in which mental disorders are socially patterned. Over the years social and epidemiological research has discovered numerous variations in prevalence rates of mental disorder by social location. Some of these have turned up so consistently that they are considered established patterns. I have singled out a few of these well-documented patterns in order to facilitate our examination and discussion of the abstract issue of social causation.

- *Gender*: Contrary to the popular belief that women are more prone to mental illness, there appears to be no significant difference in the overall rate of mental disorder for men and women (Busfield 1996). There are, however, marked gender differences in the prevalence of specific types of disorders. Women, for example, have much higher rates of depression and other mood disorders than men. Antisocial behaviour and other forms of personality disorder, however, are significantly more prevalent among males.

- *Marital status*: Marital status has repeatedly proven to be associated with rates of mental disorder. Generally speaking, studies indicate that married people enjoy better mental heath than unmarried people. Persons who are married and never divorced or separated have the lowest prevalence of mental disorders. Interestingly, people who are cohabiting, but never married, have the highest rates. The incidence of mental disorders among persons who are single, divorced, or separated falls somewhere between the other two categories (Frankel, Speechly, and Wade 1996, 149). I should perhaps add that research on this topic seems to suggest that the positive mental health benefits of marriage are greater for men than for women.

- *Social class*: Social class, or socio-economic status, is another factor that we know is frequently correlated with rates of mental disorder (Stolzman 1994). In general, research has documented the presence of an inverse relationship—that is, rates of mental disorder are higher among persons of lower socio-economic standing. While this generalization applies to the overall picture, certain types of disorders (e.g., mood and anxiety disorders) tend to be more prevalent among members of the middle class. A major disorder that does conform to the general pattern is schizophrenia, which disproportionately afflicts lower-class people (Kohn 1981).

- *Unemployment*: As you might expect, unemployment is closely related to the prevalence of mental disorder. Indeed, some years ago Brenner (1973) demonstrated that changes in the level of unemployment were the single best predictor of fluctuations in the rate of admissions to mental hospitals in New York state over a 120-year period. More recent research has reported that people who are unemployed present at least twice as many psychiatric symptoms as employed persons of otherwise similar social backgrounds (Frankel, Speechly, and Wade 1996, 149).

Social Selection and Social Causation

Familiarity with these patterns is a useful point of departure for discussing the issue of whether social factors qualify as causes of mental disorder. No one disputes that there is a correlation between mental illness and the sorts of variables I have just identified (gender, marital status, and so on). But correlation does not signify causation; it merely tells us that two or more variables occur together in some unspecified manner. In truth, either of the two associated variables might be the cause of the other. In the social patterns singled out above, it must be realized that, on the face of it, we cannot ascertain whether mental disorder is a cause or consequence of the different social factors. Except for the gender example, the direction of causation in each of the other patterns is unclear. Thus, in the case of marital status, it is plausible that the correlation is at least partly due to the fact that people's mental condition affects whether they get and stay married. The same is true for the association between social class and mental disorder. It is likely that persons who suffer from a debilitating disorder like schizophrenia might, as a direct or indirect result of their mental impairment, experience a decline in socio-economic status. Similarly, having psychiatric symptoms, or even a proneness to developing them, might well contribute to a person's inability to obtain and hold a job. These are what is known as social selection interpretations; all of them posit that something about mental disorder affects the social position of the persons who have the disorders. Discovery that social selection is operating does not necessarily mean that no causal connection exists between the two sets of factors. In order to establish the presence of a causal link between the social factors and mental disorder a researcher is obliged to demonstrate that something about these factors is responsible for variations in the occurrence of mental disorder even after one has factored in the effects of social selection processes.

If one wants to argue that a causal connection exists, a number of other things also need to be checked first. For instance, one always needs to examine the possibility that the correlation between the two sets of factors might be caused by some as yet unidentified third factor. This is what is known in research as a "spurious" relationship. At one time researchers in the United States thought they had identified a number of patterns linking race with high rates of mental disorder (Weiss 1994). However, upon closer inspection the association turned out to be a by-product of social class differences between black and white Americans. The fact that many blacks were poor and few, at that time, were affluent, gave the impression that racial minority status was a causal factor, but when middle-class blacks were compared with middle-class whites the rates were essentially the same. The lesson here is that it is hazardous to presume that one has found a causal relationship unless potential sources of spuriousness have been ruled out.

Inappropriate research methods can also lead to unwarranted or false conclusions about the social patterning of behaviour. For example, a lot of older studies used admission to a mental hospital as the index of mental disorder. This research design was later recognized to be seriously flawed on at least two counts. One of the defects is that those admitted to mental hospitals represent only treated cases. As I mentioned at the beginning of the chapter, it is well known that a certain percentage of people with mental disorders never enter treatment facilities. It is not valid to offer generalizations about mental disorder based on data that systematically excludes untreated cases, who may or may not conform to the same pattern as treated cases. Moreover, mental hospital admissions is not even a good measure of treated cases inasmuch as many persons, especially the well-to-do, seek help for their problems from psychiatrists and psychologists in private practice outside hospital settings. Hospitalized mental patients are thus unrepresentative of all persons under treatment for psychiatric disorders.

Researchers eventually realized that the best way to remedy these deficiencies was to develop a procedure for assessing mental health in the general population. Several community studies were undertaken with this objective in mind. These studies included persons who were receiving treatment for psychological problems in all types of facilities and settings. In order to identify and incorporate the untreated cases of disorder that usually escape detection, these community studies enlisted the aid of psychiatrists and psychologists in devising interview schedules and questionnaire items that elicited information about various symptoms of mental disorder. Interviews were administered to a random sample of community members. Once these results were obtained, psychiatrists evaluated the mental health of each respondent. These studies consistently revealed that a relatively large proportion of community members qualified as at least moderately psychiatrically impaired, though only a small minority of these cases had ever been psychiatric patients (see Srole et al. 1962).

All of these considerations should encourage sociologists to exercise caution when we attempt to draw inferences about causation from knowledge that rates of mental disorders are socially patterned. However, let us assume that the data we have on these social patterns is derived from research that has successfully avoided the kinds of methodological shortcomings just outlined. What kinds of evidence would then be needed to corroborate the proposition that the association between social factors and mental disorder can properly be characterized as causation?

Let me begin my answer to this question by re-asserting that I think social causation implies something more substantive than what the societal reaction model has addressed. To reiterate, the labelling perspective helps us understand who gets identified as mentally ill and why. It is particularly useful for explaining why, in the community studies just cited, an inventory of persons socially defined as mentally ill and an inventory of persons who have symptoms of mental illness would reveal only partial overlap. Results of such studies indicate that many persons, possibly a majority, would qualify for both lists. By the same token, they also suggest that a number of the individuals on each list would not be included on the other one.

I believe that differential societal reaction, on the part of both community members and mental health professionals, explains most of this lack of correspondence between the lists. What it can't explain are variations in the prevalence of mental disorder that remain after the vagaries of differential labelling have been taken into account. The claim that various social factors are a cause of a certain level of mental disorder, be it high or low, implies that something inherent to the social position or social conditions actually contributes to the impaired mental state of the persons who comprise the pattern. There is obviously a big difference between saying that social factors are the reason why some people are identified as mentally ill and saying that social factors are the reason why some people manifest a degree of psychological impairment sufficient to warrant being classified as mentally ill. I trust you will appreciate that the latter is clearly a sterner, and better, test of causation. Let us thus consider the issue of whether sociological analysis points to ways in which features of the social environment may be said to contribute to mental disorder in the sense of fostering impaired mental functioning.

Macro-Level Sources of Social Stress

One argument in this vein emphasizes social stress. Originally conceived of as a physiological state, in recent decades scholars have increasingly viewed stress as a social phenomenon. An army of researchers and writers have popularized the idea that a whole catalogue of life stresses are responsible for a vast array of human maladies, including psychological distress and symptoms of mental disorder. A lot of theory and research have gone into formulating and refining a model of the "stress process," specifying the linkages between the different sources of stress, the factors that mediate the experience of stress, and the various manifestations of stress. This work has produced a voluminous and incredibly detailed literature on the various parameters and outcomes of social stress. Stress and stressful events abound in social life. Many of these stresses manifest themselves in small-scale social units such as families, workplaces, friendship networks, and neighbourhoods. If stress permeates the routines of everyday life, why not simply adopt the "microsociological" approach currently in vogue among stress experts?

According to Pearlin (1989), a sociologist who has himself been a major contributor to this area, the inordinate attention paid to the details of this process has led stress researchers to lose sight of the structural features of society that predispose people in certain social positions and social contexts to life experiences that are more stressful than those associated with other social locations and social circumstances. Pearlin laments that these structural features of the larger society have come to be viewed as mere "background factors." If the idea of social stress is to be of value in explaining variations in rates of mental disorder, I concur with this author that we should put the structure of society in the foreground of analysis. Accordingly, I wish to highlight two macro-level sources of distress that have been identified by traditional sociological theory—namely, socially structured inequality, and what I will call **socially structured ambiguity**. I will argue that both of these aspects of social organization produce stresses whose impact on the individual members of society is not randomly distributed but rather is concentrated among persons in particular social locations and social positions.

Structured Social Inequality

Throughout this chapter I have proclaimed that sociology's distinctiveness as a perspective on human behaviour is founded on the observation that the way in which groups and societies are organized significantly influences how its members think, feel, and act. A key aspect of a society's structure is its system of stratification. This term refers to the social arrangements whereby positions in society receive unequal amounts of, and have unequal access to, valued goods and resources (e.g., wealth, prestige, and power). In effect, this creates a hierarchy of positions, called strata, arrayed above and below one another according to the amount of property, power, and honour they command.

The structure of social inequalities is important because the level of valued resources that people have access to and command over determines a great deal about their lives. Where people are located in the hierarchy of positions will tend to strongly influence what they strive for, whom they associate with, the kinds of opportunities available to them, the satisfactions and achievements they are able to gain, and the deprivations they experience. Expressed another way, people's position in the stratification system greatly affects their "life chances"—the probability of procuring resources that will promote and enhance the quality of their life. The chance of enjoying good mental health is one such resource.

Structured social inequality generates stresses and, by its very nature, virtually guarantees that they will be most heavily concentrated in the lowest strata. Positions in the higher echelons are by no means immune to social stress; indeed, they feature certain kinds of stressors that are relatively uncommon at lower levels. However, recognition that privilege has its burdens should not blind us to the fact that all systems of stratification bestow those at the top with a host of advantages that enrich the quality of their lives in fundamental ways. Conversely, multiple disadvantages accrue to occupants of positions at the bottom of the hierarchy that fundamentally diminish the quality of their lives.[2]

At the risk of overstating the obvious, let me nevertheless delineate some of the major inequities that differentiate the life circumstances of high- and low-status positions in a stratified society. In this regard I would cite the following:

- *Material deprivation*: Except for positions at the very pinnacle of the hierarchy, occupants of positions at all levels below can claim to be, and may genuinely see themselves as being, relatively deprived compared with those in higher positions. But there are also grades of *absolute* deprivation involved in a system of unequal rewards. Chronic hardship is a reality in the lowest strata, but rare among occupants of high-ranking positions.
- *Autonomy*: Autonomy refers to the ability to control one's life and living conditions. Occupants of top positions have many resources that enable them to exercise a high degree of control. The autonomy of persons in the bottom strata is far more limited, particularly when they act individually rather than collectively to extend such control over their circumstances.
- *Social opportunity*: Occupants of higher-status positions face fewer barriers to advancement or achievement. Persons occupying lower-status positions encounter greater obstacles in efforts to improve their social status.
- *Disrepute*: Stratified societies always make invidious distinctions between positions at or near the top and those at or near the bottom. Honour and notoriety tend to be accorded occupants of high-status positions. Occupants of low-status positions generally receive little prestige or social recognition; worse yet, they are often despised or pitied.

For analytical purposes we have treated the above elements as separate entities. In real life, of course, they are overlapping and intertwined. I would also hypothesize that the interaction between these elements tends to have mutually reinforcing effects for occupants of positions at both extremes of the hierarchy. If so, this adds weight to the conclusion that while stressors and stressful life events exist at all levels of the stratification system, they are felt most intensely by persons occupying low-status positions.

Social and Cultural Sources of Ambiguity

Human beings depend on society and culture to guide and channel their behaviour. Peter Berger (1963) has persuasively argued that compared to other species of the animal world, human behaviour is only moderately governed by biological instincts. To be sure, there are promptings emanating from our biology that impel us to seek food, drink, sexual gratification, and so on. But, notes Berger, these instinctual impulses, unlike those of other animal species, are very undirected. In other words, our bodies may generate a need for food or sex, but they do not specify any particular method of satisfying the need. Because humans do not have highly developed biological instincts to channel our behaviour, our lives could easily turn into an endless series of quandaries that would absorb most of our individual and collective energy. To oversimplify, Berger believes that humans have compensated for the lack of inner guideposts for their behaviour by constructing social systems. In effect, culture and society provide us with elaborate guidelines for our behaviour. Consequently, most of the potential dilemmas of everyday life do not overwhelm us; humans undergo a lengthy and extensive socialization process that enables most of us, most of the time, to successfully negotiate the routine exigencies of daily life. Culture provides us with socially shared ideas—customs, beliefs, knowledge, values, and norms—that expedite these negotiations.

Social structure also lends stability and regularity to human behaviour. As Johnson (1991, 51) has remarked, "For individuals, the most immediate and important structural aspects of a social system are the positions (statuses) they occupy in relationships and the roles they are expected to perform as a result." Two of sociology's most elementary principles are (1) that each person occupies many statuses, and (2) that at least one or more roles are attached to each of these statuses. These principles may appear trite, but it can be argued that society is only possible because its members are able to rely on people in various statuses to act in more or less predictable ways. If we could not count on other people to carry out the roles connected with their statuses, social life would become uncertain and chaotic.

To the extent that they make life in the everyday world more orderly, coherent, and predictable, society and culture operate to reduce and prevent social stresses. But the cultural beliefs we have internalized, the social positions we occupy, and the roles we perform can, under certain conditions, themselves be sources of stress. A rough set of guidelines for behaviour comes with membership in society, but these guidelines do not always give clear directions for how we should think, act, or feel in given social situations. Sometimes the directions are ambiguous; they convey mixed messages or contradictory expectations. People caught in this predicament generally experience a sense of ambivalence, of being simultaneously pulled in opposite directions. Ambiguity and ambivalence have traditionally been thought of as individual psychological or emotional states. Sociologists certainly do not dispute this characterization, but they do assert that a lot of the ambiguity and ambivalence experienced by individuals is built into social systems and social relationships. Following Merton and Barber (1982), here is a brief survey of some of the ways ambiguity can inhere in certain social locations:

- There may be conflicting expectations associated with two or more of the positions a person occupies (i.e., his or her "status-set"). Cases of conflict between a person's status in the occupational sphere and in the family domain illustrate this point. Different statuses that make incompatible demands or are significantly discrepant in the level of valued social goods they offer produce *status inconsistency*.
- The norms or expectations of a particular role attached to a social position are sometimes contradictory. Psychotherapists, for example, are expected to be both impersonal/detached and personal/concerned in their relations with clients.
- The demands and expectations of two or more of the roles accompanying a particular position can be at odds. University professors, for instance, often find that the roles of teacher and researcher make competing claims for their time and energy.
- Society may encourage its members to respect certain cultural values that are contradictory. For example, the dilemma facing a person called upon to testify against a friend in court will not be eased by a culture that values both honesty and loyalty.
- Strain occurs when there is a disjunction between culturally prized values and the availability of socially approved avenues for achieving them. Robert Merton's (1957) famous anomie theory of deviance is founded on this notion. Merton highlighted a key contradiction of American society: On the one hand, American culture

extols the values of achievement and material success to all its citizens, while on the other hand, its social structure limits the opportunities of persons in the lower class and other disadvantaged groups for realizing these goals by legitimate means.

• Ambiguity also develops among people who have lived in two or more societies (or in two radically different locales within the same society) with the consequence that they oriented to divergent sets of values. The classic example is of course immigrants who are torn between the ways of their country of origin and those of their adopted society.

Social Ambiguity and Psychological Distress

The above list is by no means exhaustive, but it will suffice to identify some ways in which cultural beliefs and social organization engender stress by placing people in circumstances where their behavioural options are fraught with ambiguity. This aspect of social systems is, I believe, especially germane to the study of psychological distress and mental disorder. Analysis of the role of socio-cultural factors in generating ambivalence is reminiscent of the once-fashionable countercultural thesis that mental disorder is a mystifying, humane reaction to the allegedly pervasive social and political madness of modern society. More specifically, R.D. Laing, Gregory Bateson, Jules Henry, and other authors affiliated with anti-psychiatry proposed that schizophrenia and other types of insanity often have their origin in a certain type of destructive family dynamic (see Laing and Esterson 1970; Bateson et al. 1956; Henry 1965). These authors maintained that some families heap impossible and destructive demands on an emotionally vulnerable member, usually a child, who effectively becomes the scapegoat for assorted family problems. The confluence of the parents' inconsistent behaviour and bewildering communications make it exceptionally difficult for the child to act other than in a seemingly irrational manner. According to Bateson's **double bind hypothesis**, schizophrenic thought disorder may develop when children are constantly exposed to contradictory demands from their parents. These mixed messages are particularly damaging if they occur in a context where the child cannot withdraw from the situation or respond to the dilemma in a manner that avoids parental rejection and disapproval. Children caught in such "no-win" situations face a double bind, since they are "damned if they do and damned if they don't." In short, there is no "rational" way for the person to either apprehend or respond to what is happening; only "irrational" behaviour makes sense in such twisted circumstances.

This way of looking at psychopathology appears to have few adherents today. If mainstream psychiatrists and psychologists now mention these ideas at all, it is apt to be as an example of the preposterous theories that prevailed before biomedical science supposedly established that schizophrenia is an illness. The polemical character of this alternative approach to insanity made it easy to dismiss, especially during the more conservative political climate of the 1980s. Rejection of these ideas as the explanation of schizophrenia was no doubt warranted, but I believe they contain an important kernel of truth which, stripped of the radical hyperbole, merits revisiting. As should be evident from the foregoing commentary, I do not believe there is anything far-fetched or implausible about the proposition that certain kinds of social environments are conducive to distorted thought or emotional confusion. For a number of reasons (e.g., their level of intimacy, the intense emotional investments they entail, their susceptibility to the myths of popular culture) family relationships offer particularly fertile soil for the production of so-called **crazy-making situations**.

A classroom exercise I have conducted tends to confirm this point. I have occasionally invited students in my mental disorders class to recall situations in their own lives that may have caused doubts, however fleeting, about their own sanity. Most of the experiences they recount involve their families and scenarios in which they encountered real or suspected dissonance between their personal views and those of other family members on some matter heretofore believed to be unproblematic. It should also be noted that this assignment usually elicits a few examples drawn from other domains of students' lives—religion, friendships, or jobs—suggesting that family relationships do not have a monopoly on crazy-making situations.

Incidentally, I also think it is telling that most students have absolutely no trouble grasping what is being asked of them in the exercise I have just described. What it means to say that something made us "feel crazy" is commonly understood in our culture to involve unanticipated incidents of dissonance. That is, our intuitive sense of what it is like to be mentally ill ("crazy") as well as what kinds of factors precipitate the experience of becoming mentally ill ("going crazy") correspond to perspectives on mental disorder that seek to relate it to social sources of ambivalence and ambiguity.

Linkages between Stress and Mental Disorder

Until this point, I have identified and discussed some of the major social sources of stress that help to explain socially patterned differentials in the prevalence of mental disorder. I have singled out two features of social structure that affect the level of stress associated with a given position. The first of these features is a position's rank in society's system of stratification. Other things being equal, positions high in the status hierarchy are relatively less stressful, whereas positions at the low end of the hierarchy tend to more stressful. The second feature is the degree of cultural or structural ambiguity associated with positions. In general, positions that provide their occupants with relatively clear expectations and demands about their behaviour are low in stress; positions that involve vague or conflicting expectations and demands are apt to be high in stress.

You will remember that sociological analysis is aimed at trying to explain variations in rates or patterns of mental disorder. Knowledge about the level of stress associated with a social position only permits us to estimate the probable odds that the person who actually occupies the status will think, act, or feel in a particular manner. Even if we had precise quantitative measures of a position's "stress quotient," such information still would not enable us to explain the behaviour of the individuals who occupy these positions.[3] Just as the stress level associated with different positions varies, the individuals who occupy any given position are not uniformly susceptible to the effects of stress. A host of biological, psychological, and sociological variables combine to make some people more resilient and resourceful in the face of stress than others. Thus, an individual who is relatively "stress resistant" may occupy a stressful position without experiencing negative psychological consequences. Likewise, a "stress prone" individual occupying a relatively low stress social position may find the experience excruciating. In order to assess the consequences of social stress on people's psychological well-being, we must take into account both the objective features of their social location and any factors that render individuals differentially vulnerable to stress. It is very well documented, for example, that the amount of social support individuals have can

What Proportion of Psychological Distress Is Due to Social Factors?

Community mental health studies have repeatedly established that indicators of psychological distress and well-being are not randomly distributed in society; rather, they form social patterns. The mere fact that symptoms of distress are socially patterned strongly suggests that social factors have at least some effect on the overall level of distress found in society, but just how important are they? Do social factors contribute marginally or substantially to the total pool of distress symptoms found in society?

Two sociologists at the University of Illinois, John Mirowsky and Catherine Ross, figured out a way to investigate this question statistically. In 1985 they conducted a survey of a random sample of 809 adults in Illinois. The interviews included questions about specific symptoms of both depression and anxiety. The researchers also collected data on various social characteristics of the respondents, especially traits known from previous studies to be associated with psychological distress. Each respondent was assigned a score that was a tally of the predicted risk of depression for someone of their gender, minority status, age, family income, education, sense of personal control, and social support.

The sample was divided into ten groups (deciles) of roughly equal size based on these scores. The top 10 percent of the sample thus consisted of persons whose combined social traits indicated they had the lowest risk of distress. At the other extreme, the bottom 10 percent of the sample possessed the greatest number of traits associated with a high risk of distress. There were of course eight other deciles arrayed between the top and bottom groups. The groups with lower risk of distress tended to include respondents who were male, married, did not belong to a minority group, were employed full-time with high incomes and educational levels, and had a strong sense of personal control and social support. The deciles at higher risk included more respondents whose social traits were the opposite of these.

As expected, Mirowsky and Ross found that the average number of symptoms in each decile increases when you array the groups from top to bottom. They decided to use the average number of symptoms of the top group as a baseline for estimating how much distress is a result of social factors. The logic of this research strategy should perhaps be spelled out. Respondents in the top decile, like everyone else, possess some symptoms of depression and anxiety. Having the "best" social traits minimizes, but certainly does not eliminate, the risk of distress. Mirowsky and Ross reasoned that the number of psychiatric symptoms

(continued)

(continued)

found among this least vulnerable 10 percent of the population can be regarded as the "base"—that is, the level of distress one expects to find in a group even when the respondents have optimal social characteristics. The "excess" refers to the portion of symptoms over and above this base level. The excess represents a measure of the proportion of each decile's symptoms attributable to its respondents *not* having, or having fewer, of the traits known to reduce the likelihood of being distressed. In effect, the base and excess represent indicators of the percentage of the total pool of psychiatric symptoms that may be assigned, respectively, to both non-social (biological and psychological) and social causes. Dividing the symptoms of depression in this manner, Mirowsky and Ross discovered that 48.6 percent were in the base category, the remaining 51.4 percent were classified as excess. They conclude from this that "at least half of all the symptoms of depression are attributable to social factors" (1989, 17). The results for symptoms of anxiety yielded a similar pattern.

Mirowsky and Ross also wanted to know whether the impact of social factors extended to severe cases of distress. They had anticipated that one reaction to the findings above might be to concede that social causes may figure in everyday, "garden variety" types of symptoms while expressing scepticism that they have any influence on more extreme forms of distress. Such reservations would be in keeping with the biomedical perspective, whose advocates tend to argue that serious psychiatric disorders are organic in origin and are therefore unrelated to social factors. In order to examine this issue, Mirowsky and Ross's analysis singled out the respondents in their survey who might be said to suffer from severe psychological problems. Extreme or severe distress was operationally defined as persons who have a level of symptoms greater than that found in 95 percent of the general population. According to previous community mental-health studies, at least 61 percent of people with this number of symptoms meet the criteria for a psychiatric disorder; stated conversely, of people who do not qualify for a psychiatric diagnosis, only 3 percent have this level of symptoms.

The number of respondents in the study exhibiting this extreme level of distress was too small to permit meaningful comparisons by deciles. Hence Mirowsky and Ross used socio-economic measures to divide the respondents into two halves, the advantaged and the disadvantaged. They found that 83.9 percent of all severe distress was located in the disadvantaged half. Expressed another way, the odds of being severely distressed were almost six times greater among the "have nots" than the "haves." These findings clearly suggest that, as with milder forms, severe distress is strongly related to social factors.

I believe this ingenious research presents fairly compelling evidence that the contribution of social factors to the overall amount as well as the intensity of the psychological distress people experience has been vastly underestimated. The fact that findings such as Mirowsky and Ross's commonly receive relatively little publicity in the media, compared with research that links psychiatric problems with genetic or other organic factors, certainly adds to the public's lack of appreciation for the effects of the social environment on our mental health.

Source: Based on a reading of John Mirowsky and Catherine Ross, *Social Causes of Psychological Distress* (New York: Aldine de Gruyter, 1989), pp. 172–76.

significantly help or hinder their ability to cope with stress. The amount and quality of a person's "coping resources" is thus a key factor mediating the relationship between social location and psychological outcome (Kohn 1981).

The connection between stress and mental disorder is obviously less than straightforward. Stress per se is simply tension. In principle, the effects of such tension on people's physical and mental well-being can be either beneficial or harmful. Psychological distress, following Mirowsky and Ross's usage (1989, 21), is an unpleasant subjective state that may take the form of either depression or anxiety. Distress has both emotional and physical components, which they refer to as mood and malaise, respectively. The severity of distress people experience is wide-ranging. In Mirowsky and Ross's words, "only the more extreme levels would be considered mental illness.... Much distress is the psychiatric equivalent of the common cold" (1989, 24).

To review, it seems that social stress does not necessarily create psychological distress, and even where it does, being psychologically distressed usually does not indicate the presence of mental disorder. The relationship of stress to psychological distress as well as the relationship of psychological distress to mental disorder are what philosophers of science describe as "necessary but not sufficient conditions." To say these conditions are "necessary" means that psychological distress only occurs if some degree of stress is present, and mental disorder only occurs if some degree of psychological distress is present. The qualifier that these conditions are "not sufficient" means that stress alone is not enough to produce psychological distress, and psychological distress alone is not enough to create mental disorder. This being the case, analysis and empirical inquiry are required in order to specify under what conditions (1) stress does or does not translate into psychological distress and (2) psychological distress does or does not develop into mental disorder.

I would like to conclude this chapter by suggesting that the challenge of identifying the salient conditions and factors linking social systems, stress, mental anguish, and psychiatric impairment is to bridge the differences between biomedical and social conceptions of mental disorder. Dialogue and the sharing of research may yield a degree of rapprochement, but anything more than this is, in my opinion, extremely unlikely. The gulf dividing the basic standpoint of these approaches is simply too great. To proponents of the medical model, psychological distress and mental illness signify a problem that is confined to the mind and body of the person afflicted. The view expressed in this chapter, by contrast, is that the patterning of mental distress and disorder is normally a sign of social problems. Mirowsky and Ross express this point rather eloquently:

> The misery, demoralization, or distress a person feels are not the problem. They are consequences of the problem. Misery is not only real, it is realistic. Suffering contains a message about the causes of the suffering; a message that can be read, understood, and acted upon. We are not looking for a drug to suppress the misery. While such drugs have humane uses, they are palliative. A drug that suppresses anguish does not remove its cause. We are not attempting to find a way to talk people into believing things are better than they seem. An illusion cannot dispel a distressing reality; it just makes the reality more perplexing. (1989, 5–6)

I believe this point of view is and will remain anathema to adherents of the medical model. What do you think?

Summary

- Although it is customarily viewed as a psychological and/or biological phenomenon, mental illness also has many social dimensions.
- Psychiatric conceptions of mental illness emphasize that it is a pathological condition of the body unaffected by what either the individual afflicted or other people think and feel about it. Sociologists argue that mental illness is also a social state based on cultural standards of normality and evaluations of other people that carry consequences for how persons defined as mentally ill are treated.
- Biomedical views of mental illness arose historically as a reaction to theological conceptions of madness, which viewed the mad as wicked sinners in the grip of supernatural forces. Medicine's authority as the agents in society responsible for mental disorder derived more from the key role physicians played in reforming mental asylums than from the scientific superiority of their ideas and treatments. The recent drug revolution in treating mental disorder was instrumental in winning public acceptance of the medical model.
- The anti-psychiatry movement of the 1960s and 1970s challenged the conceptual integrity of the psychiatric enterprise. Psychiatry has attempted to minimize diagnostic bias by emulating the scientific procedures employed in other areas of medicine. The viability of this strategy is questioned because it neglects the influence of contextual factors in psychiatric assessment.
- The way society reacts to certain kinds of unusual behaviour may or may not result in designating them as "mental illness." Such labelling can lead to a transformation of identity and an adoption of the social role of mental illness. The stigma attached to the label of mental illness has negative consequences, but the labelling perspective overestimates the extent to which the process is self-fulfilling and underestimates the extent to which psychological impairment is a reality independent of social definitions and reactions.
- Sociological analysis seeks to explain variations in the rates or social patterning of mental illness. Psychological analysis, in contrast, addresses the question of why some individuals are mentally ill while others are not. Many of the established social patterns of mental disorder appear to reflect the amount of stress associated with different social positions. Two macro-level sources of stress have been identified—namely, socially structured inequality and socially structured ambiguity. Social positions that are low in the status hierarchy or provide their occupants with conflicting expectations and demands are associated with high levels of stress.
- Analysis and empirical inquiry into the connections between social stress, psychological distress, and mental disorder are required to specify under what conditions social stress does or does not translate into psychological distress and the latter does or does not develop into mental disorder. People's vulnerability to stress and distress is not only a matter of their personal characteristics; it is also affected by social location and features of their social environment.

Questions to Consider

1. What is the difference between the kinds of questions sociologists and psychologists seek to answer about mental disorder?

2. In the Rosenhan study, the psychiatrists and other hospital staff members failed to recognize that the pseudopatients were impostors. In what sense might it have been a more remarkable result if the staff *had* detected them?

3. Do you think psychiatry's recent efforts to make diagnosis of mental disorders more objective and unbiased by adopting the scientifically based procedures used to assess physical illness are apt to succeed or fail? Why?

4. Mirowsky and Ross's research suggests that at least half of the symptoms of depression and anxiety may be attributed to social factors, yet the public tends to view mental illness as mainly a biological and/or psychological affliction. How do you account for this discrepancy?

5. What are the characteristics of "crazy-making situations"? Can you relate this concept to a personal experience?

Suggested Readings

Conrad, Peter, and Joseph W. Schneider. *Deviance and Medicalization: From Badness to Sickness*. Expanded ed. Philadelphia: Temple University Press, 1992.

Kirk, Stuart A., and Herb Kutchins. *The Selling of DSM: The Rhetoric of Science in Psychiatry*. New York: Aldine de Gruyter, 1992.

Mirowsky, John, and Catherine E. Ross. *Social Causes of Psychological Distress*. New York: Aldine de Gruyter, 1989.

Rosenberg, Morris. *The Unread Mind: Unraveling the Mystery of Madness*. New York: Lexington Books, 1992.

Scheff, Thomas J. *Being Mentally Ill: A Sociological Theory*. 2d ed. Chicago: Aldine, 1984.

Glossary

anti-psychiatry A school of thought, popular during the 1960s and 1970s, that was critical of the medical conception of mental disorder and psychiatry's function as an agency of social control.

crazy-making situations Circumstances of unexpected dissonance that cause persons to question their sanity.

deinstitutionalization The policy of shifting the setting of treatment of mental disorders from hospitals to the community by releasing large numbers of patients to live in the outside world.

demonic perspective The view of mental disorder as madness caused by evil supernatural forces.

double bind hypothesis A theory of schizophrenia that attributes disordered thought patterns to family interactions in which children are repeatedly exposed to contradictory messages and demands that invite rejection no matter how they respond.

labelling perspective An approach to the study of deviance that focusses on the selective reaction of society to certain kinds of rule-breaking and the effects of this response on the self-concepts and future behaviour of the people so labelled.

medical model of mental disorder The view of mental problems as a disease of the body that can be treated by medical means in much the same manner as physical illness.

residual rule-breaking The transgressing of norms that govern basic aspects of everyday interaction for which the culture provides no explicit label or name.

socially structured ambiguity A condition in which the expectations for behaviour are inconsistent or incompatible owing to features of the social environment.

stigma Personal characteristics that others treat as a mark of disgrace or unworthiness that deny a person's claim to a "normal" identity.

true prevalence The total number of cases of an illness or disorder that exist at any given time irrespective of whether or not they are receiving treatment.

Notes

1. Many mental health professionals think this formulation of the model goes too far in equating mental and physical illness. The prefer a "softer" version that admits a number of significant differences between the two types of illness. Unlike the "hard-liners" they are more receptive to the notion that psychological and social factors figure prominently in the development and experience of mental illness. They adhere to the medical model as a useful metaphor rather than as a doctrine of scientific belief—even though they recognize that mental disorder is unlike physical illness in important respects, they still believe it makes practical sense to conceptualize and treat mental problems as if they resulted from afflictions of the body.
2. Incidentally, I consider these statements sociological descriptions, not ideological prescriptions. Ideology only rears its ugly head when someone puts a particular "spin" on them in order to either justify or condemn the existence of such inequality.
3. It is of course true that the behaviour of many individuals who make up the patterns sociologists analyze does not conform to the pattern. For example, although the rate of schizophrenia is relatively high among the poor, it is nevertheless the case that (a) most poor people do not suffer from schizophrenia, and (b) some very wealthy people do. Any social pattern is bound to include individual cases that are "exceptions to the rule." Perhaps you are saying to yourself, if this is so, why not simply forget about the stupid patterns, and try to understand the behaviour of the different individuals, whether they fit the pattern or not? This strategy is fine if you believe the only questions worth answering about human behaviour are psychological ones. But sociologists believe questions about rates, patterns, and trends of human behaviour are equally worth answering. The fact that some individuals do not conform to these rates, patterns, and trends negates neither the rationale nor the need for sociological analysis.

References

Bateson, G., et al. 1956. "Towards a Theory of Schizophrenia." *Behavioral Science* 1: 251–64.
Bayer, R. 1986. *Homosexuality and American Psychiatry: The Politics of Diagnosis*. Princeton: Princeton University Press.

Berger, P. 1963. *Invitation to Sociology: A Humanistic Perspective*. New York: Anchor Books.

Bolaria, B.S., and H.D. Dickinson, eds. 1994. *Health, Illness, and Health Care in Canada*, 2d ed. Toronto: Harcourt Brace.

Breggin, P. 1991. *Toxic Psychiatry*. New York: St. Martin's Press.

Brenner, H. 1973. *Mental Illness and the Economy*. Cambridge: Harvard University Press.

Busfield, J. 1996. *Men, Women and Madness: Understanding Gender and Mental Disorder*. London: Macmillan.

Cockerham, W. 1996. *Sociology of Mental Disorder*, 4th ed. Englewood Cliffs, NJ: Prentice-Hall.

Conrad, P., and J. Schneider. 1980. *Deviance and Medicalization: From Badness to Sickness*. Toronto: Mosby.

Frankel, B.G., M. Speechly, and T. Wade. 1996. *The Sociology of Health and Health Care: A Canadian Perspective*. Toronto: Copp Clark.

Freidson, E. 1973. *Profession of Medicine: A Study of the Sociology of Applied Knowledge*. New York: Dodd and Mead.

Grusky, O., and M. Pollner, eds. 1981. *The Sociology of Mental Illness: Basic Studies*. New York: Holt, Rinehart and Winston.

Henry, J. 1965. *Pathways to Madness*. New York: Random House.

Isaac, R., and V. Armat. 1990. *Madness in the Streets: How Psychiatry and the Law Abandoned the Mentally Ill*. New York: Free Press.

Johnson, A. 1991. *The Forest for the Trees: An Introduction to Sociological Thinking*. Toronto: Harcourt Brace Jovanovich.

Kirk, S., and H. Kutchins. 1992. *The Selling of DSM: The Rhetoric of Science in Psychiatry*. New York: Aldine de Gruyter.

Kohn, M. 1981. "Social Class and Schizophrenia: A Critical Review and a Reformulation." In Grusky and Pollner, *The Sociology of Mental Illness*. 127–43.

Laing, R. 1969. *The Divided Self*. New York: Pantheon.

Laing, R., and A. Esterson. 1970. *Sanity, Madness, and the Family*. New York: Basic Books.

Merton, R. 1957. *Social Theory and Social Structure*, rev. ed. Toronto: Collier-Macmillan.

Merton, R., and E. Barber. 1982. "Sociological Ambivalence." In *Sociological Theory: A Book of Readings*, 5th ed., ed. Lewis Coser and Bernard Rosenberg. New York: Macmillan. 493–507.

Mirowsky, J., and C. Ross. 1989. *Social Causes of Psychological Distress*. New York: Aldine de Gruyter.

Pearlin, L. 1989. "The Sociological Study of Stress." *Journal of Health and Social Behavior* 30: 241–56.

Pfohl, S. 1994. *Images of Deviance and Social Control*, 2d ed. New York: McGraw-Hill.

Preskorn, S. 1995. "Mental Disorders Are Medical Diseases." In *Mental Illness: Opposing Viewpoints*, ed. W. Barbour. San Diego: Greenhaven Press. 29–36.

Rosenberg, M. 1992. *The Unread Mind: Unraveling the Mystery of Madness*. New York: Lexington Books.

Rosenhan, D. 1975. "On Being Sane in Insane Places." In *Labeling Madness*, ed. Thomas J. Scheff. Englewood Cliffs, NJ: Prentice-Hall. 54–74.

———. 1981. "The Contextual Nature of Psychiatric Diagnosis." In Grusky and Pollner, *The Sociology of Mental Illness*. 319–29.

Scheff, T., ed. 1975. *Labeling Madness*. Englewood Cliffs, NJ: Prentice-Hall.

———. 1984. *Being Mentally Ill: A Sociological Theory*, 2d ed. Chicago: Aldine.

Spitzer, R., and P. Wilson. 1975. "Nosology and the Official Psychiatric Nomenclature." In *Comprehensive Textbook of Psychiatry*, Vol. 1, 2d ed., ed. A. Freedman, H. Kaplan, and B. Saddock. Baltimore: Williams & Wilkins. 826–45.

Srole, L., T. Langner, S. Michael, M. Opler, and T. Rennie. 1962. *Mental Health in the Metropolis*. New York: McGraw-Hill.

Statistics Canada. 1981. *The Health of Canadians: Report of the Canada Health Survey,* Cat. no. 82-538E. Ottawa: Minister of Supply and Services Canada.

Stolzman, J. 1994. "The Distribution and Treatment of Mental Disorders by Social Class." In *Sociology of Health Care in Canada*, ed. B.S. Bolaria and H. Dickinson. Toronto: Harcourt Brace Jovanovich. 261–77.

Stouffer, S., et al., eds. 1949. *The American Soldier*. Vols. 1 and 2. Princeton: Princeton University Press.

Szasz, T. 1961. *The Myth of Mental Illness*. New York: Harper and Row.

———. 1970. *The Manufacture of Madness*. New York: Dell.

Weiss, G.L., and L.E. Lonnquist. 1994. *The Sociology of Health, Healing and Illness*. Englewood Cliffs, NJ: Prentice Hall.

PART VII

The Welfare State and Social Policy

INTRODUCTION

The analysis of social institutions and structural contradictions illuminates how these institutions and contradictions cause and perpetuate inequalities in this society. These inequalities are likely to be exacerbated by shifts in both the economy and state policy. Economic restructuring in the context of globalization of production and the need to become more competitive internationally is responsible for economic dislocations and job losses in some sectors of the Canadian economy. At the same time, the adoption of neoconservative state policies has hastened the diversion of state priorities and resources from social and human services to the enhancement of labour productivity and capital accumulation. It is argued that excessive social expenditures are responsible for budgetary deficits and need to be cut back in order to avert economic collapse. The welfare state, which was at one time seen as the most important instrument to ameliorate inequalities and solve social problems, has itself become the focus of criticism that it requires overhauling. Readings in this section address these issues.

Gary Teeple, in the chapter entitled "The Decline of the Canadian Welfare State: Policies and Implications of Retrenchment," examines the nature of the welfare state and discusses the common elements in the history of social reform and the significance of such policies in industrial nations. He pays particular attention to the development of the welfare state and social legislation in Canada. Teeple explores the reasons for the present decline in the welfare state and the consequences of this retrenchment in Canada, which are already very visible in a number of areas. The retrenchment of social programs is discussed in the context of the North American Free Trade Agreement. Teeple states that, concomitant with cutbacks to the public-sector provisions, private-sector provisions are growing, in the form of charitable donations or voluntary services (charities) and in the systematic privatization of services and programs. In general, Canada is moving away from the state provision of social services and programs, especially universal programs or those characterized as social rights. This undermines the principle that the state has a social responsibility to its citizens and puts an end to the principle and practice of social citizenship. Teeple argues that the interim goal of the provincial and federal retrenchment appears to be a minimalization of the state's social responsibilities; for those aspects of the welfare state that are not yet abolished, the state is developing dual systems: private but publicly supported programs for the well-to-do and a degraded state program for those who cannot afford the "private." Teeple concludes that the forces of global capitalism that underlie this retrenchment are being resisted around the world. This resistance will continue to grow as economic inequality deepens and the ability of capitalism to provide for the material and human needs of the populace further declines.

In the concluding chapter, entitled "Social Issues and Social Policy," B. Singh Bolaria examines the policy implications of interpreting and analyzing social issues and problems within individualistic and structural frameworks. The discussion indicates that dramatically different solutions flow from these analyses. A number of policy alternatives, such as individualization of social problems, their medicalization, and reforms that do not disrupt existing power relationships, help to "manage" the contradictions without solving structural problems. While piecemeal solutions may be ameliorative and provide immediate relief to individuals, they do not address the underlying basic social–structural causes of social problems. These policy issues will become even more prominent in the context of current attacks on the welfare state, the politics of retrenchment and deficit reduction, and their impact on the lives of Canadians.

Internationalization of capital and globalization of production has meant not only economic dislocations, layoffs, and declining social wages, but also less national sovereignty and political leverage on public policy. Global corporate demands and increasing pressure for harmonization of all regulations, standards, laws, and social programs make it implausible that the Canadian welfare state in its present form will be maintained. The national social policy debate cannot be divorced from these global capital and multinational corporate demands for economic restructuring and harmonization.

CHAPTER 16

The Decline of the Canadian Welfare State: Policies and Implications of Retrenchment

Gary Teeple

Learning Objectives

After studying this chapter,[1] you should be able to
- Define the term "welfare state" and analyze its component parts.
- Delineate the common elements of the history of social reform and the significance of such policies in industrial nations, with particular attention to the development of social legislation in Canada.
- Outline the main principles of the modern welfare state and their relation to **Keynesianism**.
- Outline, with examples, the reasons for the dismantling of the welfare state in Canada.

Introduction

Hardly any aspect of life in the modern industrial nation-state is not affected by the policies, programs, and regulations that make up the so-called welfare state. Indeed, so extensive are these reforms—yet so taken for granted—that few citizens of these countries realize how profoundly their lives are influenced by them.

"From the cradle to the grave" is the dusty cliché that was often employed to describe the extent of the influence. Merely to be born into a modern industrial nation-state is to become the recipient of numerous goods and services and the beneficiary of many standards and regulations, all associated with the welfare state. In one way or another these "reforms" have a profound impact all through one's life, and even beyond. And all for very important reasons, as we shall see in this chapter.

Since the late 1970s, a transformation of the welfare state has been underway. In virtually every country that claims to have extensive social reforms, governments have made conscious efforts to undermine, retract, retrench, or eliminate them (Mishra 1984; Banting 1987; Kamerman and Kahn 1989; Sulieman and Waterbury 1990). Nonetheless, despite more than a decade of these efforts and repeated declarations that "welfarism" has lost public favour, that "big government" must be cut back, that state regulations inhibit economic growth, and that **neoliberalism** has created a new morality, the reforms that comprise the welfare state have maintained a remarkable level of popular support—everywhere (Mishra 1990, chap. 2; Navarro 1985/86; Therborn and Roebeck 1986).

That the majority of citizens continue to look positively on social policies, programs, and regulations should not be surprising. Imagine a society without these reforms. In the labour market, there would be no legislated minimum wage, or limits to the working day, or employment health or safety standards, or restrictions on hiring and firing, or unemployment or accident insurance, and so on. People would have to do without state pensions, social services, hospital and medical insurance, public education, and income supplements. This list could easily be extended. Such a state of affairs is difficult to imagine because these reforms have become part of an accepted standard of living: they are essential to the way of life that has come to be a norm in the industrial world.

Even in capitalist societies that have all these reforms, however, people live in fear, particularly of unemployment and of the financial consequences of illness, injury, childbirth, and old age. This is because reforms are still just reforms; that is, they rarely provide more than minimal support and certainly give no guarantee that membership in society will bring employment, decent housing, accessible education, a living retirement pension or disability benefits, an unpolluted environment, employment standards, or freedom from poverty. For the most part, social reforms offer only limited security or standards for whatever need or issue they are intended to address; and while these "minimums" can be raised, they can also be lowered. Given rising unemployment and the present retrenchment of the welfare state, the above fears are becoming more deep-seated for growing numbers.

There can be little doubt about the consequences of cutbacks or elimination of social reforms. Capitalist societies with minimal or no reforms are close at hand. Here will be found workplaces without standards, child labour, high rates of illiteracy, environmental degradation and destruction, pervasive poverty, and enormous disparities in the wealth of citizens.

These social conditions appear to be typical of the direction in which industrial nations are moving, and they place the question of the nature of the welfare state and the reasons for its decline at centre stage.

The Welfare State

What Is the Welfare State?

Considerable debate has taken place over the definition of the welfare state, and several authors have attempted to forge its many characteristics into a coherent concept (Titmuss 1958; Gough 1979; Carrier and Kendall 1986; Quadagno 1987; Esping-Andersen 1989).

It cannot be said, however, that any general agreement came out of this controversy. For our purposes the following definition will suffice: The welfare state refers to a capitalist society in which the state has intervened in the form of social policies, programs, standards, and regulations in order to mitigate class conflict *and* to provide for, answer, or accommodate certain social needs for which the capitalist mode of production in itself has no solution or provision.

The main elements of this definition, common to all welfare states, should be spelled out, since they are important to an understanding of what the welfare state is, not to mention why it is being dismantled. First, it is a product of a capitalist society, which is characterized by commodity production, by contradictory interests (in particular between workers and the representatives of capital), and by the profit motive as the purpose of production. Second, the role of government, as the political embodiment of the system as a whole, has been to ensure its maintenance and reproduction. The government must fulfil this role because such a system has no inherent design, aside from the production of commodities for sale, for coping with potentially destabilizing social needs or class conflict. Third, the welfare state is delimited by the boundaries of the nation-state, the geographic territory under the jurisdiction of a given government.

The nature of the social reforms at the centre of this definition should be further specified. In general, these comprise state interventions in four key overlapping arenas of societal reproduction. The one most commonly associated with the welfare state is that of the physical propagation of the working class and its preparation for the labour market. Included here are the health-care and educational systems and many of the non-contributory social benefits (the largest recipients of which are women and children), which include subsidized day care, child/family allowance, food stamps, transfer payments to single mothers, and so on.

Another arena is the labour market and here the state has intervened not only to mitigate the extent of leverage that capital has over labour, but also to prepare fresh workers for the market and to ensure an "adequate" labour supply. Typically, this arena includes regulations on the minimum wage, hours of work, child labour, retirement age, education and training, injury insurance, immigration, and so on.

The third arena is the point of production, that is, the point of contact between workers and the representatives of capital, and the point where labour has submitted to the dictates of capital. Here the state intervenes to provide the institutional framework for class conflict (collective bargaining) and to protect the workers from the worst effects of exploitation by capital. Collective bargaining rights are central here, but employment and health and safety standards are also very important.

The fourth arena is the provision of income assurance for the "unproductive," in a word, retirement and other pensions and social assistance of all kinds for those unable, for whatever reason, to work in the system.

Just how these social reforms are carried into effect can be briefly categorized as follows. The most commonly recognized form of implementation would likely be the provision of services, such as education, health care, and child day care. The second most significant form of realizing these reforms is probably income transfers, such as pensions, unemployment or injury insurance, social security, and so on. In some countries the supply of "goods," for example in the form of public housing, comprises an important aspect of social reform. Lastly, there is the large category of laws, regulations, and standards that the state has promulgated in order to institutionalize inherent conflicts and to protect the disadvantaged in a system based on inequalities.

When State Intervention Becomes "The Welfare State"

If many of these social reforms, along with the modes of implementation, seem to have accompanied the long development of capitalism and the modern state, the question has arisen about just when a society can be defined as a welfare state. Is it the amount of reform or the sort of reform that is necessary for a regime to be so classified?

If it were possible to give a short answer, the following would likely suffice: When class conflict, reduced to the contest between workers and the representatives of capital, presents a chronic threat to the stability of the system and has to be institutionalized (i.e., placed within a legal framework of industrial relations) *and* when the majority of social needs pertaining to the reproduction of the working classes are addressed formally (i.e., by the state via "public" policies, etc.) rather than informally (i.e., via the community, family, friends), the welfare state has arrived. Such a definition, of course, leads one to question why and how this happens, not to mention when in history.

Why and How the Welfare State Comes About

The introduction of social reforms varies across nations in time, circumstances, and kind. While one cannot identify all the specific reasons and how they contribute to each coming of the welfare state, one can isolate a common premise and other factors general to the development of all national reform programs in the nineteenth and twentieth centuries.

The shared premise of national reform programs was the development and rise to pre-eminence of industrial capitalism within the nation-state. It was the consequences of the breakdown of the old mode of production and the coming of this new one that laid the ground for the social reforms that followed sooner or later.

The fundamental outcome of the destruction of precapitalist modes of production was twofold: (a) the creation of a capitalist labour market and working class, or the "freeing" of labour from its means of production and existing forms of bondage; and (b) the breakdown of social institutions, labour processes, and communities that embodied to a considerable degree an integrated social, political, and economic life. The significance of this transformation was that it gave rise to objective needs that had formerly been integral to a way of life. It also created new needs and new problems, which arose from and were associated with the capitalist labour market, the "freedom" of the worker, and new labour processes. In itself, capitalism had no answers for these needs and problems, aside from the wage relation and the purchase of commodities. The "answers" were to come as imposed reforms.

The "freed" working class, after it became entirely dependent on employment for its livelihood, found it necessary to defend itself against the depredations of the capitalist class and the vagaries of the labour market. The consequent attempts at self-protection and resistance by sections of the working class brought trade unions into being, which were to become the principal force behind the introduction, defence, and extension of many social reforms. Class conflict of one sort or another, or its potential, has been the common context for all reform.

Far from homogeneous, however, the fragmented and stratified working class produced corresponding fractures in its organized representation. As a counter-force to capital, trade unions were perpetually weakened in most countries by irresolvable sectionalism and the narrow interests and cautiousness of unions representing certain strata. In part because of this lack of a militant, united, and class-conscious trade union movement, class conflict, which is intrinsic to the system, was increasingly expressed in "gradualist" terms and the outcome limited to forms of compromise and accommodation (Kirk 1985).

This same organized resistance spurred the struggle for universal enfranchisement, and gave rise to political parties representative of certain strata of the working population. Such changes broadened the institutional political choices, allowing for a modicum of access to state power and the public purse, and for more political leverage for reform legislation. The number and inclusiveness of reforms owes much to these extra-parliamentary struggles and to the nature of political expression for the working class within the nation-state.

Out of the resistance to industrial capitalism came theories of socialist alternatives. The "spectre" of socialism or communism, a direct consequence of the coming of capitalism and the organized working class, has always been part of the motivation for the introduction of systematic reform programs (Mommsen 1981; Whitely 1981). All the industrial countries in the late nineteenth and early twentieth centuries had working-class parties and trade unions well versed in socialist theory and aware of the potential for revolution. Many actual attempts at revolution and numerous examples of general strikes appeared the world over. The success of the Bolshevik revolution was no minor inspiration to reforms in the West. Even after much of the political theory of the working class turned from revolution to reform and social democracy, spurs to reform included ongoing wars of liberation and the examples of the Soviet Union, China, and Cuba as "workers' states." In short, they served as reminders to the representatives of capital who might resist reforms.

Another consequence of industrial capitalism was increased productivity and the consequent need to expand overseas, producing colonial or imperial systems to "complement" the productivity of the industrial metropole. This expansion of capitalism brought with it the possibility to ameliorate its inherent conflicts. Among the effects of this export-led growth was the rapid increase in capital accumulation in the metropolitan countries. In turn, this allowed for a rise in the general standard of living. Capital accumulation expanded, confirming the legitimacy of the system and generating sufficient revenues for the creation of a **social wage**, the fiscal foundation of modern social reforms.

By the late nineteenth century, new technology, increased productivity, and expanded markets had begun to increase the segmentation, stratification, and social mobility of the labour force. The resulting complex hierarchies and numerous strata created a multitude of varying immediate interests within the working class, many of which actually depended on the continuing expansion of capitalism. Divisions along many lines fractured the working population, and the grounding of the interests of some strata in capitalism itself made substantial sections of the class more amenable to reform than revolution.

With industrial capitalism also came the "business cycle": the periodic rise and fall of economic activity and employment. In times of economic slumps, the working population, with no alternative to employment for its livelihood, suffered profoundly. These periodic deprivations frequently produced civil unrest, threatened social stability, and at times even piqued the conscience of members of the middle-class and corporate leaders. Organized and unorganized social disruption (and, to a small degree, charitable sentiment) during recessions or depressions have been the motivation for some reforms.

Another general aspect to the origin of the welfare state is the concessionary and even promotional attitudes on the part of organized capital. The former is explained in part by the delimited national labour market and relative immobility of national capital in the relatively "closed" national economy prior to the 1970s. The latter is explained by the desire of the corporate sector to "socialize," and thereby limit, some of the costs to industry that are "incidental" to its operations. In various countries, the introduction of seniors' pensions, hospital insurance, and even public education are illustrative of this point. The origin of industrial accident insurance schemes, while not without the component of working-class demand, lies largely in the efforts by corporations to create a system both limiting their liability for industrial accidents and "socializing" the costs through industry-wide insurance premiums and chronically inadequate compensation to workers and their families (Tampke 1981; Lubove 1986).

Although these are the principal reasons for, and conditions underlying, the coming of the welfare state to all industrial countries, it is important to stress that they comprise a multidimensional rationale, in the context of the contradictions of nationally structured capitalism. While throughout the industrial world, reforms attempt to address broadly the same needs and problems intrinsic to capitalist society, the specific forms they take as **policy regimes**, and when they develop, depend on a host of historically specific national factors. (There is a specific literature for each country. See Domhoff 1990; Rimlinger 1971; Kohler and Zacher 1982.)

By the first decade of the twentieth century, as a result of the forces outlined above, many of the reforms we now identify with the welfare state had been instituted in a limited way in most of the industrial nations. The reforms were not comprehensive because in these industrial countries large percentages of the labour force remained "on the land" outside the wage relation, and large-scale emigration and colonial expansion relieved much of the social pressure from "redundancies" in the labour force.

Only in the aftermath of the Second World War did all the conditions that underlie the modern welfare state fall into place, and the welfare state, as defined above, come into being.

The Modern Welfare State

In light of conditions in the post–Second World War period, the welfare state became a political and economic necessity. The industrial economies, with the exception of the United States, lay exhausted or in ruins, and the experience of the 1930s and the collective war effort made socialism an attractive alternative to the fear and indignity the working classes experienced in the capitalist labour market.

In order to reconstruct national capitalism in Europe and to resist widespread popular support for socialism in the industrial world, the state had to be employed (Hirschman 1988), to a degree not seen in earlier decades, to socialize the costs of reconstruction and to circumvent a repeat of the Depression and its consequent class struggles. So began almost three decades of unprecedented state intervention in the arenas comprising the relation between labour and capital.

The modern welfare state is often referred to as the Keynesian welfare state (KWS). The name derives in part from the economist John Maynard Keynes, whose theories came to dominate in the industrial countries during and after the Second World War (Schott 1982). His principal assumption was the existence of a national economy, in which, he argued, the state could intervene to effect levels of investment and domestic income, and thereby partially regulate unemployment by these national "demand management" policies. Such intervention represented a certain socialization of the costs of production (state credits, guarantees, grants and concessions) and of working-class reproduction ("public works," and aspects of the welfare state), as part of a political compromise with the working classes. This compromise included the goals of moderating the business cycle (to prevent a repeat of the unrest of the 1930s), helping rebuild the war-destroyed economies of Europe (to ensure the re-establishment of capitalism), and containing or diminishing the growing interest in socialism stemming from the experience of the 1930s and the devastation of war (Winch 1969, 221, 349).

This rationale for state intervention in the economy was complemented by several other postwar developments, which combined to create the general conditions demanding and allowing for the construction of the welfare state in this period. These conditions were many and interrelated, but it is possible to identify and isolate some of the important ones.

The most significant was the persistence of the national state, the political counterpart to national corporate enterprise. Here lay the political and operational framework of the welfare state. That is, social reforms have been defined and administered as national programs. Social reforms have represented the political compromise between the power of a national capitalist class and resistance to its particular forms of exploitation by sections of a national working class or social movements. Social reforms have depended partly on the kind and degree of political alternatives historically evolved in particular nations.

The state's ability to finance the programs of the KWS rested on several economic prerequisites. Among them were massive state indebtedness and expenditures during and after the Second World War (lend-lease for the war effort, the Marshall Plan for reconstruction, then the Korean and Vietnam wars, etc.); decolonization, which created new markets and cheap labour; and the "deepening of the domestic market," consumerism by another name, which depended on the vast expansion of ever-cheapening domestic commodities. In these ways, during this period, enormous surplus-value was generated, Gross National Products (GNPs) expanded relatively constantly, high wages could be paid, and, it followed, the tax-base in the industrial nations grew in concert.

Advanced Fordism[2] transformed the capitalist labour market, expanding and consolidating it with dramatic reductions in farm labour and the rapid growth of unproductive sectors. A relatively consistent high demand for labour and corresponding rises in wages and salaries in these postwar decades laid the basis for the growth in the number and size of trade unions. Accompanying this increasing union strength, there arose new and more comprehensive institutions of collective bargaining. The importance of collective bargaining for maintaining the system in the form of the nation-state, where the organized working class presents a threat to state power and capitalist hegemony, is much underrated (Harbison 1954).

The concomitant development of huge numbers and many layers of technical, para-professional, and administrative workers in both the private and public spheres substantially increased the strata of the working class, whose immediate interests rested on employment hierarchies, growth of the state sector, and national economic expansion. Here were the ingredients for the political platform promoted by social democracy as its vision of "reformed capitalism."

It is in this postwar period, then, that we find the culmination of social reform in the shape of the KWS. The overwhelming majority of the labour force had become working class, with sizeable percentages organized into trade unions. Class conflict now implied a chronic threat to the reproduction of the system and so had to be contained by institutionalized legal means. Moreover, with the transformation of the labour force and demise of precapitalist modes of production, the majority of social needs necessary to the reproduction of the working class (health, education, and social security) were not met by the private sector and could only be met formally by the state through "public" policies, programs, and standards, that is, macroeconomic policies based on state indebtedness and the "social" wage.

Redistribution

Most aspects of the welfare state were designed to redistribute a portion of wages and salaries, collected by the state in the form of tax revenues, premiums, and deferred income. They were not intended to redistribute social wealth, the accumulated capital assets of society. To do this would have contradicted the essence of the system, the private accumulation of capital, and thereby challenged the powers vested in such private ownership.

In redistributing the "social wage," the function of the welfare state has actually rested on a prior distribution of total income, determined by existing property relations and by the ongoing struggle between the working class and the corporate sector over their respective shares of the social product. These shares are determined more specifically by a number of variable factors, namely, historical and current expectations, the legislated minimum wage, the supply and demand for labour, the degree of unionization, the restrictions on collective bargaining, the business cycle, and so on. Such factors determine the initial distribution of the social product, which takes the form of wages/salaries and profits. It is from a divided and distributed pie, then, that the state collects its tax revenues, premiums, and deferred income.

If we examine how components of the welfare state are financed, the nature of redistribution can be seen more clearly. Certain programs in Canada, such as workers' accident and hospital insurance, unemployment benefits, and pension plans, are state-run indemnity schemes financed by premiums or deferred income paid by the working class out of wages and salaries. Some costs are often shared in part by corporations, their portion of the premiums calculated as part of the wage bill or the *faux frais* of doing business, like fire and theft insurance. Other programs, such as public education facilities, family allowance or child benefits, social assistance, public housing, and so on, are usually paid out of general revenue, but the lion's share of general revenue comes from taxes on wages and salaries.

It is possible, then, to say that the welfare state represents two forms of redistribution. One is the general redistribution of deductions from wages and salaries in the forms mentioned to pay for schemes that assist the working class to reproduce itself. The other is a certain redistribution of revenues upward in the social strata since the well-to-do make proportionally greater use of the more costly programs (for example, health care and public education) but contribute proportionally less income in their support because of the structure of the tax regimes.

It can be said, moreover, that the redistribution associated with the welfare state has had little effect on economic inequality, mainly because it was never intended to level economic differences. Although a degree of levelling may take place because of the "averaging" of a portion of labour income, it does as an unintended consequence of the principal goal of such programs, namely, to ameliorate the worst effects of economic inequality and to placate resistance to all the political and social implications of such inequality. A modicum of social security, certain minimum standards, and containment of class conflict, as opposed to economic equality, have been the intent of the welfare state. The existence of social policies and programs has not threatened the basis of inequality, namely, the structure of ownership and control, and it has not changed the necessity for workers to sell themselves in a competitive labour market.

Social Citizenship and Decommodification

If the foregoing is the negative evaluation of the impact of the welfare state, the positive evaluation must bring into focus the concept of social rights, or **social citizenship**[3] (Marshall 1963). Here is contained the notion that all members of society have an innate claim to certain social services and programs such as health care, education, seniors' pensions, unemployment insurance, and so on. The degree of universality of these reforms is the degree to which the concept has been realized. Social citizenship implies an equality of status in the social realm, in the same way that citizenship denotes equality in the political realm: just as there is universal enfranchisement, there has been, with conditions, universal entitlement to certain social guarantees with the welfare state.

Like the historical struggle for universal suffrage, driven by the aspiration of the working population to have control over their lives, so the demand for universal social security is the implicit desire of the working classes to be free from the insecurity of the labour market and the bondage of wage labour. The only recourse from the instability of the labour market and the servility of employment—in a word, to the commodification of labour power—is to organize into trade unions to secure concessions from corporations or to obtain, through protest, state-sponsored social and economic reform. Such reforms and union rights to bargain collectively, to strike and to organize, however, are never more than conditional concessions against the insecurities of the competitive labour market. In other words, they represent a qualified decommodification of labour power. The degree to which the reliance on the labour market for one's livelihood is supplanted by reforms is the degree to which social rights have been established in labour law and social benefits. The less universal and less comprehensive the welfare state, the less social citizenship can be said to exist (Esping-Andersen and Korpi 1984).

In other words, decommodification, whatever its degree, runs counter to the principles of the capitalist labour market. The existence of a social net and union rights undermine the negative effects of competition, powerlessness, fear, and poverty for the working class, which are part and parcel of the labour market. To go further, social citizenship represents the highest development of the principle of welfarism or social reformism. Just as universal enfranchisement marks the completion of politics, the concept and limited achievement of social citizenship marks the completion of social welfare, that is, the final result of a citizenry's struggle to have social security and meaning in an alienated society. Within capitalist social relations, the working class can achieve no more.

The partial and conditional achievement of social citizenship in the Western welfare states, however, helps clarify the limits of reformism. Even in those countries in which social and union rights have gained wide application, they have always remained provisional. That is, first, they often do not apply to certain categories of the population outside the labour force or marginal to it. Second, the boundaries of application are continuously subject to a fluctuating balance of class power. Third, social citizenship is only a compromise offered by a state and capitalist class, a response to the demands of subordinate classes. Fourth, it does not bring economic equality and presents no fundamental challenge to existing power relations. It rests, moreover, on several economic and political preconditions, which, as we shall argue, are rapidly disappearing.

This delineation of limitations is not intended to disparage legislative attempts at redistribution of income for economic security. In fact, it should be strongly asserted here that these are positive gains for the working class. They are not gifts from anyone, and, as such, they should be defended (and will have to be defended) as gains, however paradoxical their nature may be. We are simply attempting to uncover what "redistribution" is actually redistributing and to question the prevailing myth surrounding welfare-state expenditures. In a word, all of these programs, from unemployment insurance to state pensions to health care, are financed by deferred or diverted component parts of wage income, not by deductions from the profits of capital, although they do presume wages high enough to allow for deductions. They are forms of state-controlled redistribution of a portion of working-class income intended to facilitate the reproduction of wage-earners, to provide limited economic security, and to serve as emollients for the denial of economic privilege.

The Welfare State in Canada

Background

The history of social reform in Canada before the 1940s possesses no single moment of introduction and no developmental continuity or comprehensiveness. Many of the reforms that preceded the Second World War were specific and limited responses to trade union pressure, corporate desire to socialize costs, and the destabilizing effects of unemployment and worker unrest. The most significant arenas of state intervention throughout this period were in formal education and in relations between labour and capital at the point of production.

From the early 1870s the legislative results of pressure for educational reform begin to be seen. An Ontario act proclaiming compulsory education was promulgated in 1871 but its realization was limited. These nineteenth-century efforts to introduce state-sponsored elementary education came in response to the growth of industrial capitalism and to the need to prepare the working class for the factory work place. Literacy, numeracy, and respect for authority all had to be instilled at an early age. But the unintended consequences proved to be equally important to the system, namely, the provision of an "official" route for working-class upward mobility and legitimation for economic inequality and the role of the state (Spring 1972; Schecter 1976).

Also from the early 1870s, successive attempts were staged to restrain and contain the growing powers of the trade unions, to institutionalize class conflict[4] as it became more destabilizing (Logan 1956, 7–10; Woods and Ostry 1962, 18–87). To prevent, moreover, the utter degradation of workers in the factories of the late nineteenth century, several provincial factory acts were put in place attempting to regulate hours and conditions of work. Although varying considerably in their terms, they were similar in their lax enforcement (Kealey 1973).

Also from the late 1880s, limited efforts were made to introduce industrial accident insurance (workmen's compensation). For the most part, the intention of these acts was to limit the liability of corporations in the case of work-related injury, disease, or death. The level of compensation was dismally inadequate until their revision and standardization across Canada in the late 1920s. Industrial standards acts specifying minimum wages and hours of work, with designated boards and agents for enforcement, became a reality only in the second half of the 1930s.

With respect to the labour market, the state could not ignore the periodic rise of unemployment to levels that produced social unrest. Prior to the 1930s, high unemployment was dealt with primarily by means of increased "public works" and municipal relief payments (Struthers 1977). Unemployment insurance, although frequently a political issue from the turn of the century, was not to come into being until the 1940s (Cuneo 1979). What did come instead, in the depths of the Depression, were legislative and coercive suppression of unions; imprisonment of Communist party members; deportation of foreign-born militants; *and* in 1932 the "relief camps," established as a form of **workfare** for single, homeless, and unemployed young men. When closed down in 1936, these camps had "taken in" over 170 000 unemployed men (Liversedge 1973; Brown 1987).

Despite widespread unemployment and poverty, many demonstrations and strikes by workers, and numerous reform proposals from the business sector (not to mention legislative attempts) during the "dirty thirties," little was introduced by way of social reform aside from the "relief camps" (Finkel 1979).

Present Structure

The present structure of the welfare state in Canada has been described as a "'patchwork quilt' of programs" (Banting 1982) or as a "hodge-podge" of policies, programs, and laws and standards "that vary across political jurisdictions (federal, provincial, and municipal), categories of people," and types of need (Ismael 1985, xi). This patch-like structure, not in itself different from most other welfare states, is indicative of the nature of these social reforms as national attempts to respond to developing social needs not met by the wage relation, to contain the class conflict that is inherent in this same relation, and to maintain a labour force available for capital.

Such a motley array of social reforms, however, makes a coherent description very difficult. They have been ranked by amount of expenditure, periodized by date of enactment, categorized by constitutional division, and described by type of "delivery system," among other approaches (Armitage 1975). Probably the most common methods of grouping the programs are by (a) the mode of financing and (b) the nature of the recipient (Banting 1982).

Modes of Financing

The modes of financing social reform in Canada reflect the unsystematic introduction and nature of the reforms themselves. If the many forms of federal government funding have anything in common, it is that they represent attempts to moderate provincial disparities and maintain national standards across the country (Hess 1992).

One of the most important means by which Ottawa accomplishes these goals is through the transfer of funds in the form of equalization grants. These comprise unconditional payments given to "have not" provinces on an unconditional basis (the amount determined by a formula); they derive from general tax revenues and are intended to allow the same quality and kinds of public service across the country.

National standards in health care and post-secondary education, the two most expensive components of the welfare state, were maintained between 1977 and 1996 by a funding arrangement called "Established Programs Financing," sometimes referred to as block funding. This involved transfers to the provinces of federal funds, which were supposed to increase with the growth of population and GNP and were conditional on meeting certain criteria. In the terms of the Medical Care Act (1966), for instance, the provinces had to meet five criteria for the funding; namely, accessibility, universality, portability, comprehensiveness, and public administration. Although intended to contribute to the financing of health care and education, these federal block grants were not program specific and therefore the provincial governments had considerable leeway in their disposition.

National standards were also maintained in the sphere of welfare and social assistance by the funding arrangement known as the Canada Assistance Plan (CAP).

Established in 1966, CAP was a cost-sharing system in which certain terms were specified for the social programs by the federal government and provinces meeting them could be reimbursed for half the cost. This system lay at the heart of what was colloquially known as welfare, the mainstay in the attempts by federal and provincial governments to ameliorate the worst effects of poverty. (Dramatic changes to the EPF and to CAP came in 1996–97, and they are described later in the chapter.)

Premium payments, which are deductions from income, usually "at source," represent a sizable source of funding for significant components of the welfare state. Under this category may be placed such programs as unemployment insurance, medicare, and the Canada Pension Plan. Such components may include funds from general tax revenue but for the most part they are financed by the premiums paid.

Federal grants for specific programs (concerning, for example, literacy, drugs, job strategies, etc.) also constitute a source of federal transfer payments, although not as large as the above transfers.

In addition, the income tax system is employed to finance social benefits through tax credits and deductions or exemptions, sometimes called "tax expenditures." The tax credits are intended to boost indirectly the income of those with children or of retirement age whose incomes are below certain levels. The exemptions and deductions, on the other hand, for the most part further the incomes of the relatively well-to-do, and properly belong to a hidden welfare system for the rich (NCW 1976; 1979), not to mention being in part a Trojan horse to the existing welfare state, as we shall see.

Despite the fact that these forms of funding of the welfare state in Canada went a long way to establishing a relatively unified set of national standards and programs, it could not be said that there was a genuinely national system of social reform. The jurisdictional lines of different levels of governmental responsibility and the sources of funding have always been, and remain, divisive matters. The trade union movement has never been sufficiently united to wrest a more coherent system of reform or indeed a national system of industrial relations from the powers that be.

Categorizing social reform by the mode of financing reveals some essential features of the welfare state. It does not embrace, however, certain arenas of the welfare state, such as the labour market, employment standards, or the volunteer sector. It remains, moreover, descriptive and offers no explanation for the motley nature of social reform, the varied forms of funding, or the present retrenchment of the welfare state.

The Nature of the Recipient

If we examine the nature of the recipient as the criterion for attempting a coherent description of social reform in Canada, we find that the following categories are usually employed: (a) universal programs, or "demogrants," which apply to all individuals of a given unit (e.g., Old Age Security, veterans programs, public education, etc.); (b) social insurance programs, which provide benefits to those who have made contributions or premium payments (e.g., workers' compensation, unemployment insurance, Canada Pension Plan, medicare, etc.); and (c) social assistance programs, which are based on needs or income assessment and provide income supplements to those whose income falls below a certain level (e.g., Guaranteed Income Supplement, Refundable Child Tax Credit, welfare, etc.).

This way of grouping the programs of the welfare state, however widely used, does have significant shortcomings, some similar to those of the mode of funding. First, the categories are usually restricted to income security systems, which do not usually include education or health care; or an array of social services, which do not easily fall into one of the categories; or those privately run programs encouraged by the state through income tax exemptions and deductions (in particular, pensions, but increasingly education and health); or those programs financed and run by the volunteer sector. Second, the categories do not include any of the broad range of reforms dealing with the labour market or the point of production, namely, minimum wages and hours, collective bargaining, employment standards, and so on. Third, the categories have no underlying rationale; they are essentially descriptive, and while they reveal roughly who gets what, there is no explanation of why these programs were implemented, what role they serve in the system as a whole, and why they now appear to be on the wane. The categories are not anchored in the nature of the system itself.

The Welfare State and the Capitalist Mode of Production

If we return to our definition of the welfare state, it becomes possible to relate its component parts to the capitalist mode of production and thereby introduce an element of explanation into the categorization. To recapitulate, the welfare state refers to a capitalist society in which the state has had to intervene to ameliorate the contradiction between labour and capital and to ensure the reproduction of the working class and of the system as a whole.

As we have seen, historically one of the earliest arenas of intervention was at the point of production, the most immediate sphere of class conflict between workers and the representatives of capital. There are two main elements to this arena, namely, the bargaining relation between the union and corporation, and the need to impose elementary standards on corporate power in the workplace. The first is institutionalized in industrial relations acts or labour codes, which set out the terms for collective bargaining, intended to reconcile irreconcilable differences (Weiler 1980). There are ten provincial codes and one federal code that govern the structure of these relations in Canada (Sethi 1989). The second refers to those standards and regulations that are imposed by government on capital because of the unmitigated power it holds in the workplace. These would include health and safety standards, minimum wage and hours regulations, and other employment standards. All of these have both provincial and federal jurisdictions.

Aspects of these forms of intervention overlap in their implications with state activity in the arena of the labour market. Here the state is concerned in part with setting the broad parameters for the supply and demand of labour power; that is, of course, the supply *for* and the demand *by* capital. The parameters are established by immigration policies, which are used to add selectively to the labour force, and by numerous programs aimed at developing the skills, training and education, and mobility of the existing work force. Besides these boundaries to the labour market, the state must concern itself with the maintenance of the existing labour force, ensuring a constant and adequate supply of fresh workers for the market. Unemployment insurance, workers' compensation, and legislation covering statutory holidays, paid vacations, and other employment standards are the main forms of intervention here.

The existing labour force, however, must also be replenished with new generations of workers, and this necessity involves the propagation of the working class and its preparation for the labour market. One of the earliest forms of social reform falls into this category, namely, public education, which served to socialize the costs of training the working class to be literate, disciplined, and respectful of authority (Schecter 1977). Access to hospital and medical care was greatly increased in the late 1950s and 1960s (Swartz 1977; 1987) in an attempt to address the significant and growing problems of disease and injury resulting from the passive, consumerist society and the advanced Fordist mode of production. The supply of subsidized housing, a very important aspect of the welfare state in some countries, has always been limited mainly to the elderly and the lowest strata of the working class in Canada, but this amounts to about 15 percent of all households. Other means of supplementing wages that have been employed include offsetting the costs of maintaining a family with the "family allowance," the child tax credits, the child care expense deduction, and so on.

The fourth arena of intervention concerns the provision of income assurance for the "unproductive" (mainly the physically and mentally challenged and single mothers) and for people whose "productive" life is over. Most of the varied programs for the former are financed through the Canada Assistance Plan. For the latter, the Canada Pension Plan (premium financed in the main), Old Age Security (general revenues), the Guaranteed Income Supplement (for those over 65 with very limited other income), and the tax-assisted Registered Retirement Pension Plans (RRSPs) are the principal means of providing for those past productive age as defined by the capitalist mode of production (Phillipson 1982). Despite these income security programs, a

Figure 16.1   Unemployment Rates, 1946–1992

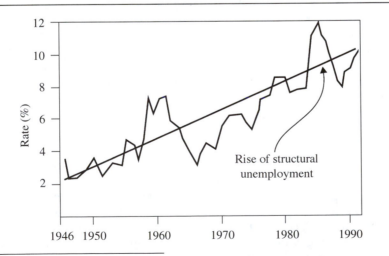

Sources: Statistics Canada, *Annual Labour Estimates*, 1946–1990, 1991, 1992 (Ottawa: Minister of Supply and Services); Statistics Canada, *Canadian Social Trends* 20 (Spring): 30.

substantial percentage of the "old" and "unproductive" live in relative poverty with subsistence incomes, inadequate housing, and poor medical care.

Despite the relative comprehensiveness of the programs of the welfare state and the huge state bureaucracies dedicated to their functioning, poverty has never been eliminated and indeed is growing. Unemployment has risen inexorably since the 1960s to persist at about 10 percent of the labour force, employment standards are being reduced, literacy rates are failing, demand for health care is expanding, the rates of certain chronic diseases increase, and on and on. In short, whatever amelioration of the worst effects of capitalism, redistribution of income, and containment of class conflict the welfare state may have proffered, it has neither changed the fundamental nature of the capitalist mode of production nor provided permanent immunity from its effects.

The Decline of the Welfare State

"Necessary" though it was, the KWS could only be developed after the Second World War under certain conditions, which have been briefly sketched earlier. Economic reconstruction carried out with advanced Fordism in national economies, a consistent demand for labour, rising real wages, expanding trade unions, and growing social strata and employment hierarchies were some of these interrelated prerequisites. Here were the ingredients for widespread support among the representatives of labour and capital for state intervention in practice and even as a political philosophy in the form of social democracy.

All this began to change, however, in the early 1970s. The productive power of advanced Fordism had already long outgrown the national market, but now it was being replaced by computer-aided processes whose productive capabilities were far superior. In concert with these changes, the structure of capital itself began to shift from a national to an international base. Under the auspices of the General Agreement on Tariffs and Trade, the World Bank, and the International Monetary Fund, systematic pressure was gradually applied to level national social and economic policies to facilitate world trade. Changes in the labour market followed, not so much for the workers, who remained restricted by national boundaries, but for capital, which now began to search for ways to escape the high wages necessary to maintain the KWS. As real wage rises began to stagnate and then to fall in the 1970s and 1980s, often owing to state intervention, trade union membership followed suit, also often "assisted" by restrictive government legislation. As national policies, regulations, and standards began to be usurped by their international counterparts, the sovereignty of the nation-state began to wane. Trade union leverage on the national state and capitalist class could no longer be maintained. "Real existing socialism," moreover, became exposed as corrupted state capitalist regimes, and so the socialist alternative to the capitalist mode of production could no longer be presented as a goal worth fighting for.

Neoliberal policies, variously labelled as Thatcherism, Reaganism, neoconservatism, and the New Right Agenda, began to become visible by the mid-1970s and became formal government policy in many countries by the end of that decade. They were, we suggest, the policy side of the "new reality"; they represented the political

Figure 16.2 Federal Transfers to Provinces for Health and Education, 1989–2004

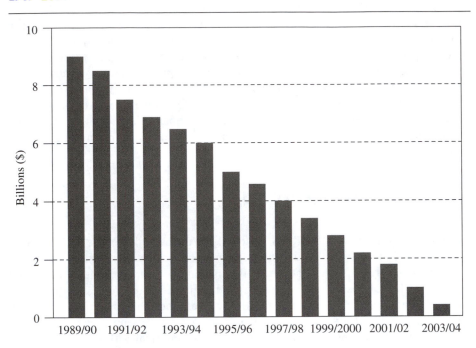

Sources: Canadian Council on Social Development, "Canada's Social Programs Are in Trouble," *Newsletter for the Campaign Against Bill C-69* (Ottawa: CCSD, October 1990).

requirements of capital internationalized, highly centralized, and global in perspective. In attempting to transform all forms of state intervention into market functions, these policies are intended to level national distinctions for global investment. They also represent the last truly national policies to be promulgated, the final act of the independent nation-state, because with their acceptance the economic and political barriers to production and distribution around the world will have been minimized. With their adoption they in effect harmonize the national with the global economy.

The possibility of national management of national economies is now increasingly abridged, and national forms of the welfare state are now more and more difficult to maintain. In all the industrial nations and in most of the developing nations, these neoliberal policies continue to be legislated, and with their promulgation social reform as we know it is being transformed. Social democracy as embodied in the New Democratic Party in Canada, it follows, is losing its meaning and purpose. All political parties, the social democrats included, increasingly find themselves obliged with greater or lesser resistance to carry out the agenda.

For Canada, as for all industrial countries, the coming of the global economy has meant relatively less corporate tax and declining wages and so a declining social wage. It has also meant less national sovereignty and so less union or political leverage over policy. Global corporate demands for access to the public sector and for the "level playing field" have come to prevail.

> "Treat us nice or kiss us goodbye," warns mining mogul. B.C. should give its mining companies a break or watch as they seek a warmer climate in countries like Chile, says Cominco Ltd. President. (*BC Business*, April 21, 1992)

North American Free Trade

Co-terminous with these global demands and policy reflections that are cutting back Canadian social programs are the pressures arising from the Canada–United States Free Trade Agreement (FTA) and the North American Free Trade Agreement (NAFTA). These treaties, which are intended to create a single continental economy, present two areas of threat to the Canadian welfare state. First, the treaties themselves contain no explicit safeguards for the multifaceted social programs and standards of this country. In light of the marketplace principles underlying the accords, all aspects of the welfare state may well be considered "unfair subsidies" or "barriers to trade." Under the terms of the FTA, furthermore, should the Canadian government wish to establish either new social programs that are universal or new Crown corporations, it must "notify and consult" the U.S. government. Not only, then, are the present programs unprotected, but also any possible extensions or new programs are made conditional on "consultations" with Washington.

Second, there are the broad implications of a unified economy: increasing pressure for the harmonization of all regulations, standards, laws, programs, policies, and so on that pertain to the labour market, the workplace, the reproduction of the labour force, and the "non-" or "unproductive," not to mention fiscal and monetary policies. Differences do exist and will persist among political jurisdictions, but where they create overriding economic disadvantages government will maintain higher-than-average standards and policies at the risk of declining investment and their own political doom. It is, to say the least, implausible that the Canadian welfare state can be maintained as we have known it in the face of these free trade agreements (Drover 1988).

The Decline of the Welfare State in Canada

By the late 1970s, the attack on the welfare state in the United Kingdom, the United States, and Canada had become visible, and by 1980 it had become government policy in the former two. As in these two countries, the dismantling of the welfare state in Canada went on in a patchwork manner throughout the 1980s; in the early 1990s, however, the Government of Canada passed Bill C-69, which began the progressive, systematic, and comprehensive withdrawal of federal monies from national social programs.

Even when countries are not asking for financial aid, the IMF apparently gives unsolicited advice: "The International Monetary Fund secretly urged the Canadian government this year to freeze public servants' wages, slash unemployment insurance in poor regions, and stop protecting inefficient farmers, confidential documents … reveal. In [the] report … the UN agency also urged Ottawa to axe a staggering $6 billion from next year's projected $30.5 billion deficit." (*Vancouver Sun*, November 1991)

The earliest stages of retrenchment in Canada were most easily seen in the arena of state intervention at the point of production. In the 1970s the increasing use of back-to-work legislation and the Anti-Inflation Program of 1975–78, which enabled the federal government to roll back wage increases that went beyond certain guidelines, set the stage for a much more comprehensive assault on collective bargaining rights (Panitch and Swartz 1993). From the early 1980s on, the federal and provincial governments embarked on changes to labour legislation that were to diminish significantly the established rights of trade unions. Provincial wage restraint laws were also promulgated; the right to strike was restricted, and for some workers even eliminated; union organizing and certification regulations were everywhere made more difficult; and "right-to-work" (anti-union) laws began to make their appearance in several provinces.

Gradual improvement in employment standards came to a halt by the early 1980s and many began to be cut back. Hours of work, minimum wages, vacation time, termination regulations, restrictions on child employment, the right of appeal, and so on, all were subject to gradual retrenchment by provincial and federal governments (Fawkes 1983).

Figure 16.3   Real Annual Wage Increases, 1920–1990

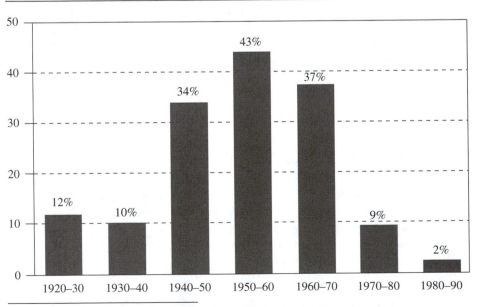

Source: Adapted from Statistics Canada, *Canadian Social Trends* 32 (Spring 1994): 18.

With respect to the labour market, two major programs have been undergoing curtailment for several years. Workers' compensation boards have allowed a relative decline in assessment rates for the corporate sector and have cut back on benefits and services to ill or injured workers. Less emphasis is being paid to prevention and monitoring, and inspection has been downgraded. Significant changes to the unemployment insurance system have been made since about the mid-1970s. In several stages, the qualifying periods have been lengthened, other eligibility criteria have been tightened, the benefits have been cut back, maximum time for benefits has been reduced, penalties for voluntary quitting have been introduced, the federal contribution has been withdrawn, some of the funds have been reallocated to wage subsidization, and the premiums paid by employees and employers have been raised. Increasingly severe restrictions continue to be legislated.

Of the welfare state, the principal component for preparing the working class for the labour market is the educational system. Primary and secondary education is funded provincially and all the provinces have engaged in cutbacks since at least the early 1980s. This has resulted in teacher salary freezes, program cuts, fewer extramural activities, and larger class sizes. Post-secondary education was financed largely under the block-funding arrangements mentioned earlier whereby the federal government contributed according to a formula based on growth of the GNP and population. Since the mid-1980s, however, the formula has been cut back, the increases frozen, and the funding reduced annually. In 1996, the nature of funding changed, as described later.

These same retrenchments apply to the medical care system, which was financed in the same way but similarly changed in 1996. Medicare remains central to the maintenance and propagation of the working class, but as the method of funding changed the results of the cutbacks were exacerbated: national standards have declined as have the accessibility and comprehensiveness of the services offered.

Federal contributions to subsidized housing have also suffered cutbacks since the mid-1980s. During the latter half of this decade the overall funding was reduced, including finds for co-operative housing and "low-cost" rental shelter.

For those considered "unproductive" or "non-productive" in light of the capitalist mode of production, namely, those over 65 years old, those under employment age, and those receiving social assistance, the retrenchment has been similarly consistent over the past decade. Both the family allowance and Old Age Security were subject to clawbacks starting in 1989, so ending their universality in all but name. The Canada Assistance Plan, the only shared-cost national program intended to alleviate poverty (until it was folded into the CHST in 1996), has had limits put on increases to the three richest provinces, Ontario, British Columbia, and Alberta, where it so happens that most of the poor in Canada live. It should not be forgotten that a sizable percentage of welfare recipients, about 40 percent, are children; they will experience the impact of these cuts most dramatically.

Across the levels of government there has been a systematic divestment of the role and responsibilities previously assumed by the state. This divestment encompasses the increasing introduction of user fees, the reduction of subsidies and grants, disentitlement by the re-definition of state responsibilities, contracting out to private enterprise, and the cancelling of non-statutory services such as family support, child abuse programs, and so on (Ismael 1988).

While the retrenchment was systematic and continuous in the 1980s and early 1990s, there was a significant change in the method of federal funding in 1996 that opened the possibilities for a wider range of cutbacks at a quicker pace. The introduction of the Canada Health and Social Transfer (CHST) combined the federal Canada Assistance Plan (CAP) and the Established Programs Financing (EPF) into one fund. Among other consequences, it brought an immediate cut in cash transfers to the provinces, with projected additional annual cuts to the year 2001.

The CHST is another step in the general dismantling of the social and economic responsibilities associated with the KWS in Canada. The KWS represents state-sponsored compromise in a class-divided society: "public" interests, truncated as they may be, were and are embodied in state or Crown corporations, trade union rights, and the broad range of rights and entitlements that comprise social services, social insurance, and social assistance.

Globalization, as argued earlier, brought pressure to transform the entire sphere of public property into corporate private property. Such a transformation required an enormous ideological shift for a government and citizenry that had come to expect state intervention as the "human face" of a capitalist system that was otherwise unable to provide the necessities for all its members. On the ideological front, the pervasive mind-set that accompanied the KWS, assuming and demanding state responsibilities, had to be changed. This was done in part through a systematic and conscious transformation of the dominant political party platforms and mass media perspectives that redefined society as merely the sum of its individual members. The social responsibilities of the state were attacked and in their place individual and family responsibilities were asserted as paramount, while state assistance was recast as a last and negative resort. The private sector, or the "market," was presented as the solution to social problems, but social problems were re-asserted as individual problems and the individual defined as "economic man"—the human being as consumer and commodity. These changes were the rationalization for the policy changes and political assault on the entire range of public forms of property.

With the coming of the CHST in 1996, federal funding for health and post-secondary education and the shared-cost social assistance programs would be combined in one block fund. Aside from serious cuts to spending in these social programs, the CHST also embodied a significant devolution of powers to the provinces over the programs and services previously funded in part through the CAP and EPF. There were several implications to this devolution.

One of the most important of these flows from the fact that the KWS had become central to the definition of the nation itself. In most industrial nations in which the KWS developed, the national identity was to some degree embodied in state-sponsored forms of public property. To the extent that a public medicare system, public education, employment standards, unemployment insurance, and state-run corporations and so on existed, the nation created a sense of itself. Canada was no exception. The CBC, medicare, the former UI, and the standards associated with the CAP need only be mentioned to make the point. With the financial cuts and changes to these state-sponsored corporations and services, a significant part of the foundation of national distinctiveness begins to wane. National identity gives way to regionalism, to multiculturalism, to racial/religious supremacism, and to a vacuum.

Another implication concerns the decline or loss of national standards associated with the previous form of federal funding. With the CHST and its devolution of administrative powers, all but two standards have declined or disappeared: the

Canada Health Act retains its five principles and the prohibition of a provincial residential qualification remains on welfare. Even these are enforceable, however, only as long as federal funding continues and the will to defend the standards persists.

A good example of the elimination of most of the standards associated with social assistance is the rather rapid rise in the introduction of provincial experiments in workfare, the requirement to work for some categories of recipients for a welfare allowance. Under CAP the recipients of social assistance could not be obliged to work for this minimal stipend; it was legislated as a social right based on the assumption that everyone desires a dignified and worthy relation to society and that welfare is a last resort in a system whose structure does not allow adequate provision for everyone. It must be remembered that the overwhelming majority of recipients have been the elderly, the disabled, and single mothers and minors—those who are defined as outside the labour market. While workfare does not apply to all social assistance recipients, it does represent a shift away from welfare as a social right and an erosion of social rights in general. Workfare also translates into much tighter control over the lives of recipients than before, into a tacit form of coercive labour as the state-sponsored introduction of cheap and flexible labour to the labour market, and into an implicit definition of the cause of poverty as the individual inadequacies of the poor themselves.

It is worth noting that the tax concessions advanced to RRSP contributors each year nearly equals the total amount spent on welfare in Canada. Needless to say, the treatment of welfare recipients and RRSP contributors is vastly different; yet, both receive transfers of state revenue. How to explain this obvious inequity? Welfare recipients are judged as unworthy because they are without a source of revenue and therefore without practical rights in a private property system whose morality rests on money and its associated power. RRSP contributors are treated with deference because they have more revenue than is required for immediate consumption and so are able to defer a portion of their revenues for the future. In a system of private property they are citizens who have the wherewithal to exercise their rights, and for that reason are judged as worthy.

Aside from the changes brought on by the CHST, the unemployment insurance system first promulgated in the 1940s and expanded in the 1960s has suffered from continuous tightening of the rules for eligibility and declining benefits relative to the cost of living. Because of long-term structural unemployment, a growing number of uninsured contract workers, and tougher qualifying regulations, a *record low number of unemployed* received benefits in 1996. Only a little over a third of the unemployed in that year were able to draw on unemployment insurance, according to Statistics Canada; and this compares with more than 80 percent before 1990–91 and the coming of increased restrictions (Statistics Canada 1998). In form, the elements of an unemployment insurance system persist, but in practice, Employment Insurance (EI), as it is now called, is moving more or less rapidly toward a system of minimal income protection against unemployment.

Another significant change that has taken place recently has to do with the Canada Pension Plan. The CPP and its counterpart the Caisse de dépôt et placement du Québec embody the employment-related deferred income part of retirement pensions for Canadians. For many years the Caisse has been employed as a source of investment funds by the government of Quebec. But the CPP has always been structured mainly as a pay-as-you-go system, relying on the premiums of present-day workers

What Is Welfare?

Social assistance, or welfare, is the income program of last resort in Canada. It provides financial assistance to individuals and families whose resources are inadequate to meet their needs and who have exhausted other avenues of support.

Until recently, welfare was paid under the terms of the Canada Assistance Plan (CAP), an arrangement that allowed the cost to be shared by the federal government and the provinces and territories. In April 1996, CAP was replaced by the Canada Health and Social Transfer.

Although people talk about welfare as a single entity, there are really twelve welfare systems in Canada—one in each province and territory. Some would say there are hundreds of welfare systems, because of the leeway allowed to municipalities, which run welfare programs in Nova Scotia, Ontario, and Manitoba.

Despite the fact that each of the twelve main welfare systems is different, they have many common features. They have complex rules regulating all aspects of the system, including eligibility for assistance, the rates of assistance, the amounts recipients are allowed to keep from outside earnings, and the way in which applicants and recipients may question decisions regarding their cases.

Eligibility

Eligibility for welfare is based on some general administrative rules that vary widely throughout the country. For example, applicants must be of a certain age (usually between 18 and 65). Full-time students of post-secondary educational institutions may qualify for assistance in some provinces only if they meet stringent conditions. In other provinces, they cannot apply for assistance without leaving their studies. Single parents must try to secure any court-ordered maintenance support to which they are entitled. Individuals who are disabled require medical certification of their conditions. Strikers are not eligible in most jurisdictions. Immigrants must try to obtain financial assistance from their sponsors.

Once these administrative conditions are met, each applicant goes through a "needs test." This test compares the budgetary needs of an applicant and any dependents with the assets, and income of the household; needs, assets, and income are defined in provincial and territorial welfare laws. In general, welfare is granted when a client household's non-exempted financial resources are less than the cost of regularly recurring needs, that is, food, shelter, household, and personal needs (and special needs, in some jurisdictions).

First of all, applicants' fixed and liquid assets are examined. In most provinces, fixed assets like a principal residence, furniture, and clothing are considered exempt. Most provinces also exempt the value of a car, although some jurisdictions take into consideration factors such as the need for a private vehicle and the availability of public transportation. Property and equipment required for employment are generally considered exempt. Applicants are usually required to convert any non-exempt fixed assets into liquid assets and to use any non-exempted liquid assets for their ongoing needs before qualifying for welfare.

Source: National Council of Welfare, *Welfare Incomes 1995* (Ottawa, 1997).
Reproduced with the permission of the Minister of Public Works and Government Services Canada, 1998.

to finance the pensions of the retired. The small fund that has accumulated, about two years' worth of benefits, has been lent to the provinces at less than market interest rates over the years. This arrangement naturally benefited the provincial governments but clearly not the intended beneficiaries, the retired men and women whose deferred income it represented. To the degree that provincial governments used it for the benefit of the corporate sector, these loans represented a shift of wealth from one class to another by means of institutionalized government control over a pension plan.

In December 1997, however, a law was passed to put the accumulating CPP fund more decisively into the hands of the corporate sector. With minimal debate among Canadians over the fate of their pensions (discussions were limited to Parliament and its committees) and premised on questionable arguments about the future of the CPP, it was legislated that the fund should be invested in the stock and bond markets. Beginning in 1998, an investment board is to be set up to take over this investment of a large and growing fund.

The membership of the board is to be chosen by the finance minister from a list prepared by a senior corporate official. The administration of the fund will then rest in this board and be out of the hands of government. In other words, the disposition of the fund will be depoliticized and rely on ostensibly strictly economic criteria and the rise and fall of the market. This means that the pensionable earnings of the working class have been put at the disposal of the corporate sector, whose only morality is that of the marketplace; because it will be made subject to the vagaries of the market, this deferred income will suffer the same fate as the market.

An alternative vision for the disposition of the CPP fund does not seem to have been considered. Most obviously a mechanism for some democratic accounting of the disposal of the fund should have been included. Second, some guidelines or principles for investing the fund should have been established. And third, consideration should have been given to investing the fund in the public domain; in other words, the fund could be invested in public housing, medical clinics, co-operative food supply and other amenities for the elderly, as guarantees for a decent life outside the labour market. None of these things have been done.

Official Alternatives

Coincident with these cutbacks to the public-sector provision of all aspects of social welfare has been the active encouragement of private-sector provision in the form of charitable donations or volunteer service and through privatization.

The Rise of Charities

There are many hundreds of "charities" in Canada and many more are added each year, including educational facilities, hospitals, and a range of social services previously funded by the state. The size and role of such umbrella organizations as the United Way has grown enormously since the late 1970s when this retrenchment first began to be felt.

Several important trends comprise the context for this vast growth since 1980 in size and number of charitable institutions and non-profit organizations, and for the conscious efforts by government and the corporate sector to promote it. One such trend has been the rapid increase in social needs, which has accompanied increasing long-term structural unemployment, among other forms of social disintegration. Another has been the growing limits on further expansion of the social wage;[5] a third has been the planned reduction of the services of the welfare state. As these trends accelerate, the entire sphere of social reproduction, embracing all aspects of health, education, and social services, will increasingly be moved into the realm of the private market, one part of which takes the form of charities or trusts. The fostering of such institutions and agencies is but a means of "privatizing" public facilities; and their expansion is an attempt to shift the responsibility for the human costs of an inhuman system from the state to the individual, and to transfer the means of redress from the "social wage" to private "gifts."[6]

Although charitable donations at present comprise only a small fraction of state social expenditures, they play an increasingly larger role as the above trends continue to unfold. To the degree that they replace state provision, they make it evident that society as a marketplace does not provide for all of its members such basic elements of life as employment, housing, food, health care, and so on. It has no mechanism, aside from social reforms, charity, or volunteer work (i.e., anomalies to the system), to provide such "amenities" to those who are not working or, for that matter, even to the growing numbers of working poor. With the decline of the welfare state and the growth of charities, the marginalized will increasingly become dependent on the purported benevolence or good will of others; and this in a society that looks upon altruism as abnormal.

It also becomes clear that society as marketplace relies mainly on individual donations and tax revenues, that is, on deductions from the wages of those working, to shore up the chronic social destruction that takes place under capitalism. But now, increasingly in the form of charity, social redistribution becomes a voluntary matter and indeed is tax deductible. This last point means that the more that is given to charity, the less goes to the state for redistribution. It is a planned paradox: charities are both a substitute for and an instrument in the decline of the welfare state.

To the degree that charitable institutions and non-profit or volunteer organizations become significant forms of social redistribution, moreover, the existing "social rights" and universal entitlements to state-funded social services will be narrowed. In part in the name of charity, the elements of "social citizenship," though never fully realized anywhere, have begun the process of erosion everywhere.

Systematic Privatization

Aside from the active promotion of charitable and volunteer organizations to compensate for the conscious discharging of the role and responsibility of the welfare state, policies of systematic **privatization** are becoming commonplace.

The least visible and yet widely employed process of privatization is the policy of incremental degradation of benefits and services. Public services are increasingly restricted by rising eligibility criteria, cancellation, disentitlement, contracting out, redefinition, transferred responsibility, or declining quality. Income benefits are rolled back, taxed back, or allowed to fall behind the rate of inflation. The objective of such policies is that, over time, pressure to meet minimum standards or fill omissions will be met by the private sector. The public health-care systems provide good examples of this form of privatization with the growth of user fees, deductibles, and restricted treatments, operations, and facilities, while at the same time private insurance and medical treatments are encouraged by a variety of incentives.

Other examples can be found in social assistance programs and insurance for unemployed and injured workers, wherein qualifications and restrictions increase and payments do not keep pace with the cost of living. Government restrictions on grants to public schools have multiplied, while increasing government funding encourages the growth of private schools. Similarly, universities have experienced restrictions on grant increases, causing a rise in student fees, larger classes, declining facilities, restricted eligibility, and a need to pursue greater links with private enterprise.

In contrast to these undeclared policies of erosion, the government makes use of open incentive policies. The use of tax deductions is a widely employed form of inducement to move to the private provision of benefits, and the privatization of pension plans and medical insurance are the common objectives of such schemes. Included here might also be the use of education vouchers, which can be used in the public or private schools, with the ultimate goal of undermining the public system and providing the private sector with state funding, making a universal social program of benefit to the private sector. These incentives all involve a form of subsidy to those who can afford private provision at the expense of those who are and will be completely reliant on state provision. They will, moreover, encourage existing two-tiered systems in which those who have the means to set aside money or afford private fees are assisted in doing so.

The Poor and Transfer Payments

The differences between the average incomes of the poor and of all Canadians are sometimes striking. Poor couples under 65 with children under 18 had an average family income of $19 691 in 1995, for example, while the average income of all couples with children under 18 was $62 116 (or three times as large).

The differences were much less in the case of unattached seniors and single-parent mothers, because average incomes were much less. The average income for poor single-parent mothers under 65 with children under 18 was $14 696 in 1995, but the average income of all single-parent mothers was only $25 122—much less than average incomes for all husband–wife families.

Obviously, many poor Canadians rely on government programs of one kind or another to help make ends meet. In some cases, the amounts provided by governments are surprisingly modest, and the amounts provided by earnings and non-government sources of income are substantial. In other cases, especially in

(continued)

(continued)

the case of poor seniors, governments provide a very large portion of total income.

The table below shows the average amount of transfer payments received by poor families and unattached individuals in 1995. Transfer payments include Canada and Quebec Pension Plan benefits, unemployment insurance, welfare, the federal Old Age Security pension and Guaranteed Income Supplement, the federal Child Tax Benefit, and the federal GST credit. The Canada and Quebec Pension Plans and unemployment insurance are government-run programs, but the money comes from contributions by workers and employers, not from government.

The family types in the table are ranked according to the average size of the transfer payments, with the smallest amounts first. The second column gives the average incomes of poor families and unattached individuals from all sources; the third gives the percentage of total income from transfers.

Government programs of one kind or another provided less than half of the total income for the first four family types, 70 percent of total income for single-parent mothers under 65 with children under 18, and 91 to 92 percent of total income for the three family types 65 or older.

Average transfer payments to poor families and unattached individuals were generally down in 1995 from the previous year's levels. The average losses between 1994 and 1995 were $507 for poor unattached men under 65, $556 for poor unattached women under 65, $86 for poor childless couples under 65,

Transfer Payments to the Poor by Family Type, Canada, 1995

Family type	Average transfer payment	Average income from all sources	Percentage of total income from transfers
Unattached men under 65	$ 3 674	$ 8 022	46%
Unattached women under 65	3 682	8 271	45
Childless couples under 65	6 275	12 828	49
Couples under 65 with children under 18	8 488	19 691	43
Single-parent mothers under 65 with children under 18	10 233	14 696	70
Unattached women 65 and older	11 248	12 422	91
Unattached men 65 and older	11 265	12 184	92
Couples 65 and older	16 503	17 905	92

(continued)

(continued)

$619 for poor couples under 65 with children under 18, and $293 for poor unattached senior men.

These losses may seem small in absolute terms, but they are relatively large when compared with the low incomes of those affected by them. The loss of $556 by poor unattached women under 65, for example, represents 7 percent of their total average income of $8271.

The only family types to get higher transfer payments in 1995 were poor unattached senior women, with an average gain of $65, and poor married couples 65 and older, with an average gain of $674.

Source: National Council of Welfare, *Welfare Incomes 1995* (Ottawa, 1997). Reproduced with the permission of the Minister of Public Works and Government Services Canada, 1998.

Implications

In general, the three levels of Canadian government are moving away from state provision of social services and programs, especially those that are universal or characterized as social rights. In place of these "rightful" entitlements, government is re-instituting and reinforcing the principles of the "poor laws," the welfare schemes of pre-industrial times and the Third World (Midgley 1984). The current trends in Canada represent a revivification of the concept of the "deserving" versus the "undeserving" poor, and of the principles of means testing, of familial liability and responsibility, of qualifying moral conduct, of temporary benefits, of deterrent eligibility criteria, of "targeting the needy," and of the workhouse ("workfare"). The more that these principles come into practice, the more the principles of universality and social right are undermined, and the more the failures and omissions of the system are presented as the responsibility of the individual rather than of the state or the corporations—and the more every aspect of the welfare state can be made into an instrument of social control.[7]

There are many reasons for these changes in policy, for the encouragement of charities and the privatization of social services and benefits. Among them are the following political goals: to "downsize" the role of government by reducing state responsibilities and the number of employees; to "open up" state sectors to private accumulation; to divert the revenues spent on health, education, and welfare, which represent a large percentage of national budgets, to the private sector; and, not least, to attempt to "discipline" the working classes by undermining union achievements and eroding their social security in the face of rising permanent unemployment.

There are, of course, broader material causes behind these changes. The decline in state revenues, for instance, is no small factor, but this is only an immediate cause because it in turn is due mainly to recurrent recessions, the shift in tax burden, and greater demands from capital. The global context of these changes is the economic necessity to "harmonize" national social security reforms, which constitute barriers of varying degrees to the needs of the international market.

In a society that can now provide employment only for a diminishing number of its citizens and that has no inherent mechanism for providing for those without work, the rescinding and downgrading of those parts of the welfare state that offer a modicum of support have consequences that are now visible throughout Canada. Unemployment presently stands at about 10 percent with much higher rates in the Maritimes and Quebec; and, given free trade, new technology, and global production, it is unlikely that this chronic rate will decrease. The demands on unemployment insurance will continue to rise and the welfare rolls increase: the system has no intrinsic morality and sloughs off human beings as so much waste (Burman 1988), and, for a growing percentage of youth, provides no future. Today over two million Canadians receive social assistance payments (about 8 percent of the population), a figure that does not include large numbers who fall outside increasingly strict rules, not to mention the homeless and the working poor.

Such social assistance, which does not even keep pace with the cost of living, is not extended to everyone without work or means of support. Over the past decade the need to supplement welfare and to provide for those who have no other means of income has given rise to food banks, an institution dependent on charitable, private donations. The first opened in Edmonton in 1981; by 1991 there were almost 300 of them across the country. In that year about two million individuals received food from a food bank at least once; about 600 000 were regular monthly recipients and the numbers have grown markedly every year (Oderkirk 1992; Riches; 1986; 1987).

The past decade has also seen a large and growing number of homeless. Unemployment, welfare retrenchment, a shrinking rental market (especially in the low-end), abolished social programs, redefined state responsibilities, privatized social services (Ismael 1989), and discharged mental patients without services or care (Ismael and Vaillancourt 1988) have all contributed to social disintegration. Far from seeking an answer to this problem, the federal government has continued to cut back its support of affordable housing. In 1990 it cut funds for low-cost housing; in 1992 it terminated the co-operative housing program; and in 1993 it froze expenditures for social housing at 1993 levels. Estimates of the number of homeless are difficult to make, but in 1986, more than a decade ago, it was estimated that between 130 000 and 250 000 people were homeless at any given time that year (Begin 1989).

Conclusions

Both of these developments, the privatization and the shifting of the social services and income security programs to charitable organizations, share a common rationale. They undermine the principle that the state has social obligations to its citizens, and they circumvent the existence and fulfilment of state social responsibilities. In short, they end the development of the principle and practice of social citizenship, the foremost achievement in the long attempt to reform capitalism. They also represent the progressive abandonment by the state of significant aspects of public "property" to the private sector. Both privatization and the encouragement of charities represent the systematic abolition of the forms of collective property represented by the welfare state and its limited achievement of social citizenship, replacing these with the principles and practice of private property.

The interim goal of provincial and federal retrenchment would appear to be a minimalization of the state's social responsibilities, achieved by the various means outlined above. For those aspects of the welfare state that are not abolished, dual systems are developing already, as well as private but publicly supported programs for the well-off, and a degraded state program for those who cannot afford the other.

As long as the welfare state remains relatively intact, providing a range of services and benefits, there remains a political aspect, albeit modest, to the determination of the kind and nature of these policies and to the disposal of the necessary public funds. With charities and a privatized system of welfare, this element of political determination is replaced in theory by moral sentiment (in a society whose highest virtues are egoism and selfishness) and market principles (impersonal, apolitical forces beyond the control of the state, especially when stripped of its economic management policies). Not only, then, does the goal of a privatized welfare system remove the future possibility of political control, it also makes the provision of essential aspects of the reproduction of the working class subject to the vagaries of market forces. As the market follows its booms and slumps, so too will rise and fall the benefits and services so necessary to a healthy working population. Just as stock markets can collapse, businesses go bankrupt, corporate theft and embezzlement on a grand scale continue, and unemployment remain chronically high, so will the elements of a privatized welfare system bear not only the consequences of the business cycle, but also those of a system of contradictory class interests.

The forces of global capitalism that underlie this retrenchment, however, are not the only forces presently at work. Numerous experiments in alternative modes of production and new forms of resistance to capitalist expansion have begun to develop around the world. In the industrial countries, the resistance appears in a number of forms as yet poorly organized and with consciousness limited to particular issues, but it is unmistakably there. The most prominent actions are those of the trade unions, the environmental organizations, aboriginal alliances, and the women's movement; but to these can be added consumer protection groups, old age advocacy coalitions, unions of the unemployed, cultural forms of protest, civil liberty associations, and antinuclear groups. In the Third World, organized armed resistance to repressive regimes is once again growing.

Resistance and co-operative alternatives will necessarily grow as economic inequality deepens and the ability of capitalism to provide for the material, let alone the human, needs of the populace declines and the experience and recognition of this inability expands.

Summary

- We begin with a definition of the welfare state, analyzing its component parts and, briefly, its historical development.
- The main principles of the modern welfare state and their relation to Keynesianism are outlined.
- Social citizenship and decommodification are examined as the central considerations in the contemporary welfare state.
- The character of the welfare state in Canada is described and analyzed.

- The reasons for the dismantling of the welfare state in Canada are explored and examples are given.
- The so-called market alternatives to this dismantling and their negative consequences are described briefly.

Questions to Consider

1. What is the definition of the welfare state? At what historical moment can it be said to have come into existence, and why?

2. What are the general preconditions of the welfare state? What are the post–Second World War conditions of the modern welfare state?

3. What are the two most common ways of categorizing the Canadian welfare state? What are their shortcomings?

4. Why can we say that social citizenship "represents the highest development of the principle of welfarism"?

5. Describe the consequences of the decline of the welfare state and suggest what might be the logical conclusion of present developments.

Suggested Readings

Blake, R., P. Bryden, and F. Strain, eds. *The Welfare State in Canada: Past, Present and Future*. Toronto: Irwin, 1997.

Deaton, R.L. *The Political Economy of Pensions: Power, Politics, and Social Change in Canada, Britain and the United States*. Vancouver: UBC Press, 1989.

Doern, G.B., L.A. Pal, and B. Tomlin, eds. *Border Crossings: The Internationalization of Canadian Public Policy*. Toronto: Oxford University Press, 1996.

Guest, D. *The Emergence of Social Security in Canada*. Vancouver: University of British Columbia Press, 1985.

Mishra, R. *The Welfare State in Capitalist Society*. Toronto: University of Toronto Press, 1990.

Moscovitch, A., and J. Albert, eds. *The Benevolent State: The Growth of Welfare in Canada*. Toronto: Garamond, 1987.

Pulkingham, J., and G. Ternowetsky, eds. *Remaking Canadian Social Policy: Social Security in the Late 1990s*. Halifax: Fernwood, 1996.

Glossary

Keynesianism A set of economic policies attributed to the British economist John Maynard Keynes intended to offset the business cycles of capitalism. This would be done by deficit spending in recessionary periods to promote public works, offset corporate expenses, and provide unemployment insurance.

neoliberalism A comprehensive set of policies, presently being adopted by governments around the world, that seeks to change every aspect of state intervention in society with the goal of privatizing all forms of property that embrace collective or co-operative elements. (For a comprehensive analysis, see Teeple 1996.)

policy regime A system of governance for capital accumulation in a given era, which includes all the forms of state intervention intended to assist in the reproduction of the corporate private sector and the corresponding structure of the working class. In any particular period, this regime would have a certain coherency, changing incrementally in keeping with progressive changes in the mode of production, and radically transforming with revolutions in production.

privatization From the perspective of property rights, a "reassignment of claims to the control and use of [state] assets." In this sense, privatization (or "deregulation") is intended to undermine "the foundation of claims for public purpose and public service" (Starr 1989, 42).

social citizenship The notion that all members of society have a right to certain social services and programs such as health care, education, old age pensions, unemployment and injury insurance, housing, welfare, and so on. This principle of social welfare is achieved by undermining the negative effects of the capitalist market, namely, competition among workers, powerlessness, poverty, and unemployment.

social wage State-sponsored partial socialization of income from wages and salaries by means of premiums, taxes, and deferred income. The funds so created are used for redistribution from one social strata or class to another through transfers such as pensions, income supplements, or social insurance schemes.

workfare A state policy requiring certain categories of recipients of income support to perform some kind of labour or participate in some kind of training, ostensibly to increase their employment potential. It challenges the notion of social citizenship, embodies an element of coercion, contradicts the notion of the "free labour market," implies an individual cause of poverty, and usually causes an increase in costs to the state, with little or no proven success rate (see Shragge 1997).

Notes

1. Parts of the argument of this paper are drawn from my book, *Globalization and the Decline of Social Reform* (1996).
2. Fordism arose out of the cauldron of the First World War to become the prevailing mode of production in the industrial world. It is generally seen as a system of production employing semi-automated assembly-lines and giving rise to rapidly expanding domestic and external markets for "cheapened" consumer goods, that is, a system of mass production and consumption. It is also associated with large production units and complex work hierarchies.

    Advanced Fordism arose out of the forced industrial growth of the Second World War. Here science and technology, once subordinated to capitalist production and increased automation, vastly expanded the quantities and improved the qualities of goods and services. It co-existed with a delimited national labour market, a protected product market, and growth based on extranational and domestic expansion. The resulting high standard of living in the industrial nations for the majority of the working class allowed for a grand compromise between the trade unions, corporations, and government, which took the form of the KWS.
3. The increase in these social rights, "the revolution of rising entitlements," as D. Bell put it, became an issue for debate and one of the reasons the Trilateral Commission raised the spectres of "excess democracy" and "ungovernability" (1974, 39). Social citizenship contradicts the principle of corporate private property, that is, the rights associated with ownership of the means of production. It is mainly for this reason that social citizenship comes under attack as a social form

of property, although it remains always a reformist measure because it merely attempts to ameliorate the worst effects of the exercise of the rights of corporate private property.

4. The attention paid by the federal and provincial states to class conflict was far more extensive than that paid to any other arena of intervention. At the federal level the reforms began as early as 1872, with The Trade Union Act, then the Conciliation Act of 1900 and 1906, the Fair Wage Resolution, the Railway Labour Disputes Act of 1903, and the Industrial Disputes Investigation Act of 1907 (extended in 1916 and 1918). Very little changes until 1940 (PC2685) and 1944 (PC1003), which established the foundation of the modern labour relations system in Canada (Logan 1956).

5. The movement to "world wages" in the industrial nations means the gradual reduction of the "disposable" portion of income and of taxable portions, which in turn results in the decline of the social wage. Indeed, wages and salaries increasingly become sufficient only to reproduce labour power during periods of employment, leaving periods of unemployment, invalidity, old age, maternity, and so on, with increasingly only private, limited resources.

6. The most significant umbrella charity in North America is the United Way. Promoted vigorously by corporations, its annual drive for funds amounts to another tax on the working class, while corporate donations remain *very* limited.

   Recognizing the decline in corporate tax revenue and its implications in declining social reforms, the corporate sector in Canada has initiated a Centre for Philanthropy and a program of corporate charity called Imagine, intended to stimulate corporate but mainly employee donations of time and money to charitable and other non-profit organizations.

7. The element of social control is not generally visible: deterrents to benefits can force people to work for subsistence or below subsistence wages; qualifications can counter the readiness to go on strike by making the benefits conditional on reasons for being out of work; conditions for benefits may include retraining, moving, menial work, or eventual acceptance of low paid jobs; and so on.

References

Allen, R.C., and G. Rosenbluth, eds. *1986. Restraining the Economy.* Vancouver: New Star Books.

Andrew, C. 1984. "Women and the Welfare State." *Canadian Journal of Political Science* 17: 667–83.

Aquan-Yuen, M. 1991. *Homelessness in Canada: A Selected Bibliography.* Waterloo: University of Waterloo Library.

Armitage, A. 1975. *Social Welfare in Canada.* Toronto: McClelland and Stewart.

Banting, K. 1982. *The Welfare State and Canadian Federalism.* Montreal and Kingston: McGill-Queen's University Press.

———. 1987. "The Welfare State and Inequality in the 1980s." *Canadian Review of Sociology and Anthropology* 24, no. 3: 309–28.

Begin, P. 1989. *Homelessness in Canada.* Ottawa: Research Branch, Library of Parliament.

Bell, D. 1974. "The Public Household: On Fiscal Sociology and the Liberal Society." *The Public Interest* (Fall): 29–68.

Briggs, A. 1967. "The Welfare State in Historical Perspective." In *The Welfare State*, ed. C.I. Schottland. New York: Harper and Row.

Brown, L. 1987. *When Freedom Was Lost.* Montreal: Black Rose.

Brown, M.K., ed. 1988. *Remaking the Welfare State: Retrenchment and Social Policy in America and Europe.* Philadelphia: Temple University Press.

Burman, P. 1988. *Killing Time, Losing Ground.* Toronto: Wall and Thompson.

Carrier, J., and I. Kendall. 1986. "Categories, Categorizations, and the Political Economy of Welfare." *Journal of Social Policy* 15, no. 3: 315–35.

Cuneo, C.J. 1979. "State, Class, and Reserve Labour: The Case of the 1941 Canadian Unemployment Insurance Act." *Canadian Review of Sociology and Anthropology* 16, no. 2: 147–70.

Dickinson, J., and B. Russell, eds. 1986. *Family, Economy, and State.* Toronto: Garamond Press.

Djao, A.W. 1983. *Inequality and Social Policy.* Toronto: John Wiley and Sons.

Domhoff, G.W. 1990. *The Power Elite and the State.* New York: Aldine De Gruyter.

Drover, G., ed. 1988. *Free Trade and Social Policy.* Ottawa: Canadian Council on Social Development.

Esping-Andersen, G. 1989. "The Three Political Economies of the Welfare State." *Canadian Review of Sociology and Anthropology* 26, no. 1: 10–35.

Esping-Andersen, G., and W. Korpi. 1984. "Social Policy as Class Politics in Post-War Capitalism: Scandinavia, Austria, and Germany." In *Order and Conflict in Contemporary Capitalism*, ed. J.H. Goldthorpe. New York: Oxford University Press.

Fawkes, T. 1983. *Assault From the Right*. BC Federation of Labour and BC & Yukon Building Trades Council.

Finkel, A. 1977. "Origins of the Welfare State." In *The Canadian State*, ed. L. Panitch. Toronto: University of Toronto Press. 344–70.

———. 1979. *Business and Social Reform in the Thirties*. Toronto: James Lorimer.

Flora, P., and A.J. Heidenheimer, eds. 1984. *The Development of Welfare States in Europe and America*. New Brunswick, NJ: Transaction Books.

Gough, I. 1979. *The Political Economy of the Welfare State*. London: Macmillan.

Guest, D. 1985. *The Emergence of Social Security in Canada*. Vancouver: University of British Columbia Press.

Harbison, F. 1954. "Collective Bargaining and American Capitalism." In *Industrial Conflict*, ed. A. Kornhauser, R. Dubin, and A. Ross. New York: McGraw-Hill. 270–79.

Hess, M. 1992. *The Canadian Fact Book on Income Security Programs*. Ottawa and Montreal: Canadian Council on Social Development.

Hirschman, A.O. 1988. "How Keynes Was Spread from America." *Challenge* (November–December): 4–7.

Ismael, J.S., ed. 1987. *The Canadian Welfare State*. Edmonton: University of Alberta Press.

Ismael, J.S., and Y. Vaillancourt, eds. 1988. *Privatization and Provincial Social Services in Canada*. Edmonton: University of Alberta Press.

Kamerman, S.B., and Kahn. A.J., eds. 1989. *Privatization and the Welfare State*. Princeton: Princeton University Press.

Kealey, G., ed. 1973. *Canada Investigates Industrialism*. Toronto: University of Toronto Press.

Kirk, N. 1985. *The Growth of Working Class Reformism in Mid-Victorian England*. London: Croom Helm.

Leseman, F. 1987. *Services and Circuses: Community and the Welfare State*. Montreal: Black Rose Books.

Liversedge, R. 1973. *Recollections of the On to Ottawa Trek*. Toronto: McClelland and Stewart.

Logan, H.A. 1948. *Trade Unions in Canada*. Toronto: Macmillan.

———. 1956. *State Intervention and Assistance in Collective Bargaining*. Toronto: University of Toronto Press.

Lubove, R. 1986. *The Struggle for Social Security, 1900–1935*. Pittsburgh: University of Pittsburgh Press.

McLaughlin, M. 1987. *Homelessness in Canada: The Report of the National Inquiry*. Ottawa: Canadian Council on Social Development.

Magnusson, W., et al., eds. 1984. *The New Reality: The Politics of Restraint in British Columbia*. Vancouver: New Star Books.

Marsh, L. 1975. *Report on Social Security for Canada*. Toronto: University of Toronto Press.

Marshall, T.H. 1963. "Citizenship and Social Class." In *Sociology at the Crossroads*, ed. T.H. Marshall. London: Heinemann.

Midgley, J. 1984. "Poor Law Principles and Social Assistance in the Third World: A Study in the Perpetuation of Colonial Welfare," *International Social Work* 27, no. 1.

Mishra, R. 1984. *The Welfare State in Crisis*. Brighton: Wheatsheaf Books.

———. 1990. *The Welfare State in Capitalist Society*. Toronto: University of Toronto Press.

Mommsen, W.J., ed. 1981. *The Emergence of the Welfare State in Britain and Germany, 1850–1950*. London: Croom Helm.

Moscovitch, A. 1986. "The Welfare State Since 1975." *Journal of Canadian Studies* 21, no. 2: 77–94.

Myles. J. 1988. "Decline or Impasse? The Current State of the Welfare State." *Studies in Political Economy* 26: 73–107.

National Council of Welfare (NCW). 1976. *The Hidden Welfare System*. Ottawa: The Council.

———. 1979. *The Hidden Welfare System Revisited*. Ottawa: The Council.

Navarro. V. 1985/86. "The 1980 and 1984 U.S. Elections and the New Deal: An Alternative Interpretation." In *Socialist Register 1985/86*, ed. R. Miliband et al. 158–209.

Oderkirk, J. 1992. "Food Banks." *Canadian Social Trends* 24 (Spring).

Offe, C. 1984. *Contradiction of the Welfare State*. Cambridge, MA: MIT Press.

Panitch, L. 1986. *Working Class Politics in Crisis*. London: Verso.

Panitch, L., and D. Swartz. 1993. *The Assault on Trade Union Freedoms*. Toronto: Garamond Press.

Phillipson, C. 1982. *Capitalism and the Construction of Old Age*. London: Macmillan.

Quadagno, J. 1987. "Theories of the Welfare State." *American Review of Sociology* 13: 109–28.

Reasons, C.E., L.L. Ross and C. Paterson. 1981. *Assault on the Worker: Occupational Health and Safety in Canada*. Toronto: Butterworths.

Riches, G. 1986. *Food Banks and the Welfare Crisis*. Ottawa: Canadian Council on Social Development.

———. 1987. "Feeding Canada's Poor: The Rise of the Food Banks and the Collapse of the Public Safety Net." In Ismael, *The Canadian Welfare State*.

Rimlinger, G.V. 1971. *Welfare Policy and Industrialization in Europe, America, and Russia*. New York: John Wiley and Sons.

Russell, B. 1984. "The Politics of Labour-Reproduction, Funding Canada's Social Wage, 1917–1946." *Studies in Political Economy* 14: 43–93.

Schecter, S. 1977. "Capitalism, Class, and Educational Reform in Canada." In *The Canadian State*, ed. L. Panitch.

Schott, K. 1982. "The Rise of Keynesian Economics: Britain 1940–1964." *Economy and Society* 11, no. 3: 292–316.

Sethi, A.S., ed. 1989. *Collective Bargaining in Canada*. Scarborough, ON: Nelson.

Shragge, E. ed. 1997. *Workfare*. Toronto: Garamond.

Splane, R. 1965. *Social Welfare in Ontario, 1791–1898*. Toronto: University of Toronto Press.

Spring, J. 1972. *Education and the Rise of the Corporate State*. Boston: Beacon Press.

Stafford, J. 1986. "Retirement Pensions: Reinforced Exploitation." In Dickinson and Russell, *Family*.

Starr, P. 1989. "The Meaning of Privatization." In *Privatization and the Welfare State*, ed. S. Kamerman and A. Kahn. Princeton: Princeton University Press.

Statistics Canada. 1998. *The Daily* November 24.

Struthers, J. 1977. "Prelude to Depression: The Federal Government and Unemployment." *Canadian Historical Review* 58, no. 3: 277–93.

———. 1983. *No Fault of Their Own: Unemployment and the Canadian Welfare State, 1914–1941*. Toronto: University of Toronto Press.

Sulieman, E.N., and J. Waterbury, eds. *The Political Economy of Public Sector Reform and Privatization*. Boulder: Westview Press.

Swartz, D. 1977. "The Politics of Reform: Conflict and Accommodation in Canadian Health Policy." In *The Canadian State*, ed. L. Panitch. 311–43.

———. 1987. "The Limits of Health Insurance." In *The "Benevolent" State*, ed. A. Moscovitch and J. Albert. 255–70.

Tampke, J. 1981. "Bismarck's Social Legislation: A Genuine Breakthrough?" In Mommsen, *The Emergence*.

Taylor, M.G. 1987. *Heath Insurance and Canadian Public Policy*. Kingston and Montreal: McGill-Queen's University Press.

Teeple, G. 1996. *Globalization and the Decline of Social Reform*. Toronto: Garamond.

Therborn, G., and J. Roebeck. 1986. "The Irreversible Welfare State." *International Journal of Health Services* 16, no. 3.

Titmuss, R.M. 1958. *Essays on "The Welfare State."* London: Allen and Unwin.

Torczyner, J. 1987. "The Canadian Welfare State: Retrenchment and Change." In *Modern Welfare States*, ed. R.R. Friedmann, N. Gilbert, and M. Sherer. Brighton: Wheatsheaf Books.

Wallace, E. 1950. "The Origins of the Social Welfare State in Canada, 1867–1900." *Canadian Journal of Economic and Political Science* 16, no. 4.

Warnock, J. 1988. *Free Trade and the New Right Agenda*. Vancouver: New Star Books.

Weiler, P. 1980. *Reconcilable Differences: New Directions in Canadian Labour Law*. Toronto: Carswell.

Whitely, P. 1981. "Public Opinion and the Demand for Social Welfare in Britain." *Journal of Social Policy* 10, no. 4: 453–76.

Wilensky, H.L., and C.N. Lebeaux. 1965. *Industrial Society and Social Welfare*. New York: The Free Press.

Winch, D. 1969. *Economics and Policy*. London: Hodder and Stoughton.

Woods, H.D., and S. Ostry. 1962. *Labour Policy and Labour Economics in Canada*. Toronto: Macmillan.

CHAPTER 17

Social Issues and Social Policy

B. Singh Bolaria

Learning Objectives

After studying this chapter, you should be able to
- Appreciate the shift over time in the conceptualization and the analysis of social mores.
- Appreciate the important distinction between analysis of social issues solely with reference to the personal pathologies of individuals and a focus on the social structural conditions and institutional arrangements that produce social problems.
- Understand the policy implications of divergent conceptualizations and analyses of social issues.
- Understand how **individualization** and **medicalization** of social issues helps to "manage" rather than to "solve" social contradictions.
- Appreciate how medicalization of social issues helps to manage a wide range of problems that are social rather than medical in origin.
- Appreciate the distinction between **reformist reforms** and **non-reformist reforms**.
- Appreciate the implications of globalization of capital and production on state sovereignty and Canadian social policy.

Introduction

In their study of social issues, generations of sociologists have not only focussed on different problems but have also used different conceptual frameworks and perspectives. Early sociologists, who were mainly concerned with issues of deviance and criminality, analyzed the pathologies of individuals. The organismic, order, and medical models of society dominated the analysis of societal ills, which was expressed in clinical language.

Now, the study of social issues encompasses a much wider range of topics. There has also been a shift, over time, in the conceptualization and analysis of social issues. These issues are no longer analyzed solely with reference to the personal pathologies of individuals. Sociologists with a critical orientation not only question the order and stability model of society (by positing conflict rather than order as the norm), but also tend to focus on the social structural conditions and institutional arrangements that produce social problems. This **structural approach** locates the cause of the problematic conditions in the "defective" system rather than in "defective" individuals and their "defective" way of life.

The distinction between "personal troubles" and "public issues" and the division of social analysis into an individualistic versus a structural dichotomy may be an oversimplification of a complex phenomenon, but it leads us to a different perspective and allows us to conceptualize problematic conditions in new ways. As well, it helps us distinguish between individualistic and structural explanations. This distinction also has important consequences for the individual. A "personal situation" is commonly defined as a consequence of one's own failure, and so one easily falls into self-blame and self-accusation; in that case, one is likely to accept the situation passively. A more detailed discussion of this topic was presented in the first chapter of this book. This chapter examines the policy implications of interpreting and analyzing social issues within individualistic or structural frameworks. As the following discussion indicates, dramatically different solutions and policies flow from these analyses. A number of policy alternatives are discussed that are intended to help "manage" the contradictions. These include individualization of social problems, their medicalization, and the implementation of reforms that do not disrupt the existing power relationships.

Individualization of Problems

Whether such social issues as inequality, poverty, and hunger are interpreted and analyzed within an individualistic or structural framework has important consequences for their solutions.

Many people tend to individualize these issues as personal problems of the poor and unemployed by attributing them to the personal characteristics of individuals. The ideology of equality of opportunity for everyone in this society tends to promote the notion that success or failure depends on individual characteristics. Positive characteristics, such as hard work, competitiveness, and high motivation, are associated with success. Failure and poverty, on the other hand, are attributed to some personal deficiency such as intellectual inferiority, laziness, or low aspirations. Public opinion polls tend to confirm the popularity of these beliefs. A 1985 Gallup poll asked a national sample in the United States, "In your opinion, which is more often to blame if a person is poor—lack of effort on his part, or circumstances beyond his control?" Of the national sample, 33 percent responded with "lack of effort," 34 percent with "circumstances," and 31 percent felt that both lack of effort and circumstances were to blame (Gallup 1985, 24). In a 1986 *Maclean's*/Decima poll of 1575 Canadians, in response to a question about what it takes to be successful or get ahead, 82 percent replied hard work, 10 percent said luck, and 7 percent chose privilege (*Maclean's*, January 6, 1986).

Refinements of these attitudes have been the Social Darwinism of the nineteenth century and more recent theories of biological causation that put the blame for failure on inherited physical or intellectual traits (Herrnstein 1971; 1973; Jensen 1969; 1980). These perspectives have important social policy implications. From Social Darwinism it follows that the poor *should not* be helped because that would interfere with "natural selection"; the implication of arguments such as those of Jensen and Herrnstein is that the poor *cannot* be helped—they are "uneducatable" (Eitzen and Zinn 1989, 178–79).

Biological, intellectual, and cultural deficiency theories of inequality and poverty support the status quo and promote a laissez-faire policy whereby individuals are left to fend for themselves. This focus on individuals tends to strengthen the ideology of individualism by which one is responsible for one's station in life; it justifies Social Darwinism and masks the social structural conditions in societies that produce inequality and poverty (Feagin 1975; Navarro 1978; Eitzen and Zinn 1989).

A strictly individualistic and "blaming the victim" approach absolves the state, its political–economic structure, and other institutions of any responsibility for these problems. Consequently, solutions are oriented toward changing the individuals and their "defective" ways of life. Ryan calls the "blaming the victim" ideology "a brilliant ideology for justifying a perverse form of social action designed to change, not society, as one might expect, but rather society's victim" (1971, 7). If the problems are defined as a result of personal pathologies, the "treatment" may involve individual counselling and psychotherapy (Eitzen and Zinn 1989).

Uncritical use of the socialization perspective in gender studies diverts attention from the structured inequalities of the system and ends up blaming women themselves for gender inequality. This displaces not only the cause of the problem but also the solutions. Peterson and Enarson (1974, 8) conclude, "Rather than directing efforts toward radical social change, the solution seems to be to change women themselves, perhaps through exhortation ('If we want to be liberated, we'll have to act more aggressive ...') or, for example, changing children's literature and mothers' child rearing practice."

Another illustration comes from the area of medical sociology. Individual lifestyles and consumption patterns are now widely invoked as explanations of the current increase in many chronic and degenerative diseases. I have discussed elsewhere the ideological and policy implications of individual lifestyle and self-care approaches in the area of health care (Bolaria 1988). Health promotion strategies and educational campaigns are primarily oriented toward changing individuals and their lifestyles. This obfuscates the social causes of disease, shifts responsibility for health and illness back onto the individual, and individualizes what is essentially a social problem. As Berliner (1977, 119) has commented, "Focussing on lifestyles serves only to reify the lifestyles as an entity apart from the social conditions from which it arises." Berliner further argues, "Discussing changes in lifestyles without first discussing the changes in the social conditions which give rise to them, without recognizing that the lifestyle is derivative, is misleading and, in effect, is victim blaming."

The poor are blamed not only for their own poverty, lack of health and education, and so forth, but also, by extension, for fiscal crises and budgetary deficits. It is argued that excessive social expenditures are responsible for deficits and need to be cut back in order to avert economic crises. As Minkler (1983, 155) states, "A hallmark of the current politics of retrenchment has been the tendency by many policy makers to scapegoat the poor and the elderly as 'causes' of the fiscal crises."

The rhetoric of victim blaming, fiscal crisis, and individual responsibility all combine to justify cutbacks to welfare and other social programs.

Medicalization of Problems

Historically, medical jurisdiction has expanded over a number of human conditions. Medicine's domain has been extended to such areas as family life, sexuality, addiction, fertility, domestic violence, problems related to work and the life cycle, and many other areas (Cooperstock and Parnele 1982; Crawford 1980; Conrad and Schneider 1980; Stark and Flitcraft 1982; Koumjian 1981; Waitzkin 1983). Medical vocabulary is used more and more to define and analyze social problems. Many of the human conditions that were once considered "bad" are now classified as "sick" (Conrad and Schneider 1980). Illich has referred to this extension of the medical domain as the "medicalization of life."

This medicalization has mixed effects. The medical vocabulary and the definition of behaviour in medical terms tend to create more humanitarian tolerance than its definition in criminal terms. Medicalization also has negative consequences. Medical language mystifies human conditions and problems and thus removes them from public debate (Conrad and Schneider 1980). It often categorizes problems that are basically social in origin as "biological or personal deficits" (Stark and Flitcraft 1982). Waitzkin (1983, 41) states,

> As medical professionals assume responsibility for managing problems beyond the illnesses of individuals, attention shifts away from the underlying structural conditions that often are sources of individual distress. By defining social problems as medical, medicine becomes an institution of social control. Through medicalization, the structural roots of personal distress become mystified and depoliticized.

As Waitzkin points out, occupational stress becomes classified as muscular tension, a worker with black lung disease is given a medical certificate of disability, a homemaker's emotional stress related to the demands of housework is given a prescription for a tranquillizer, or a poor woman who cannot support her family receives a physician's recommendation to be sterilized. The important point to be made here is that "in each instance ... a problem at the level of social structure—stressful work demands, unsafe working conditions, sexism, and poverty—is transformed into an individual problem under medical control" (Waitzkin 1983, 41).

Thus, medical "technological fixes" are used to "cure" a wide range of problems that are social in origin. The most frequent response to many socially induced psychological disorders may be pharmacological—antidepressants, anti-anxiety agents, stimulants, and tranquillizers (Waldron 1977; Stroufe and Stewart 1973; Fee 1977). These are generally prescribed to women, who consume large quantities of prescribed drugs (Cooperstock and Parnele 1982; Koumjian 1981; Harding, Wolf, and Chan 1977; Fee 1977).

Medicine is playing an important role in some other respects, in the area of occupational health. For instance, genetic screening is being done in some petrochemical industries in order to detect those workers whose genetic make-up may make them more susceptible than others to various toxins. The assumption made in genetic screening programs is that certain workers get ill because of their genetic background and structure rather than because of the general dangers posed by exposure to toxins at the workplace. This shifts responsibility for disease back onto the individual, promoting a victim-blaming epidemiology. Thus, medical "intervention" transforms a social issue—occupational diseases affecting a large segment of the labour force, with roots in the hazardous work environment—into an individual problem of the genetic heredity of the individual worker.

Structural Changes

Both the individualistic and medical models of social problems see the solution in changing individuals, through, respectively, social or medical intervention. Within the structural framework, however, the solutions are seen to lie in transforming the political–economic structures and other institutional arrangements that produce and reproduce deleterious social conditions. Its proponents argue that equality of class, race, and gender is not possible within the existing capitalist system. Substantial evidence supports this contention. A number of chapters in this book show that many social groups continue to encounter unequal opportunities and differential life chances, correlated with gender, class, and race.

A structural explanation of poverty locates its causes in the structural conditions that produce unemployment, low-paying jobs, and unequal opportunity structures. The **segmentation** of the Canadian **labour market** along occupational, gender, ethnic, and racial lines is a structural source of inequality. Therefore, the solution to social inequality lies in the alteration of labour market inequalities rather than in changing the individuals. Individual solutions cannot solve structural problems. We conclude this discussion by quoting at length from C. Wright Mills:

> In so far as an economy is so arranged that slumps occur, the problem of unemployment becomes incapable of personal solution. In so far as war is inherent in the nation-state system and in the uneven industrialization of the world, the ordinary individual in his [or her] restricted milieu will be powerless—with or without psychiatric aid—to solve the troubles this system or lack of system imposes upon him [or her]. In so far as the family as an institution turns women into darling little slaves and men into their chief providers and unweaned dependents, the problem of satisfactory marriage remains incapable of purely private solution. In so far as the overdeveloped megalopolis and the overdeveloped automobile are built-in features of the overdeveloped society, the issues of urban living will not be solved by personal ingenuity and private wealth. (1959, 10)

Global Capital and Social Policy

The discussion of social issues and the national social policy cannot be divorced from global capital and multinational corporate demands for economic and social restructuring of national economies and social welfare programs. The increasing corporate concentration through takeovers and mergers has given a small number of managers and their corporations enormous economic and political power (Bronson 1994). **Multinational corporations** increasingly organize production on the basis of global economic strategies primarily driven by profits and capital accumulation (Banting 1996; Bronson 1994). This globalization of production has often meant transformation and declining importance of national economics and erosion of political sovereignty. Political and economic pressures emanating from the wider global context change the context of national social policy debate and constrain decision-making and policy options.

In Canada there has always been concern about foreign domination, particularly by Americans, of the economic, political, and cultural lives of Canadians. The Canada–U.S. Free Trade Agreement (FTA) and the North American Free Trade Agreement (NAFTA) have resurrected longstanding fears about foreign controls and loss of national sovereignty and have raised concerns about Canada's autonomy over its social policy and freedom to maintain existing programs and/or create new ones in response to emerging domestic issues and problems (Bronson 1995; Banting 1996; Teeple 1994; Shields and McBride 1994; Battle 1994). Pressures to harmonize all regulations, standards, laws, and social programs have increased significantly with regional and bilateral trade agreements. These trade agreements provide a legal and political framework for our trading partners to challenge the existing and new welfare programs and policies on the ground that they provide unfair subsidies and unfair advantage to Canadian employers and Canadian industries. This, in relation to the United States, means downward pressure on social commitments and social expenditures to bring our programs in line with the U.S. model. To create this convergence would require moving away from the state provisions of social services and programs, especially universal programs or those characterized as social rights. This means a loss of social protection provided by public sector programs for many Canadians and an increasing dependence on charitable donations or voluntary services.

The threat of retaliation from our trading partners puts constraint on the state from responding to the needs of those Canadians affected by economic restructuring in the context of global capital. The erosion of national sovereignty and less political leverage on public policy make it increasingly difficult to chart an independent course to protect the existing programs and formulate an independent social policy. Indeed, the Canadian welfare state and its various social programs face an uncertain future. What is certain, however, is that our domestic policies are affected by forces beyond our border and that the public policy debate cannot be insulated from these economic, political, and social forces.

Free Trade and Social Programs

As debt and taxation problems worsen, the corporate community increasingly emphasizes social service cutbacks as a solution. FTA negotiator Simon Reisman dismissed concerns over social programs in Canada, with his initial assurance that "there is no reference to them in the agreement" (1988). He avoided consideration that, for example, the FTA allows American private-profit enterprise access to hospital management, nursing homes, blood donor clinics, and most other social services.

He was thus failing to deal with questions raised by more rigorous analysis, such as the independent study by retired judge Marjorie Bowker. She noted that although the FTA makes no direct reference to social programs, it contains "indirect hazards" (1988, 3). Programs such as our health and medicare systems, unemployment insurance, the Canada Pension, and workers' compensation could all be challenged by the United States as "unfair subsidies."

Bowker's concerns soon materialized after the 1988 election. The *Business Journal on National Issues* (December 27, 1988), representing 150 large corporations, called for cuts in federal contributions to unemployment insurance—a policy that was later implemented in the April 1989 budget. That should not have been surprising, because during the FTA negotiations the U.S. side had insisted that such programs are unfair subsidies.

A similar lack of safeguards for social programs was found by Canadian Union of Public Employees analyst Matt Sanger (1992, 30) in Chapters 11 and 12 of the 4300 page NAFTA agreement. He saw "no mechanism to ensure minimum standards." That omission would allow "harmonization" of Canadian programs with inferior social programs in the United States and Mexico.

Such "harmonization" of social programs below current Canadian standards seems certain to continue as U.S. and Canadian trade deficit and debt problems worsen. Consumer advocate Ralph Nader has warned that under corporate pressure, the tendency will be toward "uniformity down" rather than at constant or higher levels (CBC, November 15, 1988).

Source: Harold E. Bronson, "Free Trade: Political, Economic, and Social Issues and Contradictions," in *Social Issues and Contradictions in Canadian Society*, 2d ed., ed. B. Singh Bolaria (Toronto: Harcourt Brace, 1995), p. 368. All rights reserved. Reprinted by permission of Harcourt Brace & Company, Canada.

Conclusions

Linking social issues and social problems to the basic underlying social contradictions also raises the question of political strategy. If various policies do not address the social roots of social problems, solutions will be piecemeal, limited, and unsatisfactory. Yet, in the absence of a radical transformation of society, these issues and problems need to be "managed," both from the point of view of the state to maintain legitimacy and social harmony and of the individuals and social groups affected by deleterious social conditions.

The state, through a number of strategies, has tried to manage these problems. These include appointments of royal commissions to further study the problem, parliamentary investigations, appointment of various committees composed of members representing various groups affected by the adverse conditions, and human rights commissions to oversee various programs.

While these strategies may give the appearance that "something is being done," the objective reality is that in spite of various royal commissions and senate committee reports, status of women committees, multicultural committees, and human rights commissions, women and racial minority groups continue to face economic, social, and political inequality. Wide income disparities continue to exist among Canadians. The welfare state has not been able to solve these problems. This is because, as some have argued, the piecemeal and technocratic approaches to social problems have dominated the social policy decisions. As George and Wilding (1976, 17) state, "To see the eradication of social problems as depending upon a range of piecemeal welfare programs is to cherish a comfortable illusion." The technocratic "approach assumes that if only we knew more about the causation of such problems and if there were the necessary resources, then these problems would be solved."

While piecemeal solutions may be ameliorative and provide immediate relief to individuals, they do not address the underlying social structural causes of these problems. In fact, as some have argued, these reforms "may reinforce the *status quo* by reducing the potential for social conflict" (Waitzkin 1983, 42). The history of welfare reforms in capitalist countries shows that these reforms most often follow social unrest and protests, make incremental changes and improvements that do not alter overall patterns of inequality, and face retrenchment when social unrest and protests recede (Piven and Cloward 1971). Gorz's (1973) distinction of "reformist reforms" and "non-reformist reforms" may help to clarify this point. "A reformist reform is one which subordinates objectives to the criteria of rationality and practicality of a given system and policy.... [It] rejects those objectives and demands—however deep the need for them—which are incompatible with the preservation of the system." These reforms, by providing small material relief, reduce discontent and leave intact the current economic, political, and social structures and obscure the basic sources of inequality. The "non-reformist reforms," on the other hand, expose the sources of exploitation and inequality and address the issues of fundamental structural changes in the system. This distinction is quite crucial because many programs that on the surface may appear to be aimed at structural changes are in reality "reformist reforms": they help sustain the current political, economic, and other structural sources of inequality.

These social policy issues will become even more prominent in the context of the global corporate demands for economic restructuring and harmonization of social programs, current attacks on the welfare state, and the politics of retrenchment and deficit reductions and their impact on the lives of millions of Canadians. We need to continue to carefully examine various reforms and their direction and potential to challenge basic social contradictions and structural changes. To paraphrase Waitzkin (1983, 43), without a careful examination of the links between social problems and social structure, "both problems and solutions will continue to float in a haze of confusion and mystification."

Summary

- The primary focus of this chapter is on the policy implications of divergent conceptual and analytical frameworks in the study of social issues.
- It is argued that whether social issues are interpreted and analyzed within an individualistic or structural framework has important public policy implications.
- Examples from various substantive areas are used to demonstrate how a strictly individualistic approach tends to support the status quo and promote a laissez-faire policy whereby individuals are left to fend for themselves and/or promote solutions oriented to changing the individuals.
- Within the structural framework, solutions are seen to lie in changing political–economic structures that produce and reproduce deleterious social conditions.
- It is argued that the rhetoric of individual responsibility, victim blaming, and fiscal crises combine to justify cutbacks in social programs.
- This chapter highlights the increasing importance of global capital and its threat to political and economic sovereignty of Canada and pressures toward harmonization of social programs. Implications of these developments for Canadian social policy and social programs are also discussed.

Questions to Consider

1. Discuss both the positive and negative consequences of the medicalization of social problems.

2. Is it possible to eliminate class, race, and gender inequality within the existing capitalist system?

3. Discuss the policy implications of interpreting and analyzing social issues within individualistic or structural frameworks.

4. Discuss how some strategies and state-sponsored programs only help to "manage" problems of class, race, and gender inequalities.

5. Examine how individualization and medicalization of social issues and problems supports the status quo?

6. Discuss how "reformist reforms" only help to sustain the current political, economic, and other structural sources of inequality.

7. Examine the impact of the internationalization of capital and the globalization of production on current social programs, and on national sovereignty in regard to political leverage on future public policy.

Suggested Readings

Blake, Raymond B., Penny E. Bryden, and J. Frank Strain, eds. *The Welfare State in Canada: Past, Present and Future*. Concord, ON: Irwin Publishing, 1997.

Bronson, Harold E. "Free Trade: Political, Economic, and Social Issues and Contradictions." In *Social Issues and Contradictions in Canadian Society*, 2d ed., ed. B. Singh Bolaria. Toronto: Harcourt Brace, 1995. 362–81.

Doern, G. Bruce, Leslie A. Pal, and Brian W. Tomlin, eds. *Border Crossings: The Internationalization of Public Policy*. Toronto: Oxford University Press, 1996.

Johnson, Andrew F., and Andrew Stritch, eds. *Canadian Public Policy: Globalization and Political Parties*. Toronto: Copp Clark, 1997.

Lo, Clarence Y.H., and Michael Schwartz, eds. *Social Policy and the Conservative Agenda*. Malden, MA: Blackwell Publishers, 1998.

Glossary

individualization An analysis that tends to attribute social problems (success or failure) to the personal characteristics (pathologies) of the individuals.

labour market Those institutions that affect the purchase and sale (price/cost) of labour.

medicalization The extension of medical domain over a number of human conditions and the use of medical vocabulary to define and analyze social issues and problems.

multinational corporations Corporations that operate in more than one country, owning or controlling branches in countries apart from their primary headquarter location.

non-reformist reforms Reforms that expose the basic social contradictions and sources of exploitation and inequality, and address the issues of fundamental structural changes in the system.

reformist reforms Reforms that are compatible with the preservation of the existing system. Usually refers to reforms that provide small material relief, reduce discontent, and leave intact the current economic, political, and social structures, obscuring the basic sources of inequality.

segmentation Occurs when the labour market is divided into separate submarkets distinguished by different characteristics, opportunities, and working conditions.

structural approach An approach that gives priority to patterned relations (structure) over individuals in analysis of social issues and problems. A structural explanation of poverty, for instance, locates poverty in the structural conditions that produce unemployment and low-paying jobs, rather than in the characteristics of individuals.

References

Banting, K.G. 1996. "Social Policy." In *Border Crossings: The Internationalization of Public Policy*, ed. Bruce G. Doern, Leslie A. Pal, and Brian W. Tomlin. Toronto: Oxford University Press. 27–54.

Battle, K. 1994. "Poverty and the Welfare State." In *Power and Resistance: Critical Thinking About Canadian Social Issues*, ed. L. Samuelson. Halifax: Fernwood Publishing. 19–38.

Berliner, H.S. 1977. "Emerging Ideologies in Medicine." *Review of Radical Political Economics* 9: 116–24.

Bolaria, B.S. 1988. "The Politics and Ideology of Self-Care and Lifestyles." In *Sociology of Health Care in Canada*, ed. B.S. Bolaria and H. Dickinson. Toronto: Harcourt Brace Jovanovich. 537–52.

Bolaria, B.S. and R. von Elling Bolaria. 1997a. "Capital, Labour Migrations." In *International Labour Migrations*, ed. B.S. Bolaria and R. von Elling Bolaria. New Delhi: Oxford University Press. 1–17.

———. 1997b. "Immigrants, Migrants and Labour Market Opportunities." In Bolaria and Bolaria, *International Labour Migrations*. 192–209.

Bowker, M. 1998. *On Guard for Thee*. Hull: Voyager Publishing.

Bronson, H.E. 1994. "Economic Concentration and Corporate Power." In *Essentials of Contemporary Sociology*, ed. P.S. Li and B.S. Bolaria. Toronto: Copp Clark Longman. 127–46.

———. 1995. "Free Trade: Political, Economic, and Social Issues and Contradictions." In *Social Issues and Contradictions*, 2d ed., ed. B.S. Bolaria. Toronto: Harcourt Brace. 362–81.

Carroll, W.K., and R. Warburton. 1995. "Capital, Labour, and the State: The Future of the Labour Movement." In Bolaria, *Social Issues and Contradictions*, 2d ed. 336–56.

Conrad, P., and J.W. Schneider. 1980. *Deviance and Medicalization: From Badness to Sickness*. St. Louis, MO: C.V. Mosby.

Cooperstock, R., and P. Parnele. 1982. "Research on Psychotropic Drug Use: A Review of Findings and Methods." *Social Science and Medicine* 16: 1179–96.

Crawford, R. 1980. "Healthism and the Medicalization of Everyday Life." *International Journal of Health Services* 10: 365–89.

Eitzen D.S., and M.B, Zinn. 1989. *Social Problems*, 4th ed. Boston: Allyn and Bacon.

Feagin, J.R. 1975. *Subordinating the Poor: Welfare and American Beliefs*. Englewood Cliffs, NJ: Prentice-Hall.

Fee, E. 1977. "Women and Health Care: A Comparison of Theories." In *Health and Medical Care in the United States: A Critical Analysis*, ed. V. Navarro. New York: Baywood Publishing. 115–32.

Gallup Report. 1985. "Poverty." No. 234 (March): 21–25.

George, V., and P. Wilding. 1976. *Ideology and Social Welfare*. London: Routledge and Kegan Paul.

Gorz, A. 1973. *Socialism and Revolution*. Garden City, NY: Anchor Books.

Harding, J., N. Wolf, and G. Chan. 1977. "A Socio-Demographic Profile of People Being Prescribed Mood-Modifying Drugs in Saskatchewan." Regina: Alcoholism Commission of Saskatchewan.

Herrnstein, R. 1971. "I.Q." *Atlantic* 228 (September): 43–64.

———. 1973. *I.Q. in the Meritocracy*. Boston: Littlewood.

Jensen, A.R. 1969. "How Much Can We Boost I.Q. and Scholastic Achievement." *Harvard Educational Review* 39 (Winter): 1–123.

———. 1980. *Bias in Mental Testing*. New York: The Free Press.

Knutilla, M. 1994. "The State and Social Issues: Theoretical Considerations." In *Power and Resistance: Critical Thinking about Canadian Social Issues*, ed. L. Samuelson. Halifax: Fernwood Publishing. 1–18.

Koumjian, K. 1981. "The Use of Valium as a Force of Social Control." *Social Science and Medicine* 15E: 245–49.

Mills, C. 1959. *The Sociological Imagination*. New York: Oxford University Press.

Minkler, M. 1983. "Blaming the Aged Victim: The Politics of Scapegoating in Times of Fiscal Conservatism." *International Journal of Health Services* 13: 155–68.

Navarro, V. 1978. "The Crisis of the Western System of Medicine in Contemporary Capitalism." *International Journal of Health Services* 8, no. 2.

————. 1986. *Crises, Health and Medicine*. New York: Tavistock Publications.

Peterson, L., and E. Enarson. 1974. "Blaming the Victim in the Sociology of Women: On the Misuse of the Concept of Socialization." Paper presented at the Pacific Sociological Association, San Jose, California, March; cited in Eitzen and Zinn, *Social Problems*.

Piven, F.F., and R.A. Cloward. 1971. *Regulating the Poor: The Functions of Public Welfare*. New York: Vintage Books.

Reisman, S. 1988. "Let Us Get It Straight," *The Globe and Mail*, Oct. 4: A7.

Ryan, W. 1971. *Blaming the Victim*. New York: Pantheon.

Sanger, M. 1992. "A Tool to Dismantle the Public Sector." *Action Canada Dossier* (December): 30.

Shields, J., and S. McBride. 1994. "Dismantling a Nation: The Canadian Political Economy and Continental Free Trade." In *Power and Resistance: Critical Thinking About Canadian Social Issues*, ed. L. Samuelson. Halifax: Fernwood Publishing. 227–60.

Sinclair, P.R. 1995. "Underdevelopment and Regional Inequality." In Bolaria, *Social Issues and Contradictions*, 2d ed. 382–401.

Stark, E., and A. Flitcraft. 1982. "Medical Therapy as Repression: The Case of Battered Women." *Health and Medicine* 1: 29–32.

Stroufe, L.A., and M.A. Stewart. 1973. "Treating Children with Stimulant Drugs." *New England Journal of Medicine* no. 291: 289–409.

Teeple, G. 1994. "The Capitalist Economy and the State." In *Essentials of Contemporary Sociology*, ed. P.S. Li and B.S. Bolaria. Toronto: Copp Clark. 104–26.

Trumper, R., and L.L. Wong. 1997. "Racialization and Genderization: The Canadian State, Immigrants and Temporary Workers." In Bolaria and Bolaria, *International Labour Migrations*. 153–91.

Waitzkin, H. 1983. *The Second Sickness*. New York: The Free Press.

Waldron, I. 1977. "Increased Prescribing of Valium, Librium, and Other Drugs: An Example of the Influence of Economics and Social Factors on the Practice of Medicine." *International Journal of Health Services* 7, no. 1: 37–62.

CONTRIBUTORS

B. Singh Bolaria is a Professor in the Department of Sociology at the University of Saskatchewan. He has researched and published widely in the areas of racial and ethnic studies, migrant labour, and medical sociology. Most recently, he has co-edited *Contemporary Sociology* (1993); *Essentials of Contemporary Sociology* (1994); *Racial Minorities, Medicine and Health* (1994); *Women, Medicine and Health* (1994); *International Labour Migrations* (1997); and *Health, Illness and Health Care in Canada* (1994); and has edited the previous editions of this book. He also co-authored *Racial Oppression in Canada*, 2d ed. (1988).

Michael Clow is an Associate Professor in the Department of Social Science at St. Thomas University in Fredericton, New Brunswick. A specialist in the political economy of resource development, community-based resource management, and sociological theory, he has completed several studies of the important resource sectors in the Atlantic region, including forestry, agriculture, and fishing. He is currently working on a volume on environmental sociology in which he examines the contribution that a critically informed sociology can make to public policy debates concerning sustainable development.

Harley D. Dickinson is Professor and Director of the Social Research Unit, Department of Sociology, at the University of Saskatchewan. His current research interests are in health policy, health reform, and evidence-based decision making in the health-care sector. He currently pursues these interests as Principal Investigator with HEALNet, a Canadian Networks of Centres of Excellence Program. Professor Dickinson has numerous publications related to health care.

Lawrence Felt is a Professor of Sociology at Memorial University in St. John's, Newfoundland. A specialist in North Atlantic maritime societies, he is the author of several books and over sixty articles in the areas of rural economic development, work, and resource management. His most recent book, *The North Atlantic Fishery* (co-written with Ragnar Arnason), examines how fishing regions of the North Atlantic have responded to severe economic and social hardship resulting from over-fishing in the region. He recently examined how knowledge of those who fish for a living can be combined with fisheries science to create more sustainable fisheries policies.

James S. Frideres is currently Associate Vice-President (Academic) at the University of Calgary. His research interests have focussed on ethnic relations in Canadian society with an emphasis on aboriginal people. He is co-editor of Canada's only national ethnic journal, *Canadian Ethnic Studies/études ethniques Canada*. His book *Aboriginal Peoples in Canada* is now in its fifth printing and is considered required reading for those studying in the area, and he has published four additional books as well as in academic journals around the world. He has acted as a consultant for various ethnic and aboriginal organizations as well as for government.

Karen R. Grant is an Associate Professor of Sociology and Associate Dean in the Faculty of Arts at the University of Manitoba. The overarching theme of her work is the manner in which social institutions and practices affect women's experiences of health. She is currently studying the impact of health reform in Manitoba on women's careers in hospitals and at home. As well, she is working on an oral history project about women's experiences of the 1997 Manitoba "Flood of the Century." Professor Grant has written on subjects as diverse as the new genetics, women's experiences using prenatal diagnosis in pregnancy, women's health policies, and equity for women in universities.

Alison Hayford is a Professor in the Department of Sociology and Social Studies at the University of Regina. She has a background in geography and her current research interests reflect interdisciplinary approaches to the study of urban society and city life, including social movements, immigration, gender roles and the family, and cultural issues. She has presented numerous papers to professional groups and has contributed to a number of edited volumes.

Leslie J. Miller is Associate Professor of Sociology at the University of Calgary, where she teaches courses in gender relations, sociology of families, and theory. Her current research is on moral reasoning and moral conduct at the boundary of family and corporate worlds.

Alicja Muszynski is an Associate Professor in the Department of Sociology at the University of Waterloo. Her previous research involved work on ethnicity, race, class, and gender among shoreworkers in the British Columbia fishing industry and resulted in the book *Cheap Wage Labour: Race and Gender in the Fisheries of British Columbia* (1996). She spent seven years at the University of Regina, where she studied farm families and rural communities. Publications included an article in the *Canadian Review of Sociology and Anthropology*. She is currently working on two textbooks in the areas of sociology of families and women's studies.

Leslie Samuelson is an Associate Professor of Sociology at the University of Saskatchewan. His primary academic area is criminology. Areas of concentration include aboriginal peoples and justice, criminal justice administration, and policy evaluation, as well as comparative research in Australia and Canada. He has recently published an article in the fiftieth anniversary special edition of *The Institute of Comparative Law* in Japan, as well as a second edition of his *Power and Resistance* reader (co-edited by W. Anthony, 1998).

Vic Satzewich is an Associate Professor in the Department of Sociology at McMaster University. He is the author of *Racism and the Incorporation of Foreign Labour* (1991), and co-author of *First Nations: Race, Class and Gender Relations* (1993). He is also the editor of *Deconstructing a Nation: Immigration, Multiculturalism and Racism in '90s Canada* (1992) and *Racism and Social Inequality in Canada* (1998). He tries to grow apples in his spare time.

James Stolzman is an Associate Professor in the Department of Sociology and Social Anthropology at Dalhousie University. His areas of academic interest are the sociology of mental disorders, social stratification, and sociological pedagogy. He teaches and writes in the area of mental health and was a contributor to *Health, Illness, and Health Care in Canada* (1994).

Gary Teeple is an Associate Professor in the Department of Sociology and Anthropology at Simon Fraser University. His current research areas are in political sociology, the global division of labour, and Canadian political economy. His publications include *Capitalism and the National Question in Canada* (1972), as editor and contributor; *Marx's Critique of Politics* (1984); and *Globalization and the Decline of Social Reform* (1995).

K. Victor Ujimoto is Professor of Applied Sociology, Department of Sociology and Anthropology, and Research Associate, Centre for Information Technology Research, University of Guelph. He has published widely in the areas of aging, ethnicity, and health. His current research is on multiculturalism and human resources development in industrial organizations.

Terry Wotherspoon is a Professor and Head of Sociology at the University of Saskatchewan. His recent books include *The Sociology of Education in Canada: Critical Perspectives* (1998), *First Nations: Race, Class, and Gender Relations* (co-authored with Vic Satzewich, 1993), and *Multicultural Education in a Changing Global Economy: Canada and the Netherlands* (co-edited with Paul Jungbluth, 1995). He has published several other articles and books on various aspects of education and Canadian society. His current research examines school-to-work linkages, First Nations students, and educational inequality.

INDEX

Reader Reply Card

We are interested in your reaction to *Social Issues and Contradictions in Canadian Society*, Third Edition, by B. Singh Bolaria. You can help us to improve this book in future editions by completing this questionnaire.

1. What was your reason for using this book?

    ❑ university course ❑ college course ❑ continuing education course
    ❑ professional ❑ personal ❑ other (specify) _____
       development   interest _____

2. If you are a student, please identify your school and the course in which you used this book.

3. Which chapters or parts of this book did you use? Which did you omit?

4. What did you like best about this book?

5. What did you like least about this book?

6. Please identify any topics you think should be added to future editions.

7. Please add any comments or suggestions.

8. May we contact you for further information?

    Name: _____

    Address: _____

    _____

    Phone: _____

    E-mail: _____

(fold here and tape shut)

0116870399-M8Z4X6-BR01

Larry Gillevet
Director of Product Development
HARCOURT BRACE & COMPANY, CANADA
55 HORNER AVENUE
TORONTO, ONTARIO
M8Z 9Z9